William Morris, T Longmore

A Manual of Ambulance Transport

William Morris, T Longmore

A Manual of Ambulance Transport

ISBN/EAN: 9783742899149

Manufactured in Europe, USA, Canada, Australia, Japa

Cover: Foto ©ninafisch / pixelio.de

Manufactured and distributed by brebook publishing software (www.brebook.com)

William Morris, T Longmore

A Manual of Ambulance Transport

All Rights Reserved.

A MANUAL

OF

AMBULANCE TRANSPORT

BY

SURGEON-GENERAL SIR T. LONGMORE

C.B., Q.H.S., F.R.C.S.,

LATE PROFESSOR OF MILITARY SURGERY AT THE ARMY MEDICAL SCHOOL; OFFICER OF THE LEGION OF HONOUR; ASSOCIATE OF THE SOCIETY OF SURGERY OF PARIS; CORRESPONDING MEMBER OF THE ACADEMY OF MEDICINE OF FRANCE, ETC.

SECOND EDITION.

EDITED BY

SURGEON-CAPTAIN WILLIAM A. MORRIS,

ARMY MEDICAL STAFF.

LONDON:
PRINTED FOR HER MAJESTY'S STATIONERY OFFICE,
BY HARRISON AND SONS, ST. MARTIN'S LANE,
PRINTERS IN ORDINARY TO HER MAJESTY.

And to be purchased, either directly or through any Bookseller, from
EYRE & SPOTTISWOODE, East Harding Street, Fleet Street, E.C.; or
JOHN MENZIES & Co., 12, Hanover Street, Edinburgh, and
90, West Nile Street, Glasgow; or
HODGES, FIGGIS, & Co., Limited, 104, Grafton Street, Dublin.

1893.

Price Six Shillings.

(Wt. 17253 1000 3/93—H & S 6107.)

CONTENTS.

	Page
PREFACE TO THE SECOND EDITION	xiii
INTRODUCTION	xv

CHAPTER I.

GENERAL REMARKS ON AMBULANCE TRANSPORT IN TIME OF WAR.

Military hospitals detached from barracks—Progress of ambulance work in civil life—Movable character of field hospitals necessitates special means of ambulance transport—Ambulance transport on the line of march—On the occasion of battle—Surgical importance of speedy removal of wounded—Influence of the ambulance service on the progress of a campaign—Ambulance transport in standing camps—Consequences of the accumulation of sick in standing camps—Experiences at Scutari and Constantinople in 1856—Consequences of deficient ambulance transport—Experiences at the battles of the Alma, Solferino, and the Franco-German War—Proposed aid by volunteers—Their practical value considered—Provision of ambulance transport by Governments—British transport service, and its peculiarities—Construction of ambulance transport conveyances—The medical officer's part in the construction of ambulance vehicles—Qualities of a good field surgeon—The responsibility of the surgeon who is placed in charge of wounded during their transport—No single point in the mode of carrying a wounded man unimportant—General Jonathan Letterman on the duties of medical officers 1-19

CHAPTER II.

HISTORY OF THE MODERN ORGANISATION OF THE MEDICAL SERVICES OF THE PRINCIPAL EUROPEAN ARMIES, WITH SPECIAL REFERENCE TO THE TRANSPORT OF SICK AND WOUNDED.

SECTION 1.—Old methods of removing wounded from battlefields—Baron Larrey's ambulance system—Larrey's flying ambulance—Its organisation—Baron Percy's ambulance system—Percy's flying ambulance—Its mode of operation in the field—Larrey's and Percy's systems compared—Percy's corps of stretcher-bearers—Principles of their organisation.

SECTION 2.—Ambulance system of the British service—Royal wagon train—Ambulance transport during the Peninsular and Crimean wars—Hospital Conveyance Corps—Land Transport Corps—Military train—Regimental hospital orderly system—The first Medical Staff Corps—The Army Hospital Corps—Control Department—Unification of the Medical Department—Abolition of the regimental hospitals—Present Medical Staff Corps—Their training—Militia Medical Staff Corps—Volunteer Medical Staff Corps—Army Medical Reserve—Volunteer Brigade-Surgeons—Volunteer brigade bearer companies.

SECTION 3.—Ambulance transport arrangements in other armies—French army—German army—Austrian army—Russian army—Danish army 20-55

CHAPTER III.

THE CONVENTION OF GENEVA AND ITS BADGE, THE RED CROSS.

No account of ambulance transport would be complete without reference to the Convention of Geneva—Most erroneous ideas exist with regard to the Red Cross—The one and only meaning of the Red Cross—The badge of neutrality itself—Formation of the National Red Cross Societies—The great ignorance of the terms of the Convention even by those who have served under its flag—No European war would take place without the Red Cross being recognised—The abuses of the Red Cross—Instances of these—Wrongful use of the Geneva badge in civil hospitals—International law suggested to suppress these abuses—The latitude allowed to Red Cross Societies in the past will not be permitted in future—The French Red Cross Society—Its intelligent and continuous activity—The Red Cross in Germany—The Red Cross in Austria-Hungary—The Red Cross in Russia—The Red Crescent in Turkey—Civil work of the Red Cross Societies in peace—Great importance of discipline without which the organisation and working in the field is much endangered—The Articles of the Convention of Geneva—List in chronological order of countries in which National Societies of the Red Cross have been formed—Aim and general organisation of the Red Cross—Relations between National Societies and Governments—Work of National Societies in time of peace—Work of the National Societies during war—Maritime activity of National Societies—International relations 56–77

CHAPTER IV.

GENERAL REMARKS ON ESTIMATES FOR AMBULANCE TRANSPORT WITH ARMIES ON ACTIVE SERVICE.

Ambulance transport on active service—Circumstances which have to be taken into consideration—On what basis is this framed?—The control of the medical arrangements of an army in the field—The Principal Medical Officer and his position in the field—General Sir Donald Stewart's opinion—Lord Morley's report—Its special value to army medical officers—Bearer companies—The difficulty in the first instance of knowing how many hospitals will be required along the line of operations—The lines of medical assistance—The regimental assistance—Assistance by the bearer company—The first English bearer company—Personnel of the present English bearer company—Bearer companies and field hospitals as permanent establishments—Mobilisation of bearer companies and field hospitals—Volunteers from the Army Medical Reserve—Militia Reserve—Reserve of the Medical Staff Corps require to be trained annually—The lifting and carrying of wounded men most irksome—The physical conditions that a bearer should possess—Mounted bearer companies—Foreign hospital service—Ambulance transport for the English army is decided by authority, and issued on scale—The decision is influenced by certain conditions—The nature and climate of the country—Character of the enemy—The nature of his weapons—Duration of hostilities—Casualties in battle—Illustrations from the Franco-German War—The American War—Mortality among Medical officers in the English army—Returns of great battles—The ill-fated Walcheren Expedition 78–91

CHAPTER V.

RECOGNISED POSITION OF WOUNDED DURING TRANSPORT AND THEIR CARRIAGE BY BEARERS ONLY.

SECTION I.—Positions of wounded men during transport—The recumbent position—Its advantages to men severely wounded—Kinds of wounds which necessitate a recumbent position—Transport in a sitting position—Wounds for which such a posture is suitable—Transport in a semi-recumbent position—Conditions where the semi-recumbent posture is particularly serviceable—Comparative merits **of recumbent and semi-recumbent carriage.**

Section 2.—Difficulties of defining the proportions of different kinds of ambulance transport—Importance in the interests of the sick and wounded to have a sufficient supply of recumbent carriage—Peculiarities and variations in the relative proportions of the two kinds of transport—Experiences in Africa and the Italian Campaign—Classification of wounded according to their requirements.

Section 3.—Concerning wounded who do not absolutely require to be carried to the stations of medical assistance—Deficiency of bearers in action—Duties of hospital attendants in the field as regards classes of wounded—Wounded who can walk unaided—Stimulus of a gun-shot wound—An example—Esmarch's crutches—Esmarch's braces for hæmorrhage.

Section 4.—Assistance by bearers to wounded men—Carriage by a single bearer—Carriage en cheval—Baron Percy's bravery—Captain Shaw's method—Fischer's method—Carriage by two bearers—Two-handed seat—Three-handed seat—Four-handed seat—Carriage by two bearers of a patient in a horizontal position—Method by which three bearers can carry a man in a horizontal position 92–111

CHAPTER VI.

AMBULANCE **TRANSPORT MATERIAL.**

Class I.—*Conveyances Borne by Men.*—*Sub-classes*—Hammocks—Dandies—Stretchers—Construction and mode of carriage of conveyances borne by men—Uses of this class.

Hammocks.—Derivation of the name—Soldier's blanket—Officer's sash—Hammocks suspended from a single pole—Sailors' hammocks—The looped blanket—Uses of hammocks after the action of the Alma—Hammocks on the Gold Coast—Ashanti cot—Mexican twine hammock—The hammock nature of the Himalayan dandy—Confusion with the Jhampan—Jhampans—Not used in ambulance transport.

Dandies.—Himalayan dandy—Staff-Surgeon McCosh's improvements—Bareilly dandy—Distinction between a jhampan and a dandy—jhampan method of carriage applied to a dandy—Lushai dandy—Experiences in Afghanistan and Burma—Leake's dandy—Collis dandy—Macpherson's stretcher-dandy—The Trag-sitze—Landa's apron—New Zealand litter—Improvised methods—Blanket stretchers—Rugs **and** poles—Greatcoat stretcher—Hill's hayband stretchers—Galton's temporary stretcher—Dhooley-wallahs, Kahars or bearers—The Palki—Muncheels—Tonjons.

Stretchers.—Derivation of the term—Primary and secondary stretchers—Necessity for this division no longer exists—International uniformity proposed—Stretchers can only be carried by Europeans and their allied races—Inventors should aim at great strength and simplicity—Remarks on models—Remarks on the construction of stretchers—Poles—Traverses—Feet—Canvas and pillow—Slings—The weight—Baron Percy's stretcher—Prussian stretcher—French stretcher—Austrian stretcher—Baron Mundy's stretcher—Italian stretcher—Mark I. British field stretcher—Mark II. and III.—Mark IV. and V.—Furley military stretcher—General observations **on** civil stretchers—The Furley stretcher for civil purposes—Stretcher with telescopic handles—The police **stretcher**—The Lowmoor jacket—Peck's stretcher—General rules for **the proper carriage** of stretchers—Crossing a fence—Carrying up steps—Crossing a ditch.

Class II.—*Conveyances wheeled by men.*—General observations—Objects aimed at in the use of wheeled stretchers—Rapid removal of the wounded—Reduction in the number of attendants—To supplement pack-animal transport—Bautzen wheelbarrows—Evans's hand-wheel litter—Ordnance ambulance barrows—Ambulance wheelbarrows in China—Macdermott's wheeled carrier—Dr. Gauvin's spring stretcher on wheels—Baron Mundy's single-wheeled stretcher—Baron Mundy's two-wheeled stretcher—**Neuss's** two-wheeled litter—Neuss-Manley litter—British regulation wheeled litter—The Ashford litter—Concluding observations on hand-wheeled litters.

CLASS III.—*Pack animal Ambulance Transport.*—General remarks—The division of ambulance transport effected by animals—Saddles—Animals under fire do not, as a rule, stand.

SECTION 1.—Elephant ambulance transport—The nature of the elephant—Pads—Howdahs—Charjamahs—The health of the elephant.

SECTION 2.—Camel ambulance transport—Dromedary and the Bactrian—The load of the camel—The gait—Riding camels—Endurance of the camel—His health and food—Larrey's Egyptian camel litters—Camel kujawahs—Brett's camel doolies—Camel saddles—Experiences in the Soudan—Italian camel saddles—Mosley's crates—The Turkestan saddles.

SECTION 3.—Mule and pony ambulance transport—Mules preferable to horses for ambulance transport—Weights carried by mules—Analysis of a regulation mule load—East Indian mules—Saddles—Not to be used for sick—Experiences in the Peninsula and the Crimea—Pillion seats—Arab mode of removing wounded—General remarks on mule cacolets and litters—The construction of cacolets—Italian mule cacolet—Mosley's **mule** crate—English mule litter—French mule litter—Pre**cautions** to be observed by patients—Mr. Hill's **two-mule** litter—Italian **sitting** litter—Shortell's mule litter—Locati's mule **conveyances**—**Woodcock's mule** litters—United States mule litter—Horse litters—The **travois**—Concluding observations.

CLASS IV.—*Conveyances drawn by Animals.*—General observations—**Wheeled** ambulance carriage must go where army transport vehicles go.

SECTION 1.—History of the fourth class of animal transport—Experiences in France in 1792—During the Peninsular war—During the Crimean war—The Paris Exhibition in 1867—The good effected by this exhibition.

SECTION 2.—Military advantages of wheeled ambulance transport—An essential part of an army—Superiority of wheeled conveyances to other kinds of transport on the line of march—The Duke of Wellington's objections to regimental ambulance vehicles—The special reasons of these objections—General summary—The neutrality under the Geneva Convention of all sick transport.

SECTION 3.—Remarks on horses in relation to their employment with ambulance transport—Kind of horse fitted for the draught of ambulance vehicles—Strength of draught horses—Limit of pace and endurance.

SECTION 4.—Requisite qualities of wheeled ambulance transport—Springs necessary—Capacity adequate to the draught power employed—Proper relation of strength, weight, and draught—Ventilation—Facilities for loading and unloading patients out of the vehicle—Carriage of water and surgical stores—Accommodation for ambulance attendants—Kits and arms of sick and wounded to be carried.

SECTION 5.—On the comparative merits of carts and wagons for the transport of sick and wounded—Wagons are safer under all circumstances—The economy of wagons—Carts more durable but less safe—Poles **as compared** with shafts—Larrey's ambulance cart—La voiture Macon—**Guthrie's** hospital conveyance cart—Tufnell's military field cart—Macpherson's Madras cart—Cherry's field cart—Maltese cart—British ambulance cart—The Tonga.

Larrey's ambulance wagon—The "Wheeling" wagon—The "Rucker" wagon—**Locati's** Vettura d'Ambulanza—**Baron** Mundy's ambulance wagon—The "Löhner" wagon—The French Red Cross wagon—The Prussian ambulance wagon—The New Zealand wagon—Macpherson's ambulance wagon—Francis' ambulance wagon—Marks I. and II.—British ambulance wagon—Marks III., IV., and V.—British ambulance wagon—"Furley" ambulance wagon—Cairo wagon—Howard's wagon—The Tortoise ambulance.

Country carts—Definition—Springs for carts—Method of supporting a stretcher by springs in a cart—The Lorraine wagon—The Araba—Indian bandy—Indian **hackery**—**Burmese** bandy—Trek **wagon**.

CLASS V.—*Railway ambulance Transport.*

SECTION 1.—General remarks on railway ambulance transport in time of war—Advantages offered by the use of railways for ambulance transport—Probable influence of railways on the surgical treatment of the wounded—Railway ambulance transport in the Crimea—The Italian campaign—The Schleswick-Holstein campaign—The Civil War in the United States—Austrian-Prussian campaign—Franco-German war—Russo-Turkish campaign—Ambulance trains in the Franco-German war—Russian ambulance trains.

SECTION 2.—Observations on the various kinds of carriages in present use upon railways, especially English railways, so far as regards their fitness to be applied to the transport of sick and wounded in time of war—Construction of railway carriages commonly used in Europe unfit them for sick-transport purposes—Sub-divisions of railway passenger carriages—Narrowness of the doors of railway passenger carriages—Goods wagons on railways—Their springs—Conversion of railway wagons into sick-transport vehicles—Urgent reasons for using only ordinary stretchers in railway ambulance wagons.

SECTION 3.—Historical resumé of railway ambulance transport—Practical experiences in Prussia in 1860—Hammocks, and the difficulties in the way of slinging them in railway carriages—Baron Mundy's experience of straw for railway wagons adapted for wounded men in the Bohemian campaign—Objections to straw—Practical experiments at Paris in 1867—United States' railway hospital trains.

SECTION 4.—On the regulations which are necessary for sick and wounded soldiers when transported by railway—Arrangements prior to bringing a convoy of sick to a railway train—Authority of the railway officials—Proper disposal of the field kits of the sick—Supplies of food, water, &c., during the transport—Inspection of the train before starting—Halts during the route—Arrangements on reaching destination.

SECTION 5.—Railway ambulance transport in the East Indies and in England—Occasions on which sick and injured soldiers require to be transported in India—The "étappen" system, as suggested by Surgeon-General Balfour—Experiments at Delhi—Indian ambulance trains—Railway ambulance transport in England—Sleeping saloons—Third class—Express luggage vans—The training of railway employés by St. John Ambulance Association.

SECTION 6.—Special systems—Peltzer's system—Morachi's system—Beaufort's system—Bey-Ammeline system—The Berlin system—Zavodovsky's system—The Gründ system—The Hamburg system—Fischer's system—Boulomie's system—The Austrian system.

CLASS VI.—*Marine Ambulance Transport.*—Definition—Red River and Nile experiences—Register of ships—Sea-going—Coasting—River—Tonnage—Hospital ships—Organisation of river vessels by the Italian Red Cross—Experiences on the Chindwin and the Irrawaddy—Barges and the French Red Cross Society—Knots—The Gorgas Lift—Macdonald's ambulance lift—Macdonald's ambulance lowerer—An extemporised lift—Mowll's folding ship ambulance chair—Macdonald's ambulance lift and stretcher—Singleton's chair—Ambulance launches—The "Red Cross" Ambulance steamer 112-410

APPENDICES.

APPENDIX	I.—The Sanitary Train of the Société Française	411
,,	II.—Ambulance Trains of the Knights of Malta	415
,,	III.—Macpherson's Dandy Drill	425
,,	IV.—Morris's Dandy Drill	434
	V.—The Tortoise Wagon Tent Drill	439

LIST OF ILLUSTRATIONS.

Fig.		Page.
I	Captain Shaw's method of rescuing from fire	103
II	Fischer's apparatus	103
III	Supporting belt used with same	103
IV	Two-handed seat, first method	105
V	,, ,, second method	106
VI	Three-handed seat	107
VII	Carriage by three-handed seat	107
VIII	Four-handed seat	109
IX	Prepared four-handed seat	109
X	Carriage by four-handed seat	110
XI	Method by which two bearers can carry a man in a horizontal position	110
XII	Method by which three bearers can carry a man in a horizontal position	111
XIII	Conveying a wounded soldier in his blanket	115
XIV	Hammock carriage, showing cramped position of patient	118
XV	The Ashanti cot	119
XVI	Chinese palanquin	121
XVII	The Himalayan dandy	122
XVIII	,, ,, with McCosh's improved method of suspension	122
XIX	Pole stanchion used with ,,	123
XX	Jhampan of the present day	124
XXI	Dandy carried jhampan fashion	125
XXII	Lushai dandy	127
XXIII	Leake's dandy	129
XXIV	,, ,, stretcher and folded up	129
XXV	,, ,, showing method of shortening and lengthening going up-hill	129
XXVI	Leake's dandy shortened	130
XXVII	,, ,, as a stretcher	130
XXVIII	Collis dandy	131
XXIX	,, ,, the framework	132
XXX	,, ,, end view showing method of supporting pole	132
XXXI	Macpherson's stretcher dandy	134
XXXII	,, ,, ,, showing construction of the sack	135
XXXIII	Macpherson's stretcher dandy as a stretcher, open and folded	135
XXXIV	Trag-sitze or bearing seat	139
XXXV	Mandil de Socorro	140
XXXVI	New Zealand Amoo	142
XXXVII	Hill's hay stretcher	144
XXXVIII	The Indian dooley	146
XXXIX	Dr. Francis' dooley	151
XL	Porter's hill dooley	152
XLI	Baron Percy's stretcher	165
XLII	,, ,, for carrying wounded	165
XLIII	Beaufort's stretcher	167
XLIV	Baron Mundy's stretcher	168

Fig.		Page.
XLV	Plan of British Mark I. stretcher	170
XLVI	,, ,, ,, with traverses unfastened	170
XLVII	Plan of British Mark I. stretcher, pillow and straps packed	170
XLVIII	Plan of British Mark I. stretcher ready for use ..	170
XLIX	Faris's field stretcher	172
L	The "Furley" military stretcher..	174
LI	The "Furley" stretcher with telescopic handles ..	176
LII	The "Lowmoor" jacket	178
LIII	Peck's stretcher	178
LIV	,, ,, ...	178
LV	Carrying loaded stretcher up steps	181
LVI	,, ,, ,, over a fence	182
LVII	,, ,, ,, over a ditch	183
LVIII	,, ,, ,, ,, ,, ...	183
LIX	Ambulance barrow	188
LX	Ambulance barrow fitted with stretcher	189
LXI	Gauvin's spring stretcher on wheels	190
LXII	,, ,, ,, removed from its wheels ..	191
LXIII	Baron Mundy's wheeled stretcher..	192
LXIV	Neuss's two-wheeled litter	193
LXV	The military wheeled litter..	195
LXVI	The Ashford litter	196
LXVII	,, ,, with cover	196
LXVIII	Larrey's camel litter	203
LXIX	Camel kajawah for sick lying down	204
LXX	,, ,, ,, sitting	205
LXXI	Camels with kajawahs on line of march	206
LXXII	Brett's camel dooley..	207
LXXIII	Italian camel saddle..	210
LXXIV	Mosley's camel crate saddle for two sick lying down ..	211
LXXV	Perspective view of Mosley's camel crate for patients lying down..	212
LXXVI	Mosley's crates for sick sitting up	213
LXXVII	Perspective view of Mosley's sitting up crate ..	214
LXXVIII	Illustrations of side leverage pressure	216
LXXIX	The Turkestan saddle	218
LXXX	Convoy of wounded on mule cacolets	230
LXXXI	Side view of mule cacolet attached to its pack saddle ..	231
LXXXII	End view of mule cacolet	232
LXXXIII	French cacolet	232
LXXXIV	Italian mule carriage	233
LXXXV	Italian mule saddle	234
LXXXVI	Mosley's mule crate..	234
LXXXVII	Mule litter attached to its pack saddle	235
LXXXVIII	French mule litter	236
LXXXIX	English mule litter, original pattern	237
XC	A sitting litter	241
XCI	Locati's side litter (sectional view)	244
XCII	Locati's single litter..	245
XCIII	United States mule litter	247
XCIV	Mule panniers	248
XCV	Larrey's flying ambulance cart	273
XCVI	,, ,, ,, end view (front) ..	273
XCVII	,, ,, ,, interior ..	273
XCVIII	,, ,, ,, end view (back) ..	273
XCIX	Guthrie's hospital conveyance cart	275
C	Tufnell's military field cart..	276
CI	,, ,, ,, side view	277
CII	Macpherson's Madras cart	279
CIII	Cherry's cart..	281
CIV	Maltese cart	282
CV	British ambulance cart	284

List of Illustrations.

Fig.		Page.
CVI	Ambulance tonga	286
CVII	"Wheeling" wagon	288
CVIII	The Rucker wagon	290
CIX	" " " cross sections of	290
CX	Locati's ambulance wagon	292
CXI	" " " interior	293
CXII	" " " end view	294
CXIII	Baron Mundy's ambulance wagon	297
CXIV	" " view of stretcher from	297
CXV	Löhner wagon	299
CXVI	Ambulance wagon of the Société Française	300
CXVII	French red cross wagon	301
CXVIII	Prussian ambulance wagon	303
CXIX	Perspective view of the New Zealand ambulance wagon with its cover	305
CXX	Perspective view of the New Zealand ambulance wagon without cover	305
CXXI	Macpherson's Indian wagon	307
CXXII	Fuller's india-rubber spring	311
CXXIII	British ambulance wagon, Mark II.	311
CXXIV	" " " Mark III.	313
CXXV	" " " Mark IV.	315
CXXVI	" " " Mark V.	317
CXXVII	The "Furley" ambulance wagon, showing interior	318
CXXVIII	" " " closed	319
CXXIX	" " " for one or two stretchers	319
CXXX	The "Cairo" wagon	320
CXXXI	Howard's ambulance wagon (outside view)	321
CXXXII	" " " (inside view)	322
CXXXIII	" " " showing arrangement of interior	322
CXXXIV	The "Tortoise" ambulance wagon	324
CXXXV	Ground plan of surgery tent of ditto	325
CXXXVI	Surgeon's sleeping tent of ditto	326
CXXXVII	Showing the interior of one-third of the "Tortoise" ambulance, ready for the reception of patients	327
CXXXVIII	Plan of "Tortoise" ambulance with wagon	328
CXXXIX	Stretcher bedstead, section of pole, showing construction	329
CXL	Stretcher bedstead, showing end of pole	329
CXLI	"Tortoise" field railway	330
CXLII	Ground plan of complete "Tortoise" ambulance camp	331
CXLIII	Stretcher supports	334
CXLIV	Country wagon, supporting stretcher by springs	335
CXLV	View of the spring	335
CXLVI	The Lorraine wagon	337
CXLVII	The Indian hackery	339
CXLVIII	The Burmese bandy	340
CXLIX	The Trek wagon	342
CL	Side view of seat in Trek wagon	343
CLI	End view of seat in Trek wagon	344
CLII	Spring with straps	344
CLIII	Arrangement of stretchers in 4th class railway wagons in Prussia	362
CLIV	Ditto	362
CLV	Side elevation of the interior of an American hospital car	367
CLVI	Perspective view of half the interior of an American hospital car	368
CLVII	Section of an Indian railway carriage	373
CLVIII	Leu's stretcher rest	378
CLIX	Zavodovsky's railway system (perspective view)	379
CLX	" " The hook	380
CLXI	" " The grummet	380

List of Illustrations.

Fig.		Page.
CLXII	Zavodovsky's railway system, showing method of attachment of pole to hawser	381
CLXIII	Zavodovsky's railway system, showing complete arrangement of ropes	381
CLXIV	Zavodovsky's railway system, showing manner of fastening stretcher to floor	382
CLXV	The Gründ system, side view	384
CLXVI	,, ,, perspective view	384
CLXVII	The Hamburg system, Griffe du diable spring and stretcher supports	386
CLXVIII	Fischer's system, upper tier	387
CLXIX	,, ,, lower tier	387
CLXX	Beaufort stretcher rest	388
CLXXI	,, ,, with stretcher	388
CLXXII	Austrian system	389
CLXXIII	I.M.S. Sladen hospital ship with flats	393
CLXXIV	Knots	395
CLXXV	Gorgas lift	396
CLXXVI	Macdonald's Naval ambulance lift	398
CLXXVII	,, ,, ,, lowerer	399
CLXXVIII	An extemporised lift	400
CLXXIX	Mowll's ambulance chair, as a chair	401
CLXXX	,, ,, as a stretcher	401
CLXXXI	,, ,, ,, ready for hoisting or lowering	402
CLXXXII	Macdonald's ambulance lift and stretcher	404
CLXXXIII	Singleton's chair, patient horizontal	407
CLXXXIV	,, ,, patient sitting	408
CLXXXV	,, ,, patient perpendicular	408
CLXXXVI	The "Red Cross" Ambulance steamer	410
CLXXXVII	Ambulance train of the Knights of Malta. Kitchen wagon	419
CLXXXVIII	Ambulance train of the Knights of Malta. Ambulance wagon	422
CLXXXIX	Macpherson's dandy drill. "Lift poles"	426
CXC	,, ,, "Lift dandies"	427
CXCI	,, ,, "Stand to stretchers"	429
CXCII	,, ,, showing stage of removing the cover	430
CXCIII	Macpherson's dandy drill, showing extension of dandy detachments	432
CXCIV	Plan of "Tortoise" wagon drill	440
CXCV	,, ,, ,,	440
CXCVI	,, ,, ,,	441

SUBJECT HEADING OF CHAPTERS.

INTRODUCTION

CHAPTER I.—General remarks on Ambulance Transport in time of war.

,, II.—History of the modern organisation of the medical services of the principal European armies, with special reference to the transport of the sick and wounded.

,, III.—The Convention of Geneva, and its badge, the Red Cross.

,, IV.—General remarks on estimates for Ambulance Transport with armies on active service.

,, V.—The recognised positions of wounded during transport, and their carriage by bearers only.

,, VI.—Ambulance transport material :—

    Class I.—Conveyances *borne* by men—

        (*a*) Hammocks.
        (*b*) Dandies.
        (*c*) Stretchers.

    ,, II.—Conveyances *wheeled* by men.

    ,, III.—Conveyances *borne* by animals.

    ,, IV.—Conveyances *drawn* by animals.

    ,, V.—Railway ambulance transport.

    ,, VI.—Marine ambulance transport.

APPENDIX I.—The Sanitary Train of the Société Française.

,, II.—Ambulance Trains of the Knights of Malta.

,, III.—Macpherson's Dandy Drill.

,, IV.—Morris's Dandy Drill.

,, V.—The Tortoise Wagon Tent Drill.

PREFACE TO THE SECOND EDITION.

THE revision of Sir T. Longmore's work on Ambulance Transport, in order to bring it into accord with ambulance matters as they are at the present time was entrusted to me by the Author, with the sanction of Director-General Sir W. A. Mackinnon, K.C.B., upon whose recommendation to the Government an issue of a second edition was approved and ordered.

The system upon which the Author, in the first instance, founded the work has very greatly facilitated my labours in connection with it, and though the period embraced in the revision is twenty-one years, the original form and system of the book has been rigidly preserved. It is only on these lines that a work of this class could be laid, in order to be of practical value to those for whom it is intended.

"A Treatise on Ambulance Transport," published in 1869, was the first complete work devoted exclusively to this very important subject. It is true that there were some orders and regulations bearing upon the carriage of the sick and wounded in the time of war, and writers on military surgery referred to this subject in a more or less perfunctory manner, but it is since that time that Ambulance Transport has grown to importance. The experiences of the Franco-German and the Russo-Turkish Wars, and of our own campaigns in Zululand, Afghanistan, Egypt, and the Soudan have more than proved the absolute necessity of rendering, in as perfect a manner as circumstances will permit, relief to the soldier when he is wounded, with the result that much attention has been directed to this important service, with great advantage to the individuals concerned, and economy to the State. In the first edition of this work, the necessity for the development of the Medical Service was noted by the Author, and the absolute necessity of improving the conditions of the sick and wounded prominently indicated. During the period embraced in the revision many works on Ambulance Transport have appeared, especially on the continent, and in all of them, references are made, and extracts quoted, from the first edition so that for this reason, and for the "perfection of the system of transporting the sick and wounded of armies in time of war,"* this second edition is considered well-timed and expedient.

---

* See Introduction, p. xv., by Author.

The title of the book has been changed from "A Treatise on Ambulance Transport" to "A Manual of Ambulance Transport;" the change is for no reason beyond the fact that the word "Treatise" has fallen into disuse, and the expression "Manual" has taken its place in works of this class. A new feature will be observed in the introduction of a special chapter on "The Convention of Geneva." This forms a complete history of the Convention to the present year, and is written by Mr. John Furley, whose knowledge and personal experience of the "*working value*" of the Red Cross in many campaigns stand almost unrivalled. The history of the British Medical Service commenced by the Author has been completed by Brigade-Surgeon-Lieutenant-Colonel W. Johnston, Army Medical Staff, and forms a most interesting and accurate record of the various phases through which our Service has passed. Chapter VI., with the several sections referring to Ambulance Transport Material has been, for the greater part, rewritten, but all the interesting historical matter relating to the work of earlier inventors and exponents of systems, has been carefully preserved. An Appendix, containing the various drills connected with ambulances, and a description of the Ambulance Trains of the Knights of Malta (Austria-Hungary) complete the work.

The Author has liberally supplied me with papers and notes which he had collected from time to time, with a view of bringing out the work himself, had he had the required leisure.

I take this opportunity of thanking Mr. John Furley for the great assistance he has given me in the preparation of this edition. He has, in the kindest manner, allowed me, at all times, to avail myself of his counsel and advice, with great advantage to myself and the work, as it passed through my hands.

To my wife I am indebted for sixty new sketches. She has devoted much valuable time to them, and I think they form an artistic and important feature in illustrating the text.

The work of revision has necessarily entailed a very large correspondence; and I beg here to thank many foreign Officers, and especially my brother Officers of the Army Medical Staff, for the kindness and promptness with which they replied to my inquiries, often, I fear, entailing much inconvenience to themselves.

WILLIAM A. MORRIS.

INTRODUCTION.*

The best method of transporting sick and wounded soldiers from one place to another in time of war is one of the most important questions to be studied, as it is one of the most difficult problems to be solved among the subjects which concern the medical service of armies. On numerous occasions in campaigning, the safety of the lives of soldiers disabled by injury or disease, and on all occasions, the abridgment of their sufferings, must depend upon the means of effecting their removal being proper in kind, efficient in condition, proportionate in amount to the need, and upon its being close at hand so as to afford relief, when required, without unnecessary delay. But the importance attached to this service is not confined to the interests of the sick and wounded. The tone of **moral** feeling and degree of confidence among the troops, the preservation of due order in the ranks, are influenced by it; and even the strategical designs of a commander may **be** aided or thwarted on occasions of urgency according as this duty is well or ill provided for and carried into execution. As a matter of economy, too, the subject demands attention. The direct loss, when the conveyances for the sick and wounded sent with an army prove useless; the greater indirect loss from the failure of their services; and the necessary expenses, under all circumstances, involved in the maintenance of a hospital transport establishment, sufficiently indicate the importance of securing for adoption the **best** system of sick transport, both as regards the matériel and the administration, that can be devised and adapted to the exigencies of warfare.

Yet, valuable on the one hand as a good system of hospital transport is, and, on the other hand, worse than useless the reverse of a good system, the established arrangements for this service are generally regarded, notwithstanding the many improvements which have been made in them of late years, **as** the most defective part of military organisation, as they certainly are of the medical departmental organisation in armies. The author of the most recent work on military surgery in France has written:—" L'enlèvement des blessés du champ de bataille et leur transport à l'ambulance sont la partie la plus

---

* The former edition, to which this Introduction was prefaratory, was published in 1869.

défectueuse du service de santé en **campagne."*** The **alterations** which have been made from **time to time during the** last few years in the organisation of **the** personnel, **the repeated** failures of old forms, and **the** constant efforts **made for discovering** better forms **of** ambulance vehicles, **not to mention** the expressed opinions **of** many experienced **officers, confirm this statement as regards** this country; just **as changes and experiments of a** corresponding nature point **to the same fact in other countries.**

It is not surprising that this part of the military system should **be still in** an imperfect state. **There has** probably never been **a time** when endeavours **have** not been made **to** improve the destructive implements **of** war and to ascertain the most effective methods of employing them. These are subjects in which the community at large take interest, for it is felt that power as well as protection are involved in their possession; but it is comparatively a short time ago since attention **was** first given to determine practically the best means of meeting the pressing necessities, in respect to transport, of those who are disabled by the effects of war, and even during the interval of time which has since elapsed, interest in the question has been limited, with comparatively few exceptions, to the persons officially concerned with the special duties belonging to it. There is not a systematic work published on the subject in any language, as far as I am aware. The subject is casually referred to in almost all modern works which treat on the duties of army medical officers, but usually only very briefly and superficially, unless some particular system of transportation, or special form of conveyance, is advertised by the writer; while what is felt to be wanted by everyone taking a practical interest in the question is a work of reference in which may be found, without much **loss** of time, an account of what has hitherto been **done towards** its solution, an explanation of existing arrangements, and such guiding principles as may not only serve the purpose of preventing a repetition of former failures, but also of steering the way to future improvements. This is the information which I have attempted to furnish in the present work.

The personnel of ambulance establishments—the men to whom the duty is entrusted of picking up and carrying the wounded to the field hospitals, of attending upon them under the directions of the surgeons while they are in hospital and during the subsequent removals, are so inseparably connected with the appliances which are placed in their hands for carrying on this service, that a description of the one would necessarily be very incomplete without a description of the other. I have therefore traced the history of **this** branch of military service through its successive changes to **the** present time. I have

---

* *Traité de Chirurgie d'Armée, par M. le Dr. Legouest, Professeur au Val de Grâce,* page 904.

more particularly shown the successive improvements made in the organisation of the Army Hospital Corps of the British service: at the same time I have not omitted to sketch the constitution given to similar corps in other countries, under the belief that this information may be useful as well as interesting for purposes of reference and comparison. The arrangements and regulations for their field duties, more particularly for those connected with the transport of the wounded have been almost exclusively kept in view in these descriptions of the ambulance personnel of different armies.

The various forms of ambulance conveyances hitherto used will be found to be systematically classified, and each class separately described under its respective heading. The general plan adopted is first to indicate the objects sought to be attained in each class, and then to describe particular examples of the class; at the same time, when seeming necessary, the merits and deficiencies of each example are pointed **out**, and the extent to which it has been found to answer its intended purposes in practice is noticed. Mention is made of all the examples of each class of conveyance that have attracted attention, or that appear to be noteworthy on account of any peculiarity in their design or construction.

In describing the qualities of particular conveyances whenever I have not had the opportunity of personally observing them, I have made every endeavour to obtain the results of practical observations made by others; and whenever I have been able to obtain them the authorities are mentioned. Nothing **but** actual use and observation can determine truly the merits **or** defects of particular inventions; ambulance conveyances constructed on the best principles theoretically have over and over again proved failures when subjected to the rough tests of service, to the great disappointment of their designers.

When the carts and wagons constructed for the conveyance of the sick and wounded were sent out with the army to Turkey in the year 1854, the Director-General of the Army Medical Department, anticipating that many defects would be discovered in both, from such appliances at that time being only known theoretically in the British service, issued a Departmental Memorandum,* requesting medical officers to suggest whatever alterations and additions they might think calculated to render them more suitable and efficient. This request produced some reports on the subject, but not so many, nor those so full, as would have been desirable, for the subject in respect to service in any country excepting India was a new one to most army medical officers. At the same time, while the war in the Crimea was in progress, various persons in England, actuated by patriotic motives, turned their attention to devising new forms of conveyance for the sick and wounded in the field, and brought them to the notice of the War Department. Many of these supposed improvements of the then existing forms of ambulance

---

* 20th **June**, 1854.

transport were rejected at the first examination from their evident unfitness for use under the circumstances of campaigning. Others, after examination and approval of the designs by committees of competent persons, were ordered to be constructed, and were then sent to the seat of war, and to camps and garrisons in England, to be subjected to the test of actual employment in the purposes for which they were designed. The results of these trials are only to be found by reference to the multifarious correspondence with which the various public offices connected with the administration of the army at that time abounded. I have had the opportunity, through the kindness of the late Director-General, Sir James Gibson, at whose suggestion this work was first undertaken, as well as of the present Director-General, Dr. Logan, of making myself acquainted with the reports and decisions which have been preserved among the records of the Army Medical Department on some of these inventions. Records of this kind are calculated to be valuable not only as regards the general consideration of the subject of ambulance transport, but also for preventing useless repetition of experiments of a similar nature on future occasions.

Unfortunately, the decisions in many instances are limited to a declaration of opinion as to the fitness or unfitness for service of the particular invention which has been submitted to the judgment of the reporters, without at the same time the reasons on which the decision has been based being recorded. But in others this information is furnished, and the reports are proportionately all the more instructive and valuable.

During the year 1867 the Universal Exhibition at Paris gave a fresh stimulus to the study of the questions involved in the subject of ambulance transport. A committee of persons, deputed from the "Societies for Help to the Wounded in Time of War," of different countries, brought together and deposited in the Exhibition Park a large collection of conveyances which had either been used, or had been suggested for use, for the carriage of sick and wounded troops, and offered prizes for the best forms of hand litters, wheeled litters, and wagons. Several Governments also exhibited the authorised ambulance conveyances of their respective countries. I was fortunate enough to have an official opportunity of examining this large collection, and of assisting in practical trials of many of the conveyances included in it, and thus of further adding to my knowledge of the subject.

The ambulance arrangements of the British service require not only that the kind of transport most suited for use in European warfare should be studied, but also the best kind for use in India, and in the various colonies of the Empire. The transition state through which India has been passing as regards road improvements, railroad communication, and steam conveyances on its great rivers, but more especially the changes which have taken place of late years in respect to opportunities of employment for the labouring population, have exerted an influence which has tended to curtail the old, almost exclusive use of the dhooly system of transport for sick and wounded; while special features in the climate, of the surface of the country in certain districts, in the habits of the natives, and in the usual characters of Indian warfare, have made it difficult to decide upon any suitable form of sick transport to take its place. There is every reason to believe that eventually the system of ambulance transport in India will be adapted in principle to the system which is now in force in the general British; that is, to certain proportions of hand, bât-animal, and wheeled transport being allotted to every field force, the forms of the conveyances being severally modified to suit them to the climate and adapt them to the habits of the natives. This question is, however, still under discussion, and remarks upon it will be found incidentally in the chapters describing the conveyances which have been hitherto employed in India, and those which have been proposed either as substitutes for them or as supplementary to them.

Nor is the question of the best forms of ambulance transport for other parts of the British empire one easy of settlement. Each colonial possession presents such peculiarities, either in its climate, or in the character and general features of the country, its soil, its mountains, ravines, valleys, the habits of the people, the kind of draught usually employed, that it is more than probable that a special modification of the common forms of ambulance conveyances will be required for each. This, again, is a subject considered at some length in the chapters on special conveyances.

It would be scarcely possible for any written description to convey an accurate knowledge of the forms of the vehicles and appliances to which reference is made in the course of this work. Numerous illustrations have, therefore, been added, and although these are not drawn to any general scale, it is believed they will answer the purpose proposed, which is not so much to afford plans and drawings for the construction, as to furnish general ideas of the design and forms of the conveyances described in the text.

I am aware that many deficiencies exist in the work, but I trust it will be found to be so methodically arranged that the task of improving what it contains, and adding what is deficient, will be comparatively an easy one. It will, at any rate, serve to show what difficulties exist in devising such a system of ambulance transport, and such conveyances as will be thoroughly serviceable under all the varied circumstances of field-service; how many efforts have been made by the authorities in England, since attention has been turned to the subject, to overcome these difficulties; and it will, I hope, have the additional advantage of assisting in the attainment of the main object which all have in view, namely, the perfection of the system of transporting the sick and wounded of armies in time of war, and of advancing the economical administration of this important branch of military service.

CHAPTER I.

GENERAL REMARKS ON AMBULANCE TRANSPORT IN TIME OF WAR.

THE necessity for providing suitable and adequate means for the transport of those who fall sick, or who are wounded, exists under all the circumstances of military life, in time of peace, as well as in war.

During peace, both on home and on foreign service, military arrangements require that the hospital in which the sick and wounded soldiers of a force are treated shall be detached from the barracks in which the men ordinarily live; and, as a matter of course, from time to time instances occur of soldiers being too weak, or too disabled by injury, to make their own way from one building to the other. Provision has therefore to be made for the conveyance of these helpless individuals. The same rule requires a detached position for the hospital, when the troops are encamped or hutted, and the same need exists for providing means of transport to those who are disabled by casualties from reaching the hospital without assistance. No difficulty is experienced in the execution of this service, under any of the circumstances just mentioned. Whether the troops are quartered in barracks or are encamped, a certain number of hand conveyances are always issued, and assistance from their comrades may always be obtained. Appropriate wheeled conveyances of an authorised pattern are furnished if the distance from the barracks to the hospital, or the nature of the ground, necessitates such a mode of transport, and if a soldier meets with an accidental injury of a serious kind, or is suddenly seized by illness at a distance from his comrades and the regular military means of transport above mentioned, he has the same opportunities of being removed to hospital which are open to all other persons of the civilised community in which he is for the time placed. The progress in London and the large cities of the continent during the last ten years in applying ambulance aid, and making arrangements for the transport of persons suddenly disabled by injury or sickness and for the carriage of patients labouring under infectious maladies, has been considerable. Notably, the Invalid Transport Service of the St. John Ambulance Association, organised by Mr. Furley,

Military hospitals detached from barracks.

Progress of ambulance work in civil life.

CHAP. I.

the Wiener Freiwillige Rettungs Gesellschaft, organised by Baron Mundy at Vienna, and the present admirable system for infectious cases of the Metropolitan Asylums Board of London. The soldier has the same advantages as the civilian under these circumstances, and no practical impediment is ever met with as regards the accomplishment of the main object, his removal to hospital.

Change of circumstances when troops take the field.

But when troops are called upon to take the field, leaving behind them all the resources of civilised life, and exchanging for them the limited resources available under the conditions in which armies are placed in time of war, then the question of the proper provision to be made for the carriage of the sick and wounded becomes involved in many difficulties. All the conditions are changed. An army in movement is compelled to carry with it all that is necessary to supply its wants, and is therefore dependent for the most part on its stores and transport, whatever may be the circumstances of season or locality, or the chances of exposure to the sudden exigencies which spring from battle. The hospital is no longer a fixed building, but is as movable as the troops to whose service it is devoted; it is, in fact, an ambulance.*

Movable character of field hospitals necessitates special means of ambulance transport.

The means of transporting the sick and wounded of armies must be of a peculiar nature; these must possess the construction, capacity, and all the other qualities essential to fit them for ambulance purposes. Although in peace time and on home service it is best for many reasons, to employ the ambulance convey-

---

* The term "ambulance" has been adopted in English from the French language, and is derived from the Latin "ambulare," to walk. The word has, however, a different signification, among all continental people, from that which is frequently applied to it by English writers. An *ambulance* never means, among foreigners, anything else but a *field hospital* attached to an army, and moving with it—hôpital ambulant—for the primary reception and care of its sick and wounded. The "ambulance" of the "Quartier Général" is the field hospital at Head Quarters. The "Ambulance Volante" (Larrey) is a field hospital fitted for very rapid movements; Soldats d'ambulance" (Percy) are infirmary-men attached to the field hospital; les caissons d'ambulance, les voitures d'ambulance, are respectively the store-transport and the sick-transport carriages of a field hospital. In England the term ambulance is very often applied to the *conveyance* itself, by which the sick and wounded are carried to or from the field hospitals or elsewhere, a sense in which it is never used in any foreign writings. "The supply of ambulances;" "the ambulances for the conveyance of the sick were too heavy," meaning the transport vehicles; "the French ambulances," meaning the French mule litters and cacolets; and such other expressions are constantly met with in published documents connected with the Crimean War. The same misuse of the term has been adopted from the English by several writers in the United States.

Without the explanation just given it would be scarcely possible for an English student to understand the signification of such a French sentence as the following:— "Les secours à donner aux blessés, sur le champ de bataille, comprennent trois phases bien distinctes:—1°, le premier pansement, fait sur le terrain; 2°, le transport à l'ambulance; 3°, le pansement, ou l'opération nécessaire, à l'ambulance" (Arrault). The aid to be given to the wounded on the field of battle comprises three very distinct phases:—1st, the primary dressing on the ground; 2nd, the transport to the ambulance; 3rd, the dressing, or necessary operation, at the ambulance.

In this book when the term "ambulance" is used as a noun substantive, the signification of a field hospital is preserved, and when employed adjectively, as in "ambulance arrangements," "ambulance wagons," it implies that the arrangements or wagons have connexion with a movable field hospital.

ances which have been adapted for meeting the wants of an army in the field, yet any conveyance suitable for the carriage of sick would fulfil the object equally well; but for ambulance purposes in war, special vehicles, specially contrived, are matters of absolute necessity. The material of the sick transport is not the only part of the subject demanding particular consideration; the nature, amount, and organisation of the personnel employed in the transport of the sick must be equally considered, for the system on which the ambulance transport service is to be conducted, can only be properly regulated when the material and personnel are mutually adapted to each other. To determine these matters so that this service may be satisfactorily and at the same time economically performed during a campaign, is a subject full of difficulty. Yet under no circumstances can the need for perfect arrangements, and for adequate means of transporting sick and wounded men, be so urgent as it is when troops enter upon a campaign, and this can be easily rendered evident, and it can equally be shown that the general good, as well as the interest of the individuals immediately concerned, demand that this need shall be suitably provided for.

It will be useful briefly to consider the manner in which the want of proper hospital transport particularly makes itself felt under some of the circumstances of active service; namely, with troops on the line of march, on the field of battle, in standing camps, and at the several military posts established along the lines of communication with the base of operations of an army.

On the Line of March.—When bodies of troops are marching under the circumstances of warfare, they are necessarily separated for periods of greater or less duration, and by certain distances, from direct communication with the principal points on the line of operations in the rear. Under such conditions, in a strange or intricate country, in one nearly destitute of inhabitants, and in tropical or other unwholesome climates, there is little hope of saving men who are rendered incapable of marching through sickness or wounds except by carrying them on with the main force. If it be a hostile country through which the troops are marching, men left behind may be exposed to death from the enemy, as well as from the effects of neglect or starvation.* On the line of march of an army, there-

CHAP. I.

The need of suitable ambulance transport considered under the varied circumstances of field service.

Ambulance transport on the line of march.

Disabled men must be carried on.

---

* Baron Larrey mentions that this must have been the fate of the wounded with the French army that had to retreat after the abandonment of the siege of St. Jean d'Acre, owing to the total absence of any kind of conveyance for the wounded, had it not been for the order issued by General Bonaparte on that occasion, that all the horses of the staff officers were to be employed as substitutes for the deficiency in regular means of sick transport, an order which he enforced by example in giving up his own horses, and marching on foot like the rest of the army. The wounded must otherwise have been left in the field hospitals or abandoned in the desert, where they would have perished either from hunger and thirst, or from having their throats cut by the Arabs. (Campagne d'Egypte, p. 312; Mém. de Chir. Mil., tome 1, Paris, 1812).—Deputy Inspector-General Dr. Gordon, who was in medical

CHAP. I.

Transport of wounded in battle.

fore, it is essential that a due proportion of ambulance transport should accompany the troops to carry on those who become disabled by the way.

On the occasion of battle.—In the case of a general action, the possession of an adequate amount of carriage for transporting the wounded to the various stations of medical assistance is always a matter of vital importance, not only to the troops, but occasionally it may be necessary for the accomplishment of the purpose for which the war has been undertaken.

Importance of speedy removal from field hospitals.

The importance of the transport from the field to the field-hospitals being well performed can scarcely be overrated as regards the interest of every officer and soldier who falls wounded on a field of battle. Every man who is rendered helpless by a severe wound naturally feels an urgent desire for surgical aid as quickly as possible, as well as to be removed from the place of fighting, where he can no longer be of use, to a place of comparative security. But it is not merely the gratification of this longing for help that has to be thought of; it is the more serious fact that the safety of lives and the preservation of limbs in many instances will depend upon promptness and proper means of transport. Moreover, in almost all cases, the efficiency of the surgical assistance rendered will be materially influenced by the time which has elapsed before the patient is brought to hospital and the care with which the transport is conducted. Nor is the manner in which this duty is performed without influence on the combatant ranks generally; the inconvenience and disorder which are apt to result when no systematic plan for its execution exists, or when the plan is injudiciously conceived, or insufficiently or otherwise ill-provided, are indeed sufficiently notorious.

Surgical importance of speedy removal of wounded.

The late General Lord Strathnairn when Commissioner at the French head-quarters in the Crimea, in a report on the military transport of the French army, forcibly described the importance of a well organised system of ambulance transport on the occasion of battle in the following words:—

"Transport of the wounded from the field of battle to a good ambulance, besides satisfying the rights of humanity and sustaining that spirit of confidence in the soldier which, like discipline, should never leave him, has another admirable effect; it obviates the incalculable disadvantage of troops engaged in action leaving their ranks for the purpose of carrying off the wounded,

---

charge of General Lugard's field force during the operations for the suppression of the Indian Mutiny in 1857-58, mentions that on more occasions than one it occurred that the numbers helpless from sickness or wounds were larger than the regular means of transport could accommodate. To have left the sick and wounded behind would have been to have doomed them to atrocities too horrible to contemplate, yet a continuance of the advance through the rebellious districts was imperative. Under these circumstances every available kind of conveyance was occupied, a strong escort of cavalry obtained, and a rapid retreat made to the nearest existing general field hospital. The patients having been safely deposited in this asylum, and the escort having returned, the main body was enabled to continue its advance. (Army Hygiene, by C. A. Gordon, C.B., p. 217.)

Certainly, good soldiers have no other motive in leaving their ranks for this purpose than sympathy for a suffering comrade. But on the other hand, all know that on a field of battle there are at times men of a different description, who either seek rest or refreshment, or are as desirous of placing themselves, as their comrades, in a place of safety, and four or five such men may be seen assisting to the rear a man for whom one attendant would be sufficient. Nothing is so likely to ensure a reverse in action as the want of confidence caused by men leaving their ranks to carry away the wounded. This is most practised at the time when it is most prejudicial and at places where the enemy has caused the most casualties, when every available man should be present and ready to fill up broken lines and assist, by his concurrence and example, in resisting or attacking the enemy." *

Chap. I.

The progress of a campaign may even be affected by the presence or absence of the necessary amount of transport for the wounded, especially if the engagement be on a large scale, for important strategical advantages which would probably be attained by a rapid onward movement may be lost if the means of speedily disencumbering the force of its wounded are inadequate. The absence of sufficient ambulance transport must necessitate delay while the wounded are being sent to a place of safety in the rear or otherwise disposed of. It would be an outrage on humanity to leave the wounded behind on the field without the requisite professional care and means of surgical treatment, and without the necessary protection against attack; and it is not likely that an army advancing upon an enemy could spare this aid from its ranks and move on, consistently with a due regard to its own safety and requirements.

Influence upon the progress of a campaign.

It is equally important that the transport service from the field hospitals to the general hospitals in the rear of an army should be accomplished with due skill, judgment, and regularity. The best methods to be adopted for diminishing the pain and injurious consequences which result from badly contrived vehicles, careless attendants, and ill-trained drivers, is a subject deservedly worthy of earnest consideration for the sake of the sick and wounded; but a still more serious matter is the extent to which the general welfare of a military expedition is involved in the division of the hospital transport duties. The establishment necessary for this service is a source of general evil or general good in proportion to the manner in which it is organized and conducted. An ignorant, undisciplined personnel and unsuitable conveyances obstruct the progress of a campaign and act as a constant drain on the resources of the army; while a well-organized personnel and a good system of ambulance transport are calculated to clear the way for active movements

Transport from the field hospitals to hospitals in rear.

Influence of this service on the progress of a campaign

---

* Extracted from Appendix 28 to the Report (1867) of the Committee on the Administration of the Transport and Supply Departments of the Army, pp. 469, 470.

CHAP. I.

Transport of sick from standing camps.

Consequences of the accumulation of sick in standing camps.

Consequences of crowding the general hospitals in rear.

Illustrations of the evils

by ridding it of incumbrances, as well as to minister to its strength by rapidly restoring to its ranks the men who had been only temporarily disabled for duty in them.

In Standing Camps the want of an adequate amount of transport for ambulance purposes usually becomes the cause of inordinate demands upon the commissariat or means of transport required for other services. If these demands cannot be complied with, and the sick cannot be conveyed with regularity, they must necessarily accumulate in the camp hospitals, and, in order that they may be treated so as to afford a reasonable prospect of being restored to health and efficiency in the ranks, in the same proportion as they accumulate, the demand on other departments must be proportionately increased for tents, medical comforts, hospital stores, &c. If such an accumulation of sick should occur at an inclement season of the year, or on an unhealthy site, then the restoration of the sick to a condition of strength to fit them for duty will be rendered very problematical, although the increased necessities of the field hospital establishments as regards stores and supplies may be fully met.

An adequate amount of ambulance transport is not only necessary to prevent the evils on the line of march of an army, on the field of action, and in camps, which have been just mentioned, but also to obviate those which spring from the accumulation of wounded men at the depôts and in the buildings occupied as hospitals in its rear. The ill effects of collecting large numbers of soldiers with suppurating wounds in one locality, **the** development and spread of infectious diseases, the depressing moral influences, the increased mortality, were long since sufficiently demonstrated in numerous instances during the Peninsular campaigns, and have been strongly remarked upon by all the eminent British surgeons who have recorded the surgical experience which was gained in the wars of that period. Almost all the great battles in which the troops of Napoleon were engaged furnished illustrations of these results. The first Baron Larrey, in his memoirs, sufficiently shows that he fully appreciated the necessity of not leaving large numbers of wounded soldiers in one place when it could be avoided, and it was only the absence of sufficient means of transport which prevented him from dispersing them. The mortality at one time in the general hospital at Scutari, the spread of pyæmia and hospital gangrene in the French general hospitals at Constantinople, and of typhus in the French field hospitals during the latter part of the campaign in the Crimea, demonstrated still further the evil effects of crowding together masses of sick and wounded men. Acting upon this experience, the present Baron Larrey, when surgeon-in-chief of the French army in Italy in 1859, took especial pains to scatter the sick and wounded in small collections as widely apart as the means of transport at his disposal would permit.

These ill effects have fortunately been much lessened by the introduction of railways, and the increased facilities of communication of later years, and, as a consequence, the terrors alluded to hardly exist at the present time. Sick and wounded who are not likely to be able to serve any more during a campaign are sent away to their own homes as soon as it is possible to remove them.

The necessity for ambulance transport with an army being provided in sufficient proportion for its wants, under the several circumstances which have just been noted, may be best established, perhaps, by illustrations of the effects of the insufficient supply which has occurred. It would be easy enough to note numerous instances of the sufferings and losses of armies in the latter part of the last and beginning of the present century from the same cause; but it is more instructive to refer to examples which have taken place, for the systematic transport of the sick and wounded has only lately been a subject to which particular attention has been generally given.

The consequences of the absence of proper means of transport for sick and wounded *on the march* and *on the field of action* were made manifest in the early period of the Crimean war, notwithstanding the close proximity of a large fleet and comparatively easy communication with it; and in the Italian campaign of 1859, and in some of the battles of the American War, the results of deficiencies of a similar kind have been exhibited in startling relief. In the year 1855 a report on the state of the hospitals of the British army in the Crimea was presented to Parliament by command of Her Majesty. This report was based upon inquiries made from commanding officers and surgeons on the spot by commissioners despatched from England. Sir John Hall, the principal medical officer with the army, informed the commissioners that he had made requisition for 42 wagons for conveyance of stores and wounded men, **336** stretcher bearers, and 672 men, but that only three wagons **were** embarked, and that these had no horses, harness, **or** drivers.* And the commissioners were led to report that they had reason to fear that men were lost in consequence of the want of means for carrying those who fell ill on the march.

After the first action which caused any considerable number of wounded, viz., the battle of the Alma, the evil results of the absence of the necessary means for quickly carrying the wounded from the field of action to the ambulances, and from these again, after the first dressing of their wounds, to the vessels in which they were to be conveyed to the principal general hospital at Scutari, were again particularly experienced. "The want of "the ambulance wagons," say the commissioners, "was much "felt on this occasion, and we believe that great delay in "collecting the wounded and dressing their wounds was the "consequence." †

---

* Report **upon the** State of the Hospitals in the Crimea and Scutari, 1855, p. 339.
† Report, supra cit., p. 4.

CHAP. I.

Deficiency of ambulance transport in the Crimea.

The Director-General, in his surgical history of the Crimean campaign*, has also recorded the disastrous effects which resulted from deficiency of ambulance transport in the following words:—

"Of these (peculiarities of the Crimean war) the first felt was the deficiency of conveyance for wounded, and for the transport of hospital stores during the early part of the campaign. It is now pretty generally known that the army landed at Old Fort with no other hospital transport or ambulance than one pack pony per regiment, for the conveyance of what are called the field panniers, small basket-work cases, intended to contain the surgeon's instruments, a few of the most requisite dressings and appliances, and a few medicines most likely to be needed on an emergency, the whole being limited by the weight-carrying powers of the sorry animal generally furnished for this duty. To this were added ten canvas stretchers per regiment for the conveyance of sick or wounded men on the shoulders of their comrades. For all other means of transport, whether of wounded, of instruments, of medical comforts, or surgical appliances, the army was left entirely dependent upon the resources of the country. These, it is now a matter of history, failed to supply what was needed, and consequently after the first general action on the banks of the Alma, the want of ambulance conveyance or of any description of vehicle suited for the transport of the wounded men was severely felt, and had it not been for the assistance afforded by the sailors of the fleet, and the loan of a portion of the ambulance material of our French allies, the British army must either have remained several days longer than it did on the field of battle, or have left a large rear guard to protect the wounded."

The action on the Alma was fought on the 20th September, and, according to the report of the principal medical officer of the army, it was not until the evening of the 22nd that all the wounded were dressed and sent on board ship.

Want of ambulance transport after the battle of Solferino.

This battle and those which occurred in that war were not to be compared, in the number of their wounded, with the battle of Solferino on the 24th of June, 1859. At Solferino 300,000 men stood opposed to each other, the line of battle was five leagues in extent, and the fighting continued for more than 15 hours. The regulated numbers of ambulance conveyances were in the field on this occasion, but neither they nor the attendants whose duty it was to pick up and remove the wounded were in numbers at all adequate to meet the wants of the enormous masses of wounded who lay scattered over that extensive field of action. The fearful suffering from thirst, from want of surgical attention, from the direct results of a large proportion of the wounded being unremoved from the places where they fell until many hours had elapsed after the receipt of their injuries, and the evils which resulted from the blocking up of the temporary hospitals near the field from the absence of the means of

---

* Director-General's Surgical History of Crimean Campaign, Part II., p. 253.

transporting them to a more distant hospital, have been fully described in a work entitled "Un Souvenir de Solferino," by M. Dunant, a Swiss traveller, who happened to be in the neighbourhood of the scene of action, and who afterwards assisted in the hospitals.

We learn from official statements emanating from the Ministry of War at Paris, that the total number of infirmiers militaires sent into Italy during the whole period over which the campaign of 1859 extended, from the beginning to the close of the war, was 2,186*. A certain proportion of these would be rendered ineffective by sickness and injuries during the progress of the campaign, and those remaining effective would be distributed, partly with the troops in the field and partly among the numerous small hospitals (more than 200 in number according to Dr. Chenu)† established at the various bases and along the several routes by which the armies in the field operated. It is not possible from such data to estimate the proportion of infirmiers to the total number of troops, nor how many of them were actually available for the removal of, or attendance upon, the sick and wounded, on any given date during the war. But when the strength of the French army in Italy on this occasion is remembered (the French field-states show that on the 24th of June the effective strength of the army in Italy was 118,019 infantry and 10,206 cavalry, in all 128,225 fighting men); when the number of wounded is taken into account (in the three battles of Montebello, Magenta, and Solferino, the total number of French wounded amounted to 12,322, excluding those returned as killed and missing); when the number of wounded Austrians that fell into the hands of the French army as prisoners of war is added to this number; when the large numbers of sick that had become inmates of the French hospitals are also remembered, it is obvious that the provision above mentioned of trained attendants for removing the wounded from the battle field and for ministering to their wants in the hospitals would be quite inadequate to meet the requirements of the army during even the campaign of 1859, comparatively brief as it was, unless largely supplemented by assistance from other quarters. These numbers of sick and wounded, as will be seen later, were greatly exceeded in the Franco-German war, especially in the three days' fighting before Metz, before the battle of Gravelotte. The transport establishment (Corps des Equipages Militaires), large as was the number of vehicles and conductors which were sent into Italy during the war, was also quite inadequate to meet the wants of the sick and wounded. In explanation it is stated, in the official report before named, that the reductions of the personnel during the peace could not be suddenly com-

CHAP. I.

Official report of the number of infirmiers sent to Italy in 1859.

Causes of these deficiencies.

---

* Campagne de l'Empereur Napoléon III. en Italie, 1859. Rédigée au Dépôt de la Guerre d'après les Documents officiels, 3me édit., Paris, 1865, p. 34.
† Rapport au Conseil de Santé des Armées, &c., par J. C. Chenu, Méd. Prin., Paris, 1865, p. 2.

CHAP. I.

pensated, and that the supply was therefore not equal to the demand at the commencement of the campaign;* and, again, when referring to the hospital supplies of means of dressing the wounded, it is stated:—"The privations of certain corps in respect to these things can only be explained by deficiency of transport vehicles, and the necessity for giving preference to the carriage, sometimes of subsistence, sometimes of artillery materials and shot, &c." †

Means of sick transport in the Austrian army in 1859.

The difficulties which resulted from the want of sufficient transport for the sick and wounded in the *Austrian* army were also very great. Professor Parkes, when referring, in a paper published in the Army Medical Reports in 1864, to the spread of hospital gangrene and typhus in the Austrian hospitals during the Italian war of 1859, remarks, on the authority of Dr. Kraus,‡—" After Solferino the influx of sick and wounded augmented still more; at the same time, especially at Verona, two great armies were in the neighbourhood; the police con-**servancy** was bad, and the heat was excessive. As the **railroad to** the Tyrol could not be used for strategical reasons, the sick were sent on the route of Casarsa and Palmanuova to Nabresina: 1,200 sick and wounded daily traversed this road. The railroad, however, from Casarsa to Nabresina broke down, and the men were conveyed on bad country carts, and soon the cattle fell sick, and transport became still more difficult. At Palmanuova Kraus saw 1,300 men, almost all wounded, who had no shelter, and for whom nothing had been prepared; two surgeons only were available for this mass of patients, and there was want of material of all kinds. Only an eyewitness, we are told, could form any conception of the misery of these unhappy men."

Sick transport during the war of the Rebellion in the United States.

We find again that the Americans suffered severely in the early periods of the civil war on account of the deficiency in numbers of the ambulance conveyances and the want of a trained ambulance corps for carrying the wounded off to the field hospitals. It has been sufficiently shown by some official correspondence which has been published that considerable loss of life, aggravation of suffering, and other evils were due to the above-named deficiencies.

• • • •

Surgeon-General Hammond, U.S.A., reports,—" In no battle yet have the wounded men been properly looked after; men under the pretence of carrying them off the field leave the ranks, and seldom return to their proper duties;" and again, just after the battle of Bull's Run, in a letter, dated September 7th, 1862, he writes—" the frightful state of disorder existing

---

* Campagne de l'Empereur Napoleon III. en Italie, 1859.
† Op. cit., p. 34.
‡ "Das Kranken Zerstreuungs-System," von. Felix Kraus, K. K. Ober Stabarzt, Wien, 1861.

"in the arrangements for removing the wounded from the field of battle; the scarcity of ambulances, the want of organisation, the drunkenness and incompetency of the drivers, the total absence of ambulance attendants, are now working their legitimate results." "Up to this date* 600 wounded still remain on the battle field, in consequence of an insufficiency of ambulances and the want of a proper system for regulating their removal in the army of Virginia. Many have died of starvation, many more will die in consequence of exhaustion, and all have endured torments which might have been avoided."

Dr. Agnew, a member of the United States Sanitary Commission, estimated that 500 lives were lost from want of proper transport at the battle of Antietam alone.†

It is well known that the suffering and loss of life which resulted from the want of an efficient ambulance organization in the early part of the war of the Rebellion in the United States, so strongly attracted public attention that the most energetic efforts were made to remedy the defect. In the course of the war the ambulance system of the northern armies became thoroughly organised, and both the material and personnel were established on a footing proportionate to the great demands made on this branch of the military service.

It will here be not out of place to glance at the aid which has been developed to assist the regular ambulance corps in removing the wounded from a battle field, and in the field hospitals, by means of trained volunteers. The fitness for service of volunteer hospital attendants in hospitals remote from the scene of active hostilities is not now alluded to.

Proposed aid by volunteers in removing the wounded from fields of battle and in the field hospitals.

The attention which was attracted by M. Dunant to the great amount of suffering and loss of life resulting from the deficient means of transport for the wounded, and from insufficient hospital care after the battle of Solferino in 1859, led to the formation of a committee at Geneva, which undertook to try and obtain a remedy for the evils described. This committee, which was under the honorary presidency of General Dufour, the Commander-in-Chief of the Swiss army, called together an international conference to consider the subject in all its aspects. This conference took place in October, 1863, and lasted several days. It was finally resolved that the best means to assist the wounded in time of war, so as to meet the case of the regular military establishments being inadequate to the demands on their service, would be to establish in each country a central as well as sectional committees for organizing a system of volunteer aid. All these national committees were to keep up communication with the International Committee at Geneva, and through it to make

Geneva International Conference of 1863.

---

* Amer. Med. Times, Oct. 4th, 1862, p. 193.
† The Battle of Bull's Run, to which this refers, was fought on the 30th August, eight days before the date of this letter.

known to each other their respective proceedings and progress. Each national committee, according to the plan suggested, was to be placed in communication with the Government of the country to which it belonged, and was in time of peace to be occupied in devising improvements in ambulance transport for time of war, as well as in organizing and instructing volunteer hospital and field attendants. In time of war the central committees of the belligerent nations were to furnish assistance according to their means to the armies of their respective countries, and to arrange with the military authorities, for the disposal and distribution of the volunteer assistants to attend on the wounded. They were also to ask aid from the committees established in neutral nations. The volunteer infirmary attendants were to transport the wounded from the field of battle, if called upon to do so, under the direction of the regular military authorities, and to serve in the field hospitals. The necessary maintenance and equipment of these volunteer attendants were arranged to be provided through the agency of the central committees, so as to relieve their respective Governments of all charge in these respects.*

Volunteer associations for aiding wounded soldiers in time of war.

Numerous national associations for assisting wounded soldiers in time of war have been formed in response to the resolutions of the International Conference of 1863. Each of these associations has its own particular set of rules, although, in general principles, they all accord with the conclusions come to at the conference just mentioned.

Questions of volunteer aid in time of war considered.

Objections have not been wanting against the plan of organizing the volunteer aid just described. It has been argued that it is equally questionable how far such a voluntary system is either desirable or practicable, so far as an army in the field is concerned. Desirable,—for may not, it is said, the greatest evils result from the mere facts of removing from the Governments which contract wars the responsibility of providing for the wants of the sick and wounded produced by them? Practicable,—for is there not a reasonable doubt whether any voluntary organization can possess those elements of certainty which are absolutely necessary in order that dependence may be placed upon its assistance in the time of supreme need? and whether, if forthcoming, corps of volunteers, such as have been contemplated, could be incorporated with the military organization of armies, or would submit to the strict rules of discipline enforced in war time so as to carry out their proposed work efficiently?

Again, in campaigning, in what way can any body of men attached to an army provide itself, as proposed, with food, transport, forage, and its other daily wants, excepting through the military administration of that army? Such are the chief arguments and objections that have been urged against the proposals of the Genevese International Committee for affording

---

* See Chapter on the Red Cross.

voluntary aid to wounded in time of war in the field itself, and they are not without importance.

It is an admitted fact that the hospital establishments maintained in time of peace, whether as regards the personnel or the matériel of those hospitals, even though furnished on a liberal scale, must be always inadequate to meet the exigencies of war. If the establishment be very small, the system of arrangement must be one which admits of expansion in any given section without inconvenience to the general working of the whole. Then, on the breaking out of war, additions will be made in each section wherever required, according to necessity. Each increase will be intimately blended with the previously existing nucleus, and the same machinery will continue in operation, only on a larger scale.

But presuming that the additions when required can be obtained, the doubt remains whether there will be then time and opportunity for that training which is so absolutely necessary for men who will have to discharge the delicate and responsible duties of carrying wounded and of hospital attendance upon the sick,—duties which, if executed without knowledge and practice, are fraught with serious dangers to disabled patients, just as they are of benefit to them when performed with skill and intelligence. This is an anxious question, but, after all, it must be acknowledged to be the *duty* of the **Government** of each country that embarks in war to provide for all the necessities which war calls into existence, and for the right execution of this duty the Government is, as it ought to be, generally held responsible. The conferences at Geneva, and the national committees which have been formed, have done and are doing good service to humanity by directing general attention to the wants of the wounded in battles, and of the sick who always accumulate in time of war, as well as by their endeavours to effect improvements in the field hospital conveyances and appliances of all kinds for their benefit. It is also beyond doubt that volunteer surgeons, nurses, and attendants have done invaluable service to sick and wounded collected in hospitals to which they have been removed from the scene of military operations, and also in the field itself; but it is obvious to all who have considered the subject that the **volunteer** system will have to rest on a more assured basis than it at present does before reliance can be placed on it for assistance, so far as its action with an army *on the line of march in a hostile country, or in the hour of battle*, is concerned.

But whether the proposed system of introducing volunteer aid for the wounded in the field in time of war be brought into practical operation or not, there can be no question that by whatever Government a regular army is maintained, whether it be for defensive or offensive purposes, that Government must also provide and keep ready for use some means of transport for sick and wounded. Economy as well as good order demands that a certain amount of this transport shall be maintained in time of peace, so that the best system of transport may

CHAP. I.

Provision of ambulance transport by Government must be maintained.

Its maintenance in time of peace.

Amount of ambulance transport to be maintained.

not merely be theoretically considered, but that the vehicles themselves when devised and constructed may be subjected to the test of experience; desirable improvements effected; conductors practised in their management, and thus difficulties and losses be avoided which would inevitably be created on war breaking out if no such forethought and experiments had been instituted. It is not desirable that the full amount which would be required, or even that proportion which may have been determined to be allotted to individual regiments, in time of war, should be kept up in time of peace; for, not being required for service, such a plan would entail a constant unnecessary loss from disuse and decay, and the establishment would prove an encumbrance as well as an expense. If a certain amount of ambulance transport be maintained in camps of instruction, general hospitals, and garrison towns, where the vehicles can be employed in a manner similar to that in which they would be employed in campaigning, and to a certain extent subjected to similar tests of fitness for their special purposes, the transport vehicles so used will serve for patterns which, on war arising, can be rapidly multiplied to any required number. By such a method economy in expense is maintained, at the same time that due regard for present and future efficiency is not neglected. This is the system which is now ordered, and is to some extent in operation in Great Britain.

Importance of specially studying the best forms for ambulance transport in the British service.

It is especially important that the best forms and kinds of field transport for use in the British military service should be thoroughly tested, so that, as far as possible, all questions connected with the subject may be settled on a satisfactory basis. It is also important that the supply available for use after the need is rendered apparent should be sufficiently ample. No dependence can be placed upon finding means of transport in any country against which British troops are directed; for, from their having to cross the sea, and generally to effect a landing on the shores of a hostile country, all the available transport vehicles there would most probably be removed before the troops arrived at their destination. And even if such casual conveyances were to be obtained, it could scarcely be expected that they would be found to have the special qualities necessary to fit them for carrying sick or wounded men, however suitable they might be in construction for the carriage of ordinary stores. Without possessing such special qualities, or without some means being devised for supplementing the qualities which are deficient, as will be shown hereafter, every vehicle, whatever its kind, must be regarded as a most imperfect and undesirable substitute for a regular ambulance conveyance.

Peculiar description of transport vehicles required for

The insular nature of the kingdom, moreover, prevents an English army from being able to use and carry on with it the ordinary carts and means of conveyance used by the population of its own country, as may be done to a great extent by nations on the Continent when they are at war with each other. Means of transport for the sick and wounded have therefore to be devised which are not only well fitted for their immediate objects, but which, in addition, shall be themselves easily carried on board ship, and rendered available for use immediately that the forces have landed and are in movement, or otherwise serious inconveniences to the troops may be expected to result.

The extent of the outlying dependencies of the empire, and the varieties of climate, involve other subjects for consideration if a kind of transport adapted for general use be sought for; but, as will be remarked hereafter, it is questionable whether any kind of transport available for universal use is attainable.

The subject of the construction of transport vehicles suitable for use in campaigning is involved in many more difficulties than might at first be imagined. It is like many other military matters which are rendered difficult owing almost entirely to circumstances which are inseparable from the organization and movable character of armies. The means for accomplishing almost any mechanical object may be well understood, and easily carried into operation under circumstances which admit of the employment of any appliances, however complicated or varied they may be in their nature; but it is evident that the conditions become altogether changed when the problem to be solved is how to provide for these very requirements under circumstances where the same, or similarly varied and complicated appliances are quite inadmissible, and where, therefore, a system of taking the mean of advantages and disadvantages, of compromise as it were, can alone be resorted to. Yet this is the problem which has to be solved as regards ambulance transport. Let us briefly glance at the principal subjects which have to be taken into account in designing and constructing a suitable field conveyance for wounded men, to whatever class of ambulance transport vehicles it may belong. It is at once evident, on first consideration, that the artificer constructing such a conveyance will require the combined ability of:—

> Firstly. A surgeon acquainted with the requirements of the wounded who are to be carried.
> Secondly. An officer experienced in the circumstances of campaigning as regards stowage, liability to damage, opportunities of repair of the conveyances, &c., the protection and maintenance of the bearers, and the transport animals. And
> Thirdly. A mechanic who shall be capable of appreciating the surgical objects sought for, as well as the military circumstances and limitations already alluded to, and then be skilful enough to construct the conveyance in accordance with them.

All of these must be forthcoming in order to obtain a good field conveyance. I* have placed the skilled judgment of the surgeon first, because it is manifestly the most essential. How-

---
* The Author.

Chap. I.

British military service.

Ambulance transport in the British Colonies and in India.

The problem of properly constructing ambulance transport vehicles a very difficult one.

Subjects to be taken into account in designing and constructing an ambulance transport conveyance.

CHAP. I.

Surgical and military exigencies must be mutually subordinate.

ever ingeniously a transport vehicle may be contrived, and however well adapted to meet the military exigencies of field service, if, after all, it be unsuitable for the support and carriage of a sick or wounded man, it is useless so far as regards the purpose which it was designed to fulfil. But still even the surgical exigencies cannot be permitted to overrule the military, any more than they can the mechanical limitations; and the practical army surgeon will never fail, therefore, to consider the whole together when weighing the merits of any contrivance for the carriage of sick or wounded in time of war which may be submitted to his professional judgment.

The surgeon's province in the construction of an ambulance conveyance. The mechanic's part in its construction.

The surgeon's part in this combined work is by no means a simple one; on the contrary, for the reasons named as soon as he enters upon the undertaking he finds it beset with obstacles. Just as the mechanic is restrained by the requirements of the surgeon and the combatant, so the surgeon is restrained by those of the mechanic and combatant also. **He must consult** the ability of the mechanic to fashion **the conveyance according to** his wishes; he must respect, just as much **as the mechanic, the** limits of bulk and weight prescribed by military arrangements; the necessity for contrivances to ensure portability of the conveyance itself on board ship; for unity and simplicity, so that parts may not be separated or lost; for strength, in order to resist the shocks and accidents it will be liable to meet with in campaigning, and other necessities of a similar nature. At the same time he must devise, in one and the same conveyance, fitness for the reception and transport of soldiers labouring under injuries differing greatly in their nature, and almost equally different as regards their requirements for proper support, and for the precautions necessary to guard against the ill effects of motion during the act of transportation.

A sick-transport vehicle perfectly free from objections unattainable.

It is not possible to comply thoroughly with all these demands by any one contrivance. The mode of carriage which will be best adapted for one set of injuries during transport, will be in some respects more objectionable than some other arrangements as regards another set of injuries. The mechanical contrivances to enable the conveyance to be folded up, to be separated into several parts, or otherwise to be adapted for occupying diminished space when stowed away on board ship, will to a certain extent interfere with its strength and simplicity. Hence the surgeon must content himself with trying to obtain a mode of transport which shall meet the greatest number of wants, and, at the same time, offer the least number of objections. A sick-transport conveyance may be likened to the soldier's knapsack. Under any circumstances the knapsack must be an incumbrance; but, as military exigencies determine it to be a necessary one, the object in respect to finding a good knapsack is to seek for such an one as shall least injuriously affect the soldier's strength and health. So in regard to an ambulance conveyance, however it may be contrived, the removal of wounded in it over ground which is usually rough and uneven, must always be attended with a certain amount of pain and of other objectionable circumstances; and the object, therefore, should be not to strain after the total removal of these, which is unattainable, but to seek for that kind of transport which shall answer the purpose of conveying the greatest number of wounded in the shortest space of time to a place of shelter, or post appointed for surgical aid, at the same time that it reduces the risk of increasing the injuries of those carried by it, whatever their nature, to the lowest limits. This is the course the practical field surgeon will endeavour to follow in devising the various forms of ambulance transport.

Indeed, the idea that these objects can be attained by any one kind of transport has been almost universally abandoned. In European warfare, at least, it is not advisable to employ the same kind of conveyance for short distances as for long distances. On the field of action itself, and along made roads, a certain limited number of varieties of conveyance, designed for the purpose of meeting these several conditions, are now authorised for use in the British service, and are generally employed in all armies. Certain forms of hand conveyances, of conveyances carried on the backs of animals, and of wheeled transport vehicles drawn by animals, form portions of the ambulance equipment of nearly all civilised armies.

No single form of conveyance can be adapted to meet all the wants of field service.

In the preceding remarks a sketch has been given of the considerations which are demanded from the surgeon who attempts himself to devise ambulance conveyances, or who is called upon to give advice in respect to their construction. Before concluding this chapter, I * will say a few words as to the knowledge of the subject which is required from the surgeon whose duty it becomes to superintend the use of ambulance conveyances on actual service or who happens to be placed in charge of the sick transport.

A field surgeon's duties as regards ambulance conveyances.

A good field surgeon will not permit himself to remain contented with knowing merely the principles on which the particular vehicles for transport which are placed under his charge are constructed, but he will also make himself acquainted with the details of their construction, and the purposes of each portion. Although it is not his province to assist in carrying a wounded man under ordinary circumstances, he should be capable of practically showing the use and application of every part of the conveyance which is used, and, if necessary, of demonstrating to the bearers the purposes of each part, should they fail to understand these by description. In a moment, without such precise supervision and direction, a set of careless bearers, in lifting a stretcher with a wounded man upon it into the carriage which is designed to receive it, may convert an injury of a comparatively simple nature into one which places the life of the patient in great jeopardy.

He should understand their construction as well as their general principles.

It is to the surgeon that the wounded officers and soldiers,

Responsibility of the surgeon

---

* Author.

CHAP. I.

who is placed in charge of wounded during their transport.

as well as the bearers who are to carry or otherwise transport them to the place where their wounds can be treated, must look for direction and instruction in regard to every minute circumstance of the transport. The position of the wounded man or of an injured limb, the mode of progression of the bearers, the steps to be taken in case of the occurrence of a variety of accidents to which each particular kind of injury may be specially liable, are to be determined and prescribed by the surgeon. At a moment which to the patient is one of alarm, suffering, and anxiety, the surgeon should be self-possessed and unfailing in decision, and these qualities can only result from previous study and thorough acquaintance with the duties and responsibilities he has in hand. To be cool and determined under such circumstances, he must feel that he is thoroughly acquainted with the mechanical qualities and proper use of the conveyance by which the wounded man is conveyed, and by what arrangements the inconveniences connected with the conveyance itself may be diminished. He must be acquainted with the evils attending untrained or careless carriage (and here not merely the torture, sometimes almost intolerable, of the wounded man is referred to, but the ulterior ills which bad transportation is liable to produce), and be ready at once to give the necessary directions to obviate them, should he perceive a necessity for doing so.

No single point in the mode of carrying a wounded man unimportant.

No single point that has relation to the manner in which a wounded man is carried from the field should be regarded as trifling; nothing is trifling if regard be had to future as well as to immediate results. And, in addition to the direct benefits resulting from the application of this knowledge and experience, there will be also this important indirect advantage,—the wounded as well as the bearers will not fail to observe the surgeon's calmness and decision; will not fail to be impressed by this result of superior knowledge, and will in proportion have confidence in the propriety of his directions.

A thorough and practical knowledge of ambulance transport can, of course, only be regarded as a portion of the duty of medical officers, but at the same time a very important one. The late General Jonathan Letterman of the Medical Service of the United States, who organised the medical department of the army of the Potomac, wrote—" A corps of " medical officers was not established solely for the purpose of " attending the wounded and sick; the proper treatment of " these sufferers is certainly a matter of very great importance, " and an imperative duty, but the duties of medical officers " cover a more extended field. The leading idea which should " be constantly kept in view is to strengthen the hands of the " Commanding General by keeping his army in the most " vigorous health, thus rendering it, in the highest degree, " efficient for enduring fatigue, and privation, and for fighting. " In this view the duties of such a corps are of vital import-" ance to the success of an army, and commanders seldom " appreciate the full effect of their proper fulfilment. Medical

"officers should possess a thorough knowledge of the powers
"and capabilities of the human system; the effects of food,
"raiment, and climate, with all its multiplied vicissitudes; the
"influences for evil which surround an army, and the means
"necessary to combat them successfully . . . . When
"medical officers consider this subject, all their high, special,
"and important duties will naturally occur to them."

CHAPTER II.

HISTORY OF THE MODERN ORGANIZATION OF THE MEDICAL SERVICES OF THE PRINCIPAL EUROPEAN ARMIES, WITH SPECIAL REFERENCE TO THE TRANSPORT OF SICK AND WOUNDED.

CHAP. II.

In taking a retrospective glance at the history of the modern system of transport of sick and wounded soldiers of European armies in the field, and more particularly the successive improvements which have been made in this branch of service in the British army, it necessarily happens that both the personnel and the material employed in the performance of the duties referred to are brought together into notice. Not only the conveyances employed in the transport, but also the arrangements made for carrying the wounded to them and for safely conducting their subsequent removal, have to be considered. The two divisions, the personnel and the material, on which the transport of the sick depends, are, in fact, so intimately associated that it is scarcely possible to review the one without marking the progress of the other. A good organization of the corps to which the administration and conduct of the sick-transport system is confided, thorough acquaintance on the part of the men of the corps with their duties, a conscientious discharge of them, perfect discipline and subordination, activity, bravery, and other soldierly qualities, are even more essential for accomplishing successfully and satisfactorily this very important branch of service in the field than the provision of the right kinds of carriage for effecting the transport itself. The rise and progressive improvements of the personnel and material used for ambulance transport are therefore glanced at together in the remarks which follow.

SECTION I.—ACCOUNT OF LARREY'S AND PERCY'S AMBULANCE SYSTEMS.

Barons Percy and Larrey founders of the modern system of ambulance transport.

It is not necessary to give a history of the particular systems of transport and ambulance arrangements adopted by the several leading powers of Europe, but two eminent French army surgeons, Barons Percy and Larrey, are so conspicuous as the originators of the modern plan, which prevails in all armies, of removing wounded soldiers from the field of battle by trained attendants in conveyances specially designed for their transport, that it is impossible, consistently with the objects of this chapter, to avoid giving a short history of the systems which they introduced. The circumstances of the revolutionary period in which these surgeons lived, the disruption of established systems and ideas which took place at that time, the scope consequently afforded for setting forth fresh views and inaugurating new methods of action, together with the remarkable series of warlike operations in which their country was constantly engaged, sufficiently explain how it happened that the personal energy and character for enterprise which distinguished Barons Larrey and Percy came to be directed into the channels of invention with which their names are now so intimately associated. The improvements which they effected in the French service have attracted more notice among English surgeons than the systems adopted by other European powers for effecting the same objects, owing to the frequency with which French and English armies were opposed to each other in the field on the continent of Europe subsequently to the period of the French Revolution. It seems not improbable also that the observations which were made during the Peninsular campaigns have ever since had an influence on the views which have been held by English surgeons in reference to the subject of transport of wounded in time of war. Each of the eminent surgeons just named originated a separate special feature in ambulance organization. On the one hand, it was Baron Larrey who first introduced the use of light ambulance conveyances specially fitted for following the movements of the advanced guard of an army, and so constructed as to be capable of rapidly transporting the wounded from the place of fighting, as soon as the first dressings have been applied, to the hospitals in rear of the scene of conflict. On the other hand, it was Baron Percy who first introduced into any army a regularly trained corps of field litter-bearers, soldiers regularly formed and equipped for the duty of picking up the wounded during the progress of an action, and of carrying them on stretchers to the place where the means of surgical aid are provided.

Notwithstanding that the introduction of fire-arms had caused the occurrence of fractures of bones and of extensive mutilations with so much greater frequency than they had been met with when wounds were chiefly made with such weapons as swords, spears, and arrows; notwithstanding that these injuries, from their nature, had rendered the wounded much less able to assist themselves and less capable of being readily assisted by others; yet no fresh system had been introduced for the transport of these helpless men from the scene of action until the period of Larrey's innovation. Either their comrades assisted them from the field, carrying them in the best way they could on their backs, in sashes, great-coats, or on extemporised stretchers during the action, or they remained unaided where they fell till the fighting was over, when they were

CHAP. II.

The influence of the improvements effected by these surgeons.

The ambulance conveyances of Baron Larrey

The litter-bearers of Baron Percy.

The introduction of fire-arms necessitated a more efficient system of transporting the wounded of armies.

CHAP. II.

Origin of Larrey's improvements in ambulance arrangements.

carried to the field hospitals which were stationed at a distance in the rear.

The introduction of Baron Larrey's system of flying ambulances preceded that of Baron Percy's system of trained stretcher-carriers. It was in September, 1792, when Larrey was serving as an aide-surgeon-major in the French army of the Rhine, under General Custine, that, he tells us, he first conceived the idea of a new system of ambulance arrangements for active service in the field. In December of the same year he made a formal proposition through the proper channel to General Custine for the establishment of a field hospital capable of active service in *front* with the advanced troops of his army, so that the ordinary field hospitals, and the heavy hospital carts employed with them, all of which were stationed at a considerable distance in *rear* of the army, might no longer constitute the first line of surgical assistance. The requisite authority was given, and Larrey at once was ordered to organise his proposed ambulance. Larrey has himself recorded in a few words the state of the field hospitals and ambulance transport at that time, and the views which led him to effect the change mentioned. "At the time I proposed my "plan," Larrey writes, "the military regulations ordered that

Regulations of the French service for transport of the wounded previous to Larrey's invention of "ambulances volantes"

"the ambulances (movable field hospitals) should constantly "be posted at one league distant from the army. The custom "was to leave the wounded on the field of battle until after "the combat, and then to gather them together in a favour-"able place to which the movable hospital establishment was "brought as quickly as possible; but the quantity of military "carriages which were placed between the ambulance and the "army, and other difficulties, retarded its movement to such "a point that it never reached the place in less than twenty-"four hours, so that some of the wounded perished from want "of assistance. The capture of Spires having given us a rather "large number of wounded, I had the distress of seeing several "die, victims of this inconvenient arrangement; and this gave "me the idea of establishing a new system of ambulance for "carrying prompt aid to them on the field of battle itself.

Larrey's voitures d'ambulance volante.

"My proposition was accepted, and I was authorised to "organise this movable field hospital, which I named the flying "ambulance (*ambulance volante*). I then conceived the idea of "a system of carriages (*voitures d'ambulance*) suspended on "springs, which should combine solidity with speed and light-"ness. This institution created a sensation among the soldiers, 'and they now felt confident that they would receive succour 'at whatever moment they might be wounded." *

Larrey was not able to complete the entire organisation of his ambulance system at that time; but, imperfect as it was, the prompt relief which the surgeons were enabled to afford to the wounded by their presence in the immediate neighbourhood

---

* Mém. de Chirurgie Mil., par Baron Larrey Tome i., p. 64

of the scene of conflict, and the services which were rendered by the light ambulance vehicles in rapidly carrying them away to the hospitals, were considered to be most important, not only by the troops, but also by the General in command. In consequence, Larrey was sent to Paris to organise similar flying ambulances for the other armies of the Republic which were then in the field. Various other employments, however, arose to occupy the time of this distinguished surgeon after his arrival in Paris, so that it was not till 1797 that he was able to give his attention again to the subject. In the spring of that year, while engaged as Professor of Anatomy at the Military Hospital of Instruction of the Val de Grâce, he received orders from the Minister of War, at the demand of General Buonaparte, to proceed to Italy to form and direct a system of flying ambulance for the army in that country, like that which he had established with the army of the Rhine in 1793. It was on this occasion that he perfected the organisation of his ambulance system, not only in respect to the vehicles for transporting the wounded, but also by the formation of an ambulance corps organised for rapidly carrying surgical aid to the wounded in all parts of the field of action.

Larrey's ambulance establishment was now composed of three divisions. Each division comprised 12 spring vehicles for the transport of severely wounded men, four store wagons, and a personnel of 113 officers, non-commissioned officers, and soldiers, under the command of a surgeon-major of the first class; the whole being under the direction of the principal medical officer in the field. Fourteen surgeons of different grades, all mounted; a lieutenant and sub-lieutenant for maintaining order and discipline; paymaster; quartermaster and clerks; 12 mounted ambulance orderlies and 25 orderlies on foot, with their proportion of non-commissioned officers, and 25 conductors and others for the service of the vehicles and horses, constituted the personnel of each division. A trumpeter among the mounted soldiers, and a drummer among the infantry ambulance men, acted also as carriers of surgical instruments. The officers and men of the ambulance wore special uniforms, which not only distinguished their different classes of occupation and grades among themselves, but also served to indicate the common service in which they were all engaged. The distinctions were generally made by means which had the additional advantages of serving some useful purpose in the duties for which they were specially organised. Thus the uniform of the ambulance surgeons differed from that of the army surgeons generally by the addition of a shoulder belt and pouch, the latter containing some portable instruments and some few objects essential for the first relief of wounded on the field of battle. Both the mounted and foot orderlies carried a red woollen waist-scarf, which in case of need would serve to carry a wounded man; the foot orderlies carried a leathern knapsack, divided into compartments (sac d'ambulance), and containing the materials for dressings. So also, **fixed** to each saddle of the mounted officers and orderlies, was a leathern valise, arranged to be opened without detaching the straps by which it was fastened, and destined to contain also apparatus and materials necessary for dressing wounds.

The 12 spring conveyances for the wounded were of two sorts. Eight were two-wheeled vehicles drawn by two horses, and arranged for carrying two men at full length; and four were four-wheeled, destined to carry four men lying down. The 12 carriages were capable of removing 32 men at one time. These vehicles will be again referred to in the chapter on wheeled ambulance transport.

Larrey's system combined two principles; one that of a light field hospital the other, that of a field conveyance corps.

From the description given it will be seen that Larrey's ambulance volante, when completed, combined two principles; the first being a flying field hospital organised for affording instant attention, and allowing the application of the first dressings to the wounded on the field of action itself, the second an arrangement for rapid transport to the field hospitals of the first line by means of specially adapted vehicles, with trained conductors. The conveyances were so constructed, and the personnel so constituted, that the whole was capable of following the movements even of an advanced force, however rapidly the movements of that force might be made. Each division, moreover, was capable of being sub-divided, and sent into a dozen directions, thus affording aid over a wide area; for each medical officer, being mounted, could take one of the spring vehicles and a mounted orderly with him, and thus ensure both the presence of all that was necessary for administering the necessary surgical attention, and arranging the means of subsequent transport to the rear, for two or more wounded men. A special code of regulations determined the order of march when the ambulances were moving with the army, the internal economy of the corps, and the functions of each individual belonging to it. The ambulance orderlies were daily exercised in their duties, so as to be expert and dexterous in giving the assistance to the surgeons which was required from them when assisting the wounded.

Shortly after the establishment of this corps in Italy peace was made with Austria, and Larrey was then chosen to accompany Buonaparte to Egypt and Syria.

Percy's system different from Larrey's.

While Larrey was absent in Egypt another system of ambulance carriages, differing entirely in their principles and objects from those of Larrey's system, was organised in another army of France. This army was known as the Army of the North; it was under the command of General Moreau, and Percy was the chief medical officer.

Baron Percy's movable ambulance.

It was in the year 1799 when this distinguished surgeon,[*] under the auspices of the general commanding, devised a light kind of conveyance capable of rapid movement from place to place, and carrying with it all the requisites of a field ambulance,

---

[*] Histoire de Percy, par Laurent, p. 161, &c.

including hand-litters, surgical dressings and apparatus, surgeons and hospital attendants. This conveyance consisted of a long carriage on four wheels, built in many respects like the carriages of light artillery, and was drawn by six horses. It was commonly known by the name of a "wurtz,"* after the German wagon, to which it bore a general resemblance, and is still referred to by this name; but at the time of its use it was also sometimes spoken of as a "char de chirurgie," or surgical cart. Along the body of each of these carriages was a long narrow case containing surgical materials, and of such a form externally that eight persons could sit astride on it. This was intended to carry eight surgeons of different grades. In front and rear of the carriage were two smaller chests, and on these, four *infirmiers militaires*, or hospital corps men, sat, two on each box; while four other attendants sat on the four leading horses. Eight surgeons and eight attendants were thus carried, as well as a driver; and, further, the chests on the "wurtz" contained dressings calculated for 1,200 wounded. Supplies of stretchers were carried under the long case on the body of the wagon.

CHAP. II.
The peculiar construction of Percy's ambulance vehicles.

In the language of M. Percy, the intention of this carriage was that by its means "the art of preserving life should contest in activity and celerity with the art of destroying life." It was to obviate the necessity of soldiers leaving the ranks to attend on the wounded, because it was prepared for distributing assistance at all points on the field of battle.

The objects of Percy's ambulance system.

Its mode of **action was** the following:—Each *wurtz* was to keep up as **close as** possible with the division to which it belonged. As soon as the action began, and some of the soldiers were wounded, the attendants took their stretchers, ran and picked up the fallen men even though still under fire, and brought them to the *wurtz*. The surgeons then applied the first dressings, assisted by some of the other attendants. If from changes in the movements of the combatants, the wounded become numerous at other parts of the field, too distant for their rapid removal on the stretchers then the *wurtz* itself was despatched to their assistance, and the same **plan** of aid repeated as far as its capabilities admitted.

Its mode of operation in the field.

Each division of the Army of the North in the year 1800 had its movable corps of surgical assistance of this kind, and there was a reserve of the same establishments at the head quarters. This institution **seems to have** well answered **its** intended purpose at **the time it was** employed, **and to** have given great satisfaction **to** the officers and troops. **It was** spoken of with praise by general officers on several occasions. In April 1800, General Lecombe published a general order and reported to the General Commanding-in-Chief. **"We all give** a **tribute of**

---

* The word spelt in French writings "wurtz," is spelt "wurst" in its original German. When used alone in the German language it signifies a thick and short sausage, a cylinder, but when joined to the word "wagen" signifies a long wagon somewhat similar to it in form, an omnibus. The French word is therefore an abbreviation as well as corruption of the German "wurst-wagen."

CHAP. II.

"praise to this new institution created by Citizen Percy—the movable corps of surgical aid. The medical officers of these corps have succoured the wounded on the field of battle itself, and have so distinguished themselves by their zeal and devotion that the soldier reverences them, and consoles himself when he is wounded, because he sees that assistance is given to him with a rapidity hitherto without example."

Distinguishing features of Percy's ambulance system.

From the description thus given it will be seen that the ambulance carriage of Baron Percy did not supply transport for the wounded,* beyond the conveyance on stretchers from the places where they fell to the place where the wurtz was stationed, and where their wounds could be dressed. It was solely a flying hospital, or means of affording speedy attention to the wounded, but not intended for removing them to the rear.

The wounded after being dressed at the wurtz would have to remain grouped on the ground around it until other steps were taken for their removal. It was thus constructed on principles altogether different from the light transport carriages used in the ambulance volante of Baron Larrey. As before described, Larrey's ambulance vehicles were accompanied by the means of affording the necessary first dressings and surgical assistance, but were themselves built only for the purpose of quickly carrying the wounded away from the scene of conflict, so that they might not be **left** long on **the** field of action, or be liable to fall into the hands of an enemy.

Comparison between Percy's and Larrey's ambulance systems.

In Percy's system the quickness of movement of the medical officers and attendants, and the certainty of their having at hand what they required for professional use, were provided for by their being carried on the same conveyance that carried the surgical appliances and dressings; in Larrey's system the same object was attained by the officers and attendants being mounted on horseback, and by their carrying on their own persons, or on their horses, the necessary surgical appliances and materials. One obvious disadvantage in Percy's system was that a casual shot or other accident which disabled one carriage would place out of active service for the time, at least for such service as could not be accomplished on foot, sixteen officers and orderlies; while, by Larrey's system, **the** effects of

---

* Sir George Ballingall has described the ambulance of Baron Percy as a "four wheeled carriage of a very simple construction, consisting chiefly of a sort of ridge-pole raised upon the framework of the carriage, upon which *the wounded are placed astride* as if on horseback, and here they sit protected by a sort of canopy."[1] This curious error as to the intended use of the carriage has probably arisen from the surgeons, who are represented in the drawing of the vehicle at the end of the first volume of Larrey's memoirs as sitting upon the *wurtz*, having been mistaken for soldiers. A consideration of the drawing is sufficient to show how entirely unsuited the position would be for wounded men, and a full account of the objects the carriage was intended by its inventor to fulfil may be found in the life of Percy, by Laurent, already quoted.

---

[1] "Outlines of Military Surgery." Edinburgh, 1838, p. 91.

a similar accident would be limited to disabling the means of carrying a few wounded, or else to disabling an individual officer or orderly. It is evident that Percy took his idea of it from observation of the artillery carriages; and, as these were constructed to carry not only guns and ammunition, but also the men who were to use them, so, in like manner, Percy not only made his carriages to carry the materials of surgical practice, but the officers and men also who were to employ these materials in use.

The *surgical conveyances* of Percy fell into disuse after peace was declared and the Army of the North was broken up, the **support** and influence of the general officers under whose **direction** they had been employed was then lost, and they were never again resorted to. His institution of field attendants for carrying the wounded on stretchers from the places where they fell to the surgical carts was also discontinued at the same time, and when peace was once more at an end, and war again declared, the custom of the wounded being carried to the rear by their comrades in any available way again came into use. The "soldats d'ambulance" of that period only served in the hospitals. Subsequently, when Percy was with the French army in Spain, he again turned his attention to providing a special field corps of stretcher-carriers for removing the wounded from the scene of action. He no longer advocated the use of it, no doubt from the system of the "ambulance volantes" of Baron Larrey having been found so much more generally efficient for field hospital purposes in the armies in which it had been employed (for Larrey's system continued in use until the time of the Restoration); but Percy now confined himself to forming, equipping, and training a corps of foot soldiers, whose particular duty was to pick up the wounded on the field, and to carry them to the field hospitals on stretchers, and afterwards to assist the surgeons in attending upon them. This was the commencement of an institution which has continued to the present time; indeed, a combination of this institution with the use of light spring ambulance carriages similar to those first introduced in the **ambulance** system of Larrey, though variously modified, **essentially constitutes the** plan on **which the** ambulance arrangements of all modern civilised armies are now organised.

The principles on which Baron Percy, who was then Surgeon-in-chief of a Corps d'Armée, founded and organised his trained corps of bearers, and the circumstances by which his attention was first turned to the subject, are briefly related by himself. He remarks on the necessity for the men of the corps being skilful and practised in their duties, and these remarks are equally applicable to the men composing the army hospital corps instituted for service in our own or any other army.* "Tired of the ceaseless disorder," writes Percy,

---

* Laurent, Vie de Percy, Part II., p. **391**.

"caused by assemblage of undisciplined hospital attendants; distressed at seeing the deaths on the field of battle of so great a number of soldiers whose lives might have been preserved and limbs saved if they had had the help of a commodious and well-organised mode of transport; having seen, moreover, the necessity of having as near as possible to the line of battle men specially destined to carry off the wounded instead of leaving them to the care of soldiers who too often seized this opportunity for leaving the ranks; I took upon myself to organise a regular corps of army hospital attendants (soldats infirmiers) to whom I gave the name of Companies of Brancardiers (bearers of stretchers).

"I selected a hundred soldiers from among the bravest, strongest, and most adroit, and, as soon as they were completely equipped, put them on duty. The service of the sick and wounded, so neglected and abandoned before, soon changed its appearance."

Character of men to be selected as bearers for ambulance purposes.

"Companies of ambulance bearers," again says Percy, "must be composed of chosen men, uniting in their characters courage, strength, and address. A certain skill is necessary for raising a wounded man, for placing him upon a stretcher, and for carrying him; it is not so much by strength as by address that these objects are successfully accomplished, and this address can only be acquired by practice.

Evils arising from want of skill in bearers.

"The bearers of stretchers, if they march carelessly, painfully jolt the wounded lying upon them, and if these men place the wounded roughly upon the stretcher instead of laying them down skilfully and gently, what torture they may inflict! and much worse again, if no stretchers being at hand, they have to carry the wounded across muskets, or by their clothes, to the ambulance, as I have frequently seen done. One cannot too often repeat, the chief consolation, and the assistance of first importance, to a wounded man, is for him to be carried promptly and properly away from the scene of conflict."

The principles on which the institution of stretcher-bearers by Baron Percy was founded were adopted by an imperial decree for the whole French army in 1813.

SECTION II.—HISTORY OF THE AMBULANCE SYSTEM OF THE BRITISH SERVICE.

Old arrangements for transport of wounded on the field of action.

Until a comparatively recent period no ambulance system corresponding either with that organized by Baron Larrey or by Baron Percy, existed in the British military service. At the close of the last century, when a man fell wounded, the officer commanding his company ordered one or two of his comrades to take him to the rear, or, if the troops were actively engaged, he remained unheeded on the ground until the fighting was over. It was not only in the field that no regularly trained men were provided for meeting the wants of disabled soldiers, but, until recently, no special corps existed for ministering to the wants of the sick or wounded, or for assisting the surgeons in attending upon them, even in the stationary military hospitals; the only plan being for a certain proportion of soldiers from the ranks to be sent, as occasion might require, to act as attendants upon the sick. While engaged in this duty the soldiers were styled "hospital orderlies," and this name still retains a hold in military hospitals. There was no efficient system of hospital transport, no specially constructed vehicles for the surgical and medical stores, nor trained soldiers to take charge of them had they been provided, and no regular ambulance conveyances for the removal of the sick or wounded to the hospitals in rear. The long Peninsular campaign, which commenced in the year 1808, produced so many battles and created so many hospital establishments, that improvements in the care and management of the sick and wounded, the want of which became demonstrated by experience, necessarily grew up in many directions. These improvements were, however, chiefly confined to the interior economy and administration of the general and regimental hospitals; while the organization, personnel, equipment, and general character of the ambulances, or field hospitals, underwent scarcely any change. Sir James McGrigor made attempts to get an ambulance establishment sanctioned, based on similar principles to those on which the ambulance system in the French army was framed, but his endeavours did not meet with success.

During the latter period of the Peninsular War the wounded were carried from the field on stretchers by the bandsmen of regiments, or by some of their other comrades, to the first line of surgical assistance, and afterwards transported to the hospitals of the second line or further in rear, either in return carts of the commissariat train,* or in hired bullock cars, or in spring wagons. The regular wheeled transport of the army at that time was under the management of a corps designated the Royal Wagon Train. This corps had been organized in the beginning of the war for conducting the whole of the transport service of the army, and formed a branch of the Quartermaster-General's Department. It was supplied with several distinct kinds of carriages, each being constructed for a specific service. But in a short time it was found that the Wagon Train was so constituted as to be unequal to supply the transport which was required even for its own support, that is, for the conveyance of its baggage, the rations consumed by the officers, men, and horses of the corps, and its other daily wants. The constitution of the corps was then changed; its store transport was reduced to one store wagon per troop, and its own supplies were ordered to be furnished by the magazines, and to be conveyed by the commissariat cart train and hired

CHAP. II.

Arrangements of the sick and wounded transport during the Peninsular War in the British service.

Organization of the Royal Wagon Train.

Change in its organization during the Peninsular War period.

---

* Organised in 1812.

CHAP. II.

transport of the army: at the same time all other carriages under its charge were changed to spring wagons, and it was strictly prohibited that these should carry anything except sick or wounded men. There was still no ambulance corps on service with the British army corresponding with the Medical Staff Corps of the present time, or with the French "Brancardiers," nor was any formed during the whole period of the Peninsular War.*

Peninsular ambulance conveyances defective in several respects.

The three kinds of transport referred to in the previous paragraph were defective in several respects. The stretchers consisted merely of two poles, between which a piece of canvas ticking was fixed. They were very faulty,† inasmuch as they were without traverses. The weight of a wounded man caused him to sink down in the yielding canvas between the poles, and, in consequence, when the bearers became fatigued and laid the stretcher on the ground to rest themselves, the canvas and the body of the wounded man came into direct contact with it. Looped blankets were occasionally substituted for regular stretchers, the pikes which sergeants then carried being employed as the side-poles. These presented the same objections as the canvas stretchers.

The return commissariat carts were ill-fitted for carrying sick and wounded, being constructed without springs, and the supply of them was uncertain. The hired bullock cars were still more unsuited for ambulance purposes.‡ They were only employed, however, when a sufficient number of spring wagons were not available for use.

The spring wagons were calculated to carry seven or eight men sitting, or two men lying. They were drawn by four horses, and were conducted by two drivers. Their chief disadvantage was their weight, and their being so broad as not unfrequently to lead to encumberment and blocking of the roads. The several kinds of field conveyance just named will, however, be more particularly considered hereafter.

Veterinary-surgeon Cherry's suggestions.

In the year 1825, Veterinary-surgeon Cherry published an able pamphlet § on the subject of field transport, founded

---

* The then Director-General, the late Sir Andrew Smith, mentioned in a note to a departmental memorandum, dated 20th June, 1854, referring to the personnel and matériel of the Medical Department with the army ordered to Turkey, that his predecessor "Sir James McGrigor, Bart, K.C.B., made, while he was chief of the Medical Department of the army in the Peninsula, repeated efforts to have an ambulance corps, similar to what he saw in use with the French, attached to the British force, but without success."

† Millingen's "Army Surgeon's Manual," p. 21.

‡ Inspector-General Wm. Fergusson, whose long and varied army services in the Peninsula and other parts of the world between 1794 and 1817 give great weight to his opinion, in his "Notes and Recollections of a Professional Life," has recorded, "Our means of transporting sick and wounded have ever been deficient and cruel, as all can testify who attended the bullock cars of the Peninsula." London, 1843, p. 62. In Major-General Bell's "Rough Notes by an old Soldier," London, 1867, the manner in which the transportation of the wounded was carried on during the Peninsular War is equally shown to have been extremely defective.

§ "Observations on the defective State of Army Transport: with suggestions for its improvement," by F. C. Cherry, Veterinary-Surgeon in the Army. London, 1825.

on his experience in the wars in the Peninsula, Holland, the Netherlands, and other countries. The object of this work was to suggest a remedy for what had been found to be defective in the organisation of the Wagon Train.* Mr. Cherry's plan was to substitute an establishment of general staff transport, under the superintendence of a director of military transport, who was to be under the orders of the Quartermaster-General. He also advocated the use of a peculiar description of one-horse cart, invented by himself. These carts were so arranged as to be fitted, either without springs for the conveyance of commissariat and hospital stores, or with springs for the conveyance of sick and wounded. One of Mr. Cherry's carts was sent to Chatham for trial, and a committee ordered to make a report upon it. The construction of this cart will also be more particularly described in a future chapter.

The experience of the British Legion, which was raised by Sir De Lacy Evans and others to assist Queen Isabella of Spain against the Carlists in 1835, added somewhat to our knowledge of the qualities necessary for ambulance transport in European warfare. It also served to test practically the efficiency of Cherry's system of transport of wounded under the actual circumstances of campaigning, twelve of Cherry's carts having been employed with this force in the field. Sir Rutherford Alcock, who acted as principal medical officer of the Legion, published in 1838 a volume of "Notes on the Medical History and Statistics of the British Legion in Spain," and in this work discussed at some length the advantages and disadvantages he had observed in the construction of Cherry's carts. He also made suggestions as to the best method of rapidly withdrawing wounded from the scene of action to the first line of surgical assistance, and of afterwards conveying them to the field hospitals. Some of the improvements which were effected in the system of ambulance transport in the course of the Crimean war, and which still form part of the authorised system of the present day, accord with the plan recommended in this work.

Ambulance transport of the British Legion in Spain in 1835.

The outbreak of the Crimean War in 1854 found this country with not even the nucleus of an ambulance transport establishment in existence. Both conveyances and drivers had, however, to be procured without delay. Accordingly a Hospital Conveyance Corps† in some respects resembling the Royal Wagon Train as it existed at the latter part of the Peninsular War, when most of the wagons under its charge were spring wagons for the use of the sick and wounded, was hastily formed for the occasion. The Director-General of the Army Medical Department, Sir Andrew Smith, had advised that able-bodied soldiers should be selected for service in this

Transport of sick and wounded in the Crimea.

The Hospital Conveyance Corps.

---

* The Royal Wagon Train was broken up in the year 1833.
† For a history of the corps see p. 194 of "Appendix to the Report of the "Commission of Inquiry into the Supplies of the British Army in the Crimea."

CHAP. II.

First brigade of hospital conveyance vehicles.

corps; but objections were made to taking from the ranks effective fighting men, and military pensioners were therefore employed instead. The corps was under the orders of a captain as commanding officer, having an adjutant-quartermaster as an assistant. At the same time a brigade of hospital conveyance vehicles* was formed under the direction of the Quartermaster-General, by Lieutenant-Colonel Tulloch, R.A., and the eminent Peninsular surgeon Mr. Guthrie. This brigade was despatched to the expeditionary army in the East. It consisted of twenty carts, each drawn by two horses, five store wagons, each drawn by four horses, one forge cart, and one portable forge, each drawn by two horses. Ten of the carts were made each to carry sixteen persons sitting inside; and ten others to carry two men lying on stretchers, nine men sitting before and behind, while a twelfth might be added lying on a stretcher slung from the roof. The store wagons were spring vehicles, and on occasions of necessity could be used for ambulance purposes and were each made to carry ten persons. This brigade was calculated to be sufficient for two divisions of the army, and was sent complete in every way for duty in the field.

Second brigade of hospital conveyance vehicles.

Another brigade of hospital conveyance vehicles, of a different construction, was at the same time despatched as additional means of transport of the sick and wounded with the army in the East. This brigade consisted of twenty spring wagons on four wheels for carrying men, and nine Flanders wagons for carrying hospital stores. These vehicles were built according to plans recommended by Sir Andrew Smith. The spring wagons were each capable of carrying six slightly wounded men sitting, and four badly wounded lying. The Flanders wagons, though intended for the carriage of bedding and other stores for the field hospitals, were built with springs and could also be used in case of necessity for carrying wounded. In the same way, the spring wagons were so built, that the parts on which the wounded were to be placed could be removed; they then became available for supplying any deficiency that might exist in the means of transporting stores.

Explanation of two sets of differently constructed vehicles having been despatched to the seat of war.

It will appear strange that the War Department should despatch at the same time vehicles very differently constructed, yet intended for precisely the same purposes, for service with the army under the command of Lord Raglan. But the explanation is sufficiently given in a circular memorandum signed by the Director-General,† who makes it clear that they were intended not only to meet the immediate necessities of the war, but also to test practically the respective merits of the

---

* For a description of this brigade *see* a pamphlet published on the subject in 1854, entitled "Some Account of the Brigade of Hospital Conveyance Carts, &c., formed on Improvements suggested by Lieut.-Col. Tulloh, R.A., and Mr. Guthrie."

† Departmental memorandum, dated Army Medical Department, 13 St. James's Place, 20th June, 1854, by Director-General Sir Andrew Smith, on the subject of the carts and wagons sent to the Crimea.

different forms of vehicles. A brief quotation from the memorandum referred to will afford a full justification of the course pursued:—"Special attention," writes the Director-General, "is "requested to the carts and wagons which have been furnished "for the conveyance of sick and wounded. No doubt many "defects will be discovered in both; therefore the medical "officers serving with the army will, in all probability, have an "opportunity of improving upon appliances that are known "*theoretically* only to the British army, though *practically* to the "French since 1792, when a supply of light wagons, accom-"panied by a corps of disciplined attendants, was sent into the "field on the recommendation of the late renowned Baron Larrey "But notwithstanding the French have used so long what we are "now only beginning to employ, still there is reason to believe "much must yet be effected before we shall be able to consider "the object in view to have been satisfactorily attained.

"Medical officers will therefore be pleased to report, through "the Inspector-General of Hospitals, whatever defects they may "discover in the vehicles which have now been supplied, and also "**to** suggest whatever alterations, additions, &c., they may think "calculated to make them more suitable and efficient."

The organization of the Hospital Conveyance Corps soon broke down, as might well have been anticipated. The duties of the men comprised both what have been before described as the duties of the "brancardiers" organized in the French army by Baron Percy, and those of the soldiers of the "ambulance volante" of Baron Larrey. They were, in case of action,* "to "carry the wounded as soon as possible from the field of battle "to the nearest eligible place of safety;" to supply the general hospitals, if possible, with non-commissioned officers and orderlies, so as to prevent the necessity for efficient soldiers being taken from their regiments for these services; to take care of the carts and horses necessary for the conveyance of the sick and wounded; and to furnish servants for the officers of the general medical staff of the army.

This establishment failed owing to the total want of training of the men of the corps for such varied service; to their not having been accustomed to work together; to their loss of activity from age, and their general drunken and disorderly habits; partly also to over-weight and other imperfections which were found to exist in some of the conveyances, and lastly, to absence of the necessary tools and of skilled workmen in the corps for repairing ordinary damages at the time of their occurrence, for want of which a carriage was often rendered useless by **an** accident of the most trifling character. Neither the men nor the conveyances of the Hospital Conveyance Corps were much employed in the Crimea itself. None of the carriages moved with the army to Sebastopol, and those which were landed at a later date, subsequently to the opening of the siege

CHAP. II.

Failure of the Hospital Conveyance Corps.

---

* *See* the pamphlet before quoted by Lieut.-Col. Tulloch, R.A., and Mr. Guthrie, page 3.

operations, were quickly rendered useless by the state of the roads, as well as by the causes before mentioned.

On the occasion of the Crimean war sufficient time elapsed before hostilities actually commenced, and the war was sufficiently prolonged to admit of the ambulance arrangements being altered, fresh men being enrolled, and a new system organized. Had the army been put early in movement, and the campaign rapidly conducted, no regular means of transporting the sick and wounded would have been available, owing to this collapse of the Hospital Conveyance Corps.

The Land Transport Corps.

From the time that the Hospital Conveyance Corps broke down, the removal of the sick and wounded and the conveyance of medicines and medical comforts depended on the Land Transport Corps. Originally the duties connected with the transport and supply of the army had been performed by one body, viz., the Commissariat Department, though without any organized train of vehicles or trained drivers; but during this campaign the two duties were separated, and the whole of the organized transport service was placed in the charge of combatant officers under the orders of a distinct head, called the Director-General of Transport.

The Military Train.

In the beginning of 1857 the Land Transport Corps was re-organized, and a still more military character given to it, it being in many respects assimilated to a cavalry corps. It then received the name of the Military Train. The organized transport for the sick, as well as that for the warlike stores and supplies immediately accompanying the army, was placed under its charge. The Military Train had, among its other duties, that of providing the wheeled conveyances and all transport animals for the ambulance and hospital purposes of the army, as well as the non-commissioned officers and drivers in charge of them. Thus, one of the functions of the Hospital Conveyance Corps devolved upon the Military Train; its other functions, viz., those of conveyance of the wounded from the field of battle on stretchers, and of attending to the sick and wounded in the hospitals, remained to be provided for in other ways.

Regimental Hospital orderly system.

After the Hospital Conveyance Corps was disbanded, the ambulance duties, as well as the nursing in the intermediate and general hospitals in rear, were entirely performed, as they had always been prior to the institution of that corps, by soldiers taken from the ranks of the regiments of the army. Now the "hospital orderly" system, although in individual cases often providing most kind and considerate nurses, men who felt as comrades as well as acted from motives of a conscientious discharge of duty, was generally acknowledged to be, as a whole, faulty and inefficient. On the one hand, the commanding officer was deprived by it of a number of men from the ranks of his fighting force, and the worst of it was that, the more his force was weakened by wounds or sickness, the more it was still further weakened by the abstraction of the men who were taken from the ranks to attend upon them. At the general

hospitals in rear, soldiers who had recovered from sickness or slight wounds were detained to act as hospital attendants, who, under other arrangements, might have been sent back into the field to increase the fighting strength of the army. The evil was further increased by the extra labour which was thus thrown upon those who remained at their regular duty in the ranks. On the other hand, the surgeon too often found his hospital attendants deficient in those qualities of intelligence, tenderness, and activity which are essential for the well-doing and comfort of the patients. As Sir G. Ballingall has remarked,[*]
"It is not indeed to be expected that commanding officers of "regiments, upon whom the surgeon is dependent for this kind "of assistance, should be disposed to part with that description "of men best qualified for the duties we have in view. The "number of men often withdrawn from the ranks by duties of "fatigue, and casualties incident to the service, is materially "increased by the number necessarily employed in attendance "upon the sick, an attendance which should not be left to be "provided for on the spur of the moment, but should be estab-"lished and organized on a liberal scale."

To obviate the evils which were experienced in the working of this system, the Medical Staff Corps, consisting of nine companies, each company being 78 strong, was organized in June, 1855,[†] "to be employed in any way that may be required "in the performance of hospital duties." Each company was calculated for attendance in a hospital of 500 patients. The duties of this corps included not only those which belonged more particularly to the Medical Department, such as the superintendence of wards and the duties in the wards, but also those which were afterwards transferred to the Purveyor's Department, such as the charge and issuing of stores, the cooking, washing, and all other non-professional occupations appertaining to hospital service. The men of the corps were, as regards their distribution, under the Director-General of the Army Medical Department, and were detailed by him or his officers for the different hospital duties. The corps was placed generally under a military officer at Chatham, and locally under the immediate orders of the Purveyor, and the men were only under the general supervision and control of the senior medical officer of each hospital. There was, moreover, scarcely any military feature in their organization. The larger proportion of the men who were enlisted into it came directly from civil employments, without any of the previous drill and training in discipline to which all soldiers are subjected. No provision was made that the orderlies of the corps should be employed in field duties. The men were liable to be discharged from the service at any time the authorities might think fit, and without any claim to pension until after a service of 15 years. In September

CHAP. II.

The first Medical Staff Corps.

---

[*] "Outlines of Military Surgery," Edinburgh, 1838, p. 87.
[†] Royal Warrant, 157,717/1 of June 11, 1855.

CHAP. II.

of the same year a second warrant was published,* increasing the strength of the corps to 10 companies, and the strength of each company from 87 to 120 men. By this warrant an attempt at a military character seemed to be given to the corps, for it ruled that every man enlisted into it was "liable to be "sentenced for misconduct by court-martial to be reduced to "the ranks of the army and to be sent to any regiment of the "line, to serve therein with the rank and pay of a private "sentinel." Practically it was found, however, that this provision could not be carried out, on account of the majority of the men not having been previously "enlisted for general service" or into any regiment of the army.

Practical defects in the organization of this corps.

The Medical Staff Corps as thus organized did not prove satisfactory. In a somewhat doubtful and anomalous position in respect to their relations with the combatant authorities, and acting, as the men of the corps for the most part did, in hospitals under medical officers who were not invested with military authority, and had no power of awarding punishment for offences; being, in a considerable proportion of their numbers, undrilled and untrained in the strict requirements of discipline, and this not only as regarded the men of the corps, but also the stewards and wardmasters under whose supervision they immediately performed their duties, and who, though having the relative rank of non-commissioned officers, neither wore the ordinary distinctions of those ranks on their uniforms nor had corresponding powers of command; it is hardly to be wondered at that the rules for the conduct of military hospitals were constantly infringed, and that absence from duty, insubordination, and drunkenness on their part were frequent sources of neglect of the sick and vexation and trouble to all concerned.

The Army Hospital Corps.

In consequence of these difficulties and irregularities the Medical Staff Corps was disbanded, and by a Royal Warrant dated 1st August, 1857, a new corps of attendants for military hospitals was organized in its stead, under the name of the Army Hospital Corps. To this departmental corps a completely military constitution was given. Its ranks were ordered to be filled, as a general rule, by soldiers volunteering from the combatant ranks after a certain length of service in them. At least two years' regimental service was to be insisted upon under ordinary circumstances, and men who had less regimental service were only to be allowed to join it as exceptional cases, on account of some particular qualifications and by special authority of the Secretary of State for War. The volunteers were moreover required to be men of good character, to be recommended by their commanding officers, and were not to be transferred to the Army Hospital Corps until after a period not exceeding three months passed on probation in an hospital. It was also provided that misconduct or incapacity after transfer

---

* Royal Warrant, No. 157,717/145, September 20th, 1855.

to the corps, would render them liable to be re-transferred to the fighting ranks by proper authority. The ranks of the corps were assimilated to those of the line, the non-commissioned officers and men being designated sergeant-majors, sergeants, and privates, instead of stewards, wardmasters, cooks, barbers, and orderlies, as was the case in the old Medical Staff Corps. The non-commissioned officers took rank with the non-commissioned officers of other corps, wore the same distinctions on their uniforms, and both they and the privates were made subject to all the rules and regulations affecting the rest of the army, with the exceptions of a few points having reference to their particular duties, rates of pay, and pension. In this warrant it was expressly defined that, in addition to the performance of all hospital duties, the non-commissioned officers and privates of the corps " when on duty with " an army in the field will be liable to be attached to the " ambulances, and to attend on the wounded, carrying them " off the field, and performing any such like duties."

The Army Hospital Corps underwent from time to time important modifications in its organization, without altering the essential principles on which the corps was constituted. Some of these changes were made in accordance with the recommendations of a committee appointed by the Secretary of State for War in the year 1860,* to consider and report upon the working of the regulations as they then existed, and to suggest such amendments as might appear calculated to increase the efficiency of the corps. At the time the corps was originally constituted it was intended to supply trained and efficient attendants not only for "general" but also for the "regimental" hospitals of the army. But after a time it was found unequal to accomplish this end from deficiency of numbers; and, for certain reasons, even had the establishment been inadequate, it had come to be believed that such an admixture of the general and regimental system would not work smoothly and efficiently over the wide area which such a mixed service would cause the men to be distributed. The principle of attaching non-commissioned officers and men of another corps to regiments for hospital duty was very unsatisfactory to the commanding officers, medical officers, and patients of regiments; while the men of the Army Hospital Corps themselves disliked being separated so completely from the officers of their own corps, to whom they had to look for the advancement of their interests, and upon whom they had to depend for the rewards of good conduct and efficiency. For these and other reasons the committee were led to recommend that the attempt to draw the entire supply of attendants for service in all military hospitals, including regimental hospitals, from the Army

CHAP. II.

Its military organisation.

Duties on field service.

Changes in the constitution of the Army Hospital Corps.

---

* See "Report of a Committee assembled by order of the Right Honourable the Secretary of State for War, dated War Office, 26th November, 1860, No. 20/Hospital Corps, &c./196. Colonel Clark Kennedy, C.B., Commandant Military Train, President." (This report contains Draught Regulations for all ranks of both the Medical and Purveying branches of the Army Hospital Corps.)

Hospital Corps should be discontinued, and that the duties of the men of this corps should be confined to service in the general, depôt, and field hospitals of the army. The hospital attendants for regimental hospitals, the committee recommended, should as before be taken from the ranks of the regiments themselves. They advised that they should continue to form an integral part of the regiments to which they belonged, and should wear the same uniform as the other soldiers, with certain distinctive badges, but that they should in all cases be supernumerary to the combatant establishment of the corps, and, indeed, should be unarmed, except with a sword for self defence. These recommendations were approved and embodied in a warrant dated 27th September, 1861. This warrant also so far reconstituted the Army Hospital Corps that it divided it into two branches with distinct duties and regulations, one for the Medical, the other for the Purveyor's department, the former being placed under the direction, so far as regarded distribution, of the Director-General of the Army Medical Department, the latter under the direction of the Purveyor-in-Chief. It also provided that sergeants in the medical branch, on passing a certain examination, might be employed in dispensing medicines, and that, like all others in the corps who were employed in any responsible capacity beyond the general duties in which the men were habitually employed, these sergeant-dispensers, or Compounders, as they were and are still called, should receive additional pay. Under this system, therefore, the hospital attendants of the British Army consisted of two divisions corresponding with the two principal classes of hospitals then in vogue, viz., regimental hospital attendants and general hospital attendants. The former consisted of sergeants and privates who were told off by the commanding officer for duty in the regimental hospital, while the latter were drawn from the Army Hospital Corps; the medical and purveying duties being performed by distinct branches of this corps. From the date of this warrant until 1873 no essential change was made in the constitution of the Army Hospital Corps, but regulations were from time to time framed to secure a better educated class of men, as well as to ensure their training in hospital duties, and in the use of stretchers and other field medical equipment after they had joined the corps.

The Army Hospital Corps divided into two branches, a medical branch, and a purveying branch.

By Royal Warrant, dated 12th November, 1869 (Army Circulars, Cl. 1, of 1870), the various departments, dealing with the supply and transport services of the army, were consolidated into one department, designated the Control Department. The officers of the Purveyor's Department, which, by Royal Warrant of 24th December, 1860, had been reconstituted and greatly extended for duties connected with hospital supplies, were with the officers of the then existing Commissariat, Military Store, and Barrack Departments, merged in this huge new department. On the same date another Warrant (Army Circular, Cl. 2 of 1870) appeared, abolishing the Military Train referred to at page 34, and creating in its stead a special corps

The Control Department.

The first Army Service Corps.

for duty in connection with the transport and supply services of the army, styled the Army Service Corps. This corps was placed under the command of officers of the Control Department, and was in the first instance formed of volunteers from the Military Train, Commissariat Staff Corps, Military Store Staff Corps, and from the Purveyor's branch of the Army Hospital Corps, all of which from this date ceased to exist. Thus, the duty of supplying the transport required by the Medical Department, which has hitherto devolved on the Military Train, fell to the Army Service Corps.

In 1873, the same War Minister, Mr. Cardwell, afterwards Viscount Cardwell, who not only had created the Control Department, but had succeeded in abolishing the purchase of commissions in the army, now introduced a radical change in the constitution of the Medical Department.

This department, under the Royal Warrant of 1st October, 1858, consisted of regimental and staff medical officers, but on the 1st March, 1873 (Army Circular, Cl. 22, of 1873), a Royal Warrant introduced what was called the Unification Scheme, placing the medical officers in one staff or department, and abolishing the regimental medical system.

Another Warrant of the same date (Army Circulars, Cl. 23, of 1873) organised the Army Hospital Corps "for extended duties in connection with the hospital service," and the strength of the corps was increased from 671 to 1,088 non-commissioned officers and men. This Warrant created two ranks of officers in the corps, "Captain of orderlies" and "Lieutenant of orderlies," who were given the relative rank in the army of Captain and Lieutenant respectively. The ranks of these officers were, in the first place, filled by the appointment as Captains of Orderlies of the "Quartermaster and Adjutant of the Army Hospital Corps" at Netley, the "Captain of Orderlies" at the Herbert Hospital, Woolwich, and six of the more senior Apothecaries, who, under the provision of the Warrant, volunteered for service in the reconstructed corps.

Three Apothecaries were appointed Lieutenants of Orderlies, and the remaining appointments in the grade of Lieutenant of Orderlies, as well as all future vacancies, were filled by selection from the non-commissioned officers of the corps. From this date no more appointments in the rank of "Apothecary to the Forces," which had been created under a Royal Warrant, dated 23rd October, 1854, were made.

On the 6th March, 1873, a special Army Circular (Cl. 44 of 1873) was published, directing that in future, military hospitals should be organized and administered either as general hospitals, station hospitals, or field hospitals, and regimental hospitals then ceased to exist.

It was laid down that these hospitals were to be administered by the officers of the Army Medical Department under the supreme authority of the Governor or Commandant of the hospital, or of the General or other officer in command of the troops. This circular also directed that the Army Hospital

Chap. II.

Corps should perform all subordinate hospital duties under the officers of the Medical Department, and that the duties hitherto performed by the Purveyor's Department should, in future, be distributed, according to certain defined principles, between the Medical, Control, and Royal Engineer departments respectively.

Command of Army Hospital Corps given to the Medical Officers.

The next great change which was made in the administration of the medical service was the granting to medical officers, under Royal Warrant, 14th August, 1877 (Army Circular, Cl. 125, of 1877), authority to command the officers, non-commissioned officers and men of the Army Hospital Corps, and also all patients in military hospitals, as well as soldiers attached thereto for hospital duty. Thus the command of the Army Hospital Corps was transferred from the Officers of Orderlies to the Medical Officers, and the former were relegated to the performance of duties in connection with pay, clothing, equipment, and hospital supplies.

Captains and Lieutenants of Orderlies made Quartermasters.

When the Royal Warrant, for Pay and Promotion, of 25th June, 1881 appeared, the Captains and Lieutenants of Orderlies found their designation changed into that of Hospital Quartermaster of the Army Hospital Corps, but by Royal Warrant of 22nd February, 1882 (Army Circulars, Cl. 37, of 1882) this designation was modified to Quartermaster Army Hospital Corps, and eventually these officers were so gazetted with effect from 1st July, 1881, and placed on the same footing as regards pay and retiring allowances as the Quartermasters of infantry.

The present Medical Staff and Medical Staff Corps.

On 20th September, 1884, another Royal Warrant * (Army Circulars, Cl. 182, of 1884) was signed by the Queen, which directed that the officers of the Army Medical Department and the Quartermasters of the Army Hospital Corps should, from that date, be designated the Medical Staff, and the warrant officers, non-commissioned officers and men of the Army Hospital Corps should be designated the Medical Staff Corps. The organization then introduced still obtains. This Warrant also created the rank of first class staff-sergeant—equivalent to quartermaster-sergeant in other branches of the service—and by it was abolished the intermediate grade of second corporal, which had existed in the Army Hospital Corps.

Breaking up of the Control Department.

By Royal Warrant, dated 27th November, 1875 (Army Circular, Cl. 2, of 1876), the Control Department was abolished and divided into the Commissariat and Transport Department and the Ordnance Store Department, and by Royal Warrant of 31st January, 1880 (Army Circulars, Cl. 52, of 1880), the former became the Commissariat and Transport Staff. By Royal Warrant of 11th August, 1881 (Army Circulars, Cl. 214, of 1881) the Army Service Corps was similarly divided into the "Commissariat and Transport Corps" and the "Ordnance Store Corps."

With Army Circulars, Cl. 77, of 1877, tables had been published showing, for the first time, the transport required for the bearer companies and field hospitals of an army corps, which was

---

* This Warrant was issued after the report of a Committee on Army Hospital Services presided over by the Earl of Morley, 1883.

Constitution of the Army Service and Medical Staff Corps. 41

to be furnished by the Army Service Corps, and in future regulations, until the date of the change noted in the next sentence, this transport was supplied by the Commissariat and Transport Corps.

By Royal Warrant, 11th December, 1888 (Army Order 3 of 1889), the Commissariat and Transport Staff was abolished, and the Commissariat and Transport Corps was once more designated the Army Service Corps, the officers of the Commissariat and Transport Staff being transferred to the new corps as its officers, and ceasing to be departmental officers.

On this corps now devolves the duty of supplying transport for the Medical Department, and it is laid down that the transport officer of the Army Service Corps is to take orders from the Medical Officer Commanding the bearer company or field hospital to which the transport is attached. In brief, the mode of transporting the wounded from the battle-field to the rear according to the existing regulations may be summarised as follows. The bearer companies, assisted by trained stretcher-bearers of the regiment or corps engaged, remove the wounded from the field to the collecting station, thence they are removed by wheeled transport to the dressing station, and after their wounds have been dressed they are taken to the field hospitals in the ambulance carriage of the second line of assistance. In mountain warfare, pack transport (cacolets and litters) is substituted for wheeled transport.

The organization just described represents the final results of the successive changes which the British medical service has undergone since the Crimean War. Great progress has been made in the hospital administration of the army, and in organizing a system for the removal of the wounded from the field of battle. Much care is now bestowed on the training of the men of the Medical Staff Corps. Every recruit, or transfer from another corps to the Medical Staff Corps, undergoes a systematic course of instruction at the Training School at Aldershot. The course of instruction which he there receives is calculated to fit him for the practical duties which are required of him in hospitals and in the field. He is taught how to tend sick men, to apply dressings, to administer medicine, to clean the wards of a hospital, and, in addition, he is put through a very instructive course of ambulance drill. When the recruit has completed his course at the Training School, he is drafted into one of the larger hospitals, there to be taught the practical duties of a sick attendant. The establishment of the corps is now 2,396 of all ranks, and in consequence of the introduction of the short service system, there is also a very large and ever-increasing reserve of trained men, whose services can be demanded when emergency arises.

In addition to this corps, there is also a body of 1,200 non-commissioned officers and men of the Militia Reserve, who are annually trained in the duties of the Medical Staff Corps, and by Royal Warrant, dated 6th June, 1891 (Army Order 140, of 1891), the formation of a Militia Medical Staff Corps was approved. This Corps comprises the ranks of Surgeon-

CHAP. II.

Formation of the present Army Service Corps.

Present system of moving wounded from the field.

Training of the Medical Staff Corps.

Militia Reserve of Medical Staff Corps, and Militia Medical Staff Corps.

42 *Volunteer Medical Staff Corps.*

CHAP. II.

Volunteer Medical Staff Corps.

Lieutenant-Colonel, Surgeon-Major, Surgeon-Captain, Surgeon-Lieutenant, Sergeant, Corporal, Bugler, and Private.

Another large and important auxiliary to the Medical Staff Corps is furnished by the Volunteer Service. Ever since the commencement of the Volunteer movement, medical officers have been attached to each Volunteer corps, or battalion, but on 13th March, 1886 (Army Circulars, Cl. 59, of 1886) a Royal Warrant was published, which enacted that, with a view to the further development of the medical organization of the Volunteer force, a corps, to be designated the Volunteer Medical Staff Corps, should be formed. This corps comprises the following ranks—Surgeon-Lieutenant-Colonel, Surgeon-Major, Surgeon-Captain, Surgeon-Lieutenant, Quartermaster, 1st and 2nd class staff-sergeant, sergeant-bugler, sergeant, corporal, bugler, private. Like other Volunteer corps, the Volunteer Medical Staff Corps has a permanent Staff from the Regular army, consisting of an adjutant, who is a Surgeon-Captain of the Medical Staff, an acting sergeant-major, and sergeant-instructors, who are non-commissioned officers of the Medical Staff Corps. Originally the Volunteer Medical Staff Corps consisted of only one division of four companies in London, the Officer in command of which was designated Surgeon-Commandant, but is now styled Commandant. At present there are in addition companies in Edinburgh, Woolwich, Manchester, Maidstone, Leeds, Aberdeen, Norwich, and Glasgow.

Volunteer Medical Staff.

Nothing has as yet been done to unite into a homogeneous body the regimental Volunteer medical officers, unless the circumstance of their names having been published for the last three years in the Army List, in a general seniority list, headed Volunteer Medical Staff, can be considered a step in this direction.

Organization of the Militia and Volunteer Medical Staff Corps is in advance of the Medical Staff Corps of the Regular Army.

It is worthy of remark that the organization of both the Militia Medical Staff Corps and the Volunteer Medical Staff Corps is in advance of that of the Medical Staff Corps of the Regular Army, in so far, that in the Militia and Volunteers, the Officers are a component part of the corps, whereas in the Regular Service the Officers belong to the Medical Staff, and the Corps consists of only the non-commissioned ranks. The amalgamation of Officers and men into a corps was recommended by Lord Morley's Committee in 1883, and has since been strongly advocated by many Medical Officers, as well as by some of the most distinguished members of the civil profession, in the discussion which preceded the issue of the Royal Warrant of 7th August, 1891 (Army Order 187 of 1891), which "altered in some respects the designations of the departmental ranks" of the Medical Staff. It is not too much to say that this development, which would conduce so greatly to efficiency, is only a matter of time.

Army Medical Reserve.

By Royal Warrant, dated 18th February, 1888 (Army Order 56, of 1888), amended by Royal Warrant of 14th December, 1891, (Army Order 1 of 1892) an Army Medical Reserve of Officers was established. In the Secretary of State's instructions on this

Warrant, it was laid down that medical officers of the Militia, Yeomanry, and Volunteers, on electing to join this reserve, should undertake to perform army duties at home, at the rates of remuneration laid down for civilian medical practitioners in the Pay Warrant, and that officers of the Army Medical Reserve would have a prior claim to employment in the district in which they reside to other medical officers of the auxiliary forces, or to civilian medical practitioners. As an inducement to medical officers of the Militia, Yeomanry, and Volunteers to join this reserve, the Warrant promises that officers of the Army Medical Reserve shall be given the rank of Surgeon-Major on completion of twelve years' service from the date of their first **appointment** to the auxiliary forces, and also that honorary **assistant surgeons** of Volunteers permitted to join the reserve shall be granted the rank of Surgeon-Lieutenant therein.

Following the organization of the Volunteer service into brigades in 1888, a Brigade-Surgeon-Lieutenant-Colonel has been appointed on the staff of each Brigadier-General, who is responsible to the Director-General, through the Principal Medical Officer of the division, and has under his orders the regimental Medical Officers of the several corps forming the brigade.

Volunteer Brigade Surgeons.

Under this system also brigade bearer companies have been formed. These are composed of men taken from the fighting ranks, and they are only trained in ambulance work as a secondary duty, a plan which seems to have all the disadvantages of the old army system, which the formation of a special corps was intended to do away with.

Volunteer Brigade Bearer companies.

SECTION III.—EXISTING AMBULANCE TRANSPORT ARRANGEMENTS IN OTHER ARMIES.*

In order that we may be able to add to the efficiency of our ambulance system by utilizing the experience of other nations, it is useful to take a glance at the existing ambulance arrangements, especially those which relate to the transport of the wounded, in the armies of some other countries. It will be seen that the organization differs very materially in some of them, both as regards the constitution of the personnel by whom the transport is carried out, and the duties and responsibilities of the medical department in superintending the professional duties connected with this service, as well as in the material by which the conveyance of the wounded is effected. Special peculiarities as regards this last division of the service, the particular construction of the transport material, whether stretchers, mule or wheeled conveyances, will be more particularly noticed when the conveyances themselves are described. Only the general features of the system on which the transport and other ambulance duties are carried out by other nations will be described in the following remarks.

* The details contained in this section are for the most part derived from the latest editions of the "Armed Strength" of the various countries, prepared for the Intelligence Department of the War Office, and Lord Morley's Committee, 1885.

44 Ambulance Transport in the French Army.

Chap. II.

Ambulance transport arrangements of the French Army formerly.

French Army.—The organization of the ambulance service in the French army so far as refers to the care and transport of the wounded in the field was formerly as follows:—Young soldiers of the annual contingent, and steady soldiers selected from the men in the ranks, robust in frame and intelligent, were trained by medical officers to act as attendants and carriers of the wounded. These soldiers were designated "soldats infirmiers." Their duty was to collect and remove the wounded from the field of battle under the direction of the officers of administration of the hospital service, and under the surveillance of the deputy military intendants. The stretchers for carrying the wounded formed part of the contents of the field hospital store wagons (caissons d'ambulance). Seats and litters fixed on pack saddles borne by mules, with conductors, were also provided for carrying the wounded from the field of battle to the ambulances. These were supplied by the train on the requisition of the intendance. When a soldier fell in the ranks he was led or carried by the soldats infirmiers to the rear, where the medical officers attached to the regiment to which he belonged, and attended to him. He was then carried to the provisional post where the regimental ambulance was established, or else to the ambulance of the division. When the wounded were discharged from the ambulances to the stationary hospitals in rear, the caissons, or military wagons, were generally employed for the transport.

Ambulance transport arrangements of the French army at the present time.

Until the year 1882 the medical staff in the French Army had nothing to do with the organisation or administration of any of the material, transport or other, of the ambulances or hospitals. The surgeons only attended on the sick and wounded, and helped to train the infirmiers militaires for the subordinate duties of attendance which devolve upon them. The movements of the hospital staff, the transport of the wounded from the field to the flying hospitals, and then to the stationary hospitals, and even the position and arrangements of the first lines of surgical assistance, were all arranged and directed by the superintending military officer (officier de l'intendance militaires) and his subordinates.

In that year the medical officers were given command of the Infirmiers, whilst the officiers d'intendance still retained control of the supplies.

By the law of June 13, 1889, full control of the stores and of the money was given to the medical officers, thus giving a complete autonomy to the medical service of the French army.

Ambulance and hospital arrangements in the French Army.

In the field the arrangements of the Service de Santé for the care of the wounded are as follows:—

There are first the regimental surgeons and soldats infirmiers who attend the wounded where they fall, and transport them to the Poste de Secours, or collecting station, which is placed under cover about 1,500 yards in rear of the position. Here is a reserve of bearers, who relieve the regimental bearers, and convey the wounded to the Station de Voitures, where pack and wheeled transport are stationed. By these means the wounded are taken to the **Ambulances Divisionnaires**, or flying hospitals, which constitute the second line of medical assistance, and are formed at selected positions during the progress of the battle. These ambulances have each medical and surgical provision for 100 men for six months, and the necessary transport; but they are not equipped with tents, such shelter as may be required being obtained or improvised on the spot. Here dressings are applied, and urgent operations performed. The personnel comprises 6 medical officers, 12 infirmiers de visite, and 113 infirmiers d'exploitation, of whom 92 are brancardiers, i.e., bearers. Two ambulances divisionnaires are allowed to each division of infantry; a brigade of cavalry has one, and there is also one attached to the corps troops.

The preceding arrangements form part of the Service d'Avant as distinguished from the Service d'Arrière, to which the remainder of the medical arrangements in the field belong.

The Service d'Arrière comprises the Hôpitaux temporairement immobilisés, or advanced stationary hospitals, and the Hôpital d'Evacuation, from which the patients are sent to their own districts. Railways are largely utilized in the transport of the wounded.

Great pains are taken that the French infirmiers shall be well instructed. Their professional tuition is given to them at the Val de Grâce by the Médecin-en-chef and the surgeons under his direction. The instruction is both theoretical and practical, and lasts two months. The first month is devoted to explanations and exercises in classes, the second is practical **work in the wards** of the hospital. Minute regulations are **issued for their** guidance. The infirmiers thus become very reliable aids to the Medical Department, both in the home and field hospitals. The proportion of non-commissioned officers in the corps is large, there being one sergeant infirmier to six soldier infirmiers (infirmiers soldats), and **one** corporal infirmier to three soldier infirmiers.

The medical establishments of the territorial army are trained in the spring, and in the autumn those of the active and reserve armies. The training lasts 10 days, and is complete and thorough.

German Army.—The organization for the transport of **the** wounded from the field of action in the German Army embodies the experience gained in the wars of 1864 and 1866 and in the war with France in 1870. The plan of medical assistance with troops in the field is almost identical with that now in force in our own army, and comprises a regimental aid, bearer companies and field hospitals, with hospitals on the lines of communications, as well as organised ambulance trains for the conveyance of the sick and wounded back to the home hospitals.

Each battalion of infantry, of four companies, **has** two medical officers attached, with one hospital assistant to each company. Two men per company are trained **as** stretcher-bearers, and a medical store wagon is included in **the** regimental

Ambulance arrangements of the French Army.

Ambulance transport arrangements of the German Army.

transport. A regiment of cavalry has three medical officers and four hospital assistants—one per squadron—and its medical store wagon. The field artillery has two medical officers to each *Abtheilung* of three or four batteries and a hospital assistant to each battery; the garrison artillery, two medical officers in a battalion of four companies and a hospital assistant to each company. The pioneers have a medical officer and a hospital assistant with each field company

This regimental aid forms the first line of medical assistance in the field.

The second line consists of the bearer companies, of which there **are three to** each army corps of about 36,000 men in two **divisions**.

One bearer company of each army corps is permanently attached to each division, and the remaining one is kept at the disposal of the corps commander, and is attached to the field artillery.

Ambulance arrangements of the German Army.

The bearer companies form part of the military train of the army corps, and each consists of 7 medical officers with 16 hospital assistants and 166 stretcher-bearers. The company has 8 **ambulance** wagons, which carry 2 severely or 3 slightly wounded **men**, 2 medical store wagons and 2 baggage wagons, each drawn by 2 horses. There are 56 stretchers with each company, of which each ambulance wagon carries five. Two tents for the dressing station are carried in each baggage wagon. Officers, under-officers, and men of the train are attached to the bearer company for transport purposes.

Each company can be divided into two sections, each complete in itself.

The bearer company follows the troops into action, and the divisional commander decides whether one or both sections shall form dressing stations.

When the action begins the ambulance wagons and bearers of the **company** work between the minor field dressing stations, established by the medical officers of regiments, and the central dressing station formed by the bearer company, whilst the bearers of **the** bearer company and those of regiments search the **field for** wounded.

After **their wounds** are dressed, the severely wounded are sent to the nearest field hospital in requisitioned wagons, the slightly wounded proceeding there in detachments on foot.

The field hospitals form the third line of medical assistance. An army corps has 12 field hospitals, providing for 200 patients each. The personnel of each field hospital consists of 5 medical officers, 4 officials (apothecary, accountant, &c.), and 47 non-commissioned officers and men, including 9 hospital assistants and 12 sick attendants with 14 transport non-commissioned officers and drivers. The hospital may be divided into two sections. The field hospitals receive the wounded from the dressing stations of the bearer companies, and as soon as possible evacuate their sick and follow the troops; those patients who are unfit to travel to the rear, when the field hospital moves, are taken over by an permanent war hospital formed on the spot.

Hospitals are established on the lines of communication under the supervision of the Surgeon-General of the "inspection" (the line of advance of the army), and in each inspection there is a committee for the transport of the sick and wounded, consisting of 7 medical officers, 6 hospital assistants, and 9 sick attendants.

In each "inspection" also there is a hospital store depôt with 2 officers, 12 officials and 12 under-officers, with a transport column of 20 carriages, with 2 under-officers, **20** train drivers, and 42 horses.

The men composing the bearer companies do not perform the duties of hospital attendants in time of peace; they are taken from the reserve, selected men of which **are** trained for 14 days each year with the other reserve men of the army.

Every year, two men of good conduct in their second year of service from each company of infantry and rifles, and one under-officer of each battalion, are selected for a course of instruction as stretcher-bearers. The course includes anatomy, first aid, and stretcher drill, and lasts **from** January to March, with about three lectures or drills a **week**.

If in a garrison where there are several battalions, the instruction is given by a surgeon and two assistant-surgeons selected by authority for the purpose. If only one battalion is present the battalion medical officer is the instructor. In the month of May all the instructed bearers of a division, some 250 in number, are concentrated at the head-quarters of the division for ten days; during this time they are drilled together in practical exercises as bearers, and in the establishment and organisation of dressing stations. These men form in war the regimental stretcher-bearers.

Each company, squadron and battery has also one hospital assistant, whose duties are to assist the regimental medical officers in the hospitals. They are chosen by the medical officers from men of good character who have served six months in the ranks, and who volunteer for this service, and may be sent back to the ranks if found unfit. They are instructed in minor surgery, nursing and first aid; they always accompany their company on the march, at manœuvres, &c., and are provided with a case of surgical appliances.

Another class of men employed in the hospitals are the sick attendants (Krankenwärter), of whom every year 26 men per army corps are trained by the medical officers. They are chosen from men with at least **a** year's service, or from **recruits** who, from bodily defects, are not fit for the ranks. They **act** as assistant dressers, nurses, &c., in hospitals.

Societies for aid to the sick and wounded are widely spread and well organised in peace in Germany, and assist the medical department in time of war, especially in connection with the sick train service and the reserve hospitals.

Chap. II.

Ambulance arrangements of the German Army.

CHAP. II.

Ambulance arrangements of the German Army

The transport of the wounded from the battle-field and their distribution among the field hospitals, is under the general direction of the chief medical officer, who is on the staff of the General commanding the army corps. His orders are countersigned by the General, and therefore in force throughout the corps.

The only authorised conveyances for transporting the wounded in the German service are stretchers, and two-horse wagons. Mule litters and cacolets do not form part of the German ambulance transport. The Prussian* was the first army in which hand-wheel litters were used, but these were given up after 1866. All horse vehicles are four-wheeled. In addition to the regular ambulance transport, a portion of the transport common to the whole army may be employed for the conveyance of sick and wounded under unusual pressure. The officers, men, horses and vehicles which are included in the composition of the transport all belong to the "military train." The material of the train of the whole army, like all the army stores, is under the custody and control of the "Intendant-General." When, however, a portion of the material of the train is issued and attached for service to a particular department of the army, that part of the army has entire charge of it.

Ambulance arrangements of the Austrian Army.

Austrian Army.†—Special arrangements are made in the Austrian army, so far as the personnel is concerned, to provide for the duties of transporting and assisting the wounded on the field of battle. These duties are performed by the class of men who act as dressers and attendants in the fixed military hospitals, and by an establishment distinct from the nursing staff. The wounded are transported by soldiers formed into sanitary, or bearer, detachments. All the soldiers thus detached are specially trained to carry wounded men systematically, as well as to be competent to attend to their first necessities before a surgeon can be reached; most of them are taken from the general ranks of the army.

Constitution of the Austrian sanitary or bearer detachments.

The plan of organizing and mode of training the bearer detachments is as follows:—In time of peace each infantry regiment is required to have at least one non-commissioned officer and three privates per company under sanitary instruction. The original course of training lasts for six weeks, and during this period they are supplied with the equipment issued to sanitary detachments on field service, so that they may become practically acquainted with it. This training is

---

* A very complete description of the whole hospital system of the Prussian army, at the time of the war with Austria, is given in the interesting and valuable "Report on the Medical and Sanitary Services of the Prussian Army during the Campaign in Bohemia in 1866," by Surgeon-Colonel J. A. Bostock, C.B., in the 7th volume of the "Army Medical Reports."

† A very complete account of the Sanitary Department of the Austrian Army is given by Captain W. S. Cooke, in Part II. (p. 21) of the "Armed Strength of Austria," published by the War Office.

rehearsed from time to time subsequently. The men thus become qualified either (a) as bearers of wounded from the line of battle to the brigade dressing station; or (b) as bandage carriers to be about the persons of the surgeons with the necessary apparatus and appliances, ready to assist at the surgical operations which may have to be performed. Under ordinary circumstances these men remain with their respective corps. In time of war and in the field a detachment of these bearers is formed from each brigade of infantry, and placed under the command of a subaltern officer, who is told off for this service by the Brigadier-General from the strength of one of the battalions. The detachment is thus formed of one officer from each brigade, one corporal and three privates from each brigade and company respectively.

When an engagement is expected the detachment falls in together as a distinct body, separate from the combatant troops. An Austrian brigade consists of six infantry battalions and one rifle battalion of six companies each battalion, and 250 men each company; so that when thus assembled the strength of the brigade sanitary, or bearer detachment, is, one officer, seven non-commissioned officers, and 84 privates. Of the privates, 70 are intended for transporting the wounded, and 14 as bandage carriers.

The uniform and accoutrements of the men of the bearer detachments are the same as when they are on duty with their respective corps, excepting that they all wear a band of the national colours (black and yellow) on the left upper arm as a distinguishing badge, and that in the case of the privates no firearms are carried. The non-commissioned officers are armed with their rifles; the privates only wear a sapper's sword. The privates have to carry a second havresack filled with bandages, and a large pattern **canteen** with **water** for the use of the wounded.

These arrangements ensure a proportion of bearers of the wounded being with every single battalion, or even a smaller body in case of such a small force being engaged independently; and at the same time provide for a systematic and orderly removal of the wounded in case of a general engagement. After having been concentrated, as soon as their functions with the brigade are terminated, the detachment breaks up, and every man returns to his respective corps. If military or strategical reasons necessitate the detachment being kept together for a longer period, the Brigadier-General, by whose order only it is concentrated, has to make the necessary arrangements for the pay and rations of the men to be drawn at the head-quarters of the brigade.

The system just described comprehends the ordinary plan adopted for the transport of the wounded from the field of battle; but over and above these special bearer detachments there are the regularly organized sanitary corps of the army, one company of which is attached to every corps d'armée in

Marginalia: Chap. II. Bearers of wounded. Bandage carriers. Plan of performing the field duties. Ambulance transport in the Austrian Army. The "Sanitary Detachments" not to be confounded with the "Sanitary Corps" of the Austrian Army.

Chap. II.

Ambulance arrangements of the Russian Army

the field. These sanitary companies are part of the permanent hospital staff of the Austrian army.

Russian Army.—In Russia every fraction of the army, whether in peace or war, has a hospital supplied with wagons for the conveyance of the sick; the medical personnel and the number of wagons vary according to the number of troops.

A regiment of infantry of four battalions has five surgeons (a surgeon-major and four assistant-surgeons, according to the number of battalions), five aide-chirurgiens, or dressers, one aide-pharmacien, or apothecary, six hospital orderlies (or nurses, of which one is a superior), a hospital sergeant, and 16 company dressers (one to each company), with four ambulance wagons, four medical store carts, and a cart to carry the stretchers, of which there are eight, being two per company.

A regiment of cavalry of four squadrons has two surgeons, an apothecary, two aide-chirurgiens, and four squadron dressers, with two ambulance wagons, a medical store cart, and a cart carrying (four) stretchers. During peace time a hospital sergeant and two hospital orderlies are added.

A rifle battalion of four companies has two surgeons, a hospital sergeant, two hospital orderlies, two aide-chirurgiens, and four company dressers; one ambulance wagon, a medical store cart, and a cart carrying two stretchers per company.

A brigade of artillery of six batteries has two surgeons, an apothecary, a hospital sergeant, and six aide-chirurgiens, with one dresser and two hospital orderlies per battery, one ambulance wagon, a medical store cart, and two stretchers per battery.

The regimental hospitals form part of the establishment of the various corps, and follow them in the field. During the march they receive the sick, treat them, and hand them over to the nearest hospital on the line of march or to the divisional hospitals.

A regimental hospital on a war footing contains 84 beds, 21 being apportioned to each battalion. Each reserve battalion maintains hospital appliances for 45 beds, *i.e.*, nine for each battalion formed on mobilization.

In addition to the sanitary means for each corps, an army on an active footing in time of war has for each infantry and cavalry division, a divisional, and for each rifle brigade, a brigade supply and transport column, the sanitary condition of which consists of a divisional mobile hospital and a bearer company. For batteries of artillery these join the train of the infantry or cavalry division to which they are attached. The sanitary division of the train is organised only on mobilisation, and on the march follow immediately in rear of the troops, and transport the sick to hospitals in rear as soon as the divisions to which they belong, halt. In action they organise dressing stations, and render first assistance to the wounded.

Each hospital has room for 6 officers and 160 men, and can be divided into two sections. The personnel consists of 8 surgeons, 16 dressers, and 50 hospital orderlies, with the necessary officials. In the transport section are 108 drivers, with an officer in charge. The bearer company comprises 1 officer, 1 sergeant-major, 8 sergeants, and 200 bearers. With the sanitary train are 24 ambulance wagons and 24 other wagons, of which 2 are for medical stores; 6 stretcher carts, and 2 medical store carts, with 144 stretchers in all. As each company of infantry and battery of artillery has two stretchers, there are available, in an infantry division of about 2,000 men, 284 stretchers. All ambulance wagons have four horses.

During a battle these movable field hospitals (or ambulances) are established behind the line of battle. Each regiment supplies them, according to the orders of the Director-General of hospitals, with a certain **number** of surgeons and assistant-surgeons; the hospital carriages, assisted by those belonging to the regiments, convey the wounded to the field hospitals. The hospital orderlies **or** attendants, in common with those belonging to the field hospitals (or ambulances) give the first attention to the wounded, and carry them on stretchers towards the carriages and wagons. It is the Director-General of Hospitals who makes all the arrangements and gives the necessary orders for the sanitary service of the army.

The field hospitals in European Russia are 84 in number, and are permanent formations. In time of war they follow a few marches in rear of the army. Each field hospital is organised for 30 officers and 600 men, and can be divided into three equal sections. The establishment consists of a Commandant, 1 principal and 9 other surgeons, an apothecary, 2 compounders, and a total of 304 non-commissioned officers and men, of whom 63 belong to the transport section.

Each hospital has a train of 27 carriages, which may also be employed to transport the sick to the hospitals further in rear. Both matériel and hospital stores are kept in peace at the intendance depôts, the personnel and horses are only organised on war breaking out.

A field dispensary **is** also attached to every army or army corps operating independently. Each consists of 28 wagons, which carry a supply of medical stores calculated at four months' consumption. Some of the wagons follow the army in its advance, and the remainder are distributed between the base and other convenient points. The establishment consists of 4 apothecaries and 3 assistant apothecaries, a clerk, 2 sergeants, and 6 privates, with 30 transport and non-commissioned officers and drivers.

All the temporary hospitals, as also the movable field hospitals or ambulances, are under the orders of the Director-General, who is attached to the Etat-Major of the army. It is his duty to clear out the sick and wounded from these establishments as quickly as possible, and to cause them to be transported to the permanent hospitals. If the means of conveyance of the ambulances should be insufficient, or should be entirely wanting, recourse can be had to the wagons, &c., of the intendance for the transport of the sick, &c.; or the country in which

CHAP. II.

Ambulance arrangements of the Russian Army.

operations are being carried on can be called upon to supply the necessary means of transport on requisition, whether it may be required for the conveyance of the wounded from the field of battle, or to transport them from the field hospitals to the permanent hospitals in the interior of the country.

The permanent hospitals are 44 in number, and are established in the different military arrondissements, principally towards the frontiers. Those which are established at the base of military operations are destined to receive the sick of the active army.

The permanent hospitals are classified in four categories.

	Officers	Other ranks	With a reserve of Officers	Other ranks
The hospitals of the 1st class for 5	..	150	.. 2 ..	50
,, ,, 2nd ,, 10	..	300	.. 5 ..	100
,, ,, 3rd ,, 33	..	500	.. 15 ..	150
,, ,, 4th ,, 38	..	600	.. 20 ..	300

Whenever it is necessary to have a sanitary establishment of less than 150 beds, either a half hospital or a section is formed.

The Director-General of Hospitals receives his orders from the Chef d'Etat-Major, who notifies all movements of troops to him, whether of the army as a whole or a separate detachment.

The Director-General is in immediate communication with the Minister of War for the supply of all medical wants. It is his business to establish new field hospitals, on being required to do so by the chief of the staff, to move others elsewhere, and to control and superintend the supplying and keeping in a state of efficiency the hospitals, and the care of the sick. He is assisted in his duties by the principal medical officer as regards the medical details. The personnel of the hospitals is under the orders of the Director-General, with the exception of the Medical Officers, who are only subordinate to him as regards matter of discipline or administration.

Ambulance arrangements of the Danish Army.

The Danish Army.—The supreme administration of all army medical and sanitary matters is—like all other military matters—in the hands of the Minister of War. The military medical and sanitary duties are performed by a special force, consisting of: The medical officers, who form the Army Medical Staff, and non-commissioned officers and privates constituting the Medical Staff Corps. A great part of the economical affairs of the Army Medical Department (especially those concerning military hospitals) is, however, under the administration of the commissary department.

The Medical Staff.—The Medical Staff (*Hærens Lægekorps*) consists of: (*a*) 39 regular medical officers (*militære Læger*) all nominated by the Crown, viz.: 1 Director-General (*Stabslæge*), who is the chief of the Medical Staff, having the rank of a General; 14 medical officers of the 2nd class (*Overlæger*), of whom the 5 senior have the rank of Lieutenant-Colonel, the other 9 that of Captain; 24 medical officers of the 3rd class individual wearing the uniform of the army to which he is attached.

Excessive zeal is a hindrance to volunteer helpers.

The first object of a commander in war is to win battles, and however humane he may be, the victims are, for the moment, of secondary consideration. Philanthropists and humanitarians may condemn such a principle, but it cannot be changed, and the advocates of the Red Cross must start with a proper appreciation of this obvious truism, or they will soon be grievously disappointed in their efforts. Hitherto, volunteer helpers, urged on by benevolent enthusiasm, have been apt to forget that they only form a subordinate supplement to the official service which is responsible for the care of the sick and wounded; and starting probably without any knowledge of military regulations, and in entire ignorance of the exigencies of a state of war, they have had their eyes opened to the truth in the most unexpected manner, and have been greatly disappointed at the apparent want of sympathy displayed by commanding officers and by the heads of the medical department during the serious crises of a campaign. But the truth is, that at such times these officers have more than enough to occupy their attention, and the less the volunteer element is *en evidence* the better it will be for all concerned. The more this point is considered the more fully will it be understood, that if Red Cross volunteers are to be of use, and not an encumbrance, they must be thoroughly instructed during peace in the work they will be expected to perform in time of war; and from the appointed delegate of the society at head-quarters down to the humblest bearer there must be a thorough appreciation of discipline and a determination to submit to it. Unfortunately, many of the Red Cross Societies were formed, and their ambulances were organised, on the eve or after the commencement of war, and the consequence has been that there was no time for preparation, but crowds of persons, with willing hearts and full hands, have rushed off in the belief that they were about to fulfil a mission to which no objection could possibly be raised.

The abuse of the Red Cross.

It may be of advantage to introduce here a few remarks on the abusive employment of the Red Cross badge. As has been already stated, this badge had the misfortune to be adopted in some countries at times when war was imminent, and as a consequence the military authorities, who might otherwise have devoted some attention to the national relief societies in course of formation, were compelled to permit much to be done in the name of the Geneva Convention which would not bear a critical examination. In many cases there was a complete departure from the terms of the treaty, and official eyes were closed to many things on the plea that they involved no positive objection and were done with the best intentions, and to a few other things of a more doubtful character, perhaps on the principle that *inter arma silent leges*. Endeavours have been often made to rectify this state of affairs and to bring back the societies into the channel from which so many of them wandered. On

CHAP. III.

The abuse of the Red Cross.

the other hand, it would seem of equal importance that the armies which were to become familiarised with the Red Cross should also be instructed as to its meaning and as to the rights attaching to it; but there is perhaps only one army—that of Germany—in which men of all ranks possess a knowledge of the Convention of Geneva and the meaning of the badge. What is known of these matters among the officers and rank and file of the British Army? If one of them were asked the meaning of the red cross on the arm of a sick bearer or on the side of a wagon, he would probably reply that it is the badge of the Medical Staff Corps, and his knowledge of the matter is limited to this. If our army were engaged in an European war the orthodox armlet, stamped at the War Office, would have to be worn by all ranks in this corps, as experience has proved that it is the most distinctive sign and the only one that can be at once detected on a uniform, without the necessity of walking round the wearer.

One of the greatest difficulties with which Red Cross Societies have had to contend has been the unauthorised use of this badge. The Franco-German war was particularly favourable to its deceptive use, and at one time it seemed as if the whole organisation—both national and international—would be paralysed, owing to the conduct of those who were using it for improper purposes.

Briefly stated, the principal abuses of the badge which have been noted in time of war have been its adoption for purposes of espionage and pillage, or to enable soldiers who have recovered from wounds to return from the enemy's lines on parole and to rejoin the ranks of their army; but such cases have not been so numerous as to merit serious consideration, although they cannot be entirely ignored.

An instance.

One of the most flagrant attempts to employ the Geneva badge in a fraudulent manner was that of the Irish Ambulance. This so-called ambulance was composed of about 300 Irishmen, who landed in a body at Havre in August, 1870, to the great astonishment of the inhabitants. When next heard of, these men were assisting in the defence of Châteaudun, having discarded the neutral badge, and joined the combatant ranks of the French Army.

The writer has seen a soldier on outpost duty wearing a Red Cross brassard, but he was not able to obtain any satisfactory explanation of this anomaly. He has also seen a similar armlet given to a commercial traveller who was anxious to obtain facilities to reach the head-quarters of the German Army for purposes of business. It is perhaps necessary to add that in this case the badge had no real value, as it was without any official stamp; but in those days there was seldom time for the verification of such details.

The cases in which the flag has been used to obtain certain immunities in towns and villages occupied or threatened by an enemy are too numerous to mention. We remember to have seen streets in which from almost every house was displayed a

Red Cross flag, the plea being, that if there were not any wounded actually in it, the owners were quite willing to allow it to be used for hospital purposes (although it was not likely their permission would be asked); and if any member of the family were sent out to procure food or forage, it was considered quite the legitimate exercise of a right to put on the arm a white linen band with a red cross upon it; and this was often done by quite young children. These acts of self-protection were quite natural on the part of people whose country was invaded, and who had a confused notion of the rights attaching to this neutral badge, but who had never heard anything about the International Treaty by which such rights were defined.

To meet conduct of this kind the Prussian Society, in July, 1870, made a rule that an ambulance could not be established for less than twenty beds; and in September of the same year the French Government of National Defence determined that an ambulance to be seriously entitled to protection must shelter at least six invalids; and at Dijon the Germans came to the same decision.

But whilst there is some justification for ignorance such as that above referred to on the part of poor civilians frightened and harassed by war, there is none for the manner in which the Red Cross is abused during peace, a time which should be utilised in spreading correct information as to the true meaning of an International Treaty which is of such vast importance to humanity.

There is justification for ignorance, but none for the abuse of the Red Cross.

Very frequently the Geneva badge is wrongfully used in civil hospitals, and in London, notice boards may be seen in conspicuous places, where, under a Red Cross, the public are informed that ambulance material can be obtained in case of accident. Hospital nurses, also, often adopt this badge, and some invalid attendants go so far as to introduce it in their advertisements. Surgical appliances and dressings, bandages, medicines, preserved food, aërated waters, soap, and all kinds of useful and useless things bear the same sign, and, in the event of war, the general ignorance which already prevails on the subject of the Geneva Convention would be emphasized by this wholesale and unauthorised adoption of a recognised international badge.

If steps be not soon taken by all the Governments, signatories of the Convention, to protect the badge to which their authority was solemnly given, there is no doubt that some States will withdraw from the treaty. Up to the present time there are only two or three countries in which any endeavour has been made to make it generally known; and in Germany, for instance, the members of the Army Medical Service are systematically examined on the clauses of the Treaty and their effects in war.

The subject of the wrongful use of the Geneva badge was discussed at the International Conferences of Red Cross Societies, held at Geneva in 1884, and at Carlsruhe in 1887. Subsequently to these meetings prizes were offered by the

International Committee at Geneva for the best essay on the Abusive Employment of the Badge and Name of the Red Cross. The result was published in July last, and the prizes were awarded to Dr. Jules César Buzzati, Professor of International Law at the University of Macerati, and M. Constantin Castori, Avocat and Professor of Criminal Law at the University of Padua.*

According to M. Buzzati, it appears that the only countries in which serious efforts have been made to repress by law the abuse of the Red Cross are Belgium, Italy, Portugal, Russia, and Sweden; but these endeavours have not been adequately sustained.

Both authors agree that the best and only satisfactory course would be for all Governments which have signed the Convention of Geneva to agree to add to this document an additional article, to the effect that in every State the protection of the badge shall be enforced. It should then be left to each Government to pass such a law as may best suit the conditions of their respective countries.

Surely, as laws already exist for the protection of names, commercial titles, trade marks, and patents, it would be easy and proper to make it a penal offence to use, without legal authority, a badge and a name which have done, and can continue to do, so much for the cause of humanity. A law to this effect would also be a safeguard in other respects to numbers of Volunteer Aid Societies in war, as its existence would make them careful to abstain from such a use of the badge as might render them amenable to military law of the severest character.

It may be considered as conclusive, that in no future war will the same latitude be allowed to the Red Cross Societies as has been permitted in the past, and those who have at heart the interest of these useful institutions would be the last to desire a repetition of such inconvenient freedom as has been witnessed in some modern campaigns. The representatives of the Volunteer Societies will not again be permitted to exercise their functions at the front, but their services will probably be confined to the lines of communication from the second line of medical assistance to the base, where, if perfectly organised, they will prove inestimable.

France, for instance, which possesses a Red Cross Society second to none for intelligent and continuous activity, has set an example which, in case of war, will be of the greatest benefit to her sick and wounded soldiers. The Central Committee of Paris has, since its formation, maintained friendly relations with the military authorities, and it corresponds directly with the Minister of War through the medium of its president, and with

---

* De l'emploi abusif du signe de la Croix Rouge. Deux mémoires de M. le Dr. Jules César Buzzati, Professeur de droit international à l'université de Macerati et de M. l'avocat Constantin Castori, professeur libre de droit pénal à l'université de Padua, Couronnés et publiés par le Comité international de la Croix Rouge.

(*Korpslæger*), of whom the 8 senior have the rank of Captain of the Militia, the other 16 that of Lieutenant. Besides these, there are (b) medical officers of the 4th class (*Reservelæger*), who have the rank of Sub-Lieutenant; these are not regulars, being only appointed for a limited period by the Minister of War after having been nominated by the Director-General. Of these there may be up to 16 serving at the same time.

Duties.—The Director-General (*Stabslægen*) has, under the Minister of War, the supreme management and supervision of all army medical and sanitary matters. He inspects all medical and sanitary arrangements, supervises professionally the medical officers and the military hospitals, and inspects the sanitary equipment. He is professionally the superior of the other medical officers, appoints medical officers of the 4th class (*Reservelæger*), and nominates medical officers for appointment as regular medical officers of the 3rd class, and for promotion from the 3rd to 2nd class. He is also the chief of the Medical Staff Corps and has the supreme management of its administration, the details of which are in the hands of the commander of the Medical Staff Corps, who is under the Director-General. He is the adviser of the Minister of War in all medical and sanitary matters, as also of all superior military authorities.

Of the 14 medical officers of the 2nd class (*Overlæger*) two are Principal Medical Officers (*Generalcommando-Læger*) for each of the two military districts into which the country is divided. The Principal Medical Officer is under the General commanding the district, whose adviser he is in all sanitary matters, especially those concerning the district. Professionally he is under the Director-General, whom he assists in the supervision of sanitary arrangements and the professional work of the medical officers, especially in regard to the preparation of the medical statistics and the administration of the sanitary equipment.

The other medical officers of the 2nd class (*Overlæger*) and those of the 3rd class (*Korpslæger*) are employed either with the troops or in military hospitals, there being, as a rule, no difference between the employment of the medical officers of these two classes.

When with the troops the medical officer is, in the performance of his military duties, under the Officer commanding, being his adviser in all sanitary matters. Professionally he is under the Principal Medical Officer and the Director-General. He is charged with the care of the health of the troops, examines the sick and has to attend them, when he does not send them to the hospital. He furnishes statistical and other returns, and assists the commandant of the barracks in the sanitary inspection of these, when detailed for this duty.

On the employment of medical officers at the military hospitals, *see* below.

The medical officers of the 4th class (*Reservelæger*) are only appointed on probation for a limited period; they assist the

Chap. II.

Ambulance arrangements of the Danish Army

regular medical officers with the troops or in the military hospitals.

The medical officers are alternately detailed for duty at the annual *sessions* of the six conscript districts,* into which the country is divided. Here they have to examine the conscripts, and to give their opinion as to the military ability of these, whereupon the *session-committee* decides the enlistment. All matters concerning the conscription do not, however, come under the Ministry of War or the Army Medical Department, but are under the Ministry of Justice.

Those conscripts, who are either qualified medical men or are medical students who have acted as clerks and dressers at one of the large metropolitan hospitals for at least two years, are, if they are physically fit, enlisted as Assistant-Surgeons (*Underlæger*). Of these four-fifths are sent off for duty in the Army and one-fifth in the Navy. The former have to undergo the following training the next summer:—(1) During a fortnight a preparatory military training with the troops. (2) During four weeks a training in the military hospital of Copenhagen (clinical demonstrations of sick, training in medical inspection of recruits and invalids, training in general military and in special medical and sanitary matters, in military hygiene, and use of medical and sanitary military appliances, as also in medical assistance during action.) (3) During four weeks training in practical medical service with the troops during the manœuvres (in September), having then the rank of corporal, while they up to this time only were privates. The assistant-surgeons have then finished their duty, and have not to enter any more during peace, but may, if desirous, obtain an appointment as medical officers of the 4th class (*Reservelæger*), being on probation for a year at a time.

In case of vacancy any assistant-surgeon, who is qualified at the Copenhagen University, can be appointed regular medical officer of the 3rd class, those who have acted on probation as medical officers of the 4th class having, however, the preference.

Medical Staff Corps of the Danish Army

The Medical Staff Corps.—The Medical Staff Corps (*Sundhedstropperne*) consists of ward orderlies and stretcher-bearers.

The ward **orderlies'** (*Sygepasserne*) duty is to personally **attend the sick in** the military hospitals according to the **directions and** under the supervision of the medical officer in charge. It is also their duty to act as "Canteen-Soldiers" (*Kantinesoldater*), i.e., to accompany the medical officers with the troops in field, carrying the surgical haversack, and assisting the medical officers when affording temporary assistance to sick and wounded by means of the medical and surgical appliances of the surgical haversack.

Like the assistant-surgeons, the ward orderlies are conscripts, especially fit for this kind of service, 120 being annually enlisted.

---

* In Denmark military service is compulsory. All men having attained the age of 22 have to appear before the *sessions* for examination as to military ability. They may, however, appear as early as 18 years of age, but not later than 25.

They enter in four batches, 30 in each, their training **lasting seven** months. The ward orderlies of each batch go through a preliminary class of instruction lasting two and a half months, being trained here in general military and professional duties, after which they undergo a final training for four and a half months at the military hospitals, being distributed in the different hospitals. They are then dismissed, but enter again one of the following years, serving at the hospitals and with the troops (as "canteen-soldiers") during the manœuvres in September. Of the ward orderlies the one quarter most able are promoted from privates to sub-corporals, after having been trained for five months, and of these any number up to 15 may be promoted **to corporals** and appointed for one year at a time. Among the ward orderlies there is no rank higher than that of corporal. The **school** of the ward orderlies, **as** well as all matters pertaining **to** them outside the hospital, **is managed** by an officer, who is under the Director-General.

Stretcher-bearers' (*Sygebærere*) duty at the ambulances or with the troops in search for the wounded during action, afford them, if necessary, the first temporary assistance (by arresting bleeding, applying temporary dressings, &c.), and transport them on the stretcher or otherwise to the dressing-station.

The stretcher-bearers are not enlisted at the *session* to perform this duty, but chosen amongst the soldiers with complete military training. 92 privates being chosen each year. They are trained during the manœuvres in September, and are called out one of the following years to go through what they have learned. Besides these stretcher-bearer privates, 31 sub-corporals, with special ability in this kind of work, are chosen amongst the infantry troops to undergo a three months' training as bearer corporals (*Sygebærerførere*). These are also called out at the manœuvres to go through what they have learned.

CHAPTER III.

THE CONVENTION OF GENEVA AND ITS BADGE —THE RED CROSS.

CHAP. III.
The special significance of the Red Cross.

No account of the ambulance of an army or of ambulance transport material, its various kinds and its uses, would be now complete without some reference to the Convention of Geneva and its badge—the Red Cross.

Notwithstanding all that has been said and written on this subject, the most erroneous ideas still exist with regard to it, and the general impression seems to be that the Red Cross is a badge which any society or individual is at liberty to adopt, though it more especially distinguishes hospitals, civil or military, and the personnel attached to them.

Once again it must be emphatically declared that the Red Cross badge has no significance except as denoting the personnel and matériel, both official and unofficial, of military hospital and ambulance service in time of war. For this reason, therefore, it is an indefensible usurpation to employ it in civil hospital, or for civil purposes, in time of peace; and even in time of war it should not be so used, **unless** such institutions are in some degree, if not entirely, **placed at the** disposal of, and accepted by, the military authorities.

A **red cross on a white ground was** adopted **as a** badge of **neutrality by the International Conference,** representing sixteen **States, which framed the Convention** of Geneva in August, **1864.** This Treaty, which has done so much to mitigate the **sufferings caused** by war, was signed, within six months of its **conclusion, by** eight European States, including Great Britain, and at the present time it has been accepted by thirty-six Governments.

Since 1864 thirty-four National Red Cross Societies have been formed, each with an independent national existence, but with one international object, namely, the amelioration of the position of the sick and wounded soldiers in war. Some of these Societies are organised, as will be presently shown, in the most complete and practical manner, and they are ready to accomplish their humane mission to the fullest extent in their power. They also combine with this work the relief of **suffering** arising from **great** calamities which occur in time of peace. The machinery required is thus always kept in order, and it enlists the sympathy and co-operation of all classes whose interest in it could not be maintained if it were only to be used during a period of war—a time which civilians seldom anticipate. Germany, France, and Russia, as might have been expected, have been the principal leaders in this great movement, but many other States which have not had so much cause for activity have followed their example in the most liberal and disinterested spirit.

It is a matter for surprise that the Convention of Geneva, which has had such important results, and under the sanction of which so many thousands of persons of various nationalities have been enrolled, should be so little known. Hundreds of persons have worn the Red Cross badge, have served under its flag and contributed to its support, and yet remain in the most complete ignorance as to the terms of the Convention which authorises its use. There are many who still think that, in time of war, they can wear a Red Cross armlet which, whilst denoting their neutrality, will ensure their comparative safety. This feeling derived much encouragement from the great liberty allowed to volunteer societies during the Franco-German war. A belligerent army, rejoicing in overwhelming and continuous victory, can afford to permit the utmost freedom to those who can materially assist in the care of its own wounded or of those of the enemy with whom it may be encumbered. A defeated army also will naturally welcome such assistance, the more readily, perhaps, if it be given by those who are not connected with the conqueror by ties of nationality. But in a campaign, when successes and reverses are more equally balanced, the "benevolent neutral" finds himself in a very different position, and he is compelled to act more or less with and in subordination to the military authorities of the army to which he is attached, or he will inevitably incur risks from which a Red Cross badge will not save him; and, in addition to the ordinary dangers inseparable from war, he may be considered and treated as a spy.

Undoubtedly, many Red Cross Societies have suffered from the too great success and extent of their first efforts. In the absence of proper supervision, and amidst the dislocation of official means and organisation, some of the societies of neutral States were allowed a freedom of action which frequently took the place of, instead of supplementing, the military departments they were charged to assist; and, as may be supposed, the good work done was marred by acts which, if repeated, will most certainly bring them into collision with the military authorities of belligerent States. On this account it has been predicted that such an institution as the Red Cross will not be recognised in future wars. This suggestion is utterly groundless. All wars on a large scale have proved that the official means of an army organisation, however perfect they may be, must prove altogether inadequate to the requirements of the wounded on a vast battlefield, and, sooner or later, recourse

CHAP. III.

The National Red Cross Societies.

The neutrality of the Red Cross.

Chap. III.

The want of knowledge regarding the Red Cross is considerable.

must be had to volunteer aid. Without going further back in history, our own wars, from that of the Crimea to the present time, have sufficiently demonstrated the truth of this assertion. The press and the telegraph have brought even the most distant of our battlefields into such rapid communication with the base of operations that everthing is immediately known, and much is exaggerated. Enthusiastic friends imagine, in their inexperience, that the treatment of the sick and wounded can be as completely administered in a foreign land and in the midst of a campaign as it would be at home, and if it is not done they find fault with everybody whom they may consider in any degree responsible. Comparisons are drawn between the ambulances* at the front and the admirably kept wards of hospitals in our large towns, and naturally they are not in favour of the former. Angry murmurs, and letters to the newspapers follow, and very often the criticism is as unwise as it is unfair to the medical staff. *On ne peut faire une omelette sans casser des œufs.*

It is quite impossible that on a battlefield, or in close proximity to the active operations of war, such perfect arrangements can be made for a large number of sick and wounded men hastily brought into a temporary hospital as will satisfy newspaper critics or the wishes of relatives and friends at home; but there is no limit to what may be done in this direction by proper and intelligent preparation and organisation in time of peace of those voluntary and unofficial means which the public are only too anxious to place at the disposal of the military authorities.

In peace, and during periods of comparative calm, it is easy to define the position which a Red Cross Society should occupy in war, but experience has proved what a hopeless task this is during the turmoil and agony of a campaign, and to what waste and extravagance an absence of system inevitably leads.

All volunteer ambulances should be under military control.

It is not surprising, therefore, that the great continental powers, who have had ample opportunities of estimating the good and evil effects of amateur intervention in the management of ambulances and hospitals in war, should have determined that, in the future, they will not sanction the same amount of freedom and irresponsible activity as that which has been permitted in the past, but that volunteer services and gifts shall henceforth be placed under an authority not only nominal, as heretofore, but absolute. In fact, the volunteer ambulance, for the time being, will be as much under military control as any

---

* The word "ambulance" is most improperly used. Too frequently it is applied to a stretcher, a wheeled litter, or a carriage for invalids drawn by a horse; and it is impossible sometimes to understand what is wanted when an enquiry is made for an ambulance. It should be understood that an ambulance really includes everything necessary for the establishment of a temporary hospital, *personnel* as well as *matériel*. When employed in any more limited sense, the article it is intended to qualify should also be named; for instance, "Ambulance Carriage," "Ambulance Litter," &c.

the Generals Commanding Army Corps by means of delegates officially appointed. In 1884 a decree was passed with the object of bringing the society into harmony with the military changes that had taken place since the war of 1870-71, authorising the *Société de Sécours aux blessés des armées de terre et de mer* to supplement in time of war the military sanitary service, to distribute gifts offered by public generosity, to establish hospitals in places that may be indicated as requiring them, to render assistance in the transport by railway of sick and wounded soldiers, in the railway station infirmaries (a creation of the Franco-German war), and in all the auxiliary hospitals at the seat of war. Since the decree of 3rd July, 1884, two others have been passed, dated respectively 16th November, 1886, and 21st December of the same year. The first recognises *l'Association des dames françaises*, and the second *l'Union des femmes de France*. These decrees limit the co-operation of the Aid Societies with the military medical services to the rear of active hostilities and to the National Territory.

CHAP. III

The National Aid Societies of France.

Independently of this assistance the Societies are authorised to distribute to the sick and wounded the gifts they have collected. The relations of the Societies with each other and with the Official Directors of the medical service are defined by the above-mentioned decrees. Every establishment of the Aid Societies is under the surveillance of the principal medical officer of the district in which it is situated, who also superintends all the documents and registers prescribed.

The personnel of the three Societies is authorised to wear a uniform and the badges recognised by the Minister of War. All associations in France which, more or less, pursue the same object and which cannot be recognised as independent societies, are required in time of war to become merged in the Central National Aid Society; there is only one exception to this rule, and that is in favour of those strictly local ambulances whose action does not extend beyond the communes where they are established.

Their personnel is recognised.

Already at many of the most important railway junctions on the principal lines between Paris and the frontiers of France, not only have certain rooms been apportioned for the use of the Société de Sécours aux blessés, but a large *personnel* and everything required for hospital use have been allotted for the same purpose. On the outbreak of war each of these temporary hospitals could be established and placed on an active footing as rapidly as the mobilisation of the Army can be effected; and besides this the delegates of the society are charged with the useful duty of bringing back invalids from the front and accompanying the railway ambulance trains. These movable and stationary hospitals form the special work of the Société de Sécours aux blessés militaires in time of war, and they offer a large scope for the exercise of national philanthropy without the danger and inconvenience to which reference has already been made.

Great attention is being paid by the French society to the

CHAP. III.

constant improvement of ambulance material, depôts have been established in 39 towns corresponding with 39 territorial divisions of the Army, and trials of this material are annually made at the period of the great manœuvres. For the *personnel*, schools of instruction for ambulancers and nurses have been formed in Paris, and also at Marseilles, Lille, and Nancy.

The National Aid Societies in Germany.

In Germany, in time of peace, the fullest independence is allowed to the various aid societies which exist in all the States, but the moment the country is engaged in war the direction of all the different branches is brought under the Central Committee of German Associations of the Red Cross, a body composed of delegates from the societies of all the States in the Empire, acting under the control of a Commissary Inspector on behalf of the Government. Many hundreds of committees working in correspondence with the Central Committee of Berlin are scattered over Germany, and the result of this system is evident in the numerous admirable institutions which do so much good during peace whilst preparing for the eventuality of war.

One very important branch has been the formation, as in France, of depôts of ambulance material, divided into four distinct categories and placed under the management of a Commission of Surgeons and lay delegates of the central and ladies' committees. The articles contained in these stores are again subdivided into such as are absolutely necessary and those which may be useful. Models and patterns are from time to time issued for the use of all the affiliated societies and, in the same manner, instructions are given as to the changes and improvements to be made.

In Austria-Hungary.

In Austria-Hungary Red Cross work is under the dual direction of two central committees, one at Vienna for Austria and one at Buda-Pesth for Hungary. In addition to these, two ancient orders of nobility also devote their personal efforts and a large portion of their wealth to the same object. The Teutonic Order can place in the field without delay forty-three columns, each consisting of three ambulance carriages, one fourgon, and one cooking wagon, all completely fitted for a campaign. Of these columns two are adapted for mountain warfare, and each corresponds with a territorial division of the Army, the military authorities providing the necessary complement of men and horses. The Malteser Orden, on the other hand, possesses six complete railway hospital trains, each composed of sixteen carriages, and these are ready to be sent over any line in the Empire where such form of assistance may be needed.

These two illustrious orders and the National Red Cross Society work under an agreement which clearly defines their respective functions.

In Russia.

In Russia also the position of the National Society with regard to the Head-quarter Staff and the Medical Department of the Army is well laid down. During the war in the Balkan provinces in 1876–78 the work of the society was carried out on a magnificent scale as is proved by the fact that in December, 1877, it was employing 90 doctors, 10 apothecaries, 120 dressers, 90 students of both sexes, 500 sisters of mercy, 500 male nurses; and there was a reserve of 400 persons which could have been readily increased to any extent on application to the auxiliary societies scattered over the empire.

CHAP. III.

The National Aid Society in Italy.

In Italy the National Society is in a condition to pass in the shortest possible space of time from a period of peace to one of war, and for this purpose it has adopted for its various sections the same territorial divisions as those of the Army, with a sub-committee in each of the twelve towns occupied by the head-quarters of an **Army Corps**.

Want of **space** will not permit of more than this rapid **glance** at the nature of the work which has been severely **tested in** some of the large States of Europe. It would be **easy to** amplify these details and also to point out what has been done in other countries.

Even in Turkey, where the Red Crescent has been substituted for the Geneva badge, the latter has been recognised **for** all practical purposes, and it has been estimated that in 1877–78 at least 30,000 sufferers experienced the benefit of the protection of the Red Crescent. The smaller States also have **vied** with their larger neighbours, and their efforts in the same direction have been equally successful though on a more modest **scale**. But the above examples, briefly as they have been treated, are sufficient to indicate what is being done by the different National Societies, and it would be outside the province of this brief paper to enter upon any detailed criticism of their labours or to suggest rules for their future acceptance.

In Turkey.

It must, however, be noted that each of the National Red **Cross Societies has, or** should have, its own organisation and method of working in time of peace. In certain States, **as has** been seen, this system, as far as it relates to invalid soldiers, **is** under military control and in complete harmony with official rules, whilst in others more latitude is permitted. Some societies strictly confine themselves to the preparation of such means **as** will enable them, in case of war, to furnish a valuable supplement to the official sanitary service of their own Army; others **do** not limit themselves to the anticipation **of** war, but **extend practical sympathy to** the victims of great **calamities in civil life, and afford** prompt relief to those who **suffer from** famine, epidemics, fire, railway, and colliery accidents, **and** other disasters. Such calamities should, no doubt, **claim** general sympathy and charity, and they offer the best opportunities for the exercise of the machinery of these philanthropic institutions; but it must be remembered that the liberty which **is tolerated in the administration of** relief in ordinary times **cannot be sanctioned during a** campaign when military authority must be paramount.

This last point is one of such absolute importance that it cannot be insisted on too strongly. Perfect as a system may be for civil purposes, it may be found utterly wanting if applied to military hospitals and ambulances in time of war unless military discipline be accepted as its first condition. It is

CHAP. III

better to have obedience with inefficient means than the greatest wealth of means coupled with independence of official control. For this reason no volunteer aid society, whose object it is to give hospital and ambulance assistance in war can accomplish its mission unless it be so organised during peace as to be ready to fall into its proper place on the outbreak of war. To assist it to do this, an active and competent delegate of the National Red Cross Society—an officer of rank and military experience if possible—should be attached to the headquarters of the army, and it should be his duty in peace time to see that all the personal and material resources of the society are carefully registered and periodically inspected, and to make arrangements for their proper distribution in such a manner as to cause no inconvenience or friction at the critical moment when the greatest strain may be imposed on the War Office authorities.

Importance of discipline in furthering the objects of the Convention.

A National Red Cross Society thus constituted may be of the utmost value, and the daily exercise of its functions for the relief of the victims of disease and accident in civil life will be the best school for those who desire to assist in some degree in lessening the sufferings incidental to war. Then, when war occurs, the transition will be a comparatively easy one for those who have been trained in that vast field of civil ambulance work which is open to all; and a valuable nucleus of experienced men and women can be rapidly mobilised to give their aid under military conditions in which, it must never be forgotten, the first indispensable quality is absolute obedience.

CONVENTION OF GENEVA.

For the amelioration of the condition of Wounded Soldiers in Armies during War.

(August 22nd, 1864.)

The Articles of the Convention.

Art. 1.—Ambulances and military hospitals shall be acknowledged to be neuter, and, as such, shall be protected and respected by belligerents so long as any sick or wounded may be therein.

Such neutrality shall cease if the ambulances or hospitals should be held by a military force.

Art. 2.—Persons employed in hospitals and ambulances, comprising the staff for superintendence, medical service, administration, transport of wounded, as well as chaplains, shall participate in the benefit of neutrality whilst so employed, and so long as there remain any wounded to be brought in or to succour.

Art. 3.—The persons designated in the preceding article may, even after occupation by the enemy, continue to **fulfil** their duties in the hospital or ambulance which they serve, or may withdraw in order to rejoin the corps to which they belong.

Under such circumstances, when those persons shall cease from their functions, they shall be delivered by the occupying army to the outposts of the enemy.

Art. 4.—As the equipment of military **hospitals remains** subject to the laws of war, persons attached **to such hospitals** cannot, in withdrawing, carry **away any articles** but such as are their private property.

Under the same circumstances, an ambulance shall, on the contrary, retain its equipment.

Art. 5.—Inhabitants of the country who may bring help to the wounded shall be respected, and shall remain **free**. The generals of the belligerent powers **shall make it their** care to inform the inhabitants of **the appeal addressed to their** humanity, and of the neutrality **which will be the consequence** of it.

Any wounded man entertained and **taken** care of **in a** house shall be considered as a protection thereto. Any inhabitant who shall have entertained wounded men **in his** house shall be exempted from the quartering of troops, **as** well as from a part of the contributions of war which may be imposed.

Art. 6.—Wounded or sick soldiers shall be entertained and taken care of **to** whatever nation they may belong.

Commanders-in-Chief **shall** have the power to **deliver** immediately to the outposts **of the** enemy soldiers who **have** been wounded in an engagement, when circumstances permit this to be done, and with the consent of both parties.

Those who are recognised, after their wounds are healed, **as** incapable of serving, shall be sent back to their country.

The others may also be sent back on condition of **not** bearing arms again during **the** continuance of the war.

Evacuations, together **with** the persons under whose directions they take place, **shall** be protected by an absolute neutrality.

Art. 7.—A distinctive and **uniform flag** shall be adopted for hospitals, ambulances, and **evacuations. It** must on every occasion **be** accompanied by the **national flag**. An arm-badge (brassard) **shall** also be **allowed for individuals** neutralised, but the delivery thereof shall be left to military authority.

The flag and the arm-badge shall bear a red cross on a white ground.

Art. 8.—The details of execution of the present convention shall be regulated by Commanders-in-Chief of belligerent armies, according to the instructions of their respective governments and in conformity with the general rules here laid down.

Art. 9.—The high contracting powers agree to communi-

CHAP. III.
The Articles of the Convention.

cate the present convention to those Governments which have not sent plenipotentiaries to the International Conference at Geneva, with an invitation to accede thereto. The protocol is for that purpose left open.

The present Convention will be ratified, and the ratification will be exchanged at Berne within four months or sooner if possible.*

LIST IN **CHRONOLOGICAL** ORDER OF THE STATES WHICH **HAVE** ACCEPTED THE CONVENTION OF GENEVA OF AUGUST 22ND, 1864.

France	September 22nd	1864.
Switzerland	October 1st	1864.
Belgium	October 14th	1864.
Netherlands	November 29th	1864.
Italy	December 4th	1864.
Spain	December 5th	1864.
Sweden and Norway	December 13th	1864.
Denmark	December 15th	1864.
Baden	December 16th	1864.
Greece	January 17th	1865.
Great Britain	February 18th	1865.
Mecklenburg-Schwerin	March 9th	1865.
Prussia	June 22nd	1865.
Turkey	July 5th	1865.
Wurtemburg	June 2nd	1866.
Hesse (Grand Duchy)	June 22nd	1866.
Bavaria	June 30th	1866.
Austria	July 21st	1866.
Portugal	August 9th	1866.
Saxony	October 25th	1866.
Russia	May 22nd	1867.
Pontifical States	May 9th	1868.
Roumania	November 30th	1874.
Persia	December 5th	1874.
San Salvador	December 30th	1874.
Montenegro	November 29th	1875.
Servia	March 24th	1876.
Bolivia	October 16th	1879.

---

* The nine powers who attached their signatures to this Treaty at Geneva on the 22nd **August**, 1864, are—in the chronological order of their respective ratifications—France, Switzerland, Belgium, the Netherlands, Italy, Spain, Denmark, the Duchy of Baden, and Prussia. Twelve other Governments subsequently signed at different times, namely, Sweden and Norway, Greece, Great Britain, Mecklenburg-Schwerin, Turkey, Portugal, Russia, Roumania, Persia, San Salvador, the Argentine Republic, and the United States of America. Eleven other States only signed under pressure of **war** in which their armies were engaged **or** were about to enter. These are Wurtemberg, Hesse, Bavaria, Austria, Saxony, the Pontifical States, Montenegro, Servia, Bolivia, Chili, and Peru.

The Convention of Geneva.

Chili	November 15th	1879.
Argentine Republic	November 25th	1879.
Peru	April 22nd	1880.
United States of America	March 1st	1882.
Bulgaria	March 1st	1884.
Japan	June 5th	1886.
Luxemburg	October 5th	1888.
Congo	December 27th	1888.

LIST IN CHRONOLOGICAL ORDER OF COUNTRIES IN WHICH NATIONAL SOCIETIES OF THE RED CROSS HAVE BEEN FORMED.

Wurtemberg	December	1863.
Oldenburg	January 2nd	1864.
Belgium	February 4th	1864.
Prussia	February 6th	1864.
Denmark	May	1864.
France	May 25th	1864.
Mecklenburg-Schwerin	June 24th	1864.
Spain	July 6th	1864.
Hamburg	October 18th	1864.
Hesse (Grand Duchy)	December	1864.
Portugal	February 11th	1865.
Sweden	May 24th	1865.
Norway	October	1865.
United States of America	January 26th	1866.
Saxony	June 7th	1866.
Baden	June 29th	1866.
Switzerland	July 17th	1866.
Russia	May 3rd	1867.
Austria	May 18th	1867.
Holland	July 19th	1867.
Bavaria	January 5th	1868.
Turkey	June 11th	1868.
Great Britain	September	1869.
Luxemburg	July	1870.
Portugal (re-constitution)		1870.
Italy (re-constitution)	May 31st	1873.
Denmark (re-constitution)	June 18th	1875.
Montenegro	January 15th	1876.
Servia	January 21st	1876.
Roumania	July	1876.
Turkey (re-constitution)	February	1877.
Greece	June 22nd	1877.
Peru	April	1879.
Austria (re-constitution)	March	1880.
Argentine Republic	June 13th	1880.
Hungary	April 15th	**1881.**
United States (re-constitution)	June 9th	**1881.**

Switzerland (re-constitution)	June 9th	1882.
Balgaria	May 4th	1885.
Portugal (re-constitution)	May 27th	1887.
Japan	June 22nd	1887.
Congo	December 31st	1888.

RESOLUTIONS PASSED AT INTERNATIONAL CONFERENCES HELD BY THE FOUNDERS AND REPRESENTATIVES OF THE RED CROSS.*

At Geneva	1863
Paris	1867
Berlin	1869
Geneva	1884
Carlsruhe	1887

I.—AIM AND GENERAL ORGANISATION OF THE RED CROSS.

1. There exists in each of the contracting States signatories of the Convention of Geneva, a society called the Red Cross Society, whose duty it is to do its utmost in time of war to aid the official sanitary service of armies in the field.

2. It is desirable that this society should be the only one authorised by the State to use the Red Cross as a badge and that it should be protected against abuses which might prove detrimental.

3. The offices of the society should be distinguished by an external sign in order that public attention may be called to it.

4. There is no general scheme for the organisation of volunteer aid adapted to all the States. Such organisation must depend on national and local circumstances. Every National Society, therefore, should be organised in the way which may appear most useful and convenient to itself.

5. Each society shall have at its head a central committee, to which the general direction will belong.

6. Sections, unlimited in number, may be formed in support of the central committee.

7. Sections shall be formed throughout each country.

8. The assistance of ladies' committees is indispensable.

9. In large states, provincial or district committees can be

---

* If the following paragraphs appear somewhat disjointed it is due to the fact that they are literal translations of resolutions passed at meetings spread over a period of 24 years.

created as links between the central committee **and the local** sections. [Chap. III. Aim and general organisation]

10. **The central committee of a** small State can be placed in relation with that of a large State, in the same manner as provincial committees stand in regard to the latter.

11. It is desirable that local committees, whilst devoting a portion of their annual receipts to the fund of the central committee of their own country shall be autonomous with regard to the administration and disposal of their own resources.

12. In this respect the central direction—in which the local committees participate through delegates having the right to vote—can only indicate to the local committees in time of peace, its actual requirements and solicit assistance for work undertaken in common, without having the power to dispose independently of their personal and material resources.

13. National Societies, whilst remaining, as far as concerns internal organisation and administration, absolutely independent of each other, recognise that they have the same object in view. This community of work creates amongst them a moral solidarity which is **so necessary** to the accomplishment of their humanitarian mission.

II.—Relations between National Societies and Governments.

14. Each society should place itself in communication with the Government of its own State, in order that its offers of assistance may be accepted should the opportunity arise. [International relations.]

15. It is desirable that Governments should give their patronage to these societies and facilitate to the fullest extent the realisation of their objects.

16. Each society should obtain official and legal recognition.

17. The relations between the societies and the military authorities in time of war should be officially determined, and all regulations should be as uniform as possible.

III.—Work of National Societies in Time of Peace.

18. During peace the societies should prepare with a view to making themselves useful in time of war, especially in the manner indicated by Articles 19 to 46 hereinafter mentioned. [Work during peace.]

(a)—Arrangements for Mobilisation.

19. The societies should come to an understanding with the military authorities in order to define their relations in time of **war.**

20. They should arrange their organisation and **draw** up a precise and detailed plan of their action in time of war.

Chap. III.
Work during peace.

(b)—Preparation of Material.

21. The societies should prepare material aid of every description.

22. The societies, especially those on which devolve the exclusive charge of an important portion of the sanitary service, should take necessary measures so that material sufficient in quantity as well as in quality and suitable to the exigencies of war, shall be ready in case of mobilisation, more particularly for the first requirements; in default of this, they should at any rate assure themselves by previous arrangement of the possibility of obtaining this material in such a manner that the general organisation at the opening of a campaign may not be thrown into confusion.

23. It is not necessary during peace to have depôts of material. It is, however, expedient to procure models of articles necessary for the comfort of the sick as well as stretchers, and to arrange with the committees of different countries for the mutual exchange of objects of this kind.

24. It is desirable that in every State or in a union of States there should be formed a permanent exhibition of sanitary material.

25. It is advisable that **each society should** form an album **or a** collection, illustrating, **by** drawings, engravings, or photo-**graphs,** the whole of the ambulance material as well as the corresponding material used by the War Department of its own country, and that it should send a copy to each of the other societies as well as to the Governments which have accepted the Convention of Geneva. Such an exchange would take the place of an international museum.

26. An International Commission should be appointed for the examination of models of ambulance material.

27. The societies should procure tents or portable barracks adapted for the relief of sick and wounded in time of peace as well as during war.

28. The societies, during peace, should make preparation for military reserve hospitals, undertaking to establish or administer them in time of war. Such preparation should include the selection of localities, material, and administration.

29. The societies should also obtain during peace information as to the experience acquired, and all the new inventions and suggestions relating to military hygiene and the relief to be afforded to the sick during a campaign.

30. Antiseptic dressings should be adopted, by order, in all the Societies.

The societies are advised to take the necessary steps, as far as they are concerned, that antiseptic and conservative surgery shall be employed in all armies, even in the first line and on the field of battle.

(c)—Organisation of the Personnel.

31. The societies should endeavour to form and instruct volunteer ambulancers.

(1)—Men.

CHAP. III.
Work during peace.

32. The selection and equipment of a sanitary corps, composed of active and vigorous men, is as useful to the societies during peace as in war.

33. It is desirable, wherever societies of military pensioners exist, to obtain their assistance for the transport of the sick.

34. The personnel of the sick transport corps, which ought to be formed during peace, should have a proper training, as much for the purpose of maintaining the instruction already acquired as for habituating the men to that discipline which is absolutely indispensable.

35. It is advisable to form professional associations of men employed in the service of the sick: 1st, in order to maintain amongst them the sentiment of professional honour; 2ndly, in order to make provision against an uncertain future for those who in the exercise of their duty may become partially or totally incapacitated from gaining a livelihood. This object could be obtained by mutual assurance in case of accident.

(2)—Women.

36. It is part of the duty of the societies to provide for the instruction of female nurses.

37. This duty cannot be fulfilled unless those who desire to become nurses undergo a strict examination as to fitness, and are trained and exercised by experience in nursing the sick poor.

38. In examining the capacity of nurses, not only should their moral and intellectual qualities be considered, but attention should be given to their health, in order that they may be physically competent for the services which will be required of them.

39. The societies are recommended to undertake during peace the development or establishment of a system of instruction for ladies who might be commissioned to superintend the local ambulances or stationary hospitals of the Red Cross, and thus enable them to give efficacious assistance to physicians and surgeons by the intelligent execution of directions relating to the hygiene of hospitals and the treatment of the sick.

(d)—General Service.

40. It is necessary, during peace, to designate for the special branches of service to which they will be attached those persons who will be called on for active duty at the time of mobilisation, and at once to instruct them in the work which they will have to perform.

41. The nursing staff should be instructed during peace in the application of antiseptic dressings.

42. It is necessary to organise beforehand a sufficiently

numerous reserve to supply any vacancies which may occur, and thus avoid interruption in the service.

43. A pension ought to be assured not only to persons who, whilst devoting themselves to the care of the wounded in war, may become incapacitated from gaining a livelihood, but also to the families of those who may succumb to the same causes.

(e)—*Mark of Identification.*

44. The societies should endeavour to obtain by all the means in their power the adoption in the armies of their respective countries of a mark which will enable them easily to distinguish the identity of the dead and wounded.

(f)—*Catastrophes in Time of Peace.*

45. The societies should, as far as possible, associate themselves with humane works corresponding to those which they undertake to fulfil in time of war, and give their assistance in those public **calamities** which require, as in war, prompt and organised **relief**.

46. The societies should undertake the care of the sick, especially in conjunction with deaconesses, Sisters of Charity, the Orders of St. John of Jerusalem and Malta, and other similar bodies.

IV.—THE WORK OF THE NATIONAL SOCIETIES DURING WAR.

47. In time of war, the national societies of the belligerent States, in proportion to their means and in conformity with military regulations, shall furnish aid to their respective armies, particularly in the manner indicated by Articles 48 to 61.

(a)—*Auxiliary Personnel.*

48. The societies shall organise and place in the field volunteer male nurses.

49. On the demand or with the consent of the military authority, **they** shall send these male **nurses** to **the field** of battle under the direction of military officers.

50. **At the theatre** of war, in a foreign country, **the** sanitary service of armies shall be personally and materially assisted by the societies—

    (a) On the field, after a battle.
    (b) In the transport of sick and wounded.
    (c). In the hospitals.

51. The societies shall endeavour to establish good relations

and a common agreement with other aid societies acting at the theatre of war.

52. The volunteer male nurses on active service should be provided by their respective societies with everything necessary for their maintenance.

53. They shall wear in all countries, as a distinctive uniform mark, a white armlet with a red cross upon it.*

(b)—Sites for Hospitals.

54. The societies, acting in conjunction with the military authority, shall fix on sites for the care of the wounded.

55. They shall, on principle, avoid everything which may draw their members into a fight, and consequently they shall abstain from forming ambulances in the first line.

56. As a general rule, they shall not establish or undertake any hospitals outside their own country.

(c)—Depôts of Material.

57. The societies shall establish at home and abroad central and subsidiary depôts of sanitary material.

58. For this purpose they shall give special attention to the fortresses at home which are menaced.

59. Gifts of material shall be submitted to the most careful examination before being forwarded to the seat of war.

60. Purchased material shall conform as closely as possible to the patterns approved by the Government.

(d)—Hygiene of the Battle-field.

61. The societies shall arrange for the disinfection of fields of battle to the best of their means.

V.—MARITIME ACTIVITY OF NATIONAL SOCIETIES.†

62. The Aid Societies shall arrange with the Societies for the relief of shipwrecked mariners, in order that these bodies, in case of a naval war, and in consideration of higher payment than usual, shall place their lifeboats at the disposal of the former, and shall also hire a sufficient number of other boats.

63. Before engaging vessels intended for the relief of the shipwrecked in a maritime war, it will be necessary to settle

---

* In accordance with Article 7 of the Convention of Geneva of 22nd August, 1864, the military authority only has the power to give such an armlet.

† The international conference at Carlsruhe in 1887 decided that it was necessary to submit this to a complete revision. The question is now undergoing consideration, and it is probable that at the next conference, the date of which has not yet been fixed, new articles will be substituted for those which are here given.

Vide also, on the maritime activity of the Red Cross, Article 13 proposed to be added to the Convention of Geneva.

CHAP. III.
Maritime activity.

the question as to who shall bear the expense occasioned by damage to or the loss of such vessels.

64. Relief vessels shall operate during and after a battle. They shall follow the belligerent fleets, and shall be under the orders of the Admirals commanding.

65. During a battle and immediately after a signal of distress shall be hoisted, they shall go to the relief of all ships, to whatever nationality they may belong.

66. The relief vessels, immediately after a naval engagement, shall signal that they can and will receive sick and wounded.

67. For this service steamboats should be selected of a certain speed, good sea-goers, easy to handle, and spacious between decks.

68. The preparations concerning the personnel and the organisation of the relief vessels should be settled during peace, and should also conform to the military organisation of the different States.

69. For commanders of relief vessels preference should be given to retired naval officers, or to master mariners and pilots who have served in the Navy, and a pension should be assured to them, and their families should be provided for in case of need.

70. The Relief Societies shall place delegates on board, whose orders, as far as relates to destination and the object of the vessel, shall be followed by the Officer Commanding.

71. It is not necessary that the rest of the crew of relief vessels should be selected during peace. It will be quite sufficient to engage them before the outbreak of hostilities.

72. The selection of the personnel (Nos. 69 and 71) shall be left by preference to the relief societies established in maritime towns.

73. The material intended for relief vessels ought to be provided from a special list. During peace patterns can be obtained and notes made of the manufactories where such articles are produced.

74. This material will be as far as possible acquired according to the regulations and patterns of the War Marine.

VI.—INTERNATIONAL RELATIONS.

(a)—*International Committee.*

International relations.

75. In the general interest of the Red Cross, it is advisable to maintain the International Committee of Geneva in the same way as it has existed since the origin of the work.

It will continue in particular—

(a) To endeavour to maintain and develop mutual relations between central committees.
(b) To notify the constitution of new national societies, after having satisfied itself of the conditions under which they are formed.

(b)—Bulletin.

76. It is advisable to support the "Bulletin International," which is published at Geneva, as the recognised organ of the societies of the Red Cross.

77. The national societies should co-operate as actively as possible in its compilation, and should endeavour to obtain subscribers.

78. In case the subscriptions should be insufficient to meet the cost of publication, the International Committee shall have the right to refer the matter to the Central Committee.

(c)—Conferences.

79. The societies of different countries shall assemble in international conferences in order to communicate their experiences, concert as to the measures to be adopted in the interest of the work, and to develop the personal relations of their members.

80. In ordinary times it is **desirable that these** conferences should be held at intervals **of five years**.

(d)—Mutual Assistance.

81. In case of war, the societies of belligerent States can solicit the assistance of those of neutral States.

82. In case of war out of Europe, for all States which signed the Convention of Geneva having Red Cross Societies, aid to sick and wounded soldiers from the national societies of other States is assured on the terms which have been generally accepted.

83. Neutral societies which desire to give aid, either personal or material, to one or the other of the belligerent armies shall submit without reservation to the orders of the military authorities, especially in countries where the action of neutral delegates is subordinated to the direction of the national society; these delegates shall accept the regulations of the central committee of the said society.

(e)—Agencies.

84. In case of war the International Committee **shall** create one or more agencies, on the assistance of which **the** national societies can rely for the purpose of forwarding relief in money or kind to the wounded of the belligerent armies.

85. If required to do so, it shall also give its help, or that of its agencies, to the national societies of the belligerents, for the transmission of correspondence, without prejudice to the direct correspondence which these societies may establish between themselves, under the authority of the military commanders **and** the conditions determined by them.

(f)—Convention of Geneva.

86. The International Committee is invited to take active steps in order to obtain for the Convention of Geneva the adhesion of all States which have not yet signed it.

CHAPTER IV.

GENERAL REMARKS ON ESTIMATES FOR AMBULANCE TRANSPORT WITH ARMIES ON ACTIVE SERVICE.

CHAP. IV.

THE ambulance transport which has to be estimated for an army taking the field, comprehends not only that which will be required for the removal of the wounded from the field of battle, but includes also the transport which will be necessary for the use of the sick, from the fighting line in the front to the base of operations. The conveyances and the number of the bearer companies for the transport of the wounded from the scene of action to the collecting and dressing stations; the mule litters and cacolets, or other carriage for the transport of the wounded to the field hospitals and base hospitals, or to ports of embarkation, over country too broken for carts or wagons, when the distances are not very remote from the position of the army operating in the field; the wheeled conveyances drawn by animals for the carriage of sick and wounded along the roads in the rear; all these have to be taken into account in the estimate, and the numbers required of each description of transport have to be separately calculated according to the nature of the military undertaking in which the troops are about to be engaged.

There are so many circumstances which have to be taken into consideration in forming an estimate of the amount of transport matériel and of the strength of medical establishments required to accompany a force of any given strength that is about to proceed on a hostile expedition that it seems doubtful whether anything beyond an approximate calculation for *all* the wants of the army can be framed. Say that an army corps is ordered to embark on a hostile expedition and the question is put to the medical department, what strength of ambulance transport and hospital establishment will be required to accommodate the sick and wounded, and accompany the force to provide for the casualties which may be expected to take place, from conflict with the enemy, and disease. On what basis is the answer to be framed?

Before entering further into the detail of this question it is necessary to indicate the general idea of the control of the medical arrangements of an army in the field.

The Principal Medical Officer of a force in the field should

These, in the first instance, are made by the **Director-General**, who nominates a principal medical officer to the Commander-in-Chief, who appoints him. This medical officer should be on the staff of the General Officer Commanding

when such has been the case it has invariably worked well.* In the Egyptian Campaign of 1882, where the Principal Medical Officer was not on the staff, the result of the medical arrangements, excellent as they were subsequently proved to be, was nothing but confusion and disaster. If the Principal Medical Officer is not on the staff, that is to say, is not the assistant to the General Officer Commanding in matters relating to the health and efficiency of his troops, he should be relieved of all responsibility in case of failure of the medical arrangements. General Sir Donald Stewart, G.C.B., speaking at the Royal United Service Institution, on the Medical Service in Modern War, said "Dr. Marston again observes that in the new Queen's Regu-
"lations the principal medical officer is not mentioned as belong-
"ing to the staff of the army. I must confess to not having had
"an opportunity of reading up the new regulations, but I am
"sure of this, that a General Officer who is not in the closest and
"most intimate relation with his Principal Medical Officer cannot
"be surprised if the medical arrangements are not as perfect as
"they might be. My own experience is that if the head of an
"important department is not in the confidence of the General
"in command, it is absolutely impossible for him to carry on his
"duties efficiently."†

[margin: Chap. IV
be on the Staff of the General Commanding.]

The report of Lord Morley's committee, after the Egyptian War, to investigate the organisation of the Army Hospital Corps, hospital management, and nursing in the field fully corroborates the above statement, and should be well known to all medical officers in order to guide them in the future. It is, perhaps, the most valuable report that has ever been rendered on the medical service of the army. If the Principal Medical Officer of a force is not in the closest relation with the General, there is the chance of the medical service of the force failing.

[margin: Lord Morley's Report.]

The men of the Medical Staff Corps Bearer Companies, whose duty it is to render aid to the wounded on the field and to carry them on stretchers to places of safety are, in the British army at any rate, also the men who attend upon the sick in the field and other hospitals. But it is not always possible to say how many hospitals will be established along the line of operations of an army, when the very line which the army may follow, like the numbers who fall sick and non-effective, is dependent on a mass of circumstances, the degree of potency of which cannot be accurately determined beforehand. The fatigue to be endured, the loss of rest, insufficiency of shelter, exposure to the vicissitudes of temperature, the miasmata, the occurrence of epidemic disease, and other influences affect the ratio of sickness to a marked degree, and equally the strength of the bearer company and hospital establishments necessary. On the field of action itself the proportion of casualties is found to

---

* Since this was written the P.M.O. has been included in the Staff of the G.O.C. on the lines of communication.
† Lecture on Medical Service in Modern War, by Surgeon-General Marston, M.D., C.B., *Journal of Royal United Service Institution*, Vol XXXIV., p. 457.

CHAP. IV

Ambulance transport on Active Service.

vary so much in different battles that it is hard to form an estimate of the amount of ambulance transport that will be required for any particular engagement. It is not an easy matter to ascertain, even with an approach to accuracy, the number of casualties, including killed and wounded, which have hitherto occurred in particular battles; and it is still more difficult to arrive at a knowledge of the number of the wounded who require to be carried to the field hospitals for treatment. On looking back to the principal battles of the earlier part of the present century it is remarkable how frequently it is difficult to obtain information beyond the general fact that of a given number such another number were "killed or wounded"; and equally remarkable how discordant the accounts of these particular numbers are, in the records obtained from different sources.

Again, the difficulty is increased on account of the numbers of the wounded of the vanquished force left on the field, who equally have to be transported for care and treatment with those of the conquerors. This difficulty is now removed by the terms of the Geneva Convention of August, 1864; for by the articles of this treaty it is provided that wounded prisoners may either be given up for care and treatment to the countries to which they belong, or surgeons and attendants belonging to their own country may be left with them to provide for their wants without being subject to the risks and penalties attached to prisoners of war.

It is now proposed to indicate the methods by which ambulance transport is applied to a force in the field, and in the light of previous campaigns and opinions expressed by those best qualified to judge, the average amount of sick and wounded in a force for whom provision has to be made.

The lines of medical assistance.

In war there are three lines of medical assistance.

The 1st line consists of (1) officers attached to corps; (2) bearer companies.

The 2nd line consists of field hospitals.

The 3rd ,, ,, hospitals on the line of communication, and the base hospitals.

The main principle of this organization is that disabled soldiers should be passed as rapidly as possible from their regiments through the field hospitals to the base, so that the fighting line may be at once free to advance without being hampered by the care of its sick and wounded.

1st Line.—1. An officer is attached to each regiment, battalion, battery, troop, or company of Royal Engineers on active service in the field, as shown in field army establishments, to afford such temporary assistance to sick and wounded as may be required in camp, on the line of march and in action. The duty of these officers is to treat trivial cases of sickness, and to render such temporary aid to the wounded as may be necessary, until the bearer company arrives. A field stretcher is provided for each company, and two men per company are trained as bearers, and act under the orders of the medical officer. Every soldier carries, as part of his field equipment, a bandage with lint for the first dressing of wounds.

The supplemental regimental aid consists of the two **men per company** drawn from the regiment, giving 16 men to **carry 8 stretchers**. This number is quite insufficient for the purpose, and as commanding officers naturally do not like to let good men out of the ranks, these men should come with the rest of the regimental aid, except the medical officers only from **the Medical Staff Corps Reserve**.

2. The duties of a bearer company are to render the first assistance to the wounded, and to collect and remove them to the **dressing** stations, which are established by its medical officers, **and thence** to the field hospitals.

Bearer companies in the English army date their origin from the report of the Committee* of the Brussels Exhibition in 1876, and tables showing their personnel, camp equipment, and transport were first published with Army Circulars, Clause 77 of 1877.

The first bearer company actually employed in the British service was one organised during the last phase of the Zulu War. It was composed of a few non-commissioned officers, and men of the Army Hospital Corps, and of line regiments, largely supplemented from native sources. It was commanded by Surgeon-Major J. Hector, and under him did excellent service at the storming of Secocoeni's stronghold in 1879.

It was not, however, until 1881 that a bearer company was organised for war, complete in personnel, and equipment according to the existing regulations. This company under the command of Surgeon-Major W. Johnston was in January of that year sent to Natal as a reinforcement during the Transvaal War, but owing to the cessation of hostilities was never actively engaged.

The personnel was **originally laid** down as follows :—

Medical Officers	8
Captains and Lieutenants of Orderlies ..	3
Non-commissioned Officers and men Army Hospital Corps	36
Bearers (drawn from Reserve)	95
Bâtmen (drawn from Reserve)	11
1 Officer (Army Service Corps)	1
Non-commissioned Officers and men (Army Service Corps)	9
Drivers (partly A.S.C., others locally supplied)	47
Total strength **of all ranks**	210

In 1883, on the recommendation of Lord Morley's Committee on the medical service, the strength of a bearer company was very greatly reduced.

---

* Under the presidency of the Author. See "Report on the Appliances for Aid to the Sick and Wounded in War, in the Brussels Exhibition of 1876. London, H.M.'s Stationery Office, 1876."

Bearer Companies in the British Army.

CHAP. IV.
Bearer Companies.

The personnel of a bearer company is now as follows:—

	Personnel						Horses		
	Officers.	Warrant Officers.	Staff-Sergeants and Sergeants.	Artificers.	Buglers.	Rank and File.	Total	Private or provided under Allowance Regulations.	Public.	
									Riding.	Draught.
Medical Staff.										
Surgeon-Major	1	...	...	...	...	...	...	1	...	...
Surgeons	2	...	...	...	...	...	...	2	...	...
Medical Staff Corps.										
Warrant Officer	...	1	...	...	...	...	...	1	...	...
Quartermaster Sergeant	...	...	1	...	...	...	...	...	...	...
Compounder	...	...	1	...	...	...	...	...	...	...
Sergeants	...	...	4	...	...	...	...	...	...	...
Bugler	...	...	...	...	1	...	...	...	...	...
Rank and File.										
Corporals	...	...	...	...	...	6		...	...	...
Privates	...	...	...	...	...	8		...	...	...
„ as Cooks	...	...	...	...	...	3		...	...	...
„ as Bearers	...	...	...	...	...	32	} 53	...	...	...
„ as Servants	...	...	...	...	...	3		...	...	...
„ Supernumerary	...	...	...	...	...	1		...	...	...
Total	3	1	6	...	1	53	64	3	1	...
							64		4	
Officer, A.S.C.	1	...	...	...	...	...	1		1	...
Sergeants	...	...	1	...	...	...	1		1	...
Bugler	...	...	...	...	1	...	1		1	...
Corporal	...	...	...	...	...	1	} 2		1	...
2nd Corporal	...	...	...	...	...	1			1	...
Collar maker	...	...	...	1	...	...	1		...	...
Farrier	...	...	...	1	...	...	1		1	...
Privates as Drivers	...	...	...	...	...	29			...	...
„ as Batmen	...	...	...	...	...	1	} 34		...	58
„ as Cook	...	...	...	...	...	1			...	...
„ as Supernumerary	...	...	...	...	...	3			...	...
Total	1	...	1	2	1	36	41	...	5	58
							41		63	

The bearer companies are apportioned one to each brigade, but do not form an integral part of it, and they will be fully at the disposal of the divisional authorities, who will detach them or mass them as necessity may require. (Reg. Med. Services, Part I., para. 663.)

Organisation of Bearer Company on too small a scale.

The organisation of a **bearer** company is on too small a scale to be effective, and for the reason that the amount of work which might be produced with the excellent material and appliances, is lost because there is not sufficient "strength" to work it. Expense also prevents the organisation of bearer companies as permanent establishments, and it is this fact, as much as anything which militates against their efficiency.

There should be a permanent bearer company and field hospital at Aldershot, which should work at all manœuvres, and in the winter time be utilised for hospital work.

Through this depôt bearer company and field hospital all medical officers and men should pass, in order to be practically familiar with their working.

It can scarcely be expected that the officers, non-commissioned officers, and men, who are suddenly mobilised at Aldershot, on the outbreak of a war, can acquire a knowledge of their duties in the short time before embarkation. In the first place the drill and the hospital training are generally forgotten, and this is not the fault of the men so much as of the system which divides them up into such small detachments, and in the second place, neither officers nor men have the slightest idea of their various capacities for their work. Lastly, with regard to the reserve, where they have been employed they have not answered as well as was expected. One witness before Lord Morley's Committee stated that several of the men who volunteered for duty as stretcher bearers had such bad characters that they were sent back to their corps. It would appear then to be absolutely essential to have a permanent establishment sufficient, with a thoroughly competent militia reserve, to supply the 1st Army Corps, and this should be kept up to the highest state of efficiency. All reserve men should be told off to their respective duties, and might be inspected each year by the officer detailed to command them, or mobilised for ten days' training, in the same manner as in Germany. At any rate the militia is the source from which the medical service should obtain its reserve. We cannot rely on a volunteer reserve, such as was drawn upon in the Egyptian war, and which proved how utterly worthless it was.

The reserve of the Medical Staff Corps require to be trained annually, as by regulation it is ordered, or otherwise the Medical Staff Corps Reserve becomes practically valueless. The special nature of their duties **are** forgotten, and the results **are** disastrous.

The lifting and carrying of wounded men requires **much** attention and care, and it is always of the most irksome and fatiguing character. What, then, are the conditions physically that a bearer should possess? A bearer should be strong, well made, and average 5 feet 6 inches in height, and not more than 5 feet 8 inches, with a chest measurement of not less than 35 inches, and a weight of 150 lbs. This will give a muscular powerful man of exactly the mould required for a bearer's duties. The chest measurement is a most important matter, the value of which is considerably under-estimated. Energy, or that force which is put out to make work, or in other words bodily material convertible into force, which is work, results in strain or tension on all the large vessels in connection with the heart and lungs, and unless these are proportionately equal to the strain thrown upon them, and have a strong "roomy" thorax or chest cavity to assist them, and in which to work, failure will result and consequent inefficiency. The present standard of 5 feet 3 inches in height, and 33 inches chest measurement, is too low, and when a stress of work does occur,

CHAP. IV.

Bearer Companies.

The physical conditions a bearer should **possess**.

CHAP. IV

Physical standard of Medical Staff Corps recruit too low.

from this cause alone the bearers will be rendered non-effective and will fill the hospitals. Men of this size are not strong enough for the duties in the ward of a hospital, much less for the work of those of a bearer company.

The transport of bearer companies and field hospitals should be, as at present, supplied by the Army Service Corps, and only removable from the medical establishments by the General Officer Commanding. Quartermasters of the medical staff should be specially instructed in transport duties, and be able to take charge of the transport while it is attached to bearer companies.

Mounted Bearer Companies

Mounted Bearer Companies.—The application of ambulance transport to cavalry in the field is a most difficult problem, and never has any bearer company been able to follow their very rapid movements, and as at present organised it is unlikely that they ever will. Mounted bearer companies were tried in the Egyptian campaign but the results are doubtful. The late Sir Herbert Stewart in **Appendix 39** of Lord Morley's Report writes: "With regard to a bearer company, I consider the "present organisation of a bearer company absolutely unsuit-"able to cavalry.

"It seems to me that in the future not only must cavalry "be called upon to fight on foot, but this at considerable "distances from the main body of the army, and that often "they must move rapidly to these distances. A bearer com-"pany can, under present circumstances, make no pretence of "keeping near cavalry, as was exemplified specially on the "25th August and the 9th and 13th of September. I think "that a mounted bearer company should take the place of "the present bearer company, so far as cavalry is concerned. "For this I should suggest two classes of transports:—

"1. Cacolets carried by stout horses.
"2. Very light ambulance (carts).

"I should employ the first to follow cavalry wherever they "may go, and the second to follow so far as may be possible, "and to relieve the first.

"With reference to the present pack saddles and cacolets, "they are made for mules, and are not suited except on an "emergency for horses. I should suggest, of course, proper "pack saddles, and more comfortable cacolets. . . . One "man should have charge of two horses. He would thus be "able to pick up three disabled men. One of the two pairs of "cacolets should be fitted with a seat in the front part of the "cacolet upon which the man in charge could ride either "before he has taken up any one or after he has taken up two "men. As a matter of fact the transport men in charge of the "three cacolets rode to Cairo, sitting in the centre of the "cacolet when necessary, without much inconvenience.

"I do not know that I could exemplify the class of ambu-

"lance I should propose better than by likening it to an Irish
"car. I would suggest a conveyance of this sort with a driver,
"and two places on each side where men could partially lie
"down. I should suggest the lines of an Irish car as near as
"possible, as with two wheels being the most comfortable
"conveyance for five people. This could be drawn by one or
"two horses, according to the nature of the country, one in
"shafts, and the other attached by a splinter bar.

"I should not have any covering. Any covering, even
"canvas with the necessary fittings, adds weight to a great
"extent, and the very essence of these ambulances for cavalry
"should be their lightness; this even at some risk to the
"patients.

"Given the percentage of wounded to be provided for,
"two-thirds might be provided for in these light ambulances,
"and one-third in cacolets. The Army Hospital Corps orderlies
"must be all mounted.

"It seems to me that on these lines a bearer company could
"be established which would be really suitable for employment
"with cavalry."

This is an ingenious and clever idea, of applying ambulance transport to cavalry; but though this report was made eight years ago there has been nothing done. In fact, at the extended manœuvres of the cavalry at Uffington in 1890 no attempt was made to solve this difficulty. If such a bearer company were ever tried, it must be distinctly understood that it is necessary that it should at least be permanent, and retain its own transport. In the light of what has passed it is very unlikely that even horses to carry the weights of the loaded cacolets will be forthcoming, much less that an expensive unit such as this would be, kept up solely for this purpose.

The remedy would appear to lie more in the direction of increasing the regimental medical aid. If two medical officers, and double the number of trained orderlies, and all well mounted, follow each regiment of cavalry, and some light ambulance wagons be kept as far in advance as possible, and their position signalled, it is possible to do much,—and the following methods may be suggested:—

a. A wounded trooper being taken to the rear by two regimental bearers, supporting him on each side on his horse.

b. A rough litter made after the fashion of the Arabs (*see* p. 224), by which, if well done, and with a quiet horse, the injured man can be conveyed a long distance as comfortably as though he were on a stretcher.

c. A certain proportion of single mule litters allowed.

There are many rough and ready methods of relieving a wounded man under these circumstances which would readily suggest themselves at the time; but this must be borne in mind, that it is necessary for the cavalry officers to train their men and horses to many of the attitudes required, and also to know their quiet and suitable animals. There has always been, and there always will be, certain risks with cavalry, but as far as

CHAP. IV.

Collecting and dressing stations are formed by the Bearer Companies.

their scouting and reconnoitring is concerned, they suffer very little when detached, while during or after a general action help is usually forthcoming.

The bearer companies form the collecting stations, or advanced posts of pack animals, and for ambulance wagons, and dressing stations, and they carry the wounded from the front to the rear. At present there is no bearer company detailed for the communications specially, though there is in reserve one which might be so used. The wounded are either returned to the front from the field hospital, or sent to the base, and invalided to England.

Considerations, therefore, of ambulance transport cover a very large area, practically from the fighting line to England, and it will be on the efficiency of this transport that will depend, not only the front being less hampered by non-effectives, but expense avoided, and last, though not least, many lives saved.

Before quitting this portion of the subject, it may be useful to notice generally the manner in which Continental nations apply their ambulance aid to their armies. The importance of it has been very much brought home to them in the terrible battles which have occurred during the last thirty years. A direct comparison with our system is not a fair one, for the requirements of our army, for obvious reasons, do not call for quite such an extended system. Our wars are on a smaller scale, and not usually against civilised nations; but small as our establishments need be, they should at the same time be perfect.

The Constitution and Practice of the Hospital Services of the Great Powers in the Armies of France, Germany, Austria, Italy, and Russia.

A report on this matter was compiled by the Intelligence Department, and is to be found in detail in Appendix 24 of Lord Morley's Report. For the purpose of this work it is necessary merely to indicate the broad lines of the investigation, as laid down in Major-General East's memorandum in the same Report. It is as follows:—

The Hospital Service of the Great Powers.

"1. A perusal of the accompanying reports on the Hospital Service in the armies of France, Germany, Austria, Italy, and Russia will show that, as a general rule, the system in force combines the advantages of the departmental and the regimental systems. Every battalion has its own medical officer, and to this there is no exception. In Germany and Austria the regimental medical officer does departmental duty in the general hospital, while in France, Italy, and Russia he attends the sick in the regimental hospitals or infirmaries, which are established for the treatment of minor cases.

"2. Thus a certain proportion of the medical officers have a regimental connexion, and yet frequently perform general duty; apparently just the contrary to the system prevailing in our service, which attaches all medical officers permanently to the general hospital, and some of them only temporarily, and on an emergency, to the regiment.

"3. With regard to the question of discipline Austria takes one extreme, and France the other. In Austria doctors act simply and purely as doctors, while in the French service they are given command over the personnel of the hospital, including the transport in time of war, and the power of giving minor punishments to soldier patients. In Germany, soldiers in hospital cannot be punished by medical officers except in time of war, when the senior medical officer of a field hospital is given the disciplinary powers of a company commander.

"4. In the European armies under report the medical service is organised to meet peace requirements, with equipment in store to provide for the preparation of field hospitals. This transition from a peace to a war footing is comparatively easy, as the general hospital at the home quarters of a division or army corps, as well as the branch hospitals, are no longer required when the corps takes the field, and consequently the personnel is almost entirely freed for active service, their places being, to a certain extent, filled up by reserve medical officers and civil practitioners.

"5. The first and second lines of ambulance are the same in principle in every service. The first line consists of the bearer company, with ambulance wagons of service pattern, horsed by the train, and working between the army and the field hospitals; and the second line of requisitioned wagons evacuating the field hospital into the etappen hospitals. Russia is a slight exception to this, in keeping up during peace a small establishment of regimental ambulance wagons.

"6. Medical officers are in no way responsible for the movement of field hospitals, except in the French service; nor is there any special transport for this purpose. A section of the train is attached for this duty to each field hospital, and except in the case of France, the responsibility devolves on the transport officers acting under the orders of the divisional commander.

"7. Nursing in Germany and Russia is performed by orderlies detached from regiments, while in France, Austria and Italy there is a special army hospital corps. All the men of these hospital corps, however, have been drawn in the ordinary manner by conscription, and for the most part trained as soldiers for one year. Sisters of mercy and ladies from kindred societies are employed to assist in nursing, &c., and are under the orders of the medical officers.

"8. Soldiers do not generally take their arms to hospital. During peace, in Germany, they leave them in barracks, and

CHAP. IV.

during war send them to the reserve ammunition column, receiving a fresh supply on resuming duty. In Russia there is a non-commissioned officer at hospital specially charged with the care of sick soldiers' effects."

The amount of ambulance transport for an English army is decided by the authorities, and is issued on the scale laid down in Regulations.

This judgment will be formed in each case according to the probable exigencies of the campaign, the nature and climate of of the country expected to be the seat of war, the character of the enemy, the nature of his weapons, and the probable duration of hostilities.

Ambulance transport determined to a certain degree on the nature of the enemy's weapons.

The character of the enemy and the nature of his weapons is an important item of information to be obtained before allotting carriage for sick and wounded. The weapons of offence may be classed primarily guns and rifles, and secondly swords, spears, arrows and knives. The first class include the weapons of precision used by civilised nations; the latter represent those of the savage tribes who live in and upon the confines of British territory. The casualties we may expect from the latter will not compare in any way with the destruction of life that will take place in the former, that is, in any conflict between European nations—indeed, the Franco-German War of 20 years ago yields sufficient evidence on this head, and at that time machine guns, smokeless powder and other later forms of war material were unknown. "In our wars we "have not been pitched opposite an organised rifle fire, but "mainly against savages, who, though presenting great diffi- "culties and requiring much courage to withstand, have not "caused the losses to our side which exposure to volley fire "from modern rifles would involve. Generally it may be stated "that the idea is to concentrate rapidly a large force on a "given point, the weakest that the enemy presents, and "literally sweep him there with bullets. Whether the actual "attack will take place in extended order or in close order "remains to be seen. This rapid concentration of force, added "to the destructive nature of the implements of modern war, will "result in large numbers of men being wounded in an almost "incredibly short space of time, and within a limited area, or at "that point upon which the enemy has concentrated his fire.

Numbers wounded in Franco-German War.

"The following battles are illustrations of this:—At the Battle "of Borny, August 14, 1870, the Germans lost 5,000 and the "French 3,800 in 5 hours. At the battles Mars-la-Tour, Vion- "ville and Rezonville, August 16, the Germans lost 17,000, the "French 16,954—duration, 9 hours. A most fearful battle had "come to an end. Everywhere lay heaps of dead and wounded, "for this day had demanded as great, if not greater, sacrifices than "most battles of modern times" (Surgeon-Major-General Franklyn). It was during this battle that the Todten-ritt, or death-ride, occurred, when 6 squadrons of 900 men were killed to 3 troops. At Gravelotte, St. Privat, on August 18, the Germans lost 21,000 men, and the French 12,273, in 8 hours. At one period of this battle the Germans were exposed to a fearful fire from the French, and are reported to have lost 5,000 men killed and wounded in 15 minutes.

"At the assault by Grant on the enemy's lines at Cold-harbour, in 1864, over 10,000 men were wounded, besides the killed, the greater part in 10 minutes, and all in an hour's time" (Swinton's "Army of the Potomac," page 485). He adds: "Under such circumstances, every resource of the medical department is brought into requisition, and must be at hand."*

These references are sufficient to show what is to be expected when civilised nations meet one another. Not only does the force concentrate, but the medical aid must be sufficient to concentrate too, and succour the wounded, and to enable that to be done there must be reserves of officers, and these reserves should be composed of those serving in the regular army, or who have served in the regular service. The volunteer force of the English army is deficient of medical officers, and their duties should be confined entirely to it, and they should not be taken on as a reserve for the army for which they are quite untrained.

With regard to the second class of offensive weapons which are used by uncivilised nations, the number of wounded is comparatively trivial, and the forces weakened more by disease than by wounds in fighting under these conditions. The spear of the Arab, the assegai of the Zulu, the poisoned arrow of the tribes of Central Africa, and the dahs and knives of the Burmese, and the weapons of other Eastern races, though formidable in themselves, do not affect appreciably the amount of transport required.

The nature and climate of the country in which the campaign occurs.—It may at first sight appear irrelevant to discuss this matter in a work on transport, but in reality it is not so, for it is all-important to understand the precise physical and climatic conditions for which ambulance transport must to be estimated. Wars, and especially those waged by England, are liable to take place in the most diverse and different regions of the world. The mountains of India and Thibet, the plains of the Soudan, the veldt of South Africa, and the snow regions of Canada are all examples of this diversity. Last, though not least, the influences of heat and cold, of malaria and epidemic disease, have to be considered. These are some of the principal points under this heading that would be taken into consideration by the officer estimating the sick transport for any campaign.

The probable duration also will materially affect the estimate, for reserves must be sent to make up the casualties from wounds or sickness. The longer the campaign the more perfect should

---

* From "The Transport of the Wounded in Modern War," by the Editor. *Journal of the Royal United Service Institution,* Vol. XXXV.

CHAP. IV.

Mortality among the Medical Officers of the English Army.

be the regular ambulance men and material sent out, and these must be supplemented by resources obtainable in the country itself. Particularly should be noticed the heavy mortality among army surgeons in the English forces. It is nearly double that of any other branch, and only the strongest and most healthy should be selected for field service. The proportion is 7 to 13 (Q. 1,370, Camperdown C.).

Lord Wolseley writes :—" The proportion of wounded to be calculated for previous to a battle is very difficult to determine, as every action would seem to have its own special rate, the loss on the losing side being generally much the heavier; and the more decisive the action the more this fact becomes apparent. When the ground is soft and deep, as is generally the case after very heavy rains, the loss is less than when it is hard and stony, and some generals, either from recklessness of life or from ignorance of their science, lose more men than others. Then again the nature of your enemy's arms, and their dexterity in using them, will always affect the rates of killed and wounded in any engagement. The statistics of wars prior to the introduction of the breech-loader are of little value in calculating the probable proportion of losses in an action between two European armies of the present day. During the great battles of the Franco-German War, the numbers engaged were so great that seldom more than two-thirds of those present were ever under fire at all. On the data afforded by a large number of recent battles, the rate of total loss may be fixed at 81 per 1,000 men of those actually exposed to fire, whose number may be fairly arrived at for one or more army corps by deducting 360 from every 1,000 soldiers present on the field."

"As a rough calculation you may assume that in a battle between two European armies the total loss will never, as a rule, exceed 10 per cent. on either side, whilst frequently it will be less than half that amount, and that if you provide for the care and transport of wounded men at the rate of 6 per cent. of the total force you take into action, irrespective of whether they may or may not be exposed to fire, you will have done all that is necessary. According to the German medical returns, the number of all ranks in the German army killed and wounded by rifle-bullets, during the War of 1870, was 6,969 killed and 49,093 wounded, whilst by artillery fire the numbers were 695 killed and 4,389 wounded; that is, out of every 100 men 91 were hit by infantry and only 9 by artillery fire."

The following list is taken from Sir T. Longmore's list of battles, in his work on "Gunshot Injuries":—

Hospital Service.

Name.	Number Engaged.	Killed.	Wounded.	Missing.	Proportion of Wounded to Killed.	Remarks.
Alma	21,480	337	1,546	13	1 to 4·6	
Magenta	48,090	657	3,223	655	1 to 4·9	French Returns.
Solferino	138,234	2,343	12,102	2,756	1 to 5·2	French Returns.
Konigratz	220,984	1,929	6,948	276	1 to 3·6	Prussians.
"	129,000	1,929	6,948	276	1 to 3·6	Prussians.
β	215,028	5,793	17,805	7,836	1 to 3	Austrians and Saxons.
c	150,000	5,793	17,805	7,836	1 to 3	Austrians and Saxons.
Weissenbourg	106,928	293	1,082	153	1 to 3·7	
Saarbruck	119,053	862	3,632	372	1 to 4·2	
Woerth	167,119	1,628	7,570	1,444	1 to 4·7	
Vionville	151,868	3,289	10,282	1,240	1 to 3·1	
Gravelotte	278,131	4,449	15,180	939	1 to 3·4	
Sedan	190,239	1,637	6,483	912	1 to 3·9	
Orleans	56,553	170	662	87	1 to 3·9	
Coulmiers	38,951	69	573	621	1 to 7·6	
Amiens	52,630	181	1,022	31	1 to 5·7	
Le Mans	123,749	289	895	118	1 to 5·8	
Lizaine	64,735	236	1,678	227	1 to 3·1	
Turco Russian	300,000	32,752	71,268	...	1 to 2·2	Russian Return for 1st and 2nd Armies.
Plevna	75,000	3,300	9,500	...	1 to 2·88	

The proportion of wounded to be arranged for can be calculated in two ways, either upon the numbers likely to be engaged or upon the whole force. It may be safely stated that when a small force takes the field the whole of it will be exposed to fire, and, considering the nature of the wars of this country, even when not exposed to the enemy, they will be exposed to the influences of the climate, and these have to be reckoned with, in arranging the medical transport for an army. Disease resulting from fevers and climatic influence are far more potent factors in rendering an army helpless than is often supposed.

The Walcheren Expedition of 1809 is an example in point. An officer, writing to the *Army and Navy Gazette*, states that in a magazine of 1846 he found the following:—" The late Lord Chatham took from England the finest army (39,000) that ever embarked from its shores. From want of military knowledge and delays he lost the chance of a ' coup de main,' and returned home." The writer adds: " Really not much more seems to be remembered than that 8,000 men perished by ague fever in the swamps of Walcheren, and for some twenty years after that this malady haunted the survivors."

CHAPTER V

RECOGNISED POSITIONS OF WOUNDED DURING TRANSPORT AND THEIR CARRIAGE BEARERS ONLY.

CHAP. V.

BEFORE proceeding to consider the various kinds of conveyances which have been either proposed for carrying disabled soldiers, or are actually employed for that purpose, some few general remarks appear to be necessary respecting the positions most suitable for the wounded themselves during the act of removal, having due regard to their safety, comfort, and the prevention of aggravation of the injuries which they have sustained; for on the nature of these positions, it may be presumed, will depend, to a certain extent the forms of the vehicles designed for their transport. It will also be useful to add in this chapter some observations on the circumstances of wounded men who do not require transport, or who are able to make their own way for a limited distance without being carried; and lastly, to consider the manner in which the Medical Staff Corps can most efficiently render assistance to other wounded men who are unable to march alone, but who are not so far disabled that either litters or wheeled carriages are absolutely required for their safety, or who, although requiring such conveyances, are unable from accidental circumstances to obtain them.

SECTION I.—POSITIONS OF WOUNDED MEN DURING TRANSPORT.

Positions of men with recent wounds during transport.

It is with reference to recent wounds that it is chiefly of importance in these remarks to consider the position proper for patients during transportation. It may be that the patients have only to be carried a very short distance from the place where they have received their injuries to the place appointed as the first line of surgical assistance. Even under these circumstances the position in which a wounded soldier is carried may have an important influence on his present safety or future welfare. It is of the utmost importance to a recently wounded man that he receives prompt and skilled attention from a medical officer immediately, for the longer he has to wait for treatment the greater is the risk he incurs. It cannot be too strongly impressed that there shall be a sufficiency of medical officers in the fighting line, the supports, and the reserves, to render with their own hands the "first aid" to all cases approaching severity. It is not suggested or supposed that every case can be dressed by the surgeons, but it should be well understood that the less the first dressings are relegated to the bearers the happier will the result be to the wounded. Alarming hæmorrhages and specially urgent symptoms arising in the absence of the surgeon, alone should be treated by the bearers, who should, as their title expresses, be utilized only for the carriage of patients, and for performing the many various duties in connection with the hospitals, under the direction and supervision of the medical officer responsible for the sick and wounded.

CHAP. V.

Ambulance conveyances, whether they are intended to be carried by bearers, borne by animals, or are of the wheeled kind, are ordinarily constructed for carrying wounded **men in one** or two positions, either lying down at full length or sitting. Experience has shown that these positions meet all the usual requirements of wounded men. Some light field hand-carriages have been designed by continental surgeons in which the patients are carried half sitting, half reclining, and **which do** not admit of being used for either a wholly recumbent or wholly sitting posture; but they have not yet been brought into general use; other conveyances have been invented, admitting a recumbent position, but at the same time capable, by means **of** mechanical contrivances, of assuming a form suited for supporting **a** patient in a semi-recumbent posture.

Ambulance conveyances usually constructed for patients in either a recumbent or sitting position.

It will be convenient to consider the nature and effects of these several positions, viz., 1, the recumbent; 2, the sitting; and 3, the semi-recumbent position, separately.

Transport in the recumbent position.—The recumbent position is undoubtedly the best position in which to place all men who have received severe wounds, and even those who appear to have been but slightly hurt, if their injuries are complicated with faintness, tendency to bleeding, shock, or any other constitutional symptoms. It is at once the most easy and the safest posture for the patient. In the recumbent posture every part of the body is equally supported, no part has to bear the weight of another part, the necessity for all muscular exertion ceases, and there is perfect repose. If the balance of the circulatory system has been disturbed under faintness, from the effects of chills, or from any other cause, it is the position most favourable for its restoration. If hæmorrhage from divided vessels has been arrested by some of the ordinary natural methods through which this is accomplished, or temporarily stopped by the formation of clot, the horizontal position is the most effective for preventing disturbances to these favourable circumstances, by doing away with the need of moving the injured parts, and by lessening the weight of the column of blood in the vessels leading to them. Moreover, it is the posture in which, during the act of transport, the several parts

The recumbent position.

Its advantages to men severely wounded.

Its advantages in case of shock, faintness, &c.

CHAP. V.

of the body are subjected to the least amount of concussion, and in which that amount of shaking which does take place is most evenly distributed over the whole frame without shock to any one part, from the tread of the bearers or the motion of the carriage, provided the movement be judiciously effected.

Kinds of wounds which necessitate a recumbent position.

Fracture of any of the bones, wounds of the articulations, of the lower extremity; severe wounds of the head, chest, or abdomen; and generally extensive injuries of the shoulder-joint, usually completely disable men from removing themselves for help. Such patients should always be transported to the **rear in** a horizontal posture. If the means of conveying them in this manner be not at hand on the field at the instant of need, the best plan is to arrange temporarily a place of shelter until the necessary conveyances can be obtained for their use. To carry such patients far in a sitting position would inevitably lessen the chances of recovery, **even** if their condition admitted of the attempt being made.

Economy dictates that the use of recumbent conveyances should be as limited as practicable.

Essential, however, as the recumbent position is for patients labouring under certain wounds, and advantageous as it is in almost every description of recent injury, there are inconveniences connected with it when considering the means of transport in campaigning which cannot be overlooked. The recumbent position, as a matter of course, involves the necessity of a greater amount of space being appropriated for the accommodation of a given number of patients, and consequently causes a greater number of vehicles to be required for them than would be required if the accommodation to be provided were for a similar number in a sitting posture. The conveyance of patients in a recumbent position, moreover, entails more labour on attendants than carriage in a sitting position. For these reasons, as patients with some wounds can be nearly as well transported, so far as their injuries are concerned, in the sitting as in the recumbent position, a certain amount of means of transport in a sitting posture is always provided, and it becomes only right, for the sake of economy on the one hand, and for the due protection of patients on the other, to consider **and determine those** cases which **are** applicable to transport in a sitting posture.

The sitting position.

Transport in a sitting position.—As a general rule, only those patients can be safely carried in a sitting posture whose wounds or **injuries are of** a comparatively slight nature. With the exception of wounds of the foot, wounds of the lower extremity usually cause this mode of carriage to be altogether objectionable, especially if they are complicated with injuries to some of the bones. It is for injuries in the upper part of the body that transport in a sitting posture is more particularly applicable.

Wounds for which a sitting posture of the patient is suitable.

However severe a wound of the forearm or of the hand may be, even though bones are fractured or a considerable part of the limb carried away, when there is no hæmorrhage and the patient is strong enough, it does not render removal in a sitting posture objectionable in any respect. The wounded extremity should be properly slung and supported by means of a bandage, and the patient may then be removed in a sitting posture as advantageously practically as in the recumbent posture. In like manner uncomplicated wounds of the head, face, and upper part of the trunk, if they are unattended by any urgent constitutional symptoms, offer no features to contra-indicate the removal of the soldiers suffering from them by transport in a sitting posture.

Transport in a semi-recumbent position.—In this position the trunk of the patient is raised and supported at an angle with the lower part of the body and lower extremities; the knees are also raised, and the thighs bent and the legs semi-flexed. This position of the lower extremities is rendered necessary when the trunk of a recumbent patient is maintained in an inclined posture for two reasons. The first is that the weight of the upper part of the body tends constantly to gravitate downwards, and to push the legs onward; the second is that the extension of the thighs and legs speedily becomes irksome when the body is so raised, probably to a certain extent from muscular tension intended to resist the pressure. The flexed position of the legs removes the need of any such efforts. The fixed position of the pelvis and thighs as they rest against the mechanical support provided to sustain them, counteracts the pressure and tendency to descent of the trunk; all feeling of need for muscular exertion is taken away, and as the lower limbs are everywhere supported, none of the irksomeness is experienced which would be felt if they were kept extended.

There are few recent injuries for which an entirely recumbent position is not sufficient, or cannot be readily made to answer, the purposes fulfilled by the semi-recumbent posture. In some cases of wounds in the region of the chest a semi-recumbent posture is very desirable. The patients suffer so acutely from dyspnœa that they not only cannot bear to remain in a completely prone position, but they require the back and chest to be very considerably raised to relieve them. At the same time such patients will be quite unable, from prostration and other causes, to remain upright or bear the jolting which almost invariably attends removal in a sitting posture. In such cases, if the lower part of the body and extremities retain a horizontal direction, as on an ordinary stretcher, and steps have been taken to raise and support by temporary expedients the back and head of the patient in a sufficiently inclined position, then the inconvenience will not infrequently follow of the patient rolling over to one or other side, not to mention the risk of his slipping down towards the feet of the stretcher, especially if the ground be steep or much broken. A support calculated to maintain such a patient securely in a semi-recumbent posture is therefore a decided advantage.

These, however, are special cases, and even in these the

CHAP. V.

The semi-recumbent position.

Kinds of wounds for which a semi-recumbent posture is particularly serviceable.

Objections to ambulance

CHAP. V.

Carriages specially constructed for maintaining a semi-recumbent posture.

the inconveniences referred to may be materially lessened, if not prevented altogether, by care and management on the part of the bearers. For all ordinary cases of wounds it is obvious that nearly all the advantages alleged to belong, or belonging, to a semi-recumbent position can readily be given by the aid of pillows, or by the use of other substituted means of support, to a patient placed recumbent; while it seems equally obvious that it occasionally must be a source of inconvenience, whatever may be the nature of the injury, not to be able to place a patient in an entirely recumbent position in case of faintness supervening or other need.

Comparative merits of recumbent and semi-recumbent carriage.

Therefore, it may be said of patients recently **wounded,** that if they be in a condition which unfits them for **walking,** or for being carried in a sitting position, and if the **transport** be only for a short distance, conveyance in a recumbent posture will best answer their requirements, and best meet any accidents that may arise incidental to their condition. If a wound be of such a nature that the **chest** requires **to be** much raised, this can be effected by means of a greatcoat, or the addition of any other temporary support properly applied, with sufficiently good results for the occasion.

Under other circumstances than those above named, special consideration is required. If the transport, for example, be for a long distance and in a wheeled vehicle, it will often be needful, or at any rate very advantageous, for support in a semi-recumbent posture to be afforded to patients; and that support should be more firm and fixed than can be obtained from temporary appliances, which are liable to be shifted by the jolting of a carriage in motion. Here the different effects of transport in wheeled conveyances drawn by horses over rough roads as compared with hand carriage have to be taken into account, as well as the fatigue which attends a long journey, especially to enfeebled patients. But even under these circumstances, having regard to the general purposes of ambulance transport, it seems desirable that all such doubly-inclined litters, if employed, should be made capable of being lowered into a perfectly horizontal position in case of need.

SECTION II.—DIFFICULTIES OF DEFINING THE PROPORTIONS OF DIFFERENT KINDS OF AMBULANCE TRANSPORT.

The proportion of accommodation required for recumbent patients to that required for patients able to sit up, becomes a matter of consideration when ambulance transport has to be provided. It is not easy to define with exactness what the proportion is which the one kind of accommodation should bear to the other, for variations in the relative numbers of severely and slightly wounded take place in all engagements. From what has been already said it must be sufficiently evident that it is very important in the interest of the sick and wounded to have a *sufficient* supply of conveyances in which the recumbent position can be assumed. The difficulty of providing proper substitutes for litters for those who are dangerously or severely wounded in the head, body, or lower extremities, and the fact that many men whose injuries are of a less serious nature, or who have sustained fractures of the upper extremities, either from weakness, resulting from loss of blood, or from shock, are unequal, for some time at least, to assume the upright position without risk, have been already referred to. Those of the wounded, on the other hand, who are liable to be removed without harm in a sitting posture will generally be able to find other means of removal, should there not be sufficient sitting conveyances at hand, and they can always be carried in a recumbent position if there is spare carriage available. Could the necessities of the wounded only be consulted, were it not for the unavoidable restrictions of bulk and weight, and the other strategical circumstances which limit as far as possible, in all armies, the supply of conveyances occupying so much space as those designed for carrying men in a recumbent posture, the proportion of carriage for patients in a sitting position would be probably considerably less, and the recumbent considerably greater, than it usually is.

Patients who can be carried sitting can always be carried recumbent.

We see this fact illustrated in a marked manner in the French service. In expeditions in Algeria, owing to the nature of the country and the military service, it is felt to be very important to reduce the bulk of sick conveyances as much as possible, and at the same time to have the mules available for other transport, such as stores, when no sick have to be carried. This can be done with cacolets, which fold up into a very small space and lie close to the sides of the pack saddles, but cannot so conveniently be done with mule-litters on account of their size. The proportion was very different in the French army during the Italian campaign of 1859, when the necessities referred to were felt less strongly. In that war the numbers were fixed at fifteen litter mules and thirty cacolet mules for the headquarters' ambulance, ten litter mules and twenty cacolet mules for the ambulance of an infantry division, five litter mules and ten cacolet mules for a cavalry division, and two litter mules and five cacolet mules for the ambulance of a reserve park of artillery.* Here the proportion of provision for recumbent patients is seen to have been one-half instead of one-tenth of the provision of carriage for patients sitting; and, judging from the evidence of professional returns, which tend to show that about one-third is the proportion of severe to slight wounds inflicted in battles, this would appear to be a much fairer average of the recumbent accommodation likely to be required than the former estimate.

Peculiarities in the nature and circumstances of military operations lead to variations in the relative proportions of the two kinds of transport. Examples in the French military service.

Wounded may practically be divided into four classes:—

---

* "Legouest, Traité de Chirurgie d'Armée," par L. Legouest, Paris, 1863, p. 968.

CHAP. V.

1. Mortally wounded ⎱ Will require comfortable lying
2. Dangerously do.   ⎰ down accommodation.
3. Severely wounded ⎱ Will probably all require lying
                     ⎰ down accommodation.
4. Slightly wounded   Any form of transport suitable.

It must not be forgotten that in addition to their injuries all the wounded are more or less fatigued and exhausted, suffering from pain and shock, and depressed by their misfortune, and by the necessary reaction after the battle. It may be taken that on an average one man in every **five will be** placed in the first and second category, and two **in five in the** others.

It will be seen, therefore, that **in** reality a larger proportion of lying-down accommodation is required than is at first apparent, and the result of not supplying an army, especially in a European war, armed with modern rifles, would certainly be productive of a considerable increase of severity in the nature of the wounds and aggravation of their pain, and even of an increase in the mortality from the injuries themselves.

The **settlement** of the question on a fixed basis though a desideratum, is a most **difficult** matter, and there is no definite standard, in the British army at any rate, which would **answer** its purpose, in the many various conditions under which war is waged.

SECTION III.—CONCERNING WOUNDED WHO DO NOT ABSOLUTELY REQUIRE TO BE CARRIED TO THE STATIONS OF MEDICAL ASSISTANCE.

Deficiency of bearers of wounded after actions.

One of the great wants experienced in every action is the want of a sufficient number of bearers to carry off the wounded. The demand suddenly created for help is usually under such circumstances so great that it is hardly to be expected that any establishment of bearers could be regularly maintained in strength sufficient to meet it.

Duties of hospital attendants in the field as regards classes of wounded.

If there were sufficient assistants at hand no wounded man, not even those with the simplest flesh wounds, should be permitted to go to the hospital unattended. Under the movement and exertion a blood vessel may give way, and hæmorrhage occur; faintness that has passed off for a while may recur after the patient has been a short time in the upright position; with an apparently slight wound of the scalp giddiness may come on, the patient become unconscious, and fall; and so on with every wound **and** injury that firearms or cutting weapons are liable to produce. But the amount of help which would be required for every wounded man requiring to be accompanied by an attendant, or to **be** carried or otherwise assisted to the rear, is much greater than can ever reasonably be expected to be found; and it is the duty, therefore, of such attendants as are present on the field of action, first, to attend upon and select for transport to the rear those patients whose wounds appear to have most urgent need of surgical attention, and next, when these have been taken to hospital, to assist in turn the less severe cases which remain on the ground.

Fortunately, in every action there is a certain proportion of wounded men, not only those with trifling, but some with comparatively severe wounds, who do not absolutely require transport, either recumbent or sitting, but who are able to make their own way on foot to the stations of medical assistance without help from the bearers.

Here again, no precise rule can be given with regard to the relative numbers of this class of wounded in any given action, nor even as to the nature of the wounds which permit the subjects of them to walk unaided to hospital. No such power can, of course, exist after wounds directly disabling any of those structures upon which the function of locomotion essentially depends, and very rarely after any injury that necessarily entails fatal consequences. But, with these exceptions, no general statement on this head can be made. The ability or inability to walk unsupported for help after a gunshot wound often appears to depend upon personal peculiarities, the force of character, intelligence, and moral control of the individual, as much as, or more than, upon the nature of the wound or injury which has been inflicted. One man will contrive to walk to a field hospital for assistance and exhibit comparatively little signs of distress after the loss of an arm or some other wound of similar severity; while another man, with a comparatively trivial injury, will be utterly overcome and absolutely require to be carried.

Again, if there be no means of carriage ready at hand, no prospect of speedy relief obvious, after the gravest injuries, the stimulus of self-preservation will often wonderfully assist wounded men in walking, or, if mounted soldiers, in riding, to places appointed for giving surgical aid. A man who has received a wound and who is not altogether disabled by it from moving away is first prompted to escape from the area of danger and conflict in which he is no longer of use as a combatant, in the next place he is prompted to pursue his way till he arrives at an hospital by a natural desire for relief, and not improbably also from being urged by a pressing desire to be made aware of the real extent and consequences of the injury which he has sustained. He is alarmed as to the nature or consequences of his wound, and his alarm urges him on. Under the nervous excitement resulting from these mental emotions, wounded men will often perform acts, such as walking or riding long distances, which it might well be supposed beforehand they would be physically incapable of performing. Instances have frequently been known of men with the severest wounds of the upper parts of the body, with the loss of an arm, a fracture of the skull, even with a serious

CHAP. V.
Example.

wound of the brain, walking long distances to surgeons for assistance. Among the drawings by Sir Charles Bell of the wounded which he took at Brussels after the Battle of Waterloo, was one of a sergeant of the King's German Legion who had had his right arm carried off close to the shoulder-joint by a cannon ball.* Nothing remained of the limb but the torn stump which was left attached to the trunk and about two inches of the shattered arm bone. Yet, without any dressing being applied or aid of any kind, this man rode all the way from Waterloo to Brussels. On reaching the St. Elizabeth Hospital and being placed on a bed the excitement which had enabled **this man** to perform so long a ride in such a terrible condition immediately collapsed, he fainted, and for a long **time remained in** an unconscious condition. This is not an exceptional, though, perhaps, considering the distance of the ride, an extreme example of the exertion which a wounded man is capable of making when stimulated by sentiments of self-preservation.

Patients with uncomplicated flesh wounds can generally find their own way to hospital.

It is, however, ordinarily after wounds of a mild character only, after uncomplicated flesh wounds, that men are able to get to the field hospitals for help, especially when the distance of the hospital from the scene of conflict is at all considerable. Such patients may at first be disabled by a certain amount of faintness or shock, by the severity of the pain, but, after a short time has elapsed, they will frequently find themselves able to walk to the rear with more or less activity, perhaps with the aid of a sheathed sword or a rifle in their hands for support.

Artificial appliances suggested for the use of such patients.

It has been thought that artificial appliances specially designed for the purpose might be issued with advantage for the use of such patients. The stretchers, litters, and cacolets would be more completely at the disposal of those for whom transport is absolutely necessary, delay would be prevented, and the services of attendants would not be required for those who, with such artificial supports, could make their own way to the hospitals. The contrivances referred to have been designed more particularly for use after wounds in the leg or thigh; for these, even if only flesh wounds, much more if one or more bones be broken, as a rule prevent the subjects of them from walking unaided for assistance.

Esmarch's crutches for aiding wounded men from the field to field hospitals.

Dr. Friedrich Esmarch, Professor of Surgery at the University of Kiel, and one of the pioneers of ambulance improvements on the continent, has, among many other appliances, invented various kinds of crutches to assist men wounded in the lower extremities in walking to the field hospitals without attendance.† Esmarch's crutches are jointed so as to be

---

* *See* the large framed drawing, No. 14, in the Pathological Museum at Netley.
† Specimens of these crutches may be seen among the articles of surgical field equipment (No. 831) in the Museum of Military Surgery at Netley.

capable of adjustment for the use of persons of different heights. Attached to them are various appliances to fit them not only for bearing the weight of the body, but also to afford local support for particular parts of the limbs which have been injured. Thus, if the foot or leg have been much injured, there is a projecting ledge to the crutch, on which the knee can rest, so that the leg and foot are kept from the ground during the progression; for other cases there is an iron plate at the bottom of the crutch to support the foot. Again, if necessary, movement in a leg or thigh may be prevented by securing the limb to one of the crutches by means of certain **straps** attached to them. The crutches are fitted with cross pieces at the lower ends to prevent them from slipping, or sinking in soft ground. Such assistance could, of course, only avail when the arms and hands are uninjured, and they have never been popular. Professor Esmarch has also invented a tourniquet brace, which, if it can be supplied at the same rate to the soldier as those at present in use, would be invaluable on the field of battle in arresting hæmorrhage, and supporting

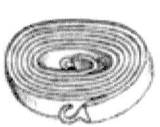 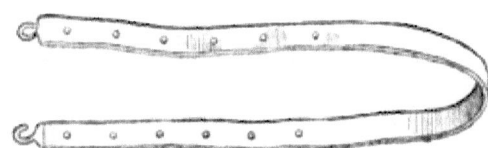

Esmarch's braces for hæmorrhage.

splints. The chief constituent of the tourniquet brace is an elastic band 58 inches in length, which can serve to check dangerous bleeding from wounds in the limbs. It is most simple in its application, merely requiring to be wound tightly round the limb above the wound and hooked.

SECTION IV.—ASSISTANCE BY BEARERS TO WOUNDED MEN.

The proper modes of proceeding to lift and transport wounded men on stretchers, and other regular field conveyances, will be considered elsewhere; but it may be advantageous to notice here some of the methods by which bearers can best give help to wounded when the stretchers are occupied or not available for use on some other account. Some special contrivances have been designed for economising the labour, and lessening the fatigue of bearers under such circumstances, and these also may be worthy of description.

There are various methods by which the transport of a wounded man, who is too weak to walk alone to the rear, may be effected by trained attendants when no litter or conveyance is disengaged, or near at hand, for use. Transport of this kind should only, however, be attempted

CHAP. V

Such help should be systematically conducted.

when the wounds are not grave in their nature, and when the distance is not very great. And in any case suited to transport of this kind, in order that the patient may receive the full benefit of such assistance, it must be given systematically according to the nature of the injury.

It will be useful, therefore, to give a few hints on the best and readiest means by which attendants may assist wounded men according to the site or nature of the wounds which they have sustained. It will be convenient to mention first some methods of affording help when only *one attendant* may be at hand.

Assistance when only one bearer is available.

With patients wounded in the head or upper part of the trunk.

If the wound be in the head, neck, or upper part of the trunk, the patient should partly support himself by his rifle in one hand used as a walking stick, while his other arm and hand lean upon the upper part of the back and distant shoulder of the attendant who walks by his side. At the same time the attendant should place his near arm across the back of the wounded, reaching round and partly encircling his body with the forearm and hand, so as to assist in supporting and keeping erect the upper part of the patient's trunk. The attendant should carry the wounded man's accoutrements in his disengaged hand.

With patients wounded in an upper or lower extremity.

The same relative position of the patient and attendant will answer when the wound has been inflicted in any part of either an upper or lower extremity, after proper temporary protection has been applied to the injured limb. If the wound be in the lower extremity the patient will be enabled by such assistance to walk without throwing the weight of the body upon the foot of the injured side, or may hop along along with less exertion and fatigue. If it be in the upper extremity the patient will not be able to avail himself of any support which requires to be held in the hand; but the injured arm should be slung in a handkerchief so arranged as to fully support it. In all other respects the assistance will be best given in the way already described.

Caution necessary in descending a declivity with such patients.

Should the patient have to descend a declivity the attendant should take special care to hold him up as he walks down the slope, not only by encircling the back and chest, but also at the same time by supporting the patient's arms under the armpits. This is necessary in order to guard against the accident of the patient suddenly slipping or falling forward from an accession of weakness.

Carriage of a patient pick-a-back fashion, or "en cheval."

If the upper extremities be uninjured as well as the thighs, and the attendant be strong enough, he may take up the patient on his back and so carry him to the hospital. In this case the patient places both arms round the neck of the attendant, while the latter supports with his own arms on either side the corresponding thigh of the man he is carrying. It is evident that the bearer cannot, with this arrangement, carry a knapsack, neither can the wounded man's rifle be taken on unless it is capable of being slung. It was in this manner that the distinguished surgeon Baron Percy, the same who designed and organised the French companies of "brancardiers," carried an officer, who had been dangerously wounded, across a pontoon bridge over the Rhine. The case was one of extreme urgency, for, at the time Baron Percy carried the disabled officer over, twelve Austrian guns were directed against the bridge, and it was being broken up under their fire. This pick-a-pack fashion was a common mode of carrying off wounded soldiers from all fields of battle until stretchers were regularly supplied in sufficient numbers for the necessities of warfare.

CHAP. V.

Example of Baron Percy

A method of carrying an injured man is credited to Captain Shaw of the London Fire Brigade. This is an excellent manner of carrying provided the patient is sensible, though even if he is not, the bearer is able to hold the patient very safely.

Messrs. Fischer and Co., the well-known manufacturers of surgical appliances and ambulance conveyances at Heidelberg, have invented a special apparatus, a shoulder litter (Schulterbahre mit Rückensitz),

Fig. I.—Captain Shaw's method of rescuing from fire.

Fischer's apparatus for carrying a wounded man "en cheval."

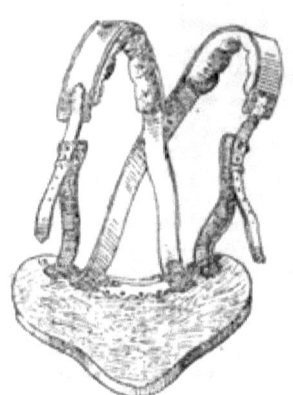
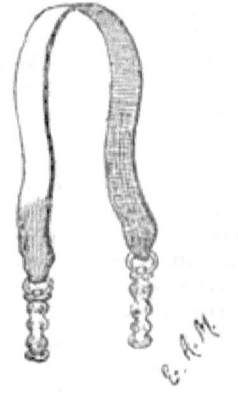

Fig. II.—Fischer's Apparatus for carrying a wounded man *en cheval* on a bearer's back.

Fig. III.—Supporting **Belt** used with the same.

for carrying a wounded man in a sitting posture on the back of a bearer:—

CHAP. V.

The apparatus consists of two parts, viz., (a), a seat, made of wood, and hollowed out, for the patient, and (b), a detached supporting belt. (See Figures 1 and 2.)

The weight of the seat, with the belts and straps attached to it, is 3 lbs. 4 oz.

The following is the method of using this form of conveyance:—

Fischer's apparatus for carrying a wounded man "en cheval."

The board is placed so as to rest on the small of the back of the bearer. The shoulder-belts are adjusted in the manner of a pair of braces, forming a cross behind the bearer's back, passing over his shoulders to be secured to the adjoining short straps by the buckles, and leaving the chest free. On taking up a patient, the bearer is to kneel down on one leg, keeping the other leg stretched out. One or two men then lift and place the patient in a riding position on the board. The loose supporting belt is adjusted under the patient's arms, and its handles are given over to the bearer. This belt serves to secure the patient in his position while the bearer is rising from his knee, and also during his transport. On arriving at his destination the bearer is to go down on his knee again, and the patient taken off in the same manner as that by which he was assisted upon the seat at starting.

Results of trials of the apparatus.

The following points were noted in the experiments made with this appliance:—

1. It is not practicable for the bearer upon whose back the appliance is placed to assist in raising a disabled patient upon it.
2. When the bearer is standing up, no wounded man could get upon the appliance.
3. Two bearers are required to place the patient upon the appliance, the apparatus thus employing three men before the bearer can start with the patient on his back.
4. When the patient has once mounted the seat the bearer finds the use of the appliance convenient. He could march farther with a patient sitting on the seat, than with one placed on his back without it.
5. If the bearer happens to slip he is liable to fall back upon the patient in consequence of the position and weight of the latter.
6. To place a patient safely on the ground from off the appliance without additional help is almost impracticable.

Conclusions regarding the apparatus.

On considering the various practical points enumerated above, all of which were observed during the experiments at Netley with this contrivance, the conclusion arrived at was that the necessity of the additional aid required for its use neutralised its alleged advantage as regards economy of labour; and that the other objections adverted to above precluded it from being suitable for general use in the British military service.

It is advantageous for military surgeons to be acquainted with all the various resources of this nature which from time to time are brought into notice; for on the one hand, this knowledge may sometimes be turned to useful account, and on the other hand it is useful to be aware of the practical objections to their employment when, as will often happen, their adoption is advocated by interested persons, or by others who have not sufficiently studied their qualities. It is questionable whether it would be desirable under any circumstances, even if the experiments had proved more satisfactory, for the Government to make provision of any such kind of special apparatus. At the best it must ever be but a very imperfect substitute for the more regular forms.

A few methods of assisting a wounded man may next be mentioned, when *two attendants* are available, and no stretcher or regular conveyance is at hand. A convenient substitute for a stretcher capable of being carried by two men is so easily improvised that it would be profitless to make efforts to assist a weak or disabled man by any other means; unless these articles are not forthcoming, or the place to which the patient is to be removed is very close at hand. When the necessity arises, however, the support of a patient may be accomplished by the two bearers in several ways.

1. He may be carried in a sitting position by the two bearers joining two of their hands beneath his thighs, while their arms which are not thus occupied are passed round his loin, in the manner shown in the illustration. (Fig. IV.)

Fig. IV.—Two Bearers carrying a wounded Man between them.

In this instance the fingers of the left hand of one of the bearers are interlaced with the fingers of the right hand of the other bearer, and a seat so formed. The patient, if he be able, helps to support himself by clasping the bearers with one or both arms.

For marching or advancing with wounded supported in this manner, the bearers are formed in line and numbered, the odd numbers are right fi'es, and the even numbers are left files.

Chap. V.

One right and one left file carry a patient, and having lifted him from the ground advance by a side pace, the right file starting with right foot, and the left file with the left.

Objections to this mode of carriage.

This mode of conveyance is very trying to the bearers, and could not be endured for any long distance. The defect of the procedure, compared with others, consists in the strain which results from nearly the entire weight of the patient being thrown on two of the arms and chiefly on the interlaced fingers of the two bearers, and only a comparatively limited number of muscles being called into action to meet it; while by other plans the weight may be thrown and distributed more evenly over the whole of three or four arms of the two bearers, at the same time that the arms are so arranged as to give each other mutual support, and all the muscles acting upon the upper extremities, as well as those directly belonging to the extremities themselves, assist in sustaining them under the burden which they are required to bear.

Second Method. Two-handed transport for patient semi-recumbent.

2. A better plan of joining two hands for the support of a patient is shown in the following drawing, Fig. V. The advanced right and left hands of the two bearers are closely locked together, and the wrists brought into contact, and not merely the fingers

Fig. V.—Two-handed Support by two Bearers for carrying a Patient in a semi-recumbent position.

interlaced, so that a firm junction of both hands is established. At the same time the other hands of the two bearers are made to rest upon and in a certain degree to grasp each other's shoulders on the same sides respectively. When a patient is carried according to this method, the weight falls chiefly upon the two arms behind him, but to some extent also upon the chests of the two bearers; while that portion of the weight which falls upon the arms in front does not bear upon

CHAP. V.

Three-handed seat.

Fig. VI.—Three-handed Seat.

the fingers and hands so much as in the former case, but is distributed over the forearms and shoulders. The patient is

Fig. VII.—Patient on three-handed Seat.

not carried in a sitting position, but lying back. It is therefore well adapted for removing a patient who is so weak as

Comparison between this

absolutely to require complete support at the back to prevent him from falling, or is quite helpless, or disabled in both upper extremities. It is not so easy for two bearers to assume the relative positions just described when they have to pick up a patient lying upon the ground as it is to take the former one; but the art can be acquired by a little training and practice, and the labour is fully repaid by the advantages to both patient and bearers. If the bearers are untrained it will be better, if it can be done, for them to stand in the position shown in the drawing, while two other bearers lift and place in their arms the man who has to be carried away. A disabled man of moderate weight may be carried to a considerable distance without extraordinary fatigue to the bearers in the way described.

To form three-handed seat the right file seizes with his right hand the thick part of his left forearm, and with his disengaged hand seizes the thick part of the left forearm of the left file. The left file with his left hand seizes the thick part of the right forearm of the right file, and the seat is made. The left file places his disengaged hand on the left shoulder of the right file forming the back and completing the seat. (*See* Figs. VI. and VII.)

3. If a wounded man be able to sit upright, and is able to assist in holding himself up by his own arms, the bearers may then employ all their hands and arms in forming a seat for him. This is sometimes done by the bearers crossing their arms and then grasping each other's hands. A space is thus left between the bearers' hands and forearms, upon which the patient may be supported for a time with tolerable security. The objection to this method of supporting a wounded man is the pain that is caused after a time to the bearers at the points where their arms are crossed one upon the other. The weight of the patient acts constantly upon these particular parts, for when once he is "settled" in his place, the relative position of the bearers' arms cannot be shifted, at least not without the patient is laid down upon the ground while the change is being effected. The portions of the arms which lean upon each other are also those where the bones of the forearm are not provided with much muscular covering, so that the painful effects of the continued pressure are very speedily, and soon painfully felt.

4. A better way of effecting the removal of a wounded man, if he is to be transported on all four arms of the bearers, is represented in the following drawings, Figs. VIII., IX. The mode of forming a seat is known among schoolboys under the name of the "sedan chair," and it is remarkable how well the weight of a person sitting is borne when the hands and arms of the bearers are so placed; for with each arm engaged in composing the support, the muscles that are ordinarily employed in effecting its various movements now all act in concert to enable it to resist the strain which is cast upon it. The arrangement, moreover, forms a very easy seat for the person carried, and a very secure one also if he is in a state to give himself the necessary additional support by placing his arms over the shoulders of the

bearers. As seen in drawing No. 6, the backs of the bearers' hands are turned uppermost, while the palms rest upon the adjoining arms.

Fig. VIII.—Four-handed Seat formed by two bearers, the arms being crossed. A A, Right Forearm. B B, Left Forearm.

Each file seizes his own left forearm and with the disengaged hand seizes the right forearm of the opposite file. The patient

Fig. IX.—Prepared four-handed Seat.

supports himself by placing his arms round the necks of the bearers.

Fig. X.—Bearers marching with four-handed Seat.

Fig. XI.—Method by which two Bearers can carry a man in a **horizontal** position.

Figures XI. and XII. show the manner in which two or three bearers can carry a wounded man in a horizontal position, and they sufficiently explain themselves.

No reference has been made in the preceding observations nor will be hereafter made, unless incidentally, to the necessity for first removing the arms and accoutrements, and setting free the chests of patients; to the particular supports to be given to fractured limbs; or to various necessary dressings and means of local protection which have to be applied to wounds preliminary to the transportation of wounded soldiers from a field of action to the rear. These are subjects which belong to the study of

CHAP. V.
———
The surgical treatment of field injuries not discussed in this work.

Fig. XII.—Method by which three Bearers can carry a man in a horizontal position.

field surgery in general, and of the proper treatment of special injuries. The modes of effecting the transportation itself of the wounded men, irrespective of the surgical treatment of their injuries, are alone intended to be discussed in this work. This, however, includes rules for *safely conducting* the transport, and these will be noticed hereafter in succession as each class of conveyance is described.

CHAPTER VI.

AMBULANCE TRANSPORT MATERIAL.

GENERAL CLASSIFICATION.

Class I. Conveyances *borne* by men.
Class II. Conveyances *wheeled* by men.
Class III. Conveyances *borne* by animals.
Class IV. Conveyances *drawn* by animals.
Class V. Railway Ambulance Transport.
Class VI. Marine Ambulance Transport.

Some of the classes naturally become divided into certain sub-classes—having marked and distinctive features. The six classes above enumerated will now be successively considered.

CLASS I.—CONVEYANCES BORNE BY MEN.

This class is sub-divided into the following sub-classes:—

A.—Hammocks.
B.—Dandies.
C.—Stretchers.

One general principle as regards the mode of carriage prevails in all the conveyances of this class. The patient is supported either upon a netting or canvas cloth, or in a cot of more substantial construction; he is usually able to lie down at full length, seldom having to adopt any other position; and while thus reclining he is borne between two or four men who are called the "bearers."*

Distinction between the terms "stretchers" and "bearers." Sometimes indiscriminately used. Probable source of this error.

* The terms *stretchers* and *bearers* are not unfrequently used synonymously in published works, and misapprehension and confusion have occasionally arisen in consequence. In page 21 of the pamphlet entitled "Personnel and Matériel of the Medical Department of the Army of 30,000 Men ordered to Turkey," among the means of conveyance of wounded are mentioned "*bearers or stretchers* . . . 780." Similar indiscriminate use of the two terms occurs every now and then, even in official documents. In circular No. 856, 31st March, 1864, page 3, it is remarked, "two at least of the *stretchers* shall be conveyed in the ambulance waggon." In the descriptive plate G to the same circular, the drawings representing the very articles of equipment referred to are designated "*bearer* open for use" and "*bearer* packed for transport." This want of discrimination has probably arisen from the fact of the patient being practically borne by the stretcher just as both the stretcher and patient upon it are by the men who carry the conveyance. But it is evidently more explicit, and therefore more convenient, to maintain in English

One of the bearers, if only two are employed, sustains the front of the conveyance, while the other sustains the hinder part; if four are employed, two bear the conveyance in front, and two behind.

The conveyance is either carried by its two extremities, or by appliances attached to them, or suspended from a single pole, on the *shoulders* of the bearers; sometimes, though in like manner carried on the shoulders, it is borne between two poles, **or** the suspension is effected by a framework, part of which is made to project for the purpose of affording the necessary means of support. Occasionally the conveyance is arranged to be placed between two side-poles, **the** supporting bottom **being** either left slack, or expanded and tightened by means of movable cross-pieces or **by** being **connected with** a permanently fixed framework, **and the** extremities **of** the poles are held in the *hands* **of the bearers, with** or without **the** additional support of straps passing **round their necks or** otherwise attached **to** their persons. The **height from** the ground at which **the** patient is carried **is** determined partly by the construction of the conveyance, partly by the manner in which it is borne. The risk of falling during the transport is obviated in some forms by the bed or sacking bottom upon which he is placed dipping below the level of the framework; in others, in which the support is firm and level, by the framework being raised above it; occasionally a strap, or two straps, are passed across the body of the patient so as to guard against the possible occurrence of this accident. In all cases the comfort of the patient during his transport depends on the manner of movement adopted by the bearers. When the conveyance itself is suitable, and the bearers are skilled in their work, this mode of conveyance becomes the most easy that can be devised for the carriage of an invalid through a hilly country or over uneven ground, and perhaps it is also over made roads.

In European armies conveyances borne by men are generally employed under circumstances in which the distances to be traversed are very short, and in situations where other modes of carriage are absent.

In the East, as will be explained in describing the dooley and dandy, they form one of the ordinary means of conveying the sick and wounded for all distances. This difference of feature in the two modes, habitually adopted in the East, and in Europe, of employing these conveyances leads to a great difference as regards the economy of their use for military

---

phraseology the same distinction which is made in other countries between the passive conveyance and the agents by whom it is carried. Just as the dooley and dooley-bearers are spoken of in India, as brancards and brancardiers in France, so stretchers and stretcher-bearers should be distinguished in the military language of this country. Moreover, "stretcher" is the name by which soldiers generally speak of this conveyance—not bearer; and it seems, therefore, in every way better to adopt the same signification exclusively in English phraseology.

purposes. In the one case, when they are only employed for short distances, if the bearers are well trained and active, two men bearing one stretcher will carry a considerable number of wounded in succession to the dressing station, and when not thus employed will be available for other duties; in the other case, when the conveyances are employed for all distances, not only must a certain number of men be entirely devoted to the duty of bearers, but they must be accompanied, in addition, with a proportion of reliefs. A large body of bearers is thus brought together, who, of necessity, must continually weigh upon the commissariat resources of the country through which they are passing, and in other ways increase the impediments of the army to which they are attached. Other points of interest to the army surgeon on this subject will be noticed in the course of the description which follows of the special qualities of each form of conveyance.

A.—HAMMOCKS.*

This section contains the simplest forms of conveyances borne by men; they may, in some instances, be said to be devoid of any distinct forms of construction, nothing more than a simple piece of cloth being occasionally used, hammock fashion, for a litter. Whatever may be the material of which they are composed, it is used in a more or less loose and pliable condition—not stretched out—and, therefore, yields to the weight of the patient, and assumes whatever form the position of his body may give to it. The soldier's blanket, when used as a conveyance for a wounded man without the addition of a pole or side supports, the broad officer's or sergeant's sash, as formerly made, offer examples of the hammock in its primitive state. The sailor's hammock, Indian hammock, Ashanti hammock, severally supported by an overhead pole, exhibit a step in advance of construction. The so-called "stretchers" as formerly used without traverses, and the looped blanket, are examples of the same kind of conveyances; but they show a still further advance in construction, inasmuch as they are adapted for carriage by side poles, and are **thus** sustained with less difficulty by the bearers. A still more perfect form of this conveyance, so far as the transport of a wounded man is concerned, is the New Zealand litter (p. 142).

---

* The word "hammock" is generally supposed to have been brought into use in Europe from the American Indians, by whom it is applied to the kind of hanging bed suspended between trees, which is in ordinary use among them. In support of this origin, some dictionaries quote Columbus, who, in the narrative of his first voyage, speaks of Indians in canoes coming to the ship to barter their cotton and "hamacas," or nets, in which they sleep. Dr. Johnson, however, derives it from "hamaca," a Saxon word.
I found the following in the library of the British Museum. "At our landing we met a widow carry'd in a net with a pole through it by two black slaves" (P. 659. A curious and exact account of a voyage to the Congo in the years 1666 and 1667, by Fathers Michael Angelo and Denis de Carli-Capachino).—EDITOR.

The Soldier's Blanket as a mode of conveyance.—The blankets which soldiers carried with them into the trenches before Sebastopol were sometimes employed after a sortie of the enemy, or on any occasion on which the killed and wounded surpassed the average of ordinary days, and when, therefore, a sufficiency of regular stretchers could not be immediately obtained. In using it, the blanket must be spread fully out upon the ground, the patient laid gently upon it in a suitable direction, and four men laying hold of the four corners of the blanket then raise it together, and march with it, as nearly as practicable, in the same manner as if they were bearing a stretcher. The great-coat may be employed in a similar way.

CHAP. VI.

The soldier's blanket used as a hammock.

Fig. XIII.—Conveying a wounded soldier in his blanket from the trenches before Sebastopol to the "ambulance de la tranchée." From a drawing by M. Durand-Brager.

It is scarcely possible for a less number than four bearers to convey a wounded man away by these means; should the attempt be made by two bearers, each bearer sustaining two corners of the blanket, the inconvenience of the position as regards the bearers in front, the constant drag of the weight on one part of the body, the shoulders, of each bearer without any intermission, the liability of the knees of the bearer marching behind to strike against the back of the patient, will be found to be serious impediments to progress. The officer's silk sash, as formerly made, did not present the same objections to being borne by two men. At the same time that the netting of which it was composed became readily stretched out laterally to a sufficient width to hold the person being carried, it was long enough for one end to be passed over the shoulder of the foremost bearer, and to be held in front of him. The weight was, therefore, more evenly distributed over his whole body, and his position for marching rendered in all respects more easy. The woollen scarf worn round the waist of each of the privates

Officer's sash as a hammock.

employed in Larrey's ambulance volante was adapted to be used in a similar manner, and was made broad and strong for the purpose.

In whatever way, however such conveyances without poles are carried, they should be regarded in no other light than as expedients only admissible in the unavoidable absence of better means of support. They have nothing to recommend them beyond being slightly better than no means of support at all. They are no less irksome and unsuited to the patients than they are burdensome to the bearers. After injuries in which fractures of the bones have been produced, more especially of the long bones of the lower extremities, blankets should never be employed with a view of saving time in reaching an ambulance or place of surgical aid; for, without the greatest care, as regards provisional support to the broken bones, the mischief done to wounded limbs will be immensely aggravated by this mode of carriage, partly owing to the doubled-up position of the patient's body, partly to the pressure upon him of the sides of the blanket, which are drawn unavoidably together by the pull and efforts of the bearers, and in great part also owing to the disturbance resulting from the unrestrained movements of the conveyance as it becomes alternately shortened and lengthened under the impulse of the transport. The safety of the patient with a gunshot fracture of the thigh or leg will be better provided for by his removal being delayed until a stretcher can be procured for his conveyance, even though many hours may elapse before one can be obtained.

Hammocks without poles should only be used for short distances, unless under circumstances of extreme risk in other ways. Bearers become more quickly fatigued with them than with any other kind of carriage. The form of the human body causes a heavy weight to be most easily carried, and to be sustained for longest distances, when the pressure resulting from it is directed upon, and distributed evenly, over the arch which is formed by the pelvis, and lower extremities. The weight may be carried on the head, and conveyed in the upright position down the vertebral column to the pelvis; or it may be thrown directly upon it, the body being bent for the purpose, according to custom of the porters of Constantinople and certain parts of India, who are remarkable for the heavy burdens which they carry upon the upper part of the sacral region, or, as it were, upon the key-stone of the arch just described. The carriage of a weight upon the shoulder is an imperfect application of this principle, but the element of imperfection which exists in it, is counteracted to a certain extent by a proportionate inclination of the body, so as to distribute the weight from the shoulder in as nearly a vertical direction as possible along the vertebral column. In proportion as this is effected, the burden, whatever it is, can more easily be carried. But when two men have to bear the weight of a man in a hammock without the aid of poles, the mode of sustentation, for which the human frame is adapted, as named above, is completely departed from, and, as a consequence, fatigue quickly ensues. The weight is applied to the upper part of the body on one side, at a considerable angle, as it were, to the end of a long lever, the action of which is to exert a constant tendency to pull the bearer over, and this can only be overcome by continued muscular effort of a severe kind. In estimating the amount of fatigue produced, this effort must be taken into account as well as the mere weight to be carried. Moreover, the bearers cannot rest from their labour by laying the hammock on the ground without risk of injury resulting to the wounded man whom they are carrying, for it is destitute of any sort of protection suitable for such a position. These several conditions are sufficient to show the impropriety of making an attempt to carry a patient to any lengthened distance in such a conveyance as a sash, blanket, or other such contrivance unless under circumstances of extreme necessity.

Hammocks suspended from a single Pole.—A hammock of regular construction has at each end several small lines, which are either looped together at their extremities, or terminate in rings, so that it can be readily secured and suspended between two solid supports, by means of hooks, screws, or any convenient fastenings. Such are the hammocks used on board ship, the grass hammocks made by the natives of South America, and others. In the sailor's hammock the lines, or *clues* as they are called, meet at each end in an iron ring, or *grummet*. When it is in use on board ship, a mattress and pillow are placed in it for a bed, and the whole is then hoisted up into its place between the deck beams by means of laniards. It will be at once seen that such hammocks can be readily adjusted so as to be suspended from a single long pole; the points of suspension being established by either the loops or rings, or secured by the laniards. By a little management again they can also be arranged to be carried between two poles, one pole being secured to either side.

In the same way two poles are sometimes adapted to a soldier's blanket to convert it into a somewhat similar kind of conveyance. The blanket does not admit of being suspended from a single pole for ambulance purposes, for it is not sufficiently long, but if a loop be sewn at each corner, and the blanket be then doubled over so that the two loops at each end are brought together, a pole, or even a rifle, can be passed through the four loops on one side, and another passed within the doubling of the blanket on the other side, and in this way we get the conveyance which was formerly commonly known as the "looped blanket." If the loops have not been previously added to the blanket, a small slit may be made in each corner as an impromptu measure instead of the loop, and the blanket can thus be used for the same purpose if the material be sufficiently strong and resisting. Such conveyances correspond in their nature with the hand litters which were formerly used without cross-pieces or traverses. They are an important step

CHAP. VI.

Rationale of the advantages resulting from the suspension of conveyances of the hammock kind from poles.

in advance, as regards efficiency, beyond the sash, blanket, or hammock used without poles.

The advantages arising from the suspension of the hammock from a pole will be at once understood on recollection of the disadvantages which have been just described to result from its absence. The bearers, carrying the pole on their shoulders and steadying it in position by their hands, support the weight with less difficulty, and can sustain it for considerable distances. The carriage is more easy for the patient, because the distance between the two points of suspension remains unaltered during the transit. The irregular movements from head to foot of the hammock, caused by the distance between the two bearers in marching occasionally varying, as well as from the frequent alterations of direction in the "pull" of the conveyance as the bearers seek to relieve themselves from the effects of the strain upon their arms, are in a great degree avoided by the hammock being suspended from a fixed and comparatively rigid support.

Use of hammocks after the action at the Alma.

After the battle of the Alma a large number of wounded officers and soldiers were conveyed in hammocks, suspended in the manner described, from the field of action to the shore, a distance of about two miles, for removal to the transports which were to convey them to Scutari. The inconveniences chiefly

Fig. XIV.—Hammock carriage showing the cramped position of the patient.

experienced in their use in carrying wounded are the difficulty of giving a proper rest or support to any injured part or limb, from the rounded form of the canvas, and from its closely adapting itself to the general outline of the body; the pressure of the sides of the hammock against the person within it; the difficulty of maintaining a horizontal posture of the patient in moving over uneven or sloping ground; and the absence of all provision to act as a guard against the effects of placing the conveyance temporarily on the ground. These inconveniences equally exist whether the hammock be borne suspended from one pole or between two poles, though some of them are felt in a somewhat less degree in the latter case.

On the Gold Coast there is no animal transport. All impedimenta are carried on the heads of natives, as the climate is so inimical to most domestic animals (horses and mules, donkeys, horned cattle) that they rapidly deteriorate after importation. These remarks do not apply to Accra, 80 miles below Cape Coast Castle, as horses and cattle seem to thrive pretty well there. The usual mode of conveyance at Cape Coast Castle is a hammock slung on a pole. Any sick or wounded must be conveyed into the castle, either on these or stretchers, and as the natives carry these on their heads, four bearers are required for each.*

The ordinary hammock consists of a bamboo pole supporting a net or cloth, in which the patient reclines, and is carried by two men, or four when the pole rests on the heads of the bearers. In his Report on the Ashanti Campaign, Surgeon-General Sir A. Home, V.C., K.C.B., writes, " hammocks carried by four men, not, as would seem natural, on their shoulders, but on their heads, for which purpose the hammock pole is fitted at each end with a piece of board placed transversely; a movable canvas-covered frame, from which hang side curtains, rests on the pole, and serves as a roof to protect from the sun. Much of the comparative comfort of this kind of conveyance depended on the native carriers being trained and matched in size and strength, the motion was easy or painful in proportion as these points could be secured."

In this campaign conveyances known as the Ashanti cot were largely used. These were a modification of the ordinary hammock, intended to prevent the discomfort of the "doubling up" of the person carried, from the strain of its fastenings at the head and feet, and was obtained by using a ship's cot (which is essentially a hammock stretched out by a light wooden frame) and it answered admirably. Director-General Sir W. A. Mackinnon, K.C.B., who was Principal Medical Officer after Sir Anthony Home was invalided, speaks highly of the Ashanti

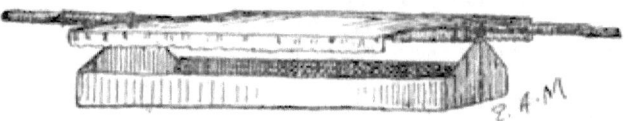

Fig. XV.—The Ashanti Cot.

cots, and also of extemporised cots in which he directed the natives should be carried. The following, which is "interesting to notice, is the kind of transport which had been used for the wounded of distinction amongst the Ashantis; * * * * the stalks of the male bamboo, or the long centre ridge stalks of the leaves of certain palms which grow **every**where in the forest, were bound together with tough sedges,

---

* Surgeon-General Sir Wm. Muir, K.C.B., A.M.D. Reports, 214, 1873.
† A.M.D. Reports, p. 243, 1873.

and formed convenient cradles in which the wounded chief was easily carried on the heads of a couple of his followers."

The numerous sick with Mr. Stanley's expedition for the relief of Emin Pasha were carried, by Surgeon-Captain Parke's directions, in hammocks, and, for natives, answers well. The cramped position is a position of rest to a native, but to Europeans a "full length" attitude is always necessary for repose.

The Mexican twine hammocks are light, portable, and pack into a small waterproof bag, fairly durable, and capable of being turned to many useful purposes. They are known in England as the "Ashanti hammocks," but were not used to any great extent in that campaign. The Ashanti hammock is furnished with two spreaders and four poles with pegs, and makes a very excellent bed. It consists of a strong net attached by several strings to a "grummet" at each end. A strong cord is attached to each "grummet," and the hammock can be either tied up between two trees or passed over two crossed poles and secured to the ground. The net is spread by two traverses or "spreaders" as they are called. An awning is supplied with each hammock to protect the individual from the sun or rain. The weight of the hammock, with awning and poles complete, is 11 lbs.; of the hammock alone, 2 lbs. This hammock is a registered pattern for the English army, and has been used during recent campaigns. They are available for a variety of purposes. Slung from a pole they can be used in the fashion of the dandy to be described, on the line of march for the sick and wounded, or for general purposes of transport. They are particularly well adapted for use on board ship, and they have been used for the transport of sick and wounded by railway (*see* transport by rail). This carriage labours under the usual disadvantages of hammocks for the carriage of wounded, previously described, but commends itself admirably for the transport of slighter cases, and the other various uses to which it may be put, by its lightness, portability, and durability.

There is a conveyance of the hammock nature met with in the remote districts in the Himalayas, and known as the Himalayan dandy (*see* p. 122). In its early form it is not often seen, but its descendant in the present jhampan (a misnomer) is the ordinary conveyance among Europeans in the hill districts, and the most recent is the Lushai dandy, which possesses all the advantages of a dooley and to a large extent the lightness of its prototype.

For the purposes of ambulance transport the jhampan is not used at the present time, though there are many practical ideas to be collected from it, and for that purpose, as well as to avoid a confusion in terms, the true jhampan will be described, and it must be carefully borne in mind that that which is commonly called a jhampan in the hills to-day by Europeans is really a dandy, and is called by this name by the bearers themselves.

Jhampans.—These are conveyances which are seldom, if ever, met with in the plains of India. They are modes of transport ordinarily employed in the hill countries, and are specially contrived for the easy carriage of persons up the steep roads, as well as down the abrupt descents, which have to be traversed in travelling through mountainous districts. The jhampans are so contrived that the part of the conveyance on which the person carried is reclining or sitting may be kept level without any part of it being brought into collision with the road, or with the detached pieces of rock which are usually scattered over its surface—for the beds of winter watercourses not unfrequently form the roads which are travelled over at other seasons in the hill countries—at the same time that the weight is evenly distributed between the front and rear bearers, whatever may be the inclination of the road over

Fig. XVI.—Chinese Palanquin, carried Jhampan fashion.

which they are travelling. These purposes are accomplished by having the poles or points of suspension placed nearly in the same plane with the part on which the person is supported, and by having the shoulder supports movable. With this arrangement, when the inclination is great, the bearers at one end can lower the part of the jhampan which they are carrying to the degree which is necessary for keeping it level with the rest of the conveyance, and thus avoid any impediment to their progress, at the same time that the pole still maintains a position at right angles to the shoulders of the bearers. The native jhampan in ordinary use is not unlike an ordinary couch, and is provided with a cover and side curtains. The couch itself is secured between two side rails made of wood. These side pieces are connected at each end by strong cross-bands of leather, or flexible traverses, and in the middle of each band, at right angles to it, is secured a short piece of bamboo. These two pieces of bamboo rest on the shoulders of the four bearers, two bearers being at each end, one inside, the other outside the flexible traverse, when the conveyance is carried. It will be seen that these short poles are neither fixed nor even in contact with the body of the jhampan. They are only connected at the middle with the bands before mentioned, so that both their ends are left loose; and the partial freedom of motion which is thus left to them enables the level of either end of the conveyance to be altered according to circumstances with greater facility, without changing the relative position of the short poles to the men who are supporting them.

122 *The Himalayan Dandy.*

CHAP. VI.

Its construction.

B.—DANDIES.

The Dandy.—The original Himalayan dandy consists of a large piece of strong cloth secured by bands at its four corners, to four rings fixed in a long pole. The pole is about 10 feet in

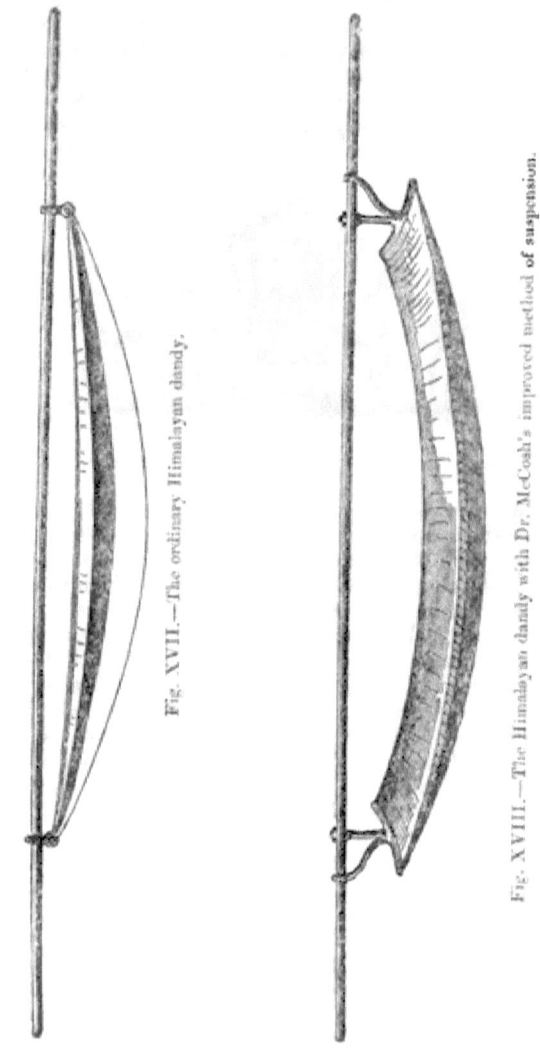

Fig. XVII.—The ordinary Himalayan dandy.

Fig. XVIII.—The Himalayan dandy with Dr. McCosh's improved method of suspension.

length, and the rings are placed in pairs, nearly opposite to each other, at about two feet from the ends of the pole. Sometimes a dandy is suspended from two iron stanchions, as shown in Fig. XVIII. The dandy is carried on the shoulders of two men; but four men usually accompany it, two acting as reliefs and carrying it in turn. It has this peculiarity that it does not admit of the person conveyed in it lying down, or occupying the conveyance in the direction of its length; he must sit crosswise in the middle of it, resting his feet on a loose rope slung beneath the hammock part, and steadying himself whenever necessary by grasping the pole with his hands. The sides of the dandy are therefore kept apart principally by the back and thighs of the person who is being carried upon it. Occasionally, as when it is used for the carriage of European ladies, a sort of basket-work chair is placed in the dandy to form a seat for the occupant. The person carried still sits crosswise.

Staff Surgeon J. McCosh, of the Bengal Army, when stationed in the Himalayas, at Almora, in 1847, made what appeared to him to be a great improvement in the hill dandy, by adding to it two stout iron stanchions to which he attached the hammock. This alteration caused the

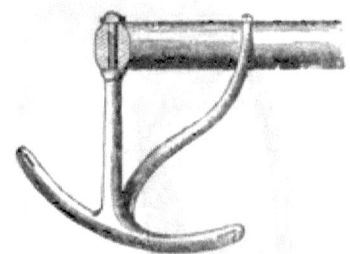

Fig. XIX.—One of the pole-stanchions used in suspending the Himalayan dandy on Dr. McCosh's plan.

dandy to be capable of being used for a patient in a recumbent position, and also allowed a small awning for protection from the sun or rain to be thrown over the person lying in it. Dr. McCosh mentions that he used it arranged as described, on many occasions in travelling, with very favourable results, and expresses his belief that from its lightness and portability it would in its improved form serve as a valuable addition to the usual mode of transport in the field in India, especially during an action.

Primarily it will be observed that this is the first step in advance from the original, and that lightness has, to a large extent, been obtained by lessening the diameter of the pole, and consequently its weight. It is a fatal mistake, even if it were possible to obtain sufficient rigidity, to have the poles thin. It is the most prolific cause of sore shoulders, and it may be laid down definitely that the heavy female bamboo poles are invariably the best for carriage of this class. The secret of correctness in construction is to observe closely the habits of the natives, and in this case they will be found to always select a rigid thick bamboo. It steadies them passing over rough ground, and there is no springing motion conveyed

CHAP. VI.
The dandy.

to those carried, as invariably occurs when thin poles are used. Secondly will be noticed the iron transverse "spreaders," giving the character of the bed as in the true jhampan, and which may have been one of the sources of original error. The objection to this part of the conveyance

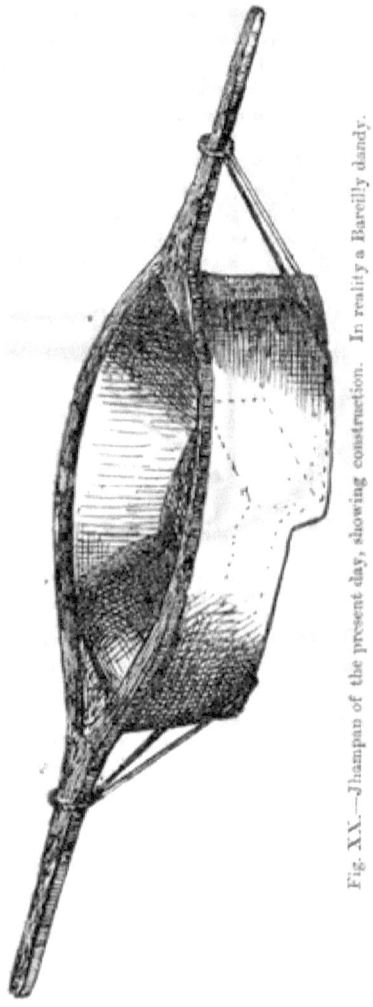

Fig. XX.—Jhampan of the present day, showing construction. In reality a Bareilly dandy.

are the projecting corners, which are most inconvenient passing along narrow mountain paths. Thirdly, it will be observed that the hammock portion is bolted on to the pole. Perforation of the pole, especially if bamboo, by an iron screw is a great weakness. Iron clamped to bamboo rots it, and lessens its durability, rendering it liable to short fracture. The intervention of thick leather washers would obviate this to a large extent.

The principal difference between the jhampan and the dandy in their original forms is that there are two poles in the former, and one pole in the latter.

We now come to the consideration of the modern form of dandy, or jhampan, as it is sometimes, though erroneously, called. The first well-known form was the Bareilly dandy. This conveyance consists of an oval frame of wood, prolonged, at the two opposite ends of the oval, into two single straight poles. The whole frame really consists of two pieces placed side by side, open at the middle, and closely applied to each other at their extremities, forming a single pole to rest on the shoulders of the bearers. This divided nature of

CHAP. VI.

The main distinction between a dandy and a jhampan.

Fig. XXI.—The dandy carried like a jhampan.*

the pole may historically associate the dandy with the jhampan. The **seat** or support is contained in the oval space between the poles, and is formed of a light open kind of basket-work. but in the modern form, which, in every other respect is similar, there is a wooden framework with a seat, allowing the person carried to occupy a sitting up or semi-recumbent position.

The drawing shows the features of the modern dandy used in the hills of India, and it also shows a method not unlike, in its physical aspects, the jhampan system of carriage. A stout bamboo pole 4 feet long, is tied on to the dandy poles in front and behind, and four bearers carry the conveyance. It is a

The jhampan method of carriage applied to a dandy.

---

* Perhaps it is not clearly shown in the figure, but dandy bearers invariably break the step, when travelling.

CHAP. VI.
The dandy.

...le method when crossing dangerous ground, as well as the usual method adopted when carrying heavy passengers, or heavy weights, up steep ascents. The bearers who carry the dandy are called jhampanis, and are strong, athletic hillmen.

A person carried in a dandy is well protected against falling, whatever may be the inclination or irregularity of the ground over which the bearers have to pass, by the oval frame within which the seat is placed. He is at the same time carried at such an elevation, and in such a position, rather semi-reclining than completely sitting, that there is no likelihood of any part of his person being brought into collision with inequalities of surface, or scattered boulders of rock, over or between which the bearers may have to pass. Lastly, the conveyance is so narrow that it can be readily carried over a ledge, or along any mountain path, however contracted in width, along which the bearers themselves can pass. There is no provision to facilitate lowering or raising either end of this conveyance for the purpose of keeping the sitter level, when ascending or descending steeply inclined paths; this can only be effected by carrying the person riding head first up hill, and feet first down hill, and also by the bearers altering their relative heights, one bearer stooping more or less according to circumstances, when such a necessity arises.

The dandy just described has never been utilised to any great extent—the occasion not having occurred. They would be suitable for cases of slight injury or sickness, and in mountain warfare are eminently more suitable than cacolets or litters; but both the Bareilly dandy and the common dandy have been condemned for ambulance transport purposes.

The Lushai Dandy.

The Lushai dandy.

The Lushai dandy, though commonly associated with the dhooly, belongs to this class of ambulance transport, and has replaced the latter, and is a much lighter and more economical form of transport.

This dandy consists of the following parts:—

    a. Pole and cover.
    b. Framework, canvas bed, and feet.
    c. Canvas bottom and sides.
    d. Suspension strings.

The pole is 12 feet long, and is cut from the stems of the full grown female bamboo, indigenous to the country where this form of carriage is used. The pole selected should be straight, fairly even in its diameter throughout its whole length, well seasoned, and not elastic. The steadier the pole, the more efficient will the carriage be.

The framework consists of two long pieces of hollow bamboo forming the sides, and two short pieces forming the ends. These four pieces are joined together to form the framework by the feet, which are specially constructed for this purpose.

Each foot is 6 inches long, and slightly flattened at its lower extremity, the upper end divides into two parts, branching at right angles to each other but lying in the same plane, and both are at right angles to the foot. These branches or arms pass into the hollow ends of the bamboos which form the frame, thus consolidating it. In the centre of the frame a piece of canvas is tightly laced to the sides and ends, and in this manner firmly brace the structure. Thus a low bed is formed 6' × 2' and 6" from the ground.

Underneath this framework is another piece of canvas, having roughly the same area, with four pieces of canvas prolonged for 6 inches at the sides and ends. These being turned up form the sides, and can be laced to each other at the corners. In the upper hem of each end of this canvas is inserted a piece of split bamboo, and from these several pieces of string, about 8 to 10 inches long, are attached, which converge to a ring.

Suspension is effected by passing the rings over the pole, and raising the latter, as in the Bengal pattern; and this is the best form of this carriage; or the ring may be placed on a hook

Fig. XXII.—The Lushai Dandy.

permanently fixed to the pole, as in the Madras pattern. The latter has the great objection of iron clamping bamboo, previously noticed.

A light framework of split bamboo is attached to the pole by three straps to support a canvas cover intended to protect the person carried from the effects of the sun, and other atmospheric influences. The canvas fits this light framework, and at this part is painted white and thickly varnished; while from it, at the sides and ends, hang curtains, divided at the latter to facilitate the passage of the pole.

The weight of the Lushai dandy is 52 lbs. to 58 lbs., the variation being due to the pole (20–25 lbs.).

The advantages claimed for the Lushai dandy may be enumerated as follows:—

(1) Economy in cost, and simplicity of construction.
(2) Four bearers only necessary instead of six.
(3) Form excellent beds for field hospitals.
(4) Extremely portable and easily packed.
(5) When broken can be readily repaired from materials close at hand.

The question of the number of bearers alone requires consideration, for the results of the experience of the wars in

Chap. VI.

General remarks on the number of bearers allowed to each dandy in Afghanistan and Burma.

Afghanistan and Upper Burma have not been as satisfactory as might have been wished. The analysis of the weight carried will be found fully discussed in the section treating on Indian ambulance transport. Generally the untrained nature of the coolies (for the majoriy are not kahars), which are detailed for work with dandies, prevents any possibility of their ever becoming efficient. In Burma this was particularly noticeable among the temporary bearers and the coolie bearers. The permanent bearers were equal to the work, but even for them it was hard. With reference to the war in Afghanistan, Sir Thomas Crawford, K.C.B., the late Director-General, writes: "The kahars and dhoolie-bearers were, for the most part, physically unfit for the work to which many of them were wholly new; clothing was very tardily issued to them; and instead of a body of carefully selected men fitted for arduous work, the majority of them had never been properly inspected. Such is the general tenor of all the reports received from medical officers."* In the Burmese Campaign it was some time before the effect of the direct control over the ambulance transport, instituted by Surgeon-Major-General G. Farrell, C.B., the Principal Medical Officer, began to be felt, but which was without question one of the most valuable administrative acts of this officer. He took over from the military authorities the entire strength of bearers in the country, and the material, which consisted for the most part of Lushai dandies, and under his management the clothing, feeding, payment, and forwarding of the family remittances was undertaken. Surgeon-Major-General Farrell appointed a medical officer to act as ambulance officer, and he had a separate office near the depôt, where stores, drill, and instruction were fully carried out. The personnel of the ambulance office was: one surgeon (the ambulance officer, as he was called), four transport staff sergeants, one gomastha, and one baboo clerk.

Four men to a dandy is too small a number for continued exertion, and even for short distances only the strongest men would be efficient, and extra help must be added in pairs, i.e., one man at each end of the dandy at the same time. The addition of one man is no relief, and he can only be considered as spare carriage.

Disadvantage of the Lushai dandy.

There is one disadvantage of the Lushai dandy, which occurs when the conveyance is placed on the ground, namely, that there is some difficulty in adjusting the pole. It is a very slight matter and should be obviated by removing the pole and cover, or directing two bearers to support them.

A second disadvantage is that at the point where the branches of the iron feet corner enter the bamboo the latter becomes rotten. All Lushai dandies before being taken over should be carefully examined and tested at these points 6 inches to 8 inches from each corner on the ends and sides.

A chagul or canvas water-bag is carried slung on the pole.

---

* A.M.D. Reports, 1880.

Leake's Dandy.

CHAP. VI.

This conveyance was invented by Surgeon-Lieutenant-Colonel Leake of the Army Medical Staff, and was designed by that officer

Leake's dandy.

Fig. XXIII.—The Leake Dandy.

Fig. XXIV.—Leake's Dandy (No. 2).

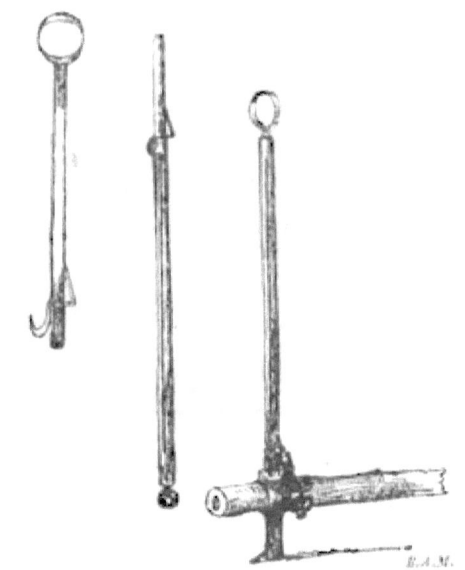

Fig. XXV.—Leake's Dandy (No. 3).

with a view of lessening the weight for the bearers to carry, and to increase the comfort of the patients carried, especially in hilly districts. It packs into a small space, and is very light and portable. It also possesses the advantages of a field stretcher.

The general appearance is shown in Fig. XXIII, and partakes of that of the Bengal dooley. It consists of the following, which will be described separately:—

 (1) Pole and cover.
 (2) Frame and canvas.
 (3) Mode of suspension.
 (4) The stretcher.

The pole is of bamboo, and is the same as that ordinarily in use in India. The top is made of split bamboo, after the

Fig. XXVI.—Leake's Dandy (No 1).

manner of a window blind, and rolls up for packing. The cover is laid over the top, and hanging down on each side closes in the whole conveyance. The side and end curtains are divided, and can be fastened back to admit light and air. There is a small window in the curtain, and the patient can be communicated with without raising the canvas.

The frame consists of two stout male bamboos passed through two hems in the canvas, and extended by two jointed iron traverses. In this way a light field stretcher is formed. This is suspended

Fig. XXVII.—Leake's Dandy as a Stretcher.

to the pole by four solid lengths of iron 2 feet 6 inches long, and ¼ inch diameter, with a loop at their extremities. These are fastened down by a strap to the poles when not required for use. There are four iron feet 6 inches long.

The mode of suspension is very simple, and is achieved by passing the pole through the loops on the iron lengths. These are tubular, and inside a spring hook works, and which allows of shortening and lengthening as may be required when going up or down hill. Fig. XXV and Fig. XXVI.

Chap. VI.

Leake's dandy.

The weight of the dooley stretcher is 52 lbs., but this varies with the weight of the bamboo pole.

This dandy has not received the notice it deserves. It is a strong, cheap, and durable article. The field stretcher, which is formed by its framework, only weighs 20 lbs., and is much more adapted for natives than the Regulation Mark V. Army Stretcher. The mode of shortening and lengthening is ingenious, but the ordinary mode of turning the stretcher and carrying the patient head first up hill, and feet first down hill, would appear to meet all requirements. Lastly must be noticed the small space into which this dandy packs. The stretcher folds as an ordinary conveyance of that class, and the canvas is lapped round. The top and canvas are rolled on the stretcher and pole and fastened off by leather straps, thus forming a light package. Fig. XXIV.

The Collis Dandy.

The Collis dandy is the invention of Surgeon-Major General W. Collis of the Army Medical Staff, and was designed by that officer to overcome the many objections already considered in the Regulation dhooly, and the Lushai dandy.

The Collis dandy.

The frame is made of good and sound male bamboo, and both side and end pieces are doubly ferruled; the legs and pole support **rings** are made of iron. The pole supports consist of two **pairs** of male bamboos 3 inches in circumference, and 3 **feet** 4 inches long. They are ferruled at the

Fig. XXVIII.—The Collis Dandy.

upper ends, **and** each pair is joined by a galvanised iron wire "seizing."* They are ferruled and iron-pointed at their

---

* Extracted from the official specification. The term "seizing" refers to the thin galvanised wire wrapped round the splices of thick wire which support the dandy.—Ed.

lower ends, and pass through rings on the legs of the frame. The bottom is made of sootli, well woven, and can be tightened as required by means of a log line, and a light piece of strong male bamboo, to which the lacing is attached. The sides are strong, supported by a malleable iron band, which passes underneath the bottom, and the canvas sling passes through it between the lacing and iron band, and is suspended to the pole by a hook attached to the centre of the sling.

There is a strong canvas suspender for raising a man up who is wounded in the chest; it will also take the place of a

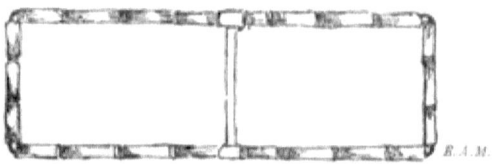

Fig. XXIX.—The Collis Dandy.

pillow, and it is provided with three pieces of log line for adjustment.

The bed is attached to the pole by means of a circular wire rope, with ends spliced into a heart-shaped cringle. It is to the cringle that the sling and centre log line of the suspender are attached.

The dandy is suspended from the pole by a manacle or compass-jointed hook band, which can be fitted to any sized

Fig. XXX.—The Collis Dandy.

pole, and can be removed without difficulty. The bamboo top of the dandy is bound together with galvanised wire and attached to the pole by means of strong log line and both ends and centre.

The cover is made of doosootie, and can be laced up by 26 eyelet holes under log line.

The cover and pole when removed from the dandy and placed on the pole supports form a small tent for the four bearers. For this purpose there are two guy ropes of thin galvanised wire, ten small square iron pegs with rounded necks, and a small hammer wrench to be carried in a canvas bag, which fits in a pocket of the dandy sling.

From the pole a small net is suspended to hold sundries, and two canvas slings to fasten the patient's rifle to the pole if necessary.

The whole of the ironwork is of the best Swedish iron.

Measurements.

Length of pole	13 feet 10	inches.
Height from ground ..	2 ,, 4½	,,
Length of top frame ..	6 ,, 1	,,
,, bottom frame ..	6 ,, 6	,,
Length of pole supports ..	3 ,, 2	,,
,, ,, suspender..	2 ,, 8	,,
Width	1 ,, 11	,,
Height of ends of sling ..	1 ,, 8	,,
Width	2 ,, 3	,,
Height of legs	4½	,,

The weight is 71¼ lbs.

Directions to put the Dandy together.

1. **Let two** bearers hold the pole at each end.
2. Hook on the dandy to the manacles on the pole.
3. Place the pole supports over the pole, cross them, and draw them towards the end of the pole; pass the lower iron-shod ends through the rings on the legs of the frame; push the upper part of the pole supports close to the manacles on the pole and fasten firmly with a few turns **of the** rope attached in the middle of the curtain frame support.
4. If the canvas sling pillow is required, attach it to the **end** bamboos in the canvas frame sling and by the middle rope to the pole of the dandy at the angle required.
5. Place the curtains over the dandy, resting on the bamboo top, the ends of the curtain frame supports must be firmly tied **at** each corner to the legs of the dandy.
6. **To** form a shelter tent, place the pole supports at each end of the pole, take a turn of the guy ropes round the pole near the manacles and attach the guy ropes to the pegs on the ground. The curtains can then be pegged out at any angle required.

NOTE.—All the parts of this dandy are interchangeable.

A committee of officers reported on this dandy at Calcutta on February 10, 1888, and approved the invention of Surgeon-Colonel Collis, and recommended the manufacture of a proportion for the Indian Army.

The advantages of this dandy are obvious, and by no means the least is the fact that shelter is afforded for the bearers. To any one acquainted or who has had experience of the native bearers in Indian warfare, will at once recognise the great importance of sheltering the bearers. As a rule they are treated very indifferently in this matter, and at the same time **it is** well known that their work requires quite as good men as **ever carried a** rifle in an Indian regiment. This dandy, equally

CHAP. VI.

The Collis dandy.

with others, would be on service insufficiently manned by four men; at least six are required.

The Collis Dandy is the Indian Regulation pattern, and all other forms are now obsolete.

MACPHERSON'S STRETCHER-DANDY.

Macpherson's stretcher-dandy.

This dandy was invented by Surgeon-Captain W. G. Macpherson, A.M.S., and designed to obviate the disadvantages of the Lushai Dandy.

The component parts of this conveyance are—(1) A canvas sack, open at both ends; (2) A canvas hammock, passing

Fig. XXXI.—General view of Macpherson's Dandy.

underneath and attached to the canvas sack; (3) A pair of

round poles, the ends being shaped as stretcher handles; (4) pair of jointed iron traverses and roller legs formed in the same piece; (5) A pair of iron rings for suspending the stretcher as a Lushai dandy; (6) A sufficient quantity of thin, strong hempen rope.

Description.

(1). *The Canvas Sack.*—*Material*—any suitable canvas material. *Dimensions*—Transverse diameter = width of regulation pattern stretcher canvas, *i.e.*, 23 inches. Long diameter = length of regulation pattern stretcher canvas, *i.e.*, 72 inches.

Mode of Making the Sack.—The sack is made of two pieces, which may be described as a *top piece* and a *bottom piece* (see Fig. XXXII.) The ends of the bottom piece are to be sewn on to the top piece with stout hempen cord, so as to form a sack of

Fig. XXXII.—Macpherson's **Dandy, showing the construction of the sack.**

the required dimensions. **The** ends of the top piece project for inches beyond the **sack,** so as to form side flaps. The arrangement of these **flaps is** shown in the figures. They form the side of the cot, **when the** stretcher is used as a Lushai dandy.

The transverse strain **on** the sack should be **in** the line of the long axis of the pieces of canvas out of which it is made. Consequently, as the width of canvas is not manufactured equal to the required length of the sack, a sufficient number of pieces (usually three) must be firmly sewn together to form the top and bottom pieces of required length.

Rope Holes.—There is a rope hole (eyelet or bound with leather) at each corner of the side flaps and two pairs of similar holes on each flap at equal intervals (see figure). There is a leather-bound hole on the top piece at each corner of the **sack** for the reception of the pins attached to the traverses.

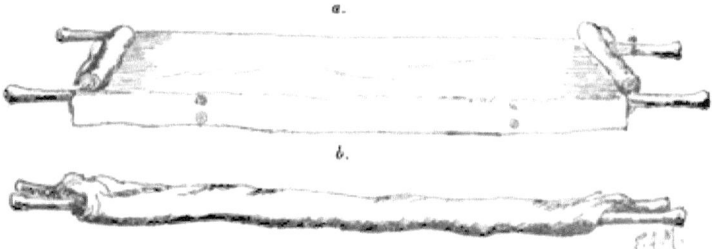

Fig. XXXIII.—Macpherson's Dandy as a stretcher, open and **folded.**

(2). *The Canvas Hammock.*—*Material*—Any **suitable** canvas material. *Dimensions*—Width = width of sack. Length = length of sack + projections at each end of 6 inches each.

Arrangement and Mode of Making.—The canvas hammock consists simply of a strip of canvas sewn on to the bottom piece of the sack, with its free ends projecting beyond the sack and shaped so as to pass between the legs, round underneath the traverses and up between the handles. These end pieces are firmly hemmed, bound with leather where there is friction or extra strain, and they have a piece of split bamboo let into each end hem. The longitudinal strain on the canvas is in the long axis of the piece out of which it is made.

Rope Holes.—Five or more (eyelet or leather bound) along each end, just below the hem, and therefore below the pieces of bamboo let in to the hem. These holes are for lacing the suspending rings to the canvas. There is a hole also on each border of the ends at the level of the rope holes in the corners of the side flaps of the sack. These holes are for lacing the flaps to the ends of the canvas hammock.

(3). *The Poles.*—*Material*—Any light strong wood. The wood used for the poles of the original stretcher is a kind known in Himalayan districts as "*Hulda*" wood. *Dimensions*—The same length as the poles of the regulation pattern stretcher, *i.e.*, 7 feet 9 inches. *Make*—The poles are round. The projecting ends, when they are placed *in situ* inside the canvas sack, form the handles and are shaped as such, *i.e.*, as the handles of the regulation pattern stretcher. The remainder of the pole is round, the diameter increasing slightly towards the centre, but equal to   inches, where the traverse is fixed, *i.e.*, just beyond the handles. *Pin holes*—One at each end, corresponding to the position of the corners of the sack, and to the position of the traverses, *i.e.*, about 11 inches from the ends of the handles.

(4). *The Traverses.*—*Material*—Iron or steel. *Dimensions*—Length = to width of stretcher between the pin-holes of the poles. For other dimensions *see* below.

Description.—There is a pair of traverses for each stretcher. Each traverse is in one piece and consists of two cylinders, through which the poles pass, two brackets, containing rollers of boxwood or other material, forming legs to the stretcher, and a cross-bar, jointed at the centre with a hinge joint (like that of the carpenter's rule), and attached to the cylinders and legs by pivot joints, pivoting round the pin connecting the cylinders and legs.

The cylinders have an inside diameter equal to the diameter of the pole, *i.e.*, sufficiently large to enable the traverse to be slipped on to the poles, and rest *in situ* at the site of the pin-holes in the poles. There is a hole in the top of each cylinder, corresponding to the pin-holes in the poles and the holes at the corners of the sack. An iron or steel pin, to fix the sack and cylinder to the pole, is attached by a light chain to each cylinder.

The axis of the cylinder is 2 inches. The cylinder and

bracket for the roller, and the pin connecting them, round which the cross-bar pivots, are forged out of the same piece of metal. The pin is cylindrical, and the bracket an ordinary stirrup bracket. The height from top of cylinder to lowest point of roller = height of regulation stretcher, i.e., 5¾ inches. The roller is very much smaller than the regulation stretcher, but is equally efficacious for the purpose of rolling the stretcher on the floor of an ambulance wagon, &c., or for acting as a leg for the stretcher.

The cross-bar is in two equal halves, joined at the centre by a hinge joint. The section of the bar is square, but the sharp edges are rounded off to prevent cutting of the canvas, which is in addition lined with leather where it rubs against the traverse. The ends of the cross-bar surround the pins connecting cylinders and roller brackets, and so form pivot joints.

When the traverse is *in situ* on the poles it breaks outwards in folding up the stretcher, and the pivot joints enable the axes of the two cylinders (and therefore the two poles) to remain parallel in all positions, and it thus forms a conveniently shaped package, the diameter of which is at the thickest point about 6 inches. (*See* Fig. XXXIII *b*.)

The length for the purpose of packing and transport could be reduced by having the poles jointed with hinge joints at centre or at the handles; but loss in strength, facility of repair, and simplicity and cheapness of manufacture is not equal to the gain.

The ironwork should be japanned or otherwise protected against rust. The woodwork should be varnished or painted.

The *advantages* claimed for the stretcher are :—

(1) Its *portability*. It can be easily transported by rail, cart, steamer, pack animal, &c., to any base or depôt where it is to be used as Lushai dandy, stretcher, or camp-bed.
(2) Its *lightness* when used as stretcher or dandy.
(3) Its *simplicity* in both material and arrangement.
(4) *Ease with which it can be repaired.* This depends—
 (*a*) On the simplicity of material.
 (*b*) On the immediate removal of any part broken without interfering with the other component parts.
 (*c*) On the ease with which temporary means can be adopted for immediate repair, while wounded or sick are being carried on it.

e.g., if the canvas sack splits the canvas hammock continues to suspend the apparatus as a dandy. If the canvas hammock gives, the apparatus can continue to be used as a stretcher till repair is effected. If the rings break, rope rings can be used. If a pole breaks an improvised pole (bamboo, &c.) can take its place temporarily. If a traverse breaks, the canvas hammock continues to suspend the patient as in a hammock, and the poles can be kept separate by lashing a stick between them. The traverse can be repaired at the nearest forge, or spare traverses might be kept at depôts, field hospitals, &c., to replace any that might break. One pair of spare traverses for each stretcher should last a campaign, because the broken one could always be repaired at a field forge, so that the balance would be maintained.

(5) *Strength.* The canvas is treble, and is therefore stronger in every way than the regulation stretcher, which has only a single piece of canvas.

(6) *Economy and Ease of Manufacture.*

(7) *Adaptability for Disinfection, &c.* The canvas can be removed from the poles in a few seconds, rolled into a small space, and placed in any form of disinfecting apparatus, or spread out and exposed to sun, fumes, &c., as required. The canvas can be replaced as rapidly as it is removed. Each component part can be separated and replaced by anyone.

(8) In use as a Lushai dandy the *handles* are no disadvantage, but are, on the contrary, very useful for steadying the stretcher in hilly country.

(9) The *dimensions* being the same as the regulation stretcher, the stretcher can be used in all conveyances fitted for the reception of the regulation stretcher.

(10) It has **uni**versal application both in peace and military operations as a camp-bed or stretcher; and in countries where proper bearers are obtainable, it can be used under all circumstances as a Lushai dandy, which **is** recognised **as** the lightest and best form **of** dandy.

(11) In military operations on the Indian scale of equipment it forms an apparatus which can be used temporarily as a stretcher in action and afterwards as a Lushai dandy for conveyance of wounded, &c., to field hospitals, or stage by stage to the base. It can, therefore, entirely replace the stretcher at present required at the front. It is no heavier and takes up no more room in transport than the regulation stretcher; and at the same time it can be employed for evacuating hospitals in movements of retreat, under circumstances when the ordinary stretcher would only be encumbering the ambulance wagons or other forms of transport.

This stretcher-dandy is *par excellence* the best form of Indian carriage that has been brought to our notice. While it preserves the type of carriage so suitable to the climate, and so well understood by the bearers, it also has precisely that amount of value as a stretcher that could be ever applied to natives.

The exact weight of the pattern we have examined, including the pole, is 46 lbs. With this dandy four bearers (Kahars) would be sufficient under all circumstances.

Trag-sitze.—Some simple conveyances, known under the name of "bearing-seats" (trag-sitz), are commonly used in Bavaria and other parts of Germany. They are occasionally supplied as supplementary to other conveyances of a less portable kind, Neudörfer's and Perigoff's two-wheeled litters, for example. These are really stretchers without side poles, designed for the removal of wounded men in a sitting position by two bearers. Though very different in appearance, they closely approximate in nature to the "mandil de socorro" to be described later, in which the body of one bearer acts as a traverse to one end of the apron, while the wooden traverse in the hands of the second bearer stretches the other.

The bearing seat consists of a piece of stout canvas doubled

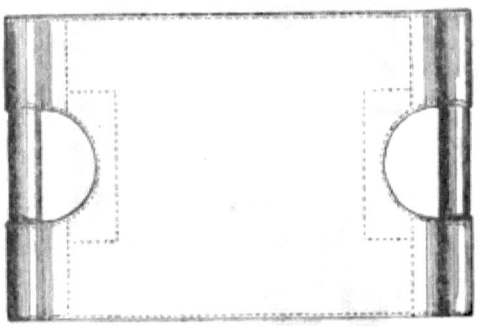

Fig. XXXIV.—The "Trag-sitz," or Bearing Seat.

over at the two ends, the whole being 22 inches long by 14 in breadth. It is stretched out crosswise at each end by a round piece of wood secured within its folds. Each of these pieces of wood is left exposed at the middle, so that it may be grasped by the hand of a bearer. Thus a seat is formed on which a patient may be placed and conveyed by two bearers, each using one hand to carry the seat, while the other is left free to support the patient's back, or otherwise to assist him during the transport.

The weight of the bearing seat in the Military Surgery Museum at Netley is 19 ounces.

Closely allied to conveyances of the hammock order are aprons. They have not any degree of popularity at the present time, but are merely noticed in order to fulfil the object of this work—to obviate the repetition of unpractical invention.

Landa's Apron, or the "Mandil de socorro," or apron of succour, was the invention of Dr. Landa, a distinguished army surgeon of the Spanish service. It is made of stout canvas, and is carried by and upon a bearer much in the same way as a pioneer's leather apron. The main part is oblong in shape, about two feet broad and three and a half long. It terminates at the upper end in two triangular bands about a yard in length, which cross over the shoulders, and are buckled together upon the back of the bearer. The lower, which reaches down to the middle of the bearer's legs, is fitted with a stitched fold or loop, intended to receive within it a strong rounded piece of wood or staff, one yard in length. When placed in the fold its two ends project so as to form two handles. If a second bearer, turning his back upon the first bearer, now lays hold of these handles the apron is raised in an inclined direction. It then constitutes a litter upon which a wounded

Fig. XXXV.—Manner of wearing the "Mandil de socorro." The staff is inserted in its hem.

man can be carried, with his head and shoulders resting upon the chest of the first bearer, and his two legs passed between the arms and body of the second bearer.

Dr. Landa's apron.

The advantages claimed by Dr. Landa for this kind of conveyance are the following:—It is of the simplest construction, so that it is not liable to derangement. It is very light, not weighing more than 500 grammes without the staff. It does not require to be specially carried to the place where it is required for use, as framed stretchers do. It does not distress the bearer who carries it, or prevent him having his arms and accoutrements. It is complete in itself, and very cheap and economical. The transport is easy for a wounded man; involves him in little fatigue, obviates all risk of his falling off, and it supplies, what to him is a matter of the first necessity, a ready means of withdrawing from the scene of conflict to the ambulance. No kind of wound is likely to be aggravated by the sole fact of the transport, excepting certain fractures of bones of the lower extremity.

There can be no doubt that some of the advantages claimed by Dr. Landa for this system of carrying off wounded men really belong to it. Its simplicity, lightness, cheapness of cost, are qualities which cannot be disputed. But the alleged ease to the wounded man carried, and the ease to those who have to carry him, are attributes essentially important to those concerned, and the possession of these by no means appears to be so well established. On the contrary, judging from personal observation of the experiments made with these aprons at the trials which were instituted during the International Exhibition of 1867 at Paris, it was in these particulars that they were so defective as to cause them to be held, by most of those who assisted at the trials, to be unsuited to the purposes for which they were designed. The person carried was "huddled up" in a very constrained and oppressive posture, while the bearers had great difficulty in making progress with their charge. The "drag" of the apron upon the shoulders of the first bearer was very severe. The conclusion arrived at by those who observed them was that these aprons were unsuitable for the general purposes of transport of sick and wounded. They hardly appeared to be as effective as some of the modes of carrying off wounded by two men unaided by any artificial appliance.

New Zealand litter.—The native litter of New Zealand, or "Amoo," is a netted hammock stretched out to a certain extent by side poles and short cross pieces near their ends, but still pliable and bellying downwards like the other conveyances of this section. It is intermediate in its nature between the ordinary hammock and the stretcher. It is quite peculiar in the manner in which it is carried, no other conveyance being carried precisely in the same fashion.

The network of this litter is made of cord or strips of the common flax, which is very abundant in the country, and hangs loosely downwards. It is supported at the sides by two slight poles, about eleven feet long, placed very nearly parallel with each other. The poles are kept about a foot and a half apart from each other midway of their length, but from that point they gradually approach each other, until they are only about four or five inches apart at their extremities. The poles are maintained in this relative position by two transverse pieces of wood, which are fastened, the one at the head, the other at the foot of the place in which the patient is laid, and again, by the extreme ends of the poles being tied together to the degree of closeness above mentioned. This last is a feature quite peculiar to these conveyances. The length of the litter between the two transverse pieces of wood is generally little more than five feet; this distance sufficing in consequence of the patient sinking down and becoming, as it were, shorter from his bent

CHAP. VI.

Peculiar advantages of the New Zealand litter.

condition while lying in the hammock. The distance between each transverse piece of wood and the connection at the corresponding extremity of the two poles is about two and a half feet. Two spaces are thus formed, one at the head, the other at the foot of the litter, in addition to the middle compartment for the reception of the sick or wounded man, and through these two end-spaces, when the litter is in use, the bearers thrust their heads. The united side-poles then descend and rest, one upon the right, the other on the left, shoulders of the bearers. It is obvious that by this arrangement an advantage is at once gained, as regards distribution of weight, over any litter which is suspended from a single pole, the weight of which must press on one side of the body of the bearer only. The peculiar mode of carrying the New Zealand amoo causes the weight of the whole conveyance to be exerted as nearly as

Fig. XXXVI.—The New Zealand Litter or Amoo.

possible in accordance with the principle on which, as already explained, the human frame can, for the longest time and with least inconvenience, sustain and carry heavy weights. Moreover, by the arrangement of securing the poles together at their ends the necessity of constantly holding them in position does not exist, the fatigue from continued elevation of the arm is avoided, and the hands are left free for occasionally raising the litter and temporarily taking the pressure off the shoulder, or for any other purpose. Another advantage of the amoo is that it can be made in a very short time in the bush, or near any place where fighting is likely to take place. The poles are made from branches of trees of convenient size; the native flax, which is very strong, and grows to a height of several feet, is torn into strips; and these form all the materials necessary for its construction. Extempore litters were constantly made in this way of the green flax by the natives during the recent campaigns in New Zealand.

The natives have generally two bearers, and one or more reliefs according to distance and the kind of country to be passed over, for each litter; but they can be made to be carried by four bearers by merely increasing the length of the poles. When only two bearers at a time are employed, the bearers in waiting can relieve them without halting. The fresh bearers, keeping pace with the movement of the bearers about to be relieved, insert their heads between the poles either before **or** behind the other bearers, who then slip away. Cords are sometimes passed between the poles above the patient to prevent the chance of the patient being thrown out by any sudden jerk during the transport.

Improvised Methods.

These are many, and include all the varieties of extemporised stretcher carriages. They do not fulfil all the conditions of a stretcher, and they are in some respects in advance of the hammock. In towns and crowded thoroughfares there are plenty of materials at hand, and such articles as shutters, doors, rugs, broom-handles, may be noticed, while in the country, light gates, tail boards of carts, shafts, and many others can be turned to good account when the necessity arises.

There are, besides, certain articles readily obtainable, but which cannot be used without a special knowledge of the manner in which they are prepared. The most important are:—

Blanket stretcher.—A rug or blanket placed on two poles of sufficient length and thickness, and the sides rolled in and tied, with two pieces of wood attached to them, to keep the sides from approximating one another, forms a reliable conveyance. It is, of course, open to the objections enumerated in this section, being merely a modification of the looped blanket.

Rugs and poles.—This is a stretcher conveyance formed more or less in the preceding manner. Rifles with the bayonets fixed may be used, but they are not available for this purpose, and any idea of utilising them in this manner is more fanciful than **real.** In **the** Appendix will be found the **rug** and rifle drill, but **poles, hedge** stakes, are recommended, **and not rifles,** which **may be** damaged by being used in this manner.

Greatcoat stretcher.—A greatcoat with the **sleeves** turned inside out, and buttoned up, and through which two rifles, pikes, or poles are passed, forms a very excellent improvised stretcher.

General Jackson recommended and adopted in his campaign against the Indians that a bull's hide fastened to two rifles should be used, and carried by two or four men as the case **required.**

CHAP. VI.

Hill's stretcher.

Surgeon-Major Philip E. Hill's hayband stretcher consists of a band of hay or straw, two stout poles of larch, ash, or any such material handy.

The poles are kept in the required position by nailing or tying two pieces of wood to their sides, and the hay band is wound tightly round them. A rolled coat forms the head to the stretcher and makes a convenient pillow.

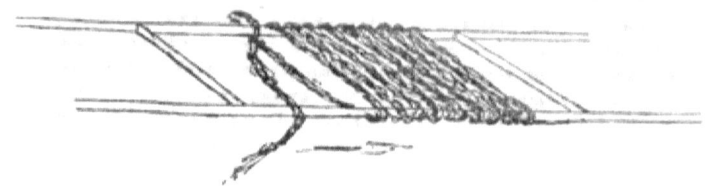

Fig. XXXVII.—Improvised Hay or Straw Stretcher.

Measurements { Length .. .. 8 feet 2 inches.
               Width .. .. 2 „ 4 „

This stretcher is admirably adapted and readily improvised in agricultural districts for accidents which are especially liable to happen now machinery is so generally in use.

Galton's stretcher.

Galton's temporary stretcher.—"Cut two stout poles, each 8 feet long, to make its two sides and three other cross-bars, 2½ feet each, to be lashed over them. Then supporting this ladder-shaped framework over the sick man as he lies in his blanket, knot the blanket well to it, and so carry him off, palanquin fashion. One cross-bar will be just behind his head, another in front of his feet; the middle one will cross his stomach and keep him from falling out, and there will remain two handles for the carriers to lay hold of. A kind of wagon top can easily be made to it, with bent boughs, and one spare blanket." It is not at all unlike in many respects the New Zealand "Amoo," which, however, is carried on the shoulders, and the outside traverses are at the ends of the long poles.

Varieties of improvised stretcher carriage can be multiplied to any extent. The best are those which are constructed for a wounded or sick man, on the spot, at the time, and efficiently. They demand energy and ingenuity, as well as resource, and determination to overcome all the obstacles, and they are many, which may arise.

Dooly-Wallahs, Kahars or Bearers.

This division of ambulance transport consists for the main part of a native race of men who carry conveyances (doolies, dandies, &c.) which present principally, though not exactly, the features of carriage of the hammock class. They are almost exclusively used in the East, and at one time were strongly recommended to be introduced into England. Perhaps it is fortunate that this **did not** occur, for independently of the difficulties which would be met with in the employment of natives, by reason of disease which would be certain to prevail among them in a northern climate, their religious prejudices and peculiar habits, the large multitude of them which would be required, almost completely preclude such an idea being entertained.

This class of conveyance is the oldest in the world, and is the most comfortable and efficient carriage for sick and wounded. In India, which is par excellence the home of this form of transport, it is being driven gradually off the face of the land by the rapid advance of railway enterprise, and before long it will only be found in those more remote parts of the country which still lack the modern facilities of communication.

The dooly-wallahs, palki-bearers, bearers, or kahars, are the various names by which the men who carry these conveyances are known. They belong principally to the Hindoo race, but a large number of Mussulmans and others are to be found in their ranks. They are a low class of individual; ignorant to a degree, and considering their position in the social scale have very strong caste prejudices, but they are willing and faithful, and when treated firmly, kindly, and with tact, repay rapidly any trouble that is taken with them. The best type of these men is to be found near the Himalayan ranges towards Nepaul and Thibet, in the North-West Provinces, Oude, and the Punjab. The Hyderabad State in Madras also furnishes very good men. The kahars, drawn from Upper India, are fine, stalwart men, often with a good record of service, and a wholesome and loyal nature, but those from Madras are often of a low moral type, and addicted to drink and its associated vicious habits. Kahars formerly served on an enlistment service for 30 years, but that has been changed in recent years, and the term of service is for three years, and that period is extended or not according to the state of the man's health and the actual requirements of the State. Naturally it is a very unpopular order among the men themselves, for they feel that they are liable, at any time after three years, to be thrown out of work, and the Government, as a result, obtain coolies instead of kahars for this work. This, as will be shown later, is a retrograde step, when it is desirable to improve the ambulance transport of the Indian Army.

There is no difficulty in explaining the sources of the extremely high estimation in which the dooley* has always been held as a means of transporting sick by those who have been practically acquainted with it. The patient while carried along has all the comfort and advantages, before described, belonging to the horizontal position, which are so essentially necessary for ease and repose in an Indian climate; he can freely turn and move his limbs; in the daytime he is

CHAP. VI.

Kahars.

Explanation of the great estimation in which dooly and dandy carriage are held as sick conveyances.

---

* The dooley is quite obsolete, having been replaced by the dandy, which possesses all these advantages. Dooley is said to be derived from the Persian "dhulin," a bride, from the fact that the lady is usually carried to her husband in this form of carriage.

CHAP. VI.
Doolies.

protected from the sun, **at the** same time that he can admit any breeze that may be stirring; at night it is not only a bed, but a place of shelter also to protect him from dews and cold, in case no tent or bungalow is at hand. It admits of **the** carriage of beverages, food, medicine, or any small article that may be necessary for the patient's use **during** the transport. The well-trained, easy, and yielding tread of **the** native bearers obviates any jolting or unpleasant jerk, and simply conveys to the bamboo pole from which the conveyance is suspended the slightest undulatory movement in harmony with their step; so slight, indeed, that it is only just perceptible to the recumbent patient within when his attention is directed to the subject. In

Fig. XXXVIII.—The Indian Dooley.*

watching the progress, however fast, of a train of dandies, nothing can be more remarkable than to observe the extremely little motion which is manifest in each single conveyance itself. There is no swinging from side to side, or rocking; the bearers have no "high action;" their feet just clear the surface of the ground, and the idea is conveyed that they are rather *pushing along* the dandies than carrying them. An almost perfect level, so extremely important as regards the ease of a patient, is preserved by the peculiar broken step with which the four bearers march. The hardly noticeable elastic movements of the bearers, together with the monotonous chant which they usually maintain on the line of march, often prove to be a source of beneficial influence; for they not unfrequently serve to soothe into sleep the invalids to whom the blessing would be denied in a hospital on an ordinary bed. Contrast these advantages with the usual sensations experienced in the other conveyances for the sick in use in India—the various kinds of carts, the conveyances borne by elephants and camels—and all surprise at the very great partiality expressed **for** this form of carriage will cease.†

---

* The dooly is usually carried by four bearers when loaded.
† The dooley-bearers of India have been noted for being a most willing and laborious class of men, exhibiting bodily endurance indeed to a surprising extent, and almost always well behaved and faithful when treated with due consideration and a little kindness. During the Indian Mutiny the dooley-bearers attached to the European regiments were generally faithful, and frequently exposed their lives on the field of action, although at this time, on account of the great and widely

Although the deficiency in the available numbers of the bearer class, and the improvements in means of communication along the principal routes of India, will prevent this transport from ever again being used in the same proportion as formerly, it is not likely that it will ever be wholly dispensed with in field service in India. When troops are moving otherwise than by railway, so long as they are marching along grand trunk lines, and the roads are good, wheeled ambulance conveyances may be found to meet all the necessities of service. But when the troops are engaged in hill or jungle warfare, or are dispersed over the country in movable columns, as they were throughout the period of the Indian mutiny, marching across districts in the plains without any regular means of internal communication, without roads or bridges, and meeting with all kinds of impediments to oppose their progress, wheeled transport would be little better than an incumbrance, and the dooley would remain the only kind of carriage to be depended upon for the safe conveyance of those who fall sick or are wounded on the way. The habits of the people of India; the ease with which the men who form the class of bearers manage to provide for themselves under circumstances where great difficulty would be experienced in procuring the necessary forage for transport of animals; the facility with which the difficulties interposed by the absence of regular means of communication are overcome by natives trained from infancy to meet them and to understand signs which are meaningless to strangers; these are all greatly in favour of the use of the native hand-litter, as compared with any other mode of conveyance, under the circumstances just described.

While Sir P. Grant observes* of the ambulance transport for the army : "But there are still divisions where the practicability of bringing it into use is more than questionable. Those who have shared in the campaigns in the Kimedy and Goomsoor jungles are aware of the utter hopelessness of attempting the use of any description of sick carriage but the muncheel. The same may probably be said of North Canara, and unfortunately, those engaged in this jungle warfare generally need carriage more than the sharers of any other campaign, for though there are fewer who suffer from the hands of the enemy, there are few indeed who do not succumb to the deadly influence of the climate," &c.

---

extended demand for these men, labourers were sometimes hired and employed who had not been regularly trained for the occupation. The late Duke of Wellington showed his appreciation of their services in the Mahratta war, in 1803, by issuing a general order in which he desired that "in consequence of the great labour of dooley-bearers in the public service, and the important services they have rendered in removing the wounded men to the hospitals after the late battles of Assaye and in the plains of Argaum, a donation of two star pagodas will be given to each maistry, and one star pagoda to each dooley-bearer in the public service in the Madras establishment."

* Remarks by the Commander-in-Chief, Sir Patrick Grant, transmitted by letter from the Quartermaster-General of the Army Head Quarters, Ootacamund, 30th July, 1858, No. 170, to the Secretary to Government, Military Department.

CHAP VI.

Disuse of doolies in India impracticable.

General **Sir William Mansfield** has also strongly argued against changing the system of employing dooley conveyances for ambulance purposes in India. He has objected even to reducing the numbers of the doolies and dooley-bearers ordinarily entertained by Government. And not only has Sir William Mansfield advised that these means of sick conveyance should be maintained to their full complement, but that dooley-bearers should be specially nurtured and supported by the Government to prevent them from decreasing in numbers and perhaps becoming, as a race, almost extinct.

Sir H. Rose, when Commander-in-Chief in India, entirely coincided in the views expressed by Sir W. Mansfield. Sir H. Rose **wrote**: "There can be no doubt that for the requirements of India no system can be introduced more effectual than the doolies or dandies as heretofore employed, by which means wounded men could be transported from the hill side, broken ground, or other locality, where they were struck down, to their respective hospitals, and that too, over ground of any nature."

Supplies of doolies advised by Bengal Sanitary Commission.

The recommendations of the Bengal Sanitary Commission in the report of January, 1865, already cited, so far as the question of the number of doolies to be issued for the service of British troops in India, irrespective of any wheeled ambulance conveyances which might be added to them, is concerned, were the following:—That the two doolies allowed by regulations to regiments in cantonments should continue to be issued as before. That each battery of artillery should be allowed one dooley to itself, instead of one dooley to two batteries, where two batteries are brigaded together. That on an ordinary line of march the proportion which doolies should bear to other kinds of sick transport, such as ambulance wagons, is one-half. Taking, therefore, the average number of sick for whom transport is necessary at 5 per cent. of strength, 25 doolies would be the complement for a regiment 1,000 strong. Lastly, the Commission recommended that the number of doolies allowed by regulations for troops on field service should not be reduced, as no wheeled ambulance conveyances could be safely and advantageously substituted for them.

Dandy carriage would never be advantageously replaced by stretchers in tropical and sub-tropical countries.

It has been urged by prominent authorities to abolish dooley and dandy carriage altogether, and establish the Army **Regulation** stretcher, to be carried by four bearers. Is this **feasible?** Admitting the value which would accrue by diminishing the numbers of followers with an army, the risk of the transport not being sufficient, for reasons already indicated, must be discounted. In tropical and sub-tropical countries sickness is the most common cause of non-effectiveness, and the dandy or dooley is the only form of ambulance carriage that could carry a patient suffering from fever, or dysentery, with any degree of comfort. Indeed, for this object alone a proportion of this class of carriage must, should be, and is rightly retained. Indian ambulance transport cannot be assimilated to the English Army method—the conditions, circumstances, and surroundings being so widely diverse.

Conditions of Enrolment.

Every bearer who is entertained for three years has to be certified as medically **in a** sound state of health, and thus **is** entered in his service book. There is no standard of height or chest measurement, no practical limit to age, and there is very little doubt that only extremes of age, deformities, or very apparent disease, "cast" the bearer on his entertainment. It is no fault of the medical officers that the examination is so slight, for the nature of the examination is not laid down, and "fit" or "unfit" are merely general expressions. The result is a loss to the State, not only from the physical incapacity for the work the bearers have to do, but also from the large non-effectiveness from sickness which accrues to the ill-bred, under-sized starvelings who rush to obtain employment as coolies when the Government require their services.*

There are three classes of bearer transport. 1. Permanent. 2. Temporary. 3. Cooly Bearers.

The *Permanent Bearers* belong, for the **most** part, to the caste which has furnished this form of carriage from times immemorial, and they know no other occupation. Fine up-standing men are to be found among them, and they can readily be recognised by the huge development of the deltoid muscle. They serve on the three years' agreement, which they can renew from time. Formerly they were enlisted for 30 years, for which period they were compelled to serve before becoming entitled to a pension. The latter plan is unquestionably preferred by the men.

The *Temporary Bearers* are coolies engaged to carry sick for **the** time the expedition lasts.

The *Cooly Bearers* are drawn from the same class as the latter, but are only used for sick transport purposes on special occasions, at other times performing ordinary transport duties.

As far as ambulance transport is concerned the two latter proved a failure in Burma. Many of them had never carried a dandy in their lives, and were not in any way adapted either by nature or physique for this work. They had been drawn from the "lowest of the low," from the northern ports on the Coromandel coast, and were a most difficult class to manage. Desertion and drunkenness were their principal characteristics, and **they** were perfectly useless in the capacity for which they were required.

It will be useful here to consider the conditions which should be required on the medical examination for the bearers of the Ambulance Transport Service.

a. Age.—As at present; that is, over 18 and under 25 years. Natives, as a rule, have no idea of their age, therefore, this part of the examination must be qualified by other signs.

b. Height.—This should be over 5 feet 2 inches and under 5 feet 8 inches; 5 feet 4 inches is a good average.

---

* By a recent order it is directed that all dooley bearers who from age or any other circumstance are "unfit" for active service, shall be "weeded" gradually out of the ranks.—ED.

c. *Chest Measurement.*—At the very lowest not less than 31 inches.

d. *Weight.*—115 lbs. as a minimum.

Conditions equivalent to these should, *at the very least*, be possessed by every bearer for the work he is expected to do.

The work performed by bearers is considerable, and in order that it may be efficiently carried out, the men should be carefully selected. It should be considered a more important service than it usually is. The following extract from a letter to the principal medical officer of the Upper Burma Field Force from the ambulance officer, will show this work analysed in detail:—

"No. $\frac{9}{239}$. * * AMBULANCE OFFICE,

"MANDALAY, 7th *May*, 1887.

"SIR,

* * * • *

"3. With reference to the number of men that should be allowed to each dandy, on analysing the weights carried, and at the present rate (four men per dandy) it is found that each man carries $62\frac{1}{2}$ lbs. The total average weight being 250 lbs., and it is made up in the following manner:—

Average British infantry soldier	150 lbs.
Arms and accoutrements	11 ,,
Sixty rounds of ammunition	10 ,,
Havresack and contents	2 ,,
Water bottle	1 ,,
Clothes	8 ,,
Blanket and greatcoat	8 ,,
Lushai dandy (average)	60 ,,
	250 lbs.

I would add that the Lushai dandy only weighs 60 lbs. in the dry state, but when it is wet the increase in weight is nearly 35 per cent.

Gunners and heavy cavalry weigh rather more, and light cavalry and the other branches rather less than the infantry soldier of the line.

The average weight of a Sepoy is 1 maund and 25 seers, *i.e.*, 130 lbs; in other respects he weighs the same as the British soldier, his clothes being 1 lb. lighter and his rifle 1 lb. heavier. The total weight of a Sepoy when carried by bearers is equal to 230 lbs., or $57\frac{1}{2}$ lbs. per man.

A cooly on the plains in India carries 40 lbs. (by regulation), so that it is evident that the bearer carries 50 per cent. more than the cooly, but there is more than this to be considered. The cooly applies his power to the weight at the most favourable point to preserve equilibrium, and works **under his load** with the least possible expenditure of energy to himself. **A** bearer, **on** the other hand, especially if he happens to be taller than his fellows, works at a disadvantage, by having to stoop or bear the greater part of the weight. Natives adjust themselves fairly, but it is a common observation to see at least one out of every five dandies, with its bearers working **at a** disadvantage, viz., in addition to supporting the weight, they would, from want of harmony in their action, tend to neutralise each other's power. It has been estimated that the weight, under these conditions, averages 70–75 lbs. per man.

To carry the dandy on service six men are required, that is four to carry, and a relief at each end by the two spare.* "Puccka," dooley-bearers, will not fail with four men per dandy, and they will work one man at each end, with reliefs for many miles, but these men are not to be found in large numbers in the ambulance transport, and inefficient men take their place. Kahars have their price, and unless that is given, they seek employment in other places, to the detriment of the interests of the State.

The following sketch (Fig. XXXIX) represents a form of **dooley** suggested **by** Dr. Francis, and is merely shown to **illustrate** the peculiar form of carriage.

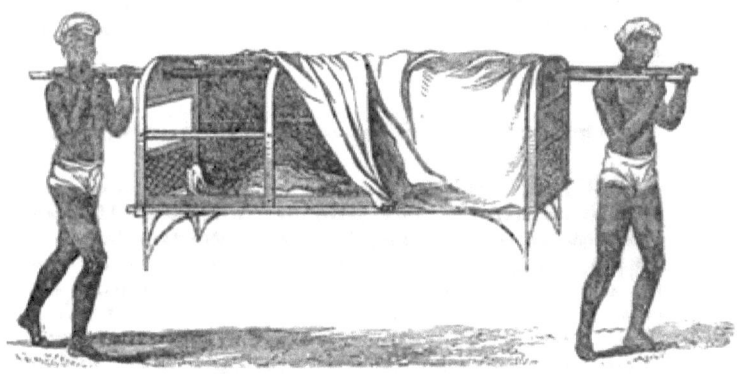

Fig. XXXIX.—Dr. Francis' Dooly.

With the single-pole dooly the bearer is enabled to relieve

---

* On one occasion I transferred 40 lying-down cases in dandies from No. 5 British Field Hospital, and No. 20 Native Field Hospital, from Mandalay Hill to the Irrawaddy, a distance of two miles. The number of bearers employed was 160, and out of them two fell down completely exhausted, and nine were seized with "fever," and were sent to hospital. The day was hot, but natives should not have broken down. I attributed their failure entirely to excessive work.—EDITOR.

each shoulder alternately, and the pressure is never of such a fixed character as it must be with the double-pole arrangement, notwithstanding that the poles can be supported from time to time by the hands. In the hills the constantly shifting inclination of the surface of the ground prevents an uniform direction of the pressure. This method of carriage must be regarded as unsatisfactory.

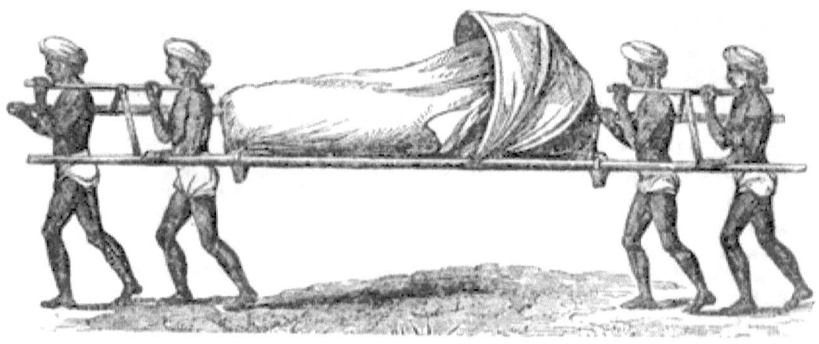

Fig. XL.

The Jhampan method, as advocated by the late Surgeon Major Porter, has never become popular, and is of doubtful value.

ON SOME OTHER FORMS OF EASTERN CONVEYANCES.

Palkis. — *The Palki.*—This conveyance is usually known among English persons by the name of *palanqueen*. Its general arrangement is the same, but its construction has a more solid and permanent character. The entrance is effected by a double wooden door in the side. Each panel of the door is made capable of sliding in a groove up to the end of the conveyance; thus affording a wider opening for getting in and out, at the same time that both panels are under the control of the person within the conveyance for opening or closing. Palkis sometimes have panes of glass inserted in the end panels, and, being chiefly intended for civil life, are often fitted with drawers and other conveniences inside, and are highly ornamented.

Muncheels. — *Muncheels.*—These differ from doolies in being unprovided with a fixed framework above the cot. Instead, the cot is suspended by cords, chains, or other means of a flexible kind from a pole, over which a curtain is thrown and extended to the sides of the cot, so as to screen the person within from the glare of the sun, or from damp. The flexible nature of the ends by *Their construction.* which the muncheel is carried renders the conveyance very portable.

portable. The chief inconveniences connected with them is the absence of the fixed support for the pole. The result of this is that when the muncheel is placed on the ground the ends sink, and care has to be taken that both they and the pole are placed outside the cot part of the muncheel to prevent them from sinking and pressing upon the patient. When thus at rest, the patient is necessarily deprived of the protection of the cover and sides, which are of such great advantage in the several forms of doolies, especially at night, by rendering them competent to act as substitutes even for the shelter of a tent or hospital of a more permanent kind. At all times the curtains of the muncheel fall comparatively closely upon the patient who is carried in it, owing to the triangular form assumed by the pole and ends over which they are placed. The inconvenience here described is one which attaches to some of the models of suggested improvements for doolies in the Museum of Military Surgery at Netley, in which ends of pliable leather straps and other such materials have been proposed for use for the purpose of giving to the conveyances greater facility of package. Muncheels are much employed by the natives in some parts of India, but seem to be ill suited for the military purposes of sick transport. They closely approach in their nature to conveyances of the hammock kind when carried from poles, the chief distinction being only the more substantial cot possessed by the muncheel.

Ton-jons.—These closely resemble the muncheel class of conveyances, the only difference being that the person is carried in a sitting instead of a recumbent posture. They are never systematically used for military purposes, and in no respect require any particular remark.

C.—STRETCHERS.

Stretchers derive their name from the fact of the sustaining canvas being *stretched* within a frame so that the whole constitutes a tolerably firm support when a patient is carried upon it. The strong and almost unyielding nature of the means of carriage which is thus afforded forms the chief distinction between it and any of the more or less loose and impossible conveyances described in the preceding section. Stretchers closely resemble in their nature the temporary wooden supports for wounded persons, such as hurdles, ladders, doors taken off their hinges, and the other improvised expedients of a like kind, which are employed in cases of emergency and in the absence of mechanical ambulance aid in civil life; the chief difference being that they are just sufficiently yielding not to require the soft materials upon them which are necessary in these harder kinds to moderate the effects of pressure. The stretching of the canvas is produced by cross-pieces of metal or wood riveted or hooked to the under surfaces of the poles forming the sides. These "cross-pieces" are called the "traverses" of a stretcher.

The French expression for a stretcher is "brancard," this term being derived from the two poles or shafts (les branches) between which the supporting canvas is held. The poles of a stretcher are sometimes also designated the arms (les bras), a word evidently of the same derivation as "branche." In this sense the poles are spoken of as the "brancards," so that "brancard," the ordinary name employed in France for the whole conveyance, appears to have been adopted in accordance with the same figure of speech which has produced the English appellation "stretcher," in which a part of the appliance is equally employed to signify the whole.

Stretchers of a great variety of form have been used at different times in armies, and even in our own military service; and still greater have been the number of those which have been proposed for use, and for which special advantages and merits have been claimed and advocated by their respective inventors.

Original division of stretchers into primary and secondary.

It was the rule in the civilized armies of the earlier part of the present century to employ two distinct classes of stretchers under the circumstances of campaigning. The stretchers of the first class were those intended for use on the field of action itself, and between it and the ambulances or movable field hospitals, and were known as "primary" or "ambulance stretchers;" the second comprised those designed for use in the stationary hospitals and in the ambulance wagons attached to them. These were designated "secondary" or "hospital stretchers." Field or primary stretchers required to be light and portable, while hospital or secondary stretchers were more complicated, and being made of heavier material could be used as beds for the sick. Not infrequently these two forms would become mixed, to this there was one special objection, namely, that a wounded man had to be moved from one stretcher to another more often than was good for him. This distinction

Necessity for division no longer exists.

no longer exists, and in most armies there is but one form of stretcher, and the uniformity thus obtained enables a stretcher to be used without change from the fighting line to the base of operations. The importance of this uniformity is being gradually recognised, and inventors and those who work at this subject have, as far as England is concerned, settled the most convenient measurements of a stretcher suitable for the requirements of both military and civil life. This uniformity might with advantage be extended if it were made an inter-

International uniformity proposed.

national question. It was, indeed, proposed at the International Conference of Red Cross Societies, held at Carlsruhe in 1884, that much suffering would be avoided if nations would come to an agreement as to the dimensions of the military stretcher to be universally employed. A uniform pattern might be impossible, but to obtain similar dimensions in all cases is not an insurmountable difficulty. For instance, had such uniformity existed in 1870–1 it would not have been necessary, as was often the case, to change wounded French soldiers from their own stretchers to others because the former could not be conveyed in German carriages, and *vice versâ*.

All field stretchers are made to be carried by the hands of bearers, including those which have arrangements for adapting them to be carried in carts or wagons; hence they were originally designated "hand litters." This designation has no value at the present time, and, as far as ambulance transport is concerned, is now obsolete.

It is the mode in which they are carried which limits the use of stretchers principally to Europeans and their allied races. Such conveyances are of questionable value if placed in the hands of Eastern bearers, who never support heavy burdens by the strength of their arms. They were never seen in India until a comparatively recent date, and it is very unlikely that the native dooley-wallahs **will prove** efficient stretcher bearers, so wedded are they to **their own** habits and intolerant of innovation. The editor **trained 24** detachments at Mandalay during the Burmese campaign with light field stretchers weighing 10 lbs. each, and though the men acquired the drill with more or less precision, they never were of the slightest use. Two natives of the average size are not physically able to carry 225 lbs. at the length of their arms any distance.

The stretchers which were sent with the troops engaged in the **war** with China in 1860, had to be provided with poles and bamboo supports, "the Chinese being incompetent for any other mode of carriage than that by means of a pole borne on the shoulder." * The ordinary forms of hand conveyances for the sick in India, previously described, have been in a great degree determined by the prevailing habit in the East of supporting burdens *upon* the shoulders, instead of sustaining them *from* the shoulders and carrying them in the hands.

The exigencies of military service limit the construction of field appliances to extreme simplicity, and, at the same time, demand for them much strength. Inventors seldom sufficiently comply with the requirements in these respects; but, too often, on the contrary, from designing in the study, and contriving in the workshop, mechanical adjustments calculated to answer a variety of adaptations, render the whole machine when completed unserviceable for the main purpose intended to be fulfilled. They lose sight of the fact that the men who will afterwards have to use their contrivances on service are, for the most part, not drawn from the class of society which includes skilled mechanics and artificers, but from that of ordinary labourers; and that, consequently, with comparatively few exceptions they **are** apt to be rough, devoid of neatness and manual dexterity.

---

* A. M. D. Reports, 1860, page 379.

CHAP. VI.

Inventors should aim at great strength and simplicity.

and, too often, especially under excitement, careless. They do not take into account the violence to which stores of all kinds are subjected in being put into and stowed in the holds of ships, during gales at sea, in transfer to lighters, in disembarkations, in being piled on landing places, in being carried in all kinds of land transport vehicles over all kinds of ground, in exposure to all sorts of weather, in frequent unpackings and packings amid the bustle and excitement of a campaign. Let inventors remember the violent usage which ordinary baggage receives in a long journey along comparatively smooth roads when there are many changes in the conveyances, when the packages transported are specially adapted for movement and made to withstand shocks, and the conveyances are expressly built for the reception of such articles, and notwithstanding too that throughout the journey they are moved by porters under the supervision of guards whose daily business it is to handle such packages and to protect them against injury in the transit. They may then imagine what would be the fate of their packages were they subjected to such continued removals with scarcely any similar preparation or precautions. But though the effects in such a case might be fairly guessed at, still, without being familiar with the actual transit of army stores under the circumstances of warfare, it would be difficult to realise the amount of additional risks and shocks to which they are then continually exposed. Yet without this knowledge it is scarcely possible to understand why such simple uniformity and such solidity are absolutely demanded for field appliances. It must be also remembered that it is essential to have these articles at all times in a thoroughly serviceable condition, so that they may be ready to meet urgent wants which may occur at any moment, and which, when they occur, no other means will probably be available to supply. If an engagement takes place, and any considerable proportion of the stretchers which were depended upon for carrying away the wounded are found to be broken or unserviceable from any cause, experience teaches that great suffering, and perhaps loss of life, will not improbably result. Hence it is that army medical officers are so prone to reject all contrivances for the first conveyance of sick and wounded in the field which are either at all complicated in construction or which do not appear to contain sufficient elements of resistance to the exposures and violence they know by experience

The contrivance which answers the greatest number of purposes not always the best suited for field service.

such conveyances will be subjected to. Inventors, who are informed that the principles of their inventions are approved, and who yet find that the inventions themselves have been rejected, are too apt to conclude that the officers whose reports have led to the rejection are overfastidious or prejudiced. Inventors find articles sanctioned for use which are manifestly imperfect in some respects, and incompetent to fulfil some of the purposes which their own improved contrivances answer, and they are led to complain that they are not supported in their efforts at improvement.

They do not see that the less perfect contrivance, if its continued serviceable condition can be relied upon with fair amount of certainty, is a more valuable article for use in the field than the most perfect machine with a liability to get out of order. If the circumstances of British service were different from what they are; if the proposed conveyances were intended for such use as they would meet with when handled only by practised and careful mechanics, in countries where well-made roads would be constantly met with, and under circumstances where opportunities of repair, or the means of speedy restoration of missing parts existed, then there can be **no** doubt but that the decisions pronounced by committees of survey would occasionally be reversed. Practical acquaintance with the exigencies and actual circumstances of a state of warfare, joined with a proper understanding of the best method of achieving the particular objects in view, can alone enable a right judgment to be formed respecting the fitness, **or otherwise**, **of any** special contrivances which are **proposed for** use in campaigning.

<small>CHAP. VI.</small>

<small>Practical acquaintance with the actual circumstances of warfare can alone decide on the utility of proposed appliances for field use.</small>

These reflections have been induced by studying the many inventions which were advocated as substitutes for the stretchers in ordinary use during the period of the Crimean and more recent wars, and from being aware of the comments which were made by some of the inventors when they found their inventions disapproved.

We find the complica**ted nature** of the design, and want of sufficient **strength in the** construction, advanced by committees of officers **as causes of** rejection of most of these inventions.

<small>Complicated construction and insufficient strength.</small>

Remarks on Models of Proposed Conveyances.

With reference to *models*, in which form **many** inventors find it convenient to exhibit their designs, and especially with regard to *models* **of complex** conveyances, may be observed that, useful as such miniature representations are for explaining the principles and illustrating the details of construction in the lecture room, it should always be remembered that they usually prove exceedingly fallacious guides when solely depended upon for arriving at conclusions on the actual fitness for service of the machines which they are made to represent. They are apt even to deceive inventors themselves as to the precise qualities and capabilities of the particular contrivances which they design them to illustrate, and should never be accepted by critical observers as sufficient for forming a reliable judgment of their practical merits. It is only by much greater care and nicety than are usually given to such articles, that models can be made strictly to scale, so that the proportionate relations **of** dimensions may be accurately preserved in all of their parts. It would surprise, perhaps, no less than disappoint, many inventors, were the models which they exhibit to be employed, **with** all their relative proportions preserved, as **the** standards

<small>Remarks on models of proposed conveyances.</small>

<small>Their use for purposes of illustration.</small>

CHAP. VI.
On models.

of measurement for the construction of *patterns* for actual use of the vehicles they represent; so obvious do small errors, which are scarcely noticeable in a model, become when they are magnified to the dimensions of the full-sized object. Many models are little better than toys, because they are not made to scale. Other matters besides form and dimensions, such as strength of material in relation to weight to be carried, effect of increased mass, the relative bearing of the several portions in the machine itself, are also subjects which can seldom be rightly estimated in models. A complete *pattern* can alone enable committees who are ordered to pronounce opinions on the merits of such inventions as conveyances, of whatever kind they may be, to do their duty with equal justice to the inventors and to the public service; for only a pattern can be subjected to tests corresponding **with the** work in which the article will be actually employed on **service** in campaigning.

Remarks on the Construction of Stretchers.

A military stretcher requires to be simple in construction, light and durable, strong, easily manipulated, and portable. There should be no separate pieces, and all the parts of the conveyance should be interchangeable. In addition the stretcher must be capable of being used as a bed in the field hospitals.

A stretcher is composed of—

(1) Poles.
(2) Traverses.
(3) Feet.
(4) Canvas **and Pillow.**
(5) Slings.

The poles.

The poles.—The poles **are** the side supports to which the canvas or other material, upon which the patient lies, is attached, and by means of which the conveyance is carried by the bearers. Consequently the steadiness and efficiency of a stretcher depends to a large extent upon the poles, which must not be too light, or too heavy, and which must be of solid construction and of an even consistence throughout their whole length.

If **the** poles are too slight, **even though** sufficiently strong to support the weight carried on **the** stretcher, an elasticity, or "*sponginess,*" occurs, most detrimental to the safe transport of a wounded individual. This springing motion may be compared to the feeling **which** is experienced by a person walking over a plank bridge **that** bends under the weight. Further, it may be added that the bearers are not so well able to support their burden under these conditions, and their already laborious work is rendered still more irksome and difficult.

The poles must not be too heavy, and yet sufficient steadiness of the carriage cannot be obtained without a certain amount of solidity, a relative term for weight. As it is, the heaviest part of a stretcher is the poles, and in constructing conveyances of this class, it is desirable to obtain as nearly as possible the exact mean equivalent, which will procure the least weight on the one hand, compatible with the greatest efficiency on the other.

The following woods have been used in the construction of stretcher poles:—

Oak.—Rarely; it is too heavy.

Beech.—Not uncommonly used, but requires additional strengthening. It is a light wood.

Ash.—Is the wood usually chosen, and most generally used. It is a heavy wood, but is durable, sufficiently strong and effective.

Pitch Pine.—Is a light wood, but not durable. It is used in the construction of some varieties of French stretcher.

Lance wood.—Is heavy, and too elastic for the purpose, besides, when old, it is liable to break with a short fracture.

Bamboo.—Enters largely into the construction of temporary appliances for transport in the countries where it grows. The male variety, which is so much used for the handles of lances, and spears, is too elastic for the purpose of stretchers, and the female variety is too large and unwieldy. Bamboo is one of the lightest woods, but for the above and other obvious reasons cannot be recommended. It is to be noted that when iron is clamped on to bamboo, the latter rots, so there should invariably be leather placed between the wood and the metal.

The length of the poles.—The length of the poles must be that of the sides of the bed of the stretcher, to which is added sufficient at each end to enable the bearers to step in between them, and when the stretcher is raised, to allow the No. 1 bearer to incline slightly forwards, and the No. **3** bearer slightly backwards, to counteract in the most convenient and natural manner the resultant force of the combined centres of gravity of the two bearers, and the weight supported, which tends **in a** direction directly downwards to a point between them, and nearest to the weight.

Experience has shown that 8 inches to 1 foot is about the proper estimate for those parts of the poles which project outside the canvas of the stretcher, the most convenient length of a pole being 7 feet 9 inches. Any length over 8 feet is practically unnecessary, and any length under 7 feet 6 inches is undesirable.

In some forms of stretcher **the** poles consist of two parts, being joined together at their centres by a hinge, or the two inner ends running into, and being fixed by, a metal tube. Extra portability is claimed for this class of conveyance, but the advantage apparently obtained is in no way proportionate to the want of security in the poles, and a weakness at the point

CHAP. VI.
The poles.

where strength is most necessary occurs, under these circumstances. The opinion of those best qualified to judge is directly opposed to a division in the poles. The poles, however, can be effectually shortened, and with comparatively slight, if any, weakening in the construction of the stretcher. In these cases the pole runs in one piece the length of the canvas, and the handles slide underneath, this will be described under the head of civil ambulance material.

The shortening of the poles to 6 feet has many advantages, and not the least among them is the fact that stretchers of that length can be accommodated in any railway carriage running on the narrow-gauge system, the width of these vehicles being 6 feet 6 inches. In this way two stretchers can be supported on two improvised traverses across the carriage, with an interval of 2 feet between each patient for the ingress or egress of an attendant.

The traverses.

The traverses.—The traverses are the stays or cross pieces which separate and keep apart the poles, stretching the canvas and preventing the person carried from sinking in between the poles, and the sides of the conveyance enveloping him, as in the case of transport by conveyances of the hammock class. It is the presence of the traverses which constitutes the principal difference between hammocks and stretchers.

The simplest form of traverse is a cross piece of wood or stick tied or nailed to the poles on each side; (2) a traverse made of wood or iron, with a hole at each end, for the handles of the pole to pass through; and (3) a similar construction to which are added feet. These forms have been tried, and, one by one, discarded for various reasons, which may be summarised thus:—

a. The light material of which these traverses were usually constructed, rendered stretcher carriage more or less insecure.

b. They usually formed separate pieces, and were liable to be lost.

c. They were only interchangeable to a certain degree.

d. When the poles passed through the ends of the traverses it was difficult to fix them, and a "*sawing*" motion was conveyed to the carriage by the swinging of the arms of the bearers.

e. When feet were, in addition, attached to the traverses, there was, unless the parts fitted exactly, considerable movement, though, to a certain degree, this might also be ascribed to the elasticity of the poles, which were thinner, and less substantial, than those in use at the present time.

With the development of the stretcher, the traverse came to be regarded as one of the most essential parts of the conveyance. It was found that they required strengthening, and that it was necessary to apply them in a different manner to the poles. But for a long time the opinion of those who considered this matter was satisfied with the traverse to be found on the Mark I. old pattern British Army, namely, an iron ⅜-inch rod working in a staple and hooking into another on the opposite pole and fastened off by string, and for the field work for which this stretcher was only intended it answered very well, but was liable to get out of order. It is comparatively recently that the strong traverse of the present stretcher has been brought into general use, and it is necessary to have one as strong and heavy as this is, to meet the many conditions demanded of the present conveyance.

It is upon the length of the traverse that the width of the stretcher depends, and the question then resolves itself into a consideration of the width of the stretcher. The greater the width of the conveyance, the stronger and heavier must the traverses be. The poles and their traverses alone form the framework **of the** stretcher, and it is on these that the strength of the stretcher principally depends. The weight of the patient acting directly downwards does so at a less advantage the nearer the poles, *i.e.*, the power, is brought to it, and *vice versâ*. All that is required is that the person carried should be able to lie comfortably on his back with the head raised, and experiment has proved that 21 inches between the poles, and an outside measurement of 22½ inches, is about the least that can be allowed, and the best for all practical purposes. Any excess, however small, at once increases the strain.

The traverses of modern stretchers (Mark V.) are for the most part made of flat galvanised iron, locking with a scissor joint at the centre. An iron plate is riveted on to the under surface of the stretcher pole, at about 12 inches from each extremity. Working on a pivot is the transverse portion of the traverse, which is hinged at its centre by a joint, breaking inwards, and prevented from being displaced outwards by the addition of a bent flat hook, into which the traverse locks.

In the Mark IV. stretcher this hook was not made, but there was only a lip of the traverse side turned up to act as a stop.

By the traverses being detached altogether or so fixed as to be capable of being laid parallel with the poles at the option of the bearers, the stretcher is rendered **more** portable. When not in use the traverses are usually stowed away within the canvas, or they are folded up alongside of the side poles when they are brought into contact, and the whole is then secured together into one long narrow package.

Occasionally, however, the traverses are solidly united to the two side poles, so as to form a strong frame within which the canvas is stretched. These stretchers have been designated "framed" stretchers, and though in more or less general use at one time have long been superseded by a superior class of conveyance. The side poles of stretchers are used parallel with each other, not curved, as in the New Zealand litter previously described.

The joint of the traverse in its simpler form has no means of preventing injury to the hands of the bearers. In the exercise of preparing and folding up stretchers, not infrequently the fingers get nipped between the parts of a traverse, and when the joint is stiff the bearers bruise the palms of their hands in

CHAP. VI.

The traverses.

Framed stretchers are now obsolete.

CHAP. VI.

The traverses.

their endeavours to close the joint. To obviate this Mr. Furley has introduced for all stretchers designed by him a strong ring, attached to the traverse by the joint; and the bearer is able to take a firm grip of this, and easily open or close the joint without the least risk of injury. (*Post* p. 176.) This simple and important addition might with great advantage be added to the military stretcher.

Stretcher trestles.

To enable the **stretcher** to be used as a bedstead, and to spare the surgeon the necessity of going on his knees to dress the wounds of a patient in camp hospitals, Mr. Furley lately introduced folding trestles: these are strongly built and jointed, and pack into a small compass.

The feet.

The feet.—The primary idea in attaching feet to stretchers was (1) That a patient being carried, and placed on the ground, should not risk chill from contact with wet earth, nor meet with any unevenness in the ground which might be distressing to him, and at the same time injurious to the stretcher; and (2) it was also thought necessary, since it was desirable that stretchers should be used in field hospitals as beds, to provide them with feet.

The feet of the stretcher do not form an essential part of the construction, but are to be considered as a necessary addition to the mechanism. They require to be sufficiently strong to support the weight carried by the stretcher, and to be made of a substantial material unlikely to get damaged or break under the exigencies of service in the field.

When feet were first attached to stretchers there was a tendency to make them too long and too weak, but now, with an absolutely immobile framework, the feet have been considerably reduced in length, and the probability is that the patient is as far off the ground as he ever was in the older forms of these conveyances. To obtain the greatest steadiness it is desirable that the feet form a part of the traverse, being derived from the traverse plate on the under surface of the pole. On no account should the feet be separate from the traverse, or a "wobbling" motion will be conveyed to the stretcher with the least movement of the patient lying on it. The feet are liable to spread, and the whole conveyance is unsteady. This is particularly the case with those stretchers whose inventors, with the least possible knowledge of the requirements of these **field** conveyances, but who assume that they have conquered the many difficulties that still exist, throw on the market articles with collapsing sides, self-acting automatic feet, a canvas divided into two or more pieces—in short, a stretcher containing all the faults which have been pointed out for years, and without a single feature of the requirements in stretchers at the present time. Self-acting automatic feet are merely feet which fall into position by their own weight, and are locked by a spring catch. They are useless contrivances, and should never be adopted.

The feet in most stretchers are between 5 inches or 6 inches long, made of iron, and instead of the iron being flattened out into feet, they hold boxwood rollers. The addition of rollers was a great advance, reducing the risk of injury to the feet, increasing the comfort of the patient, and facilitating the loading and unloading of stretcher in ambulance wagons.

The canvas and pillow.—The canvas of a stretcher is that part which lies **evenly** between the poles, and upon which the person carried reclines. This is not necessarily made of canvas, though all modern stretchers have adopted it on account of its lightness, durability, and strength. The white canvas has been superseded by red flaxen canvas, which does not show dirt and blood stains to quite the same extent. This canvas was introduced into the British Army on the recommendation of the Committee* assembled at the Brussels Exhibition in 1876 to report on the Appliances for Aid to the Sick and Wounded in War.

Canvases are attached in any of the following ways:—

(1.) By a hem through which the poles pass as in the Mark I. Field Stretcher. Fig. XLVIII. page 170.

(2.) By a hem through which a lath runs. (*Post*, p. **329.**)

(3.) By being nailed **along the** outer side of the stretcher pole under a strip of **leather, as in the** Army Regulation stretcher. (*Post*, p. **173.**)

(4.) By being buttoned along the outer sides of the poles to studs, as in the "Furley" Stretcher. (*Post*, p. 174.)

Of these four methods, the first is never used in the British Service, because owing to the attachment of the traverse, the poles do not admit of being passed through the hem. The second will be sufficiently discussed when writing on Captain Tomkin's invention. The third plan is a safe and durable one, but it is difficult to clean the canvas, and to replace it quickly when necessary. The fourth method allows of easy removal for cleaning, and replacing.

The canvas should **measure 6** feet by 1 foot 10 inches outside measurement.

The pillow **may be either separate** from the **stretcher, or, which** is far better, attached to and formed **out of the** canvas. In the first instance there is a comfortable pillow, but being separate from the canvas is very liable to be lost. In fact, it is rarely that the pillow is seen in the exercises with those stretchers which have them as a separate part. In the second method the canvas is merely folded double, or a piece is securely sewn on to it, forming a bag, which can be stuffed with hay, &c. It is principally met with in military and police stretchers invented by Mr. Furley, and the stretcher bedstead of the Tortoise Ambulance.

The latter method meets every contingency, and lessens the weight and bulk. Anything **that, as a** sufficient substitute, will do away **with the** pillow **as an** extra piece, **is** a step in the right direction.

The slings.—The slings help to support the weight of the stretcher on the shoulder of the bearer. In England they are

---

* Under the presidency of the Author.

CHAP. VI.

The slings.

usually made of strong leather, but on the continent of canvas webbing.

They are 5 feet long and 2 inches wide with loop at one end, while at the other there is a buckle fastening to form another loop. The object of the buckle is to lengthen or shorten the sling to the requirements of the bearer—an important one, but usually discarded. At the end opposite to the buckle is a transverse strap to fasten off the folded stretcher. There is no advantage of any value in leather slings over those made of webbing; the former require attention, are expensive, and heavy; the latter are cheap, light, and quite strong enough for the purpose for which they are required. A webbing sling with a slide buckle, such as is to be found on a haversack, would in reality be more serviceable and convenient. Medical Officers in charge of bearer detachments should insist on the slings being properly adjusted as to their length, as well as the other points laid down in the Bearer Drill. A sling is properly adjusted when the ends reach the wrists of the bearer standing at attention.

Preservation.

The preservation of stretchers is important, for when neglected they are apt to become stiff and to get out of order. They should be kept in a dry store, leaning at an angle against the wall, and from time to time should be opened and aired. When the canvas gets dirty it can be scrubbed with a little soap and plenty of water. The woodwork should be polished with some oil waste, and the hinges of the traverse oiled from time to time. Lastly, soft soap should be worked into the leather of the slings until they become soft and pliable.

It will be noticed that not infrequently stretchers are folded up with the slings lying loose upon them. This can and should invariably be avoided by directing the bearers to shorten the sling by its buckle, before fastening off the transverse strap.

Weight.

Finally, with regard to the weight of stretchers, it is unlikely that there will ever be constructed a stretcher which will meet all the modern requirements, and approach the weight of a light field stretcher of 15 lbs. Strength and durability mean weight, and cannot be obtained without it, but every endeavour should be made to prevent stretchers weighing, when complete, more than 25 lbs. The poles, if selected, might be lighter, as well as the traverses, a separate pillow might be omitted, and webbing used in lieu of leather for slings, would, to a certain extent, diminish the weight and cost, which at present, are considerable.

Baron Percy's Stretcher.

Percy's views.

This description is of historical interest. Baron Percy advocated the division of stretchers into two equal parts,

"What are wanted," he said, "are stretchers which shall always be at command, and that the men can carry in

Fig. XLI.—Baron Percy's Stretcher; Bearers in marching order.

equal divisions as easily as they can carry a firelock. These are the prime conditions to be sought for in these conveyances." Baron Percy was the first authority who recommended that stretchers should be adapted to answer the purpose of camp bedsteads when necessary.

Percy's plan. The several parts of one stretcher were divided between two bearers. Each bearer carried a pole 8 feet long, with one end adjusted for the purpose of receiving an iron lance-head with its transverse guard, and with the other end protected by a ferrule. The pole thus became a weapon of defence and

Fig. XLII.—Baron Percy's Stretcher, fitted for carrying wounded.

offence, like the sergeants' pikes which were used during the Peninsular war, or the lances which are still employed by some cavalry soldiers. The iron part of the lance was to be removed when the pole was used with the stretcher, and to be carried like a bayonet, in a scabbard at the side of the bearer. Each

CHAP. VI.

bearer also carried one crosspiece or traverse of the stretcher over his knapsack, its **feet** being fitted, for the sake of steadiness, into **two** leathern **sheaths**, one of which was placed at each **side** of the man's pack.

The sacking of the stretcher was divided longitudinally **into two** equal portions, **each** half being **folded** flat and **worn round the** waist of the bearers. When the **stretcher was put together the two** halves were **laced** to each other **by means of eyelet** holes, and a cord fastened to the sacking.

The Prussian Stretcher.

The Prussian stretcher.

This stretcher consists of **two wooden** poles **8 feet long, and separated** at each end by **two iron traverses. The width of the** conveyance is **22** inches. A canvas made of **red flax** material is stretched **over** this framework, **and forms** a secure support for wounded; in addition there are **two bands** attached to the centre of the poles on each side, **and made** of canvas. These are arranged to buckle **over the body of** the wounded and prevent **accidents** during transport. The **head rest** is **a** portion of **the canvas** working **on a** separate frame, **and by the means of a rack and** pinion movement, it can be adjusted to the elevation desired. There are four **iron feet** attached to the poles, which raise the stretcher 12 inches **from** the ground. The weight **of** this conveyance is 30 lbs.

There is a second variety of this stretcher, in which the **poles are divided** in two halves, and allow it to be folded. It **fastens by bolts.**

The French Stretcher.

The French stretcher.

This stretcher, made after the designs **of the** Comte de Beaufort, consists of **two poles, two traverse feet,** canvas and pillow, and slings, and **is a light, portable** conveyance, though weak.

The *poles* **are** made **of ash** or **pitch** pine, and are **7 feet 6 inches, and square the** length **between** the traverses but **rounded at their** ends to facilitate being grasped **by the bearers.**

The *traverses* are made of iron, and are fixed to the under surface of the left pole by a forged iron bolt, on which it turns. **The free** extremity of the traverse is slightly enlarged and is **pierced** by two holes, and a mortice arranged to receive a **copper** screw on the under surface of the right pole. The hole **nearest to the centre** of the traverse is intended to facilitate the **raising of the stretcher** when the **canvas is** damp.

The *feet* **are made of** wood and bound at their ends with iron. **They can be** raised or lowered at will, this movement being limited by **a** spring hook. The feet at the head of the stretcher are prolonged about 6 inches above the surface of the poles, to support the canvas.

The *canvas* is 6 feet long and made of white flax material. It is threaded (*see* fig.) along the side of the pole for three-quarters of its length, so that when the stretcher is prepared two small standard pieces of wood can be raised, and these form the support for a pillow for the head of the sick or wounded patient.

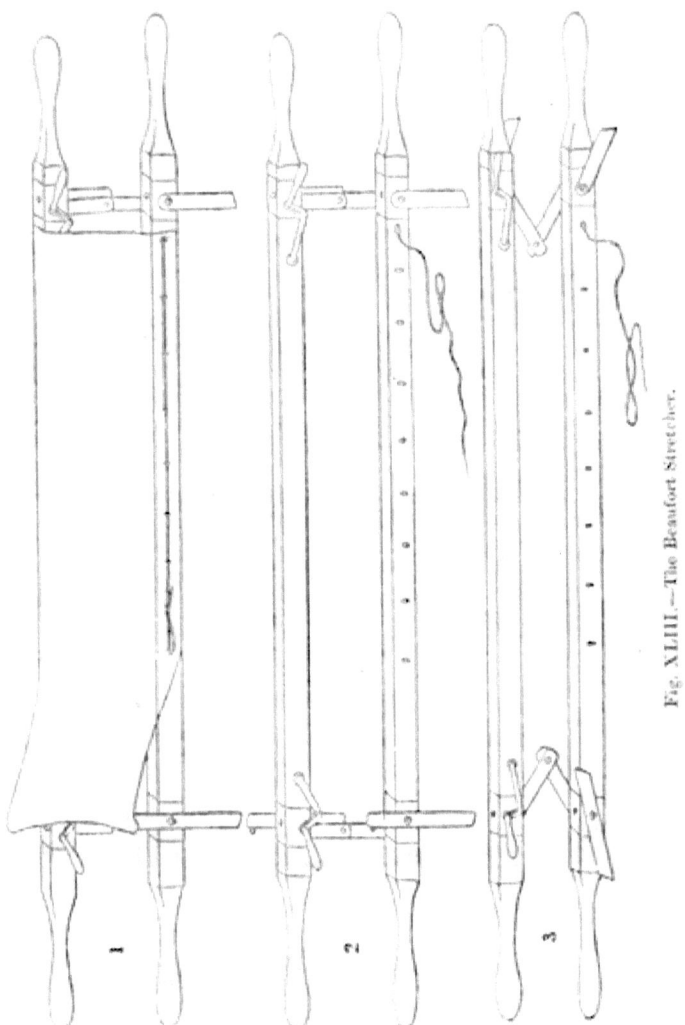

Fig. XLIII.—The Beaufort Stretcher.

The Frank Stretcher.

This stretcher is named after its inventor, and is called the Frank Stretcher. In many respects it is not unlike the Beaufort Stretcher, but is more strongly made.

CHAP. VI.

The *traverses* are made of iron, and are attached by plates to the under surface of each pole; they are curved, and break inwards when the stretcher is closed, by a flat joint.

The *canvas* is double at the head, forming a pocket which can be filled with hay, or any other material, to form a pillow. The free headpiece of the canvas is fixed to the extremities of the prolonged feet, which are raised above the poles by brass eyelets, and are fastened to buttons placed on the lower surface.

The *slings* are made of webbing, and support the conveyance when it is carried. When the stretcher is folded, the webbing sling is turned round it, and fastens the package.

The Austrian Regulation Pattern.

The Austrian stretcher.

This is a light field stretcher constructed on the same lines as Baron Percy's conveyance. It consists of two poles, two wooden traverses, to which the canvas is fastened by straps, after receiving the two poles in a hem on each side. At one end of the canvas, which is white, there is a bag forming a pillow, when filled with leaves, twigs, clothes, &c.

A second form of stretcher is also used, in which the traverse is jointed at the centre, thus allowing the poles to meet when the conveyance is folded up.

These stretchers cannot be considered anything but temporary and light articles, which would break, and parts of which would be lost on field service. They have the recommendation of being cheap, but it is doubtful whether they can be considered efficient, and at the same time economical, in a general sense. Such a conveyance would be of no value in the English service.

Baron Mundy's Stretcher.

Baron Mundy's stretcher.

Baron Mundy's stretcher, as will be seen from the sketch, partakes of the general character of Baron Percy's stretcher,

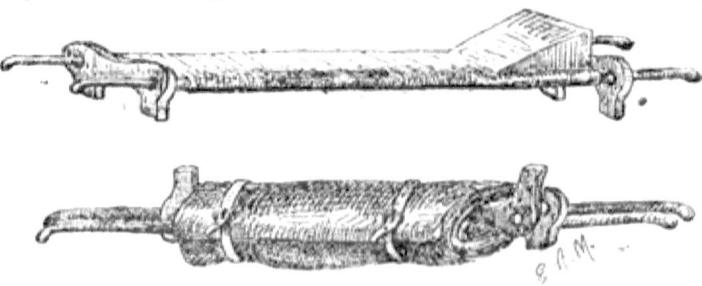

Fig. XLIV.—Mundy's Stretcher.

except that its parts are not arranged for carriage on the backs of the bearers. In the later forms of this stretcher the legs are longer. Being formed of many separate parts it is not convenient, as some of them are apt to be lost. In every other particular this stretcher is a convenient and light field conveyance.

The Italian regulation stretcher.

There are four kinds of stretcher used in Italy, and this is due to the nature of the country. It is the country, *par excellence*, for mountain warfare, and ambulance transport must conform to this, to a more or less extent.

The stretchers are—

    a. Barella pieghevole, or light field stretcher.
    b. Barella rigida.
    c. Barella degli Alpini, a folding **stretcher.**
    d. Barella arrotabile.

B. pieghevole is composed of two poles divided at their centre by a hinge, and attached to one another by a narrow iron traverse, which is permanent. The hinge allows the stretcher to fold backwards, the inner surfaces of the canvas or sacking meeting. The canvas is fastened by a cord lacing on the under surface. There are four curved handles and four small feet.

B. rigida is composed of two poles and two traverses, forming a permanent framework. It does not fold up. There is an arched head piece, and four iron rests which act as feet. The sacking is laced on with cording. The following are the measurements: length 2·45; width 0·60; height 0·15; weight 14 ks.

B. degli Alpini is, as its name implies, divided, and used in the mountains. It is readily folded up, and forms a convenient package.

B. arrotabili is not unlike the B. pieghevole, but it is raised at both ends, and buckled down the centre.

The Mark I. British field stretcher.

The Mark I. field-stretcher used in the British service at the present time is shown in the illustrations which follow. It is thus constructed:—The two poles are round, made of ash, and are each eight feet long, and one inch and a half in diameter, or nearly five inches in circumference, excepting for a short space near their extremities, where there is a slight diminution in girth to adapt them for being handled. Two plain iron rods, each 22 inches in length, three-eighths of an inch in diameter, or about one inch in circumference, and terminating in a ring at one end and a hook at the other, are attached by their rings to two staples fixed at the distance of seven inches from the extremities of the two poles, but on opposite sides and ends of the stretcher. At a corresponding distance from the end of each alternate pole is an opening in the pole itself, of a size proper for receiving the hooked end of the iron rod. The iron rods, when they are hooked across, form the traverses, and fasten up the stretcher. The sacking is made of a piece of stout canvas, and is folded over each side so as to form two plaits sufficiently large for the poles to be inserted into them. At one end is a small horsehair pillow, also covered with canvas. It is secured to the sacking by means of stout leather thongs, which are passed through openings in the sacking, and tied together on its under surface. Two stout leathern straps or slings, looped at their ends, are provided for each stretcher, but not connected with it by any fixture; they are intended to be passed round the necks of the bearers to act as braces and assist in keeping up the weight of the stretcher when in use. One end of each strap is provided with eyelet holes and a buckle, so that it may be shortened or lengthened according to the respective heights of the bearers; the other has a loop only for receiving one of

Fig. XLV.—Plan of British Mark I. Regulation Stretcher, without pillow or straps, with traverses fastened.

Fig. XLVI.—Plan of the same, with traverses unfastened.

Fig. XLVII.—The same, with pillow and straps packed for transport.

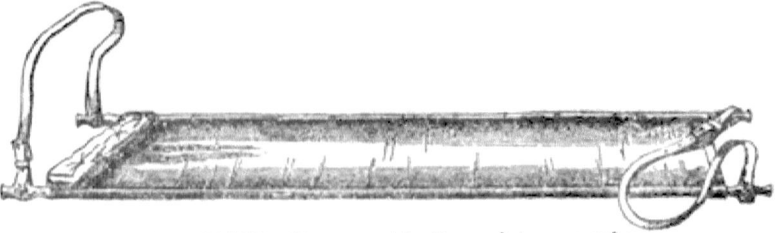

Fig. XLVIII.—The same, with pillow and straps open for use.

the handles of the stretcher. There are no feet to these stretchers. When required to be packed for transport the iron traverses are laid closely in contact with the poles, the sacking with the pillow inside and **the** poles are rolled up together, the straps of the bearers **are** laid alongside, and the whole is fastened into one package by four cords attached for this purpose to the four corners of the sacking.

The total weight of this Mark I. stretcher **is** 15 lbs. The pair of poles and connected iron traverses being 9 lbs. 5 oz.; the sacking, stays, cords, and pillow, 3 lbs. 14 oz.; the pair of leather slings, 1 lb. 13 oz. The weight varies to a slight amount in different stretchers, chiefly owing to variations in the dimensions of the circumference of the poles.

This field-stretcher has the advantage of being simple in construction, **inexpensive, and** portable. The canvas bottom is made easily **removable, so** that **it** may be **at** once washed if soiled by blood **or** dirt. **It is** questionable **whether the** cleanliness of the stretcher might not be still further secured if **an** impermeable covering of some kind were substituted for **the** plain canvas of the horsehair pillow, which cannot be **so** readily **removed to be** washed. The horsehair stuffing **would** be also **better** preserved. The separation **of** the canvas bottom, though convenient, cannot be regarded as a necessary arrangement. **Even** when removed, the canvas cannot be washed like ordinary linen by being rubbed between the hands; **it** must be laid on a flat surface and then cleaned by means of a scrubbing brush and soap, in the same way as canvas articles are cleaned on board ship. At least, this is the usual method adopted for cleaning the canvas of stretchers. It is evident, therefore, that the canvas bottom could be scoured with almost equal ease although nailed or otherwise fixed to the side **poles or** traverses.

These stretchers **are not free from important objections.** Stretchers of the same kind were **used at the commencement** of the Crimean war, with **the exception that no** straps to assist the bearers were provided **at that time.** The inconveniences then experienced during **their use** in the field were two-fold. Not unfrequently **the iron** traverse, from being too slight for the strains **to which** it was subjected, became broken, and no means of repairing the damage were at hand. More often one or both of the traverses became bent, and then there was great difficulty in forcing by manual efforts the two traverses into exactly corresponding lengths, and unless this correspondence in length were precisely **o**btained, only one traverse could be hooked into **its** place. The unprotected openings in the side poles designed **to** receive the hooks of the traverses quickly became enlarged, weakening the side poles still further at those particular points, and leading to the inconvenience of the hooks being easily jerked by accidental blows out of their places, notwithstanding the weight of a patient upon the stretcher. Another serious inconvenience **was the want of means** of keeping the patient off the wet mud in the winter time, or the hard uneven ground in dry weather, when the bearers were compelled to rest themselves during the long carriage of the patient from the trenches up to camp.

British regulation stretcher.

The British regulation stretcher, Mark V., is the latest development of this conveyance, and for strength and durability, simplicity of construction, and comfort, is not easily excelled. The Mark II. and III. field stretchers were but slightly altered from the Mark I.; it is with the Mark IV. that Surgeon-Major Faris, with great ingenuity and much thought, originated the conveyance that is now in general use. The difference between the Mark IV. and V. is very slight, and was noticed in the description of the stretcher.

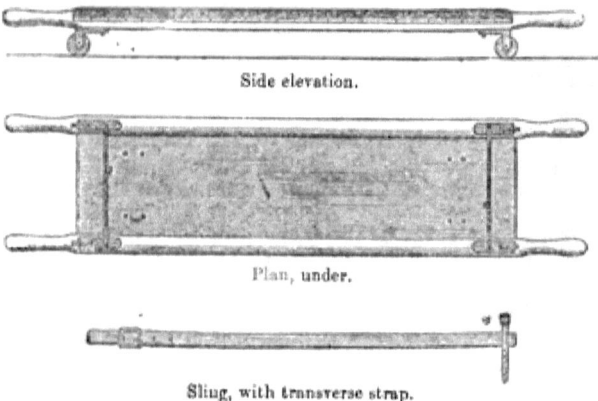

Fig. XLIX.—Faris Field Stretcher, Mark V.

The following are the dimensions of the Mark V., or Faris stretcher:—

Length	canvas		6 feet 0 inches.
	pole		7 ,, 9 ,,
Width			1 foot 11 ,,
Height			0 feet 5¾ ,,
Weight			32 lbs.
Tonnage			·08 ton.

The measurements here given were arrived at after the most mature deliberation, and may be considered as the best, and final as regards this country. It is possible that the weight may be slightly reduced at some future time, but it will not be reduced in the essential parts of the construction, viz., the poles and the traverses.

The Mark V. stretcher consists of two poles, two traverses, a separate canvas pillow, feet with rollers, and slings, **all** of which fold up into a convenient package for the purposes **of** carriage or stowage on **board** ship.

The poles are made of strong, seasoned ash, and are 7 feet 9 inches long, and square throughout their whole length except the handles, which are rounded to fit the hands of the bearers. The poles are separated the required length by the two traverses.

The traverses, which are made of iron, are fastened to two strong plates of the same material, which are riveted to the under surface of the poles 12 inches from their extremities. These traverse plates also provide for the attachment of the rollers by means of which the stretcher **is** raised from the ground or placed on the floor of an ambulance wagon. Each traverse joint, which is of the scissor variety, breaks inwards, and allows the poles to approximate **each other.** There is no protection for the hand of the bearers in locking and unlocking the traverse joint, which occasionally during heat, or **after** having **been** long disused, becomes very stiff.

The canvas is made of **red** flax **material.** It **is** very strong and durable, **and** does not show stains **so** readily as the white canvas which was formerly used. The canvas is attached along the outer side of the pole under a strip **of** leather, and is fastened by broad-headed nails. A pillow made of the same material as the canvas, and stuffed with horsehair and coir, is attached to the latter by two laces or thongs, which pass through ho**les** made for their reception, and are tied underneath.

The feet, rollers, or racquets are fixed to **the traverse** plates on the under surface of the poles, and raise **the stretcher** about 5 inches from the ground. The rollers are large, **and** **made** of boxwood.

The slings **are** strong leather straps 60 inches long and 2 inches wide, with a loop at one end and a buckle fastening **back** on the strap forms the other. The object of the buckle **is to** lengthen or shorten the sling to the requirements of the **bearer.** Close to the loop end there is a small strap 21 inches long, and placed at right angles to the sling. This is the transverse strap, and used in the following manner to fasten and secure the stretcher when it is folded. The traverses being unlocked and the poles approximated, the canvas is carefully folded over the poles. The two bearers in charge of the stretcher, standing in a stooping position facing each other, with the poles supported between the thighs, pass a sling to each other, retaining a transverse strap at each end. They then place the slings evenly along the top of the folded conveyance, pass **the** transverse **strap** through the free loop of the buckle end of the opposite sling, and buckle it off **close** up to **the** racquets.

The "Furley" military stretcher.

Furley military stretcher.

This stretcher is precisely the same in principle and of the same dimensions as the Army Regulation Stretcher which has just been described. There are, however, a **few** differences in detail which must be noticed.

The poles are made of ash, and in **order** to strengthen them, a narrow strip of galvanised iron is **riv**eted along the inner side. The handles are different in shape to those of the regulation stretcher, insomuch that while the latter are rounded off evenly the former are slightly arched, thus giving much greater **power to** the bearers holding them. When stretchers

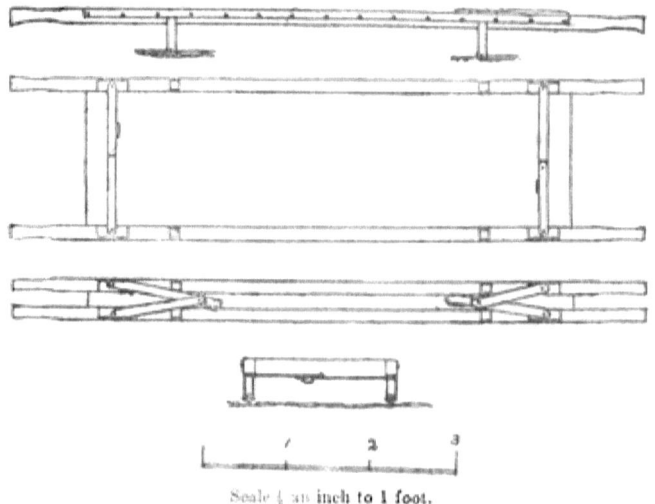

Fig. L.—The Furley Military Stretcher.

are used without slings, **as they** frequently **are,** there is the chance of the leading man stumbling and pulling the stretcher out of the rear bearer's hand. The slight change in **the configuration of the** handle of the "Furley" stretcher **lessens to a very** large extent the possibility of such an **accident.**

The traverses are provided with **a** strong fixed ring for the **bearers to seize when** locking or unlocking the joint, and this is a great protection **to** the hand, which is otherwise liable to be injured when manipulating these scissor joints; it also allows the width of **the** stretcher to be diminished without disturbing the man who may **be** on it.

The canvas is not nailed to the poles, but it is buttoned to flat-headed screws with washers, **and** by loosening these very slightly, can be **removed for** the purpose of cleaning.

The pillow also is a part of the bed, and not separate from it. It consists of a fold of canvas, forming a bag, which is closed by a leather lace; it can be filled with hay, straw, a rug or other soft material when required for use, and when not wanted it lies flat without adding to the bulk or weight.

The rollers are made of *lignum vitæ*, and are much smaller than those of the regulation stretcher, and they are fixed in lighter ironwork, which is equally strong, and gives more protection to the wheels.

The slings are made of webbing, and answer the purpose quite as well as the heavier and more expensive leather used with the army stretcher.

Weight of stretcher and slings, 28 lbs.

"Furley" Folding Stretcher.

This stretcher when opened for use is very similar to the "Furley" military stretcher, but the shafts are made of wood with fixed handles, or of angle iron jointed in two places, with handles which fold inwards. The stretcher can thus be formed into a compact parcel, 3 feet 1 inch in length and 6 inches in depth, and the weight being in iron $31\frac{1}{2}$ lbs., and in wood $23\frac{1}{4}$ lbs., six or eight can easily be carried by a mule.

General Observations on Civil Stretchers.

Red Cross Societies and other kindred institutions have made such a close connection between civil and military ambulance methods that it is quite impossible in the present day to establish any strong line of demarcation between them. From every point of view it is well that this should be so, as the advantage to be derived is reciprocal. This is especially the case with regard to transport material, and it must be admitted that the St. John Ambulance Association has largely contributed to this object. For this reason, no excuse is necessary for including a description of some civil ambulance appliances in a book which is more particularly intended for military readers. In the event of a great war the Army Medical Department should find at hand a supplement of civil aid, and it is only right that the nature of the resources from which it can be drawn should be known and tested while there is time for careful examination.

Stretchers for civil purposes, though they require a certain degree of strength and solidity, are generally made lighter than those for military use. They are not liable to the same violence, nor are they subjected to the same variations of temperature and climatic influences, and they are seldom required as field hospital beds. The use of military stretchers is, more or less, uniform, but that of civil stretchers is more complicated, and they necessarily differ in many respects from those which are constructed to meet the rougher experiences of war. For instance, stretchers which have to be daily employed in small houses with tortuous staircases, in factories filled with machinery in motion, in railway carriages with narrow doors, or in **mines**, must be adapted to all these circumstances.

The "Furley" stretcher for civil purposes.—Although Mr. **Furley**, who invented **this** stretcher for the St. John Ambulance Association, has, as far as possible, maintained one **type** with the same dimensions, certain changes have had to be made to meet the various requirements to which reference has just been made. The stretchers of this pattern principally employed may be classified as follows:—

  a. **Ordinary** civil stretcher.
  b. **Civil** stretcher with **telescopic** handles.
  c. **Police** stretcher.

(*a*) The ordinary civil stretcher is constructed on the same principle as the "Furley" military stretcher described above, but for economy and lightness the poles are generally made of selected deal, and to ensure strength a thin piece of galvanised iron is riveted on the inner side from end to end, flush with the wood. The canvas at the head is raised automatically by small iron standards which rest horizontally on the traverse until the stretcher is opened, when they are raised into a perpendicular position.

(*b*) The stretcher with telescopic handles is similar to the last, with the exception that the handles telescope below the shafts. These handles, which might otherwise prove

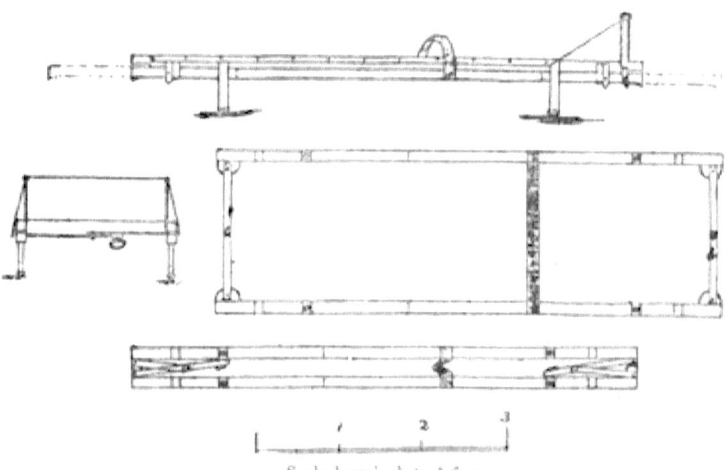

Fig. LI.—The Furley Stretcher with telescopic handles.

dangerously weak, are formed of two pieces of wood, with a thin plate of galvanized iron placed between them and firmly screwed together. One great advantage in these stretchers, perhaps, is that they can so often be used in carriages not specially built for them.

(c) The police stretcher is exactly similar to the "Furley" military stretcher (p. 174), but as it may be required for violent drunkards and lunatics, the bed is made up of doubled canvas, sewn together diagonally, and it is also furnished with strong leather straps very securely fastened to the frame.

In all of these stretchers the traverses are provided with ring handles for the protection of the bearers' hands and also to allow the traverses to be partially *broken** and thus obviate the necessity of tilting the stretcher when it has to be passed through an opening narrower than itself, which is always a hazardous proceeding.

The weight of these stretchers averages about 28 lbs., those with telescopic handles being rather heavier than the others.

A light canvas cover on a jointed frame of galvanized iron can be used with any of these stretchers, and is a valuable protection from the weather; it can be folded up with the stretcher without adding much to the bulk.

When it is considered how many conditions of a stretcher this pattern satisfactorily fulfils, it must be regarded, perhaps, as the most complete stretcher that has ever been made. It can be shortened, lengthened, or diminished in breadth; it has no separate parts and it is light and portable.

The "Lowmoor" jacket.

Special attention has of late years been paid to ambulance material for use in mines. One of the great difficulties which was formerly opposed to the use of ordinary stretchers in some pits was the narrowness of the shafts in which only small cages could be used; in order to meet this Mr. Furley invented the "Lowmoor" jacket, so called from the colliery in which it was first tried. The great advantage of this jacket is that a patient may be so securely fastened to any stretcher that he can, if necessary, be placed in a perpendicular position, and the canvas and straps adapted to meet the particular injuries from which he may be suffering, and the sound part of the body made to bear the principal strain. Thus in the accompanying woodcut it will be seen that the weight partly rests on the armpits and is partly borne by a sling used as a stirrup.

This jacket is deserving of notice here, as it may be found useful when attached to military stretchers, by enabling soldiers

---

* The expression "breaking a traverse" is the term used to describe the movement when the fixed traverse is divided by the joint, and the poles are brought closer together.

or sailors to be passed over the side of a ship into a boat or *vice versâ*, and it can be adjusted and removed without lifting,

Fig. LII.—The "Lowmoor" Jacket.

patient, so that one jacket will bring a number of men from bottom of shaft.

Peck's Stretcher.

This stretcher, for its particular work, possesses many useful features. Made of wrought steel, it is of great strength.

Fig. LIII.

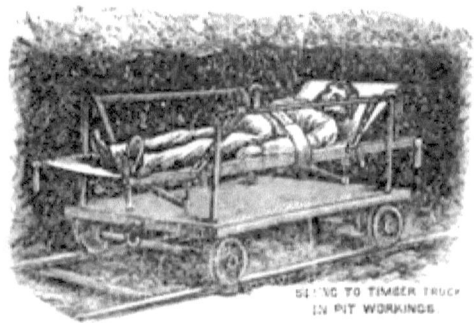

Fig. LIV.—Peck's Stretcher.

It weighs 30 lbs. It was invented for use in mines, and the above features were essential in its construction.

The Peck stretcher can be adapted to any cart, to any mine, however restricted, and to any pit cage carrying two boxes on a deck, i.e., 5 feet 10 inches by 2 feet 2 inches. There is an adjustable head rest and removable cover, so that the patient lies in contact with the canvas only.

The illustrations show how this stretcher is used in the mines, and the method of slinging it on a truck.

General Rules *for the* proper Carriage of Stretchers.

In former editions of this work rules for the proper carriage of sick and wounded were fully detailed. For the most part they were written with reference to the Mark I. Field Stretcher, and to the untrained bearers obtained from the ranks in past times. With the improved organisation and material these classical rules do not apply with the **same** force, and it is to be regretted that they should appear **as** though, written for the modern forms of conveyance in the many works, both English and foreign authors, by whom they are more or less quoted.

The main purposes to be kept in view in carrying stretchers are, firstly, that as little as possible of the impulse connected with the progression of the bearers shall be communicated to the stretcher which they are bearing; and secondly, that the stretcher may be kept level and as near the ground as is consistent with free carriage and the absence of risk of contact. If one of the conveyances be badly carried, it may be shaken in such a way by the movements of the bearers as they step along that, if it be a stretcher upon which a patient is lying, he may be rolled upon it from one side to the other alternately; or, if it be a dandy or hammock, he may be subjected to a lateral swinging movement, nearly as unpleasant and fatiguing **as** the rolling just described. Again, the machine may have such a motion communicated **to** it that the patient may be jerked *upwards* with every step, and this motion **may be** in addition to the swinging or lateral rolling before named: **or** the patient may be so placed that his head is lower than his feet or his body may be unevenly supported, in either **of** which cases the ill results of the movements just described **will** be felt with more severity. The conveyance, again, may be raised so high that the patient upon it may be kept in constant apprehension of falling off, or, in case of one of the bearers accidentally stumbling and allowing the conveyance **to** fall, he may receive such additional injuries as to lead to serious consequences. All these objectionable movements and wrong positions, which would be irksome enough to men in sound health, entail serious suffering and risks to men who are worn by illness, or who are labouring under fractures of bones or other severe wounds. Fortunately, **this suffering** may be in **a** great degree prevented by a

Objects to be kept in view in the carriage of these conveyances.

Ill consequences of a rough mode of carriage.

CHAP. VI.

systematic observance of the rules hereafter mentioned, whatever the circumstances of the locality or whatever differences there may be as to height or strength among the bearers.

One of the first things to impress upon bearers is that every movement of a man who is just wounded must be made with considerate care and gentleness to prevent pain and aggravation of his injuries. Care when raising him from the ground where he has fallen, when placing him upon the stretcher, when lifting the stretcher with the patient upon it, when halting and laying it down for the purpose of resting. In each of these cases care is as essentially necessary to obviate suffering and additional mischief as is a properly regulated step during the transport itself.

Carriage of patients with recent wounds.

Very particular care is required when the patient has had a bone recently shattered by gunshot. The proper manner of accomplishing the delicate task of lifting and removing a man with such an injury, the various modes of protecting the broken limb during the transport are subjects in which all bearers of wounded require to be specially instructed.

Carriage of chronic wounds.

But it is not only in *recent* wounds that a disciplined system of proceeding is necessary for bearers; it is equally requisite, if not more so, for those which have passed the recent state. Great as the torture is of wounded men when they are carried badly, shortly after their wounds have been received, the torture is greatly aggravated under the same circumstances after inflammatory action has set in. Nature then increases her demands for rest and quiet, in order that the processes of repair may go on, and by every means in her power makes the demand known. Interfere with her under these circumstances, and she resents the interference not simply by the infliction of pain, but, if the interference be great, by pain that is past expression, and, if sufficiently prolonged, by pain that is past endurance, for the sufferer will succumb under its overpowering influence.*

As stretchers alone are the authorised conveyances *borne by men* in the British service, the rules for the guidance of bearers during transport are given with a view mainly to the proper carriage of these conveyances.

Rule 1.—The front and rear bearers must "break" the step by starting with opposite feet. By this means the stretcher is kept level, and does not "dip" from side to side.

Rule 2.—The pace should be 18 inches, and made with a steady but easy step, particularly avoiding elevation of the bodies by springing from the fore part of the feet. The foot should be firmly planted, and the knees slightly bent. The

---

* Surgeon-Major J. A. Clark, M.S. Instructor, at the Aldershot Training School, timed 24 squads loading a wounded man, and carrying him 1,000 yards to the rear. The trial took place over rough and broken ground in the Long Valley, and the average time taken was 13·7 minutes with one change of bearers. Surgeon-Major Clark considers this a very good performance, but quite time enough for the whole party to be shot down working in the zone of concentrated fire.

gait of the hawker who habitually carries a basket of crockery, or of a man carrying a bucket of water on his head, is the most suited to the circumstances of a patient carried on a stretcher; for with such a gait the trunks and arms of the bearers, and consequently that which they are carrying, are least lifted up or moved. The peculiarity of this gait is, that in it the hip joints are used as little as possible, the advance is made with the knees kept bent, and the step is shorter. The knees are never wholly straightened as in marching. The length of the pace should be 18 inches. This is the kind of gait which is assumed by the native bearers in India when they are carrying sick, and is the most effective for stretcher-bearers too when trying to prevent undue movement of the stretcher.

The difference in the rise and fall of the upper part of the body between the regulation pace of 30 inches and a pace of

Effect of length of pace in marching with stretchers.

Fig. LV.—Carrying up stairs.

20 inches is greater than might be suspected. When two men holding a stretcher without a man upon it make together a pace of 30 inches, measured from heel to heel, the dip of the stretcher is 3½ inches; with a man upon it, the arms being then stretched to the full by the weight, the dip is 4½ inches. When the pace is 20 inches, the dip, without a man upon the stretcher, is only 1½ inches; with a man, 2¼, or about one half of the dip in the longer pace. Of course in marching at either pace there is an alternate rise and fall to the same extent. The extent of elevation and depression which has just been mentioned is irrespective of jerking or any other movement, having been carefully measured when the bearers were standing still at each position.

Rule 3.—The slings accompany a stretcher to assist the

CHAP. VI.

General Rules.

bearer in supporting the weight, therefore these should be lengthened or shortened by the buckle till the extremities of the loops reach the wrists of the bearer standing at attention.

Rule 4.—The bearers should as far as possible be of a uniform height, build, and age.

Rule 5.—As most ground over which bearers would have to carry wounded presents irregularities of surface it becomes an important matter for bearers to practise the transport of wounded under these circumstances, and so keep the surface of the stretcher level. The concerted action of the bearers is the principle upon which this rule is based.

Rule 6.—A sick or wounded person should, as a rule, be carried with his face in the direction in which the bearers walk.

Rule 7.—If the bearers have to carry a sick or wounded man up-hill, the patient is taken head first, and the reverse takes place going down hill.

Rule 8.—With fractures of the lower extremity, as a rule, the patient should be carried up hill feet first, and down hill head first, in order to prevent the weight of his body

Fig. LVI.—Crossing a fence.

pushing the upper end of the broken bone down upon the helpless and motionless portion of the limb below the seat of fracture.

Rule 9.—No attempt should ever be made, except under the most urgent circumstances, to carry a helpless patient over a high fence or wall; it is a proceeding accompanied by considerable risk, but when unavoidable is accomplished as shown in Fig. LVI.

Rule 10.—In crossing a ditch or stream, the stretcher should be first laid upon the ground near its edge. The two leading bearers descend into the ditch, and assisted by the two other bearers, advance the stretcher until the rear end rests on the ground above. The two other bearers descend, and all four raise the stretcher and carry it to the opposite side, and the fore part being now made to rest upon the edge of ground

General Rules for the proper Carriage of Stretchers. 183

CHAP. VI.

General Rules.

while the rear part is supported in the **ditch**; the two leading bearers jump **out of** the ditch, and with **the** remaining bearers carry the stretcher until the rear end **rests** upon the ground. The two other bearers **then leave** the ditch and the conveyance is carried as under.

In crossing a narrow ditch the bearers on either side jump in

Fig. LVII.—Crossing a ditch.

and steady the **stretcher so as to allow the rear** bearer to cross without shaking the patient.

Fig. LVIII.—Crossing a ditch.

Rule 11.—Patients should never be carried any distance with the stretcher supported upon the shoulder, or a dandy supported on the head. It is a most dangerous and hazardous position. There are certain times when the stretcher requires to be so raised, and then steps should be taken to be certain that the patient is securely fixed; for this the slings may be used; when loading a railway truck from the ground where there is not time to make a ramp, when carrying up a staircase, and under certain conditions over a wall.

Rule 12.—Each of the **four** bearers **to every stretcher must** understand his particular **duty** intelligently. **The front and rear** bearers attend to **the** carrying of the stretcher, and the two remaining carry the havresack and water-bottle, carefully watch the patient, and assist and change with those responsible for carriage as occasion may require.

CLASS II.—CONVEYANCES WHEELED BY MEN.*

GENERAL OBSERVATIONS.

Conveyances wheeled by men form a class which have seldom been used for the systematic removal of sick and wounded in war. The advantages of wheeled carriages moved by hand-labour for field service have been very differently estimated; by some they have been condemned as fanciful and unpractical, while by others they have been strongly advocated as a serviceable and economical form of sick transport. These opinions have, however, been put forward without much experience of their qualities or suitability for use in campaigning. Vehicles of this kind have been used from time to time under casual circumstances where other transport was not available, or where they formed an ordinary method of carriage of the country, owing to local peculiarities of ground; they have been even constructed and despatched for use in the field on a special service in which the British Army was engaged, viz., in 1860; but it was only during the Schleswig-Holstein war of 1864, and the wars of Germany of 1866 and 1870, that hand-wheel carriages, specially constructed for carrying wounded, were practically tested in active warfare.

The principal objects aimed at by the construction of these hand-wheel carriages are :—

First.—To increase the rapidity of the removal of the wounded to the rear.

Second.—To meet the want of bearers by increasing their proportion to the wounded.

Third.—To relieve the pack-animal transport as much as possible, when it forms part of the carriage of the wounded.

The first object, rapidity of removal, is gained by the use of wheels, generally high wheels, by means of which the conveyance can be caused, at the cost of slight expenditure of labour, to pass speedily over rough fields as well as over regular roads; at the same time that the whole litter is made so light that if great obstructions are met with, such as interfere with the employment of the wheels, it can then be readily carried by a couple of bearers over them.

The second object is also gained by the wheeled construction of the litter. Experience has always shown, in cases of

CHAP. VI.

Wheeled stretchers only recently introduced.

Objects aimed at by their use.

Rapid removal of wounded.

To meet the want of bearers.

---

* The remarks on some of the conveyances of this class have been previously published by the Author among the Army Medical Reports.

engagements attended with many wounded, that the number of bearers falls far short of the number required for the regular and rapid removal of the sufferers. This deficiency is made the more manifest by the length of time occupied by the bearers in the removal of a single man on a stretcher, if the distance from the first to the second line of medical assistance be considerable. The fatigue of the bearers is also increased by the continuous nature of their work; by repeated journeys for transporting the wounded between the field and the collecting and dressing stations without intermission, since so long as any wounded remain on the ground they cannot be allowed to rest from their duties. The plan of the wheeled stretcher is supposed to obviate to a great degree these sources of fatigue, by the weight being transmitted through the wheels of the conveyance to the surface of the ground instead of through the medium of the bearers; and, at the same time, by the circumstance that the slight effort which is required to set it in motion on ordinary ground can be varied, either by the act of pushing or by that of drawing the machine. One attendant is sufficient for the transportation of a patient lying on a well-made wheeled litter if the ground be favourable, and at the most, two.

To act as substitutes for mule transport.

The third object is also important. The disadvantages attending the collection of a large number of transport animals near the zone of active operations are sufficiently obvious, not only as regards their expense, but also on account of the unhygienic conditions which they tend to promote when they are placed among bodies of troops. If, therefore, a litter can be fashioned calculated to lessen the necessity for employing a larger number of transport animals, and there be no important objections to it in other respects, an undoubted improvement will be effected in the system of ambulance transport. Two bearers with two wheeled stretchers are able to do the work of a mule and its conductor with a pair of litters, with more ease and safety to the patients and with more speed. Neither wheeled litters nor conveyances borne by animals are suitable means for being brought among the ranks of fighting men while an action is going on; under such circumstances they can only be brought to convenient places in the neighbourhood, and from thence assist in the removal of the wounded. The two classes of conveyance are so far analogous. They can each also be employed in clearing a field of action after the fighting is over, and can each travel over farther distances than bearers could march with wounded men, due regard being given to efficiency and economy. The essential difference in quality between them is that the application of wheels to litters limits to a certain extent the kind of ground on which they can be employed, whereas the use of mule litters is not subjected to such restrictions. Mules are capable of service in rugged and mountainous places where no wheeled conveyances could be used.

Section I.—Description of Particular Forms of Wheel Stretchers.

Before describing the particular hand-wheel litters which have been used, it will be interesting to refer to some historical examples of this class of conveyances which have either been used or proposed for use at previous periods. They will be referred to in the order in which they have been successively brought to notice.

Bautzen Wheelbarrows (Brouettes).

Baron Larrey mentions in his account of the Russian campaign,[*] that after the battle of Bautzen, in Saxony, which was fought in the summer of 1813, two-thirds of the wounded were transported to Dresden by the inhabitants, at his suggestion and advice, in a very convenient kind of wheelbarrow which was in general use in that country for carrying provisions and merchandise. Every private person had several of these vehicles. All the road from Bautzen to Dresden, distant about 30 miles, had more or less inclination, so that the movement of these barrows met with no obstacle in the way. Baron Larrey relates that he had seen as many as 150 filing along the road, one after another; and that, from observation of them, he was convinced no kind of transport could be more favourable or more expeditious for the country. I[†] am informed that these barrows, which are in general use in the south of Germany, are usually so curved and inclined that a person lying upon one of them would find his position very much more easy than he would upon another of which the floor is straight, such as the English wheelbarrow, which requires to be tilted up considerably when put in motion. They are lower, and are also much longer than these latter barrows, being readily able to sustain a person lying at full length, with the head and shoulders slightly raised. There is only one wheel, but this is broad, and from the general width and construction of the barrow, together with the aid of two short supports near the fore part of the conveyance, they are with difficulty overturned. It is, moreover, a light vehicle, and is not fitted with sides above the shafts, so that wounded or weak persons can be readily laid upon or removed from it. It is frequently in use in this part of Germany for the removal of persons who have met with accidents in civil life.

Evans' Hand-wheel Litter.

During the period of the Crimean war, in February, 1855, a surgeon in practice in London, Mr. G. Evans, published an account of a hand-wheel litter which he had caused to be constructed as a subsidiary appliance, or addi-

---
[*] Mémoires de Chirurgie Militaire et Campagnes du Baron D. J. Larrey, Paris, 1817, tom. iv. p. 168.
[†] The Author.

tion, to the ordinary means for the conveyance of wounded from a field of battle. It was designed so as to be capable of carrying either one or two wounded men, one being in a recumbent, the other in a sitting position, and could be wheeled by one or carried by two bearers, according to circumstances. A Medical Board in the same year rejected this conveyance as unsuitable for field service.*

Ordnance Ambulance Barrows.

Ordnance ambulance barrows.

In October, 1856, two forms of ambulance barrows, one barrow having only one wheel, the other being two-wheeled, were sent from the War Department for examination and report by a Committee of Military Medical Officers. The special reasons for which the conveyances were condemned by the Committee are not stated in their proceedings, but the general principles of all such conveyances were disapproved of by these officers, so that they were induced to remark that "no hand carriage with wheels is adapted to field service."

China Ambulance Barrows.

Ambulance wheelbarrows sent to China in 1860.

In the year 1860 a considerable number of ambulance barrows with two wheels were despatched from this country to assist in meeting the requirements of the British forces then assembling in China. These conveyances have been since generally spoken of as "China barrows." When, in consequence of the disastrous affair

Fig. LIX.—Ambulance barrow (China pattern), arranged as a Commissariat Store Cart.

which occurred at the mouth of the Peiho river in the summer of 1859, it was determined to force a way to Pekin, it was found that the nature of the country, and the means of transport that could be obtained on the route from the place of landing to the Chinese capital, could not be ascertained with any degree of certainty. The immense distance of the scene of hostilities from England precluded many arrangements being

Origin of conveyance.

---

* The original litter made after the designs of Mr. Evans is now in the Museum of Mil. Surg. at Netley. Spec. No. 1,261.

made which might otherwise have been resorted to. The state of the roads that would have to be travelled over was unknown, and it seemed not impossible that all the ordinary transport animals of the country would be removed by the Chinese. It was determined, therefore, to send means of sick-carriage adapted for meeting every kind of emergency. Improved ambulance carts, as well as litters and cacolets, were provided in case horse or mule labour might prove to be available; in addition to the ordinary stretchers, doolies were sent on from India for native bearers; and the barrow which is now under consideration was also forwarded, under the idea that it might be advantageously employed, both for commissariat and sick transport purposes, with the aid of Chinese labourers collected

Fig. LX.—Ambulance Barrow (China Pattern), with the Stretcher ready for carrying a Patient, but without the hood.

in the lower provinces. The extensive and easy means of river carriage which were found, however, to exist almost up to the walls of Pekin obviated the need of using these conveyances, and, among other circumstances, prevented the opportunity being afforded of testing practically the utility of the hand-barrows for ambulance transport. The weight of these barrows **was 234 lbs.**

Macdermot's Wheeled Carrier.

Macdermot's wheeled carrier was invented with a view of applying wheels to a Lushai dandy. Two large wheels were joined together by a strongly arched crank, to the top of which was attached a powerful clamp. Into this the centre of the dandy pole was placed, and the dandy was suspended between the wheels. One man pulled the conveyance in front by a rope,

CHAP. VI.

while a second guided the pole from behind. The total weight was 240 lbs. On good roads in India they answered admirably, but absolutely failed across country. In the trials which were made with these conveyances at Delhi in 1885, it was found that they were not adapted to the carriage of unconscious patients, as there was a great possibility of their arms getting entangled in the wheels, and though two men sufficed to move the dandy on good roads, it required six to eight men to take the conveyances a day's march across the country. On a march from Gurgoan to Azaardpore, out of six, two capsized, three were broken, and one accomplished the distance. They were then returned into store as valueless.

Dr. Gauvin's Spring Stretcher on Wheels.*

Dr. Gauvin's spring stretcher on wheels.

This is the wheeled **stretcher which gained the** competitive prize offered for the best **example of this class on** the occasion of the Universal Exposition **at Paris in 1867, and is of** historical interest.

Fig. LXI.—Dr. Gauvin's spring-stretcher on wheels.

It has undergone several alterations in the details **of its** reconstruction, **and** other adaptations have been added to

---

* This stretcher was thus named at Paris. "*Brancard à roues et à bras.*" "*Brancard à ressorts, nouveau modèle, du Dr. Gauvin, conservant la suspension et l'élasticité avec ou sans ses roues.*" "Wheeled and hand stretcher. Spring stretcher, new pattern, of Dr. Gauvin, preserving suspension and elasticity without **or with its wheels.**" It was also spoken of as Dr. Gauvin's "*Brancard-lit à ressorts,*" or "spring stretcher-bed."

it, since the date when it was first brought before the observation of the Committee who adjudged to it the prize at Paris, but the essential features embodied in the contrivance remain the same. The preceding illustrations, which

Fig. LXII.—Dr. Gauvin's Spring-stretcher removed from its Wheels. The small wheeled feet shown in the drawing are to facilitate its passage over the floor of a wagon.

are copied from the second part of the report of the proceedings of the international meetings of the societies for aid to wounded troops, held in Paris in August, 1867, serve to give a fair idea of Dr. Gauvin's stretcher in its latest form, both on and off its wheels.

Baron Mundy's Single-wheeled Stretcher.

Somewhat similar to the foregoing in general form was a new wheeled stretcher shewn at the same exhibition by Baron Mundy, delegate from the Austrian Minister of War. It had the same doubly-curved form and nearness to the ground, but differed in not being capable of being folded in two, and in only having a single wheel. This wheel, which measured about one foot in diameter, was broad, solid, and turned with its axle. It was held in a central position beneath the stretcher by a triple-branched iron support. Two of the branches of this support were fixed to the side-poles, from which they curved downwards to form the axis of the wheel. The third branch, also curved, came from a concave traverse below the stretcher, and forking near the wheel formed a short arch over it. The two ends of this arch were fixed to the ends of the other two branches where they formed the axle, and the whole arch helped to keep the wheel from rocking upon the axle or swaying from side to side when in motion. The bottom of the stretcher was formed of hempen webbing interlaced. To prevent the risk of a patient rolling off the stretcher, a rail was placed on each side at the middle part of the stretcher; and in order that these rails might not interfere with the facility of placing a patient on the conveyance or taking one off, they were jointed in the middle and capable of being detached at one end, so that they could be folded back out of the way whenever necessary. Shoulder-straps were attached to the handles of the stretchers to assist the bearers in carrying, or a single bearer in drawing it.

Independently of the general objections arising from the use of low wheels, which apply to this as much as to the preceding

Chap. VI.

Bn. Mundy's one-wheeled stretcher.

Its construction.

Observations upon this contrivance.

CHAP. VI.

pattern, another defect was observed in this contrivance, owing to the presence of only a single wheel. On trying to wheel a person upon it, it was found very difficult to keep the stretcher level, especially when the weight was not distributed upon it with exact evenness. Moreover, the triple iron support which was very substantial, increased the weight considerably. The weight of the conveyance complete appeared to be about fifty pounds.

M. Devillers' one-wheeled stretcher.

A single-wheeled stretcher, constructed on nearly the same principles as the above, was also exhibited by a French exhibitor, Dr. Devillers. The wheel in this instance was expanded near its circumference, so as to offer a still broader support on the ground, and to diminish the liability to tilting over to either side.

Baron Mundy's Two-wheeled Stretcher.

Bn. Mundy's two-wheeled stretcher.

A further improvement has been made by Baron Mundy in his stretcher, the effect of which has been to make it more portable, and to do away with the inconvenience of the dragging of one wheel in turning which existed when the wheels and axle

Fig. LXIII.—Baron Mundy's wheeled Stretcher.

rolled together. In this last contrivance, made by Messrs. Fisher, of Heidelberg, under the inventor's direction, the two wheels are separately supported; the weight has been diminished to a very low limit—about thirty pounds; and the whole conveyance is so jointed that it can be folded up into a package small enough to be carried on the back of a bearer like a knapsack. The illustration which accompanies represents the general form and construction of the wheeled stretcher under description.

Neuss's Hand-wheeled Litter.

Neuss's wheeled litter.

Early in the course of the war of 1864, between Germany and Denmark, the Russian Johanniter Orden (Knights of St. John)[*] had some two-wheeled hand-litters constructed at the

---

[*] This charitable Order established an ambulance at Nübel, at a distance of three miles from the heights of Düppel, and near the road leading both to the forts and to Sonderburg. They also established, by permission of the Government, other field hospitals at the seat of war. In the campaign of 1866 the Knights of St. John equally furnished hospital aid to the Prussian Government.

factory of the Messrs. Neuss, Government carriage builders at Berlin. These carriages were constantly employed in the service of the Prussian wounded throughout the war; but their practical advantages were particularly noticed at the time of the storming of the forts of Düppel. As this was the first occasion on which wheeled carriages, moved by hand labour, were systematically employed during the active operations of warfare, a special interest is attached to them.

Neuss's conveyance consists of a litter partly made of wood and partly of canvas, stretched between two side-poles and placed upon springs; these springs being again made to rest upon an iron axle connecting the two wheels upon which the weight of the whole machine, when in motion, is supported. The side-poles are provided with handles at both ends. A single man, on grasping two of the handles at either end, can wheel

Fig. LXIV.—Neuss's Two-wheeled Litter, as seen in perspective.

the machine, either by pushing it from behind or by drawing it from the front; or two men, one in front and one behind, can together push and draw it, or can carry the litter, if required, without the wheels being brought into contact with the ground. In order to combine lightness with solidity, the framework has been made of hickory wood. The wheels are also constructed on a peculiar plan, with a view to obtain the same ends; for each nave is of unusual length, and the spokes, twelve in number, radiating from it to the circumference are alternately inclined in opposite directions, so as to cross each other at very acute angles, and distribute support evenly from whatever side pressure may be principally exerted.

Means are provided by two props to support the litter firmly when at rest, and in the absence of an attendant. The weight of the litter is 109 lbs.

Surgeon-General Manley, V.C., has made certain alterations

CHAP. VI.

in the Neuss litter, which is called the Neuss-Manley litter. Surgeon-General Manley applies the ordinary military stretcher to wheels, and arranges permanent supports to raise the stretcher off the ground when it is removed from the wheels.

An objection to the use of Neuss's wheel litter has been noticed by Colonel Beauchamp Walker, C.B., military attaché at Berlin.* It is, that though they answer admirably over favourable ground, such as a country where there are no fences, they cannot be lifted over even a low wall without an amount of hand labour not to be spared during an action. This objection applies to all wheeled stretchers. The same difficulty, though not quite to the same extent, is met with in lifting the ordinary stretcher without wheels over fences and walls; it is so great indeed, that it is an established rule never to attempt to lift a wounded man on a stretcher over a wall if it can possibly be avoided. When an opening in the fence cannot be made, or a portion of the wall be thrown down, sufficient for the stretcher to pass through, the safety of the patient requires that the bearers should traverse even a longer distance, if, by so doing, the impediment can be avoided, and a better way of access to the open ground or road be obtained.

Unfitness of Neuss's litters for general use in the British service.

This litter is not fitted for transport by sea. It could not be taken to pieces, so as to be put together into a compact package. Although the wheels are removable it is still bulky, and there remain many projecting parts, of comparatively little power of resistance, which would be constantly exposed to injury in the movements of a transport vessel in bad weather. This defect would quite unfit it, in its present state, for the general requirements of the British service. Necessity, arising from the insular nature of Great Britain, obliges such conveyances to be simple in construction, easily taken asunder and packed, to be fully capable of resisting the shocks to which they are liable during a sea-voyage, and to be fitted for being readily put together again on landing at the conclusion of the voyage. These qualities are not found in the Berlin two-wheeled litter.†

British Regulation Wheeled Stretcher.

The stretcher is the Regulation Mark V. already described. The wheeled support is composed of steel and iron throughout, and is therefore not liable to deterioration from long storage. It consists of an axletree, a pair of wheels, a pair of elliptical steel springs, with crutches on their upper surfaces to receive the stretcher poles, and a pair of legs. The axletree is made of ¾-inch square steel, with a metal cap at each shoulder. The wheels are 3 feet in diameter. Each consists of eight steel spokes, deeply hollowed on opposite

---

* Appendix No. XXXV., p. 503, Report of Committee on Transport, &c., 1867.
† Even in the passage from Hamburg to Southampton on a steamer, and carefully packed, the Neuss's conveyance obtained for the Army Medical School had one handle broken off, and was defective from the loss of two or three minor parts which had to be replaced before it could be fitted for use.

sides, screwed into a wrought-iron nave, and riveted to a T-iron tire 1 inch in width. The nave is made to secure the wheel on the axletree arm. The springs are made from 1¼ by ¼-inch spring steel, and are each two leaves in thickness. On the top of each spring is a galvanised iron crutch to receive the stretcher pole, with a hinged flap and turn-stud to secure it when in motion. When the wheeled stretcher is required to be stationary, the hinged flap just mentioned is folded back, and it then forms a stop for the wheels by including one of the

Fig. LXV.—The Military Wheeled Stretcher.

spokes in a notch on its end. At the bottom of each is a spring clip, with a stud, split key, and chain, to secure it to the axletree. The legs are attached to the rear of the springs by a double joint, and are curved so as to fold over the springs when packed. They assist in keeping the stretcher in a horizontal position when the support is stationary. When not required for use they are lifted up, and each secured to the corresponding side-pole by a shackle and a hook. The height of a stretcher, when placed on the support, is 2 feet 7½ inches. The weight of the wheeled support, without the stretcher, is 74 lbs. 13 oz.; with the stretcher upon it 100 lbs. 5 oz. The whole is made to take to pieces, and to pack up in a small space for stowage. A canvas cover or case is provided for it. As bearers must be trained in order to carry patients on hand stretchers properly, so they have to be instructed in quickly unpacking and putting together the stretcher support, and in

CHAP. VI.

using it in connection with the stretcher when a wounded man is conveyed by it, or is to be transferred from it to an ambulance wagon.

The Ashford Litter.

The "Ashford" litter.

The "Ashford" litter, which was invented by Mr. John Furley, consists of a stretcher with a pillow and removable cover, resting, without any fastening, on four iron crutches, with an under carriage of two wheels and cranked axle, to allow the rear bearer to follow between the wheels, thus preserving the horizontal position of the patient. It has been adapted to the regulation stretcher, and also to the Navy cot, and is in use at

Fig. LXVI.—The Ashford Litter.

Fig. LXVII.—The Ashford Litter, with cover.

very many home stations, and is largely used by the civil authorities of the country and as well as in India and the colonies. Each of the four iron legs which support this carriage when resting is arranged to shut up closely and to form one handle with that of the stretcher in a most convenient manner. The frame of the cover is jointed, and can be folded inside the stretcher without adding materially to its bulk.

Every hospital and main guard should be in possession of these litters, and they are peculiarly well adapted to Indian cantonments, where the roads are, as a rule, excellent. The weights of this litter are as follows:—Stretcher 29 lbs., litter 130 lbs. Two bearers can easily lift the whole with a patient in it over small obstacles.

Section II.—Concluding Observations on Hand-Wheel Litters.

For any wheeled stretcher to be accepted as a satisfactory article of field-hospital equipment, the litter part of the conveyance must possess all the qualities of a good stretcher; it must be capable of being rapidly and securely mounted on its wheeled support, and as rapidly dismounted when necessary; it should be so balanced on its wheels as to be easily drawn or pushed by a single bearer; the effect of jolting in passing over uneven ground must be provided against on the stretcher and wheels being combined; while strong enough to resist the ordinary shocks of field use. The wheeled stretcher complete must be light enough with a patient upon it to be carried by two bearers in case of ditches, or other impediments to progress on wheels, being met with; it should be capable of standing on its own support, in case the bearer has to temporarily leave his charge, as, for example, when a bearer with another wheeled litter requires assistance; it should not be costly, so that a sufficient number may be readily provided; it should be so contrived that none of the minor parts are likely to be lost or disarranged; and the whole should be capable of being folded and secured together so as to constitute a suitable package for conveyance on board ship or in store wagons. It is unlikely, however, that this class of conveyance will ever form part of the equipment for field service again.

Qualities required in a military hand-wheel litter.

CLASS III.—PACK ANIMAL AMBULANCE TRANSPORT.

CHAP. VI.

The division of ambulance transport effected by animals.

We next come to the conveyances in which the transport is accomplished, not by means of men, but of quadrupeds. These conveyances naturally become at once divided into two very distinct classes. In the first of these, not only the removal, but also the sustaining of the patients is directly effected by the animals; in the second, the patients are sustained in vehicles or otherwise, resting on the ground, and the removal only is effected by the animal. In the former, the conveyances which carry the patients are themselves *carried* by the animals; in the latter, the conveyances are not thus supported, but are *drawn* by the animals, or if partly also sustained by them, as in the instance of two-wheeled vehicles, it is only comparatively in a small degree that the powers of the animals are taxed in this respect. The first division, comprising *conveyances borne by animals*, constituting the third class of sick conveyances in general, will be now considered.

The quadrupeds chiefly used in carrying conveyances for ambulance transport are elephants, camels, mules, and horses. The two latter are employed in all climates, elephants and camels being used almost exclusively in tropical and subtropical countries. The Indian elephant has alone been employed for transport purposes, the African variety is not apparently capable of being rendered available for such a purpose. The camel is used both in Asia and in Africa, and is the only available means of transport in districts where wide sandy plains exist, or between countries divided by extensive deserts.

Saddles.

It is obvious that the conditions and circumstances of sick and wounded men render it necessary that some artificial support shall be interposed between them, and the sharp projecting spines and shelving backs and sides of the animals just mentioned, so that the patients may be conveyed with comparative ease and security. The supports or conveyances which have been devised for this purpose are of various kinds, and have certain leading varieties of form. The support may consist of a saddle or level pad, adapted to the shape of the animal's back, acting, itself, as a seat; or supporting a litter placed above it; or it may be a seat or litter suspended from a pack saddle and held in position by the side of the animal, being balanced by another similar conveyance on the opposite side; or it may be supported between extended poles or shafts, while the ends of these shafts are caused to rest upon the backs of two animals, one in front, and the other behind the conveyance.

Peculiarities in the size, mode of progression, and habits of the animals which are employed in carrying sick and wounded, lead to corresponding differences in the forms and qualities of the seats and litters for the sick which are placed upon them. Indeed, the kinds and shapes of these contrivances have usually such definite relations to the animals to which they have been adapted that, in considering them, it will be most convenient, first to take a separate glance **at** the characteristics, so far as they concern ambulance transport, of each of the animals which have been mentioned, and then to describe the particular equipment which is in ordinary use with them.

The special circumstances under which the several animals employed for carrying sick and wounded, or the conveyances borne by them, are particularly serviceable, will be remarked upon as each animal and its conveyance comes to be described. But it may be here noticed as a general rule that no conveyances borne by animals are capable of being employed during an action nearer to the fighting line than the places which have been fixed upon for collecting stations. Elephants and camels will not stand firing near them, and the steadiest and most practised mules would be rendered too restive by the noise of the rifle fire, and guns close at hand, even if other circumstances rendered their presence on such occasions admissible to allow wounded men to be laid upon the litters borne by them without the greatest difficulty and danger. But stationed at the collecting stations, this class of conveyance with good animals and a sufficiency of bearers, is capable of affording very efficient help by conveying the wounded from the field of action to the dressing station or post of surgical assistance, which would be a mile or so to the rear. It is, however, only adapted for short distances. After a combat has ceased, the animals employed in bearing litters can not only be taken close to the wounded who remain lying on an open field, but often **can** be led to situations which no wheeled carriage could approach, and **in** which **even bearers** would **find** it **difficult** to move along **with patients carried on stretchers.**

Section I.—Elephant Ambulance Transport.

The elephant is a very efficient carrier for slight cases and for convalescents. They are used principally in India, and have followed armies from the most ancient times, but being scarce and expensive they are generally required for pure transport purposes. The female is preferred to the male, which is liable at times to be "musty" and dangerous. Tractable, intelligent, powerful and obedient, the elephant is safe and reliable. The average load for an elephant is 1,000 lbs., **a** first-class animal will carry up to 1,400 lbs. His paces are even and accurate, **an**d when driven at his average rate, four or five miles an hour, the motion **is** comparatively slight; it is, however, very considerable **when** the animal

CHAP. VI.

rises from his knees or goes down on them to discharge his load.

Sick and wounded may be carried by the elephant on pads, howdahs, and charjamahs.

Pads.

Pads. These are large canvas bags stuffed with hay or grass, and neatly adapted and girthed to the back of the elephant, and they are an invariable accompaniment of the animal, the other forms of carriage being placed on the pad. On each side of the pad there is a rope fastened, and this is the only means by which those riding can hold on.

Howdahs.

Howdahs are wooden constructions placed on a pad, and covered in by a roof. For the carriage of sick they are safe, but being limited in space are not often used.

Charjamahs.

Charjamahs are double-seated benches, where the patients can sit back to back, and are kept in a safe position by resting their feet on a footboard, and being supported by a breast strap. This is the best form of carriage for sick purposes, and the load is evenly distributed over the animal's back.

For loading sick or wounded on elephants, the mahout (attendant) should invariably make the animal kneel down, and both sides should be laden simultaneously, and when loaded the animal should be at once moved off, and not kept standing.

The health of the elephant.

In health, the elephant is always swaying from side to side, the eye is bright and keen, and the white patch on the trunk is clear and distinct. Elephants are very liable to sore backs, especially when on short and irregular rations, and during the rains. Their food is a chupatti (cake) made of 20 lbs. of wheaten flour and molasses, and sugar cane, hay and green food. The mahout usually knows most about his elephant, and though it is prudent to overlook him, it is unwise to interfere.

Elephants are occasionally turned to account for hospital purposes in India, such as taking out convalescents, to give them the benefit of fresh air and change of scene.

SECTION II.—CAMEL AMBULANCE TRANSPORT.

Camel ambulance transport.

These ambulance transport animals live in a zone of about 1,000 miles in width, extending from Morocco on the west to China on the east. They are of two kinds, the single-humped camel or dromedary and the double-humped camel or Bactrian camel. The Bactrian camel is found principally in the northern part of the zone alluded to, exclusively from ancient Bactria, now Turkestan, to China. The dromedary or Arabian camel is found along the entire southern side of the zone as far as Africa and India. The Bactrian camel is the larger, more robust, and is more fitted to carrying heavy burdens than is the dromedary, which is more delicate, and is swifter and better adapted for riding purposes.

Camels are generally attached in considerable numbers as beasts of burden to armies taking the field in the eastern countries of the world. The remarkable ease and security with which they are able to travel over dry, hot, stony, and sandy regions, owing to the peculiar construction of their padded feet, enables them to be serviceable in some countries where the hoofs of horses and mules would be quickly rendered brittle and destroyed. Other advantages derived from the peculiar conformation and habits of these animals are the ease with which heavy weights, ranging from 400 lbs. to 800 lbs., are carried by them. A stout camel is said to be able to carry a burden of 800 lbs. at the rate of three miles an hour, and some camels are stated to be equal to carrying 1,000 to 1,200 lbs. The camel, like the elephant, will refuse to proceed, if loaded beyond a weight proportionate to his strength. In India the average load of a camel is 400 lbs., and the rate of movement 2½ miles an hour. With a rider only, the camel attains great speed, and is able to travel 12 miles an hour, or even faster on occasion. They have the power of abstaining from drinking for long periods together, and of satisfying their hunger by means of the wildest vegetation, so that they can travel through countries destitute of verdure, or streams of water; and lastly, their powers of endurance are very great, and enable them to keep up long marches for many days in succession without inconvenience. There are other qualities which make camels most valuable property to their owners, but which cannot be taken into account as regards their value for ambulance purposes. The special objection, as regards the use of these animals, at least the ordinary class of them, for conveying sick and wounded is their peculiar mode of progression. The camel in walking, at each step raises the two legs on the same side of the body, not absolutely at the same instant, but one so immediately after the other that they appear to be both lifted up together, and the repetition of this action, first on one side and then on the other, causes an alternate depression and elevation of the corresponding sides of its body. This up and down movement of the two sides of the animal becomes the source of considerable fatigue to a rider, especially if he is not accustomed to the motion. It is not so much felt, however, when a person is carried in a well balanced conveyance confined to one side of the animal, as it is by a person sitting on the animal's back; but still, it is usually felt sufficiently to be a source of inconvenience to an invalid. This awkwardness of gait and "rocking" movement does not, however, exist to an equal extent in all camels.

A man could ride a good saudnee or riding camel 40 miles with less fatigue than he could ride a baggage camel for five miles. It is reported that a man on a good riding camel can carry in each hand a glass full of water without any being upset, so little jolting is there in the animal's mode of movement. The ease or awkwardness of camel conveyance entirely depends on the kind of camel used. Sir Samuel Baker has noted the existence of corresponding varieties in the modes of movement of camels in Africa. "There is the same difference," he writes, "between a good hygeen, or dromedary, and a

CHAP. VI.

Camel ambulance transport.

baggage camel, as there is between the thoroughbred and the cart horse."—("The Nile Tributaries of Abyssinia," ch. 5, p. 99.)

Another disadvantage as regards the use of these animals for ambulance transport is the waste of carrying power when applied to sick or wounded requiring to lie down; for while the camel can carry as much as two or three ordinary mules when carrying stores, none of the camel ambulance conveyances hitherto constructed have enabled the animal to carry more sick in a recumbent position than would be the burden of one large mule. This, however, hardly applies to the case of patients who are able to sit up, for some conveyances are so arranged that four patients can be carried sitting; and even when carrying litters, the loss is in some measure compensated by the fact of the animal eating less than would be eaten by two mules and by his thriving on coarser foods, as coarse, indeed, as those eaten by the ass. On the whole, however, camels must be regarded as animals only to be used for ambulance transport purposes in countries where horses or mules are not procurable, or not suitable on account of the peculiar features of the country, whether as regards its soil or nature of its vegetation through which it is necessary for the sick to be transported, and where, moreover, draught carriages are not admissible. There is economy as regards labour and cost, when the use of camel conveyances is compared with the employment of dandies and ambulance bearers; but nearly all the advantages to the patients, which exclusively appertain to this latter mode of carriage, and which have been fully described in a former part of this work, are unavoidably sacrificed when carriages borne by camels are employed.

Particular Forms of Camel Carriage.

Larrey's litters.

Larrey's Egyptian Camel-litters.—In the winter of 1798–99, when the French troops in Egypt under General Buonaparte were preparing for a campaign in Syria; Larrey, the Surgeon-in-Chief, found himself obliged to organise an ambulance establishment, and to employ camels for effecting the transport, they being the only animals adapted to the country and to the habits of the natives. Speed of conveyance was an essential requisite, in order that the wounded might be removed without any delay out of the risk of casual attacks by Arabs, as well as from the chances of suffering from hunger and thirst. Larrey experienced insurmountable difficulties in his efforts to obtain some form of ready-made carriage sufficiently light for the animal to travel with speedily, and at the same time easy enough for his patients. At last he got a hundred panniers constructed for the purpose. They had the general appearance of ordinary camel-trunks, but they were made to open and fasten in such a way that sick or wounded could be easily placed and securely carried in them. When required for the carriage of a patient in a recumbent position, one end of the litter was let down and supported, drawbridge-fashion, at the requisite angle by two iron racks, one on **each** side, so as to afford the necessary length. These conveyances were suspended by flexible leathern bands, two on each side, one before, the other behind the animal's hump. By this arrangement the animal's movements in progression **were** not impeded, **while two** wounded men could be easily placed in the panniers on its two sides by making the camel kneel down for their reception, in accordance with the ordinary habit of the animal when being loaded with baggage.

The following illustrations, which are selected from the sketches in Baron Larrey's Memoirs,* will serve to show the forms of conveyance adopted by him on this occasion :—

Fig. LXVIII.—Larrey's Egyptian Camel-litter. The animal is sitting down, and the litter shown on one side is open, ready for the reception of a patient.

Kujawahs.—The name "kujawah"† has been given to this class of conveyance from a kind of hamper in which fruit and **stores are** sometimes **conveyed** to India. The kujawah **as here described is not used** so much for the transport of sick and wounded at the present time as for the stores and equipment of a force on the march, but during the last Afghan War they were resorted to in consequence of the sickness among the dooley-wallahs. They are of two kinds, corresponding with the litters and cacolets carried by mules, one kind being constructed so that the patient may be carried in a recumbent, the other kind for patients in a sitting posture.

---

* "Mémoires de Chir. Mil. et Campagnes de D. J. Larrey," Paris, tome i., 1812.

† Mr. Brett mentions that the name of "kujawah" has been given to these conveyances from a kind of hamper used in Afghanistan, in which fruit is sometimes **conveyed to India.**

204   *Indian Camel Kujawahs.*

CHAP. VI.   The following drawings exhibit the pattern of kujawahs for
────────   sick and wounded used in the Punjab :—
Kujawahs.

Fig. LXIX.—Camel Kujawah used in the Punjab for the carriage of sick soldiers lying down.

Construction   Kujawahs are constructed of very simple materials. The
of kujawahs.   kujawah used as a litter consists merely of a frame of wood,
roughly but securely put together, with the sides and bottom
filled up by stout cord interlaced or by strong canvas. Some
iron rings are fixed into the framework for holding the ropes by
which the conveyances are secured to the animal. Each recumbent
kujawah is furnished with long legs, not prolonged from
the ends, as they would then interfere with the shoulders and
thighs of the animal in walking, but from about the middle
third of the litter. These legs are an important part of this
form of kujawah, for they serve to elevate it, when the litter
with a patient placed in it is standing on the ground, to a
sufficient height to be secured to the camel after the animal has

kneeled down to receive it. The necessity of lifting it up or otherwise causing disturbance or risk of injury to the patient

*Fig. LXX.—Camel Kujawah used in the Punjab for the carriage of two sick soldiers sitting.

is thus avoided. They also assist in keeping the litter steady and maintaining it in position on the camel's back, and so lessen the amount of shaking to the patient while the animal is in motion.

The common bed, or charpoy, used by the natives of India, is easily converted into a camel litter by turning the legs upwards, and then connecting these latter together with a piece of rope, so as to form sides to the conveyance. Charpoys have not unfrequently been turned to account in the manner described in cases of emergency.

* The original drawings, from which the two engravings of the pattern kujawahs for carriage of sick soldiers in the Punjab have been copied, were kindly sent to me by Surgeon-Major-General W. M. Webb in May, 1865, then Surgeon and Secretary to the Principal Medical Officer, Her Majesty's Forces, India.

Chap. VI.

Kujawahs for patients sitting.

The kujawah for carrying patients sitting is made of similar materials to the litter kujawah just described. Sometimes it is made in the form of an arm-chair, as in the Punjab pattern, with the seat wide enough for two patients to sit upon it side by side. The seat is contrived and arranged so as to assume an inclination backwards or towards the spine of the camel, and thus to add to the security of those carried. In this form the legs of the patients sitting hang down in front of the kujawah, and foot-pieces are usually added to give them additional firmness in their seats. Cross bands are applied to prevent the patients from falling out in front.

Another kind of kujawah that has sometimes been used for the transport of sick soldiers consists of a simple square frame with a wooden floor, its sides being either made of wood or filled in with interlaced cordage. A sort of box, open at the top, is thus formed, within which the person sits in a half doubled-up position. This conveyance is really only suited for the carriage of persons in health, and during the Indian Mutiny they not unfrequently were so employed in some parts of India for hurrying forward troops to places where their services were most urgently required. They are only fit to be turned to account for invalids in the absence of conveyances of a more suitable kind.

Fig. LXXI.—Camels carrying men sitting in kujawahs on the line of march.

Position of patient in a litter-kujawah.

When the litter kujawahs for recumbent patients are employed, the patient's head is placed on that part of the conveyance which is nearest to the hind quarters of the animal, a direction opposite to that in which it is placed in a mule litter. By this rule being attended to, the patient's head is never lowered unduly, and the jolting is much lessened, when the camel is in the act of kneeling down or rising. In kneeling down, the animal descends first on the knees and afterwards on the haunches.

Brett's Camel-kujawahs or Camel-doolies.—Mr. Brett, of the

Bengal Medical Service, Surgeon to the Governor-General's bodyguard, in the year 1839, contrived and had constructed some kujawahs, which he called "*camel-doolies*," for the carriage of the sick soldiers on the line of march. Mr. Brett states that they proved most satisfactory conveyances, and that "the experiment succeeded in every way as the most comfortable and safe mode of invalid travelling I have heard or read of."*

The following is a short description of their construction:— Construction of Brett's cane doolies.

Fig. LXXII.—Brett's Camel-dooley attached to a camel by its straps, and still further secured by a strong rope passed through iron rings, and crossed over the saddle. The curtains which hang from the roof of the litter are not shown in the drawing. (*a, a,* straps; *b, b,* rope; *c, c,* iron rings.)

wooden framework, adapted by its shape to the flanks of the animal, and strengthened by iron bands in the direction of the

---

* Notes to a Practical Essay on some of the Principal Surgical Diseases of India. Calcutta, 1840, page 505.

chief strains. The framework at the bottom, and also of a portion of the sides of the litter, was filled up with canework, the remainder with strong tent cloth varnished. The inside was lined with cushions; a light framework covered with doosootie cloth and painted white formed a shade or roof over the litter, from the sides of which depended curtains like the ordinary dooly curtains. The litters were buckled on precisely in the same manner as camel trunks, by means of thick straps made of buffalo hide. Four strong iron hooks, two on each litter, and a chain would, as Dr. Brett has suggested, have probably been preferable when fastened over the saddle or pullan, being equally secure as the straps, and leaving more room for the patient. The litter was sufficiently long to accommodate a person lying at full length in it.

The sketch sufficiently illustrates the plan and construction of Brett's camel doolies.*

Camel Saddles.

Are of various forms, from the simplest native pattern to the double saddle issued by the Government. A great deal has been written, and much reported with reference to the carriage of sick by camel saddles, and the many objections to it. It may at once be stated that no man, even if he be mounted on the best hygeen, will be comfortable if it be the first time he has been in the saddle, any more than he would be at his ease the first time he is carried by a horse. Before destroying the reputation of camel carriage it is well worthy of consideration whether a little attention might not be paid to teaching officers and men the nature of the camel, and accustom them in some degree to its paces. A great deal of discredit falls on the transport, when in reality it is the person carried who is to blame.†

The native pad saddle is composed of two pads connected over the spine and supported by a framework of wood with a high pummel and cantle; it is quite suitable for footsore men, if they only knew how to ride in it.

In India there are issued large saddles carrying two men sitting astride, similar to that used by the Egyptian Camelry. They answer well, with the above reservation, for the footsore and weary.

In the Suakin expedition camels were fitted with cacolets and litters, and in the A.M.D. Reports, 1884, p. 304, Brigade-Surgeon-Lieutenant-Colonel Riordan, commanding No. 3 Field Hospital, writes as follows:—"The camel ambulance transport attached to the hospital consisted of 13 pairs of litters, and 44 pairs of cacolets. The camel cacolets consist of a pack saddle, and on either side a jointed or hinged seat

---

* The sketch is copied from the work before quoted. Three other illustrations are furnished in the same work for the purpose of still farther elucidating the construction of these litters.

† For general observations on saddles, see p. 223.

on a strong iron frame, padded, weight 112 lbs. The patient is secured in the seat by means of leather straps; he can only travel in a sitting posture. The pack saddles of the cacolet are of a universal pattern, but not so the backs of the camels upon which they are placed; in fact the shape of a camel varies much,—more so than with any other beast of burden; and to have the ambulance transport efficient much time should be spent in fitting the pack saddles to which the cacolets are attached. This should be done at the time of issue. One great advantage of the cacolet fittings is, that the camel having them on is at the same time available for carrying a load—water, tents, &c.

"The present camel litters are unserviceable as a means of transport for the sick and wounded. They are attached on either side of a pack saddle of the same pattern as that used for a cacolet, but they stand too far out from the animal's side, and the majority of camels, some more than others, give a swaying or pitching motion to the litters, so as to have the same sickening effect as caused by a ship rolling at sea. It is such as to disturb a fracture or bring on hæmorrhage from a wounded lung.

"Camels, especially when alarmed, are likely to crowd together, and when weakly constituted contrivances are projecting from their sides, they get knocked together, broken or entangled, and so the patients may come to grief. Moreover, in these litters persons on foot cannot afford assistance (owing to the height of the beast), such as might be done in the case of mule litters were an attendant walking alongside. The motion, while the animal is getting up or kneeling down is very trying to a helpless patient. This is more felt, owing to the position of the occupant in a litter than in a cacolet. The framework is too flimsy, and the bed of the litter too broad; this gives a feeling of insecurity, and alarms the patient. The hood is too near the face of the individual carried to allow a free current of air.

"The means of securing the joints with iron pins, which are frequently lost, is imperfect. These pins are attached by cord which gets cut by the hinges."

Italian Camel Saddle.

In Africa, the Italians use the camels for ambulance transport purposes, and arrange that each animal shall carry three slightly wounded or sick persons.

The carriage consists of two ordinary cacolets hung on to a pack saddle. At the part between and over the spine of the animal is arranged a saddle upon which a man can sit supporting his feet by stirrups. In front, and behind this saddle, two pairs of arms branch upwards and outwards for a distance of 4 feet. Each of these arms is jointed for the convenience of carriage. To the upper ends is attached a small "top," of

CHAP. VI.

An Italian camel saddle.

canvas, bracing them, and drooping all round is sufficient loose canvas curtain to cover the three men carried. This canvas curtain is divided down the centre for convenience in opening and closing. The men are supported in the cacolets by straps in the usual manner, and additional security is

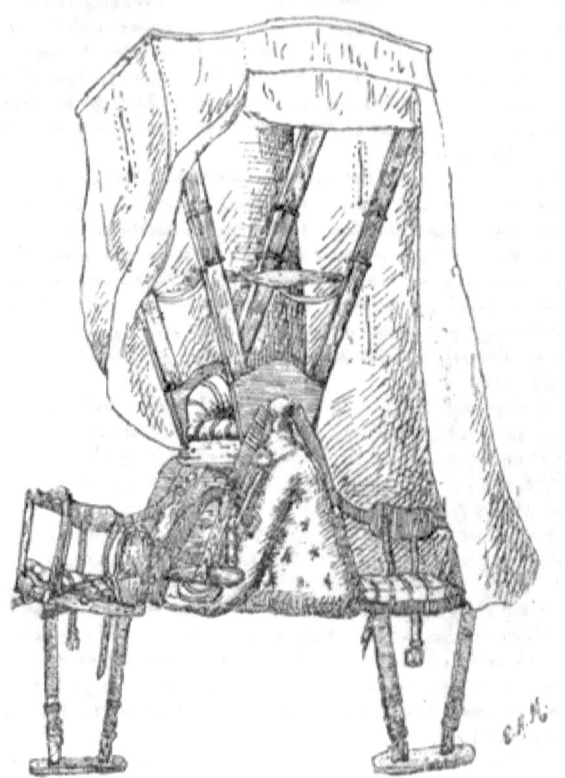

Fig. LXXIII.—Italian Camel Saddle.

arranged for **the man occupying** the saddle by similar straps arranged **round the** canvas supports.

To load this saddle, the patient to occupy the centre takes up his position first, and the cacolets are loaded subsequently and together.

Mosley's Crates.

Mosley's crates.

These are an ingenious invention of Colonel Mosley, of the Bengal Staff Corps, and are adapted for the carriage of sick and wounded men, as well as to other forms of army transport. There is no doubt, as will have been noticed from what has been alluded to previously, that there remains very much to be desired to improve camel sick transport from the point of view of comfort to the sufferer, and of ease to the camel. Mosley's crates are a distinct advance in this direction.

For sick transport purposes there are three forms of crate:—

        Lying-down crate.
        Sitting-up crate.
        Sitting-up crate for mules.

Lying-down Crates.—These consist of two crates 5 feet 6 inches long, 1 foot 10 inches wide, made of wood, both crates

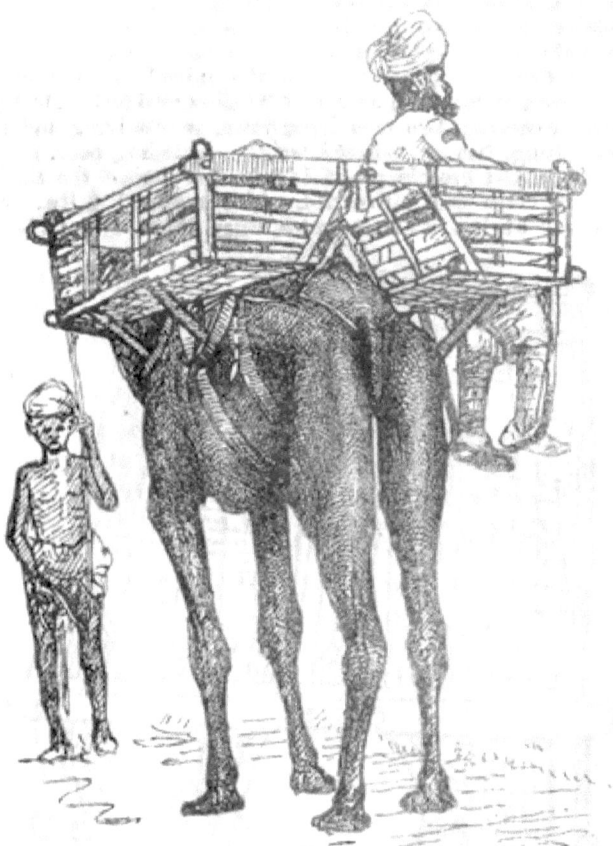

Fig. LXXIV.—Camel crate saddle for two men to lie down at full length, or for one to lie at full length, while the other sits up.

being connected in front and behind by a rigid wooden **bar** (*see* Fig. LXXIV). These are placed upon two angular supports attached to a pad which rests on the angle of the ribs of the

Mosley's crates.

camel on each side, leaving the spine free. The distance between the crates is 6 inches, but it necessitates the patients being carried rather higher than in the ordinary kajawah. For carrying two men in a lying down posture, but very cramped up, the transport department in the Punjab, and at Quetta, had a loose crate, 4 feet 6 inches in length and 5 feet 9 inches in breadth, across the camel, weighing about 105 lbs.; this, again, rode on the loose native country camel pad, the average weight of which is 89 lbs., making a total weight of 194 lbs. Owing to the native pad saddle being without girths—loose on the camel's back—and the transport crate being placed loose on this pad, there was always great risk of the whole crate capsizing; to obviate this danger in some measure the crate was made to ride as low as possible on the camel's sides, thus causing excessive breadth across the animal, amounting, in some cases, to as much as 5 feet 9 inches or 6 feet. Mosley's crates for carrying two men lying down, or one lying and the other sitting, has an extreme weight—including pads, girths, neck strap, and breeching—of 130 lbs., as against the similar transport crate and native pad, which weighs 194 lbs., or a saving of 64 lbs. These crates carry their own pads, or

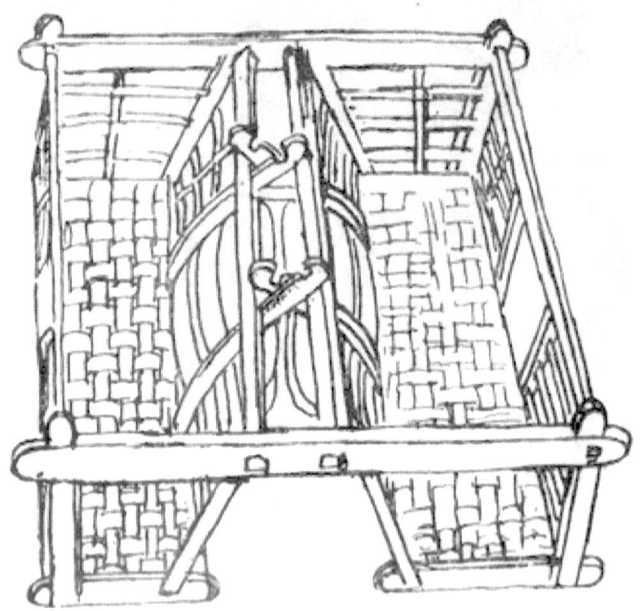

Fig. LXXV.—Perspective view of camel crate for patients lying down.

saddle, firmly sewn on to them, and being further secured by two very powerful girths, they admit of being carried high on the animal's back, without there being any chance of capsizing. About 6 inches only separate the crates in which the men lie, instead of the whole width of the camel's back, as is the case in the transport camel crate or kujawah. In fact, notwithstanding that Mosley's crates give those conveyed more space, the lateral breadth across the camel is very much reduced.

Mosley's Sitting-up Camel Crate.—This crate, constructed to carry two or four men in a sitting posture, and including all the accessories of saddle and foot-rests, weighs 88 lbs.

Fig. LXXVI.—The "Mosley" sitting-up camel crate.

It consists of two arched supports (*see* Fig. LXXVII), one in front and one behind, and to both of which are attached the saddle pads—these resting as in the former case on the angles of the ribs on both sides, leaving the spine free. At the points where the supports meet one another over the animal's back there lies a straight wooden support parallel with the camel's spine. From this, at each end, two branches of the crate fall

Chap. VI. outwards to one placed on each side and attached to the seat

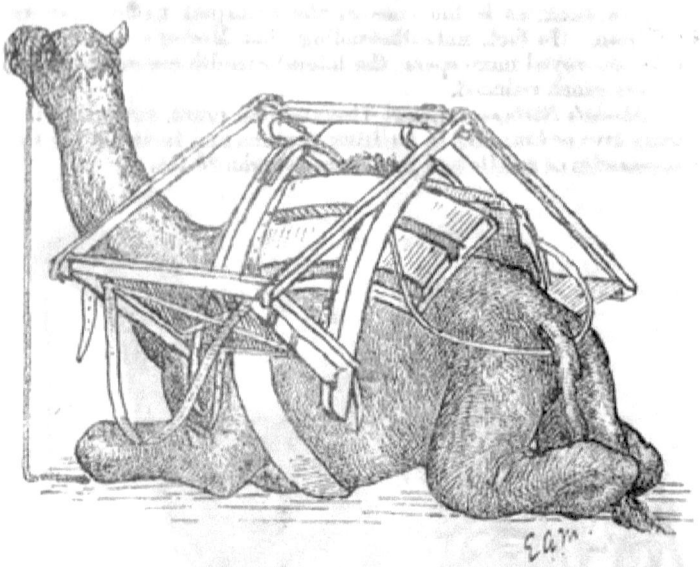

Fig. LXXVII.—Sitting-up crate, perspective view.

of the crate, which is also firmly fixed to the saddle, and form the sides. From the seat on each side foot-rests are provided.

Mosley Mule Crate.—A sketch of which is shown has an average weight of 39 lbs., and Colonel Mosley states, "That owing to the crate saddles never swinging, shifting, or being out of place, a good average mule can carry, without getting sore-backed or breaking down, a load fully double the present regulation weight for such an animal, and doing an average march (say) 15 miles every day."

Girthing. In girthing these crate saddles care must be taken that it is done correctly. The girths should be crossed X by fastening each girth on the front tongue on the one side, and on the back tongue on the other. It is best, after placing the saddle on the camel, to girth the animal as lightly as convenient by a man standing on the ground—after which the man should stand with one foot on each seat of the saddle and over the camel. By this means his weight will cause the saddle to settle well into its place, and from this position he can girth the animal securely, but care must be taken not to girth too tightly. It is well here, as in all cases connected with camel sick transport, to tie the animal's fore-leg in the usual way. One neck girth is then to be passed round the camel's neck, close to its body, and drawn tight by a leather thong passed through the iron eye at the top of the front arch of the saddle. The breech is attached to the two hooks, at the back of the saddle, passing under the tail.

Mule crates are placed on the animals in a similar manner, but must be girthed from the ground by a man standing.

There are four small holes in the arms of the mule crate intended to receive four iron pins, a few inches long. On these are carried the pieces of a tent pole, with a tent thrown over them, boxes being placed underneath all. By this means a good mule could carry the necessaries for a dressing station. At the **top** of the front arch is a hook for carrying the rein, and this used when halting, or at the end of the march, will effectually prevent the animal attempting to lie down **to** roll.

Under both camel and mule crate saddles are **four arms to draw** out when required for the foot-rest straps.

Colonel Mosley writes in reference to the many advantages of his invention as follows:—" Every animal furnished with the transport service pack saddle in addition to the actual weight of the load, is distressed by unnecessary leverage on its sides, amounting in some cases to the equivalent of doubling the weight of the load. This is no exaggeration. For example, suppose a transport pack saddle placed on a horizontal bar with two boxes of considerable size, weighing 80 lbs. each, suspended, as they would be, on the two hooks on either side of the saddle by their upper and inner edges, the lower inner edges would tend to meet one another. Then the number of pounds pressure on the centre of their inner sides required **to** separate the boxes to a distance sufficient to admit the body **of** the pack animal, will represent the amount of needless pressure that would be on its sides when standing still, and which would be greatly increased by the slight swing and jerk **of the** load when in motion over good roads, and be still further in**creased over bad** ground. In my crates not **an ounce of** side **pressure has the** animal to bear.

"**This fact,** combined with the steadiness **and non-shifting of the load on** the crate saddle, enables animals **with my saddle to** carry loads without getting galled **and breaking down under** continuous marching with loads **of double the regulation** weight.

"**I believe** I am right in supposing that in fixing the regulation weight that should be carried by an animal, the effect of side leverage pressure which, up to the present time, practically exists, was not considered, and that it has not yet been officially estimated what are the powers of an average mule, for example, supposing it to be possible to altogether relieve him of side pressure and bad loading, as I have done."

There is no doubt that this side leverage pressure has not been given the important attention it really deserves—and it appears to be a matter well worthy of the attention of those responsible for the transport of the Army.

Advantages claimed by inventor.

CHAP. VI.

Side-leverage pressure.

The importance of lowering the amount of side-leverage.

The two figures here depicted show diagrammatically the meaning of side leverage pressure. In the Fig. *a* is a load carried on a crate, and it will be noticed that the points on the animal's back on which the weight constantly rests is the angle of the ribs, which is the most convenient for the mule, and allows of free breathing; in Fig. *b* is shown the present method of loading animals. With each inspiration the over-girthed animal has to debit his respiratory powers with exactly that

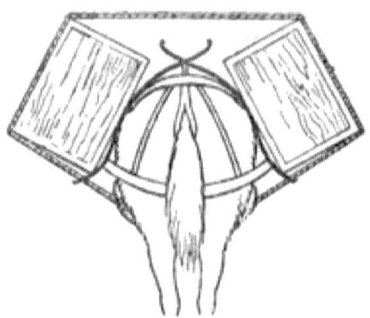

Fig. *a.*

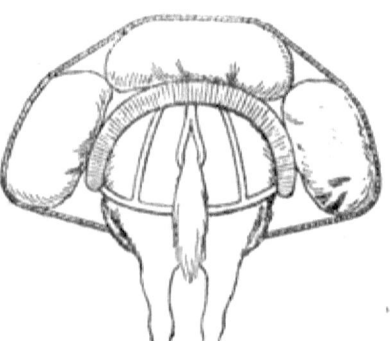

Fig. *b.*

Illustrations of side-leverage **pressure.**

Fig. LXXVIII.—Indian Pack **Saddle.**

amount of pressure that will raise the load sufficiently to allow him to expand his lungs. I[*] have constantly seen mules fail from this reason alone. The Shan tribes in Upper Burma do not girth their ponies, but carry their trade produce in long baskets hitched over the ponies' backs with breast and breeching straps to keep them in place when going over the mountain passes, and considering the size of the animals and the weight they carry; the work they do, and the distance they will travel over the roughest country without being "sick or

[*] Editor

sorry," is far greater, proportionately, than our transport animals can accomplish. Their huge saddles alone, which prevent the healthy function of a large portion of the skin area of their bodies, fill our transport sick lines with sore backs, and the other ills transport animals are subject to.

The value of the transport camel crates invented by Colonel Mosley has been shown to be considerable. At the Camp of Exercise at Delhi the Editor was entrusted by the Principal Medical Officer with the duty of experimenting with, and thoroughly testing, these crates for the purposes of sick transport. The conclusions arrived at were:—

Experiments at Delhi.

1. That the camel crates, both the lying-down and sitting-up varieties, were a distinct and considerable improvement on the kujawahs.
2. That there was no improvement in the pitching that the wounded man is liable to, when the animal rises from his knees, but that the crate being more securely fastened, there was less risk of the man being thrown out, than exists in the ordinary kujawah.
3. **That** comfort in **this or any** form of **camel-carriage** depends very much **on the** paces of **the** animal.
4. That the "sitting-up" crates were excellent, and **most** serviceable.
5. That the mule and pony crates failed only from the fact that the animals supplied by the transport department were not sufficiently large to carry the weight of two men with their rifles.
6. That the crate would be of great value, for the transport of field hospital tents and medical stores.

These crates are worthy of attention, and should sufficient encouragement be given, **there is little doubt that they could be vastly improved.** The single advantage of **the lessened pressure** should alone be sufficient to make them **the official pattern** for all future transport purposes.

Turkestan Saddle.

"A very ingenious model of transporting two men lying on stretchers on a camel was exhibited at the Brussels Exhibition by the Russian Governor and Commandant of troops in Turkestan.

Turkestan saddles.

"A framework consisting of two frames pivoted together at the top, so that they can open out to whatever width the animal's size may require, supports at the lower end of each frame a horizontal rest for a stretcher. These rests are **grooved**, and the stretchers easily inserted.

"The cloaks of the two patients are rolled and fixed round the camel's hump by two light side poles connected by lashings in front and rear. When the frame is placed on the camel it

CHAP. VI.

The Turkestan Saddle.

bears against these side poles, and the cloaks serve as a pad. The frame is secured beneath the belly by two lashings passing from one stretcher rest to the other.

"A ridge-pole resting on the top of the framework supports

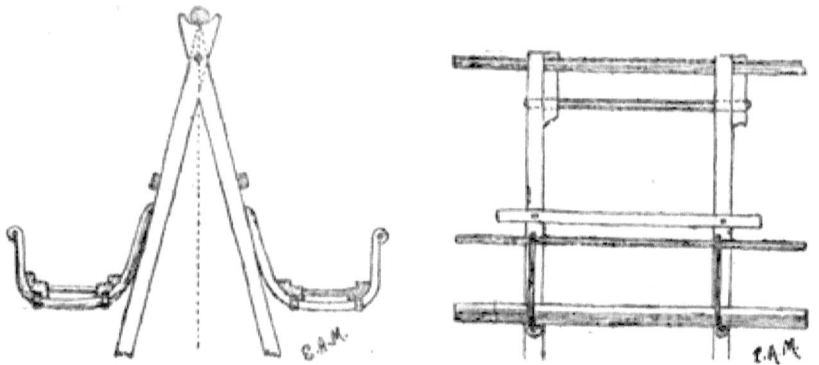

Fig. LXXIX.—The Turkestan Saddle.

a canvas covering, which, falling over the outside of the stretcher rests, serves the purpose of a shelter tent for the men lying below.

"The framework is lashed on the camel while he is kneeling, but the patients on their stretchers are not placed in the rests till the camel is on his legs, and they thus escape the swaying motion produced in other patterns when the camel rises."
—Brussels Report, 1876, p. 13.

SECTION III.—MULE AND PONY AMBULANCE TRANSPORT.

Mules preferable to horses for ambulance transport.

Mules regarded as beasts of burden for ambulance purposes.—Mules, if proper animals be selected, are to be preferred for ambulance purposes to horses or ponies, especially in mountainous districts, and over roads which are strewed with loose stones. The mule which is best fitted for carrying burdens is the produce of the male ass and the mare, and chiefly resembles the male parent in form. The mule resulting from the intercourse of the stallion and she-ass is a smaller, less hardy, and in all respects less useful animal. The countries in Europe in which mules are chiefly found are Spain, Portugal, and Italy. The Spanish mules are produced by a breed of asses of particularly fine shape and large size. Mules are also common in the East, and in the southern parts of America, but those which have been reared in the colder climates are found to be more fit for labour than those which have been reared in hot climates.

Mules walk well, and no animals, when carrying heavy

burdens, so easily pick their way, or are so sure-footed on bad roads, or can move along narrow paths and over restricted spaces with such safety. They are, indeed, independent of roads altogether. On good roads their pace is more uniform than that of the horse, and they are less liable to be startled whatever casualty may occur,—qualities of special importance where wounded or feeble patients are concerned. They, moreover, have advantages over horses of a general nature in reference to the circumstances of campaigning, for they are less subject to diseases, thrive better on rougher fare, live and work twice as long, and are constitutionally more hardy and enduring of prolonged fatigue.

CHAP. VI.

Qualities which render them preferable.

Mr. Bailey, of the Commissariat Department, who organised and conducted the duties of the transport establishments for the expeditionary force in China in 1860, testified in his report at the close of the campaign to the serviceable qualities of mules as transport animals, "Of all the animals used for transport purposes during the campaign, the mules sent from India were the best, and performed their work in the most satisfactory manner; they were hardy, and seldom afflicted with illness or other ailment."* And General Sir Hope Grant confirmed this report, stating that they were "undoubtedly the best."

In the frontier wars in India mules have been largely used for transport purposes, especially in the north-west, and also in Upper Burma. In the last country they suffered with the horses severely from "surra and kumri," a disease which affects animals in malarious districts. It was noted to occur at the same time that beri-beri affected the natives, the inference being that where the one is reported it is necessary to be on guard for the other.†

In South Africa donkeys, mules, and cattle are destroyed by the toetze fly. Dr. Geoffrey, I.M.S., recommends a hypodermic injection at the seat of the sting composed of—

R Liq. Ammon. Fort. .. .. ℥ ii
Liq. Morph. Hyd. .. .. ℥ ii
Aq. ad .. .. ℨ i

(Furse, p. 77)

The mule is deficient in speed, that is, it cannot gallop well, but this is no defect as regards the carriage of sick and wounded, whose circumstances demand a regular, steady, and even walk on the part of the animal carrying them. A more rapid pace, especially an uneven one, would be attended with intolerable jolting. Another objection frequently urged against the mule is

Want of speed and stubbornness of mules.

---

* See Mr. Bailey's report in the Appendix to the Report (1867) of the Committee on the Administration of the Transport and Supply Departments of the Army.
† Morris on Beri-beri. Transactions of Epidemiological Society of London, 1899.

CHAP VI.

its stubbornness. This quality, however, when it exists, seems usually attributable either to neglect in the breeding, or to bad after-treatment of the animal. A well-bred and properly tended mule is as thoroughly good-tempered and as easily managed as any creature employed in man's service. In Spain, where the greatest care is paid to rearing and keeping these animals, good mules are as gentle as the best horses in England.

Need of mule transport in certain positions.

In some situations, scarcely any other kind of transport can be found to take the place of mule transport. In the mountains of the Pyrenees, during the Peninsular war, no other means **were available** to the British troops for carrying away the **wounded** but the backs of mules; in some of the mountain campaigns of India mules have proved the most valuable means of conveyance; in the Crimea, in the long narrow ravines leading down to Sebastopol, along which no wheeled vehicles could pass, and over the plateau when the depth and viscidity of the mud rendered it impracticable for carts and wagons, no kind of transport proved so efficient, and at the same time so economical, for removing the wounded as the French system of transport by mules.

The French have relied entirely upon mules for transporting their sick and wounded in all their distant expeditions in Algeria, and have accorded the highest praises to their valuable services. It is, however, a point to be constantly borne in mind, that it is not every mule will answer for such service; the weight of a pair of cacolets or litters, with a couple of men lying upon them, not to mention the pack-saddle and its accessories, necessitates a certain size and stamina in the animal that is to carry them. The mules used for sick-transport in the French service are all large and robust animals, well trained, and equal in power to the demand which is made on their strength and endurance by the work in which they are employed.

Weights of loads carried by mules.

The weight which a mule can carry varies **very** much in **different** countries, and in different individuals, according to **breed.** A good Spanish mule, of proper age, is said **to be** able to travel for several months continuously with a weight **of** from **six** to eight hundredweight **on its back; but** only the best, full-sized, and well-limbed animals can accomplish this task. Mr. Darwin mentions, with regard to South American mules, that it is the custom for each animal in a troop to carry a load of 416 lbs. when the ground is level, but that in a mountainous country the mule's load is only about 300 lbs.* The Regulation weight carried by the English transport mule is 160 lbs. exclusive of pack saddle which weighs 62 lbs. Colonel Furse on page 83, in his work on Military Transport writes: "The carrying power of the mule is generally over-rated. . . . A

---

* "Narrative of the Surveying Voyages of H.M. Ships *Adventure* and *Beagle*. Passage of the Cordillera." Vol. 3.

good solid compact mule will carry 30 per cent. of its own weight." With regard to the animal's weight Harvey Riley considers that a mule 14¼ hands, to be in good working condition, should not weigh over 950 lbs., i.e., its total load should not be more than 285 lbs., but as will be shown later on, we expect efficiency in this class of transport when the mules have to carry nearly double that load, which is impossible, unless they are very specially selected, saddled, and loaded. It has been stated that 150 lbs. was found to form an average load for a mule in Abyssinia, although the mules imported for service with the batteries of 7-pounder mountain guns carried loads of 250 lbs. and upwards. The weight of the load carried by the field-pannier mule in the British service, when regiments take the field, is 190 lbs., but this is independent of the weight of the pack-saddle and harness.

Weight of mule in relation to weight it can carry.

The tendency of transport officials is to retain the better mules for army purposes, and the poorer ones for the ambulance purposes. As a consequence a first-class mule will be found carrying ammunition, and a third-class animal will be "told off" for the hospital; and this is not done with any intention, but as a consequence of a want of knowledge of the class of animal that will accomplish the work of the sick transport. There is no other form of transport that is so heavy and irksome. Analysing the weight placed upon a sick transport mule of the average size we find the following:—

Analysis of a regulation mule load.

	lbs.
Saddle and bridles	62
Cacolets 56 lb. (or litters 106 lb.)	56
Two men with field kit and rifles (at the very lowest)	300
	418

When wet 20 per cent. all round may be freely added.

It is generally laid down that the weight to be carried by horses and mules is 200 lbs., pack saddle included, and where forage is scarce or of an inferior quality, and the animals become progressively weaker, their loads must be lightened.

Only for very short journeys, and also as an occasional emergency arises, could the army mules, except those of the gun-mule type, carry 418 lbs., and it behoves every medical officer reckoning on the efficiency of his mule transport, to examine for himself whether the animals he receives are equal to their work or not.

It must at the same time always be remembered that mules are an expensive form of the carriage, that they are scarce, and that the class of animal required for hospital purposes may be more useful in some other branch, and in this way, by modifying their demands, and substituting other forms of transport, medical officers can assist the General Officer Commanding.

CHAP. VI.

East Indian mules.

Baggage mules abound in some of the mountainous parts of Eastern India, but not having the requisite size or strength, they cannot be turned to account for the carriage of European cacolets and litters, with a couple of sick or wounded men upon them. They were tried for this purpose experimentally, at Huzara in 1864, by Captain Hughes, commanding the Peshawur Mountain Battery, but were found to be quite incapable of sustaining such a load. At the Camp of Exercise at Delhi, in 1885, the mules supplied for ambulance purposes broke down entirely under the load, and were quite useless. These mules are thoroughly efficient for the tasks they have naturally to perform, for carrying supplies over rocky and precipitous defiles, or in the interior of a country where there are no roads, because their loads are properly proportioned to their size and power of endurance; but only a mule that is capable of carrying without distress a weight of from 400 lbs. to 500 lbs. can do the work required in the European mode of sick transport, and any attempt to get mules of less power to perform this service satisfactorily must always end in disappointment and loss.

The pack-saddle complete with bridle, pair of litters complete, and paillasses, together weigh 167 lbs. The weight of two men, at the moderate average of 10 stone each, 280 lbs., being added, gives 447 lbs. If the field kits, arms, accoutrements, &c., of each soldier be also carried, the weight would be increased 120 lbs. more, making a total of 567 lbs. But these articles ought not to be added to the mule's load, and the regulations arrange for spare mules to carry the knapsacks, &c., of patients under such circumstances.

Horses suitable for carrying sick men.

Horses as Beasts of Burden for Ambulance Purposes.—But if horses have to be employed instead of mules for carrying sick and wounded men, then animals of moderate size, stout-built, and compact in frame, sure-footed, hardy, and capable of enduring much fatigue, should be selected for the service when practicable. This is the description of animal which is found of most service in travelling over broken and irregular ground, and through hilly districts, and is necessarily the most suitable for carrying sick and wounded men under the ordinary circumstances of campaigning. Neither high mettle, showy action, nor speed are wanted for ambulance purposes; but a steady even gait, sufficient strength, power of endurance, with a tractable and equable temper, are the qualities most to be desired. The object in selecting animals of moderate size, such as ponies,* is chiefly to facilitate the process of putting disabled patients on their backs, and taking them off, as well as to diminish the risks of injury to them in case of accidental falls. It should

---

* A horse under thirteen hands in height, four inches being reckoned to the hand, and the measure being taken over the withers, is usually styled a pony; but in practice this definition is not always attended to. Horses of even fourteen hands in height are often designated ponies.

always be ascertained that ponies have been carefully trained before they are permitted to be employed in carrying sick or wounded patients. Some ponies are restive and unmanageable by nature, and can never be broken in to the steady and regular gait which is essential for the easy conveyance of feeble and suffering men; others, on the contrary, make good pack animals without any trouble. The same qualities which make a pony a serviceable pack animal for carrying stores, will also, as a rule, make him a useful one for purposes of ambulance transport.

Substitutes for Sick Conveyances of Regular Forms.—Saddles, or pads, of whatever description they may be, though they have occasionally under emergency been employed instead of regular conveyances, are quite unsuitable for the carriage of invalids on mules or horses. Invalids are not only incompetent for the exertion necessary to preserve their seat, but, what is of great importance, the erect position in which the trunk and head have to be maintained is calculated to induce faintness and the worse consequences to persons weakened by sickness or injury. Occasionally saddles have been employed for sick-transport purposes, but only because no better way of removing the patients concerned was at the time available. General Sir George Bell records in his published "Notes" the sufferings of the wounded of his brigade, whom he escorted, sitting on pack-saddles on mules, from one of the battle-fields high up in the Pyrenees to Alizondo, during the Peninsular war. The use of mule litters for military purposes, or of any other mode of mule carriage permitting a wounded man, even with such an injury as a fractured thigh, to assume a recumbent position, was then unknown. In a private letter, Sir George writes: "We had no ambulance vehicle—no other conveyance but the mules supplied by our commissary, with the usual common pack-saddle always in use for carrying packs of biscuit and kegs of rum. The wounded men were carried in the fashion I have stated out of the hills; two of them on a broad pack-saddle sitting astride, or both legs to one side, as the case might be, their wounds bandaged up and spliced as well as our surgeons could manage it at the time of this unexpected trial. There was no alternative—we could not afford efficient soldiers to carry the wounded."

In the early part of the Crimean war, when the sick became accumulated in large numbers, and it was necessary to remove them from the front at all hazards, and when from the state of the roads and other causes the heavy ambulance wagons could not be used, the horses of the cavalry were sometimes employed for transporting the patients to Balaklava on ordinary saddles. Under these circumstances it has happened that a debilitated man who had been carried from the tent in which he had been lying, and then lifted into his seat upon the horse, has died even before the sick from the several regiments of the division could be all got together for the cavalcade to leave the ground. Deaths also occasionally took place during the journey. These fatal events were manifestly due in a great degree to the effects produced on the very enfeebled frames of the men, by the change from the horizontal to the upright position. Unfortunately, the evil was unavoidable, for there were no other means available for the removal of the sick from camp, where to remain, under the circumstances of the time, was almost certain death for such patients. The horses in these instances were led by the dismounted cavalry soldiers. In old times, before the general introduction of wheeled vehicles, seats behind the saddles, or pillions, were often used for the conveyance of weakly persons.

Pillion seats. The pillion was sometimes made like a chair, with a support for the back of the person sitting upon it, and with a footboard suspended from it, on which the feet might rest, not unlike the seats still occasionally employed for children. In this way the invalid, sitting behind the horseman on the saddle, was relieved from all exertion in guiding or holding on to the horse, and received a certain amount of general support, which rendered his position less trying and painful. Had it, however, been possible to arrange contrivances of such a nature in the Crimea for the use of the sick, it is doubtful whether the horses, who were extremely enfeebled also, would have been able to carry the increased weight for the necessary distance, and, moreover, the evils of carrying extremely weak patients with the upper part of their bodies in an erect position would not have been remedied by such an arrangement.

Arab mode of removing wounded. The rapidity and sure manner in which the Arabs manage to carry off their wounded from a field of battle on the backs of mules or horses, without any regular mechanical conveyances, and with the aid only of the common pack-saddle, sacks and cords, which are used in carrying stores, have been a subject of frequent remark among the French during their contests with them in Algeria and Kabylia. Dr. Bertherand, Director of the School of Medicine of Algiers, has described at some length the manner in which the transport is effected.* The same method might be adapted anywhere with transport mules, in case of the absence, or of insufficiency in numbers, of the regular and authorised contrivances for removing wounded. The plan is briefly as follows :—The mule being ready saddled, two large sacks are stuffed full of straw, leaves, or grass. One of these sacks is then firmly corded on each side of the pack-saddle, and this is done in such a manner that the convexities of the two sacks, and the upper surface of the pack-saddle are all in the same horizontal plane. Any depressions between the saddle and the bags are made level by stuffing in hay and grass. This forms the litter. All that remains is to throw over all a cloak, so as to make the support soft and even for

---

* Campagnes de Kabylie. Histoire Méd. Chir. des Expéditions de 1854, 1856, et 1857, par le Dr. A. Bertherand. Paris, 1862, p. 117.

the patient, who is then placed upon it in a recumbent posture, across the animal, not parallel with the line of his walk. The litter formed in the manner described has quite length enough from side to side to carry the patient crosswise. Afterwards, as opportunity occurs, branches are arched over it, so as to protect the patient, in case of need, from sun or rain.

CHAP. VI.

Arab method of removing wounded.

Dr. Bertherand states that Europeans, as well as natives, who have travelled long distances in this fashion, declare that this mode of transport is very easy, and almost entirely free from jolts. If it be a wounded man who is thus carried, and he is suffering from a broken limb or such a severe injury as to be incapacitated from himself helping to preserve his position, so that it is necessary to take every precaution against accidental local displacement, the patient is securely tied to the litter, and, when thus fixed, he can be carried away out of reach of shot even at a gallop without risk, **or** excess of pain, from the movement.

The objection to such a method of transport would be its bulk, unfitting it for passing along narrow winding paths, or through crowded places, and the want of economy in using the animal's services for the transport of only one person. Exceptional circumstances in an open country, and the steadiness of support gained by the patient being placed across the animal, might on occasion render it desirable to have recourse to this mode of conveyance.

Mule Cacolets and Litters.

Mule-cacolets and Mule-litters.—The principal regular forms of conveyances used with mules and horses are mentioned in the Medical Regulations under the names of cacolets and litters. The former conveyances are also occasionally spoken of as mule-chairs, and the latter, using the French name, as litières. They have only been introduced among the articles of English ambulance equipment since the period of the Crimean war, and their introduction was then chiefly due to observation of the advantages of their employment by the French army in the East. The French appear to have originally derived the idea of these conveyances from the inhabitants of the Pyrenees, where the word "cacolet" is in ordinary use to signify a sort of pannier in which supplies, and occasionally persons, are carried on mules. It has been stated that the mule-chairs were designated "cacolets," from their resemblance in principle to the contrivance used for carrying milk ("càque au lait") by the peasants of Bordeaux; but good authorities consider that there is no foundation for such a derivation of the term. It has also been suggested that "cacolet" is a corruption of "cabriolet," the original meaning of which was a sort of little armchair. The term, however, is probably of local origin in the Pyrenees. Having found them of great value in their Algerian

Origin of mule-cacolets and litters.

Chap. VI

Mule-panniers.

Views of French officers on the use of mule-litters.

Mule-litters in the British service.

campaigns, the French subsequently adopted them as part of their regular field equipment for general service. This occurred some years previously to the Crimean war. In addition to the cacolets and litters here referred to, mule-panniers have occasionally been employed by the French for transporting patients. In the United States, and in Italy, special forms of mule-litters have also been employed. These several forms of conveyances will presently be described in detail.

The French officers, who have served in Africa, have always spoken in high praise of the use of mule cacolets and litters. The following passage regarding them occurs in a report by Marshal St. Arnaud on the reorganisation of the *Equipages Militaires*, dated Paris, Feb. 1852. "The use of the mule with a cacolet or litter was first adopted in Algeria. By means of these ingenious equipages hundreds of wounded, amputated, and sick soldiers have been transported in safety to our base of operations." Marshal Bugeaud was a warm advocate of the mule-litter, he compared the good they effected with what he witnessed in Spain, in 1814, when, in consequence of the want of transport suited to the ground, whole divisions had been obliged to leave their wounded on the field. So strongly did Marshal Bugeaud feel the bad effect which such neglect must produce, that he went so far as to say,—"Perhaps, the courage of our troops would not have sufficed for the conquest of Algeria, if we had not been able to save our sick and wounded from the Arabs." Marshal Bugeaud was led to recommend that the ambulance equipment of all the divisions of the French army, cavalry and infantry, should be exactly similar to that of the army of Africa, and that wheeled carriages should be attached to the reserves alone.

It was not without full inquiry and mature consideration that mule-chairs and litters were introduced among the conveyances of the British service. At an early period of the Crimean campaign it was reported home that the ambulance transport sent out with the troops had failed from various causes, and at the same time it was stated by numerous army surgeons and others[*] that the mule-chairs and litters in use by the French were acting very efficiently. In consequence of these reports the Director-General, Dr. A. Smith, sent out instructions to the principal medical officer in the field to convene a board of experienced medical officers for the purpose of reporting on the merits and demerits of the mule ambulance conveyances used in the French army. This board was composed of Inspector-General Dr. Hall, and the Principal Medical Officers of three divisions of the army. These officers made their report on the 20th of January, 1855, and it was greatly in favour of the conveyances under consideration. They reported that they considered the merits of the French cacolets and litters chiefly

---

[*] See Recommendations and Evidence in the Parliamentary "Report upon the State of the Hospitals of the British Army in the Crimea, &c." Lond. 1855.

consisted in their general applicability to the circumstances of warfare, in their admitting of the removal of sick and wounded from every description of ground, and over every kind of road where mules and horses can travel, and to the rapidity with which the removal could be effected over roads where wheeled carriages could not travel. On the other hand, the only demerits which they noticed were their uneasy motion in cases of serious gunshot injuries, and the liability of some of the animals to stumble or fall.

Col. Blane, Assistant Adjutant-General and Commandant at the head-quarters of the army, at the same time reported that "The cacolets and litters now in the French service appear to be by far the most perfect system which has yet been devised for the transport of sick and wounded with an army in the field."

Their first employment in the Crimea.

These recommendations led to patterns of the conveyances being obtained from the Director-General of Military Transport at Paris. Similar conveyances were then manufactured in England, and a supply of two hundred of them was in due course forwarded to the Crimea. After a sufficient time had elapsed, in September, 1855, the Director-General ordered another report to be furnished to him upon the qualities of the conveyances sent out from England, and the results of their use in the field. The Board, which consisted of the Principal Medical Officers of four divisions of the army, made their report on the 2nd of October, 1855. This report stated that "The Board, having personally tried the mule-chairs and litters, consider them better adapted than the wagons for the conveyance of the sick and wounded, provided that the mules are good-tempered, well-practised at the work, and sufficiently strong for it, with careful drivers;" and the Principal Medical Officer of the army, Sir J. Hall, in forwarding the report, remarked that, "if the ambulance transport be increased, I would suggest chairs and litters to be sent out in preference to wheeled carriages."

The men in charge of the mules.

The limitations and provisos introduced into the report of the Medical Board indicated defects which had been experienced in regard to both animals and drivers, principally, however, in regard to the latter, with whose efficiency the proper working of the conveyances themselves, as well as of the animals, was inseparably connected. Sir J. Hall, in forwarding the report of the Board, remarked, "The ambulance corps is imperfectly organised at present, and would not work well if the army were to take the field. It has not nearly the number of officers and non-commissioned officers that it ought to have to make it efficient. It is essentially a service of detail, and requires **not** only an additional number of non-commissioned officers, **but** that these non-commissioned officers should be sober, steady, trustworthy men." It is obvious, that however perfect may be a contrivance, the success of which depends upon the concerted efficiency and right action of other appliances or persons having to co-operate with it, the contrivance itself is

CHAP. VI.

Both mules and drivers require training.

always liable to be objected to, or even condemned, for imperfect results, which are really independent of itself, unless sufficient care is taken to investigate and appreciate correctly the sources of the failure. The Board, therefore, were only right, while speaking in praise of the mule-chairs and litters themselves, to call the attention of the authorities to the qualifying collateral provisions named in their report, for they are essential to the successful employment of mule conveyances for purposes of ambulance transport. It unfortunately has too often happened that on an emergency arising, necessitating a certain amount of sick-transport being despatched for service in the field, both animals and conductors have been without the necessary training and experience for the proper performance of their duties. The animals have been purchased in numbers at whatever market they could most readily be obtained, and the men have been enrolled in the service almost in an equally extemporised manner. But a hasty collection of animals for the purposes of sick-transport will never present the amount of efficiency which is requisite for the successful attainment of the objects for which they have been collected, nor can a body of men be found who will properly appreciate, by a rapid system of self-teaching, as it were, the necessities of the sick and wounded who are to be transported under their direction, nor can such men master the many details of attention which are essential for the proper care and preservation of the animals under their charge. Hurry in such matters invariably leads to confusion and loss, if not failure; and though after a time some of the men engaged may acquire the experience necessary for effective co-operation and right execution of duty, the experience so obtained is purchased at a high cost. But not only have ignorance of the nature of mule conveyances, and want of training in their practical employment, led to their being objected to for the transport of sick, but they have been sometimes condemned under circumstances where failure was an almost inevitable result of the manner in which they were tried. Some mule-litters and cacolets were sent to India, and were tried in the Madras Presidency. But there were no mules there to try them upon, and the conveyances were, therefore, put for observation upon a horse, and afterwards upon a camel. As might be expected, it was reported that the amount of jolting rendered carriage in them altogether insupportable. Mule-cacolets and litters were sent out to New Zealand during the Maori war in that country, but proved to be altogether useless. There were no mules in the country, nor animals suited for carrying them. To be able to judge fairly of any conveyance, not only must the contrivance itself be complete and in good order, but every adjunct that belongs to it, and is necessary for its efficiency, must be complete also, and in proper working order.

The termination of the war in the Crimea not long after the date of the report last quoted, by the medical officers there, prevented the further employment at that time of mule-conveyances; but the experience already gained was afterwards thought sufficient to warrant a decision for them to form part of the regular field hospital equipment of the British army.

It is necessary to urge the importance of ambulance mule transport being specially retained for this work when an engagement is imminent or even only probable. In the A.M.D. Reports for 1882, page 269, it is reported that, owing to the pressing exigencies of the service, the mules were often tired and overworked before starting. This should be avoided in the future.

The special construction of the conveyances themselves will now be described.

Cacolets.

Cacolets consist of folding chairs made to be hooked by pairs to the two sides of a pack saddle, and so to be carried upon a mule, or pony. Each cacolet can be placed indifferently, either on the right or on the left side of the packsaddle, but should invariably be so arranged that the patients face in the direction of the mule's head, and that each forms a seat for one patient. When the pair are secured in their places, the arrangement is such that the two patients sit one on each side by the animal's flanks, with their faces turned to their front, *i.e.*, the direction in which the mule is travelling, and their feet supported on the cacolet steps near the animal's fore-legs.

The main portions of the framework of the cacolet are made of wrought-iron: but for certain parts, such as the support for the back of the patient, the circular band attached to this back support by which the patient is secured from falling forward, and for some other minor details, straps made of leather are employed. Openings are made in the iron uprights, or "hanging bars" as they are called, so that these straps can be secured to the top at either end of the chair. The seat is covered with a leather cushion. The foot-support consists of a little plank of wood suspended by two straps, which hang vertically down from the front of the seat. The upright and horizontal rods of the framework are connected by hinged joints, and thus the whole conveyance can be folded closely together, and turned up against the boards of the saddle. The projecting vertical ribs of the pack-saddle, within which it lies when thus folded up, partly protect it from injury, while at the same time, if thought right, the saddle (notwithstanding the presence of the cacolet) is available for the carriage of packages. As the iron hooks for suspending the cacolet to the pack-saddle form part of only one side of the framework, when a cacolet that has been used on the left flank of an animal is required for any reason to be placed on the right flank of an animal, it is necessary to shift the strap by which the back of the patient is supported to the opposite part of the cacolet. In like manner the straps which support the footboard must be unbuckled and

Construction of cacolets.

To reverse a cacolet.

Chap. VI.

Cacolets.

placed over at the side where the back-strap was before fixed. These are the only changes that are necessary for reversing the

Fig. LXXX.— Convoy of wounded being removed on mule-cacolets.

position of a cacolet, or adapting one for being placed on either side of the pack-saddle.

Weight of cacolets.

The weight of a pair of French cacolets complete, when weighed in the Crimea, was found to be 89 lbs. 12 ozs. The English cacolets sent out to the Crimea from Woolwich were heavier, viz., 103 lbs. 2 oz. The weight of English cacolets has since been much reduced; the weight of a pair of present regulation, or Royal Carriage Department, pattern mule-chairs being now 56 lbs. The weight of the pack-saddle complete is 64 lbs.; the weight of the whole conveyance on the mule's back when unloaded being therefore 120 lbs. This pattern cacolet is shown in the two following drawings.

The most compact mode of folding up the cacolet for traveling is not shown in the drawing, where it appears to be only

Fig. LXXXI.—Side view of mule chair or cacolet attached to its pack-saddle.

partially folded towards the pack-saddle. In the French cacolets **the parts are so arranged as to be capable of folding quite flatly upon the side of the pack-saddle; and, when both cacolets are thus packed, a couple of boxes of biscuit can be readily placed over the pack-saddle and cacolets, and so be securely carried. It would not be easy to carry such packages without injury to themselves or the cacolets, were the latter only partially folded up, as represented in the drawing. The French pack-saddle is different to the English, and weighs more. It is a wooden arch, padded to protect the back of the mule, and held in position by one broad girth, a breast strap and breeching. When loaded, the French cacolet rides much lower than the English variety,** which, considered generally, is a disadvantage, as the weight is not so well adjusted to the power.

Great care should invariably be exercised in **harnessing sick transport animals,** either for the purpose of **carrying the wounded,** or for the transport of stores. With mules, and especially when they are carrying cacolets or litters, it is the fashion—a needless and inhuman one—to girth **extremely tight. No girths should be so tight that the finger cannot be passed in between the** skin and the girth. The breast strap in breeching should freely admit the hand, and both should incline slightly

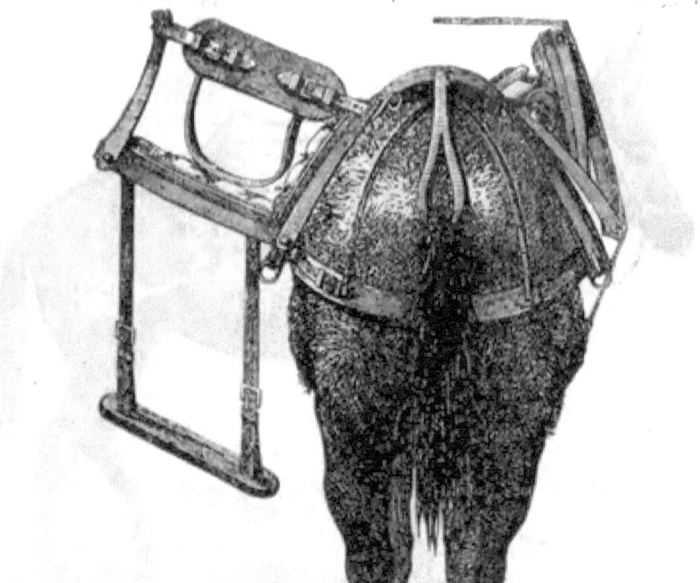

Fig. LXXXII.—End view of mule chair or cacolet, one open for use, and one packed for travelling.

downwards from the corner of the pack-saddle. With a convoy of mules it is a good plan, after they have proceeded a mile, to

Fig. LXXXIII.—French Cacolet.

halt, and examine the girths and adjust them. Over-girthing

and bad loading invariably cause sore backs, but with equable girthing and good loading the wear is inconsiderable.

A form of mule saddle to carry one slightly wounded man, and used in the Italian army, is figured in the sketch. It consists of a country wooden saddle, well padded to protect the mule's back. The front and back are similar, and are merely furnished with the means of attaching two cross-pieces of wood in the shape of the letter X, the upper parts of each side are

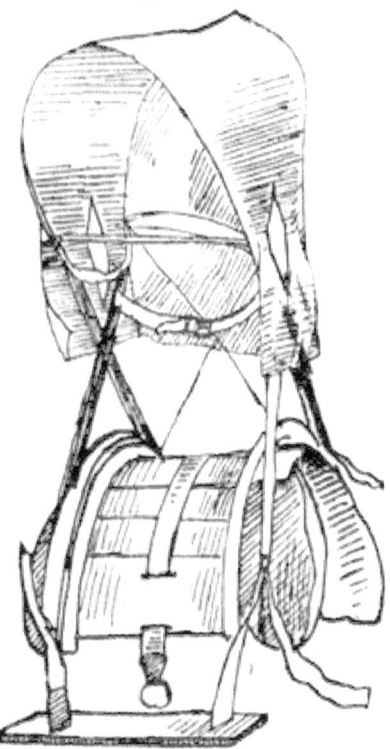

Fig. LXXXIV.—Italian mule carriage. (Copied from Dr Isnaco's work, "Manuale di Chirurgia di Guerra.")

joined by two pieces of Indian cane, over which is stretched a hood. There is a quilted cushion upon which the injured man sits, in addition there are three straps, one, the uppermost, is attached a little above where the main supports join, and forms a rest for the arms, and there are two more straps, one for the back, and one for the front of the patient, the back strap in addition supports the framework. The patient rests his feet upon a footboard, and sits sideways on the mule. This carriage folds up into a package of 1 metre long 15 centimetres wide, and weighs 4 kilos. This is an ingenious form of conveyance, and practically capable of being used in the roughest country; an important feature is, that the very largest and best mules, which are required where two men are carried, are not required, the average sized mule, provided docility is obtained, is quite sufficient.* (Fig. LXXXIV.)

The saddle shown in Fig. LXXXV represents the pattern used in Algeria and in the mountains. The position of the patient

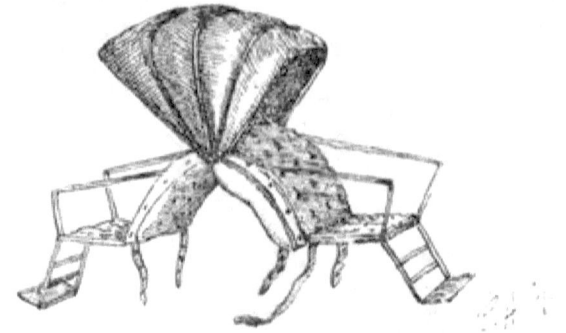

Fig. LXXXV.—Italian Mule Saddle.

is different, but does not appear to have any very superior points to the ordinary method of the English cacolet. It may be noted that sick men are more likely to lean on their sides than backwards. The weight is placed high, and the patients are strapped in.

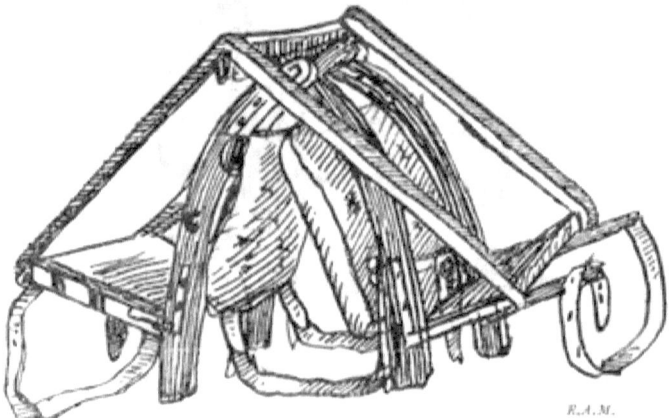

Fig. LXXXVI.—Mule crate (Mosley). *See* description, camel sitting-up crate.

Litters.

These are conveyances, as their name implies, in which patients are carried in a recumbent position. They are

---

* For a fuller description, see "Manuale di Chirurgia di Guerra," par Dottore Segre. Cav. Isaaco. Col. Med. Dept., Italian Army.

suspended, by a pair together, from the pack-saddle of a mule, in a similar way to the cacolets; but they cannot be employed indiscriminately for either side like the cacolets. They are therefore distinguished as right and left mule-litters.

Carriage of patients in mule-litters.

The form of the litter, the greater height of the mule in front, and its mode of movement in walking, render the carriage easier for the patient when he is placed with his feet toward the hinder part of the animal, and therefore with the back of his head toward the direction in which the mule is walking. Moreover, the weight of the loaded conveyance is greatest at that part where the upper portion of the patient's body rests, and this weight is most easily borne by the animal when suspended near its shoulders. The recumbent patient on a mule-litter is therefore carried in a direction contrary to that in which the sitting patient is moved on a mule-chair.

Construction of mule-litters.

The framework of the litter, like that of the cacolet, is made of wrought-iron, and jointed into three principal parts, and retained by linch pins. It is made to fold up into a comparatively compact form when not in use.

The litter used in the French army can be folded up completely, though not into so small a space as the cacolet, and when thus packed, two cases, weighing from fifty to sixty kilogrammes, can be put upon the mule and carried above the litières in the same way as when cacolets are folded upon the pack-saddle.

When fully extended, the length of the English pattern litter from end to end is six and a half feet. The bottom or bed of the litter is made of strong canvas secured to the iron

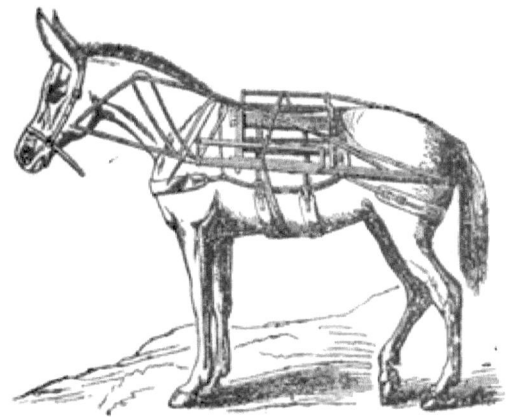

Fig. LXXXVII.—Mule litter attached to its pack-saddle (Mark III).
(*The framework only of the litter is shown*).

frame by cords in the same way as to the sides of a stretcher. This canvas has been usually pressed upon from below by the cross parts of the framework, and in consequence, a

CHAP. VI.

mattress has been added of convenient length for the patient to lie upon; but in the **latest** patterns (Mark III.) this pressure has been got rid of by altering the forms of the cross-pieces, and with these the supply of a mattress has not been found to be necessary—the canvas is soft enough without it.

At the head of the litter there is a canvas hood, which can be thrown back or raised at pleasure. Another piece of canvas **can** be attached to the foot of the frame, and this can be drawn upwards so as to completely cover the patient. When not required for use the litter can be folded up by removing the linch pins, placing head-piece over centre, and foot-piece over all, and raising the folded litter against the pack-saddle, and retaining it by the surcingle.

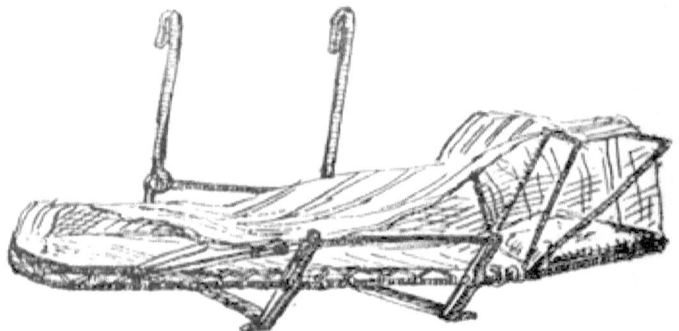

Fig. LXXXVIII.—French **Mule Litter.**

Weight of mule-litters.

The weight of a pair of French litters complete, when weighed in the Crimea, was found to be 136 lbs. The weight of a pair of English litters at that time was nearly the same as the French, viz., 138 lbs. 12 oz. The weight of a pair of litters of the present Royal Carriage Department pattern, without paillasses or the pack-saddle, is only 84 lbs.; with the paillasses and pack-saddle, 167 lbs.; the last pattern, (Mark III.) weighs 106 lbs. exclusive of the pack-saddle.

One form of English litter was secured to the saddle by a horizontal iron bar forming part of its frame, being passed **through** two openings made for its reception in the projecting **vertical** ribs of the tree of the pack-saddle. One end of this **iron bar** was furnished with a screw, and on this an iron nut **was** secured, so that the bar might be prevented from slipping back through the apertures in the saddle-tree after it had been placed in them. The present pattern is connected with the saddle by a long solid vertical iron hook-piece attached to the litter being hooked on to projections in the ribs of the saddle. One pattern of litters used in the French service are hooked on to the pack-saddle by a chain of three links, the **rest** of the attachment being a continuous piece of iron, jointed to the side of the litter-frame. The litters can thus be raised or lowered a little, according to the link used when attaching the chains to their respective hooks, which cannot be done with the solid iron hook-piece or horizontal iron bar in the English patterns. The later patterns, however, are fastened by the hook as shown in the diagram.

It is an obvious advantage to be able to adapt the height of a litter to the height of the animal which is to carry it.

By either plan, however, whether with hooks only or hooks and chains the litters can be detached from the saddle or secured to it in a few moments without any difficulty.

Fig. LXXXIX.—Mule-litter attached to its pack-saddle (original pattern).

When the litters were first made in England, they were constructed in such a way that they could not be readily detached from the pack-saddle. When a patient had to be removed on one of these conveyances, it was necessary to lift him up into it; a proceeding which, in many varieties of dangerous gunshot injuries, involved the bearers in much difficulty and greatly increased the risks and suffering of the patient. This was afterwards remedied. The litter, as at present constructed, can be at once detached from the pack-saddle by lifting the hanging bars of the litter out of their connections with the pack-saddle. When required for use the litter is laid on the ground, the wounded man placed upon it, and, as soon as he is settled in his place, the litter is raised by four men to a level with the

Mule-litters removable from pack-saddles.

saddle and hooked on; or, if of the older pattern, and provided with the horizontal connection, the bar is caused to slide through the openings made to receive it and the nut is screwed on. In either case the litter is securely fixed in its place.

Security of patients in mule-litters.

In order to secure a patient from slipping downwards beyond the end of the litter, especially in descending steep declivities, either the end of the litter for a few inches is made to turn up, or, as in the most recent French patterns, a small foot-rail is added to it. To prevent him rolling off on the outside, a double side-rail is placed along the middle compartment of the litter. The head part of the litter is always raised a little, and, in addition, the pillow obviates any tendency on the part of a feeble patient to slip in that direction. A side pad is sometimes provided to lean against the pack-saddle, and protect the patient on the side of the litter near the mule's flank.

Mode of preventing litters from swaying.

A long strap, the "back suspension strap" as it is called, is made to pass from the upper bar of the outer side-rail of one litter, *over* the litter and the patient lying upon it, and over the pack-saddle to the corresponding rail on the other litter. This strap holds up the two litters, which would otherwise by their breadth and the weight upon them, have a tendency to dip downwards at their outer margins. Another strap passes from the lower part of the same side-rail, *under* the litter, the belly of the animal, and the opposite litter, to be buckled round the lower part of the other side rail. The combined influence of these two straps is to prevent the two litters from swaying up and down during the movement of the animal, and thus to lessen the disturbance which would otherwise be caused to the patients lying upon them. A third strap passes from the inner side-rail of one litter under the belly of the animal to the inner side-rail of the other litter; this serves further to keep the two litters steady.

Peculiar motion of mule-litters

A certain amount of movement it is impossible to prevent. The kind of movement communicated to mule-litters by the action of the animal in walking is peculiar. It is totally different from the sudden jolts, or the general concussion, liable to be communicated to patients when carried on wheeled vehicles. Good mules are so sure-footed, and so steady in their gait, that they rarely ever stumble so as to jolt the patients they are carrying. But the progression of the animal causes the litter to have a movement which has something of an undulatory character, and impresses a looker-on with an idea that it would not be unlikely to cause a condition akin to sea-sickness. Some mules cause more of this kind of movement to be given to the litters than others. It forms one of the chief inconveniences connected with mule-litters, so far as the ease of the patients carried by them is concerned; but in estimating this objection to their use, it must be weighed against the necessities of the occasions which lead to their employment, and also against the inconveniences which are apt to accompany conveyances of other descriptions

Directions for the proper use of Mule Conveyances.   CHAP. VI.

Before proceeding to describe some of the mule conveyances which differ in construction from the litters at present authorised for use in the British service, which have just been described, it will be useful to mention the manner of using these latter, so that accidents from their employment may be guarded against, and the risks and inconveniences connected with this mode of transport reduced **to** the lowest limits.

STEPS TO BE TAKEN IN ORDER TO PREVENT ACCIDENTS, AND TO LESSEN INCONVENIENCE TO PATIENTS, BY THE USE OF MULE-LITTERS.

General rules for loading and unloading mule cacolets and litters.—Great care is necessary to prevent accidents during the act of raising and attaching cacolets and litters, but especially the latter, when loaded, to the pack-saddles. Without due caution it may readily happen for a patient to roll off a litter while it is in the act of being raised; and equally, without mutual understanding and concerted action on the part of the bearers, there may be a good deal of delay and difficulty in connecting **the** sliding-bar, or two hooks, of the litter to the pack-saddle, together with unnecessary jostling and disturbance of the patient. Equal caution and system are required in detaching and removing litters and patients from the animal. It is necessary to provide some one to keep the mule steady while the patients are being placed on or taken off the animal's back; for another person to steady the loaded litter on one side while its fellow litter is being detached from the opposite side; and, under all circumstances, particularly when connecting or disconnecting a litter, to ensure the bearers keeping it level, and so **to** remove all cause for apprehension to the patient of his being subjected to a fall during the operation. Particular care should also be taken that all fastenings and straps are properly secured before the mule is permitted to start with his load.

Precautions.

While either a cacolet or a litter with a patient upon it is being fixed to one side of the saddle, the opposite side requires **to** be held down **very** firmly, or **there is a** risk of the saddle turning, and the patient being upset. So when the conveyance has **been got** into its place, for the same reason equal care is necessary to provide for maintaining the balance of its weight by **a** corresponding weight on the opposite **side.** If circumstances admit of the arrangement, two patients of nearly equal size and weight should always be put on the same animal. If this cannot be accomplished, the conveyance sustaining the lighter weight should have its weight supplemented by **the** addition of a kit bag, or any other convenient article at hand, so as to obtain the necessary equipoise. If it be a cacolet, and only one patient is to be carried, then the leader of the animal must himself take the opposite seat, in order to preserve the balance. If there is only one patient to be carried, and that patient must be carried on a litter, then **a** cacolet is placed on the opposite side, and the leader of the mule takes his seat in it, if there be no attendant to do so, still with the same object in view. But under the circumstances in which these conveyances are ordinarily employed, there are usually patients enough to occupy every vacant seat and litter. As the patients carried in cacolets are usually less severely injured than those placed in a recumbent position, one leader is commonly regarded as sufficient for two cacolet mules, the leading rope of the hinder mule being simply attached to the saddle of the leading mule. But for the opposite reason, mules bearing patients on litters should invariably each have their own leader.

Special directions for the instruction of bearers in the use of mule litters, as well as in placing patients on and taking them off litter-mules.—Assistant-Surgeon Moffitt, when acting as instructor to the Army Hospital Corps, found the following plan of conducting the operation of placing patients on litter-mules and taking them off again to be the easiest for the bearers, safest for the patients, and at the same time the speediest in accomplishment:—

The mule conductor.
(1) With each mule for the carriage of litters should be a driver, whose duty it is to attend to the animal, to see that it is properly harnessed, and to drive it.

The litter-bearers.
(2) Four orderlies or bearers are required both to load and to unload the litters.*

Litters to be folded up when not in use.
(3) When the litters are not required for carrying patients, the pins should be removed, and the litters folded up and fastened close to the side of the saddle. It is easier for the mule to carry them thus packed, and the litters are less liable to be damaged.

To balance litters.
(4) Patients, if possible, of nearly the same weight should be carried on each pair of litters. When this cannot be accomplished, the heavier patient should be made to lie close to the inside of his litter, while the lighter should be placed on the outer side of his litter, a pad being placed to keep him in position; but should the disproportion of weight be so great that this arrangement will not preserve the balance of the two litters, a pack, rifle, or some other weight must be superadded to make up the difference.

Carriage of patients with broken limbs on mule-litters.
(5) When a patient with a fractured bone has to be transported on a mule litter, not only should the limb be protected by the ordinary means adopted in such cases, but any available means of support, such as straw, hay, or articles of clothing, that can be obtained should be arranged on the litter

---

* If the litter-mule can be brought to where the sick or wounded men requiring carriage are lying, the requisite number of bearers will almost always be at hand. As the sick or wounded men will have to be carried on two stretchers to the litter-mule, when circumstances render it necessary for the animal to be stationed some distance away, and, as each stretcher will have two bearers with it, these same bearers will supply the requisite number for loading and attaching the litters to the pack-saddle, whether the patients are brought to the litter-mule or the mule is brought alongside the patients. For the detail of the drill the reader is referred to the Appendix.

as padding to secure the limb in an easy position, and to prevent the movement, which is unavoidable with such conveyances, from acting locally on the injured part.

(6) It is a good practice to invariably load both sides of the litter simultaneously. This is insisted upon in the drill, and is very important.

Other forms of mule-litters.

The cacolets and litters which have been hitherto chiefly described are the mule conveyances which, according to present regulations, constitute part of the authorised field hospital equipment in the French and English military services. But other forms of conveyance of a corresponding nature have been either proposed for use at different times, or have been actually used in other armies, and some of these it will be useful to mention.

Mr. Hill's two-mule litter.

In the year 1855 Mr. Hill, a civil engineer, invented for the easy carriage of a couple of wounded men lying on a machine borne by two-mule litters. The machine was first fixed to the mules, and the patients, being placed on the litters, were then hoisted and slung within it. This conveyance was nearly as objectionable in principle as the two-horse litter elsewhere described (see page 248), for while, by the ordinary mule litter arrangement, each mule carries two patients, by this plan the proportion was only one patient to each mule. But, in addition the weight of the machine and its litters was 284 lbs.; and this fact, together with its complicated construction, and the difficulty of transporting it, caused the Committee at once to pronounce it to be unfit for military service.

The Italian Sitting Litter.

As in litters generally, it is composed of three parts head, middle, and foot pieces, which fold the one over

Fig. XC.—A sitting litter. (Drawn from the "Manuale di Chirurgia di Guerra" par Dr. Isaaco, Colonel Medical Department, Italian Army.)

CHAP. VI.

the other. The middle-piece is attached to two supports shaped like an inverted V, the legs of which fix into the (bardella) pack-saddle. The head and foot-piece are held by a chain passing over the angle of V. The head-piece is a framework of iron lined with canvas, and fitted with a hood—and the angle with the centre-piece can be increased or lessened as desired; the foot-piece is divided into two, one for each leg, and they can also be raised or lowered as desired. The patient is fastened to this litter by straps. This litter can be carried by the bearers, as well as on a mule. As the patient lies across the mule, this form of conveyance is only suitable for wide tracks, and unfrequented thoroughfares. Complete it weighs 18 kilos.*

Shortell's modification of Mule-litter.

Shortell's modified mule-litter.

It is under many circumstances inconvenient to take an ambulance mule to the place where a wounded man is lying. At the same time the patient may be a considerable distance off, and his condition may make it objectionable to place him first on a stretcher, and then to transfer him to a litter, if this double movement can be avoided. Obviously in such a case, if the litter itself could be conveniently carried and used in place of the stretcher, so that the wounded man might be placed upon it, conveyed directly to the place where the mule was stationed and, without further change, put upon the mule for removal to hospital, time would be saved, and suffering prevented. With this view, Sergeant Shortell, of the Army Hospital Corps, in 1865, placed in the Museum of Military Surgery, at Netley,† a model of a litter, the several parts of which were capable of being fixed rigidly together like a stretcher, and to which, at the same time, handles were added. The latter were attached to the four corners of the framework in such a way that when not required for use they could be folded back out of the way to avoid any inconvenience from their projecting outwards; but when required they could be at once brought forward, and be at the same time thoroughly safe for bearing the weight of the litter and patient during the act of transportation. The only additional weight was that of the small bolts used in fixing the several sections of the stretcher, and that of the handles. At the time this model was made neither the litter in use in the French service nor that adopted as the English pattern could be fixed for use as a stretcher. This adaptation has, however, as already described, been since made, and by means of small pins or bolts similar to the plan used in Shortell's model. Handles have not been added to the regulation mule-litters, probably to lessen weight, and also because it is considered unlikely that mule-litters will ever be used for the carriage of patients for any but very short distances, when the sides of the

---

* A kilo = 2·28 lbs.   † Spec. No. 1,2516.

litter-frame will answer sufficiently well to be taken hold of by the bearers.

Mule Conveyance at the Paris Exhibition of 1867.

Several forms of mule chairs and litters for sick and wounded were exhibited at the Universal Exhibition of Paris in 1867. Of the patterns exhibited the experimental trials left no doubt that the French were the most handy, best contrived for general use, and on the whole as easy as any others to the patients carried. There were Italian and Portuguese litters, as well as some from the United States Sanitary Commission, but none were so portable or capable of being folded up so thoroughly and compactly against the flanks of the mules as the French mule-cacolets and litters. In 1876, in the Report on the appliances for aid to the sick and wounded in war, by the Committee presided over by the author, it was reported—"For use on a horse or mule, we have seen nothing better than our own cacolets (English) and litters. Most of those sent by private exhibitors are too complicated for use in the field, and no Government except our own exhibits any means of transport of this nature."*

Locati's Mule Conveyances.

The Italian cacolets and litières at Paris, invented by M. Locati, of Turin, exhibited much ingenuity. The litters especially were designed for moving through very narrow defiles, and for avoiding, as far as possible, such impediments to their progress as might be met with from branches of trees in their way, whether overhead or on either side. With these objects in view, the conveyances themselves were kept within as narrow dimensions as they could be consistently made; all angles were removed, and one of the rounded convex sides of each litter was made to fit into a concave depression in the pack-saddle, so as to diminish as much as possible the projection of the conveyance beyond the flanks of the mule. It was said that the natural impediments which were met with in the transportation of the wounded along the narrow rocky paths, and through the wooded tracks of the Tyrol during the campaign in that mountain region in 1866, led M. Locati to devote so much attention to these qualities in the construction of his mule conveyances. All the Locati conveyances of the litter kind intended to be carried by mules were formed of curved steel bars, those forming the bottom or mattress, on which the patient was supported, being a little stouter in substance than ordinary hoop-iron. The object in using this material was to ensure a certain amount of elasticity as well as strength and comparative lightness in the contrivance. The sides of the litters were continued in a curve round each end, so that each litter, regarded as a whole frame, formed an elongated oval frame. This frame was divided into three hinged sections, those sections being fixed in position, when the litter was required

---

* Report on Ambulance. Brussels, 76, p. 18.

Chap. VI.

Locati's litters.

for use, by iron pins attached to small chains. The sides to which the steel ribs forming the mattress were attached, and on which the maintenance of the form principally depended, were stout and substantial. There were, in addition, two large ribs, which were made to curve outside, and at some distance from the ribbed mattress; these served to keep articles from casually coming into contact with the mattress, and also prevented the patient from coming into contact with the ground when the litter was laid down. Wooden feet were attached to these outer ribs in some examples.

The general aspect, and particularly the curved form that was given to the litters, gave them something of the appearance of a cradle. The division of the sides into three sections caused the litters to be capable of folding up to a certain extent, but under no circumstances could they be so reduced in size as to allow the mule carrying them to be used for carrying packages when the litters were not required for the conveyance of patients.

The mode of applying one of these side-litters to the pack-saddle is shown in the following sketch:—

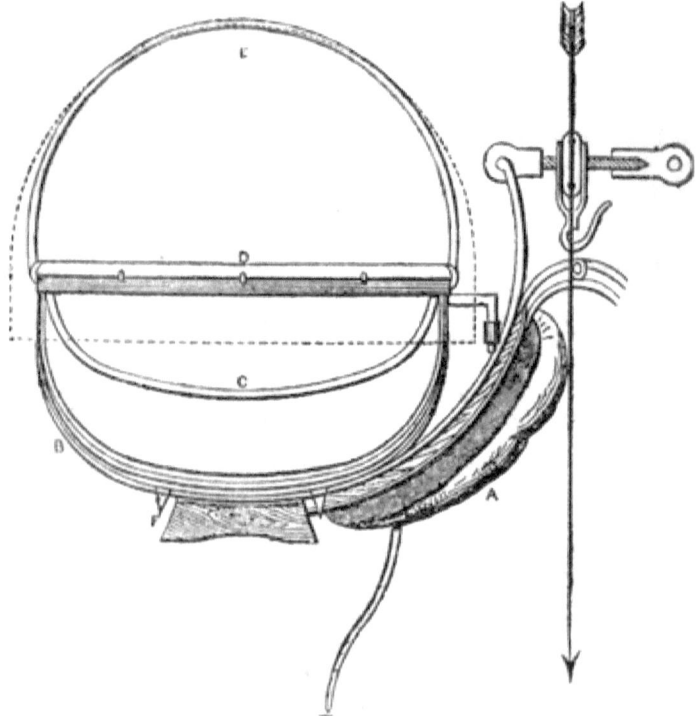

Fig. XCI. Sectional view of one of M. Locati's side-litters fixed to its pack-saddle. A, pad of one side of pack-saddle. B, outer rib of litter. C, level of ribbed mattress for patient. D, back of lateral frame of litter. E, hoop for supporting cover. F, wooden foot of litter.

M. Locati's Single-Litter Mule Conveyance.

One of the Locati mule conveyances was peculiar, the pack-saddle, and the litter carried upon it, being both designed to be borne by a mule destined to carry only a single patient. The purpose of this contrivance was to ensure the transport of a wounded man without interruption along the very narrowest passages or defiles, or along roads encumbered by numerous vehicles; in short, anywhere where the mule itself could pass. In this instance, there was upon the pack-saddle a small wooden plate turning readily upon a pivot. This revolving plate had upon

Construction of Locati's single mule-litter.

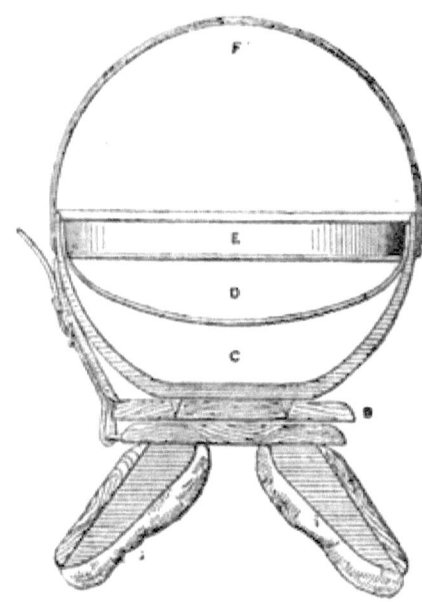

Fig. XCII.—End view of M. Locati's single-litter mule conveyance, fixed to its pack-saddle. A, space between saddle-pads. B, revolving plate. C, one of the strong supporting ribs of the litter. D, level of the ribbed mattress on which the patient lies. E, back of lateral frame. F, hoop for supporting the cover.

its upper surface four holes or sockets, and the litter was connected with it by four small iron feet, projecting from the two principal ribs which were made to fit into these depressions. The litter was no less peculiar in form than in construction. Instead of presenting a simple bed or cradle, which form would have given rise to inconvenience from the animal's head in its movement, striking against it, the litter from the middle is separated into two divisions, shaped so as to receive the legs of a patient, one in each division. The animal's head is between

CHAP. VI.

Mode of placing it on its pack-saddle.

these divisions when the litter is in a longitudinal direction in respect to the animal, as it is when a patient is being carried upon it. The pack-saddle, litter, and the hoops supporting the cover, have been all made as short from above downwards as practicable, so that when they are all in position, the whole does not exceed the height of the animal's head. Here again, the object was to obviate the risk of collision with the branches of trees overhead. The litter was made to fold in three parts for package; each leg-piece folding upon the middle part, and the head-piece over both. To place a patient upon the mule, the joints of the litter, which is laid upon the ground, are first fixed by the iron pins, and the patient is then laid upon it. When the patient has been settled in his place, the litter is raised up by two men, and laid on the revolving plate *across* the mule. As soon as the pins of the litter are in their sockets, the plate is turned round so as to make the litter take a *longitudinal* direction corresponding with that of the mule itself. The litter is further secured to the pack-saddle by side-straps. As the width of the litter in this arrangement corresponds very nearly with the outer limits of the animal's flanks, and its height with that of the animal's head, as little impediment is offered to the progress of the conveyance as can be practicable with any form of mule-litter.

The sketch shows the arrangement of the litter upon the pack-saddle, the head of the litter being presented to view.

The mule litters of other countries at the Paris Exhibition offered no special features worth description. The Portuguese, which were similar to the French in general design, were very bulky and heavy; so much so, that they could only be carried by mules of the largest and most powerful kind.

Woodcock's Mule-Litters.

Mule-litters slung from outriggers.

These mule-litters were partly supported by being suspended from wooden outriggers, one on each side, and projecting from the saddle. Leathern straps were used to connect the litters with the outriggers. The design of this contrivance was to preserve a strictly horizontal position of the two litters while patients were lying upon them. It was evident from considering the material of which the projecting supports were composed, their shape, the length of leverage, and the force which would be exerted upon them, that such contrivances would speedily become broken or otherwise disabled on active service. They were the invention of a Mr. Woodcock of New York.

United States Mule Litter.

The mule-litter which was adopted for use in the United States' army is shown in the following illustration. It is copied from a drawing kindly sent to me by Surgeon-General J. K. Barnes.

The American litter above represented is of precisely the same pattern as the mule-litter formerly used in the French army, but now abandoned. It was chiefly faulty because it could not be folded up compactly, and also, as mentioned in former remarks, because there were no means of rendering it

Fig. XCIII.—Mule-litter issued for use in the United States' Army during the war of the Rebellion.

rigid for temporary use as a stretcher. The litter frame was jointed in three sections, but the head-piece and foot-piece, notwithstanding these joints, could only be raised and approximated over the centre compartment; they could not be laid flat, one upon or within the other, owing to the strain upon the canvas, and to the fact of the head and foot-pieces being of the same width. They were tried and used in the war of the Rebellion, but were soon laid aside for more convenient forms of carriage.

Mule-Panniers.

These conveyances are simply long wickerwork baskets, with rather low sides, in the form of cradles, covered by an arched canopy of canvas supported on four hoops. They are carried in the same way that cases containing stores of matériel are carried by bât animals, and are suspended and secured in a similar manner. They do not admit of being folded up, or reduced in size in any way. Mule-panniers do not form part of the regular equipment of any army, and have only been employed in the absence of the necessary number of regular litters. Similar contrivances can readily be made in the field

CHAP. VI.

wherever the means of making gabions exist. In some respects such panniers, where sufficient bedding or other soft materials have been placed in them, answer well enough the purposes of regular litters, particularly for the carriage of men disabled by

Fig. XCIV.—Mule panniers in use for the carriage of sick and wounded.

extreme weakness, as they afford support on every side to such patients; but their cumbrous size and unyielding forms quite unfit them for general use as conveyances of the class under consideration.

Two-horse Litters.

Former use of two-horse litters.

It is necessary to notice another form of sick-transport litter issued for use in the early part of the late war in the United States, in which, instead of two litters being suspended across one horse or mule, one litter was suspended between two horses. This is a very ancient form of litter in Europe. Frequent notices of it occur, showing its common use on occasions of state and ceremony, as well as its employment for the carriage of sick persons* in the records of our own country

---

* This form of litter is referred to as late as the reign of Charles the 2nd. A quotation introduced into the first volume of Knight's "London," pp. 24, 25, mentions that " Major-General Skipton, coming in a horse-litter to London when wounded, as he passed by the brewhouse near St. John Street, a fierce mastiff flew at one of the horses and held him so fast that the horse grew mad as a mad dog; the soldiers were so amazed that none had the wit to shoot the mastiff, the horse-litter borne between the two horses, tossed the Major-General like a dog in a blanket."

prior to the introduction of coaches. It seems curious that its use should have been revived in modern times in America.

The order for the issue of these litters was first given by the United States' Army Medical Board in January, 1860, in the following terms:—"Ordered, that horse-litters be prepared and furnished to posts where they may be required for service on ground not admitting the employment of two-wheeled carriages; the said litters to be composed of a canvas bed similar to the present stretcher, and of two poles, each 16 feet long, to be made in sections, with head and foot pieces constructed to act as stretchers to keep the poles asunder."

The side poles were to be of ash, the head and foot pieces nine inches in height, of canvas stretched over strong iron wire. The canvas part to be five feet ten inches in length, two feet three inches in width.

A similar kind of conveyance is used in some parts of India, where it is called a "Tukta-rewan." The central part is more like a sedan chair than a litter, but this, inconvenient as it would be for an European, is convenient enough for the Asiatic, from the peculiar ease with which he is able to take his rest in a sitting posture upon a flat cushion. Like the two-horse litter just described, it is attached to two long poles, and is carried in the same way between two horses, one of which walks before, the other behind the conveyance. The poles rest on slings passed over the pads which are girthed to the backs of the two horses. Native ladies not unfrequently travel in these vehicles.

Two-horse litters seem to be conveyances of very doubtful expediency, if expedient at all, under any circumstances. It is a very unprofitable expenditure of labour for two horses to be devoted to the carriage of one sick man, when the same purpose can be more economically accomplished by other means. The comparatively little width of space occupied by such litters gives them some advantage in moving along narrow ways through a partially cleared country, but they cannot travel along narrow tracks presenting short turns, such as winding paths with steep acclivities on one side, which are so frequently met with in hilly districts. The conveyance is too long and unyielding for such movements. Again, it is unsuited for any but tolerably level roads. It is destitute of any provision for preserving its level in case of the leading horse elevating the fore part of the long poles, while the hinder part is depressed, or *vice versâ*, so that a road presenting either a steep ascent or descent would cause great inconvenience to any invalid in the litter during transport.

The two animals are not easily managed by a single conductor under various circumstances, and to supply a second man, so that each horse may have a conductor, would add still more to the wasteful outlay of labour which, without such an addition, is already a sufficient objection, not to mention others, to the employment of two-horse litters in military service.

CHAP. VI.

Construction of the United States' two-horse litter.

The tukta-rewan.

Remarks on the use of two-horse litters.

The Travois.

This is a kind of sleigh litter drawn by one animal, and consisting of two long poles turned up slightly at their thicker ends,—these rest on the ground, and on the traverses which bind them, the patient rides. Thin ends pass into the saddle on the back of a horse. A special feature of the travois is that when it approaches any obstacle the conveyance is lifted by hand over it. In North America it is still used by the Indians, but not to the same extent as formerly. Such a form of transport could only be used under very special and urgent circumstances for the carriage of wounded and sick men.

Concluding Remarks.

The descriptions which have been given of the several forms of conveyances under consideration have afforded sufficient means of estimating their comparative value for use in campaigning. There can be no doubt that there has been a great advance in the art of constructing cacolets and litters, and those which have been described are among the best. The English varieties for the English service are most suitable, combining, as they do, strength, durability, and lightness. The advantages advocated for these conveyances may be summed up to be:—the ease with which they can be carried on the march; their applicability under circumstances and in places where wheeled vehicles would be altogether inadmissible; the facility with which they can be taken over the most broken and precipitous ground to the very spots where wounded are lying; the ease with which wounded can be conveyed by them to distances which would be far too great and tedious for the use of stretchers carried by bearers; and, lastly, the many field uses to which the mules with their pack-saddles can be turned, when not required for sick-transport purposes. At the same time it is necessary to remember that, to ensure their efficiency, certain qualifications are requisite in the mules, which are not attainable without considerable expense and systematic care, as well as in those who have to conduct them, and to attend upon the wounded. Unless the mules possess sufficient strength to carry the weight of the two men in addition to the articles of their equipment—unless they are sufficiently docile and trained for the work—unless the corps in whose charge the animals are placed is properly organised and practised, so that the care, feeding, protection, harnessing, and working of the animals are duly attended to—and, finally, unless the men, to whose charge the wounded are entrusted are sufficiently practised in the proper exercise of their responsible duties, among others, in the best modes of loading of taking care of them during the transport, their utility is lost, for without these essential adjuncts, it is obvious that in actual campaigning the animals and conveyances will quickly become unserviceable, and their purposes have accomplished in a very imperfect way.

CLASS IV.—CONVEYANCES DRAWN BY ANIMALS.

General Observations.

We now come to a class of conveyances, the use of which has not only to be studied with reference to the intrinsic qualities of the vehicles themselves, their relations to the power by which they are set in motion, and to the other conditions which have been shown to influence the forms and construction of the several kinds of conveyances already considered, but also in respect to another circumstance, viz., the nature of the country in which they are to be employed. All the conveyances for sick and wounded which have been designed for carriage by men, as well as those borne by quadrupeds, are comparatively independent of this consideration, being adapted for use on any ground over which either men or mules can walk; and even the conveyances *wheeled* by men, which can *also* be carried **by bearers, are not liable to be** baffled by meeting obstructions or excavations which would be fatal to the employment of wheeled conveyances drawn by animals.

The **same qualities** of strength combined **with light**ness, portability, adaptation to the necessities of sick and wounded, facility of loading and unloading, and economy in cost, as regards the vehicles; the same circumstances in regard to the maintenance, protection and fitness for service in the field, of the animals and of those who have care of them; have to be taken into account, as with the several kinds of conveyances previously described; but, in addition, a tolerably level condition of the surface of the country, or, if broken into hills and valleys, the existence of made roads, is essential in order that this class of carriage may be used with advantage, and with due regard to the maintenance of efficiency. At **the** same time, a field hospital wagon should not be so constructed as only to be capable of being safely conducted **over such** well-made roads as are met with usually in this country; **it** ought to be put together strongly enough, and to be **so** mechanically arranged with regard to the maintenance of the line **of** gravity within the wheels, notwithstanding considerable deviations of the surface upon which it is moved, as to admit of its use in all places and under all circumstances in which other military wheeled conveyances can be used. Just as conveyances borne by men and animals should be competent to follow the fighting line over every kind of ground that they can move over, so it is desirable that the wheeled ambulance carriage drawn by horses should be capable of being taken with ease and security over any ground, soft, rugged, or broken, and down any declivity, over which the rest of the

Chap. VI.

Necessary qualities of conveyances drawn by animals.

Can only be employed upon ground which is tolerably level.

Should be capable of passing wherever the other transport vehicles of the army can go.

CHAP. VI.

Not to be expected that ambulance conveyances are to be capable of going wherever gun-carriages can go. Circumstances of the two kinds of carriages compared.

transport of the army can be taken. It is sometimes said that the ambulance carriages should be capable of going wherever gun-carriages can go, but this is not expected, and, indeed, cannot be carried into execution. Gun-carriages have to be forced over the most difficult places, rocky ground, ground broken into deep furrows and high ridges, and at the same time to be manœuvred in a manner that no vehicles fitted with springs could be subjected to with impunity. Such springs as are capable of affording any ease to the patients carried in an ambulance wagon would be inevitably broken, or otherwise disabled, by the violent shocks which gun-carriages must be able to withstand with impunity. If the principle be accepted that an ambulance wagon is to be capable of going wherever a gun-carriage can go, then it will have to be built of such great solidity that one of the most important qualities of such a conveyance, ready mobility, must be at the same time destroyed. It is better, therefore, to lay down the rule that an ambulance wagon should be capable of going wherever the other wheeled transport vehicles of the army can go, leaving to other forms of ambulance transport the duty of removing any wounded who may require removal from the difficult ground to which guns have occasionally to be taken on field service.

SECTION I.—HISTORY OF THE FOURTH CLASS OF AMBULANCE TRANSPORT.

History prior to the Peninsular War.

There is no distinct account of wheeled conveyances having been constructed with special adaptations for the conveyance of sick and wounded of British armies until the period of the the Peninsular campaigns. In the wars in which the troops of this country were engaged on the continent of Europe prior to that period, it seems that, so far as attention was given to the subject at all, the authorities chiefly depended on obtaining some of the ordinary vehicles of the country which formed the theatre of war for the carriage of the sick and wounded of their armies back to the base of operations or port of embarkation.*

---

* The following interesting note occurs in a history of the war in the Spanish Netherlands, 1691, which I found in the library of the Royal United Service Institution :—

"This is an impartial account of the business of that day of which the French, notwithstanding their Te Deums, have no great reason to brag.

"Before I quit this Relation of the Engagement, I can't omit the generous Charity of the Princess of Vaudmont at Brussels.

"I wish that all those of her Communion as the Popes have canonized had as good a Title to be Saints: For the number of our wounded being greater than could be contained in the Hospital which the King had at Brussels, a great many on the Monday in the Evening were lying with their wounds up and down the Streets; whereupon this excellent Princess, moved with a Christian Principle of Charity, went in her coach, attended by a great many Flambeaux, up and down the Streets to find them out, and had them conducted to the great Hall of the Palace, where she saw them dressed of their wounds herself by her Surgeons, she and the Ladies of her Attendance giving Linen and other necessaries for that purpose; And here she maintained them till they could either be removed to the other Hospitals, or till they were in a condition to go abroad themselves."—EDITOR.

In France they do not appear to have been employed until the year 1792, when Larrey had light wheeled conveyances specially constructed for removing wounded soldiers from the field as part of the organisation of his ambulance volante. It is a curious circumstance, as will be noted hereafter, that although France introduced these conveyances at this comparatively early date, for many years she abandoned the use of them; while other countries, that introduced them among their military equipment much later, have not only continued to use them to the present time but have unceasingly devoted great efforts and expense for their improvement.

Chap. VI. First employed in France in 1792.

It has been already mentioned that when the wagon train was organised at the commencement of the Peninsular war, among the carriages under its charge there were some especially constructed for the transport of sick and wounded. These were spring wagons, designed for carrying eight men in a sitting posture, or two men lying down. After the termination of the Peninsular War and the campaign of 1815, little appears to have been done in this country with a view to the improvement of wheeled ambulance transport suitable for European service—if we except the experimental trials made with Veterinary-Surgeon Cherry's carts, and the practical observations made of their qualities in the expeditionary force under Sir De Lacy Evans in 1835—until the outbreak of the war with Russia in 1854. While that war was in progress, however, much attention was given to the subject, and since its conclusion, numerous contrivances have been brought forward with a view to the improvement of the ambulance carts and wagons in use at the successive periods at which these alterations have been suggested. Indeed, the varieties of ambulance conveyances which have been brought to notice in England and on the continent of Europe, as well as in the United States, have been so numerous of recent years that it will be only possible to describe some of the most important among them in this work.

During the Peninsular war.

During the Crimean war.

In the year 1867 a large number of wheeled conveyances was collected, and for the most part placed side by side in the park of the Universal Exhibition at Paris. The Governments of England, France, and the United States exhibited the authorised wagons of their respective countries for carrying sick and wounded. Patterns of nearly all the conveyances of the same class that had been used during the war of the rebellion by the United States Sanitary Commission, were exhibited in a collection formed by Dr. Evans, the eminent American dentist at Paris. Other examples were exhibited by the National Societies for Aid to Wounded in time of War of Italy, Prussia, Switzerland, and Austria. Altogether seventeen illustrations of this class of sick conveyances were exhibited, and of this number thirteen were full-sized patterns complete in all respects, the remaining four being models. An opportunity was thus afforded of comparing one kind of carriage with

Exhibition of ambulance carts and wagons at Paris in 1867.

CHAP. VI.

Prizes offered at Paris for the best patterns of these vehicles.

Efforts of the stimulus given at Paris to the improvement of these vehicles.

another, and thus of studying their relative advantages and defects, both as to general principles of construction and to the fittings and appliances with which they were respectively furnished.

A further stimulus was given on this occasion towards the improvement of this class of conveyances by the offer of prizes for any ambulance wagons more in consonance with the principles on which it was believed all such vehicles should be constructed than any of those under observation at the exhibition. The competitors for these prizes were permitted to study all the patterns in the collection, and to apply to their own inventions any of the meritorious features they might observe among them. The principles on which the new wagons were to be constructed were defined in the terms on which the offer of the prizes was announced. The time for the competition was short, and only two fresh patterns were sent in: to these a first and second prize were awarded. These wagons will be found described among others in the succeeding pages of this chapter.

The good that was effected by bringing together so many examples of ambulance vehicles as were collected on this occasion, by the trials which were made of them, and the discussions which took place on their particular qualities, was great. The observers were so numerous that it is only reasonable to suppose that the information gathered must have laid the seeds for the production of many improvements which have occurred since that time.

Before commencing a description of special examples of ambulance carts and wagons, it will be useful to consider the general advantages and disadvantages belonging to this kind of sick transport for military purposes, bearing in mind more particularly the circumstances under which they have to be employed with troops on active service. It will also be useful to try to determine the principles on which all such vehicles should be constructed, and to note any circumstances that lead to the necessity of special arrangements as regards our own country; and further, to consider the comparative merits and fitness for service of the two leading forms of these conveyances, viz., two-wheeled carts and four-wheeled wagons.

Section II.—Military Advantages of Wheeled Ambulance Transport.

Wheeled ambulance transport an essential part of army equipment on field service.

The acknowledged necessity of having a regular and efficient system of transporting the sick and wounded of armies on the line of march as well as after an action with the enemy, has been already enlarged upon in this work. But further, it is now generally agreed that wheeled conveyances of some form or other drawn by animals constitute an essential part of the means to be provided for carrying this purpose into effect under the ordinary circumstances of modern warfare. That they are occasionally to be dispensed with when more important interests are at stake than the safety of the wounded of a particular force, as in the rapid movements of incursionary attacks or of reconnoitring expeditions, does not militate against the general principle of their regular employment with troops on active service. The conveyances carried by men, and those borne on the backs of animals, in European warfare, are usually to be regarded as expedients for meeting temporary purposes or special circumstances. The former cannot be employed for long distances owing to the limited number of bearers usually available, and to these quickly becoming fatigued; while the latter are ill adapted for the carriage of sick or wounded for prolonged periods, and should only be continuously so employed when the surface of the country or other circumstances do not admit of wheeled transport being used. But wheeled transport can be adapted to almost all the necessities of sick and wounded men over ordinary roads, and its progress can be maintained quite as well as the progress of the stores and matériel of the army. These qualities of wheeled ambulance conveyances make them peculiarly suitable for use on the line of march, and it has been long since proved that in the sustained movements of armies, especially when a force is numerically only adequate to the necessities of the occasion, the means of carrying for a few marches the men who suffer from the temporary ailments which constantly arise among troops on active service, or from slight injuries which only incapacitate them for duty for a few days, is a real military benefit. It is so, first, by preventing the strength from being diminished as it would otherwise be by such men being left behind or sent to the rear, and, secondly, by preventing the evil results which invariably follow the detachment of men from their corps when active operations are in progress. But as the ready mobility of an army is a quality which gives to the commander of it the greatest facility in handling it, commanders look generally on such incumbrances with little favour. From knowing there is so much temptation to carry a variety of things on field service they dread that if one cart be admitted for a given purpose other carts for other purposes will follow, and the impediments of the army be constantly increasing. Sir James McGrigor states in his autobiography* that when he joined the army in the **Peninsula** as Principal Medical Officer under Lord Wellington **in 1812 he** found the hospitals in rear crowded with an immense **number** of sick, or reported sick, and wounded **officers** and men. One consequence was that a disproportionate part of the medical officers of the army was detained in the stations where this accumulation of sick had occurred. To remedy these evils Dr. McGrigor submitted to Lord Wellington a proposal

CHAP. VI.

Importance of this part of field hospital equipment.

Superiority of wheeled conveyances to other kinds of transport on the line of march.

---

* " Autobiography and Services of Sir James McGrigor, Bart.," 1861, p. 265.

CHAP. VI.

Sir J. McGrigor's account of Lord Wellington's objections to regimental ambulance vehicles.

that each corps should have a temporary hospital of its own, where slight cases of wounds and disease might be treated by the regimental surgeons, and that only special cases of either wounds or sickness should be sent to the rear, and these only after examination and reports by medical boards. The same rule was to apply to officers. Lord Wellington fully approved of these arrangements, as well as of other regulations having the same end in view; but when Sir James McGrigor proposed further that each regiment and brigade should have provided for it the means of conveying its hospital establishment, Lord Wellington would not hear of it. He said he would have no vehicles with the army but for the conveyance of guns. He admitted it was lamentable to see so many men slightly ill or wounded sent constantly to the rear, and diminishing the force of the army in a greater proportion than the reinforcements from England were adding to it; but he said:—"I cannot risk encumbering the army and impeding its movements either in advancing or retiring." Notwithstanding, however, the objections which then existed in Lord Wellington's mind on this subject, and which were not improbably due in a great degree to the peculiar circumstances of the occasion, the secrecy and rapidity with which the army was moving upon Badajoz with the intention of investing the place before the French commander could get down to relieve it, the practice of having a cart to carry slight cases gradually crept in, even during this march; for the regimental commanding officers, being unwilling to part with men at a time when every bayonet was of importance, did everything they could to keep with them all sick and hurt who were likely to be able in a few days to resume their places in the ranks, and the regimental medical officers readily entered into their views. And so it came to pass, Sir James McGrigor remarks, that "few corps were to be seen without a cart to carry their slight cases with them when they marched."* The carts here referred to were those of the district. The advantages of carrying on slightly sick men was generally acknowledged during the campaigns of the Peninsular War, and spring wagons were not unfrequently ordered to be attached to regiments for the purpose from the wagon train. Subsequently hospital wagons were regularly issued to regiments as part of their field equipment. Two ambulance wagons, one for carrying sick or wounded men, the other a wagon for stores, were attached to every regiment forming a

---

* "When I passed the different divisions of the army, and saw the description of sick they were depositing at the appointed stations on the route, I entered into conversation with the regimental surgeons, all of whom agreed with me, that if they had only some kind of conveyance, such as the common carts of the country, it would be necessary to send but few men to the rear. Their commanding officers were of the same opinion, being very unwilling to part with a man in moments of emergency; but having no authority, they feared to incur censure by carrying slight cases with them. This practice, however, gradually crept in; few corps were to be seen without a cart," &c. Op. cit. pp. 267, 268.

part of the army of occupation in the year 1815. The system of regimental issue was not followed in the Crimea, owing probably to the stationary nature of the operations in which the troops were engaged; but the ambulance transport was attached in fixed proportions to divisions of the army.

To sum up the arrangements, then, the system of employing specially constructed vehicles for the carriage of sick and wounded, not applicable to the carriage of stores, is the most efficient, and therefore in the end the most economical, for an army operating in the field; while, as regards transport communication between **the** several intermediate hospitals established **along** the line **of** operations of the army, and between them **and the** base, **the** use of carriages of a mixed kind, that is, vehicles capable of being adapted both to the carriage of stores and of sick, appears to be practically free from objections, and at the same time to be more economical as regards cost, taking into the estimate the amount of work done, than the use of special conveyances for each service.

It may generally be stated that sick and wounded should only be carried in properly constructed ambulance carriages, or country carts properly improvised, and that sick carriages as a rule should not be used for any other purpose. It should be generally known that during actual fighting the Geneva Convention expressly forbids the use of any carriage forming part of an ambulance being utilised for any other purpose.

Section III.—Remarks on Horses in relation to their employment with Ambulance Transport.

Observations are elsewhere **made** on the kind of horse most fitted for *carrying* sick and wounded. A few further remarks on the quality of horse suitable for *drawing* wheeled vehicles containing sick and wounded, and on certain circumstances connected with the application of horse-power for this purpose are now introduced. In Europe the use of horses for draught labour is universal; in the East and at the Cape of Good Hope, oxen or buffaloes are largely employed instead of horses.

On considering all the circumstances of **ambulance** vehicles, the nature of the work to be done, the usual rates of progression, the fact of the same horses having to work continuously the whole day, and often for many successive days together, it becomes obvious that the kind of horse which is most suitable for their draught, approaches more closely to that of **the** best breed of cart horses than to any other sort. Some **of** the qualities which distinguish the charger, the carriage horse, and the best descriptions of coach horses,—high speed and mettle, and especially what is called good action, lifting the feet high

Kind of horse suitable.

by free movements of the knee, showy pace, elevated crest and spirited carriage of the head,—are not only not required, but, indeed, are some of them very objectionable qualities in horses destined for the draught of ambulance wagons. Strength, a moderate amount of speed, prolonged power of endurance, a sound and vigorous frame, with the other qualities common to all horses liable to be employed in campaigning, are what are wanted in draught horses for these vehicles. There can be no doubt that the strength of horses is better applied in drawing than it is in carrying heavy weights. In the one case his muscular power is more or less interfered with according to the manner in which the weight to be carried is fastened on the animal; in the other, his muscular power is almost entirely free and unfettered.

"In the English army horses and mules generally draw the ambulance carriages. The class of animal for ambulance transport work should be strong and hardy, quiet, and docile. Speed or action are not required, but a slow, measured pace, of 3 or 4 miles an hour, is quite fast enough for the purpose, and should not, as a rule, be exceeded. Led or driven horses are infinitely preferable to the postilion fashion of the Army. An interesting circumstance, which a French anatomist proved some years ago, was that a horse was a more perfect machine walking than trotting, and could accomplish more work through a longer space of time, and with less expenditure of energy, than at any other pace, from the fact that the levers of his body are more perfect and co-ordinated at that pace than at any other. This is, moreover, borne out by everyday observation, and proves the truth of the adage, ' It is the pace that kills,' and it is hardly necessary to say here that we desire our transport to last. Proportionately one horse will do more than two, and two more than four.

*   *   *   *   *

"There is a *limit* of pace, and a *limit* of endurance in every animal, and a slight excess over either, particularly if continued many days in succession will weaken, if it does not destroy, the efficiency of the transport."

Section IV.—Requisite Qualities of Wheeled Ambulance Transport.

There are certain necessary qualities in conveyances moved by draught power intended for the carriage of sick and wounded men, and certain provisions necessary to ensure their efficiency, that are common to all such vehicles whatever may be their individual forms. These may be enumerated and

---

* From "The Transport of Wounded in Modern War," by the Editor, Journal of the Royal United Service Vol. XXXV.

considered with advantage before noting the special construction of particular carriages. They are the following:—

1. The conveyance must be fitted with proper springs or other contrivances in order to prevent the force of the concussions, which the vehicle will be subjected to in travelling, from being directly communicated to the patients within the conveyance.

Springs or other contrivances necessary.

2. The conveyance should be fitted to carry the greatest number of sick or wounded that can be got along by the amount of draught power employed, consistently with due provision for all the other requisites of an ambulance vehicle.

Capacity adequate to the draught power employed.

3. Provision must be made for the conveyance of men in a recumbent as well as in a sitting position.

4. The carriage must be capable of being packed up for transport on board ship, and capable of being readily put together again for use on landing. This more particularly applies to carriages in the British service.

Portability of the vehicle itself.

5. Provision must be made for repairing parts which are liable to be damaged, and replacing those which may be lost, especially such as are essential to the efficiency of the whole conveyance, as the wheels, for example.

Means of repairing damage, to be at hand.

6. The strength of the vehicle must be adequate to the shocks it will meet with in campaigning, but this power of resistance must not be obtained by adding to its weight to such an extent as to unfit it when fully loaded for the draught, and continued exertion over all kinds of roads, of the number of animals it is intended to be drawn by. Durability and lightness of draught must be made mutually consistent.

Proper relation of strength, weight, and draught.

7. Provision must be made for the carriage of water, a few stretchers, means of artificial light, and such surgical articles and restoratives as the wants of wounded men in the field usually demand.

Provision for carriage of water.

8. The vehicle should be provided with the means of protecting those who may be carried in it from rain, dust, and the glare of the sun.

Protection from rain, sun, and dust.

9. There must be a free circulation of air in the vehicle, especially in that part where the recumbent patients are placed.

Sufficient aeration of interior.

10. Arrangements must be adopted so that patients may be lifted into and removed from the carriage with ease to the bearers, and without risk of injury to the patients.

Facility of placing patients in and out of the carriage.

11. There should be ready means of communication between the sick, and the attendants, or others, who are in charge of them.

12. A place should be allotted for the kits, arms, and accoutrements, of the wounded men who are carried in the conveyances.

Place for knapsacks, arms, and accoutrements.

Remarks on the foregoing list of requirements.—In the list of requisites just enumerated I have not included those for sim-

CHAP. VI.

plicity of design, general stability, limits of breadth and length, facility of turning in narrow roads, and other mechanical subjects of equal importance under the circumstances of campaigning, but which are common to all military wheeled vehicles, whatever may be the purpose of their construction. Qualities have only been mentioned which are of particular importance to form a good *ambulance conveyance for the carriage of sick and wounded.*

Remarks on the need of springs.

1st. *As to the springs.*—Little need be said as to the need of springs. A cart or wagon without springs has its body intimately connected by bolts or other means with the axletree and wheels so that the whole is knitted together into one piece, and a sudden stroke or jolt communicated to either wheel is directly transmitted to the floor of the machine, and to anything placed upon it. The torture inflicted on wounded men, the injury added to the wounds themselves in many instances, especially to those in which bones are broken and splintered, the consequent increase of hazard to life, equally with the suffering and irritative fever caused to patients debilitated by severe illness, when they are subjected to the incessant unmitigated jarring, and occasional violent shocks and jolts, which are inseparable from the movements of springless carts and heavy wagons over ordinary country roads, and much more over roads that have been ploughed up into ruts by the constant passage of vehicles, are apparent to all who have thought on the subject, and sufficiently indicate the necessity for means by which such evils may be obviated. But it is not an easy matter to adapt springs so that the object sought for may be equally attained under all circumstances; for the strength of springs must be adjusted to the weight which is placed upon them, and the weight in ambulance carriages cannot be calculated as a constant quantity. Again, if the road over which the vehicle is passing be very uneven, the pressure on the several springs will vary according to the inequalities of level, and their influence being proportionably disturbed, an unequal effect will be produced on the occupants of the carriage according to their position. Various plans have been resorted to for ensuring an evenness of result under all circumstances:—of breaking the concussion alike whether the vehicle be occupied by its full complement of patients or only by one or two. Some of these methods will be referred to when describing the particular carriages in which they have been employed. The material by which the elastic quality is given is not similar in all vehicles. In some ambulance conveyances the springs are made of steel and resemble ordinary carriage springs, in others they are made of vulcanised india-rubber. There is one serious objection to the use of india-rubber for springs in vehicles which are subjected to occasional severe strains and are designed for use in all climates. However elastic, and perfect in all respects, the india-rubber composition may be when first applied, it is liable to deteriorate gradually, more especially if it be employed in a hot climate. White lead,

Adjustment of springs to the weights carried.

Adjustment of springs.

sulphur, and other matters, usually constitute some among the various ingredients of vulcanised india-rubber, and, in consequence, a chemical action slowly takes place within its substance, even though the material may be lying unemployed, and the result of this action is such that the homogeneous character of the rubber is lost, it acquires more or less of a granular condition, and is easily torn asunder. This deterioration occurs more rapidly when it is subjected to much straining, and when once this change has occurred throughout the spring, it is rendered useless for the purpose it was intended to fulfil.

2nd. Proportion of capacity to draught-powers.—Economy dictates the rule that the capacity of a vehicle as regards the number of sick to be carried should be fully equivalent to the draught-power attached to it, consistently with other requisites. At the same time it must be admitted that it is very difficult to lay down distinct rules for the number of sick to be carried by conveyances according to the number of horses by which they are drawn; for variations in the qualities of the horses employed, in the nature of ground over which they may have to be used, in construction according to the positions in which they are adapted to carry the patients, and in other such circumstances, constantly occur to modify regulations formed on the subject from ordinary data. In practice we find carts drawn by two horses, which have been constructed to carry only two sick or wounded men lying, thus allowing one patient to one horse; we find others, with the same amount of draught, designed to carry two, or even three men lying, and in addition nine persons sitting, allowing even six patients to one horse. So we find wagons drawn by two horses designed to carry eight wounded men and a driver, or four and a half men to each horse; and wagons drawn by four horses, designed to carry ten wounded men and two drivers, or three men to each horse. These different arrangements serve to exhibit the varying amounts of accommodation which have been provided in different vehicles. Extended observation and experience can alone furnish a safe test of the proper proportions to be preserved for the transport of the greatest number of sick at the least possible expense of horses and drivers; but as a general rule two large horses can draw a loaded ambulance wagon over fair roads, but in districts which are hilly, or where the roads are bad, and the draught heavy, an extra pair is required.

3rd. Accommodation for recumbent as well as sitting patients.—The accommodation for the recumbent patients need never be lost; when not required for appropriate cases it can always be made available for sick or wounded men, who under ordinary circumstances would be able to sit up. By allowing for this in every carriage, all kinds of casualties are provided for, and possible contingencies met, so far as the space at command in the vehicle admits. Under any circumstances, whether the transport be only for men lying down, or of a mixed kind for both lying and sitting, it is difficult to provide for more than two patients lying, or at the most three, at full length with

CHAP. VI.

Objections to the use of india-rubber springs.

On the capacity of ambulance vehicles.

Variations in the capacities of different ambulance vehicles.

Accommodation for both sitting and recumbent patients should be provided.

safety and convenience. There are some wagons which carry four patients, and even six, but there is no accommodation for patients sitting inside under these circumstances. Any attempt to carry more lying down is thoroughly unpractical. There is the risk of the vehicle being upset, and consequently the danger to the patients within is increased by requiring an upper tier of recumbent patients to be carried in an ambulance carriage. **One form** of cart has been constructed capable of conveying **three** men in a recumbent position, one between the wheels and two over them; but it was not found to answer on field service, and, when so employed, it was not fitted for carrying any sitters. On the whole, the limitations as to width, length, bulk, and weight, as well as the safety of the patients to be carried, seem to decide that provision for two or three men lying down with a proportion of sitting accommodation cannot be exceeded with advantage, whatever the nature of the vehicle; while in a two-horse wagon, if due regard be given to economy, and the remaining available space of the vehicle be fully employed, the number of persons who can be at the same time carried sitting may be made to vary from four (two being sitting patients with severe wounds) to six (four being sitting patients with light injuries); or two may be carried lying down.

4th. *Portability of conveyance.*—The necessity for being prepared to convey on ship-board all kinds of ambulance vehicles to be used in the British service is not of the same importance at the present time as it was formerly. The English regulation wagons have not proved themselves of great value in countries outside Europe, and resort has generally under these circumstances been made to the carts of the country.* At the same time it is a great convenience for the wheels to be easily removable and interchangeable, for the cover and frame of the carriage to be easily separated, and by having certain portions previously connected by hinges, so that they may be folded down.

5th. *Capability of Repair, &c.*—To effect this object a certain proportion of artificers, as well as of carpenters' and blacksmiths' tools, must be available. These should be carried in the equipment of the Bearer Company and Field Hospital.†

6th. *Strength and Weight of the Conveyance.*—The lighter the vehicle, consistent with durability, the easier will be the draught, and, consequently, the less will be the distress and injury of the horses during a campaign, and the greater the regularity and speed with which the purposes of the carriage are accomplished. An ambulance wagon does not require to have the specific weight and solidity of frame which are necessary in wagons that are constructed for being loaded with heavy materials, such as have to be carried in the general traffic of civil life, or in the store wagons used in campaigning, but, on the contrary,

---

* See p. 313. English ambulance wagons in Franco-Prussian War.
† See British ambulance wagon, p. 310 et seq.

should never be used for any other purpose than ambulance transport.

To combine lightness with sufficient strength and accommodation constitutes one of the principal difficulties to be overcome in the manufacture of sick-transport conveyances, and how far the object is accomplished in any particular example can only be ascertained by careful examination and thorough practical trial of the vehicle after its construction.

7th. Carriage of Water and Surgical Stores.—Several methods are adopted for the carriage of the drinking water. In some it is carried inside, in others in a tank fixed to the flow and filled from the side. Below the floor is the best place, as the weight steadies the wagons and the water is kept cool. Six stretchers should accompany every wagon and four every cart, and a certain amount of reserve surgical stores may be carried on the wagon. — *Carriage of water.*

Means of light should also accompany the wagon, in case of its being used at night. Two descriptions of light should be provided; one, a fixed lamp attached to the vehicle itself, the other a lantern that can be carried to any particular object a light might be required for. The lamp attached to the vehicle should be so placed as to give light to the interior, and at the same time to indicate outside by coloured glass, or other means, the nature of the conveyance. Lamps would probably also be required to assist the driver at night. A hand-lantern should also be ready for use; numerous casual circumstances may arise to cause it to be wanted at night time. — *Carriage of light.*

8th. Protection against Weather.—This is frequently obtained by a canvas roof and sides stretched over movable supports and secured to the framework of the carriage. The material is light and efficient, resists a moderate amount of rain, and its employment facilitates package when the cover is not required for use, or when the vehicle is folded up for conveyance on board ship. Some vehicles are constructed with roofs of a more permanent nature, and are rendered quite impervious to moisture. On the whole, however, a strong canvas cover, with proper means for fixing it securely to resist the action of high winds, appears to answer the purpose of a roof best, if not to be the only kind of cover admissible, for vehicles such as British ambulance wagons, which have to be made capable of being reduced to comparatively small packages. — *Canvas roofs.*

9th. Ventilation of Interior of Vehicle.—The wounded who have to be placed in a recumbent position are frequently in a half faint condition, suffering from laboured and imperfect respiration, and, therefore, especially feel the need of a constant supply of fresh air. Without due forethought and provision in this respect, the compartments for the reception of these patients will not improbably be so hedged in and covered over that the free access of air will be prevented, and the suffering of the inmates be much increased. Even want of protection against rain or cold can be borne with more impunity than want of sufficient movement of air. Various plans are adopted for — *Ventilation of interior.*

CHAP. VI.

Ventilation often insufficient.

insuring a sufficiently free access of this requisite, such as leaving the sides of the vehicle open or only protecting them by curtains that can readily be rolled up, providing jalousied openings when the sides of the conveyance are solid, and making openings in the roof and ends. The plans employed will be again referred to when the several carriages are described, but, as a rule, it may be said that the means have not hitherto been adequate to the need, especially when the recumbent patients are not only shut in by the sides of the vehicle, but the access of air is still further prevented, as usually happens, by the patients who are carried sitting being placed on high seats in the fore part of the vehicle.

Need for ease of loading.

10th. *Convenience for Loading and Unloading.*—The **height** of the part of the vehicle on which the recumbent patients are placed must be regulated, and suitable arrangements made, so that wounded or very sick men may be got into and taken out of the places assigned to them with the utmost facility. The urgent circumstances of the wounded men, and the not improbable hurry and condition of excitement of the bearers, if the wounds be of recent occurrence; the weakness, suffering, and irritability of other patients who have been some time under treatment, whether for wounds or other ailments, before their transport, cause it to be very important for every obstruction to the ready transfer of sick and wounded into the **conveyance** to be avoided.

Risks when loading difficult.

Not only prolongation of suffering depending upon the movement, but accidents of a painful nature are not unlikely to occur if difficulty be met with, either in raising the wounded up into, or placing them in the ambulance vehicles. A want of sufficient facility of loading and unloading formed one of the inconveniences of the vehicles used in the Crimea, in which one tier of wounded was placed above another tier of wounded. The wounded destined to be carried in the upper tier could only be got into their places under any circumstances with difficulty, and, unless great care was taken, with risk of their slipping off the stretchers. The same objections equally applied when it was necessary to remove them. The height of the upper tiers for the wounded in such conveyances should never exceed the average height of the men who are to place the stretchers, upon which the wounded or sick men are lying, into them. The height of the floor of the wagon from the ground should be 3 feet, and of the upper tier 5 feet.

Communication with patients during their transport.

11th. *Access to Patients.*—The importance of the rule that there should be ready means of communication between the inmates of the conveyances and the attendants or others who are in charge of them will be at once understood, when the usual circumstances of the sick and wounded men who will be carried are remembered. On the one hand, the patients themselves should have the power of easily calling the attention of the attendants to wants which will inevitably rise from time to time, particularly if the transit be prolonged; on the other, the attendants should have every facility **for** watching their patients, and, if necessary, for handing them water, or administering help in case of hæmorrhage or **any** other emergency.

If sufficient medical attendants be available there should always be one with every ambulance wagon **of** a convoy. Six or eight patients, two of them so ill as to render a recumbent position necessary, will certainly require frequent attention under the circumstances of their transport, and **accidents** may not improbably arise that will render the prompt application of surgical aid of vital importance. If, however, it be impossible to spare one attendant for each wagon when several are moving together, arrangements should be made to ensure that ready means of communication are established between **such** attendants as **are sent** and the patients over whom they are placed in charge. A patient should on no account be allowed to feel that he is beyond the reach of help till the journey's end, but should understand the way of calling for assistance if he is in need, and have confidence that he will be attended to. This isolation was one of the **complaints** of the recumbent patients **shut** up in the tiers **of** compartments of the Crimean four-horse ambulance wagon; these compartments were sometimes likened to coffins in consequence.

A good plan for **carrying the hospital** orderly or medical attendant with an ambulance wagon was shown in some of the carriages exhibited at Paris. A seat, small in size, just sufficient to accommodate a person sitting, was attached to the back of the vehicle on one side of the door leading into the conveyance. This was designed for the attendant, who, when seated, would have his feet resting upon one of the steps of the carriage. He would thus be in the same position as the conductor of an omnibus, easily supervising the persons in the vehicle, easily called if wanted, and as easily quitting his place to render assistance. In some instances this seat remained fixed in position, in others it was made capable of folding down, or of sliding away under the body of the vehicle, when not required for use.

12*th. Stowage of Kits, &c.*—A soldier should never be separated from his kit in campaigning, and without the provision named under this clause, the kits of the sick and wounded would not unfrequently be mislaid or even lost. The importance of providing means to ensure the safety of the rifles and accoutrements is also obvious, for under ordinary circumstances the vehicles will move over ground held by the forces to which the patients belong, and their arms will have to be carried with them. The articles of the Geneva Convention, entered into **by** the European Powers to ensure the neutrality of sick and wounded troops in time of war, stipulate that the **wounded** men with their private effects and all ambulance material necessary for their care and safety, are to be regarded as neutral and covered by full protection in consequence; but equally plainly lay down the rule that no war materials of any kind shall have part in the neutrality. All that will be necessary **to** prevent

CHAP. VI.

infringement of the stipulations when ambulance vehicles are moving over ground held by an enemy, as happened in Germany in 1866, will be to leave the places provided in the wagons for the arms vacant. The military authorities in such a case will make provision elsewhere for the care of the rifles or other weapons belonging to the sick men.

SECTION V.—ON THE COMPARATIVE MERITS OF CARTS AND WAGONS FOR THE TRANSPORT OF SICK AND WOUNDED, AND ON THE SEVERAL MODES ADOPTED FOR DRIVING SUCH VEHICLES.

Wheeled ambulance vehicles are met with of two forms, and these are most conspicuously indicated by the number of their wheels, viz., those with two and those with four wheels. The former are called carts, the latter, which are in their nature only double carts, are called wagons. The carts are usually built for draught by one or two horses, the wagons by two or four horses according to the size and kind of vehicle. Provision, however, is usually made in both forms of vehicle for **supplementing** the regular amount of draught by **additional** horse power **in case** of necessity.

Merits of carts and wagons differently estimated.

It has frequently been a matter of discussion which of these two forms **is** the most convenient and the most economical for the transport of sick and wounded under the circumstances of campaigning; just as in civil life the like question has been often discussed in respect of single-horse carts and four-horse wagons for the general traffic and farming operations of the country.* The principal reasons which have been advanced against, as well as in favour of, the use of each kind of conveyance are as follows:—

Arguments in favour of the use of wagons for ambulance purposes.—1. Wagons are safer under all circumstances. A wagon cannot be upset so easily as a two-wheeled vehicle. One of the horses may stumble and fall without risk of injury to the occupants of a wagon.

Safety of wagons.

Their kind of movement.

2. The motion of a wagon is less irksome and fatiguing to a patient than the motion of a cart.

3. The rolling of one or even of two wheels of a wagon can be stopped without difficulty by various mechanical contrivances, and the progression of the whole conveyance be greatly checked at any moment by the friction which follows between each locked wheel and the ground. The risk of accidents to the patients inside when they have to be carried down hilly roads with a steep descent can be thus materially

---

* It is a singular fact, but in the English army all transport is arranged for pairs; one-horse carriage is uncommon; three-horse, very rare; the loads moreover are very unequal; for instance, a loaded ambulance on M. IV. weighs over 30 cwt., a water cart under 20 cwt., and a pair of horses is the allowance to each.—ED.

lessened as compared with the risk they are subjected to when carts are employed.

4. Wagons render a less number of vehicles necessary in a campaign.

5. The cost of the equipment is less in providing a given number of wagons than the cost would be of providing a corresponding amount of accommodation for patients in two-wheeled carts.

6. A smaller number of drivers is necessary. An increase in the number of non-combatants with an army is always an evil when it can possibly be avoided, not merely on account of the expense entailed by the entertainment of the men themselves, but also on account of the additional provision of rations, tentage, and other incumbrances.

Objections to the use of wagons for ambulance purposes.—
1. Wagons, as they have been usually built, and as is stated to be necessary to make them substantial and strong enough for their size, the weight they carry, and the usage they will be subjected to, are both cumbrous and heavy. When a wagon has broken down in a narrow pass, at the foot of a declivity, or on a bridge, it has proved itself to be a sufficient impediment to stop the progress of a whole force for a considerable time.

2. It requires time and practice to get a team of four horses to work well together; and, even when they have been well practised together, it is almost impossible to maintain with them a continued equality of exertion. One horse will pull hard, while another shirks his work as he finds opportunity; and thus calculations of power of draught, based on the multiplication of the power of draught of a single horse, becomes falsified in practice.

3. The sudden occurrence of an injury or illness to one horse of a team paralyses the usefulness of three others. If one of the four fail in health, the increased exertion exacted from the other three has a tendency to knock them up also.

4. A wagon drawn by a team of four horses has either two drivers mounted or a driver sitting on a box. In either arrangement the art of driving skilfully can only be attained by proper instruction and long practice. An unskilful driver, especially in bad roads, who has not acquired the art, not merely of conducting the carriage, but also of connecting the efforts of the animals so that they may all pull together and evenly to a given purpose, will cause each horse to be quickly fatigued, will make under any circumstances but indifferent progress, and will not unlikely disable the wagon before a long time has elapsed.

5. The capacity of wagons cannot be sub-divided. Though only one sick or wounded man may require to be carried, the transport vehicle designed for the carriage of eight or ten men must be employed for the purpose. If a regiment be divided into several detachments, the means of transport allotted to the regiment cannot be divided in proportion.

CHAP. VI.

Effect of wagons on roads.

6. The concentrated weight in wagons cuts up roads more than lighter conveyances, though the latter are more numerous.

Power of draught of riding horse in wagons.

7. If a wagon be built to be drawn by only two horses, one in shafts, the other attached to a swingletree with the driver postilion fashion, the mounted animal is caused to walk in a kind of trot, and its power of draught is considerably interfered with.

Arguments in favour of carts for ambulance purposes.—

Durability of carts.

1. Carts, from their less bulk and comparative lightness, are less likely to be injured or to break down on service than wagons; they are therefore more durable, and consequently in the end more economical, notwithstanding that, owing to the greater number required, they may cost more at first. Should such an accident occur as a breakdown, or should it be overset, a cart can be righted or removed out of the way of a column in a few minutes by three or four soldiers.

Advantages resulting from the lightness of carts.

Their lightness also makes them more manageable in other ways. They can pass over by-roads which would not be practicable for large wagons. They are moved with greater speed than wagons. They go up-hill more easily, and with less distress to the animals drawing them. The efforts of a few men can help the passage of a cart through a temporary difficulty, over an obstruction, up the slope of a ravine, and such like impediments, when they would be fruitless on a heavy wagon.

Art of leading a single-horse cart easily learned.

2. When a cart drawn by one horse is used, the horse should be led. Any steady soldier can be taught in one or two lessons to manage and lead a horse.

Advantages of leading.

3. It is an advantage for the horse to be led instead of being driven. The expenditure of force in carrying the weight of a mounted driver is thus saved, and it is no hardship for the conductor to walk his day's march, as he will be relieved of the appointments which the infantry soldier has to carry the same distance.

Economy in draught.

4. One horse acting independently will exert his strength more equally in drawing his load, and cannot shirk his work without making his failure at once obvious to the conductor.

Effect of injury to the horse.

5. If the animal in a single-horse cart meets with an injury that disables him completely from work, or dies, it alone is disabled, and its own proportion of transport only is delayed; if he is only sick or lame, he can be weighted accordingly.

One conductor may lead several carts.

6. In case of necessity one conductor can take charge of several carts, by each horse being connected by a guiding strap or rope, three or four feet in length, to the tail-board of the cart in front. This method is not recommended.

Less waste of labour with carts.

7. The use of carts obviates the inconvenience attached to wagons of not being able to subdivide their capacity. A certain number of carts can always do the work of a wagon, at the same time that they can be separated to do the work required

by a detachment, or meet **the** wants of one **or two** sick or hurt men, without unnecessary waste of labour.

8. It constantly happens, where one-horse carts are employed, **that** a partiality grows with acquaintance between the animal and its attendant. The man's inclination then, as well as his duty, leads him to do whatever work is necessary with the most ease to the horse intrusted to his keeping, to look carefully after the rations allowed for him, and to do **all in** his power towards preserving the animal's health and strength. **Besides,** the man knows that the condition of the horse will be a **test of** the attention he has given **to it.**

9. The objection to carts on account of the additional number of vehicles and drivers required when they are used **is** more apparent than real, for if it be true that single-horse carts are more durable in campaigning than wagons, then a proportionally less total amount of hospital conveyance for a campaign may be estimated for with propriety at its commencement.

10. It is stated that the weight which can be conveniently conveyed by four one-horse carts is considerably **greater** than that which can be carried by a wagon drawn by **four** horses. Mr. McAdam, the grandson of the inventor of the modern system of road-making in England, has strongly advocated that single-horse carts should be used in farming operations, as **a** much more convenient and economical method of conveyance than the wagons which have been generally used.* One of his reasons is that four single-horse loads are found practically to exceed the load conveyed by four horses in a team. According to his observations a well-formed English cart-horse, of $15\frac{1}{2}$ hands high, in good condition, can draw 25 cwt. over any hard road, independent of the weight of the cart, which should not exceed seven cwt.; so that four such loads would equal five tons of loading, while the weight usually carried by a four-horse wagon is 3 tons 15 cwt. The one wagon is about 5 cwt. lighter than the four single-horse carts together; consequently while, on the one hand, 5 cwt. in the carriage is thus saved, on the other, 1 ton 5 cwt. in the load is lost, or a clear loss **of 1 ton in** cartage results when the four-horse wagon is used.

Objections to *single-horse carts.*—These **have** been already **referred to in** the arguments urged in favour of the use of **wagons.**

The most powerful objection is that two-wheeled vehicles are insecure and liable to be upset by careless driving, by accidental irregularities of ground, by horses falling, and by the absence of any mechanical means for checking undue progression of the vehicle when its rate of movement becomes accelerated from going down a steep road. The radical source of the risk of accidents arising from **the** causes just named is the instability which necessarily results from the conveyance being

---

* Mr. McAdam's views on this subject are fully explained in a pamphlet entitled "Observations on single-horse carts," printed by H. E. Carrington, Bath, 1844.

CHAP. VI.

Care of horses with single-horse carts.

Number of single-horse carts necessary for a campaign.

Load carried in one-horse carts.

Comparison with loads carried in four-horse wagons.

Instability of one-horse carts.

CHAP. VI.

Motion of one-horse carts.

poised on a **single axle** and pair of wheels instead of being maintained in position, independently of the animal between the shafts, as wagons are, by supports placed both in front and behind the body of the vehicle.

Another objection to the use of carts for ambulance purposes arises from the intimate and rigid connection between the shafts and the bodies of these vehicles. The shafts and body of a cart form one piece as it were, and, as a consequence, when the horse within the shafts trots, or moves in any pace quicker than a walk, the body of the cart is lifted up and down with every step of the animal. Even at a walking pace, the movement, although not so objectionable as when the horse is trotting, is still greater than the movement of a four-wheeled vehicle, owing to the different manner in which the shafts are attached to the bodies of wagons; not, however, so much so as of itself to form a sufficient cause of rejection for hospital use.

The remaining objections are, firstly, the number of carts required, and consequently the greater outlay of money at starting to supply the wants of an army; and secondly, the number of men required for their care and conduct throughout the campaign. These have been considered in previous **remarks**.

General Conclusion.—It will be observed from these remarks that the most serious defect of the two-wheeled carts, and that which has chiefly prevented their general adoption, has been their want of stability. On the other hand, the strongest objections made to the four-wheeled wagons which have been hitherto employed in the field have been based on the impediments arising from their cumbrous size and weight, and the number of horses required to act in combination for their draught.

Instability a fatal objection to any vehicle.

Want of stability, or in other words, liability to be upset, must always be a fatal objection to any vehicle, more especially to one which is destined to carry disabled men who are deprived of the power of aiding themselves under any circumstances. Were it not for the conviction that this serious defect is inseparably connected with carts, a conviction deduced from experience, there can be little doubt but that the general advantages possessed by two-wheeled over four-wheeled vehicles in campaigning would have ensured their adoption for purposes of **ambulance** transport. It may be a question how much faulty construction, especially in the relation of height to width, has been the cause of the want of stability complained of; and also how far want of systematic training of the drivers, carelessness or neglect of common precautions, may have led to the accidents on account of which the use of two-wheeled vehicles has been so generally condemned for sick transport purposes.

Ambulance vehicles not subject to same conditions.

The carriages employed in transporting sick and wounded, or hospital stores, would never, as a rule, be taken over such ground as guns are liable to traverse, nor are they required to be manœuvred as artillery vehicles are. They would scarcely ever be driven over any other than made roads. The general principle is that the wagons will be brought up and remain stationary at the nearest convenient spot to the place of fighting for receiving the wounded. The men with stretchers, and the mules with cacolets and litters, can follow the troops down ravines, up steep slopes, and over ploughed **fields** with impunity; they are designed for such purposes; and the wounded will be brought on them to the ambulance wagons **to be** afterwards carried still further to the rear. Under these circumstances it appears that it would **be a** wiser plan to economise the strength of the horses, and to devote it entirely to the draught of the loads behind them. This would be accomplished by driving from **a box**, for the objectionable expenditure of force, and the **unfavourable condition** for making exertion in which a horse is placed when carrying a rider, would be avoided.

*The **use** of poles compared **with that** of shafts **for** ambulance wagons.*—The same reasons that make the plan of driving from a box more suitable also lead to the conclusion that the use of a pole would be more advantageous than the use of shafts. Under the present system, so far as the draught is concerned, the labour is very unevenly divided between the two horses. The horse in the shafts, or off-horse, has the weight of the wagon chiefly thrown upon it. In taking the wagon over an obstruction it is the off-horse which lifts the wagon; in going down-hill the weight of the wagon falls on the same horse; in backing, the same thing happens. With a pole, this labour would be equally divided between the two horses.

The pole system has other advantages over that of shafts. If a horse fall he is more easily got up again with the former than when he is in shafts, and, in case of breakage, a pole is more easily repaired than shafts. It is obvious that spare poles are more easily carried than spare shafts.

For these reasons, although the shaft system may be necessary for the rapid manoeuvres and other circumstances of artillery, the pole seems to be the best suited for ambulance vehicles.

A.—AMBULANCE TRANSPORT CARTS.

A description of particular conveyances, both two-wheeled and four-wheeled, will now follow. The patterns about to be described have been selected for one or other of the following reasons, or for several of them combined:—Either the carriage is noteworthy from historical associations; or it possesses some characteristic features of construction which have been supposed to fit it particularly for use in the field; or some alleged special advantages as regards the wounded intended to be carried by it; or it affords an example of some design which experience has proved to be defective, so that a notice of it is calculated to be useful as a means of preventing wasteful repetition of an unserviceable contrivance; or it is the kind of vehicle authorised

CHAP. VI. for use in the British army or in the service of some foreign country.

Wheeled Ambulance Transport, then, will be discussed under three heads:—

    A. Ambulance carts.
    B. Ambulance wagons.
    C. Hired or country carts.

A. AMBULANCE CARTS.

Larrey's Ambulance Cart.

Vehicles of Larrey's ambulance volante.

In the chapter on the history of the modern system of ambulance transport, the important innovation made by Baron Larrey in the medical service of armies by the introduction of his flying field hospitals (ambulances volantes) in the year 1797, has already been described. The ambulance volante included not only the means of keeping up the materials necessary for the surgical treatment of the wounded with the troops in advance, but also the means of carrying away the wounded from the field of action after their wounds had been dressed. This latter service was accomplished by means of two sets of vehicles, one being two-wheeled carts for two patients lying at full length, of very simple construction, which, while solid, yet according to Baron Larrey's description, were very light, and capable of rapid movement. They were designed for draught by two horses. The other set was four-wheeled, for four patients recumbent, and designed for draught by four horses. The two-wheeled vehicles were suitable for flat countries; the four-wheeled were designed for use in mountainous countries. These vehicles were maintained in use until the year 1811. The following description refers to the former kind.

Construction of Larrey's ambulance carts.

The body of each cart had the form of an elongated tube, rounded at the upper part. Both the front and back were fitted with folding doors, which met in the middle on being closed. On being opened, these doors admitted of being thrown back far enough to leave the whole of the space between the sides clear of any obstruction. The greatest facility was thus afforded for getting patients in and out of the carriage; for their ingress and egress could not only be effected at the back of the cart, but could also be materially facilitated by assistance from the front. Each side was pierced by round openings for air and light, with sliding shutters inside; there appear also to have been spaces for the admission of air at the two ends, between the folding doors and the covering of the roof. The floor of the interior of the cart was formed by two movable frames, each furnished

---

* Model No. 1301 in the Mus. of Mil. Surg. at Netley.

CHAP. VI.

Larrey's cart.

with a horsehair mattress and pillow covered with leather. These frames were caused to slide easily upon the two lower side-beams and a central partition within the cart by means of little iron castors. Each frame was also furnished with four iron handles fixed in the wood of its sides; these were for the purpose of receiving straps, or the belts of the soldiers, to assist in carrying a wounded man upon the frame in the same way as upon a stretcher. The sides of the interior of the cart were padded for a foot in height from the floor; there were also several pockets for carrying bottles or other articles necessary for the sick. Each

Fig. XCV.—Side elevation of Larrey's "voiture d'ambulance volante a deux roues," or flying ambulance cart.

cart was drawn by two horses; one in shafts, the other, upon which the driver sat, being attached to a swingle-tree.

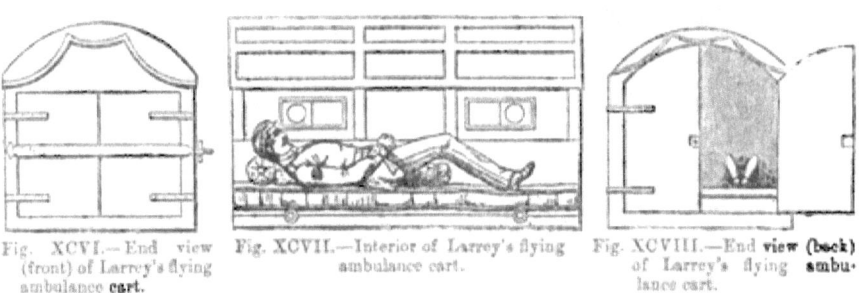

Fig. XCVI.—End view (front) of Larrey's flying ambulance cart.

Fig. XCVII.—Interior of Larrey's flying ambulance cart.

Fig. XCVIII.—End view (back) of Larrey's flying ambulance cart.

These vehicles were not carried upon springs, but were suspended *from* springs by straps at the four corners, as shown in the sketch. Excessive movement, upward or lateral, was restrained by straps and chains connected with the framework to which the springs were fixed.

The illustrations (Figs. XCV—XCVIII) of Larrey's flying ambulance cart are copied from sketches in the memoirs of the eminent military surgeon by whom the vehicle was invented.

La voiture Macon.

Chap. VI.

This two-wheeled vehicle was exhibited by the French Government in Paris in 1867. Although not forming at that time part of the regular train equipment of the French army, it was found so serviceable in Mexico, as it had been previously in Algeria, owing to its lightness, ready mobility, simplicity of construction, cheapness, and other advantageous qualities, that many trials were made with a view to its introduction.

Construction of the Macou cart.

The *Macon* carriage is so called from the name of its inventor. It has been designed for carrying **two wounded men lying** recumbent upon two stretchers, **together with a driver on a** seat in front. It is drawn by **one mule.** The stretchers, which are of peculiar construction, **can**, if necessary, be taken out altogether and placed on the roof of the vehicle. When thus removed and placed outside, the cart is empty, and can then carry from three to four hundred kilos. of materials, but there are no special adaptations to fit it for the carriage of stores. The cart is of the tray kind. The sides are formed for a limited distance of wood; the remainder, up to the roof, of canvas. The same material closes the back of the vehicle above the tailboard. The roof is solid, being formed of wood, is covered above by canvas painted white, and is supported **on four** light iron uprights springing from each side **of** the body and continued under the roof of the vehicle. The wooden part of the sides is not of the same depth throughout; **it is lower in fron**t, and **is** heightened behind in the part which corresponds with the raised heads of the stretchers in the interior. The floor of the cart behind is sunk, so as to form a well for the reception of certain articles; this well also corresponds in position **with** the raised parts of the two stretchers. When the tail-board is lowered the knapsacks of the patients lying on the stretchers can be readily placed beneath the raised stretcher-heads into the well just described. Under the floor in front is placed, on one side a water-barrel; and on the other a box for surgical materials. The seat for the driver is in front, and consists of a semicircular board with an iron rail; it is supported on three iron legs, one on each side fixed to the front board of the cart, the third in the centre behind fixed to the piece of wood that divides the two stretchers. The seat is thus within the body of the vehicle. An inclined footboard for the driver is placed **across the** shafts.

Guthrie's Hospital Conveyance Carts.

Mr. Guthrie's ambulance carts.

The carts known under this name were built according to the directions of Inspector-General Guthrie, the author of the celebrated commentaries on the surgery of the Peninsular War. The practical experience of this eminent surgeon, gained during long service in the field, gave great weight to his suggestions on the form of transport to be despatched with the army proceeding to Turkey. Accordingly, twenty carts, ten for recumbent and ten for sitting, were despatched from Woolwich, and built after his plans. They were two-wheeled **carts**, drawn by one horse, though an extra horse could **be** easily attached. The weight was **10½ cwt.** It was covered in with white painted canvas, with an **apron** attached in front and behind to a footboard. It was found

Fig. XCIX.—Guthrie's flat-topped Hospital Conveyance Cart. For carrying **two** patients lying on spring stretchers on the floor, and a third, if required, in **a** stretcher slung from the roof, with room also for nine persons sitting **on seats** before and behind. The second horse is not shown in the drawing.

that these carts were liable to be upset, and also, when heavily **loaded and going** down a declivity, to throw the horse down.

Tufnell's Military Field Cart.

This cart was designed by Professor **Jolliffe Tufnell,** of Dublin, and was based on the same principle of construction, **and had** the same outward appearance **as** an Irish "outside car" or "jaunting car." It was, however, of larger dimensions than the cars in ordinary use in Ireland.* The "well" of the cart **was divided into** two compartments, an upper and lower. **At the top of** the upper compartment **a** stretcher **was carried, ready to** accommodate a **wounded** person in a **recumbent position.** A drawer, extending the whole length **of the** car, occupied the bottom **of the** lower compartment **of** the well. This drawer contained an assortment

Construction and contents of Tufnell's field-cart.

---

* Model No. 1305, in the Mil. Surg. Mus. at **Netley.**

Chap. VI.

Capacity of Tufnell's field-cart.

of medical comforts, surgical materials, blankets, and other articles. A space existed between the drawer and the stretcher above, and here were stored iron rods which could be used as standards for supporting a waterproof cloth to form a cover for the cart in case of need. This cover when removed from the car was capable of being set up in a field, and of being used as a tent. Another tent complete, of the bell form, was carried in the same part of the car. The seats on each side of the well afforded, under ordinary circumstances, room for

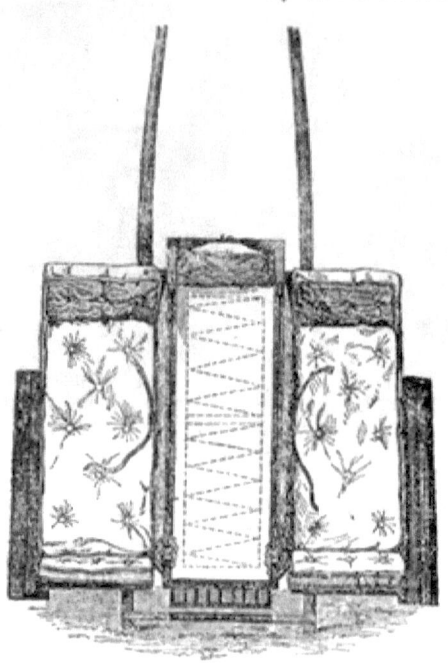

Fig. C.—General view of Tufnell's Military Field Cart. The cart has been turned up so as to show the stretcher in the "well," and the two cushioned side-seats, at one glance. The two foot-boards are seen to project on each side.

three men sitting, but the end boards of the seats were so arranged that they could be let down to any desired angle, or even could be completely lowered so as to be on a level with the rest of the seat. By this arrangement they could each, on an emergency, accommodate five men sitting, or be used as a litter with a sloping head-rest, for receiving a patient in the recumbent position. In this last-named case the foot-boards could be turned up and strapped by the side of the seats or litters, so as to secure the patients from the risk of falling off. The car could thus be made to carry three men lying down, one on the stretcher in the middle, and one on the long seat on each side. A water-cask with stopcock and two drinking vessels were carried under the driver's foot-board.

This form of carriage, as well as a similar one made by the Royal Carriage Department, was discarded after many trials.

In October, 1855, a medical board in the Crimea reported as follows on the results of the use of these conveyances at the seat of war :—

"The jaunting-cars being very narrow between the wheels, are consequently unsafe, and are reported to the Board to be very liable to be upset. The cars, with a fair load, appear to travel very easy, but are complained of, when persons are carried singly, as being rough and shaking." Sir John Hall, in for-

Fig. CI.—Side view of Tufnell's Military Field Cart.

warding the report of the Board, expressed his opinion that cars of this description would be very useful on the line of march in carrying men who were compelled to fall out for sickness or were footsore, as they could easily mount and dismount from it. The same fault, however, of liability to be upset was found at Aldershot, to which camp one of the Irish cars with india-rubber springs had been sent for trial. The principal medical officer, Surgeon-Major O'Flaherty, reported concerning it on the 8th of November, 1855 :—"This cart is not a good one, it is unsafe from being top-heavy. The breadth of the body is too great for the length of the axle, so that a trifling elevation of the wheel is apt to overturn the whole machine." Surgeon-Major O'Flaherty considered, however, that an ambulance cart on the Irish car principle might be so constructed as to be free from the liability to be upset, and that such a conveyance would "be found to be the easiest and best description of one-horse carriage for removing a number of sick or wounded men, who, although unable to walk, could sit up."

CHAP. VI.

*Inspector-General Macpherson's Madras cart.**

Capacity of Macpherson's Indian sick-transport cart.

This cart was designed to replace the old pattern of Indian hospital cart over which it possesses many advantages. It is less heavy in construction, and is suspended from two axle springs. As regards amount of accommodation, it is adapted to convey two men in a recumbent position, or one recumbent, and two sitting up back to back, or four men sitting or semi-recumbent back to back, together with the driver. It is provided with shafts, as well as with a pole, and can be drawn either by a single horse or a pair of bullocks, according as circumstances may render most convenient.

Construction of Macpherson's cart.

The body of the vehicle is formed with a double floor. The lower floor is separated from the upper by a space which is intended to receive medical stores, the men's knapsacks, accoutrements, or firelocks. This space is open at both ends, but is closed at the sides. The upper floor forms the support for the beds of the patients when they are placed in a recumbent posture, and equally supports the seats for them when they are carried sitting. The mechanical construction employed to effect these several purposes is peculiar. An upright post rises from the middle of the upper floor to the roof or frame which supports the awning of the cart; and two upright posts, at the same distance from the front and back of the cart as this central post, are fixed upright close to each side of the cart. These pillars are grooved on their opposite aspects respectively, and two frames, fitted with open canework, are made to slide up and down these grooves at pleasure. These frames can therefore be raised near to the roof of the cart, or they can be lowered to a certain depth when they form backs for sitting patients to lean against.

Before and behind the upright posts just described, four seats with arms are placed, two in front and two behind. Each seat is divided into two parts, one part being fixed to the upright posts, the other part being rendered free to move by being hinged to the fixed part. The movable part or flap of the seat can be lifted upwards, and may be so far folded back as to lie flatly on to the fixed part. Thus a patient can sit either on the double seat as on an ordinary arm-chair, or the flap may be left hanging down in front without causing inconvenience. But the movable part can also be extended and maintained in the same plane as the fixed part by a catch in front, and the patient can then recline in a semi-recumbent position, having his legs raised as on a couch. When the cart is intended to be used for carrying two patients wholly recumbent the canework backs are caused to slide up in their grooves towards the roof where they are secured. There is now an open communication between the two seats in front and the two behind the upright posts. If all

* Model No. 1304 in the Mus. of Mil. Surg. at Netley.

the movable flaps are now raised and secured, each of the front and corresponding back seats will be united in one plane, and thus a sufficiently long support is afforded on each side of the central upright post, and between it and the two side posts, for the reception of a patient lying on a mattress or ordinary stretcher.

The sides of the cart are protected by awnings. These awnings consist of four wooden flaps, two on each side, formed of light frames covered by canvas. They extend along the whole length of the cart. These flaps can be separately opened or shut at pleasure, and can be kept open at any necessary angle by iron stays. Ventilation may thus be maintained through the cart, at the same time that the glare of the sun is shaded from the interior. The front and rear curtains are made to hang

Fig. CII.—Inspector-General Macpherson's Madras Cart.

down loosely from the roof, but can be rolled and kept up when necessary.

The weight of Macpherson's cart as constructed at Madras was seven hundredweight.

Although this cart was only used for a very short period, still it marks a distinct progression in the nature of ambulance conveyances in India.

Cherry's field cart for hospital service.

This ambulance cart was designed by Veterinary-Surgeon Cherry, and is referred to by him in his "Observations on the defective state of Army Transport, with suggestions for its improvement, printed for the author in 1825." It is a single-horse cart, and when used for sick-transport purposes is intended to carry four men sitting, or one man recumbent. One of these carts was sent for trial to Chatham and was for some years in use in connection with the general hospital at that station. Twelve of them were subsequently sent from England to be used with the expeditionary force in Spain under Sir de Lacy Evans in 1835. The practical trials to which Cherry's field cart was thus subjected, while they elicited the fact that it possessed very many advantages, also served to show the defects which existed in it when employed on field service. A particular description of its construction, which **presents several special** features, as well as of the **results of the experience gained by its use**, will be useful for reference, especially if in the future it should be thought advisable to provide conveyances adapted for both ambulance and army transport purposes. The defects experienced in the field with Cherry's cart, which were chiefly want of strength in the shafts and wheels, and its being fitted as a single-horse conveyance. These can no doubt be remedied, and its peculiar mechanism adapted to a four-wheeled conveyance drawn by two horses, if circumstances should render the attempt desirable.

Construction of Cherry's carts.

The principal peculiarity in the construction of Cherry's cart is the mechanism by which the vehicle is enabled to be employed either as a cart with springs, or with the body resting directly upon the axle without the intervention of the springs, so as to fit it for carrying either wounded men or heavy stores. This mechanism, which is placed beneath the cart, but manipulated by a lever, one end of which projects behind the cart, consists of two movable blocks sliding upon the axle so as to be transferred at pleasure, either under the framework on each side, or within the hollow space beneath the floor of the cart. The handle of the lever by which the movement is effected is furnished with a stirrup-shaped iron loop, and this enables it to be secured to either one or other of two hooks which project from the two corners of the hinder part of the cart.

Mode of suspending the seats or litter in Cherry's field-cart.

Another peculiarity in the fittings of Cherry's cart is the manner in which the stretcher for a patient lying down, or the seats when the men are carried sitting, are suspended within the cart. They are slung by the following means:—Closely connected with the upper borders of the sides and ends of the cart is a continuous piece of strong rope. This rope runs along the *inner* surfaces of the two *sides*, but along the *outer* surfaces of the two *ends* of the cart. They are passed through openings made for their passage at the two ends. An apparatus is provided for bracing up this rope according to circumstances. The seats for men sitting, when not so employed, form portions of the floor of the cart, which is partly double, or rather, is provided with two wells for the reception of various articles. The planks covering these wells are removable, and at each end they are fitted with two curved pieces of iron, of a shape to fit them for securely grasping the rope fixed to the sides of the cart. A certain amount of elasticity is afforded to the seat by its suspension from the rope, as described, but a further provision is made for breaking the force of concussions by the cart, when used as an ambulance transport conveyance, being arranged to rest only on the springs. When a man is to be carried in a recumbent position, the seats are not removed from the floor, but the poles of a regulation stretcher are looped to the two side ropes, and so an easy litter is obtained for the carriage of the patient.

CHAP. VI.

Cherry's cart.

The arrangement by which the men are carried sitting is shown in the following sketch. The two side ropes are indicated by the lines proceeding from *a*; *b b* represent the two planks used as seats, which have been taken from the two wells marked *c c* in the floor of the cart. The drawing also shows the manner in which the covering of the cart is supported. The poles which form the support are carried on the outside of the

Fig. CIII.—Cherry's cart arranged for the carriage of four patients sitting. *a*. The two side ropes. *b b*. The two planks employed as seats, removed from, *c c*. Two wells in the bottom of the cart. *d*. The cover of the cart.

two sides of the cart. When mounted, the poles and cross-piece which form the ridge of the cover are supported within staples fixed to the ends of the cart; those which constitute the framework for supporting the sides of the awning pass through partitioned openings at the upper part, and are secured in iron staples on the lower part of the framework of the sides of the cart.

This cart was very favourably received, and marks an era in ambulance carriage building.

CHAP. VI.

The Maltese Cart.

The Maltese cart.

The Maltese cart is a conveyance used for the carriage of all kinds of packages and stores, whether light or heavy, and is drawn by one horse. It is exceedingly simple in its construction. Two long and strong shafts are firmly secured to an axletree which connects two very high wheels. The shafts are raised by blocks placed upon the axle, so that they rest about the height of a foot above it. Cross-bars of wood, each about 1 foot broad, are nailed at intervals upon the part of the shafts which lies between the wheels and also a little distance beyond this portion, both in front and behind.

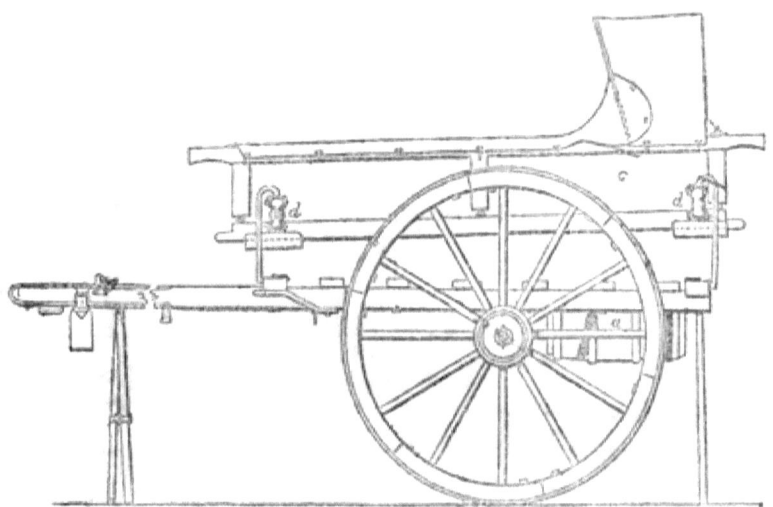

Fig. CIV.—Side elevation of the Maltese cart, with folding litters. *a.* Water-barrel. *c.* Folding litter. *d.* India-rubber springs.

The shafts and the interrupted floor just described, without any further addition, constitute the frame or body of the vehicle as it is used for the common purposes of civil life in Malta.

Manner of slinging the stretchers upon it.

To adapt it for carrying the wounded, four upright iron supports, each about 2 feet in height, are inserted into cross-pieces bolted upon the upper surfaces of the two shafts, at nearly equal distances in front of and behind the wheels. Two broad and strong cross-boards are next suspended between the iron uprights or standards, one between the two standards in front, the other between the two in rear, by means of Fuller's[*] india-rubber springs. The two stretchers are then laid upon and secured to these two boards. The sick or wounded by this arrangement are slung, as it were, in the cots, and they escape the ill effects of the concussions communicated to the frame-

---

[*] *See post*, p. 311.

work of the cart when in motion, as the shocks they would otherwise receive are broken by the intervention of the elastic springs. A barrel for four gallons of water, and a grease tin are strapped underneath the cart. Arrangements also exist for carrying the rifles and kits of two men beneath the cart. The usual draught is by one horse, but an outrigger and swingle-tree are provided to attach a second horse if necessary.

One of the Maltese carts with folding litters **was** tried for some time at Aldershot, and in November, 1855, the principal medical officer of the camp, Deputy Inspector-General O'Flaherty, reported upon it as "affording a very easy way **of** placing a patient upon a cart, and permitting him to recline, as it **were,** in a bed, on either his back, or **on** either side, in com**parative** comfort. It travels safely, easily, and for the removal of two bad cases, I cannot fancy a better vehicle. The land transport men who drive this cart, and those **who** have ridden in it, speak of it as being well adapted **for the** purposes it is intended to accomplish."

Twenty-five of **the Maltese** carts **with folding litters complete were** sent for the **service of the army in the Crimea on the 18th of** August, 1855.

British Ambulance Cart. Mark II.

This cart is descended from the Cyprus cart, constructed for one-horse draught, and intended for use in that country after the occupation. It was designed by Colonel Close, R.A.

The description **is** as follows:—

The cart is constructed to carry four patients in a **sitting** posture or two lying on stretchers.

It consists of a wooden body fitted with side springs **and front and** rear footboards, an axletree with two 4-feet 8-inch **wheels** and two removable shafts.

Spiral "draw springs," through which the loops for the swingle-trees pass, are fitted behind the splinter bar; these are intended to ease the strain of draught upon the horses, particu**larly at** starting.

The cart springs are attached to the under side of the **axletree, so as** to lower the body and increase the stability **of the cart.**

An angle steel bracket (*a*) is fitted to the "offside" to facilitate access to the front seat, and the bottom of the cart **is** fitted with two boards, provided with flaps, and hinged to centre cross-bars, so that when the cart is required to carry four patients the boards can be folded upwards to form backboards, the bottom of the cart being fitted with cushions for seats.

When stretchers are required for use the backboards **are** folded down to form the floor, the stretchers being then **secured** in position by the staple (*b*), and by the tailboard, which, **when** not in use, is carried behind the footboard at (*c*).

A removable wooden partition is placed between the stretchers to divide the patients. When not in use the partition

Chap. VI.
Mark II. ambulance cart.

and stretchers are strapped to the ball hoops at (*d*), and the stretcher-pillows to the top of the centre ball hoops. The sides of the cart are furnished with iron handles (*e*), for leather breast straps, steel staples for the ball hoops, iron hooks for the cover, iron staples, and brackets for the lamps, and wooden cleats, and iron staples for carrying two carbines.

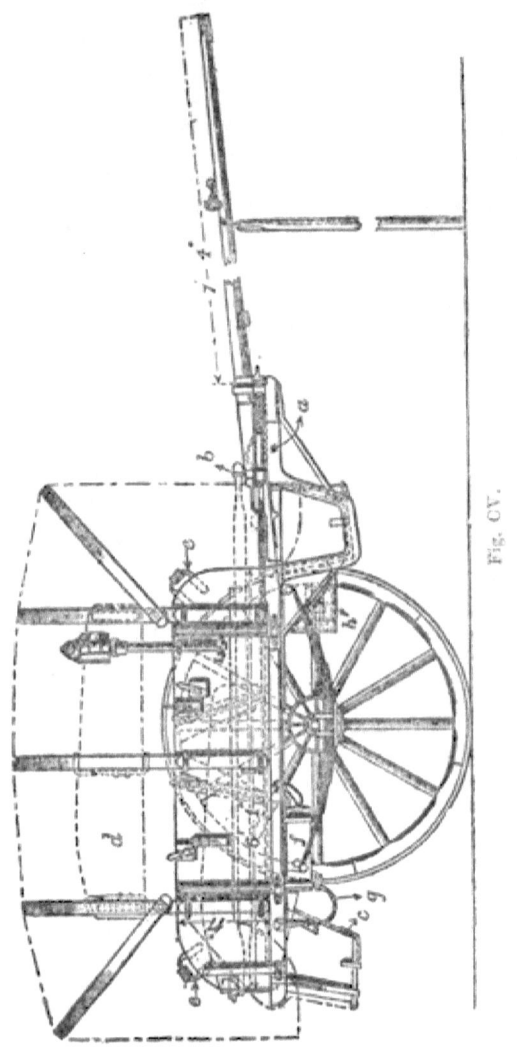

Fig. CV.

A zinc tank (*f*) for water, covered with wood, is fixed to the offside of the cart by iron bands, and is fitted with an india-rubber tube (*g*), having a tinned copper mouthpiece, which is **hung** on an iron claw when not in use.

A wooden box of the same dimensions as the tank is carried in a similar position on the "near" side. The interior of this box is fitted with cork partitions for two ordinary wine bottles, the rest of the space is utilised for packing medical comforts. A locker (k) is fixed under the front seat for the driver's use, and fittings are attached to the "near" side of it for securing a grease box.

The cover, which is of waterproof canvas, is made to fit over the footboards, and encloses the front and rear seats. The front and rear parts are slit up the centre to form flaps, which can be folded up, and fastened back by leather straps. Aprons of bleached "duck" are made to fit over the footboards, in which position they are secured by leather straps.

The stretchers used are the service pattern, Mark V. The wheels are 3rd class, with flanges of malleable cast iron, formed with ribs for lightness and strength. The tyres are 2 inches wide by half-inch thick, and the pipes are of phosphor bronze.

		cwt.	qrs.	lbs.	cwt.	qr.	lbs.
Weight	cart	8	2	14	9	0	19
	two stretchers	0	2	5			
Tonnage				3·5 tons.			
Rectangular space occupied in boats				16′·4½″ × 6′·0¾″ × 7′·9¼″			

A few carts constructed on the same principle as the cart already described, but differing in some of the details, have been manufactured and designated Mark I., but no more of that pattern will be made.

The Tonga.

This form of conveyance is very common over the whole of India, being suitable to the country and its roads, rapid in its movement, and of a light and economical construction. Although there may not be a very apparent similarity to the form of tonga about to be described, this carriage is the modern descendant of the ancient war chariot, in which the **horses** or ponies were yoked or harnessed *tonga fashion*, i.e., a bar, to which is attached the pole of the tonga, crosses the backs of two ponies, and is fixed to the saddles, traces, and pole-straps, making the furniture complete.

The Ambulance Tonga which is now the official regulation conveyance in India for the transport of sick and wounded in supersession of all other forms, which are now obsolete, is a slightly larger and heavier conveyance than the ordinary country pattern. This, of course, is necessary, in order that the carriage may have the required strength and solidity to withstand the trials of active service. It consists of a strong framework on **two** side springs, and a back spring resting **on an axle** connecting two stout wheels of the ordnance type. **The** bed of the conveyance is "roomy," and the two sides curve slightly upwards and outwards. It accommodates either four men sitting up, or two men lying down. In the first instance, there is a centre-board, forming a rest and back to the seat of those carried. There are four leather cushions—two to sit upon and two strapped against the centre-board. In the second case, when it is desired to accommodate two men lying down, the centre-board is removed, and placed on the two wedge-shaped blocks at the rear of the carriage, while in front a light framework turns down. In this way a level bed is prepared, on which the four cushions are laid, and the two patients, lying side by side, with their heads raised, and feet to the front of the carriage, are in as comfortable and convenient a position as possible. The kits can be stowed underneath, and the rifles and belts are carried strapped to the raves of the carriage on the inside. A double-varnished cover, supported by six standards, forms a roof to the conveyance, from the sides and ends of which depend curtains capable of being closely

Fig. CVI.—The Tonga.

fastened, and thus forming a complete shelter to those carried. The tonga is drawn by two bullocks yoked to a pole, and the driver sits on the pole. When the animals are taken away, the tonga can rest in the horizontal position by a support placed under, and attached to the pole.

This conveyance is adapted in every way for Indian campaigning, and is a very great advance on the forms of carriage which have hitherto been used.

It must be added, the tongas pack well and easily on railway trucks. Each truck carrying three tongas, the poles having been removed, and laid lengthwise on the floor.

B.—AMBULANCE TRANSPORT WAGONS.

Larrey's Voiture d'Ambulance Volante à Quatre Roues.

This wagon was constructed and suspended on the same plan as Larrey's two-wheeled cart already described, being only increased in length and width, so as to admit of its receiving four instead of two recumbent patients. It was drawn by four horses, and conducted by two drivers, riding postillion. The same proportion of patients to draught power and to drivers was therefore maintained in the wagon as was employed in the ambulance cart. The wagon opened, however, on one of its sides, the left, instead of at the two ends. The opening was made as wide as possible by two doors sliding in grooves up to the ends of the conveyance, and thus the full complement of wounded men could be placed on the floor of the interior while still lying down, and arranged in their places without much difficulty. The floor was fitted with a fixed mattress, and the sides were padded up to the same heights as the carts. Beneath the wagon was suspended a grating which could be carried like a handbarrow in case of need. It was employed with the wagon for the reception of various articles and to assist in fixing the centre of gravity. The front part of the vehicle turned on the axle, and the fore-wheels were made sufficiently small to pass under the body, to facilitate the movement of rotation. The wounded men lay on the mattressed floor in the long direction of the conveyance, their legs meeting and a little crossing each other in the middle. No steps appear to have been taken to separate the patients or to prevent them from coming into contact with each other, and the construction altogether was of a very simple kind.

Voiture d'Ambulance Française à Quatre Roues (modern).—At the Exhibition of 1867, the French Government exhibited an ambulance wagon differing very little from an ordinary omnibus. It was one which had been designed specially for transporting the sick of the garrison of Paris and its neighbourhood from the barracks to the hospitals. It has never been introduced into the general service of the French army, nor has it been employed on active field service. The pattern exhibited consisted of an interior compartment entered from behind, and a coupé in front, communicating with the interior by a glazed door in the partition separating the two divisions of the vehicle. The seats in the interior were placed longitudinally, and would accommodate eight patients sitting or two recumbent. The coupé seat was placed transversely, and was intended to carry two sick men and two attendants. The total charge was, therefore, ten sick and two attendants. Room was provided in a well beneath the vehicle for the arms and kits of the soldiers carried. If not required for patients, this vehicle could carry, in case of need, 500 kilos. of materials, but the benches were not removable, and there was no special adaptation to fit it for a store-transport wagon. Any other omnibus would answer this purpose equally as well. The weight of the vehicle was officially stated to be 930 kilos.; the price, 1,200 francs, or 48*l.* The opening behind was ascended to by folding iron steps, and was objectionably high, being four feet and a half from the ground. There was a central door for admission on ordinary occasions; but, if necessary, the whole of the back, being hinged on each side, could be thrown open. Without this arrangement it would have been scarcely possible to have effected the entrance of patients requiring admission in a recumbent position. Five rather small windows were provided, two to each side and one in the door behind, but these hardly appeared to be sufficient for purposes of ventilation. It was a vehicle quite unsuited for campaigning purposes, being evidently designed for the special service in which it was habitually employed.

The "*Wheeling*" or "*Rosecrans*" Ambulance Wagon.

The "Wheeling" wagon. This was the wagon most extensively used by the armies of the United States during the latter part of the late war in that

Fig. CVII.—Side elevation of the "Wheeling" Ambulance Wagon.

mostly used during the war in the United States. country. The Washington report states that it derives its name from having been first constructed at Wheeling, Virginia, according to the designs of General Rosecrans, and that it soon came into very general use. It differed in many respects from the wagon last described. It was light enough to be drawn by two horses, and was constructed to carry both sitting and recumbent patients; its capacity being for ten or twelve persons sitting, or for two or three sitting with two lying down. The accompanying drawing shows the general form and appearance of this wagon.

The weight of the wagon complete was between 700 and 800 lbs. The body, which was of the tray kind, was 7½ feet long by 3 feet 9 inches broad. The fore-wheels were 3 feet 5 inches in diameter, the hind-wheels 4 feet 1 inch. The wagon was fitted with a brake, the pressure being applied to the hind-wheels by a handle worked near the driver's seat in front. A footstep at the back was provided to help patients to mount, or bearers to carry patients into the interior.

The principal objections made to this wagon appear to have been that it was too high from the ground, especially for getting recumbent patients into their places. The motion, too, was said to be uneasy, unless there was a full complement of persons sitting in the wagon. With only two recumbent patients the action of the springs was stated to be excessively troublesome.

"Rucker Ambulance Wagon."

This wagon was constructed under the direction of Major-General Rucker, of the United States' Quartermaster's Department, at the Government repair shops, Washington, towards the close of the late war, and met with much approval. In the Surgeon-General's report, before quoted, it is stated that this conveyance has been recommended for adoption as the regulation ambulance wagon of the United States' army. The Rucker wagon is adapted for the reception of patients either in a sitting or in a recumbent position. It is so planned that four patients are capable of being accommodated in the latter posture. Eight or ten sick soldiers can be carried in it seated. It resembles the Wheeling wagon already described in several respects; in like manner, when used for the carriage of patients sitting, two cushioned seats, with cushioned flaps dropped down in front, are arranged along the two sides of the interior of the conveyance. To the stretchers are attached small wheels, which facilitate the loading of the wounded in the wagon. To accommodate the other two recumbent patients, the backs of the seats being made high, are only joined to the sides of the wagon by hinges at their upper margins, and are thus adapted for being raised upwards and inwards toward the middle of the carriage. On being elevated in the manner described, the two backs meet together in the centre of the carriage, and are now ready to be supported by some iron props, which, being hinged to their under surfaces, can readily be lowered for the purpose. There are small openings in the floor for the reception of these props. In this way a platform partition is formed in the carriage, on which two stretchers can be laid. The stretchers for this purpose are carried in the wagon. The distance between the surfaces of the

CHAP. VI. litters on the floor and of those placed on the upper platform is a little over two feet; the space between the two platforms,

Fig. CVIII.—Ambulance Wagon, **built** at Washington, under the direction of Major-General Rucker, and recommended for adoption as the regulation sick-transport wagon of the United States' army.

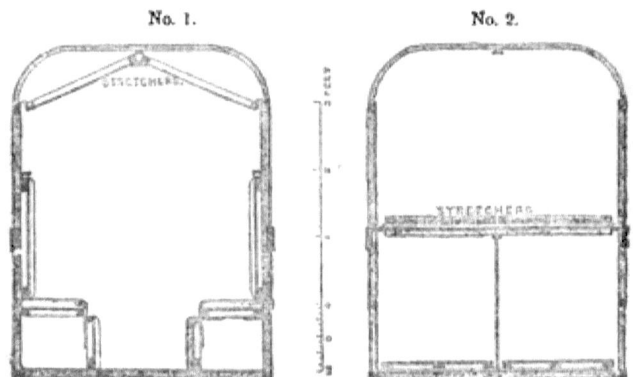

Fig. CIX.—Cross sections of the Rucker wagon. No. 1 arranged for patients sitting. No. 2 arranged for patients recumbent, the seats being detached, lowered, and acting as stretchers, the backs of the seats being raised, and supporting two stretchers brought down from the roof.

that is, between the under surface of the upper platform and the upper surfaces of the two lower litters is 21 inches. The whole arrangement will be best understood by reference to the cross-section sketches, copied from Surgeon-General **Barnes** circular, of November, 1865, which are subjoined.

The body of the wagon is similar in general construction to that of the Wheeling wagon, but is slightly longer and broader, being 8 feet long by 4 feet broad. It is supported on platform springs; there is no inner system of springs within the carriage or attached to the stretchers. The wheels are unequal in size, but the fore-wheels do not turn under the body of the wagon; they are of the same diameters as those of the Wheeling wagon. The water is carried in front, instead of at the rear of the vehicle. The weight is greater than that of the Wheeling wagon, being 1,120 lbs.

Weight of the Rucker wagon.

Locati's rettura d'ambulanza.

This carriage was designed and constructed by A. Locati, coach builder, at Turin, under the general direction of Dr. Bertain, Médecin-en-chef of the volunteers in Italy. The carriage presents a great number of very novel and peculiar features. Its chief peculiarities are: (*a*), the mode in which the recumbent patients are moved in and out of the vehicle *at its sides* instead of, *at the back*; (*b*), the number of recumbent patients (**five**) it carries; (*c*), the plan of ventilation; and (*d*), the variety of hospital purposes to which the carriage is made subservient. Everything necessary for the surgical and medical treatment of the patients, for cooking purposes, and for their dietary being carried with it. It is not merely an ambulance vehicle for the transport of sick and wounded, but it is an ambulance or moving field hospital itself, with its sick transport and store transport, and attendants, all complete; capable, therefore, of being rendered independent of aid from any other quarter for many days together, and consequently fitted for the removal of patients from a field of action to places a long distance off.

Peculiar features of Locati's Italian ambulance wagon.

The Locati wagon is a **four-wheeled** vehicle of the omnibus kind, for two-horse draught, and is divided into an interior and a front coupé. The division is effected by a **wooden** partition. There are sliding doors in the partition, so that a communication can be readily established between the two parts of the vehicle when necessary. The length of the carriage, exclusive of the coupé, **is 2** metres, or nearly 7 feet; its width 1 m. 20, or nearly 4 feet. The body is suspended upon six springs, four longitudinal, two transverse, all with double joints to break the shock of concussions as far as practicable. It is driven from **a** box, the driver's seat being separate and advanced in front **of** the coupé. Behind, near the door **at** the back **of** the vehicle, **is** a wooden slab made to slide **in** and out of a grooved recess under the floor at pleasure; this serves as a seat for a hospital attendant. Below it there is a hinged footstep, which can be folded up out of the way or lowered to act as a support for the feet of the attendant just mentioned, or to assist the entrance of patients into the vehicle. The coupé in front, which is well protected by coverings above and an apron in front, can carry

Construction of Locati's ambulance wagon.

CHAP. VI.

three persons sitting; the interior, five persons recumbent, two on each side and one at the bottom, or two only recumbent on one side and five seated on the other; or else ten seated, five on each side, besides the driver and the attendant. It is said that these wagons with a load of ten patients were proved to be capable of being conveniently drawn by two horses only, so long as they were travelling on main roads. The drawings (Fig. CX.) below represent the external appearance of the carriage and some of the appliances attached to it.

Mechanism by which recumbent patients are raised into Locati's ambulance wagon.

The manner in which patients lying down are got into the wagon is the following. The two sides of the interior are each enclosed by four folding doors. The two doors on each side of the central opening are hinged together, and these again are connected by hinges with the upright posts of the frame of the

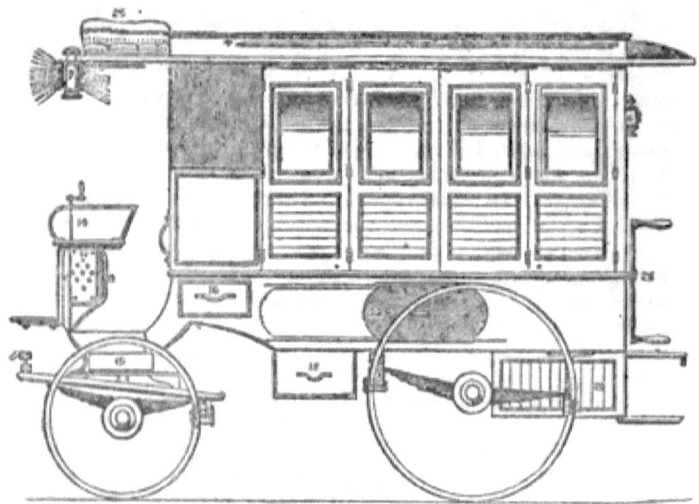

Fig. CX.—Side view of Locati's Ambulance Wagon. 1, double imperial; 2, lateral screen on roller; 3, screen behind; 4, hospital attendant's sliding seat; 5, footstep; 6, hand lantern, removable; 7, front lantern; 8, wooden sides of coupé; 9, break; 10, 11, coupé cover and apron; 12, partitioned case for various objects; 13, wooden screen to keep off mud; 14, driver's seat; 15, chest for tools; 16, medicine chest; 17, water tank and ice box; 18, drawer for surgical materials; 19, footstep to reach the roof; 20, cage for forage; 21, small door in main door; 22, doors to openings for patients' kits; 23, cover of roof; 24, entrance door to back of carriage; 25, place for horse clothing; 26, lever to lower and raise upper litter frame. These explanations also refer to the corresponding numbers on the three illustrations of this wagon which follow.

body of the vehicle at each end. Thus the two doors in the middle on being opened are capable of being folded back on the adjoining doors, and, when again the double door thus formed is turned back, the whole interior of the vehicle is exposed to view. On each side of the interior there are two frames, one above the other, for the reception of litters and mattresses. They are so placed that when the litters and mattresses are upon them they have the appearance of the **upper** and lower berths in a cabin upon board ship. There is a peculiar mechanical contrivance for placing patients upon the upper mattresses. At the back of the vehicle on each side of the entrance door are two rather long iron levers with double handles; on turning either of these levers in one direction the corresponding upper litter, with the frame on which it rests, is lowered out of the side of the vehicle until it is brought to a level with the lower litter; a patient being then laid upon it, the litter and patient are raised into their place in the interior by turning the lever in the opposite direction. The two patients for the lower tier of mattresses are easily laid on them from the outside when the side folding doors are fully opened. The litter for the fifth patient is laid on the floor of the vehicle in the centre, between and below the two tiers already mentioned. This litter is put in and out through the door at the back of the vehicle. The particulars just described **are shown** in the following illustrations:—

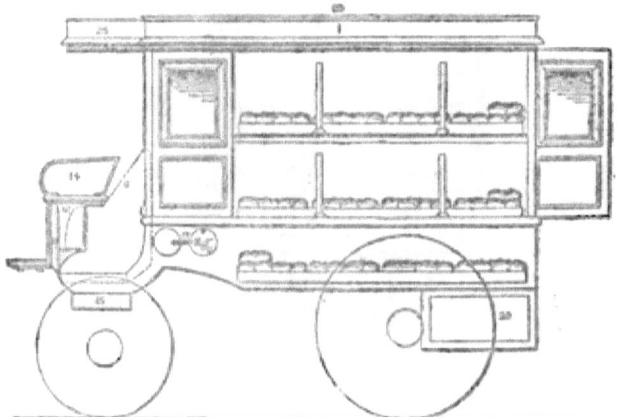

Fig. CXI.—Side view of the interior of Locati's Ambulance Wagon.

The litters used in this wagon are made so as to answer as hand-stretchers for the removal of patients, or, if need be, as hospital beds. Each is formed of an oak frame, with cross-bars of thin steel placed at intervals of 0·10 m. from each other to sustain the mattress, with light folding iron handles at the four corners, and with rather high wooden feet, which are made to fold up beneath the stretcher. Two semi-circular hoops of thin steel are attached to the sides of these stretchers, and arch over it, so as to guard a patient from falling off; when not required, they can be folded down. The advantage of a certain amount of elasticity is afforded to a patient lying on the stretcher **by** he steel bands on which the mattress rests.

The upper part of the coupé seat can also be taken **off** and used as a stretcher. It is so jointed as to be capable of carrying a patient in a recumbent, semi-recumbent, or sitting position.

Construction of the litters in Locati's wagon.

Chap. VI.

The double roof of Locati's wagon.

There are some other noticeable features in this vehicle. It has a double roof to protect the patients inside against great heat; at the same time, part of the space between the two roofs is otherwise utilised by being made to serve as a magazine to contain the arms of the wounded men carried in the vehicle. The upper roof, or imperial, is covered by oiled canvas to throw off the rain, and can be raised at pleasure at the two sides for ventilation. Along each side of the roof there is an awning; under ordinary circumstances this is rolled up and concealed from view, but it can be opened out by a mechanism provided for the purpose, when it forms a lateral tent, as it were, protecting the sides of the vehicle against the glare of the sun. Beneath the coupé, for one half of its length, is a case for medicines, arranged for being drawn out at one side of the vehicle; the other half is occupied by a box for ice and a tank for water, with a stopcock

The fittings in Locati's wagon.

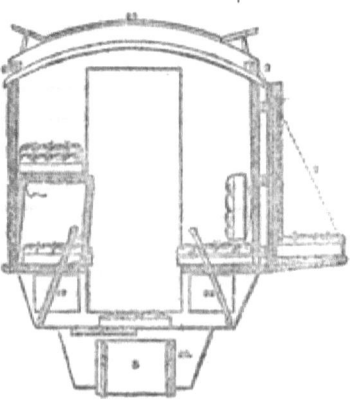

Fig. CXII.—End view of the interior of Locati's Ambulance Wagon. In this view both litters on one side are in position; in the other, the upper litter has been lowered to the outside, ready to receive a patient.

at the other side of the vehicle. At the back of the vehicle are two doors which open into vacant spaces beneath the lower litters or seats of the interior; these openings are destined to contain the knapsacks and other field necessaries of the sick. Beneath the driver's seat is a compartment arranged for carrying cases of provisions. Beneath the footboard of the coupé is a case for a few necessary tools. Under the bottom of the vehicle, behind, is a cage for containing forage; under the bottom, in front, is a chest for surgical instruments, splints, &c.; on the roof above the coupé is a place assigned for horse-rugs and other such articles. Two lanterns are supplied, one behind, removable, for the use of the attendant in helping the wounded; the other, in front, so placed as to light up the road in front, the coupé, and the interior of the vehicle, all at the same time.

The wheels are bi-rotal and underlock. The break is made to press upon the upper surfaces of the wheels, and is applied by turning a handle placed conveniently near the seat of the driver.

These ambulance vehicles, according to Dr. Appia, who assisted in using them in July, 1866, during the operations of the Garibaldians against the Austrians in the Tyrol, gave much satisfaction as conveyances for the wounded. "Not being allowed to go with much speed," he writes, "the carriage did not give rise to the troublesome rocking movement which the increase of load at the upper part might lead one to fear it would."* M. Appia also mentions that he sent away several carriage loads in these vehicles, after the battle of Bezzecca, to Storo, and that even the wounded who subsequently travelled the distance from Storo to Brescia in them, a journey of twenty-one hours, declared themselves well satisfied with this new form of carriage.

Experience of Locati's ambulance wagons in the Tyrol.

Voiture simplifiée d'ambulance Locati.

The "vettura d'ambulanza" just described, was examined by the International Committee at Paris in 1867, and while it was admitted to have many meritorious features, it was held to be too complicated and too costly for the ordinary puporses of an ambulance vehicle. M. Locati then constructed another sick-transport carriage of a simpler kind, and sent it to the Exhibition under the above title. In general external form and dimensions, and in many of its details, it resembled the original vettura d'ambulanza, but it was not fitted for the variety of purposes which that wagon was prepared to fulfil. The simplified carriage was not, like the former, a hospital complete in itself, but was built almost exclusively for sick-transport purposes. Thus a large number of cases and compartments were got rid of. It carried with it a surgical canteen, but the contents were rather intended for the first necessities of the wounded before being placed in the carriage, than for their treatment after being placed in it. The experience of the circumstances of campaigning as they are met with in such a climate as that of Italy in a summer campaign, evidently still dictated many of the leading features of this carriage, such as the double roof, side-awnings, &c., as the same circumstances had done in nearly all the arrangements of the former carriage. It was only made for four recumbent patients, and these were placed directly in at the sides of the vehicle. The mechanical appliance for lowering the upper tier of stretchers, which has been described in the account of Locati's original carriage, was not provided in this vehicle; but, instead, the places for the upper stretchers were fixed at a rather lower level, and small wheels were fitted to the framed supports to facilitate the entrance and passage over them of the stretchers.

Alterations made in Locati's simplified ambulance wagon.

---

* "Les Blessés de la Bataille de Bezzecca dans la Vallée de Tiarno" (Tyrol), 21 Juillet, 1866. Par Louis Appia, docteur, &c., &c., Genève, 1866, p. 39.

Baron Mundy's Ambulance Wagon.

Baron Mundy's ambulance wagon.

This is the vehicle which gained the prize of a thousand francs offered at the Paris Exhibition in 1867, for the best ambulance wagon, possessing certain stated qualities. It was made by M. Locati, the builder of the two carriages previously described, but was constructed in accordance with directions laid down by Baron Mundy, a well-known and distinguished officer of the Austrian army. Like the simplified Locati carriage just described, this vehicle resembles in general appearance, in its side-openings, and still more closely in its external proportions, the Locati hospital wagon used by the Italian volunteers during the last campaign in the Tyrol. But the resemblance here ceases. The internal fittings, appliances, and amount of accommodation for which it is designed, differ greatly from those of the "voiture-hôpital," sent by the Florentine Committee to the Exhibition. The prize wagon, which for brevity may be called Baron Mundy's wagon, instead of five recumbent patients, is arranged to carry only two recumbent patients.

Its amount of accommodation.

In addition, it is capable of conveying three or four sitting; or it can carry eight or ten sitting, if none are carried lying down. As the adaptation is for only two patients in a recumbent posture, the internal construction is enabled to be simpler, and the ventilation more thorough. Only a portion of the side of the carriage is enclosed by wood, namely, a space about 17 inches in depth; and of this, 14 inches can be opened at pleasure, the panels, by which it is enclosed, being hinged, so as to be capable of being let down when necessary. In the drawing which follows, one half of the wooden side is lowered, so that the position of the stretcher may be visible.

Construction of Baron Mundy's wagon.

Baron Mundy's wagon, like the rest of Locati's carriages, has an open coupé in front, and an interior behind. The roof, however, is single: it is only formed of thick sailcloth canvas. The same material falls down to shade and to protect the two partially open sides of the interior above the wooden panels before mentioned; it is used as a curtain, sliding along a rod to separate the interior from the coupé; it also closes the back part of the carriage. A considerable diminution in weight is obtained by this arrangement. The canvas behind is divided into three parts, one corresponding with the middle entrance at the back of the carriage, the other two with the end openings for the admission of the stretchers on each side. When the sailcloth curtains at the side are rolled and fastened up near the eaves of the roof, and the wooden panels are fully lowered, when the canvas at the end is also either rolled up or thrown over the roof, and the partition curtain which separates the interior from the coupé is withdrawn; then the whole interior is open to the air, with the sole exception of the roof which covers it. The front wheels are small enough to turn under the fore part of the body of the carriage, which rests on platform springs. The transverse seat in front is capable of accommodating three persons sitting with great ease, and on occasion it could readily carry four sitters. The handle of the

CHAP. VI.

Baron Mundy's wagon.

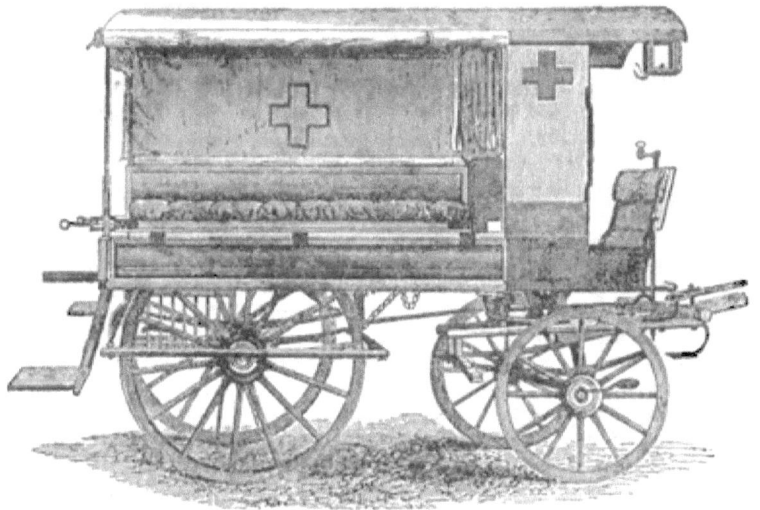

Fig. CXIII.—Side view of Baron Mundy's Ambulance Wagon.

break is placed at this part of the carriage; it acts upon the two hind wheels. The frames on which the two stretchers for the recumbent patients are placed are separated from the floor of the carriage behind by a space of seven inches. Within this space are two simple bow springs, the extreme height of each

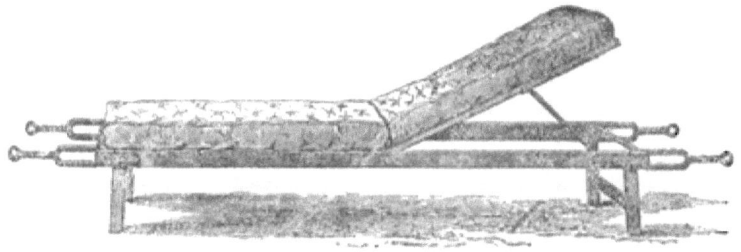

Fig. CXIV.—View of one of the stretchers removed from Baron Mundy's Ambulance Wagon.

of which is three inches. The rear ends of the two stretcher frames directly rest on these springs; the remaining four inches of the space above-mentioned are occupied by blocks of wood, on which the springs move when they are in action. The fore parts of the two stretcher frames are supported upon two corresponding bow springs; but at this part of the vehicle the floor itself is raised four inches, so that no blocks are required in this situation. The **object** of **raising the** floor at this end is **to give more space to** the compartments beneath. The stretchers can be be placed into the interior either at the back of the carriage or at the sides. They glide upon two wooden rollers; these rollers are within and slightly above the level of the framework which is destined to carry the stretchers. Outside each hind wheel, and of course completely detached from it, is a foot rail, on which a person can stand, and from which he can readily assist a patient lying upon the stretcher at the corresponding side of the vehicle. The stretchers have folding backs.

A place is provided for the **patients'** rifles under a part of the floor before the coupé seat in **front.** A cage under lock and key is placed beneath the floor **of the wagon** behind, between the hind wheels. This case is intended to receive kits, **the** opening into it being reached between the two broad steps which are fixed at the back of **the** carriage. There is a cistern for water in the fore part of the vehicle, easily accessible by a tap at one side. On the opposite side, a door, under lock and key, leads to a compartment containing surgical dressings. There are also two barrels for wine and other medical comforts in front. **The** taps of these barrels are placed immediately **under the coupé seat,** and **are** protected by a sliding **door** under lock and key.

The dimensions of the principal parts of the carriage, ascertained by measurement of **the pattern at the** Exhibition, are as follows:—Length of carriage, interior measurement, exclusive of coupé, 6 feet 6 inches; outside measurement, 6 feet 7½ inches; width of carriage, interior measurement at level of stretchers, **4 feet 10 inches**; outside measurement, 5 feet; width of floor of carriage, inside measurement, 4 feet 5 inches; height of carriage from centre **of** floor **to middle of roof, 4 feet** 6 inches; from floor to spring of arch, **3 feet 4 inches.** The full length of the carriage from end **to end, including** the coupé, was 9 feet. The diameter of the fore wheels **was** 2 feet 9 inches; that of the hind wheels 3 feet 10 inches.

The width of each stretcher bed was 2 feet 2 inches, leaving a space only of 6 inches between them, available for the legs of patients, in case of their being used by men in a sitting position. This interval of space would be altogether too narrow to allow any one **to** pass along for the purpose of attending **upon** patients lying upon the stretchers, but the arrangements **of the** carriage already explained evidently design that any such attention shall be given from the outside.

The Lohner Wagon.

This is a strongly built conveyance, carrying four patients **lying** down, or twice that number sitting. The stretchers are

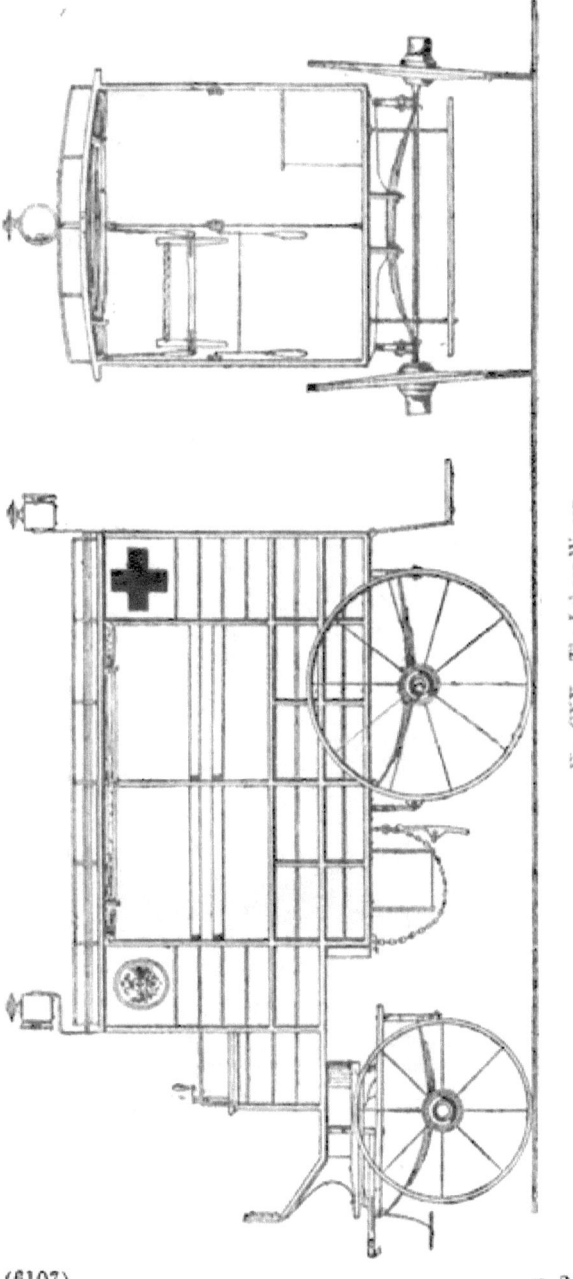

Fig. CXV.—The Lohner Wagon.

CHAP. VI.

arranged in two tiers, one above the other, and are supported by leather loops which hang down and embrace the handles of the stretcher. In front the driver sits, and two wounded men can sit alongside of him. Underneath the "box" is a receptacle for a few medical necessaries. The wagon is bi-rotal—the hind wheels = 3 feet 6 inches, and the front wheels 3 feet—and underlocks. A large number of these wagons are ready at the depôt of the Red Cross in Vienna.

These wagons are large, heavy, and the floor is high. The interior arrangement is distinctly good, and they are among the best ambulance wagons on the Continent. It will be noted that they carry a lamp in front and behind, and that the roof is flat and railed in, so that a certain amount of material can be carried.

Ambulance Wagon of the Société Française.

French Red Cross wagon.

This wagon is arranged after the method suggested by the Comte de Beaufort, and carries four lying down in two tiers.

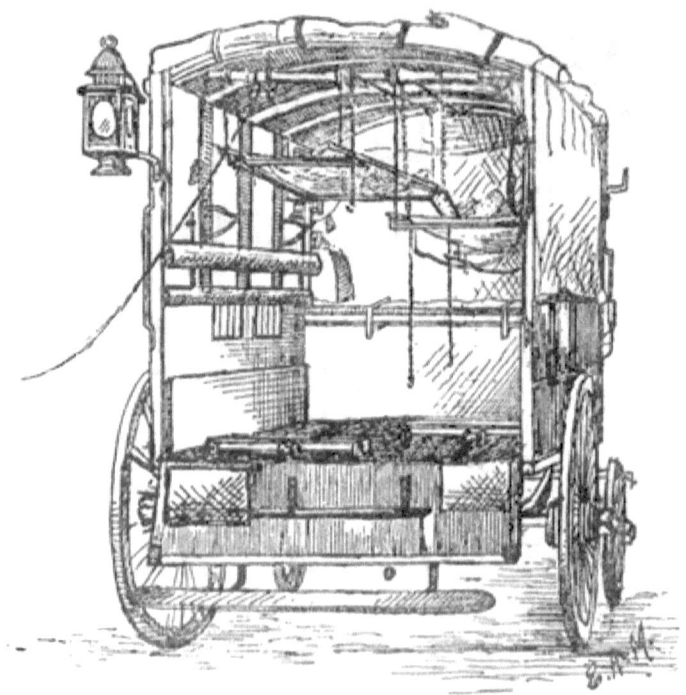

Fig. CXVI. Ambulance Wagon of the Société Française.

On the floor will be seen two traverses, one on each side, working along in two-iron grooves by single wheels at their centres. A small chain is attached to each in order to withdraw the traverse from the front of the wagon. A framework is attached to the roof, the four wheels of each side of which

Fig. CXVII.—French Ambulance Wagon.

are cogged so that the stretcher is said to be conveniently and easily raised.

The loading of this wagon is effected thus:—The traverses on the floor being drawn to the rear of the wagon by the chain and along the groove, the front end of the stretcher is placed on it and passed into the wagon, four chain hooks fixed to four wheels above are attached, and the stretcher is raised into position. The arrangement is ingenious but not practical.

The ambulance wagon shown in figure CXVII. is another form of French Red Cross carriage. It does not differ materially from the ordinary *fourgon d'ambulance*, being merely slightly larger.

Three uprights are arranged at the front and rear carrying leathern loops, into which the handles of the stretchers rest. Attendants **reach the wounded through the** canvas sides of the vehicle.

Voiture d'ambulance à quatre roues, appt. **au Quartier** *Général de sa Majesté le Roi de Prusse.*

Neuss's sick-transport wagon for a single patient.

A carriage by **the** same maker **and** constructed on the same principles was exhibited at the **Paris** Exposition of 1867 by the Prussian National Committee **for** Aid to Wounded in Time of War. This carriage had been attached **to** the head-quarters of the King of Prussia during the **war** of 1866 in Germany. It was arranged for the conveyance **of only one** patient in the interior, the place of the **two stretchers** described in the preceding carriage being occupied **only by** one bed. The coupé in front was intended for a **driver and** for attendants. The materials **of** the carriage **and all its** fittings were **of** a very **superior** quality, the object **kept in view being to provide** every convenience that might be **required for the wants of a** single patient. The bed, which was **covered with morocco** leather, could be converted into **an arm-chair,** one **end** being capable of being raised to form **the back,** the other **of** being lowered to support the legs. The lowness of the body of the carriage obtained by the bending of the axle between the hind-wheels **was** one of the leading features **of its** mechanical construction, **as it** was in the other of **Neuss's** wagons previously described.

Neuss's Prussian Ambulance Wagon.

Prussian ambulance wagon.

This wagon, designed for draught by two horses, **was** constructed for the brotherhood of the Knights of St. John, **by** Messrs. Neuss, of Berlin, the same carriage builders who constructed the two-wheeled hand-litter **for** them, described **in a** previous chapter. It was first used by **this** brotherhood in the **war** between Prussia and Denmark **in 1864**, and afterwards in the campaign **of 1866**. **It was** built, with some modifications, on the general principles **and plan of** what were held **to** be the best kind **of** German sick-transport **wagons,** viz., those made to accommodate **two** badly wounded **men on** stretchers in the body of the wagon, and a certain number less severely hurt sitting in a coupé partitioned off from the interior and formed by the transverse **seat** usually occupied by the driver in front. The patients **sitting on** the front seat were protected by a folding hood, **and the** horses, when the **seat** was thus occupied, were conducted by the driver postillion **fashion.**

Construction of Neuss's sick-transport wagon.

The weight **of** the wagon built by the Messrs. Neuss was only 6 cwt. The iron axle between the two hinder wheels was bent, as shown in the drawing at (*a*), and upon it and the fore-axle a connecting **pole** (*b*) was fixed. By this arrangement the body of the carriage is enabled to be placed at a very moderate elevation above the ground. On the hinder axle two springs were fixed longitudinally, on the fore axle one spring transversely. The fore-wheels were low and turned under the coupé. The body of the carriage had very light open sides, the upper part having only waterproof canvas curtains capable of being rolled up and fastened by straps. The hood over the seat in front was made of the same material, and the part (*f*) marked with the Maltese cross was enclosed also by waterproof canvas. Within this part of the wagon was a compartment for the reception of the men's knapsacks and for a supply of restoratives and surgical dressings. The interior of the wagon was separated into two longitudinal divisions by a partition reaching from the floor half way up to the roof. In this partition, and also at corresponding heights on the sides of the wagon, ledges (*h, h, g,* in the drawing) were fixed in order that

Fig. CXVIII.—Neuss's Prussian Ambulance Wagon. *a*, curved axle; *b*, pole; *c*, transverse spring; *d*, side curtain; *e*, folding hood; *f*, compartment for stores, &c.; *g, h,* ledges for stretchers; *i, i,* position of coupé seat.

two folding stretchers, each capable of supporting a patient in a semi-recumbent or recumbent posture, might be slid along them into the wagon.

Professor Gurlt, in his "Militär-chirurgische Fragmente," speaks, from personal observation and experience, of the lightness, ease of motion, and solidity, characterising these vehicles, as well as of the advantages afforded to the wounded from the varied postures which they were able to be placed in, owing to the peculiar construction of the stretchers. The drawing of the wagon is taken from the same source.

Chap. VI.

New Zealand Sick-Transport Wagon.

History of the New Zealand sick-transport wagon.

This was a spring conveyance introduced in 1860, during the last war in New Zealand, to take the place of the Regulation pattern ambulance wagon, which had been found to be too cumbrous for the primitive roads opened up by the troops during the military operations in that country. It was made on the principle of an American wagon; so light that a few men would readily suffice to get it out of any difficulty it might meet with in its progress. It was capable of accommodating two men lying down, and several sitting. This wagon has been reported by Inspector-General Mouat, C.B., by whom it was introduced, to have answered admirably as a conveyance for the sick and wounded on the particular service on which it was employed, and it has been supposed by some that it might be adopted with advantage as the Regulation wagon of the British army for carrying sick and wounded in time of war.

Trials of this wagon at Netley, as to its fitness for general service.

One of these wagons, which had been built at Auckland, was sent to Netley for trial, more especially to ascertain its fitness for use as a military ambulance carriage for general service. The trials were made under the observation of the author, and the following account embodies the results of them. At first starting it was found that the regulation harness was not suitable for being used with the New Zealand wagon. Some civilian cart harness was therefore obtained, and one of the army transport horses was attached by it to the vehicle.

Construction and fittings of the New Zealand wagon.

At the first glance the body of the vehicle is seen to consist of a simple light tray mounted upon four elliptical springs. These springs are all placed at right angles to the axles upon which they rest.

All the fittings and appliances of the vehicle are of the simplest character. The wheels are narrow, as in most American vehicles, and are not on the equi-rotal principle. Two plain, cushioned seats with backs are made to rest upon the sides of the tray which forms the body of the wagon. They are simply laid on the tray, so that they can be taken off or shifted along the sides at pleasure. The seat in front is single, and is calculated to accommodate three persons, including the driver; the seat behind is double, having a back between the seats common to both. This last seat is calculated to accommodate six persons, three sitting on each side. The handle of a double break acting upon the two hind wheels is placed in front near the driver's seat.

The floor of the wagon is level, and affords space enough for two stretchers or two patients to be placed upon it at full length. But should the floor be used for two recumbent patients, the back seat could not be used for patients sitting, for the legs of the latter would be resting upon the patients lying upon the floor.

The wagon is therefore fitted for carrying nine persons sitting, including the driver; or three persons sitting, including the driver, as well as two recumbent.

Fig. CXIX.—Perspective view of the New Zealand Ambulance Wagon with its cover.

Fig. CXX.—Perspective view of the New Zealand Ambulance Wagon without cover.

A water barrel is slung beneath the floor of the wagon. Hoops are arched over the whole vehicle. These support a varnished canvas cover, which is divided down the middle at each end to afford openings for ingress and egress. The cover is secured by straps and buckles to iron staples fixed on the outside of the body of the cart. The wagon is designed for draught either by one horse or by two horses; in the latter case the horses must be driven tandem fashion.

Measurements of the New Zealand wagon.

The following are measurements of particular parts of the wagon:—Extreme length, including the shafts, 16 feet 10 inches; extreme breadth, 6 feet 6 inches; height, from ground to top of cover, 8 feet 3 inches; outside length of tray including the foot-board, 8 feet 3 inches; outside breadth of tray, 4 feet 10 inches; outside depth of tray, 1 foot 3 inches; inside measurement of tray 7 feet 1 inch, by 3 feet 8 inches, by 1 foot. The height from the floor of the tray inside, to the centre of the cover, is 4 feet 10 inches. The hoops, three in number, are 3 feet 2 inches apart. The diameter of the fore wheels is 43 inches, that of the hind wheels, is 52 inches. The drawings Figs. CXIX and CXX sufficiently illustrate the general appearance and construction of the wagon just described.

Macpherson's Indian Ambulance Wagon.

Construction and fittings of Macpherson's Indian wagon.

This wagon was constructed in the year 1858, under the direction of Inspector-General Macpherson, of the Madras Medical Service, who designed the cart previously described under the same name. The experience of this officer was not confined to India; he had been the Principal Medical Officer of the Turkish Contingent and other forces under the command of General Sir Robert Vivian during the Crimean war, and, in that capacity, it had been his duty to organise the ambulance equipment for that army. Circumstances had thus led him to give attention to the subject of ambulance conveyances and their construction. Dr. Macpherson's wagon was on the omnibus plan, was supported on four double elliptic steel springs, and was intended for draught by two bullocks or horses. It was constructed to carry eight patients within the body of the vehicle, and two sitting on each side of the driver in front. Space was provided for carrying the arms and accoutrements of these ten men. The driver's box was separated from the interior by a slight open frame fitted with curtains which could be raised and fixed near the roof if desired. The weight of the whole conveyance, as made at Madras, was 15 cwt.; the cost 600 rupees (60*l.*). Two stretchers with hoods were carried with the wagon, one being fixed to each side of the body of the conveyance. The upper half of the body was open, with the exception of the upright posts employed to support the roof; but the open part was protected on each side by a framed canvas blind, hinged to the sides of the roof, so that it could be raised, or lowered, and fixed in either position at pleasure. Overhead, the wagon was covered by a canvas tilt, and this was prolonged in front so as to form a hood over the transverse seat in front. A free circulation of air, and, at the same time protection against the glare of the sun, were afforded by these means to all the persons carried on the vehicle. All the wheels were of equal diameters. The longitudinal seats in the interior were made of open cane-work, as were also the backs for the patients to lean against. The front borders of both seats were grooved, and in this way were prepared for receiving two cane-work frames, which were carried with the wagon, of proper size for fitting into and resting upon the grooves. When the frames were laid in their places, they and the seats formed a continuous platform on which two patients lying upon mattresses or stretchers might be readily placed. Under the seats were racks for the men's muskets. Beneath the upper floor was a second floor divided

Fig. CXXI. Inspector-General Macpherson's Indian Wagon.

into two wells, one rather deeper than the other, with movable lids, arranged for the reception of various articles. The two wells were separated only by a narrow space, in which the axle of the hind wheels was received; with this exception the lower floor, or the two wells into which it was divided, corresponded in size with the size of the upper floor. The under part of the driver's seat was hollowed out at the sides to facilitate the turning of the fore wheels.

The following illustration is taken from the model of this conveyance in the Museum of Military Surgery, at Netley.*

Double floor of Macpherson's Indian wagon.

---

* Spec. No. 1301.

CHAP. VI.

Result of trials of Macpherson's sick-transport wagon at Madras.

The officer commanding the 1st Battalion Madras Artillery, St. Thomas's Mount, who made a report, respecting the cart already referred to,* of Dr. Macpherson's invention, was also ordered to make a trial of this wagon. On the 11th of July, 1859, this officer stated with regard to the wagon, that he had sent it out filled with men, some of whom were sick, over the roughest ground in the neighbourhood for three days under non-commissioned officers, and that he had himself accompanied it on the fourth day. "The four-wheeled ambulance wagon," he reported, "runs very light and easy; wonderfully so, considering the load it carries. The one pair of bullocks took it over difficult ground with as much ease as the two-wheeled; but both require more cattle. The drivers were all very bad, *i.e.*, not one of them seemed to have the remotest idea of the best way of crossing a ravine or ditch, but did all they could (ignorantly I believe) to break the springs, and to give the greatest possible inconvenience and discomfort to the inmates. Yet, notwithstanding these disadvantages, the men generally express a favourable opinion of these ambulance vehicles.† Notwithstanding the general satisfactory character of this report, neither Macpherson's ambulance wagon nor the cart invented by him have come into general use in India, but his ideas are very noticeable in the later forms.

Dr. Francis' Ambulance Wagon.

This wagon, proposed for use in India, has been designed and modelled by Surgeon-Major C. R. Francis, of H.M.'s Bengal army. This officer made the hospital equipments at the 1867 Universal Exposition of Paris a subject of special study, with a view particularly to ascertaining their suitableness for ambulance service in India. The result of these observations Dr. Francis published in a quarto pamphlet, illustrated by drawings of several of the articles which had particularly attracted his notice.‡

Origin of Dr. Francis' proposed ambulance wagon for India.

With regard to sick-transport carriages, Dr. Francis mentions that he could not find any single one in the collection at Paris suitable for India without alteration and adaptation; and that he therefore endeavoured carefully to consider the advantages of each component part of those which were exhibited, with a view to the construction of a new conveyance which should embody all the necessary qualities for the transport of sick and wounded in an Indian campaign.

---

* See page 365.

† Report from the Officer Commanding 1st battalion Madras Artillery, St. Thomas's Mount, 11th July, No. 379.

‡ "An inquiry into the suitableness of certain Articles of Hospital Equipment for India." By Surgeon-Major C. R. Francis, M.B., Her Majesty's Indian Army, Bengal. Rochester: W. T. Wildish, 1867.

The following are the **principles** which, according to the definitions of Dr. Francis, **should rule** the construction **of an** ambulance wagon for India:—

"1. It should be light, elastic, and **solid** at the **same** time.

"2. It should consist of as few pieces and fittings as possible.

"3. Injuries should admit of easy and quick repair.

"4. It must be proof against the elements; and, in a country like India, the provision must be complete. At one **time** protection **may** be required from the vertical rays of a tropical **sun**; **at another** from a torrent of **rain** which, in **a** few hours, **will** cover the ground to an extent of four or five inches; and, in the cold weather, in the upper provinces, it may be necessary to shield the sick, at night, from a temperature which admits of the manufacture of ice.

"5. The wounded must be **able to get in and out of the** vehicle with facility.

"6. There should be accommodation for as large a number as possible, avoiding overcrowding, of course, and having reference to the powers of the cattle.

"7. Space must be utilized as completely as the vehicle **will** admit of.

"8. **The mode of** transporting the conveyance **must be adapted to the habits of the** natives. Thus, in India, bullocks generally will be required; and, as riding postillion is not **an indigenous** practice, provision must be made for a driver. In **some** of the ambulance vehicles at the Exhibition, the driver is supposed to sit amongst the sick on the front seat; but, as this arrangement would be manifestly objectionable in India, and for other reasons, I have provided him with a separate seat, as in the original ambulance wagon, sent by Locati, of Turin, to the Exhibition—the wagon which **was** characterised by the ' Société de Secours aux Blessés' as **a** '*type modèle*.'

"9. The vehicle should be **well** supplied **with** good water, with medical comforts, and **with the** means **of** sustaining life for a limited period.

"10. It should carry **a medical subordinate.**"

In **designing** his ambulance wagon, Dr. Francis also starts on **the principle** that men badly wounded, and therefore requiring **a** recumbent position, should continue to be conveyed in doolies **(for** which number, it is presumed, a sufficient proportion of **dooley** bearers may still be obtained); while those able to sustain **a** sitting position should be conveyed in wheeled conveyances. This is an arrangement which appears to be advocated by **not a few** who have thought much on the subject; **and** there are many arguments **in** its favour, so far as the transport of sick and wounded in India **is** concerned.

Spring Wagon used in the Peninsular War.

Chap. VI.

The Peninsular spring wagon.

I* am not aware that any record exists of the construction of these wagons, but a great amount of concurrent testimony confirms the fact of great inconveniences having been experienced from their cumbrous size and weight. They were drawn by four horses. Each wagon was calculated to carry seven or eight men sitting, but would only accommodate two men requiring a recumbent posture. There was a strict prohibition against these vehicles carrying stores, or anything but the sick men, their kits, and fire-arms.

Mark I and II. British Ambulance Wagon.

History of the present pattern British ambulance wagon.

This conveyance was styled in the Army Medical Regulations "ambulance car,"† but it is now entitled "ambulance wagon."

The unfavourable reports received from the Crimea concerning the wagons and carts sent out to that country with the Hospital Conveyance Corps in the year 1854 have been already referred to elsewhere. In April, 1855, Lord Panmure, who was then Secretary of State for War, directed a committee to consider and report upon the merits of certain ambulance conveyances which were proposed to be adopted as substitutes for those which had then turned out to be failures. This committee having met at the Royal Carriage Department, Woolwich, inspected, among other conveyances submitted to them, two hospital wagons for carrying eight wounded men each, viz., six sitting and two recumbent, and only differing from each other in the springs and mode of suspension. One of the wagons was supported on steel springs. This vehicle weighed 12 cwt., being nearly 10 cwt. lighter than the wagons which had been sent with the hospital conveyance corps to the Crimea; the other wagon was fitted with Fuller's india-rubber springs, and weighed only 11 cwt., each, or nearly 11 cwt. lighter than the original Crimean wagons.

Pattern with india-rubber springs first adopted.

The kind of wagon which was fitted with Fuller's india-rubber springs was chiefly recommended. "Although these wagons may not prove so easy for badly wounded men," the Committee remarked in their report, dated May 7th, 1855, "as those on steel springs, still considering the stretchers are also on india-rubber springs, the Committee consider them to be suitable for the majority of cases, and also to possess the advantage of accommodating a good many men; and having further ascertained that no four-wheeled vehicles of a lighter description can be constructed without a material sacrifice of strength absolutely necessary to enable them to withstand the wear and tear of field service, the Committee approve of these wagons."

---

* The author   † Med. Reg., p. 76.

The form and construction of the india-rubber spring, known by the name of "Fuller's spring," which for some years after the Crimean war was the kind of spring employed in the sick-

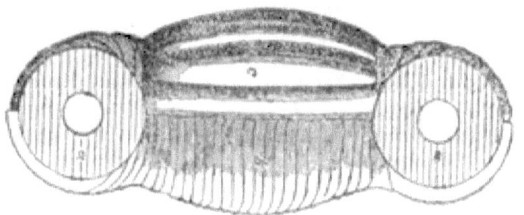

Fig. CXXII.—Fuller's india-rubber spring. *a, a*, metal rings; *b*, leather casing; *c, c, c*, india-rubber strands, half the leather casing having been removed to expose them to view.

transport vehicles constructed at Woolwich, is shown in the subjoined sketch.

The fore wheels were at that time smaller than the hind wheels, and the Committee recommended as an improvement in regard to lightness of draught and facility of movement that higher fore wheels should be substituted for them. This was

Fig. CXXIII.—Ambulance Wagon, Mark II.

afterwards done, and an appliance, known by the name of Jacob's lock, was added to lessen the inconveniences resulting from the use of the high fore wheels in turning the wagon.

CHAP. VI.

Construction and fittings of the British ambulance wagon.

An examination of the drawings will show that the wagon is a modification of the tray-form of carriage. It is built without separate compartments for the recumbent and sitting patients. The two men carried recumbent lie upon movable stretchers specially designed for the carriage, and occupy the central portion of the floor of the wagon; three of the men carried sitting occupy a transverse seat in front, the three others occupy a similar seat in rear. The driver conducts the vehicle postilion fashion. The stretchers*, as already mentioned elsewhere, are fitted with special springs and also with rollers to enable them to be moved in and out of the wagon more easily. There are four of the india-rubber springs (Fuller's) and each of these is caused to act between two curved iron rod supports; one rod being fixed to the under surface of the floor of the wagon, this being the larger and descending the lower of the two; the other being uppermost and fixed to the lower frame or bed which rests upon the two axletrees. The body of the wagon is thus suspended, as it were, from the springs, although it is carried above them. The fore and hind wheels are each 4 feet 2 inches in diameter. One of the two horses by which the wagon is drawn is harnessed between shafts; the other, the riding horse, is attached to a swingletree. A barrel capable of containing three gallons and a half of water is corded on a small platform in front of the body of the wagon; a water-bucket, grease tin, and drag-shoe are carried below. The whole is covered by strong canvas supported upon a framework of movable hoops. From the upper part of this roof a wicker basket is suspended to receive the men's knapsacks, while straps are attached to the sides of the wagon for carrying their firearms.

The India-rubber springs ordered to be discontinued in 1866.

In February, 1866, in consequence of the india-rubber springs having proved defective, principally as regards durability, steel springs were approved to be substituted. The springs then adopted and still in force are of the single semi-elliptical kind, are four in number, and are placed longitudinally. The lower frame or bed of the wagon is retained.

The space between the wheels, measured from outside of tyre to outside of tyre, or in other words, the width of track of the wagon, is 5 feet 5 inches. The wheels are moderately dished, so that a line and plummet dropped from the upper part of the circumference of either wheel falls 4 inches outside the track. The nave projects 6 inches beyond the track. The wagon, therefore, requires a clear space of 6 feet 5 inches to enable it to pass along without touching an upright obstacle on either side of it.

The drawing gives a general view of the wagon, fitted and ready for use.

---

* Wagon stretchers are now obsolete.—ED.

The Mark III. British ambulance wagon.

This wagon has been designed for draught by two horses, though appliances are provided for attaching an extra pair, in case animals of sufficient strength cannot be obtained, or on other occasions of need. The wagon is arranged for carrying two slightly wounded men, together with the driver, sitting in front; two badly wounded lying on stretchers in the body of the wagon, and three slightly wounded, or two with an attendant, seated behind, and resting their feet on the ledge of the tailboard. It can either be driven from the box or the rider can ride and drive, as is done in most other military vehicles; all the appointments are provided for either mode of conducting the wagon. The diameter of the fore wheels is 3 feet, of the hind wheels 4 feet 8 inches. The reduced diameter of the fore wheels is to enable the wagon to turn round on its own ground. This could not be done with the Mark I. wagon, as the wheels were equirotal. The increased draught, owing to the reduction of size of the fore wheels, is to

British ambulance wagon.

Fig. CXXIV.—Ambulance Wagon, Mark III.

a great extent counterbalanced by less weight being thrown on them than on the hind wheels. The springs are semi-elliptical, carefully adjusted to the weight to be carried; a cross check spring is added behind to come into play when the full complement of men are placed in the wagon. A break, acting on the hind wheels, is worked by the driver from his seat in front; and a drag-shoe is suspended near the fore carriage. A zinc water-tank, cased in wood, and fitted beneath the floor of the wagon, is capable of holding ten gallons of water.

Behind the tank is a locker for forage and utensils, and is accessible through the floor of the wagon by two padlocked trap-doors. The available space inside the wagon is 9′ 5¼″ × 4′ 3″. The height of the sides of the wagon is

CHAP. VI.

British ambulance wagon.

1 foot 8 inches, they are boarded for the first 14 inches, and open from the middle to the upper rave about 5 inches. The portion of the floor for the recumbent patients is divided longitudinally by a centre-board 14 inches high. The roof of the wagon is framed and hinged in the centre to facilitate package, and is supported on tubular iron standards. Straps are attached to these standards for carrying two spare stretchers rolled up on each side, on the top of the side rail of the wagon. The framed roof is filled in with double canvas, the two layers being fastened together by india-rubber solution. It is thus rendered impervious to rain. The sides are single canvas arranged to be fixed down or rolled up at any required height at pleasure. Places are provided for the valises of the wounded men between the stretcher handles before and behind. There are also straps fixed to the floor of the wagon for securing the rifles of the wounded men. It is necessary before depositing these weapons to *always ascertain that they are not loaded*. The weight of the wagon and fittings is 18 cwt.; the calculated weight when loaded with eight persons and their kits a little over 30 cwt. This is a manageable weight for draught by two horses; regard being had to the fact that, as a rule, the wagon will only be required to move over made roads, and not faster than at a walking pace. The wagon is "under-horsed" with one pair over unmade roads or loose soil.

In the Marks I. and II., which are varieties of the old pattern ambulance carriage or Crimean wagon, the wounded were transferred from the field stretcher to the wagon direct or to a wagon stretcher. In the converted Mark III. or the Mark IV. wagon, the principal difference is that the wagon stretcher is abolished, and the patient is placed in the wagon on the same stretcher he was laid upon in the first instance, this running into its appointed place on the wheels with which it is provided. The stretchers having been loaded, the backboard is adjusted, thus fixing the stretchers.

Must be portable and pack.

A special difficulty, which has been before referred to, exists in respect to every carriage in the British service, and influences all the details of their construction. Owing to the insular nature of Great Britain, the whole of the army equipment, including the wagons, to be available for military operations in a foreign country must be capable of being carried by sea. An ambulance wagon has, therefore, itself to be made portable. In the present instance the whole wagon is made so as to be readily taken to pieces, folded up, and to be put together into a convenient package for stowage on board ship.

Experiences in Franco-German War with English wagons.

A practical illustration will show the importance of this arrangement. During the Franco-German War the British National Aid Society obtained from the War Office twenty ambulance wagons, for use with the ambulance sent to France under the direction of Deputy-Inspector-General Dr. Guy. Eight of these wagons were for the transport of the wounded, and twelve were general service wagons adapted for the transport of stores. All these vehicles were made up into packages, and placed on board ship at Woolwich. On arrival at Havre the packages were unloaded, unpacked, and fitted together on the wharf, with regularity and dispatch, so that the twenty wagons, complete in every respect, were ready to proceed on the road—the time being under five hours. Had the attempt been made to convey them from Dover to Calais in their ordinary condition, not only would the vessel have been unable to accommodate them but they would have scarcely escaped from being damaged during the voyage.

Objections have been made to the solid, and therefore proportionally heavy, construction of British ambulance wagons. But the advantages of their solid construction were also exhibited in the instance of the wagons just noticed. They were subjected to very severe usage during the whole of several months in the trying winter of 1870-71, yet, in the following spring, they returned to England in so serviceable a condition that the Government readily consented to repurchase them from the Society to which they had been sold.

British ambulance wagon. Mark IV.

This wagon has two large wheels (56 inches in diameter) behind, and a smaller pair (36 inches in diameter) in front, and thus enabling it to turn round on a small axis, and greatly

Fig. CXXV. Mark IV. ambulance wagon.

obviating the risks of upsetting. Wagons which have equal wheels before and behind are called "equirotal wagons." The body has a floor space, 9 feet 4 inches long by 5 feet 3 inches wide, and rests upon the axletrees by semi-elliptical springs, with a check-spring under the centre of the wagon.

CHAP. VI.

Mark IV. wagon.

The wooden sides are about 20 inches high, and from them run up from sockets three iron standards on either side, supporting an angular framework of ash hinged along the centre, forming the wagon roof, which, with the sides, is covered by white canvas, dropping as curtains over the wagon, and forming also a hood to protect the driver and patients in front, and curtains to shield those sitting behind. A canvas curtain also closes the front of the wagon behind the driver's seat, preventing wind and rain entering the wagon from that end. The interior of the wagon is divided longitudinally by a partition 14 inches high, which separates the floor into two equal portions, and these portions are occupied by two stretchers of the ordinary "Faris" pattern, which are run in on their wheels into the wagon. Besides these lying-down arrangements for two patients, three individuals, viz., the driver and two patients, can sit on the front driving seat; and three more, two patients and an orderly, can sit on a hind seat on a level with the floor of the carriage, with their legs hanging out, and protected by a tail-board and leather apron. A sliding partition of wood is placed across the wagon near the rear, acting as a backboard for those sitting on the hind seat. Both seats have leather-covered cushions. Water is carried in a tank (9 gallons) under the body of the wagon, and there is also a corn locker at the rear of the floor of the wagon. A ladder, for use of the patients entering the vehicle, is carried over the fore carriage of the wagon. There are two lockers, one on either side of the sides of the wagon in front, one being used for restoratives, and the other for tools, &c. A double-screw break worked by a cranked lever handle acts on the hind wheels; a drag-shoe is also carried. The rifles and kits of the sick are placed on the floor of the wagon. The wagon weighs about 17¾ cwt., and with eight persons and their kits 30 cwt. The wagon is drawn by two horses from the seat, in double harness, or by a postillion riding one of the animals.

For shipment, the vehicle takes completely to pieces, the iron supports and the roof come off, and the wooden sides are collapsible. The wheels and the tailboard are taken off, and the whole can be packed into a ship space of about 3½ tons.

Mark V. wagon.

British ambulance wagon. Mark V.—This wagon was approved for use in the British army on the 15th January, 1889, and a drawing has been sealed to govern future manufacture.

The wagon is constructed to accommodate 12 men seated, or two men on stretchers, and four seated. It is fitted with a perch, and a "Jacob" lock fore-carriage, which reduces the strains on the body in travelling, and admits of large front wheels being used, so as to minimise the pull on the horses. It is also fitted with a pole and swingle-trees for long rein driving.

The front part of the wagon body is partitioned off, and provided with seats to accommodate two men. Entrance to this part is gained from the front of the wagon, over the driver's seat, the back rail of which can be folded up out of the way. The remaining part of the body is fitted with seats along the sides, arranged to fold upwards when not in use, to make room for two stretchers. A sliding step is fitted to the back of the wagon, which, when not in use, can be raised and pushed close up to the tailboard in guides fixed along the bottom

CHAP. VI.
Mark V. wagon.

Fig. CXXVI.—Mark V. British Ambulance wagon.

for that purpose. The sides are fitted with ventilators, staples for the bale hoops, and standards for the back rail. Fittings are attached to the back rails, and under the seats for carrying rifles, and there are a drag-shoe, a 3 lb. grease tin, and two straps attached to the back rails for the safety of the patients' seat. The stretchers used are of the service pattern, and when not in use they are packed beneath the seats.

Weight	18 cwt. 1 qr. 14 lbs.
Tonnage	11·08 tons.
Minimum space wagon can turn in	30 ft. 7 in.
Rectangular space required in boats	12' 7¼" × 6' 1" × 9' 2¼"

CHAP. VI.

The Furley wagon.

AMBULANCE CARRIAGES INTENDED FOR CIVIL PURPOSES, BUT WHICH CAN BE UTILIZED FOR ARMY REQUIREMENTS AT HOME.

The "Furley" Ambulance Wagon.

This carriage was invented by Mr. John Furley and is intended for the transport of sick and injured persons in civil life.

The framework is of English ash, with mahogany panels, pine roof and floor, seats of kowrie wood, and wheels of oak, ash, and beech. It will accommodate two patients on stretchers and four persons seated inside, or it will carry three patients on stretchers and one attendant. There is also space for two persons to be seated with the driver. The upper stretcher, as

Fig. CXXVII.—The "Furley" Ambulance Wagon (open).

shown in the accompanying diagram, Fig. CXXVII, is placed in position in a very simple and effective manner by an elevator (also invented and patented by Mr. Furley). This elevator consists of two pieces of iron bent at a double right angle, and fitting into slots in the floor of the wagon; both are connected by two lengths of wood. When required for use, the elevator is lowered on to the floor, the stretcher is then run upon it, and the whole is raised by one man into position, and secured by a screw. This action is much assisted by a strong spring fixed at the side on the floor, and this also avoids the risk of shock in case the elevator should be lowered too rapidly. The weight of the wagon is well within the capacity of one

CHAP. VI.

The Furley wagon.

Fig. CXXVIII.—The "Furley" Ambulance Wagon (closed).

horse on good and level roads, and two horses could take it over any ground.

Fig. CXXIX.—"Furley" Ambulance Wagon for one or two stretchers.

In order to provide for the contingency of these civil ambulance carriages being used by Volunteers or, in case of war,

CHAP. VI.

The Furley wagon.

requisitioned by the Military authorities, Mr. Furley has lately made certain modifications in all carriages of the above type, intended for two stretchers and attendants. By making a double floor under the driver's feet these vehicles will now take, not only the stretchers with telescopic handles, for which they were originally intended, but they can also be used with the army regulation stretcher. They are also arranged to carry soldiers' kits and rifles.

This class of wagon possesses an excellent feature, which is, that the whole of the interior can be cleared, and thus it can be used for beds, bedding, &c., and can also be easily cleaned and disinfected, especially as it presents a smooth surface of varnished mahogany.

The wheels are birotal and underlock, thus allowing the vehicle to be turned in its own length, a convenience not to be lightly estimated. The doors are of equal size, and the step is automatic.

The Cairo Wagon.

The Cairo wagon.

This wagon was built at very short notice from the designs of Mr. Furley, specially for H.R.H. the Princess of Wales's Committee of the British National Aid Society, for

Fig. CXXX.—The Cairo Wagon.

the use of the sick and wounded in Cairo during the Egyptian war.

In general construction it resembles the form of the "Furley" wagons already described, but is also provided with a double roof, which completely covers the whole carriage, and a double curtain on both sides, with a space between the outer and inner "flys" of canvas of four inches. The vehicle is provided with an elevator and a stretcher with telescopic handles (see p. 176). The weight is 11½ cwt.

This wagon has been constantly used in Cairo, and though apparently light and delicate in its construction is reported to be a strong and durable carriage, and well adapted for the purpose for which it was built.

Howard's Civil Ambulance Wagon.

Dr. Howard's wagon is practically a little compartment on wheels, 6′ 6″ × 4′ 1″, in which, on a sliding litter, a patient can lie, with an attendant seated beside him. It is drawn by one horse, and is very light; owing to the crank-axle the floor of the wagon is within 15 inches of the ground, and the tail-board drops down to form a step halfway between the distances Consequently it is essentially a civil ambulance conveyance, and is not intended for military service. The hind wheel is large and is in the centre of the vehicle. The floor is below the centre of motion, and the spring from which the body of

Fig. CXXXI.—Howard's Ambulance Wagon. (External).*

the carriage is suspended is a very long semi-ellipse. The four wheels have rubber tyres, and the carriage turns on its own axis. Beneath the driver's seat is a box for surgical appliances, and there is an opening to it from the interior of the carriage. Shafts and a pole are supplied, and either one or two horses may be utilised. In the interior, the right half of the floor is occupied by a light tramway, with india-rubber roller tyres. The tramway rests on four elliptical springs, the pair at the head being 6 inches higher than those at the foot. Between the side of the tramway and the side of the carriage are india-rubber buffers. Resting upon the india-rubber rollers

---

* From Brigade-Surgeon Lieut.-Colonel Evatt's "Handbook of Ambulance Transport."

CHAP. VI.
Howard's ambulance wagon.

is a light cane-bottomed litter with sliding handles. Upon the litter is a thin hair mattress and pillow. The front-bearer

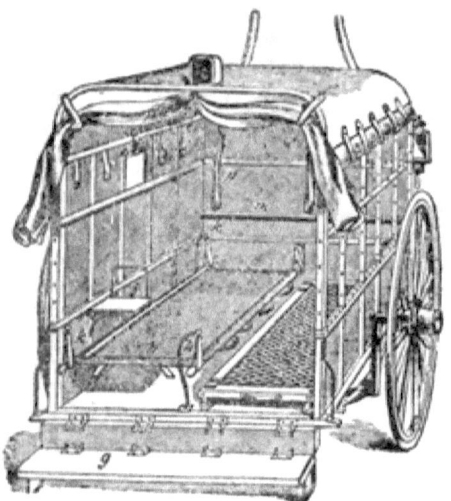

Fig. CXXXII.—Howard's Ambulance Wagon.*

walks into the carriage, and rests the litter on the rear roller, the rear-bearer then pushes the litter into position. A sus-

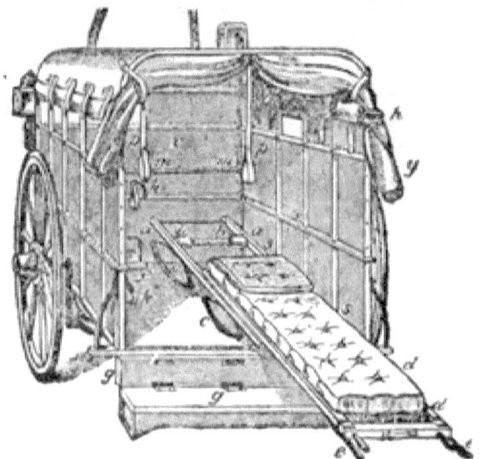

Fig. CXXXIII.—Dr. Howard's Ambulance Wagon (*a a.*) Tramway. (*b b.*) Rubber rollers. (*c c.*) Counterpoise springs. (*d d.*) Litter. (*e e.*) Sliding handles. (*f.*) Attendant's seat. (*g g.*) Tailboard. (*h.*) Folding stretcher. (*k.*) Suspension loops. (*m.*) Supporting bar for police stretcher. (*p p.*) Patient's aid straps. (*s s.*) Lateral buffers.*

---

* From Brigade-Surgeon Lieut.-Colonel Evatt's "Handbook of Ambulance Transport."

pended strap is for the patient to lift himself up by, **if** desired, **and** a corresponding strap at the lower end may **support** a fractured limb.

The other half of the interior has in it **a** seat for the attendant, **and is** otherwise clear at ordinary times; but if a second patient needs to be carried, a stretcher is kept in the roof of the carriage, and can be lowered and suspended by loops hung from iron supports in **the** floor, and lies **at** the **same** level as the left-side litter.

If four patients have to be carried, and two other stretchers are needed, these rest with their front handles on an iron bar, running across the back of the front of the carriage, and the rear handles rest on the iron-bound top of the tail-board.

For ventilation and lighting, openings covered by canvas curtains exist, but in cold climates wooden shutters should be used.

If desired, the carriage can be cleared out of **all** its contents, and will remain available for any ordinary carrying purposes.

The bed of the wagon is **so near** the ground that **the vehicle can only be** used on level and **well-made** roads.

The Tortoise **Ambulance**.*

This ambulance, which is the invention of Captain A. Savill **Tomkins of the** Victoria Rifles, is called the "Tortoise," **because, like that animal, it carries its** shell **on its back, the tent portion lying on the** hoops and raves **of the** wagon. The **Tortoise is essentially** a tent-wagon, and **is a** totally new departure in ambulance.

Universal in **its** application, the tent can be carried on wheeled conveyances, on animals, and by men; it is equally adapted for hot and cold climates, hills or plains; it therefore essentially becomes the most important invention for ambulance purposes, and for the relief of the sick and wounded in the present day, and in its complete form is literally a genuine ambulance, i.e., a movable hospital, carrying all the necessaries, surgical and material, for wounded and sick, capable of following a force wherever wheeled transport can travel, and is of equal efficiency when carried by other forms of transport.

As this system is being gradually adopted in the armies of Europe, and its convenient features recognised, it is proposed to describe this wagon-tent hospital, as it certainly must in time much modify, if it does **not** actually displace present systems. It **has** already been adapted to the regulation pattern ambulance wagon.

The wagon.—The wagon is **a** capacious strong carriage on four wheels, which are birotal, the front pair being 3 feet

CHAP. VI.

Howard's ambulance wagon.

The Tortoise ambulance.

---

* Sometimes called "Flying Field Hospital," which is an ambulance.

CHAP. VI.

The Tortoise ambulance.

6 inches, and the hind pair 4 feet 6 inches in diameter. The bed of the wagon is 4 feet 6 inches wide.

The rear half of the wagon has a well or lower floor 5 feet long 4 feet wide and 14 inches deep. The carriage body is 10 feet long. The sides of the wagon are 2 feet 4 inches high. The entire body is made of selected wood and the strength of the springs is considered with regard to the weight they

Fig. CXXXIV.—The Tortoise Ambulance Wagon packed with tent, equipment, medical necessaries and comforts, and rations for three days for twenty patients requiring lying down accommodation.*

are required to bear. Wagons are made of different sizes, but these are the general proportions.

Attached to the body of the wagon are two strong raves, one on each side, and connecting the two sides are four bale hoops, upon which a tent is laid, and folded into the raves. A row of hooks is fixed on the outside of the upper bar of each rave,—these are utilised to hang accoutrements and kits, when the wagon hospital is pitched. Near the front on each side are two long boxes, holding the tent pegs required. In front, under the driver's seat, is a large box, capable of holding the medical and surgical requisites for 20 patients confined to bed. Underneath are two long boxes to receive the side poles of the tent, and behind the fore-carriage is the water tank, which holds eight gallons, and which is filled from the front. The tailboard carries a locker, which can be used for laundry purposes or for carrying ration wood.

Inside the wagon are carried 20 stretcher beds, arranged in tiers of 10 on each side and towards the front, behind

---

* The well by an oversight is not shown in the figure.

and to the "off" side, is carried a stove capable of cooking for 50 men.

When it is desired to prepare a hospital the wagon is halted, the side poles are removed from the boxes, and four men, one at each side and end, lift the folded tent off the raves, and it unrolls itself—the men then place the pegs round the wagon. Two men then pass underneath the tent, and, assisted by those outside, fix the side-poles, and fasten them to the pegs. The windows are removed from their boxes, and fixed in the places assigned to them. The stretcher bedsteads are removed and prepared for occupation. The whole proceeding is accomplished easily in 15 minutes, even by untrained men.

When it is desired, the wagon can be removed from the tent, and its place as a support occupied by two poles and a ridge pole, the latter is to be found on the top of the bales, and the former in the raves.

The stove is easily removed from the wagon by one man,

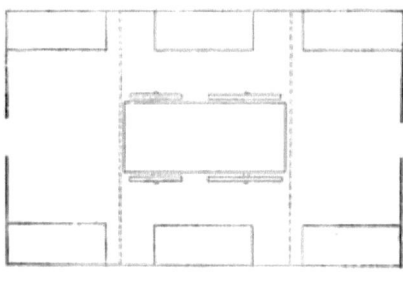

Fig. CXXXV.—Ground plan. Surgery tent. The dotted lines representing the curtains dividing the tent.

and can be replaced in the tent, or cooking can be carried on outside. The wagon is then available for transport of stores or provisions to its own particular section, and is not necessarily idle.

The wagon can carry two patients recumbent and two sitting, by the driver, and when the interior is cleared, three recumbent and three sitting can be accommodated.

The Tortoise ambulance is arranged to receive 54 to 60 patients, and is carried on three wagons, with an additional small four-wheeled wagon for the Medical Staff. This wagon contains accommodation for 4 officers, 6 non-commissioned officers and men, together with all the requisite drugs, instruments, and surgical appliances.

The tents.—The small tent is for the Medical Staff and attendants, and when pitched measures 24' long by 15' wide, is 9' high, with a 5' wall, and contains 2,700 cubic feet of space, covering 360 superficial feet of ground. It is lined

CHAP. VI.
The Tortoise ambulance.

throughout, and weighs with jointed poles, wall poles, pegs, and mallets, 252 lbs., including weight of saddle bags, 277 lbs.

It can be divided into 3 divisions, each 15' by 8'. Division 1 is the operating room, and is lighted by windows in

Fig. CXXXVI.—Surgeon's Sleeping Tent.

the roof, and in the walls of tent light frames of glass are also arranged to slide into the canvas. In this division is an operating table. Division 2.—3 bedsteads for nurses who are not on duty, and stores. Division 3 contains 2 bedsteads for administrative officers.

The total weight of this wagon, when loaded, is about 3,400 lbs., requiring 3 horses, at the rate of 10 cwt. each horse. The stretcher beds are included in this calculation.

The wagon can be removed from the tent, and used for any ambulance transport purpose.

The Surgeon's sleeping tent contains 2 bedsteads, and weighs complete about 55 lbs. It is well ventilated, and lined.

For the remainder of the hospital there are 3 large wagons,

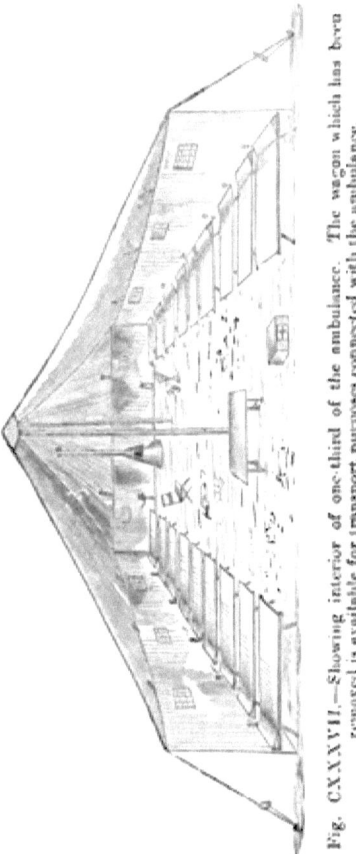

Fig. CXXXVII.—Showing interior of one-third of the ambulance. The wagon which has been removed is available for transport purposes connected with the ambulance.

which are similar in every detail, and each part is interchangeable with the other. A description of one, i.e., one-third of the complete hospital, will be sufficient here.

The tent, which is carried on the outside of the wagon, can be lifted off and transferred to 2 pack animals, and may be pitched with or without the wagon. It measures 30' long and 21' wide, is 10' high, with a 5' wall, and contains about 5,000 cubic feet of air space, covering a surface of 630 super-

CHAP. VI.

The Tortoise ambulance.

ficial feet. It is lined throughout, and weighs, with jointed poles, wall poles, pegs, and mallets, including weight of saddle bags, 396 lbs. The weight of water is not reckoned in this estimate; the tank contains 6 gallons, and would weigh 1½ cwt.

The great facility **for** ventilation and change of air at night or in rainy weather **when** the tent **is** closed, more than compensates for the **reduced** cubic space requisite for each man.

The tent is lighted by windows in the roof, and in the walls, **and light** frames **of** glass are arranged to slide into the canvas. **When not required** there is a slide box in the wagon to protect **these windows from** being broken.

In case the glass windows be broken, **canvas** flaps take their **place until repaired.**

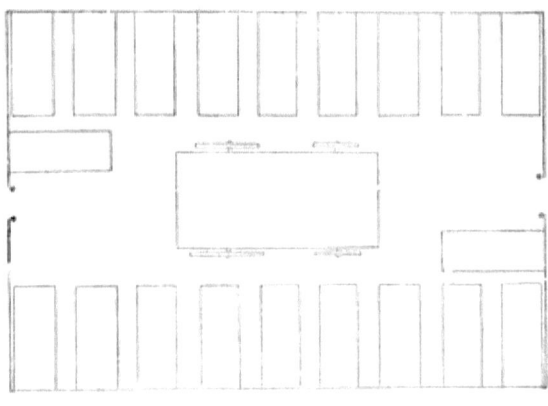

Fig. CXXXVIII.—The Tortoise Ambulance Wagon inside. Ground Plan.

The Norton Stretcher Bedstead consists **of two** poles, feet, **traverses, and** canvas, and is specially **constructed for the purpose of** making a good hospital **bedstead, as** well as a **stretcher.**

This stretcher bedstead when **folded up** occupies less space **than any** other in general use at **the present** time, forming a neat, easily stowed, and firm package, 6′ long, 5″ broad, 3½″ **deep,** and **is of** a total weight **of 30** lbs.

The poles are peculiar in construction, insomuch that they are not composed of one solid piece, but of three flat pieces joined together. They consist of two long pieces of American ash, 6′ long, 3″ deep, and ⅝ inches wide, and joined slightly below the upper surface by a wood runner 1½ inches wide, passing the whole length, and leaving a groove on the upper surface of the pole. This groove receives the canvas, by an arrangement to be described later. Between the sides of each pole, and placed at equal distances apart, are five small blocks, to keep them separated. The extremities of the poles are cut down to the level of the runner to facilitate the insertion of the lath which holds the canvas in the groove.

CHAP. VI.
The Tortoise ambulance.

Fig. CXXXIX.—Section showing 2 longitudinal pieces *l l*, and transverse piece *t*.

The pole is finally strengthened by brass bands, one at each end, and five placed at equal distances between, so that on the upper surface of the pole there are four metal bands bridging the groove between the sides and the runner. The under surface of the poles is hollow, and into this the feet are placed when the conveyance is folded. The feet, which unfold and

Fig. CXL.—Showing how the end of the poles are made with two of the brass bands (*x x*).

lock automatically, are made of wood, and are 12" long, and a person lying on the stretcher is about the same distance from the ground, when the relaxation of the canvas is taken into consideration; attached to the feet is a length of galvanised iron wire, with a loop at the end farthest from the foot, and which, when the stretcher is raised, falls into its place by its own weight, and is there fixed by a block. The foot is replaced by pressing up the wire with the hand sufficiently to raise it over the block, and it will then lie inside the pole.

The handles of the stretcher are 18" long, but only 7" project for the bearer to hold. They are so arranged that they can be passed inside the pole and drawn out when required by a piece of strong whip-cord threaded through the end, for that purpose. That part of the handle which is **always** inside the pole is square, **and** is retained in position by a **small** spiral **spring** with a button.

The traverses are precisely the same pattern as the Army Regulation stretcher, with the exception that the feet are not attached to the traverse **plate** which, consequently, is smaller.

For the purpose of passing the stretcher along the floor **of a** wagon, there **are** four wooden blocks each with **a** small wheel.

The canvas is made of the same material as in the stretchers previously described. It is 6' × 1' 11", and along the sides there is a hem divided so **as** to correspond to the intervals between the five metal bands binding the pole. In order to attach th canvas, it is laid on the opened-out stretcher, and the hem placed in the groove on the top of each pole, and between the brass bands. At one end of the pole on each side, a narrow lath, 6 feet long, is inserted through the hem, and under the brass **bands**, and in **this** way the canvas is evenly and securely **stretched**; as a result of this simple method, **the canvas is easily removed** to be **cleaned**; the laths, at the end of which are small loops of whip-cord, are drawn out, and the canvas is free. The pillow-case is made in one with the canvas, merely consisting of an extra piece of canvas sewn on at the head, forming a bag which can be filled with fern or grass. There are no slings provided with this stretcher, but these could be supplied when required.

The Tortoise Field Railway.—A valuable addition to the equipment is the field railway. This consists of rails laid on iron sleepers over which a light car can be pushed by hand.

Fig. CXLI.

Upon this wounded or stores can be carried. This car weighs 80 lbs. A mile of rails weighs 8 tons. In large encampments a portable field railway of this nature would be very efficient and useful; even in action the railway might be utilised with great advantage in transferring sick and wounded to the field hospitals, and medical stores to the front. As an ammunition feeder also it could be laid along entrenched positions: in brief, there is a large field of extreme usefulness to be developed with this carriage.

All the stores of the tortoise ambulance are arranged to be packed in valises and basket panniers, fitted with the proper attachments, so that they may be carried on pack animals when required.

The tortoise tent wagon, which has just been described, represents the most perfect military hospital wagon at the present time. The main features to be especially noticed are :—

1. Interchangeability of methods of transport and consequent economy.
2. Portability.
3. Completeness, cooking, laundry, &c.
4. Lightness.

1st. The interchangeability of methods of transport.

For a service like that of the British Army—where small forces are continually protecting the frontier in all climates and seasons, and where, unfortunately, as a rule, sickness plays a large part in rendering a force inefficient—the fact of being able to provide shelter so easily for the men is a very important consideration in favour of this system. As has been already stated, the tent can be packed in portions and removed from the wagon to pack animals or the heads of coolies. In tropical and sub-tropical countries the necessity of tenting forces in the field has been proved over and over again, and is so fully recognised that no commander, except under the most urgent and pressing circumstances, would expose his men.

The following is the plan of encampment:—

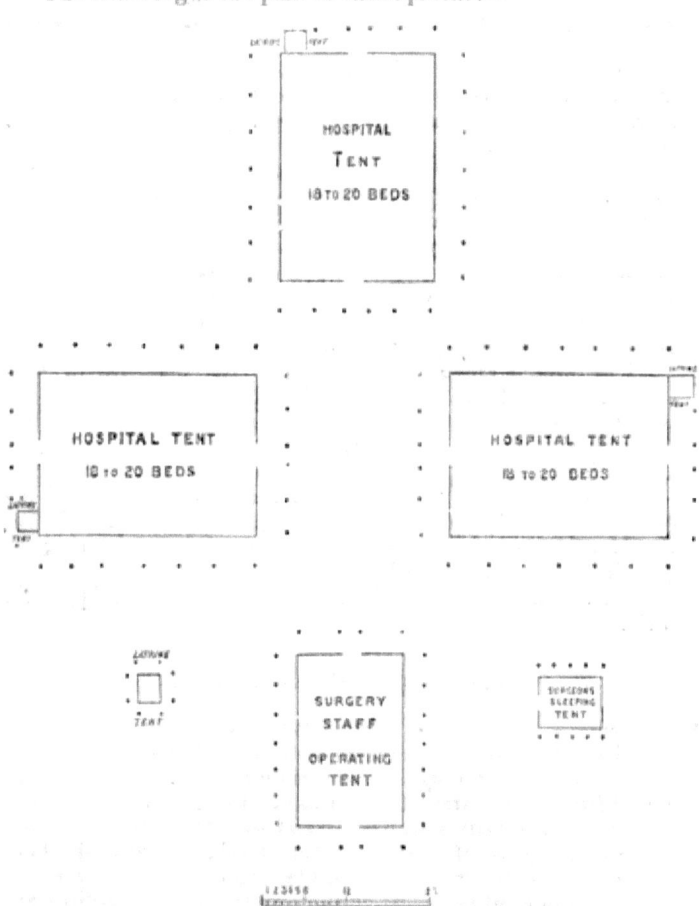

Fig. CXLII.—Ground plan of complete "Tortoise" Ambulance, comprising 4 wagons, 16 horses, and tents, with all the surgical and material requirements for 60 patients.

Apart from all considerations of ambulance transport, these tents can be fixed to any form of transport cart or wagon, and

CHAP. VI.

The Tortoise ambulance.

by the addition of one to each baggage cart with a force on the march, a shelter could be given to the men in 15 minutes. The present system rarely admits of a force being sheltered under two or three hours, and it must be remembered that the mobility of a force is always influenced in proportion to the amount of baggage accompanying it.

Further advantages may be noted as follows:—

The shape of the tents make them capable of resisting the pressure of the wind, owing to the low pitch of roof—the karki (earthy) colour renders them less visible to the enemy—and at night lamps lighted inside the tents cannot be seen by persons outside.

The tent being spread round the wagon, all stores can be unloaded under cover, and conversely when striking camp stores can be loaded on the wagon protected at the same time from the weather.

When tents are wet, they can be dropped round the wagon to dry. This is a great consideration, for tents weigh 30 to 40 per cent. over their normal when wet.

The large tent wagon or hospital wagon when packed, and including three days' rations, 20 bedstead-stretchers, cooking apparatus, stoves, plates, cups, knives and forks, &c., and allowing 200 lbs. for patients' accoutrements, weighs 4,200 lbs., and is a fair load across country for four draught horses.

The wagon stove can be utilised on the march, thus enabling the attendants to provide beef-tea, soup, and hot water at all hours; these comforts being always available, even on the march, will often be found to be the means of alleviating great suffering.

In conclusion, it must be noted that the simplicity of the arrangements of this tortoise tent wagon is such as to allow of considerable modification without in any way endangering the principle of the invention.*

For the drill to pitch and strike tortoise tents (*see* Appendix VII).

C.—HIRED OR COUNTRY CARTS.

Country carts.

Country carts possess a great many advantages to recommend them for the purposes of ambulance transport, while to the English army they are of peculiar value. The wars of Great Britain are carried on, now in one hemisphere, and now in the other, in countries so diverse and so distant, that the difficulty and expense of carrying sufficient vehicles with animals to draw them is almost insurmountable, and recourse is invariably taken to the local resources of the country where hostilities are taking place. A knowledge therefore of the broad features of the ordinary carts of different countries which may be used

---

* This ambulance can be arranged also for 12 or 6 beds, the latter being carried on a 2-wheeled cart.—ED.

for this purpose, and of ready and simple methods of arranging them for the reception of sick and wounded men, is quite in place in this manual.

The definition of a country cart here, is the cart which is in daily use for all purposes of transport, and which is employed by the inhabitants of any country. They are the carts which are indigenous to any district in any part of the globe. Observation and practical experience through long periods of time have instinctively taught the inhabitants the most convenient forms for their own countries, and their carts are no exception to this rule. These conveyances being native to the soil on which they work, fit the ruts of the track, and their build and springs are exactly adapted to the "ups and downs" of the roads of the country. As a rule, the structure of these carts is light and simple, and their transport value is very great, inasmuch as they can be drawn from any village, and the driver is usually the owner of the carts and animals, and therefore it is to his interest to make his unit of transport last as long as possible. What does he do? He feeds his animals properly and well, and he understands their ailments; he harnesses and loads well, so that the point of limit of endurance of the animals may not be exceeded. He knows the roads, and is able from materials always at hand, to repair his cart when it breaks down, and by no means the least important point in these carts is that they can be hired or discharged as required.

English ambulance wagons have answered very well the tests to which they have been subjected in England and in France, where roads exist which are suitable to them, but they have not proved so successful in other countries, when employed on service abroad. On these occasions it has almost invariably been given up in favour of the local district carts. In India, the Cape, Zululand, Egypt, and New Zealand, they have been found very unsatisfactory. In India their very solidity and massiveness appeared to be the cause of parts yielding and breaking under the shocks met with in travelling. The extreme dryness to which the wood had been brought by the heat of the climate, probably had a share also in its failure. At the Cape the wagons broke down under the violent concussions to which they were subjected in going down the precipitous cart tracks, and over the rocky drifts which constitute marked features of certain parts of that country. In New Zealand, owing to absence of roads, the attempt to use them was hopeless; while in Egypt they could not be taken with the troops owing to the loose sandy soil, and in consequence were left at Ismalia.

These examples are sufficient to show that too much confidence in the value of English wagons in foreign countries, other than those of Europe, is apt to be misplaced—and reliance is necessarily placed upon the transport vehicles of the country.

In Europe, generally, there are a large number of carriages which can readily be improvised for the reception of sick and

CHAP. VI.

Definition of a country cart.

English ambulance generally unsuited for the colonies.

On occasions of emergency private

CHAP. VI.

carriages can be easily arranged for patients.

wounded soldiers, even after exhausting the variety of invalid carriages which had been made. Private carriages require but slight alterations to make them perfect for the reception of ordinary cases. It must not be supposed that every case will require the most comfortable form of transport that there is—the wounded will receive the best the nation can give them, but there will be a great distinction between the carriage for severe cases and that for slight ones. One case may require an entire ambulance wagon, and another, having had a slight wound dressed, may be ordered to walk to the field hospital. Sentiment is all very well, but it must be absent from medical officers who are responsible for relieving not only the sick and wounded themselves, but also the fighting line of non-effectives.

Baron Mundy's work.

Baron Mundy, the distinguished Army Surgeon of the Austro-Hungarian army, has devised many clever ideas for rendering ordinary carriages available for the reception of patients in civil life.* In some of these carriages the sides open out, and

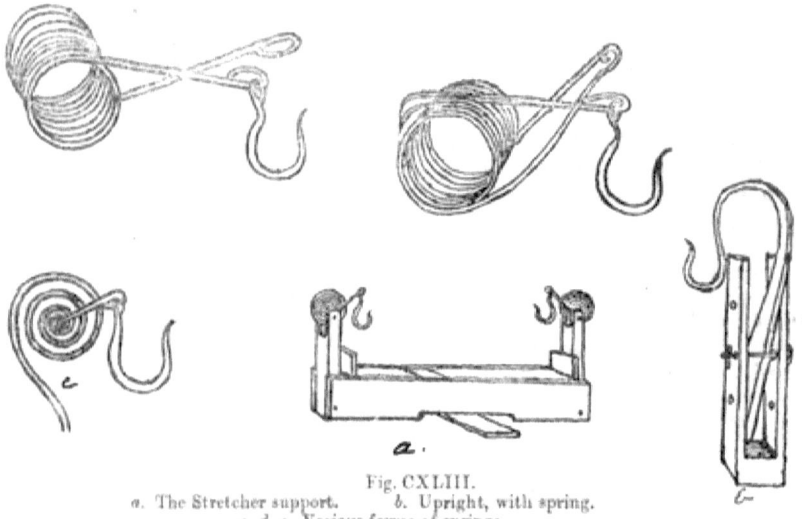

Fig. CXLIII.
a. The Stretcher support.   *b.* Upright, with spring.
c, d, e. Various forms of springs.

in others, the latest, they open at the back, and the stretchers placed in the wagon. The patients can be placed in, and removed from, the wagon with the greatest facility. There is accommodation, also, for an attendant with the necessary appliances and restoratives for first aid.

Omnibuses were largely used in Paris during the siege in

---

* During a recent visit to Vienna, the Editor had an opportunity of seeing the great work which Baron Mundy has instituted there. The Wiener Freiwillige Rettungs Gesellschaft is a masterpiece of organisation, and during the year saves a large number of lives from the perils of the streets, and of civil life.

1871. They are well adapted for the carriage of slight cases on good roads, but for *lying down* cases are not so convenient. Mr. Furley recommends and uses an arrangement by which a

Fig. CXLIV.

Fig. CXLV.

Method of supporting a **stretcher** by springs in a cart.

stretcher is suspended from a trolly running on a rail under the roof of a carriage; one great advantage being that it can be adapted to any omnibus of sufficient length without disturbing its arrangements for ordinary purposes. This is the opposite of the plan used by the French Red Cross Society, where a wooden traverse, resting on a flanged wheel, receives the stretcher, which, when pushed from behind, carries the stretcher into its place in the wagon. A small chain is attached to the trolly to draw it to its place when required. It was found that this arrangement was apt to become blocked.

The Comte de Beaufort has invented a stretcher rest, for use in a vehicle or railway carriage, or for forming a bed, in a very ingenious manner.

This stretcher support consists of an oblong box of wood, 2″ × 6″, divided at the centre by a partition, at each end of which an upright (*b*), fitted with a spring working a hook, is fixed. These uprights can be folded into the box, and the whole forms a convenient package. They are utilised in the following manner: two stretcher supports are opened and separated about 6 feet 6 inches from each other, and in the hooks are placed the handles of the stretcher. There are other modifications of this system, but they are all constructed on the same principle. The special idea is to present a portable apparatus which will render any ordinary conveyance suitable for the transport of the sick and wounded men.

The measurements are:—

Height of spring	1 foot.
Height of box	3·75 inches.
Breadth of box	1·75 ,,
Length of box	2 ft. 6 in.
Weight	14 lbs.

Mr. Furley's modification.

Mr. Furley has modified this invention, by substituting galvanised iron uprights and a chain for the springs, which are liable to break, on which the stretcher rests. They also pack better. The difficulty and delay so often met by using hooks alone is thus got rid of, and it has been found to be less liable to injury.

Fig. CXLIV shows the method of fixing a stretcher by spring hooks to a two-wheeled cart, or any country vehicle suitable for the purpose. The hook consists of a strong steel spring working inside a tube—a hook is to be found at each end. One of these is attached to the rave of the wagon, and the other to the handle of the stretcher.

The Lorraine Wagon.

The Lorraine wagon.

This large forage wagon is used in Alsace-Lorraine and the Rhenish Provinces of Germany. It is characterised by its extremely simple construction, and length. The four or six patients are most conveniently arranged on the method suggested by Major-General Christen Smith, or they may be laid on stretchers which rest on ropes tightly drawn from side to side, as recommended by Mr. Furley. In the bed of the wagon is carried forage, arms of the sick, kit, and hospital stores.

In Austria-Hungary these carts are met with, and also a **much** more solid conveyance, in which the sides can be remo**ved.**

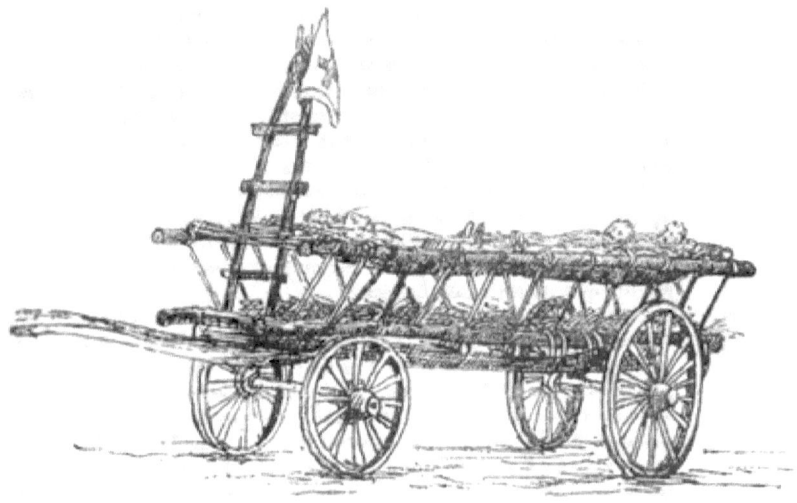

Fig. CXLVI.

In Continental armies these wagons are much used for ambulance transport purposes.

The Araba.

The araba, or Turkish agricultural wagon, which was largely employed for the conveyance of sick of the British army in Bulgaria and in the Crimea,* during the Russian war, may be taken as an example of the rudest form of a four-wheeled sick-transport conveyance. It is only noticed for its historical associations, and as a standard for comparison with other conveyances. The wheels were without tires, rather loosely put together, and, like the axles, formed only of wood. The fore-axle was not movable, so that it could not be made to turn aside to let another vehicle pass without the greatest difficulty.

The araba an example of the most primitive form of wagons.

---

* The only available wagons for carrying the wounded of the British troops to the shore, after the battle of the Alma, were the arabas, or country wagons, which had been pressed into service after the landing of the army in the Crimea. These vehicles had been chiefly obtained for the conveyance of commissariat stores. But even arabas were not present in sufficient numbers, and hence it was that many of the wounded had to be carried the whole distance from the field of action, about three miles, to the boats on stretchers or hammocks by bandsmen, sailors, and others. The arabas continued to be the only wheeled vehicles for the carriage of sick and wounded, until the arrival of Director-General Smith's wagons from Varna. The commissariat arabas were still largely used, however, even after the arrival of the ambulance wagons, owing to the limited number of the latter, viz., two to each division of the army. Many of the wounded after the battle of Inkerman were removed from the front to Balaklava in arabas.

There were no springs. The body, which constantly varied in size in different examples, consisted only of a rough frame secured together by a simple system of inserting one piece into another, or of union by wooden pegs. Two or three planks, sometimes laid loosely, sometimes pegged to the bottom of the frame, formed the floor of the vehicle. It was drawn by two bullocks;* was necessarily very slow in its movement; and was constantly accompanied by a creaking noise, as the pieces of wood of which the wheels and other parts were composed rubbed against each other. When used for conveying sick, the only means adopted to obviate its inconvenience, was a supply of straw or mattresses on the floor to form a bed, and to lessen the effects of jolting. Two, or sometimes three, patients could be placed in an araba in a recumbent position; eight or nine could be accommodated sitting.

The araba resembles the Indian hackery. The araba bears a close analogy with the hackery of India to be presently described, and, as in it, so also in the araba, only one quality can be advanced in its favour. It is this, that in a partially civilized country, with long distances intervening between the places where skilled workmen can be obtained, great difficulty would be experienced in remedying the effects of an accident to a carriage of complicated construction; while, under similar circumstances, in case of any part of an araba becoming broken or lost, means of restoring the damage can be always attained wherever wood or a tree is available. The wood being provided, the skill of the driver, with the aid of the few tools which he always carries with him, quite suffices to effect the necessary repair. The hackeries in India are sometimes four-wheeled, but no further allusion to them is necessary, as their construction is carried out on precisely the same plan as the two-wheeled hackeries.

Indian Country Cart or Bandy.†

Primitive construction of the common bandy of India. This is perhaps the simplest form of two-wheeled conveyance employed in any country. Each wheel is generally constructed of three separate pieces of flat wood, and these are of such a shape that when they are united together the whole forms a solid wheel with a circular outline. They are simply joined together by pegs of wood, nothing of the nature of a tire being employed to bind them together. These wheels are commonly called "log-wheels." They are connected by a wooden axle, which passes through openings in their respective centres, wooden pegs again answering the purpose of linch-pins. Two long poles of wood are fixed horizontally upon the axle. The ends of these poles *behind* the wheels are stretched widely apart by a cross-piece, while the ends *in front* of the wheels are brought closely together,

---

* "Militär chirurgische Fragmente, von Dr. E. Gurlt, Berlin, 1864," p. 11.
† Model No. 1,302, Mus. of Mil. Surg. at Netley. The Ceylon bandy is a similar vehicle. *Bandy* is the common Tamil word for cart.

and lashed tightly to each other by half-tanned hide cords. Thus, the two side-poles and the cross-piece at the back together form a triangle, and this constitutes the frame of the cart. At the point of the triangle the yoke is fixed for a couple of oxen. Upon this frame, projecting partly beyond the base of the triangle, and extending to some little distance in front of the wheels, is placed the body of the cart. It is broad behind and tapering in front, corresponding in general form with the frame on which it rests, and consists of bent strips of wood tied together by a lacing of split bamboo. As an additional support to the body of this conveyance, three stakes or upright pieces of wood are fixed in each of the shafts at certain intervals to strengthen it on either side. These supports are fastened together at their upper ends by cross pieces of wood, or sometimes by ropes, and thus they are not only strengthened, but an easy means of supporting a cover over the upper part of the cart from side to side is afforded.

Indian Hackery.

The hackery is the cart in common use among the natives in Bengal and other parts of India. Its construction is some-

Fig. CXLVII.—The Indian Hackery.

what more advanced than that of the bandy just described. The wheels are not log wheels, but consist of a nave with from four to six broad spokes inserted into separate pieces of wood, or felloes, to form the circumference. The several parts of the wheels are very heavy, roughly hewn, and rather loosely pegged together by pieces of wood. No iron enters into the composition of the cart. The frame of the cart rests directly upon the wooden axles, and is usually irregularly triangular, sometimes quadangular in form. The sides and ends **are** very rudely constructed. Each cart is drawn by two **oxen**.

Like the bandy, the hackery not only forms **one** of the

ordinary hired means of conveyance for heavy stores when troops are marching in India, but it is also frequently used to supplement other lighter and handier means of transport for those who fall sick or become wounded. They were very extensively employed during the Sikh campaigns and during the time of the Indian mutiny, for carrying the sick and wounded along the main roads, some of the cotton quilts of the country, or mattresses stuffed with hemp or straw being employed to soften the concussions, there being no means provided in the cart itself. Their rate of progress is very slow, and this, together with the circumstance of the wheels and other parts being joined so loosely together, causes violent concussions to be by no means so frequent during their movement as might be expected, or as would be the case were the wheels more firmly and rigidly constructed. After a hackery has been some time in use it is liable to be temporarily disabled by the loss of part of a wheel or some such accident; but on the other hand, the very simplicity of construction which leads to this liability, proportionately renders repair of the damage or restoration of the lost part an easy task. The native driver never finds himself at a loss to remedy occurrences of this kind in whatever part of the country they may happen. If a wheel-spoke or even an axle break down, the driver goes to the nearest tree and with his axe soon hews out of it a substitute for the disabled piece, and after an hour's delay or so the vehicle is able to proceed on its journey.

Hackeries easily repaired in case of accidents.

The Burmese Bandy.

The Burmese bandy, during the late war, was very largely utilised for the conveyance of the sick and wounded from the British and native field hospitals to the banks of the Irrawaddy.

Fig. CXLVIII.—The Burmese Bandy.

from whence they where transhipped to the base hospital by the hospital steamer "Sladen." They **were** not adapted to or ever used for the carriage of serious cases in the recumbent position. Those carried were obliged to sit with their legs stretched out or crossed underneath. Each bandy carried two, exclusive of the driver.

Another form of cart is found in the country districts. In its construction it was similar to the Indian hackery, but is much smaller. It is built in the simplest manner, and can be easily mended when broken.*

Cape of Good Hope Ambulance Wagon.

The experience at the Cape of Good Hope well illustrates the necessity which occasionally exists for conveyances of special construction being provided to suit particular colonies. Some of the regulation ambulance wagons built in this country, which at least appeared strong and solid enough to be turned to use in any country with practicable roads, were sent out for service to the Cape of Good Hope, but after trial, they were reported to be useless. They broke to pieces under the severe shocks to which they were subjected in travelling over the peculiarly rough and precipitous roads of that colony. In consequence, in March 1861, a Board of officers was assembled at King William's Town to consider the description of ambulance wagon which would be most suited for the country of the Cape. The Board, after full consideration, came to the conclusion that the best vehicle they could recommend for ambulance purposes was the common cartel or trek-wagon of the country, with certain modifications. The cartel was to be provided with inside fittings in the shape of cots and seats; direct concussion and lateral motion were to be prevented by such means as spiral springs, elastic bands, and other contrivances; and the whole carriage was to be furnished with a covering to shelter the occupants from wind and rain.

In order that a judgment may be formed of the difficulties which may be experienced in devising a suitable sick-transport conveyance in consequence of special features presented by the country in which it is to be used, the following remarks written when Inspector-General Taylor, C.B., was the principal medical officer at that station, and just after he had been on a tour of inspection to the frontier posts, are inserted:—

---

* A curious custom in the country districts is not to apply any lubricant or oil to the axle-boxes of the wheels. The Burman imagines that the noise of his wheels keeps evil spirits away from him as he journeys through the dense and luxuriant forests of his country. When the axle gets hot, the driver fills his mouth with water and blows it with force into the wheel. A good *trait* among the Burmans is their universal kindness to animals; it is, of course, a precept of their religion. [ED.]

CHAP. VI.

Inspector-General Taylor's experience.

"The roads through the interior of the colony are rarely other than simple cart tracks from one station to another. When the track is at any part worn so irregular as to be impracticable, a supplementary track is made, and so on. The surface soil is generally scanty, and, if the irregularities of the rock beneath, and the boulders plentifully scattered, do not from the first make the track a very rough one, the weather acting on the surface soon brings about that result.

Nature of the country over which sick-transport wagons have to pass in the Cape Colony.

"Generally between every two stations the bed of a river has to be crossed once or twice, or even as often as five times; such places are called 'drifts.' The wheels have generally to pass over large bare boulders in these places, rendering the passage very trying, not only to the wood and ironwork of the vehicle, but also to the safety and soundness of the passengers. Such is the extent and state of the roads, that it does not appear to me they are for many generations likely to be improved, so that a severely wounded or sick man cannot be conveyed over

Fig. CXLIX.—A Trek-Wagon.

them in any wheeled vehicle without much agony. I was furnished by the commissariat with their best description of two-wheeled and spring mule-cart, and, though along the edge of the roof on either side pads are fixed for the head to jerk against, yet the oscillations of the cart were frequently so violent that the buffeting was very unpleasant. The neck, too, was frequently strained by the violent concussions the cart was subjected to, even with careful driving. Such a conveyance, I was satisfied, would be intolerable to any but a sound man. The mules that I saw were much too small for the chairs or litters like those used in the Crimea."

Inspector-General Taylor thought that the plan recommended by the Board before mentioned, though not likely to prove unobjectionable, was yet the least painful mode of transport practicable under the existing circumstances of the country, and he agreed in recommending that a trial of it should be made. This recommendation was approved, and has been carried into effect. The following is an account of the construction of the conveyance which was eventually adopted. It is abridged from a description, illustrated by photographs, which Inspector-General Dr. Lawson, who succeeded as principal

Construction of the sick-transport conveyance adopted for

medical officer at the Cape Colony, was kind enough to send to the Author in the spring of 1866.*

The conveyance when complete for use is composed of a frame supporting the crate and litters, and an ordinary bullock-cartel within which the framework is suspended. On removing the frame with its seats and litter the wagon is as suitable as before for carrying ordinary loads. It is to the construction of the litter-frame that the chief attention has been given, more particularly with regard to its mode of suspension, and the best disposal of the space afforded by it for the carriage of patients.

The frame is made of wood, 9 feet 7 inches long, exclusive of footboards, and 3 feet 4½ inches wide. It consists of two side pieces and one shorter centre piece, these being connected by two cross pieces, nearly two feet apart, at each end. Upon this

Fig. CL.—Side view of the sick-Transport frame prepared for suspension in the common cartel, or bullock wagon, of the Cape of Good Hope, with stretchers and seats fixed. One strap only is shown in each spring.

frame are placed two stretchers along the middle portion, and at each end a seat for two persons sitting. Each stretcher is 6 feet long exclusive of the handles, and 20 inches broad, each seat 16 inches broad. The seats are provided with backs and footboards, as well as with leather cushions on each side to keep the occupants clear of the sides of the wagon. The stretchers are also each fenced on the outer side by pieces of wood fastened along their upper surfaces, so as to prevent the men lying on them from rolling against the side of the wagon when much inclined; while between them, fixed simply by iron pegs passed into holes in the centre longitudinal piece of the frame, is a padded upright piece of wood for the purpose of keeping the occupant of one stretcher from rolling against the occupant of the other stretcher. As thus arranged the frame is able to support two men recumbent and four sitting.

If it be desired to carry four men sitting, instead of the two

---

* The Commissariat store-transport wagons used at the Cape of Good Hope are also special wagons made from local designs at Graham's Town, in Caffraria, and not wagons suitable for general service. They are drawn by mules, and they travel from six to eight miles an hour. Commissary-General Drake has mentioned that one of these wagons went from Graham's Town to Port Natal and back, about 650 miles each way, without any injury whatever. See evidence by Commissary-General W. H. Drake, C.B., before the Transport Committee, on the 27th of Nov., 1866.

CHAP. VI.

The ambulance frame.

recumbent, arrangement is made for this being done in the following way :—The stretchers and their cushions are removed, the central upright partition between them lifted out of its holes, and these are slung up against the inside of the tilt of the wagon. Two spare seats which, when not required, are carried beneath the frame, are now fixed in the place which was occupied by the stretchers, facing inwards. The occupants of these seats use a footboard common to both (*see* Fig. CLI.), which is fixed beneath the middle of the frame. Their legs pass between the side and central longitudinal pieces of the frame. When thus arranged, eight men can be carried sitting, four in the middle, and two, as before, at each end.

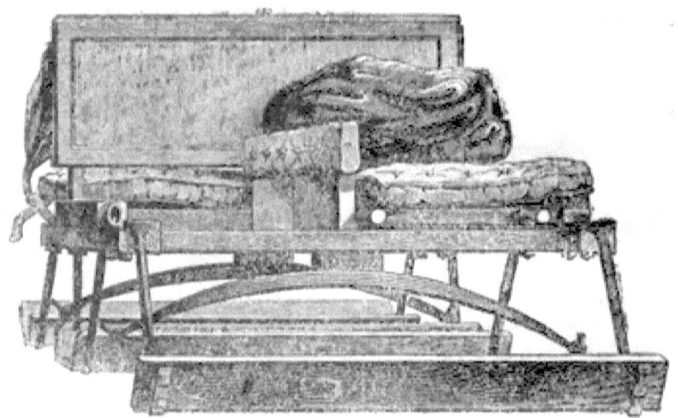

Fig. CLI.—End view of the ambulance frame; one stretcher being removed, and the straps taken out of the springs.

The framework, with its seats and stretchers, just described, is suspended from the sides of the cartel, by leather straps attached to the ends of two steel semi-elliptical springs fixed beneath the frame. The springs are fixed at their centres to the two cross-pieces nearest to the middle portion of the frame, as shown in Fig. CLII. The manner in which the strap is attached to the spring is shown in the following sketch :—

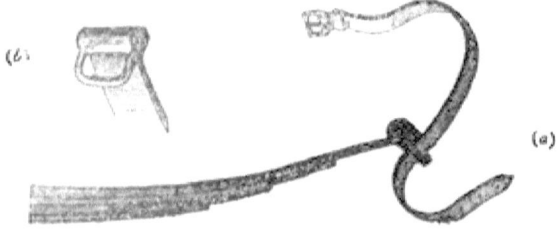

Fig. CLII.—(*a*), end of spring with suspension strap attached; (*b*), loop of spring through which the strap is passed.

The men's knapsacks are intended to be placed in the spaces between the springs and the central footboard; the two spare seats, when not in use, between the springs and the two end footboards. A place is arranged for slinging the men's fire-arms against the tilt of the wagon inside.

The report sent with the description states that:—"The frame, properly slung in a bullock wagon, and carrying six persons, was tried over rough ground, such as would be occasionally met with on service at the Cape. When the play between the frame and the sides of the wagon was sufficiently reduced to prevent lateral jerking, the springs acted well, and the motions were as gentle and easy as could be expected with any mode of conveyance over such a surface; on smooth ground, nothing could be easier."

Surgeon-General J. A. Woofryes, M.D., C.B., C.M.G., Principal Medical Officer of the Force in the Zulu War, 1877, thus writes:—"The question of ambulances caused some anxiety. In the Cape Colony campaign the ordinary ox wagons **were used,** fitted with a framework called a cartel, having **springs,** and slung inside the body of the wagon. A number of **these** cartels had been forwarded to Natal, but it was found that the wagons of this colony were of a different pattern, and were not sufficiently wide to receive them. As ambulances* were required without delay, travelling wagons with springs, such as are used by the better class of colonists, were brought up and converted into ambulances, but only a few of them could be obtained. Therefore, five store wagons with springs were procured from the Ordnance Department, and these were adapted to the purpose. As the war assumed greater proportions, however, more ambulances were required, and it was only after some difficulty that a tradesman could be found who engaged to complete and hand over one every fortnight. He constructed 12, which proved to be most serviceable. They were ordinary wagons of the country, each having on its floor a platform resting on six stout carriage springs, three on either side, leaving a space of some 18 inches between the floor and the platform. On the platform behind were arranged three hospital stretchers abreast for lying-down patients, and in front a double **row** of seats, back to back, for fourteen patients sitting up. A double tent covered the whole length of the wagon, and there **was ample** circulation of air through the open sides, while **canvas** curtains excluded the rain. The men's kits and rifles, **with** tents for use on the road, and cooking utensils, were carried in the space between the **two** floors. The length of the vehicle made its motion easier over the rough roads, and the jolting was counteracted by the springs most satisfactorily."— (A.M.D. Reports, 1879.)

Ox Wagons.—In the Galeaka-Gaika war, 1877–78, S. G. Woolfryes writes:—"The usual means of transport of the

CHAP. VI.

Result of trials with the Cape sick-transport wagons.

Experiences in the Zulu War.

---

* Ambulance wagons are intended.—ED.

CHAP. VI. country had to be used, viz., wagons drawn by 16 or 18 oxen; these were fitted with cartels on springs slung inside the body, and accommodated two lying down and six sitting, and answered fairly well; but the roads of the country are so bad that no conceivable contrivances could entirely prevent jolting. The ox ambulances were very heavy, cumbrous, and slow in their movements, only progressing 18 miles in 24 hours, and taking four days to traverse the distance between Ibeka and King William's Town, necessitating the passing of three nights on the road; and, therefore, some light wagons were fortunately obtained and substituted for the ox ambulances when the more rapid transport of sick or wounded was absolutely necessary."—A. M. D. Reports, 1878.

CLASS V.—RAILWAY AMBULANCE TRANSPORT.

SECTION I.—GENERAL REMARKS ON RAILWAY AMBULANCE TRANSPORT IN TIME OF WAR.

The universal employment of railways and of carriages drawn by steam power in Europe, and the rapid increase of this method of locomotion in all civilised parts of the world, sufficiently indicates the vastness of the extent to which this powerful means of rapidly concentrating large bodies of troops and military stores will be used in all wars of importance. Recent campaigns have, indeed, shown how much the strategical arrangements of the commanders have been bent to accord with the facilities of movement offered by following the directions of the lines of railway running through the countries which have formed the theatre of warfare, and have served to prove beyond all doubt that the positions of railways will take a very prominent part in the plans of military operations of future wars.

But however great may be the influence and importance of railway transport as regards the general movements of armies and their power of destruction, in no part of the military operations are railways capable of being employed more largely, or more usefully, if proper arrangements be previously made, than in the transport of the sick and wounded among the troops. In considering this subject from a military point of view, the urgent necessity and important strategical advantages of speedily relieving the active part of an army from its encumbrances of sick and disabled men; and, further, the advantages of rapidly removing non-effective soldiers, and placing them under circumstances where they will not only be secure against attack or disturbance, but where also they will find the best assistance as regards accommodation and hospital appliances, and where, therefore, they are most likely to be quickly restored to a capability for fresh active service, at once force themselves on the attention.

Other important advantages arise out of those which have just been named. If the sick and wounded can be quickly carried away and dispersed among hospitals in towns, camps, or other places appropriate for their reception far away from the immediate theatre of warfare, there will be, as a consequence of this dissemination, all the less risk of disease being generated and of epidemics springing up among the active portions of the army. Again, if the sick can be rapidly and regularly removed to places at comparatively remote distances from the scene of active hostilities, there will be no necessity

CHAP. VI.
Railways in time of war.

Advantages offered by the use of railways for transporting sick and wounded.

Probable influence of railways on ambulance establishments in the field.

(6107)   2 A 2

CHAP. VI.

Colonel Furse on the importance of spreading the wounded.

Probable influence of railways on surgical treatment of wounded.

Experience in Germany.

for large ambulance establishments being kept with the forces operating in the field. The hospital establishments of armies, the articles and necessary materials for the care and treatment of the sick and wounded among the troops, and the vehicles for their transport, have always been a source of difficulty and objection to military commanders, and they have become so more than ever since the progress of civilisation and science has required the sick and wounded to be provided for in a manner more adequate to their necessities than formerly was ever contemplated. But with the advantage of railway communication at hand, the amount of ambulance stores and transport may be limited to the probable wants of a single action, and only a small medical staff will be required to supplement the surgical assistance which will be always in company with the troops, either as regimental, brigade, or divisional medical officers.

Colonel Furse, in his work on Military Transport, writes: 'One of the principal aims in organising a proper communication service is to civilise war by limiting its evils. Where railways are available, the removal of the sufferers by their means is one way of carrying out this idea. Did railways offer us in war no other advantage but improved means for removing a large number of sick speedily, with ease and comfort, this of itself alone would be a great boon. The spreading of the sick over a large tract of country where a railway is at hand becomes possible, they need no longer be massed in large numbers in crowded and pestilential hospitals, and being subdivided into small groups, miles away from the front, can be better cared for.'

Many serious primary surgical operations, which had till recently to be performed inconveniently on the field itself, are now postponed until the arrival of the wounded at a fixed hospital, where they can remain undisturbed after such operations; for with good management the railway conveyance may be so arranged as to carry them there with no greater disturbance than has hitherto happened in the transport of wounded from a field of action to the hospitals in rear, while the journey can be performed with such speed that there will not be sufficient time for those symptoms of fever and irritation to arise, which, when they exist, counterindicate amputation or other surgical interference of a primary nature. Certain other surgical operations of a conservative kind, which, from their nature could hardly, under any circumstances, be attempted with propriety on the field itself, and which would be almost equally unjustifiable in hospitals, the temporary nature of which would render the patients liable to be moved to other hospitals more remote shortly after the operation, may be resorted to without any special risk if the hospitals to which the patients are at once transported possess a more permanent character. The surgeons during the wars in Schleswig-Holstein and Bohemia, and in the Franco-German War, were in numerous instances enabled to avoid amputations, and to resort to more intricate operations in the interest of their patients, owing to the speedy removal of the wounded from the neighbourhood of the scenes of action to fixed hospitals. It was not merely from the fact of these hospitals being fitted with all the necessary appliances that the surgeons were induced to undertake the special operations referred to, but what also materially influenced them was that they knew their patients could remain in hospital without any necessity for further removal until they were in a proper condition to undergo the transport without the danger of irritation to their wounds and interference with the process of healing.

The circumstance of railways being made available for ambulance transport will also probably cause intermediate field hospitals—always burdensome, costly to manage, and too often hiding-places for idleness, as experience showed during the Peninsular War—to be established in less proportion than has hitherto happened in war, for it will be far more easy and economical to add to the hospital accommodation already existing in towns and large centres of communication, at a distance from the theatre of warfare, than to open hospitals in fresh situations, a plan which necessarily involves great outlay at starting, as well as continued expense from the transport of stores, and from the loss produced by wear and tear and accidents inseparable from such movements.

In 1855, in the Crimea, after the railway between Balaklava and the camp before Sebastopol had been completed, it was occasionally used for conveying sick from the camp hospitals; but only the wagons constructed for carrying stores to the front were available for this service, and they being unprovided with any contrivances to make them suitable for invalids, no patients so infirm or injured as to require a recumbent position were sent by it. This was the first time that any railway was employed for transporting sick and wounded soldiers from a scene of actual hostilities to the rear.

The campaigns which have been undertaken since the Crimean War have afforded a regular and progressive experience of the important use which may be made of railways for the transport of wounded in the time of war. The Italian campaign of 1859, the Schleswig-Holstein War of 1864, and the Civil War in the United States of 1864, the Austrian-Prussian campaign of 1866, and Franco-German war of 1870, and Russo-Turkish Campaign, all exhibit this mode of conveyance from its simple origin to the product of an important science. In some of these instances the opportunity has been afforded of observing the application of railways to military sick transport purposes where no previous preparations had been made for this particular service; in some, of studying the advantages of certain peculiar contrivances as additions to ordinary passenger carriages, which had been expressly provided. In other instances carriages had been specially constructed with all the necessary fixtures and appliances for receiving and taking

CHAP. VI.

The need of systematic preparation for the transport of sick by railway shown by the experience of recent campaigns.

care of wounded men labouring under all kinds of injuries, and in every condition of physical prostration, and had been extensively employed, notably in the Franco-German War, for which service they were designed.

The result of this varied experience has been to show it to be particularly important, having due regard to the necessities which are liable to occur in time of war, that the methods best adapted for meeting such wants efficiently, and the most economical plans for carrying these methods into execution, should be fully considered during the time of peace. When war has commenced, and while it is actively proceeding, all military exigencies arising out of the circumstances of the time acquire special urgency; for success in any strategical operation usually depends upon these exigencies being met at the instant they occur, so that no avoidable risk may be undertaken, and no opportunity of advantage lost. If the system of railway ambulance transport be not settled beforehand, when the necessity occurs the military and medical authorities will probably be harassed by conflicting views as to the best steps to be taken to meet the emergency; and that, too, at a time when they ought to be able to give their undivided attention to the urgent need which will then press for immediate action. The sick and wounded will also not improbably suffer from the same cause, for everything under such circumstances usually has to be sacrificed to the main military object, which is to get such encumbrances away almost at all hazards. Individuals will be little regarded while the thoughts of those in authority are directed to clearing away the wounded as a mass; so long as accumulations of disabled men remain with an army, they cannot fail to fetter the movements, to detract from the strength and activity of the main body, and also, in a certain degree to distract the attention of the commander from the object of chief importance which he has in hand.

Economy of systematic preparation.

That the method to be adopted for the transport of sick by railway should be perfected in all its details before the time of need comes, is also important from pecuniary considerations. Little heed can be given, when the want presses, to suggestions for pecuniary economy. That which appears at the moment to be the most practicable, and so the most advantageous, mode of proceeding, will have to be adopted irrespective of cost. Not unfrequently it will happen that the military exigencies are such that they must be met by any method that may offer itself, even by one which is manifestly faulty, owing to there being no longer time to make any preparation for one that is known to be better, but not at the time available. It appears

Disastrous results of arrangement in the Italian war.

to have happened thus in respect to the method of railway sick-transport conveyance in use during the Italian war of 1859. No suitable provision had been previously made for the carriage of disabled soldiers by the railways, the military movements were so rapid that no time was afforded for making proper preparations for their conveyance after the campaign had opened, and the sick and wounded, who suddenly became accumulated in immense numbers at the front and in numerous improvised hospitals, must either have not been removed at all from the theatre of warfare, or have been brought away, as they were, by railway carriages in the ordinary condition in which they are used in peace time for the conveyance of persons in health and strength, and in the wagons employed for carrying goods and cattle. Unfortunately, there was a deficiency of ambulance transport in the field, as well as on the railways. The inevitable consequence was that the removal of the wounded was greatly obstructed. Many men died from being detained in over-crowded and ill-provided field hospitals, who might have escaped had there been adequate means for their transport; while those who were brought to the railways and then removed, suffered greatly during their journey, from being chiefly carried in open trucks, or in third-class carriages, without any arrangements for breaking the violent concussions arising from the oscillations, or the jostling against each other of the carriages, beyond the use of some straw placed on the floors to protect them from the hard planks upon which they were lying.

But although a large amount of individual suffering, which might have been avoided by previous arrangements and preparation was thus brought about, the general good that resulted from the opportunity of removing the wounded with even comparative rapidity from the ground of conflict by means of the railways was immense.

The very distance to which the wounded may be carried when railway transport and free communication are available, is in itself an advantage. All the inconveniences that attend the transference of sick and wounded from field hospitals to depôts and intermediate hospitals, as well as those arising from the circumstances of a retreat, or a change in the strategical positions, being liable to bring these hospitals within the sphere of military operations, are avoided. Strategical movements too are now so rapid that the concentration of detached groups of sick and wounded soldiers in intermediate hospitals is a matter of daily increasing difficulty. The town or place in which it may be to-day convenient to establish an intermediate hospital, may to-morrow be out of the line of communication with the army operating in the field.

When the base of operations happens to be a seaport, as must always be the case if British troops are engaged, as allies or otherwise, in foreign expeditions, a line or lines of railway exist between it and the front, and carriages are usually available by which the sick and wounded can be rapidly and regularly moved to the base, to be thence transferred either to hospital ships or to naval transports for removal to fixed hospitals away from the neighbourhood of the sphere of conflict. Again, when a continental power is operating from a base in its own dominions, the active part of the army, as well as the troops which have become disabled for service, will be equally benefited by taking

CHAP. VI.

Influence of the transportation of sick by railway on the active part of an army.

Chap. VI.

Experience of the American War.

advantage of the opportunities afforded by the railways for ambulance transport.

During the War of Secession in America in 1864 a large proportion of the wounded were removed by means of railways,—indeed, so well did the American rolling-stock lend itself to the purpose of ambulance trains, and so well did they work, that this campaign may be said to mark an era in their history. There were two forms (a): Passenger wagons of the long type, opening at their ends and communicating by bridges over the couplings, so that a direct communication existed throughout the whole length of the train. In these the cots were suspended by means of india-rubber loops to traverses, placed across the wagon, in a similar manner in many respects to the Système Gurlt. (b.) Goods wagons were also utilised in this war, but only those which opened at their ends. They carried nine lying down, and never more than twenty altogether. The floor of the wagon was covered with straw, upon which mattresses were laid. It is reported that when there was sufficient straw and the wounded were well arranged, the shock from the movement of the train was considerably deadened, and severe cases were comfortably transported. It was, however, very difficult to obtain a sufficiency of straw or hay, and after a general engagement the trains succeeded one another on their way to the rear so rapidly that only temporary beds could be improvised out of materials close at hand.

Battles of Gettysburg and Olustee.

After the battle of Gettysburg more than 15,000 wounded were sent back from the advanced positions by railway to Baltimore, York, Harrisburg, and Philadelphia. A large proportion of these were transported in goods wagons containing straw. After the battle of Olustee, 20th of February, 1864, 1,100 were transported in goods wagons, lying on branches of pine and a little straw, and covered over with blankets. The train was rapidly driven to Jacksonville, a distance of nearly fifty miles, and Assistant-Surgeon Janeway, who was in charge, reports that the patients who had undergone amputation and received severe wounds, did not complain very much of this primitive method of transport.

In 1864 there were three ambulance trains, each composed of ten or twelve wagons, which joined the advanced force at Nashville and Louisville. Every day a train left the hospitals at the front of the advanced line. In each train a wagon was exclusively retained for cooking purposes, and for stores, another for a dispensary, and with a large provision of medical comforts, apparatus, &c. Surgeon E. Cooper reports that a passenger train arranged for the carriage of sick and wounded by Surgeon Barnum already travelled regularly over the line, a distance of 184 miles between Louisville and Nashville. Surgeon Barnum estimated the total number carried at 20,472.

Experiences of 1870-71.

During the war of 1870-71, Germany had an admirably organised service of evacuation. During this war 21 ambulance trains were running: 9 Prussian trains, 1 Saxon, 1 Hanoverian, 1 Rhenish, from Cologne; 1 Hessian, from Mayence; 4 Bavarian,

2 Wurtemburg, 1 Baden, and 1 Hamburg. The trains were organised for the most part by the military administration, and partly by the Aid Societies, which were absolutely under military command.

<small>CHAP. VI.
German Ambulance trains.</small>

The ambulance transport evacuations, in conformity with the Regulations, were placed under the general orders of the Surgeon-in-Chief of the Staff of the Army, but the importance of the service had necessitated the creation of special evacuation committees at Weissemburg, Forbach, and Epernay.

The German ambulance trains were composed of **27** wagons, comprising 20 wagons for wounded, 1 passenger wagon, 1 provision wagon, 1 kitchen wagon, 2 baggage wagons, 1 platform wagon for fuel. Each train of the Prussian kind carried 196 patients lying down.

The Saxon ambulance train was composed of 19 goods wagons, each arranged for 8 beds; 3 fourth-class passenger wagons arranged on Gründ's system, a kitchen and provision, a baggage, and a platform wagon. There were no wagons for the "aides." It carried 182 patients.

The Baden train consisted of 2 first-class and 2 second-class carriages for seated patients, 1 kitchen and provision wagon, 1 saloon wagon for the Staff, 14 wagons for lying-down wounded **on the** Heidelberg (Fischer) system, and other wagons borrowed from the Wurtemburg lines: 220 sitting up and 140 lying down wounded were transported.

The Wurtemburg train was provided with wagons for medical officers, kitchen and provisions, and carried 120 wounded. During the war it transported 4,303 wounded, and travelled over 4,197 miles.

The Rhenish train was composed of 3 passenger carriages for sitting-up wounded, 3 wagons for the assistants, 3 for provisions and kitchen, with 16 wagons of 8 beds, each suspended by elastic rings. It could carry 152 lying-down wounded, and 96 convalescents or slightly wounded.

The Hessian train was more or less similar to the Rhenish, with 20 suspended beds for lying-down wounded.

Several trains could run from the place of actual hostility to Berlin without much delay.

A sufficient staff of medical officers, assistants and nurses, accompanied these trains.

It is to be noticed that the trains composed of wagons, which could be rapidly transformed and arranged into auxiliary trains, were the most useful in the evacuations from the battlefield after long engagements.

The *special* sanitary trains were used later on, and by reason of the congestion of the traffic could only proceed slowly to their destination. From Gomeru, the point of departure just outside of Paris, trains of wounded occupied about six days in the journey to Berlin, but they were complete travelling hospitals.

On the Nancy line Dr. Peltzer says, "From October 1st to May 5th, 1871, 15,787 wounded or sick were transported:"

<small>Peltzer's statistics.</small>

No. conveyed.	Ambulance Trains.	No. of Journeys.	Average number per train.
6,583	Prussian	32	205
3,738	Bavarian	17	219
2,245	Wurtemburg	10	224
872	Cologne	3	290
793	Hamburg	5	158
520	Saxony	3	173
440	Mayence	2	220
236	Hanover	1	236
200	Baden	1	200
160	Palatinate	1	160
15,787		75	

Average number carried by each train was 210.

Dr. Steinburg says that 26 sanitary trains arrived in Berlin from the 28th September, 1870, to the 19th May, 1871, carrying 3,255 wounded. In his report, "Contributions to the Statistics of the War of 1870 and 1871, Dr. Engel, Director of the Royal Prussian Bureau of Statistics," thus fixes the number of wounded evacuated after the great battles:—

Date.	Battle.	Officers.	N.C.O.	Men.
Aug. 2	Wissembourg	40	109	938
,, 6	Wörth	305	741	6,412
,, 5	Spicheren	134	325	3,173
,, 14	Colombey-Nouilly	119	350	3,165
,, 16	Mars-le-Tour (Vionville)	381	1,016	8,885
,, 18	Gravelotte	526	1,363	13,300
,, 13	Noisseville	74	191	1,837

Engel further states that 89,728 were altogether during the war transported by the sanitary trains.*

Russian railway ambulance transport. In Russia a complete system of ambulance train service exists, and during the Russo-Turkish War Doctor Sillèn writes: "Of the number, 190,915 wounded and sick transported from the seat of war, by January 1st, 1879, 3,218 men only, that is to say, 1·9 per cent., and consisting of the most serious cases, were transported at the beginning of the war in the ordinary trains, the remaining 187,697 were transported by the ambulance trains."

The State subsidises the railways to a certain extent, and

---

* I am indebted for much information regarding this subject to M. le Docteur Robert, Médicin-en-Chef of the French Army, in his interesting monograph, "On Railway Ambulance Transport," published under the auspices of "La Société de la Croix Rouge."—ED.

orders that each shall keep up a certain number of vehicles of the special ambulance type, and a prescribed quantity of material ready to be applied to the wagons. In the following proportions:—

Russian ambulance trains.

For railways—

150 versts long	1 wagon,	material for	10 wagons.
150 to 200 ,,	3 wagons,	,,	25 ,,
250 to 500 ,,	6 ,,	,,	50 ,,
Above 500 ,,	9 ,,	,,	75 ,,

The ambulance train is arranged in the following manner:—

1. Magazin wagon.
2. Cooking wagon.
3. Nine 3rd class carriages for seriously ill and wounded.
4. Two 2nd class for the Commandant and Medical Officers, Delegates of the Red Cross, Sisters of Charity, etc.
5. Eight carriages for those lightly wounded and able to sit.
6. One wagon for soiled linen and the dead.

The personnel consists of 1 Commandant, 1 superior officer, 2 medical officers, 20 hospital attendants, and 8 Sisters of Charity.

General remarks.

The ambulance wagons are arranged on Zavodovsky's plan, and answer very well. (*See* page 375.)

All the good which resulted from scattering the sick and wounded during and after the Italian campaign of 1859, might have been equally effected, and at the same time the suffering which attended the rough mode of transport by the railways have been prevented, had some means been provided for rendering the railway carriages employed in transporting the sick and wounded suitable to their condition. At the present time there exists, as has been shown, on the continent a more or less complete organisation of railway ambulance transport. In Germany, Austria, and France a certain number of these trains are kept up, and the staff which works them pass through an annual training. With such previous experience it is evidently most important for every European country to fix upon some regular system beforehand, so that, in case of similar necessities again arising, a recurrence of the evils which have lately been glanced at may be suitably obviated. The appliances most appropriate for converting the various classes of railway carriages into conveyances proper for the transport of sick and wounded should be determined, and certain regulations settled by which the transport may be expected to be most safely and most expeditiously accomplished.

CHAP. VI.

SECTION II.—OBSERVATIONS UPON THE CARRIAGES IN USE UPON RAILWAYS, ESPECIALLY ENGLISH RAILWAYS, AS REGARDS THEIR FITNESS FOR THE TRANSPORT OF SICK AND WOUNDED IN TIME OF WAR.

Construction of railway carriages commonly used in Europe unfit them for sick-transport purposes.

The necessity, which was dwelt upon in the previous section, for determining beforehand the best mode of transporting sick and wounded troops by railway conveyances in time of war, will be found, on a little examination, to be no imaginary one. Most of the passenger carriages in ordinary use in England, and, in general upon European railways, are quite unsuited in their actual condition for the removal of any but persons who are in the possession of the full use of their limbs and bodily powers. In addition, these vehicles are so constructed that many difficulties occur in devising efficient plans for adapting them to the circumstances of persons who are debilitated by illness or disabled by wounds. In the United States, where no distinction is, or used to be, made as to classes of carriages; where no high partitions in them, dividing one part from another, exist; where each carriage resembles a large open chamber or gallery capable of holding from fifty to sixty persons, the conversion of a passenger car into a sick-transport car has been a comparatively easy undertaking. Carriages of nearly the same dimensions and similar in general construction, though not intended for all classes of passengers indiscriminately, are in use in some parts of Europe. They are met with on some of the Austrian railways and in Switzerland. But a serious difficulty is met with at the first step in undertaking to fit the carriages in use on English railroads for the transport of sick and wounded. It is not merely that the two principal classes of carriages are divided into wholly distinct and comparatively narrow compartments, and that the third-class carriages are also partially sub-divided, but a still greater difficulty arises from the fact that the doors opening into the several compartments are of such limited dimensions, as to make it next to impossible to carry an ordinary stretcher, with a wounded man upon it, into any one of them. The doors of second and third-class carriages vary in width, from twenty to twenty-two inches; the width of first-class carriage doors varies from twenty-two to twenty-four inches. A man of average size, walking face forwards, and having command over all the movements of his body, requires twenty-one inches for a clear passage; so that it is only by assuming a certain amount of slanting direction as he moves through the doorway that a moderately stout person can enter into either kind of carriage. No class of *passenger* carriages can therefore be accepted as suitable for receiving into them badly wounded or sick persons, such as require to be carried

Subdivisions of railway passenger carriages.

Narrowness of the doors of railway passenger carriages.

into them on stretchers in a recumbent position, so long as the doorways remain as narrow as they now are. The only carriages which remain are those of the truck or goods wagon kind, and horse-boxes. Sick and wounded on stretchers can be admitted into these vehicles without much trouble or risk; but here again another difficulty occurs, for they are destitute of such springs or other adaptations as will serve to break the jars from oscillatory movements, or from the severe concussions which are induced from time to time by accidental irregularities in the joints of the rails, by the vans being brought up suddenly against each other, and by other such casualties, particularly when they are only carrying so trifling a weight as that of a few men. Hence the railway wagons constructed for the porterage of heavy stores, or for the carriage of horses, are quite unsuited for the purpose of sick-transport conveyance in their existing condition. Supposing, however, that the doors of passenger carriages could be made wide enough to admit stretchers with wounded persons upon them, and the difficulty already noticed of their entrance be thus removed, there would still remain further impediments to the reception of stretchers within the carriages. This fresh perplexity is brought about by the usual internal dimensions of the compartments of these vehicles. The length of the space occupied by two opposite seats measured from back to back, including the intervening passage, in a compartment of a first-class carriage, is greater than the corresponding space in a second-class compartment; but in the former it is under five feet, generally four feet eight inches. It would, therefore, be impossible to cause a stretcher bearing a man in a recumbent position, to rest upon the opposite seats of either a first or second-class carriage. The rounded, sloping form, and the comparative narrowness of the adjoining seats, the partitions which are usually applied to cause partial separation and to form arm-rests between them, would equally prevent a stretcher from being supported along either side of the carriage. The only plan that remains to be adopted for accommodating a patient in a lying-down position in a first-class passenger carriage, is to have cross-supports resting upon the opposite seats, and on the frame so formed to place a stretcher specially constructed for the purpose. This stretcher will have to correspond in width with the width of the interval between the seats, and one patient only can be accommodated in each compartment. This is evidently a plan not likely to be generally adopted, although special conveyances have been constructed in accordance with it, and it may be employed on certain occasions. Corresponding difficulties are met with in trying to convert third-class carriages into conveyances for sick and wounded, although they are not divided into compartments, and the interior partitions are only raised high enough to form backs to the seats. The narrowness of the doors, as well as of the wooden benches inside, are impediments both to the admission and to the support of recumbent patients on stretchers. The only wounded persons, therefore, for whom

CHAP. VI.

Goods wagons on railways.

The springs of goods wagons.

Field stretchers cannot be placed on the seats of passenger carriages.

CHAP. VI.

any of these passenger carriages can be rendered generally suitable, will be such as are capable of maintaining a sitting position; and special arrangements, in addition to the ordinary furniture of the carriages, will have to be made for a certain number of these patients, according to the nature and situation of their wounds, in order to make them suitable for their reception. Special contrivances have been devised to enable third-class carriages to accommodate recumbent patients, but it is questionable, as will be shown presently, whether any of them are suitable for practical application on an extended scale.

Conversion of railway wagons into sick-transport vehicles.

Nothing thoroughly satisfactory as regards the conversion of railway wagons into sick-transport carriages for recumbent patients can be settled without actual experiment; but one of the plans which at once occurs as both practical and expedient is the suspension of stretchers within them, such as the Zavodovsky method which appears to be the best and which will be described later. To carry out this, or any similar plan, there would be merely required a supply of ropes and holders, or iron rings capable of being screwed into the sides of the wagons, through which the ropes would have to be passed. It would apparently be an easy matter to secure temporarily iron hooks, or suspenders, to the poles of stretchers to enable them to be used with such a contrivance. Their capability of application would, however, depend upon the width of the carriages being suitable for receiving them. If not suitable, then special stretchers for the railway trucks and wagons must be constructed and kept in store, and in such a case they would have to be so made as to be available for all the ordinary purposes of stretchers for carrying patients from the field or elsewhere, when not required for use in the railway trains. Whatever plan be adopted, it is absolutely essential that the stretcher itself, or the support upon which it rests, be not fastened into the sides or floor of the carriage. As many "removes" as possible should be allowed (and these can be fairly obtained by ropes and improvised springs), to the wounded who are transported, or intense agony may result from the excessive jolting. It must be remembered that the weight carried on the springs of goods wagons loaded with sick has no comparison with the weight the springs are intended to bear, and will scarcely make any difference at all, and the wagon will run as though it were springless.

Urgent reasons for using only ordinary stretchers in railway ambulance wagons.

So much suffering is unavoidably inflicted in lifting up and placing wounded and feeble patients from one stretcher to another, and particularly in removing them from the stretchers to put them into their places in railway carriages as ordinarily constructed, that it is especially desirable to prevent the necessity of these changes. If brought from a field of action, the shattered frame or limb of a wounded man must be held in the hands of the bearers and must be moved with their movements, from the moment the patient is lifted off the stretcher until, after being got into the wagon or carriage, he is placed upon another stretcher. **Under** any circumstances, even when no such change of stretcher takes place, it is a difficult operation, and usually a very painful one, to get helpless patients into and out of a railway train, and it can be easily understood how much the difficulty must be increased, and proportionately the pain also, if the patient is to be carried to the train by one stretcher, transferred and settled in another, and again removed by a third in the course of his journey. In making arrangements, therefore, for the transport of sick and wounded by railway, the plan adopted should always include means by which those patients, whose condition is such as to render a recumbent position imperative, may remain during the whole of their transit upon the same stretchers on which they have been brought, whether from the field or from hospital, to the railway train. When the patients have arrived at the place of their destination, the stretchers upon which they have been carried should be collected by some responsible person and sent back to the quarter from whence they came, so that they may be available for further use. One advantage in connection with ambulance trains, and which should invariably be secured, is that badly wounded soldiers should not be required to leave the stretchers upon which they have been brought to the railway until they are transferred to the hospital beds which they are appointed to occupy for the remainder of their treatment.

SECTION III.—HISTORICAL RÉSUMÉ OF RAILWAY AMBULANCE TRANSPORT.

Two series of inquiries on the continent have principally served to attract attention to the subject of railway ambulance transport in Europe; in the United States it was forced into notice by the exigencies of the last civil war in that country. The first series consisted of certain experiments which were conducted for the purpose of ascertaining the best modes of transporting sick and wounded by railway in Prussia in 1860; the second was the experimental trials made at the instigation of the societies for aid to wounded in time of war in 1867, at the Western Railway at Paris, and later at Vienna in 1873, and at the Red Cross Conferences.

*Investigation concerning the transport **of** sick soldiers by railway.*

Practical Experiments in Prussia in 1860.

Dr. Gurlt, Professor of Surgery in the University of Berlin, wrote in 1860 a pamphlet, which at that time and since has attracted considerable attention, entitled, " *Ueber den Transport Schwerverwundeter und Kranker im Kriege, nebst Vorschlägen über*

CHAP VI.	*die Benutzung der Eisenbahnen dabei.*" In this paper Professor Gurlt first suggested the plan of transporting the wounded in hammocks slung to the roofs of goods wagons, and making use of suspended cradles for single shattered limbs in railway carriages. Professor Gurlt's ideas were not accepted at first, but later the success of nearly the same arrangement, proved that his suggestions were good ones, and that this eminent surgeon was in advance of the times in which he wrote. The chief feature in the plan suggested by Dr. Gurlt was that the wounded requiring to be carried lying down should be placed in hammocks or cots similar to those used on board ship, slung from the roofs of third-class carriages and luggage-wagons.
Difficulties in the way of slinging hammocks in railway carriages.	A serious difficulty was experienced, at the outset, in trying to put the system into practice. The roofs of the carriages, which had only been made for purposes of protection, not for sustaining weights, were found not to be sufficiently solid to admit of the hooks being made fast at some of the parts where it was necessary to insert them for the proper disposal of the cots; neither were they strong enough in some other parts, where the hooks could be inserted, to bear the weight of a man lying in a hammock. The screws of the hooks were drawn out and the hammocks fell. There were, however, a few positions where portions of the framework of the carriages were found to be sufficiently strong for sustaining the hammocks and men in them, but fresh difficulties then started up. Although the persons carried in the hammocks felt very little inconvenience from jolts or sudden shocks, they were subjected to a lateral swinging movement which gradually increased with the motion of the train, until it produced upon them **an uneasiness of the** same nature as sea-sickness, and occasionally caused the cots to be brought into collision with the sides of the vehicles in which they were suspended. It was obvious that such sources of disturbance would be injurious to sick and wounded men.
Plan of railway ambulance transport finally adopted in Prussia in 1860.	Efforts were then made to get rid of these objections by various changes in the mode of suspending the hammocks, but without success. Finally, the Committee recommended the adoption of a more simple plan of transport, viz., to cover the floor of each wagon with a thick bed of loose straw, to carry the patients to the trains upon ordinary straw paillasses, and then to lay the paillasses with the patients upon them on the **straw-covered** floor of the wagon. The paillasse intended for **this service** was **to be** furnished, on each side, **with three** canvas loops, these **being** designed **for the** reception **of two** stretcher-poles or lances, with a view to assist the bearers in the removal of the litter and its burden. By this arrangement a patient would be carried on the paillasse from the field or hospital, and without any change would be placed in the train, and again, without change, would be carried to his place of destination at the end of the journey. The Prussian regulations in force for the removal of wounded by railway

were based on this system at the time of the German war of 1866.

Professor Gurlt, who originated the experiments and plan above mentioned, himself assisted at the trials of railway sick-transport contrivances conducted in Paris in 1867. Among them was the Prussian system just described. Two persons, one placed on a paillasse filled with straw, and the other on an ordinary sack filled with the same material, were carried in a goods wagon. It was found in each instance necessary to employ five persons, including the bearers who had carried them, to effect the transfer of the paillasses and persons on them into the wagons. The paillasses were simply laid on the floor of the wagon. On the train proceeding it was found that the vibrations impressed on the floor of the wagon were communicated to the paillasses, and in a short time their elasticity was proved to be insufficient to prevent the persons lying upon them from suffering a considerable amount of inconvenience from the jarring disturbance to which they were incessantly subjected. As Dr. Gurlt remarked, however, the experiment was not complete, from the floor of the wagon not having been covered with loose **straw, which,** he asserted, is not liable **to become matted together, and to** be unevenly scattered **in** concrete masses, as straw confined in paillasses is apt to be. On the other hand, Baron Mundy, who had **been** charged with the direction of trains of wounded in Austria during the war of 1866, stated that his **experience** led him to regard loose straw as a very defective **material** for obtaining elasticity under the circumstances described, not because it is **liable** to become matted together beneath the patients, **but because it** becomes easily displaced **when** the body which presses upon it is moved to and fro, and because it remains heaped up in whatever direction it may be pushed aside, and also because it is quickly broken up, and then becomes close and condensed when trampled upon. On the whole, the question of success or failure attending the employment of loose straw for breaking such concussions as are met with in the rougher kinds of railway conveyances when in motion seems to resolve itself principally into one of the quantity **of** material employed. If a large quantity is available and the bed **of** loose straw on the floor of the wagon is sufficiently thick, and **if** the paillasses are large and well filled, it is scarcely possible for the straw beneath the paillasses to be so much disturbed **as** to lose its elasticity in the course of one or two journeys. A far stronger objection to its employment appears to be that **the** large amount of clean straw which would be required to ensure efficient results, for train after train, could not be obtained, or, at any rate, could not be depended **upon to** be forthcoming when required, under the circumstances **of** campaigning. It follows, therefore, that some other means of lessening the impulses of the concussions and the jarring effects of the oscillatory motion belonging to railway transport, especially such as is met with in open wagons designed for the transport of heavy cattle and merchandise, must be sought for,

CHAP. VI.

The Prussian system of railway ambulance transport tried at Paris in 1867.

Experience of Bn. Mundy in Austria in 1866, on the use of straw for adapting railway wagons to carry wounded men.

Objections to the straw-system of railway ambulance transport.

CHAP. VI.   if reliance is to be placed on these means proving effective and constantly available at the moment of need.

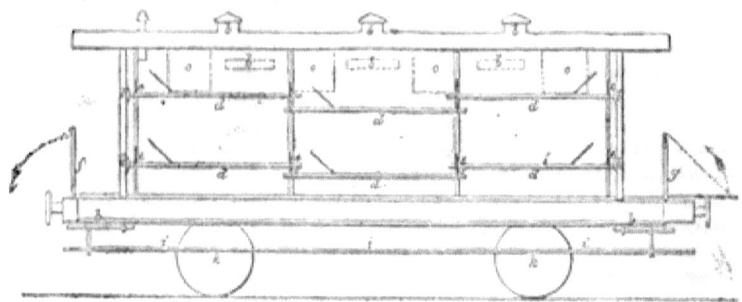

Fig. CLIII.—Longitudinal sectional sketch, showing the general arrangement of the stretchers in one of the fourth-class wagons adopted in Prussia for the transport of wounded in time of war. Scale, quarter inch to a foot. *a*, lamp; *b*, lateral and roof ventilators; *c*, windows; *d*, stretchers; *e*, suspension apparatus; *f*, bridge up; *g*, bridge down; *h*, upper step; *i*, lower step; *k*, wheels; *l*, india-rubber pads.

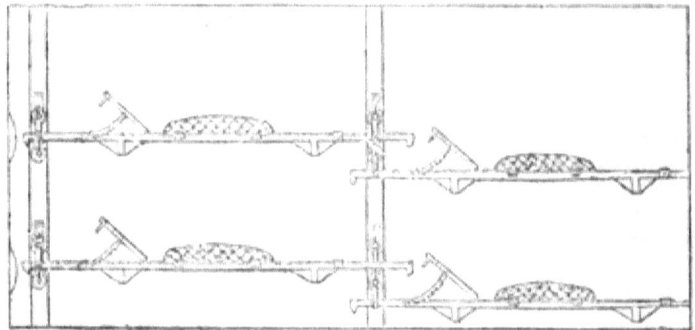

Fig. CLIV.—Sketch to show the method of suspending the stretchers in the fourth-class wagons adopted in Prussia for transport of wounded. *See* description in text. Scale, half inch to a foot.

Adaptation of luggage wagons in Prussia for carrying recumbent patients.

A subordinate part of the Prussian system has been to make preparations for the covered luggage and merchandise wagons (Eisenbahn-Güterwagen), also to be utilised for the transport of wounded in case of need. Many vans of this description are used in time of war for the transport of horses to the front, and the swinging poles, which are then employed for the purpose of separating one horse from another, are economically arranged to be turned to account as supports for stretchers when wounded are required to be sent to the rear. Under ordinary circumstances the swinging poles are connected with the sides of wagons by chains or leathern straps only, but when so attached they are under the direct influence of every concussion to which the wagon itself is subjected. To obviate this inconvenience in case of the poles being required for bearing wounded men lying on stretchers, the following plan has been adopted. The horse-pole itself is unchanged; each of its ends remains protected by its ordinary iron cover and projecting iron ring, and the same kind of staple and ring is fixed to the side of the van as is usually employed for being connected with the pole; it is the mode in which the union is effected between them, which is changed when they are to be used for sick-transport purposes. Under these latter circumstances a very stout caoutchouc ring and two short straps of leather, with buckles, are employed. The two leather straps are passed through the india-rubber ring, one strap is then buckled to the ring hanging from the wall of the wagon, the other strap to the projecting iron ring at the end of the horse-pole. The pole being thus attached at both its ends becomes suspended, and possesses the necessary amount of power of yielding to any concussions that may be impressed upon it, and so of lessening their impulse before they can reach anything which the pole may be caused to support.

A Prussian goods van will carry twelve stretchers, by their being placed in two tiers, six above and six below. For this purpose eight horse-poles have to be suspended. Four are suspended at a distance of rather more than a foot and a half above the floor, of course in the transverse direction of the vehicle, and four others immediately over them, at a height of a little more than four feet above them. The width of the wagon admits of three stretchers, with intervals of more than half a foot between them, being laid upon each pair of poles, so that twelve stretchers can be laid upon the four pairs.

It is obvious, on slight consideration, that the system just described, with its two horizontal layers of wounded, one above the other, occupying the complete width of the goods wagon, is inferior in every respect to that applied to the fourth-class passenger-wagons. Dr. Gurlt has remarked that the length of the poles of the six stretchers composing each one of the tiers leaves scarcely any space in the middle of the wagon for the access of attendants, and that the ventilation is also defective. The latter system can only with propriety be regarded as supplementary to the former, and as one calculated upon for meeting an emergency in case of a sufficient number of fourth-class passenger wagons not being at hand when required.

Observations on the Prussian plan of fitting luggage wagons for the carriage of patients.

Practical Experiments at Paris in 1867 and 1868.

Having now described the Prussian experiments on railway ambulance transport, the trials which were conducted at Paris in 1867 on the same subject have next to be adverted to. They were executed under the direction of one of the sections of the International Committee of delegates from the Societies for Aid to Wounded in time of war. The

Experiments on railway ambulance transport conducted at Paris in 1867.

section referred to was deputed to submit to examination the sick-transport contrivances of every description, which had been collected from different countries, and were exposed to view in the park of the Universal Exhibition at the Champ de Mars. Among these objects there was a large amount of material designed for facilitating the transport of wounded by the ordinary carriages and wagons met with on railways. The **chief** of these contrivances were exhibited by the **Baden National Committee**, and had all been manufactured by Messrs. Fischer, of Heidelberg. The Paris Committee being desirous of submitting some of the contrivances selected from these articles to practical trials, and of comparing them with some others proposed for similar purposes, a locomotive engine with a passenger third-class carriage and a goods wagon were placed at their disposal by the directors of the Western Railway, one terminus of which had been established within the enclosure of the Exposition grounds. An opportunity was thus afforded of subjecting not only Messrs. Fischer's contrivances, but several other plans of transport, such as the spring-stretcher of Dr. Gauvin, straw paillasses, and loose straw, to the test of a railway train in motion.

Objections to all apparatus laid upon the seats of passenger carriages.

Like the several contrivances, however, which have been already described for being laid upon and connecting the seats of first and second-class carriages, this third-class jointed litter-support depends entirely upon the springs of the carriage itself for its elasticity. The patients carried upon all such apparatus must be subjected to the same jolts and concussions as ordinary passengers **are** liable to when sitting upon the seats on which the contrivances are **made to rest**. The effect is more objectionable as regards the contrivances which cause the recumbent patients to be placed transversely to the line of movement of the carriages, than it is with those which admit of patients lying in the same direction as that in which the train is travelling. The whole of the patient's body, under the former circumstances, becomes rolled from side to side in case of a sudden jolt, in a manner which he has no power to resist; and even without any such sudden impetus a feeling of instability and discomfort is usually engendered by lying across a carriage which is not experienced when the person is placed longitudinally, *i.e.*, corresponding with the direction in which train is travelling. The **sense** of discomfort is probably due to the transverse **direction** being **contrary to** that which **is** naturally assumed by **the body in** the **act of** progression; partly it may be, also, to **some** disturbance, caused by the peculiarity of the movement, **to the** circulatory fluids of the body.

Transport of Sick and Wounded Soldiers by Railway in the United States.

United States' hospital trains.—For a considerable period of the late Civil War in the United States, the railway transport of the sick and wounded of the Northern as well as of the Southern armies was carried on in the ordinary passenger and luggage cars, and is generally described to have been attended with severe suffering, from the absence of necessary appliances, and from the motion of the vehicles. Dr. Letterman, of the United States' army, Medical Director of the Army of the Potomac, writes:—"The railway from Fredricksburg to Aquia Creek depôt had a single track, with short sidings. Over this road, had to be transported, in a very short time, more than nine thousand wounded and sick, with all the hospital tents, medical and surgical supplies, stores, &c., required for their care, together with the accumulated supplies of the Quartermaster's, Commissary, and Ordnance Departments. I sent Medical Inspector Taylor to Aquia Creek to receive the wounded, and to send them by hospital ships to Washington. The network of telegraph wires made by the Signal Corps enabled me to regulate the shipment of this large number of men without difficulty or accident. I had directed that all who could not sit up, or who would be injured by so doing, should be carried by hand upon the beds they occupied in the hospitals (some of which were more than a mile from the railway); the beds placed upon hay in the cars; removed carefully from the train and placed in the transports, so that the sufferers should not be removed from the beds on which they lay in the camp hospitals until they reached the hospitals in Washington. Medical officers, with supplies, accompanied every train, and, when required, were sent with their men to Washington. Many of those most severely wounded, cases in which the femur was extensively fractured, assured me they had not suffered the slightest discomfort or fatigue up to the time of their being placed on the transports." The removal of this convoy of sick and wounded, numbering nine thousand and twenty-five, began on the morning of the 12th of June, and before six o'clock in the evening of the 14th of June all had left the depôt at Aquia for Washington.*

Towards the end of the year 1863, the United States' Government adopted a system of specially-fitted sick-transport cars for the lines of railway running in the directions on which the armies were operating. These railway ambulance vehicles were first contrived, it is stated, at the suggestion and in accordance with the designs of Dr. Harris, a member of the

Early transport of wounded during the war of the Rebellion in the United States.

Transport of wounded of the army of the Potomac in June, 1863.

System introduced at the end of the year 1863.

---

* "Medical Recollections of the Army of the Potomac," by J. Letterman, M.D. &c., New York, 1866, p. 150.

CHAP. VI.

United States' Sanitary Commission. They were only calculated for the reception of patients who required a recumbent position. The external frame and the general arrangement of the carriage itself remained the same as when employed for the conveyance of ordinary passengers in a sitting position, but the furniture of the interior was entirely changed. A passenger car in America consists of a large carriage with a door at each end, not at the sides, and a central passage down the whole length of the vehicle. On each side of this passage there is a row of seats, each capable of accommodating two sitters. Outside both ends of the car is a platform, with steps at its sides by means of which the passengers ascend to the car doors; and the junction of the platforms, which are all made on an uniform level, belonging to adjacent cars, enables a communication to be kept up throughout the whole of the train, even while the cars are in motion. There is no division of carriages into compartments as in England. The cars which were built for hospital service were constructed with similar end doors, central passage, and communicating platforms; but on each side of the interior, instead of the ordinary seats, standing frames were erected, and the stretchers were suspended to them by india-rubber rings.

Passenger cars in the United States.

Conversion of passenger cars into sick-transport cars in the United States.

India-rubber rings employed for slinging stretchers in the United States' cars.

Objections have been raised in this manual to the use of india-rubber springs when applied to sick-transport wagons and carts. But this is one of the occasions in which no objection could be made to the use of well-prepared vulcanised india-rubber bands of proper strength and consistence. There could scarcely be time under the circumstances in which railway conveyances are likely to be employed in time of war for the molecular changes to take place, which so frequently render vulcanised caoutchouc articles useless. Moreover, any number of these bands could be speedily got ready for use, and from the facilities of communication between one part of a railway line and another there would be no risk of not being able to replace them from the stores in case of loss or injury of those which had been issued for service. Some of the india-rubber rings which had been employed in railway hospital cars in the United States were at the Paris Exhibition of 1867, and appeared to be still in perfect order.* They were not made in separate strands like the india-rubber springs of which a drawing is given on page 311, but consisted each of one solid circular mass.

Ventilation and lighting of the United States' sick-transport railway cars.

The American cars were well lighted by windows in the sides and doors of the vehicles, as well as by panes of glass along a portion of the roof, which was elevated, like a ship's skylight, above the general level. This raised portion of the roof rested upon the two central rows of posts, and corresponded in size with the central passage of the carriage. The whole of

---

* Having had many opportunities of practically comparing vulcanised caoutchouc articles manufactured in the United States with similar articles manufactured in England, the former has been invariably found more consistent and durable. Vulcanised india-rubber was an American invention.

the interior was capable of being very quickly and freely ventilated by opening the windows and doors, at the same time that the admission of rain was guarded against by projecting eaves. Each carriage was also furnished with a stove, so arranged that by its means the carriage could be both heated and ventilated in case of severe weather preventing the windows from being opened. It was essential for a good system of aëration to be provided, on account of the large number of wounded patients, thirty-two, which each sick-transport car was prepared to accommodate.

A train of ambulance cars carried with it nearly all the appliances and materials necessary for the sick and wounded that would be found in a fixed hospital. In one carriage was a specially arranged stove for heating water, and suited for such culinary purposes as preparing tea, soup, and other simple restoratives and nourishment for the patients. A certain number of hospital attendants, as well as surgeons, accompanied the trains, and even means were supplied for verbal communication between the surgeons and attendants by speaking tubes being fitted along the carriages. It is also mentioned, with regard to the hospital cars furnished by the United States' Sanitary Commission, that most of them were grooved to run upon railways of different gauges, so as to avoid needless transfers of patients. These cars and the Government cars were constructed on the same general plan.

Hospital equipment attached to trains of sick-transport cars in the United States.

The stretchers suspended in the United States' hospital cars have been the field stretchers in ordinary use since the War of Secession, so that when a patient was brought to the train there was no necessity for moving him from the position in which he had been carried to the station. The stretcher with the patient upon it was lifted into its place in the carriage, and was at once ready for the journey. No contrivance for shifting a wounded man from the field to the train could be easier for the patient or for the bearers. Uniformity of stretchers has already been insisted upon in this work. The United

Carriage of patients into the United States' sick-transport railway cars.

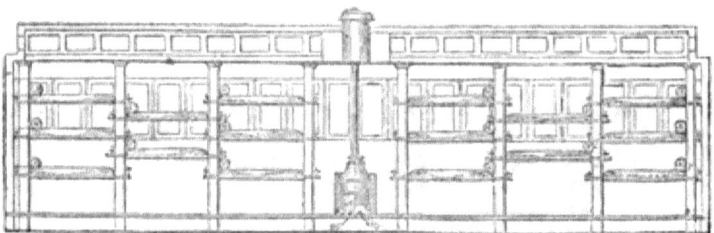

Fig. CLV.—Side elevation of the interior of an American hospital car.*

---

* This drawing is copied from one of the illustrations in a work by Dr. Evans, entitled "La Commission Sanitaire des Etats-Unis," and published by G. E. Dentu, Paris, 1865.

Fig. CLVI.—Perspective view of half the interior of an American hospital car conveying wounded soldiers.

[CHAP. VI.] States were the prime movers in this direction, and have been gradually copied by the other nations when considering the needs of the wounded in battle.

Section IV.—On the Regulations which are necessary for Sick and Wounded Soldiers when transported by Railway.

The plan for most safely conducting convoys of sick and wounded by railway should be studied by army medical officers.

Whatever may be the plan eventually determined to be adopted for the transport of wounded by railway, certain regulations will have to be enforced, whenever the necessity for applying it unhappily occurs, to ensure the safety and protection of the patients, and to maintain general order.

It may be useful to mention some regulations which will be necessary, or which, at least, will conduce to the attainment of these essential objects. This is one of the occasions on which a medical officer may have to exercise his own judgment and, in a great measure, to act on his own responsibility, and he should, therefore, have considered beforehand the leading features of the line of conduct which it will be necessary for him to pursue.

If the train be a mixed one a military officer will be in command, if an ambulance train a Medical Staff officer will command, and will have the entire responsibility of the charge. The details of the course of action laid down will be subject to alterations dependent upon exigencies arising out of **the** railway administration which the conductor of the train can alone be competent to judge of. The following directions, **however**, admit of general application.

CHAP. VI.

(1.) If it be left to the medical officer to conduct the arrangements for the transport of the sick under his charge, as soon as the order for their removal is received, he should carefully arrange with the principal railway manager, or ascertain that arrangements have been made by superior authority, as to the hour of departure, and the list of stations to be stopped at during the journey. In any case he should provide himself with a written copy of these arrangements.

Arrangements prior to bringing a convoy of sick to a railway train.

(2.) Every medical officer with **a** convoy of sick and wounded, and all who **are** in **attendance** upon them, must be made to understand **that** the utmost precision, as well as smartness, **are necessary in** all business connected with railway transport. **The want of** a due appreciation of this necessity may lead to interruption of the service, and cause delay; and this delay may interfere with the movements of other trains on the line.

Strict attention to regulations essential.

(3.) Every one connected with the train should be made aware that it is **a** duty to implicitly follow, so far as the railway administration and service are concerned, the instructions and recommendations of the railway officials whose special function it is to direct the management of the train, who are responsible for safely conducting its movements, and also for the general protection of those who are carried by it. In many respects a body of military passengers, when they are being conveyed by railway, whether sick or well, may be regarded as being in a similar position as that in which troops are placed when on board ship; for, in both cases, much of the general management and direction must be exercised by others than the military authorities.

Authority of the railway officials.

(4.) Special arrangements must be made for **the** carriage of **the** men's kits; they cannot be placed in charge of the sick, **as** they **are** with able-bodied troops. Care should be taken that **they are** protected from the effects of weather and from **dust by** tarpaulins, in case they are placed in open trucks. It **will** save time after the sick have arrived at their place of entraining, if the name and number of the patient who owns it, be chalked on the bottom of each kit bag before the men are moved to the train. It will also add to security against loss, if each pack is labelled separately by the railway officials in the same manner as is done when private luggage is moved, a number being posted on the pack and a corresponding number being given to the owner or **a** responsible non-commissioned officer. The hospital steward or sergeant, who has received the kits of the sick in charge, and who has probably given receipts

Proper disposal of the field-kits of the sick.

CHAP. VI.

for the same to the colour-sergeants of the companies to which the sick men belong, should, if possible, get receipts for the same from the railway officials who take charge of the baggage. In case of loss he will be held responsible by the military authorities for them.

Supplies of food, water, &c. during the transport.

(5.) Forethought should be exercised, and arrangements made, so that there may be no uncertainty as to the sick receiving the necessary food and refreshment during the journey, according to the distance to which they are to be transported; no dependence should be placed on supposed opportunities of obtaining anything which may be required at any of the stations where it has been arranged for the train to make brief halts, unless a definite arrangement has been made beforehand for the requisite supplies to be forthcoming at one or more of them on the arrival of the train.

When the journey to be undertaken is a long one, a supply of the usual extra medical comforts should be provided, for the progress of the train may be delayed by a failure in motive power of the engine, or various other causes, and, in case of such an accident occurring, the sick should not be left without refreshments. The disbursement of this extra supply will have to be accounted for after the arrival of the train at its destination in the usual manner. Medical Officers must, in cases where the sick are in want of any necessary that is actually required, become responsible in a pecuniary sense for the same recovering their outlay subsequently. (*Vide* Lord Morley's Report).

A supply of water for drinking purposes should be also carried, and where tanks are arranged on the train, it will be necessary to ascertain that they are filled.

Carriages to be marked.

(6.) The number of sick and wounded to be placed in each carriage must be marked with chalk upon the panels under the direction of the surgeon or the assistant. If any carriages are designed to receive special cases, they should also be marked to that effect, for the information of those who are attending on the sick. This should be done before the patients are brought on to the platform of the station.

Admission of the sick into the carriages.

(7.) The admission into the carriages should be carried out in an orderly, systematic, and expeditious manner. Each patient should be made successively to take his place, and once seated, or in his cot, should be warned not to alter his position till the rest of the sick are installed, and the doors are shut. There should be no delay, and no hurry or confusion.

Inspection of the train before starting.

(8.) When all the sick are reported to be in their appointed places, the surgeon in charge, with the officer commanding, if one be present, and the conductor of the train, should make a passing inspection of all the carriages in succession, and if any alterations are necessary they should then be made. The surgeon should on no account omit to make this inspection, so as personally to ascertain that everything connected with his charge is correct. Before taking his seat he should inform the conductor, and the officer commanding the train, or superintending the despatch, that all the sick are settled in their places and ready to start.

(9.) The senior non-commissioned officer in each carriage should be directed to keep order, and in the event of his not being well enough, the next should be warned.

(10.) A special watch should be placed over the carriages on the stoppage of a train at a station. No one should be allowed to leave his place, or to purchase or receive into a carriage any article without the knowledge and sanction of a medical officer, or, if he is not present at the spot, without the knowledge of a non-commissioned officer in attendance. Smoking should be discouraged as much as possible.

(11.) If the halt be long enough to permit it, the surgeon, who will be in possession of a copy of the route, will inform the non-commissioned officers that there is time for those who are able and desirous to get down from the carriages to do so. The men must be looked after by the attendants in charge, and care taken that none of them get beyond the limits of the station, and that they are in the carriages again before the time fixed for departure.

(12.) Notices cannot, as a rule, be given by bugle or drum, as when able-bodied troops are moving by railway, and therefore more activity is required on the part of the officer directing the whole service, and the more necessary it becomes that the non-commissioned officers and attendants on the sick should be constantly attentive and alert in seeing all orders and instructions carried out, both as regards themselves and the patients under their supervision.

(13.) On arriving at the place where the patients are to be removed from the train, no one should be allowed to leave the carriages, on any pretence, until the medical officer in charge has reported himself to the officer receiving the train and taken his orders. If this rule be not enforced, straggling will almost certainly occur, and the inevitable result will then be delay, and probably confusion, in the removal of the patients.

(14.) The more helpless and severely injured patients should be first attended to, and should be got to their destination as quickly as the arrangements render possible. Whenever practicable, these patients should remain during the journey on the same stretchers which brought them to the train, so that they may be again carried upon them to their destination, and the repetition of pain in moving from one stretcher to another be thus avoided.

It is presumed that on all occasions when sick and wounded troops are moved by railway the departure of the train and all necessary instructions will be telegraphed to the place of their destination, so that all the requisite arrangements for the reception, removal, and accommodation of the patients may be prepared and ready for them on the arrival of the train at the end of its journey.

(15.) Marching out and marching in states must be furnished

at the start and termination of the journey, also the reports required by regulation to be furnished to the Principal Medical Officer of the district.

Section V.—Railway Ambulance Transport in the East Indies and in England.

The most superficial glance at the territory under direct British Imperial administration will suffice to show the extraordinary development of railways, opening up day by day new routes for trade, or under the greatest difficulties forcing a civilisation, as in **Burma, among** the half-wild people of that **rich country.** In **India, the most** remote places of any importance **are now** within **a comfortable** journey, and the whole of **that** vast land—approaching an area **of** nearly a million of square miles—is being gradually **worked** by these wonderful strides of railway enterprise into one solid and united whole. Not only do these railways net the Empire itself, but they pass well up to the frontiers, and are constructed with the view of any military exigency.

The vast army which controls India and guards her Imperial interests, requires special consideration for the management of the sick and wounded, and arrangements for their transport by railway will be a new and prominent feature. The Indian Government have always recognised to its fullest extent the importance of *efficient* and *sufficient* ambulance transport for those sick and injured in her service, and her medical establishments and organisation are so thorough that failure can only result from maladministration.

There are three occasions upon which sick and injured soldiers require to be transported by railway, viz. :—

1. Transfer of invalids from their stations to Bombay for transport by troopship to England.
2. Transport for those invalids for whom **a change to the hills** only is required.
3. Transport in war time.

Indian railway ambulance transport.

In **addition to** these there are the series of moves made by **regiments in** the course of relief. When a regiment arrives at **Bombay it is** at once placed on a special train and taken to **Deolali,** the military depôt of the country, and then, after a rest of **a few days,** the journey up country is commenced. A special train is chartered, and a second-class compartment with sleeping berths for six patients, and with a lavatory and latrine, is provided for the purposes of a hospital; the corresponding half of the carriage is occupied by the apothecary, with a railway companion.* A medical officer is in charge. The journey is made

---

* The Railway Companion corresponds to the Field Medical Companion, vulgarly called a "Hairy."

by stages, each stage being called a Rest Camp. A start is made about 4 p.m., and the train travels steadily to the next Rest Camp, arriving there early the next morning. The men are turned out and placed in barracks or tents, and rest during the day, while the train is thoroughly cleaned and aired so as to be ready to continue the journey in the evening. At each Rest Camp fresh rations are obtainable, there is a plentiful supply of water, and the sick can be treated at the Rest Camp Hospital, and, if necessary, detained. This *étappen* system was suggested by Surgeon-General Beatson.

By adopting these precautions the dangers of travelling in this country are reduced to a minimum. The allowance— eight to ten men for each compartment—is quite sufficient for the time of the year that the reliefs occur, viz., the cold season.

The movements of invalids are effected in the following manner: a special troop train is arranged, and if the number is

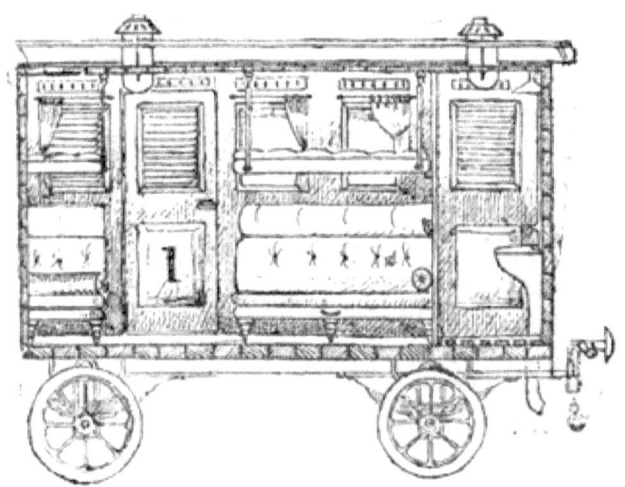

Fig. CLVII.—Section of Indian Railway Carriage.

large cots are arranged on an improvised Zavodovsky system, and this has answered well; but when a small number of patients are travelling use is made of the beds contained in all the first and second-class carriages on the principal Indian railways. Each first-class carriage has accommodation for eight or twelve beds, and there is a lavatory, sometimes a shower bath, and always a latrine; the two halves of each carriage communicate, but communication does not exist between the carriages. The Indian railways have never been thoroughly tested as to their capacity to carry sick and wounded, but they are probably very considerable.

In 1885, at the Camp of Exercise, Surgeon-General Farrell, C.B., directed Surgeon-Major S. H. Carter, A.M.S., and the Editor, to arrange a carriage for the conveyance of the non-effectives from Gurgaon to Delhi. Surgeon-Major Carter (on whom devolved the responsibility, in the absence of any recognised plans except the Russian) devised a system of suspension, similar, in some respects, to the Swiss method, and for the few journeys that the train was used it answered admirably. The dandies were brought to the side of the train and the poles withdrawn; the cot portion was then laid on two traverses, which were attached by a chain to the roof, the outer end of the traverse being hinged to the side of the wagon.

In the future, in war time, special ambulance trains, arranged to carry the Collis' dandy, will be used for the transport of the sick and wounded. The number of these trains and the number of carriages composing them will be decided when the occasion arises for their use. Each wagon, 3rd class ordinary, is 27 feet 6 inches long and 9 feet broad, 7 feet at the sides and 8 feet in the centre, high—forming a large roomy conveyance, built on the lines of an ordinary passenger carriage.* In the roof is a large tank carrying water, and there are three windows on each side and two doors. Two more doors 2 feet 10 inches wide are placed at each end of the carriage, and there is a foot plate over the couplings to facilitate passing from one carriage to another. Thus communication is available from end to end of the train and one of the most important of the many requirements of an ambulance train is attained.

In India especially is this so, on account of the long distances the trains travel without stopping, while the ready access of the medical officers to their patients, is under all circumstances a distinct advantage.

Beds are formed by the field regulation dandy (Collis), and these can be loaded on the train either from the end or the sides, the former being the most convenient where it can be practised. The dandies, the poles being removed, are placed in 3 tiers of two on each side, each carriage carrying 12 lying down cases. The lower tiers rest on the floor of the wagon and are fastened to the sides, the upper tiers are suspended from the roof by a powerful hook screwed into a wide block. They also are fastened to the sides. Upper tiers should invariably be loaded first and unloaded last.

In each carriage there is a latrine and urinal.

If feasible there should be a passage through the centre of the ambulance train from end to end.

Railway Ambulance Transport in England.

In England no special consideration has been given to this matter, on account of the extreme rarity that trains are used for this purpose and the short distance they have to run.

In 1870 the author of this Manual was requested to draw up a plan for the transport of the sick and wounded by railway from Portsmouth to Netley. A design was submitted,

---

* Saloon or bogie carriages are also available, and carry 100 sitting, or 22 lying down, patients.

and a carriage made at the Metropolitan Railway Works in Birmingham.

The wagon was of the ordinary type of a saloon carriage in its external appearance. The following were the most noticeable points in this wagon:—

(a.) A side entrance by folding doors, which allowed any stretcher 8 feet and under to be carried and turned in the carriage with ease.

(b.) There were eight bunks, four on each side, into which the stretchers were placed, and secured by a folding side board which corresponded in height with the head and foot pieces of the stretcher.

(c.) Lockers for medicines and medical materials were provided under a seat arranged for the medical officer.

(d.) A stove and kettle, by means of which hot water was constantly ready, and the carriage was evenly warmed.

(e.) Hinged seats for the attendants.

(f.) End doors with sliding bridges over the buffers were provided,—these would be absolutely necessary in a made-up ambulance train.

(g.) A w.c. connected with a water tank placed in the roof of the carriage.

(h.) A lavatory and sink, opposite to the w.c.

This carriage performed its work efficiently always, and in 1885-6 a second carriage was added arranged in a similar manner, except there was no stove or w.c. in it. Bogie wheels were applied, and wire-woven mattresses recommended.

This arrangement of the carriage has answered admirably the special service for which it was designed up to the present date; and it must be borne in mind that this train was originally intended for the long journey *viâ* Bishopstoke, from Portsmouth to Netley Hospital, which occupied some hours. Indeed the same necessity for comfortable, rapid and complete transport by rail exists, though in a modified degree, at the present time, with all the advantages of the direct extension, on account of the extreme and often critical condition of the invalids on their arrival from the tropics at Portsmouth during the winter.

Colonel G. Findlay, of the Engineer and Railway Volunteer Staff Corps, and the eminent Manager of the London and North-Western Railway, writes as follows: "I may say, however, that having regard to the large stock of sleeping carriages and invalid carriages, and the amply supply of bedding of all kinds in the possession of English railway companies, I think there is no reason to doubt that if ever the emergency should arise we should be found equal to it, and that we should be able to make up and run suitable ambulance trains for sick and wounded men, with convenient accommodation for doctors, nurses, &c., without any difficulty."

The following are the measurements of the London and

North Western Railway carriages,—the other railway companies vary but slightly:—

Sleeping saloons, 42 feet long, and from 8 feet to 8 feet 6 inches wide, with beds for 16 persons and lavatory accommodation.

Third-class.—The latest type are 42 feet long, 8 feet wide, and divided into seven compartments, each being 5 feet 10¼ inches wide.

Covered carriage trucks vary from 21 feet to 18 feet in length, and are 7 feet 10 inches in width. They serve admirably for the erection of Zavodovsky's system. As far as possible these should be limited to express luggage vans.

In addition to the actual number of carriages is the consideration of the knowledge of attending, lifting, and carrying of wounded at railway stations. It is due to the St. John's Ambulance Association to report here that they have trained many hundreds of railway employés in the application of first aid, and a large number of these pass through an annual re-examination. In the event of a large transfer of wounded this assistance would be of extreme value in relieving the overworked regular staff.

SECTION VI.—SPECIAL SYSTEMS.

Special systems.

The simplest form of arranging a goods wagon for the reception of wounded is to place straw, hay, or fern on the bottom and to lay the stretchers upon it.

Two or more trusses of straw may be so arranged to act as traverses, for the stretchers or beds laid upon them.

Mattresses may be laid upon litter material and the stretchers secured above.

A layer of fibre mats or a double layer of thick mats when the former are not at hand make a good bed for stretchers.

For every form of injury or disease transport of this kind is *eminently* unsatisfactory, and should only be resorted to on the rarest occasions.

Those who are suffering from fractures and wounds should never be carried in this way, but only those who are sick and have the power to adjust themselves more or less to the shaking of the journey.

Carriage in hammocks is unsatisfactory on account of the lateral motion, and also for the reasons stated in the chapter upon this class of conveyance.

Peltzer's System.

Peltzer's system.

Peltzer's System consists of the resting of the stretchers or beds upon C springs, which are fastened to the floor of the wagon.

Morache's System.

M. Morache's System.—This officer's system consists more of an arrangement than an invention. He arranges his beds in the following manner—the lower tiers on the Grund system, and the upper tiers by suspension; each carriage is supplied with a stove and the necessaries for patients on a journey.

Morache's system.

Beaufort's System.

The System *of suspension* by means of cords is unsatisfactory, by reason of the excessive jolting to which those carried are subjected. This system was improved by the Comte de Beaufort, who interposed spiral springs to the suspending ropes, thus breaking the shock. The arrangement is not a popular one, and could only be used in the absence of any other system.

Beaufort's system.

Bry-Ameline System.

The Bry-Ameline system **is a method of** suspension **derived from** Prof. Le Fort's system.

On **each** side of the doors of the goods wagon are **placed** two pairs **of traverses one** above the other, suspended **at their** extremities on Le Fort's spring hooks. Each pair of traverses is destined to receive three stretchers, so placed that their heads **are** to the ends of the wagon. The traverses are suspended by means of an elastic apparatus composed of a spring held in a sort of arched cover fixed over the point of suspension. The top of the suspension spring is fixed by a bolt with a screw-nut to an iron plate, which is fastened in a similar way to the wall of the wagon. The traverses have in addition six straps, which hold the poles of the stretchers in place, and at each end is a screw ring which slides vertically in a groove riveted to the iron plate.

This system allows of 12 stretchers to each wagon. The different systems of hooks, particularly those of Le Fort and Desprez, allow of the rapid and economical fixing of stretchers in goods wagons.

Bry-Ameline system.

The Berlin System.

The German railway companies, following the method adopted by the Berlin Company, in the first instance used india-rubber rings as elastic supports for their suspended stretchers (flottantes lits), but during the Franco-German War, and since that period, experience has proved them to be untrustworthy, and springs have been universally adopted in their place.

India-rubber under nearly all circumstances connected with ambulance material and construction is unsatisfactory. The

German plan.

rubber, after a comparatively short time, hardens and breaks, and when india-rubber rings suspending weights as in the systems alluded to harden, they are liable to fracture "short," with probably disastrous results.

Dr. **Leu** has invented an ingenious rest for stretchers when a temporary support is required in a railway van. It consists of a framework with two supports at each end, these being

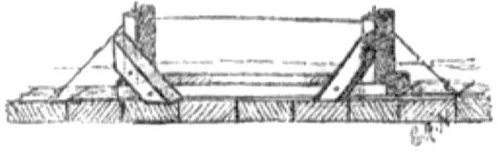

Fig. CLVIII. Leu's Stretcher Rest.

braced to the foundation by cross-pieces of wood. The tops of the supports are notched for the reception of a cord which is tightly strained across the supports between two screw hooks firmly fixed in the floor of the vehicle. The stretcher rests upon the stretched cord between the supports.

Zavodovsky's System.

This method is a most efficient, economical, and convenient form of adaptation of a railway wagon for the reception of the sick and wounded. The materials used are few in number and of the simplest nature, and by the easiest manipulation are readily put together and converted into a valuable means of transport. This arrangemement was invented in 1873 by Major-General Zavodovsky, a Russian engineer, after whom it is named.

In order to apply this means of improvision it is necessary to select wagons free from all projecting obstructions, and as a result the method has been principally used with goods wagons, but it can be applied to any covered wagon, provided all the fittings are removed. The lighter the springs and easier the carriage the better will be the transport by this plan. Unfavourable opinions to this method have been due more to the ill-selection of the wagons—or, indeed, the absolute **necessity of** using only goods wagons, **no** others being available—**and to** the arrangement being **improperly** managed, than to any defect in the plan itself.

Stretchers on Zavodovsky's plan were arranged for the transport of the sick and wounded from Wady Halfa to Cairo, in the Nile Campaign, and gave great satisfaction, as this plan almost entirely prevented the effect of vibration being communicated from the carriages.

Each goods wagon in England to which it has been applied is capable of holding eight patients, but there is no definite limit to the number carried—this depends upon the length and the width of the vehicle. Even in the goods wagon commonly used twelve patients could be accommodated if necessary.

A Pullman drawing-room car can carry 16 lying down.

A third-class car can carry 16 lying down.

A goods van can carry 8 or 12 lying down.

Wagons which open at their ends, as the Pullman car, or by wide sliding doors in the sides, as in the goods vans, lend themselves readily to this class of arrangement. The ordinary passenger carriages could not in this manner be utilised on account of the narrowness of the doors.

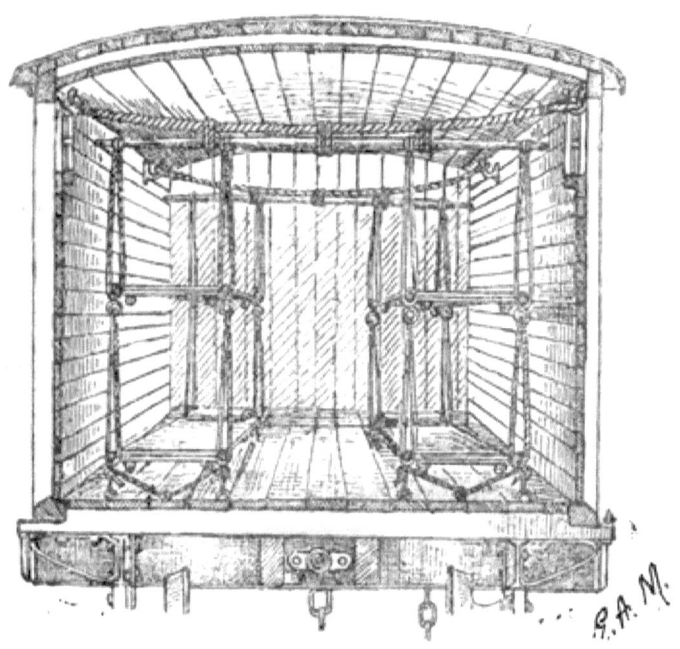

Fig. CLIX.

The material required to fit up a goods wagon is as follows:—Eight large blunt hooks with bolts, four 1½-inch cables 8 feet long with iron bound eyelet holes at each end, four 4-inch ash poles 7 feet 6 inches long, 75 yards of strong cording, a strand of cobbler's thread, and a piece of wax, and 24 iron screw rings, with 25 yards light cord.

The blunt hooks require to be made of good material, as it is upon them that the greatest weight and strain is thrown. An accident incurred by one of these snapping might—indeed probably would—be fraught with most serious consequences. The depth of the hook should be 6 inches and the width 5 inches, and it should pass into a plate which is applied to the side of the carriage, thus steadying the hook and screw which

CHAP. VI.

Zavodovsky's system.

passes through, and should be fastened on the outside by a "washer" and bolt. As an alternative arrangement a ring may be placed in the position of the hook, in which case the cable would carry the hook. Of these two the latter is the less desirable, as more security is established with a hook fixed, and not liable to be shifted by the movements of the train. When the hook is fixed, as shown in the drawing, the fastening more nearly approaches that of two rings joined together than in the other position. Lastly, this fastening may be improvised by boring holes in the side of the wagon, and tying the cable by cord round one of the beams of the framework of the carriage. The

Fig. CLX.

hooks are screwed into the side of the conveyance and should be distant 6 feet 4 inches from each other and 9 inches from the roof. When stretchers of the English pattern are used they should correspond to one another on the opposite side.

The cables should be between 7' 6" × 8' in length, but should never exceed the latter. Strong 1½-inch cable is the best material, and each should terminate in a loop with an iron bearing. On the length of this cable will depend in a large measure the effectiveness of the arrangement and the comfort of the patient. If the cable is too long the nearer will it approach the floor of

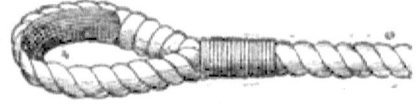

Fig. CLXI.

the vehicle, and the more confined will the patients be. This difficulty can be overcome, to a certain degree, by soaking the cable in water, and altogether by placing the hooks higher up on the sides. The cables are placed across the carriage on corresponding hooks. The accurate fixing of the hooks and the cables is of paramount importance; that which follows is most simple.

The poles should be 7 feet 6 inches long as a rule, but a slight degree longer is of no importance—single stretcher poles of ash are quite sufficient for the purpose; ash is the best wood to be used, as the weight of four to six men is considerable. The poles are bound by cord to the cable, in the manner shown in the diagram. In most drawings of this arrangement the poles taper towards their extremities. There is no advantage gained by this, but rather the disadvantage that the cords supporting the stretchers may slip off, especially when the train is in motion and travelling round a curve in the road.

A diagrammatic drawing of the disposition of the ropes supporting the stretchers, *a* upper tier, *b* lower tier, is given in Fig. CLXI.

The 75 yards of rope mentioned as one of the necessary materials for arranging this plan are utilised for the purpose of supporting the stretchers in the following manner:—

Fig. CLXII.

Lengths of 12 feet are cut and spliced, thus forming a loop. Each stretcher requires four loops. These are laid over the pole commencing 6 inches from each extremity, and the second loops are 22 inches from these and nearer to the centre.

By the means of the wax and twine the loops are tightly bound, immediately beneath the pole at *a*, and at *b* a point half way between the pole and the end of the loop *c*. There is a tendency in doing this to allow too little space for the lower

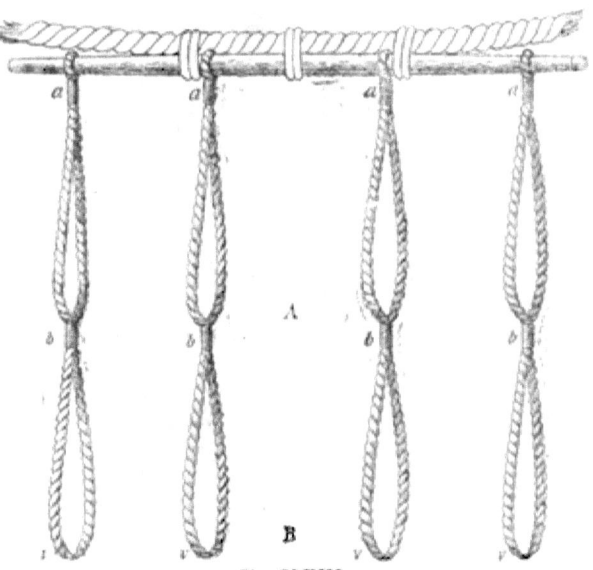

Fig. CLXIII.

tier. The length of rope mentioned must not be considered as an absolute number, but the lengths cut must be proved in the following manner. Take the rope and loop it over the pole, and draw the two pieces straight down to within 6 inches of the floor of the wagon, then, leaving sufficient length for splicing, there will remain after the shortening resulting from the binding at *a* and *b*, and allowing for the stretch of the rope, sufficient length to allow the stretcher to swing about 6 inches to 8 inches from the floor of the wagon.

Lastly, and perhaps one of the most important points as regards the security and comfort of those transported, is the accurate fastening of the tiers of stretchers to the screw rings,

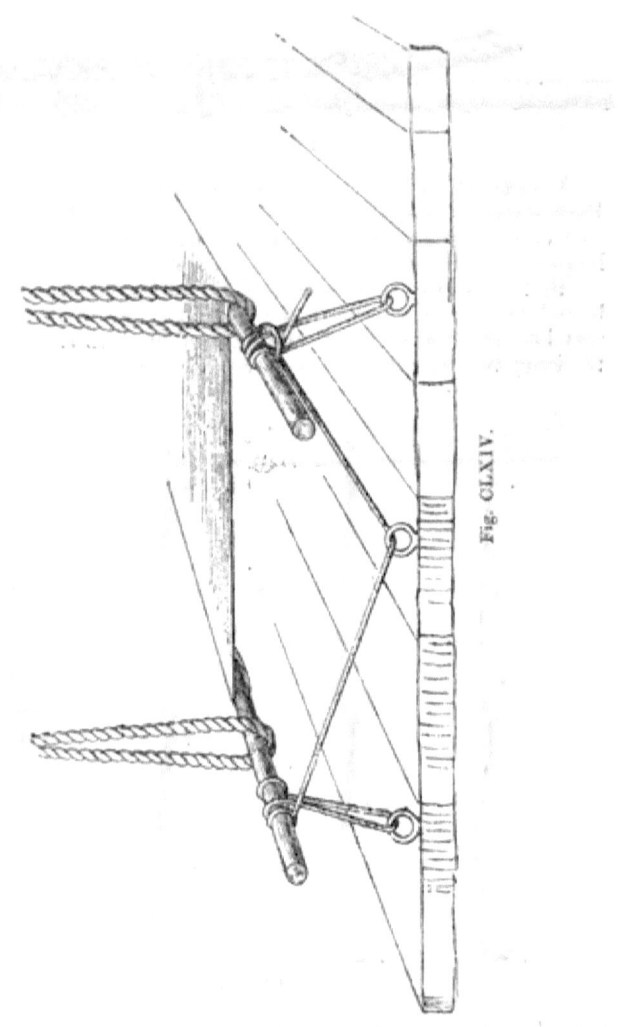

Fig. CLXIV.

or, preferably, hooks in the floor. To each tier of stretchers there are six rings arranged under the handles in threes. The three rings are disposed thus, No. 1 under the near handle, No. 3 under the off handle, and No. 2 equidistant between the others. The rope is looped at one end and laid over the near handle, and threaded through No. 1 ring, and being drawn as tightly as possible, is taken up to the same handle and turned round it twice, the second time overlapping the first; it is then taken across through the ring No. 2 and over the off handle, and directly through the ring No. 3, returning to the off handle it **makes** one turn, and at this point the whole is drawn tight, **a** second turn overlapping the first is then made, and the rope fastened off. There are two practical points to be observed here: the one is that the tiers are only tied to the floor *after* the sick are loaded—this operation should take place immediately this is achieved, and under no circumstances should a train start carrying wounded until this has been reported as finished—the other point is that the tighter these ropes are drawn the more comfortable will be the transport.

The loading and unloading of the wounded is carried out rapidly in the following manner:—The wounded having been brought to a convenient place on the railway, or, if possible, to a station, detachments of the bearer company successively load the patients on the upper tiers first, and subsequently the lower ones. The No. 4's of the last detachments should remain and **fasten off** the stretchers securely to **the** floor of the **wagon**. For unloading the converse takes place, the lashings are unfastened and the stretchers successively removed, the lower tier first. This operation requires care and attention, and is a good test of the quality of the knowledge of sick transport possessed by the bearers.

Major-General Christen Smith, Surgeon, of Norway, has described **a** modification of Zavodovsky's method. He does **not use** the cable, but attaches the poles directly to the beams of the carriage or to wooden traverses placed from side to side. In the place of the rope used for suspending the stretchers Dr. Smith uses wire rope. This is an advantage if variations in the length required did not continually occur; for that reason wire rope could not be utilised in Zavodovsky's method. By looping a rope round the upper stretchers in each tier, the risk of accident from any portion of the arrangement giving way is minimised.

Gründ's System.

This system was approved by a Commission in Germany, 1868, and was largely used in the sanitary trains of the German Army in the Franco-German War. In 1878 this system was officially adopted by the Government, and is described in the Kriegs-Sanitäts-Ordnung.

It consists of four springs and two traverse poles 7 feet 6 inches to 8 feet long, the poles of a stretcher answering admirably. The springs are arranged opposite to each other near the sides of the wagon, and are fastened by bolts to the floor. The traverses are laid across, and on these the stretchers are laid, usually in threes. The springs, one of which is shown **in the accompanying** figure, **are** made of steel, and are similar to

CHAP. VI.
Gründ's system.

the upper half of an elliptical carriage spring, and are placed on the wagon floor with their convexities uppermost. The spring is fixed by a bolt at one extremity, and this point is the fulcrum of the mechanism, the other extremity ends in a roll of metal,

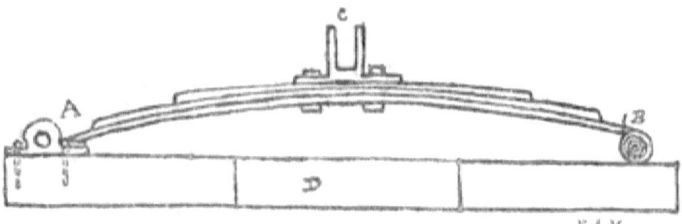

Fig. CXLV.—Gründ's system.—Side view. (*a*). Attachment of the spring. (*b*). Roller. (*c*). Slot for the reception of the traverse. (*d*). Floor of the wagon

and is free. By this means the spring is able to respond to any varying conditions of weight by the sliding to and fro of this

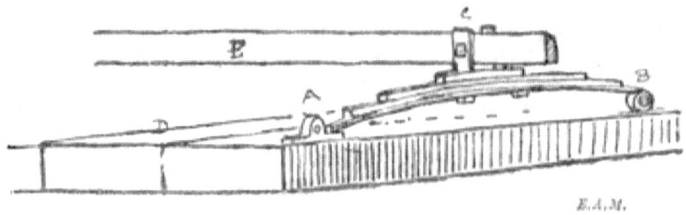

Fig. CLXVI.—Gründ's system.—Perspective view. (*a*.) Attachment of the spring. (*b*). Roller. (*c*). Slot for the reception of the traverse. (*d*). Floor of the wagon. (*e*.) Traverse.

roller. Over the convexity of the spring is a plate holding two upright pieces and forming a slot for the traverse (*see* Fig. CLXV). Into this slot one end of the traverse is laid, the other being placed in the slot of the corresponding spring on the other side.

Richter's modification.

There is a modification of the Gründ system by which a **framework capable** of supporting two tiers **of stretchers is placed on** the springs. At the convexity of each spring an upright post is fixed to a plate, and on four of these posts the framework is built, these are steadied during transit by fastenings attaching the tiers to each other and to the sides of the wagon. This is known as Richter's modification, and is the new German pattern.

In comparing the two systems just described, the differences between them are very apparent. In Major-General Zavodovsky's plan the wounded are suspended and placed many "removes" from the wagon. The author of this book, in his work on "Gunshot Injuries," p. 551, alludes to his personal experience of these systems in the following manner:—" I have personally assisted in a series of trials of it under various **circumstances.** At one time a baggage van to which the appliances had been fitted, was subjected to violent jolts and sudden halts; at another time was attached to a fast train on the South-Eastern Railway, and I found myself, while lying on one of the stretchers, on each occasion subjected to far less disturbance than I had previously supposed this or any other mode of elastic suspension of stretchers would have permitted." The Gründ system, on the other hand, rests entirely on the floor of the carriage, and is only two "removes" from the vehicle itself. A disadvantage which is manifest is that a large quantity of the springs require to be specially made—the springs have to be properly and accurately adjusted to the wagons, and in no way can the Gründ system be so readily extemporised from materials to be obtained at any village as is the case with the Zavodvosky system. The Gründ system carries few patients with a greater amount of expensive material, and in no way compares in utility and cheapness with the Russian method.

Hamburg System.

This system is the invention of Herr Hennike, it is also used in Germany, but is not generally so favourably received as the Gründ System or the Gurlt System.* The accompanying figure shows the principle, which consists of four iron clamps, four springs, four chains and steel bars, with openings to receive the handles of the stretchers.

The clamp is so constructed that the greater the weight placed upon the spring the tighter will it hold. Hence the name it has received, "La griffe du diable." This clamp is steadied by the action of a pin bolt, and for the sake of security this is very important, the jolting of the train being likely to disarrange this mechanism. Two rings connect the clamp with a coiled spring working in a cage, and at the end of the spring is a hook to receive a chain, and bar with holes for the handles of the stretchers: the first hole represents the upper tier, and the last hole the lower tier of stretchers. These can be raised, or lowered by shortening or lengthening the chain link by link. To prevent swinging from side to side the tiers of stretchers are fastened to the sides of the wagon by means of steel springs.

This system has not the practical character of the other systems described. The objections may be enumerated as follows:—

(a.) The mechanism itself is of such a nature that it could not be readily replaced in the event of any portion of it breaking or not working.

(b.) The action of clamp is that of a power which multiplies in an inverse ratio to the weight opposed to it. The condition and nature of the material clamped is of the utmost importance

---

* See description in "Kriegs-Sanitäts-Ordnung."

—only the hardest and most resistant materials affording the necessary security.

(c.) Coiled springs are invariably unsatisfactory, by reason of the fact that their strength is not uniform, and, although they will act equally to a certain degree, yet that degree is too slight to reckon for very much.

(d.) The "dead" weight is on the roof of the wagon, and this is often lightly built.

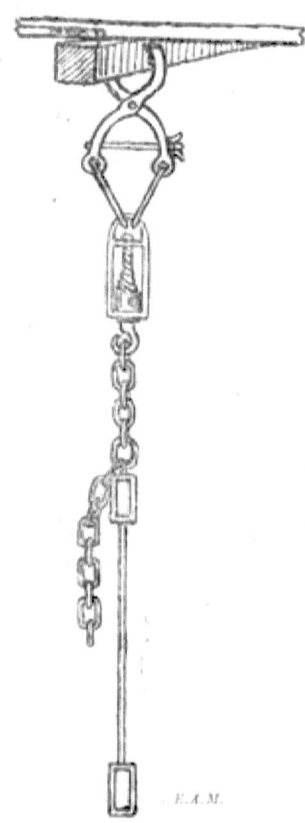

Fig. CLXVII.—Hamburg system.—The "Griffe du diable" spring and stretcher supports.

(e.) The attachment to the sides of the vehicle of each tier of stretchers is unsatisfactory.

(f.) The absence of any attachment to the floor. It would appear necessary to have an attachment, especially under certain conditions of running over a rough permanent way or passing points. The sudden jerk then experienced is directly upwards, and would tend to loosen, if it did not altogether displace, the action of the clamp.

Fischer's System.

This method of suspending the wounded in railway carriages was the invention of Herr Fischer, of Heidelberg. An iron ring is bolted into the side of the vehicle 2 inches distant from the roof on each side, and at a space 1 foot to 1 foot

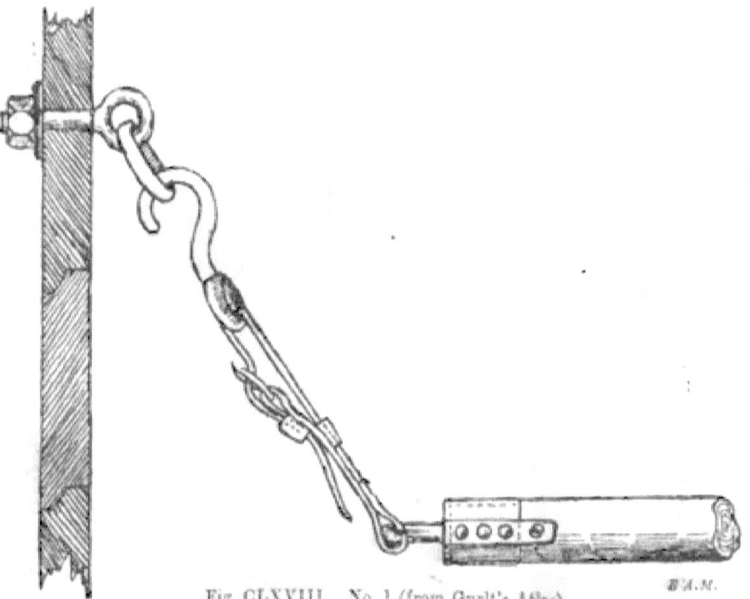

Fig. CLXVIII. No. 1 (from Gurlt's Atlas).

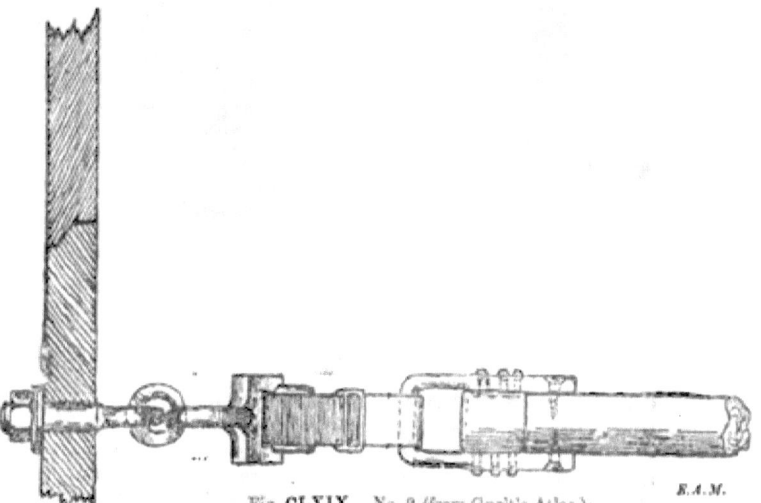

Fig. CLXIX. No. 2 (from Gurlt's Atlas.)

CHAP. VI.

Fischer's system.

6 inches from the floor; a second bolt, with an arrangement to hold a strap, is fastened to the side of wagon, on both sides. To the upper bolts are hooked two horizontal bars 6 feet long and 2 inches thick, attached by a strap buckled to a hook, which joins the ring of the bolt. Two of these bars are placed at a

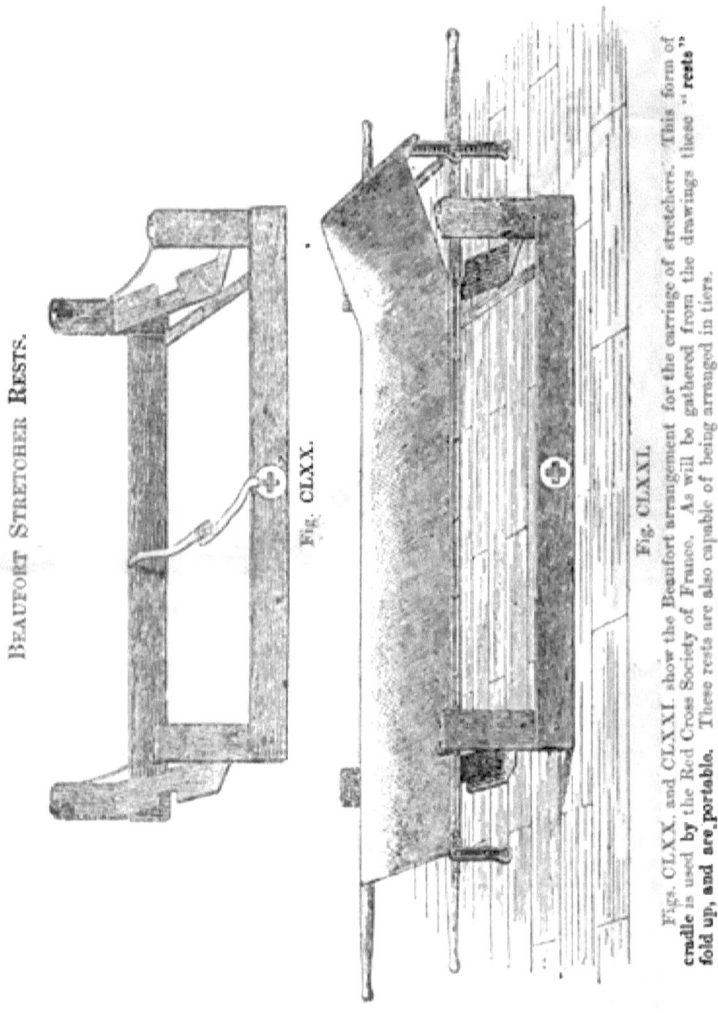

BEAUFORT STRETCHER RESTS.

Fig. CLXX.

Fig. CLXXI.

Figs. CLXX. and CLXXI. show the Beaufort arrangement for the carriage of stretchers. This form of cradle is used by the Red Cross Society of France. As will be gathered from the drawings these "rests" fold up, and are portable. These rests are also capable of being arranged in tiers.

distance of 4 feet from each other, transversely across the wagon, and upon them the stretchers supporting the patients are laid. The lower transverse bars are arranged in a similar manner, but the straps require to be pulled very tightly. The stretchers are placed on a framework, which can be utilised as a field bedstead. This system is ingenious, but there appears to be no arrangement to prevent motion backwards and forwards. The manner in which the lower tiers are arranged does not appear advantageous, and there is no apparent reason why it should differ from the upper one or indeed not be suspended from it.

Boulomie System.

This is a method of "improvising" goods wagons for the reception of sick. At each end of the carriage four posts are fixed in pairs, and opposite to each other. Two pairs are placed in each corner of the wagon, and two more are placed 4 feet from the end of the vehicle. To these posts are lashed with rope traverses of the same material as the uprights. Each of the latter are fastened by two traverses. The centre uprights are kept steady and elastic by two strong ropes, stretched from the fixed uprights; between the two sets is arranged a movable roller of wood, and this "eases" the stretcher, forming an improvised spring support. This arrangement forms four tiers of stretchers with three stretchers in each tier. There are free ropes to tie the stretchers in their places. The whole arrangement is complex even if the materials were readily to be found, which is not always the case, and is of very doubtful practical utility.

Austrian System.

The figure explains the improvised system which is used in goods wagons. The beds are slung to rings fixed in the sides

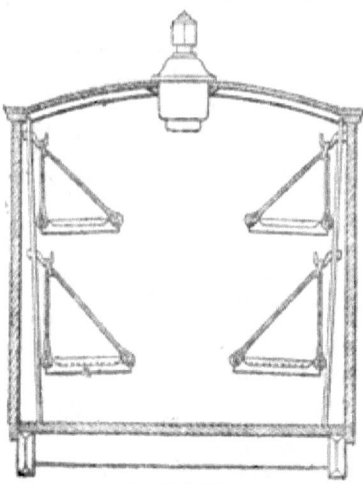

Fig. CLXXII.

of the vehicle. The method allows of eight patients being carried in one wagon, and there is ample room in the carriage for those attending to the **sick**.

CLASS VI.—MARINE AMBULANCE TRANSPORT.

Chap. VI.

Marine ambulance transport.

A KNOWLEDGE of the various methods by which marine ambulance transport is carried out is as essential to all military medical officers as a knowledge of their duties is to naval medical officers. The men of the Royal Navy are often engaged fighting on land, in fact, it has been unusual for a force to take the field without the Naval Brigade, and soldiers of Her Majesty's Army are continually being transported by sea. The services are interchangeable to a large extent, though obviously each individual officer will be more familiar with the service to which he actually belongs.

There are two branches of this subject, the one relating entirely to "Transport" and the other exclusively to "Hospitals." The first includes all the various methods of transferring a sick or wounded man from a ship to the land, or from the land to the vessel, both at sea and on rivers. It also embraces the transport of a man from the "rigging" to the sick bay of a ship. Hospital ships comprise the other part, and refer to the arrangements made for working a hospital on board ship. In this manual the former will be fully discussed, and the latter only so far as the matter relates to the subject under consideration.

Definition.

Marine ambulance transport, then, is **the carriage of** sick and **wounded men in** connection with the sea, **rivers, or any** water, **and the** vessels on their surface.

At first it would appear to be a large subject, considering the wide diversity, the various conveyances to be **met** with under these circumstances, and the many conditions under which it may be required. Fortunately, there are **few** methods used, and they are nearly always practical, simple **in** construction, and easy to manage.

The Red River and Nile experiences.

"Transport," writes Lord Wolseley, "is always **a** most **difficult** question in all military operations. Unless a railway **exists, you** have to maintain the roads along your lines of **communication** in good order and to feed thousands of animals **constantly** employed in carrying forward to the fighting army **the** provisions and various stores it requires. A navigable river **relieves** you of most of your worst difficulties. I may say with confidence that **the** Red River Rebellion in 1870 could not have been put down except by a boat expedition, and **no** army could have penetrated as far as we did in 1884 and 1885 into the hostile Soudan, except by the Nile route."

The ships, steamers, and various vessels of all kinds may be divided into the following :—

1. *Sea-going.*—Includes all ships of war, liners, and vessels that cross the sea.
2. *Coasting.*—Includes all those vessels which ply round the coast, the harbours, and the mouths of large rivers.
3. *River.*—Vessels which ply in rivers and on lakes.

A register of ships suitable for the purposes of transport is kept at the Admiralty, where are also worked out the various military units under the heads:—

1. Short voyages.
2. Voyages under 7 days.
3. Distant voyages.

The scale of tonnage allowed for a man or horse varies with the length of the voyage; for a short voyage $1\frac{1}{2}$ tons for a man, $2\frac{1}{2}$ tons for a horse. For seven days 2 tons for a man, and 7 tons for a horse. For distant voyages $2\frac{1}{2}$ tons per man, 7 tons a horse, or 10 tons for a cavalry soldier and his horse.

In round numbers, 52 cubic feet will be required for a man, 126 cubic feet for a horse.

Tonnage. The expression ton, although referring to weight in shipping, is generally used in connection with its equivalent of space, about 40 feet. The gross tonnage at which a ship is registered is taken to represent the entire cubic capacity of all enclosed space, both above and below deck, by deducting all non-freight carrying spaces, the net tonnage is arrived at, practically 40 p.c. less than the gross tonnage: thus 3,000 tons gross will be 1,800 tons net.—*Riordan.*

1. *Sea-going Vessels.*

This class includes all those ships of war and of trade which ply from continent to continent, as the troopers, transports, and mail liners.

Ships of this class are admirably adapted for the transport of sick and wounded, and there are very few campaigns in which one or more of them have not been fitted up for hospital purposes. There is, as a rule, plenty of space and ventilation, with a regularity of living, and those features of treatment which tend to restore a man exhausted by disease or injury. It has been urged that sailing ships are better than steamers, on account of the room occupied by the machinery, as well as on the score of expense in the latter, but it would be a hazardous matter to have a hospital ship becalmed in the midst of the regions in which we fight. The principal hospitals are "Queen of the South," "Victor Emmanuel," "Carthage," "Ganges," and "Tenasserim."

CHAP. VI.

It has been urged that, in addition to hospital ships, there should be transport ships fitted up for the reception of the sick, and complete in every detail. It has happened that the medical staff of a ship suddenly requisitioned for this purpose has been drawn from the Medical Officers at the base of operations, thus reducing the medical establishments at the base.

CLASS II.—*Coasting.*

Coasting vessels.

This class represents those ships which ply round the coast—passenger steamers, and so forth, and not particularly those which also cross the sea. This class may be used as feeders to larger **transports**, when the latter cannot come alongside a quay, but for ambulance transport purposes are unimportant.

CLASS III.—*Rivers, Canals, &c.**

This forms an important class, and includes all river steamers and launches, native craft, as diahbiyehs, dhows, flats, &c.

Steamers for river purposes are of three kinds—*a.* screw; *b.* paddle; *c.* stern-wheelers. Of these the paddle steamers, as a rule, are the best, as they do not draw so much water. Stern-wheelers are admirable, and were largely used in the

---

* A most interesting paper by Dr. Santini, of the Italian Navy, and Dr. Home-Rosenburg, of the Italian Army, on the organization of river vessels for succouring the wounded in war, was published in the "Revista Marittima," of October, 1890. The following is a short abstract:—

"The paper deals almost entirely with the organisation of **vessels** suitable for carrying wounded on the great river-ways connected with the seat **of** war.

"Reference is made to the use of such vessels in the Egyptian War; and the suggestion is made that an organization should be carried out by the Red Cross Societies for equipping and supplying ships on the same lines as is already done in the case of ambulances, etc. The Seine, the Rhine, the Rhone, the Danube, are referred to as rivers on which such vessels might be of great use in time of war.

"The latter part of the paper details the organization necessary for mobilization at the required moment of the various vessels plying on lakes, rivers, and canals. These vessels must be registered and devided into two categories.

"(1) Those of a tonnage of not less than 200 tons, and capable of being regularly equipped and each fitted out for a special service.

"(2) Smaller vessels not suitable for such equipment but capable of being utilized in time of need by improvised means.

"Vessels of the first class would be of three kinds—

"(*a*) Ships organized as a field hospital and complete in themselves; with surgeons, hospital attendants, stewards, etc., and fitted below with 56 cots and 25 seats, and on deck with accommodation for about 200 slightly wounded sitting down or reclining.

"(*b*) Ships of the '*Trenos-ospedale*' for the accommodation of wounded only, holding below deck 72 cots and 21 seats, and on deck about 200 less severely wounded. These ships are furnished with washing apparatus, filter, ice room, disinfecting apparatus, stores for weapons, etc., of wounded ('*effetti militari*'), bath, etc.

"(*c*) Ships for the personnel of the hospital ships of type (*b*), and the vessels of the 2nd class—and containing dispensary, surgical equipment, kitchen, and apparatus, etc., noted in **ships** of type (*b*).

"There are plans at the end of the paper which explain themselves.

upper reaches of the Irrawaddy and Chindwin Rivers during the Burmese Campaign, and also in the Nile Expedition of 1884 and 1885.

CHAP. VI.

River steamers.

River steamers, as a rule, have two decks, a main and upper

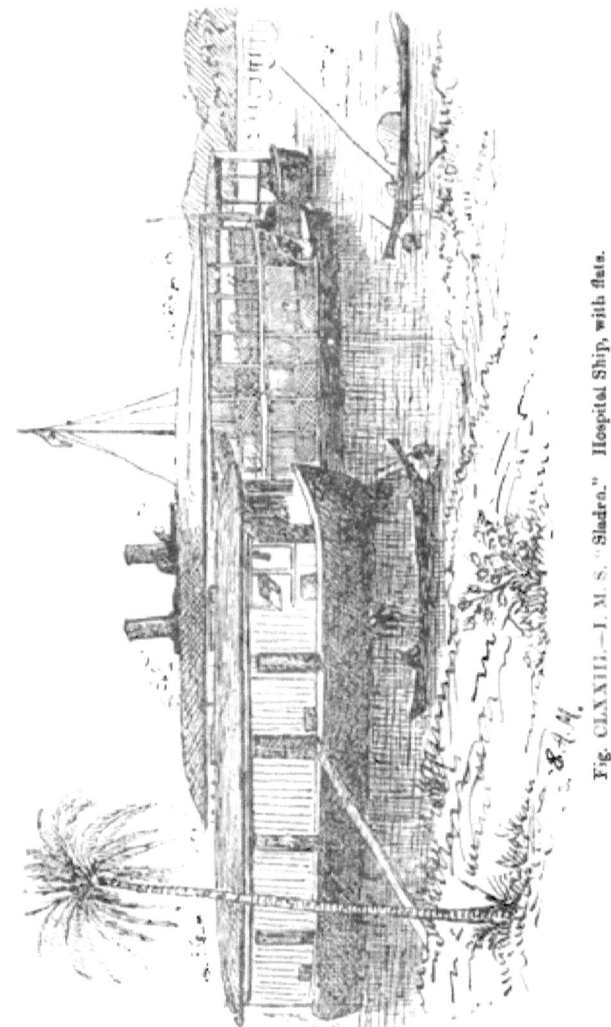

Fig. CLXXIII.—I. M. S. "Sladra." Hospital Ship, with flats.

deck, and in the tropics these are covered in by a roof and double awning on each side. Consequently they are well adapted for the transport of wounded and sick men. In some rivers the steamers take large flats in tow, and these are capable

(6107)

2 D

of affording much accommodation for sick and wounded. During the night river steamers generally anchor, and start at daybreak. In tropical rivers it is essential that punkahs should be worked by steam during the night when tied up to the bank, as the suffering and irritation to patients is by no means inconsiderable from mosquitoes and heat.

Barges, gondolas and boats.
Barges, gondolas, and boats of all description, lend themselves for easy improvisation for purposes of ambulance transport. Barges were used in the Franco-German War for the transport of the wounded, and plans exist in the offices of the French Red Cross Society for rapidly converting a barge into a comfortable hospital.

Considerations of the means of transporting sick and wounded from the shore to the ship, from one ship to another, and from one part of a ship to another part, involve many difficulties, and require no small amount of skill and resource to overcome.

When a vessel cannot lie alongside, means have to be adopted to sling patients from the shore to the ship. This may be effected in the following ways:—Placed in a suitable litter, the patient may be slung by a crane into the ship, or in a similar manner he may be passed by a life-saving rope, and, lastly, he may be taken in a small boat to the ship's side, and then taken on board. The first two considerations, when they can be used, are very efficient, but the last is more difficult. It may appear unnecessary to make these preparations, but though 200 patients can be placed on board with comparative ease, there will be one case which will cause great anxiety. The writer recollects a case of ununited fracture of the thigh, in which the limb was set at right angles to the body, and, with the patient, was firmly fixed to the bed. It was necessary to place him on the upper deck of the "Sladen," and the only means of approach was down a steep bank on to a plank which crossed from the shore to the lower deck. The gangways to the upper deck would not permit his bed to pass, and it was only with great difficulty and much anxiety to the patient that he was eventually passed outside and to the upper deck. The means of doing this were extemporised at the time.

There are many means of passing a patient up and down a ship's side, though when required are not always to be found. They are as follows:—

1. A knotted rope.
2. Gorgas ambulance cot.
3. Macdonald's ambulance lift.
4. Macdonald's ambulance lowerer.
5. The Lowmoor jacket. (*See* p. 177.)
6. An extemporized lift.
7. Mowle's folding ambulance chair.
8. Macdonald's lift and stretcher.
9. Singleton's chair.

Knots.
Before describing these various forms, it will be well to take some notice of knotting. To the Ambulance Transport Officer a

knowledge of the simple knots is indispensable when transport breaks down; or when it is necessary to extemporise saddles or litters, as well as on the occasions connected with the transport of sick and wounded by sea. The following is drawn from the "Soldier's Pocket Book":—

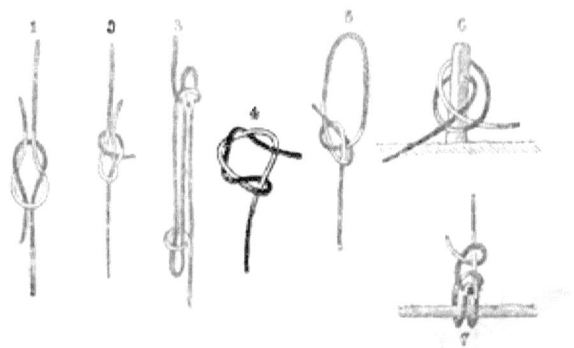

Fig. CLXXIV.

No. 1. *Reef knot*, used for lashings, when two ropes or the ends of one rope have to be fastened so as to be easily undone.

No. 2. *Single sheet bend*, for joining two ropes, or fastening a rope to a loop; it can be made much more secure by passing the lower rope twice round the loop.

No. 3. *Sheepshank*, for shortening a rope when both ends are fastened.

No. 4. *Timber hitch*; as long as a strain is maintained it cannot give way, but immediately it is taken off it comes undone easily; it is useful in dragging material from place to place.

No. 5. *Bowline.* Invaluable in making a loop at the end of a line; it is difficult to undo, it is useful for making the draw loop of slip nooses.

No. 6. *Clove hitch*, for making fast breastlines and painters; it binds with great force.

The simplest method of raising a man is by his placing his foot in a ring and holding on to the rope, and being drawn up. This is not adapted for sick men, but would be a useful way of drawing up an attendant.

THE GORGAS AMBULANCE LIFT.

This lift consists of a cot of the ordinary pattern, at the extremities of which a series of strings pass to a grummet, which in turn is attached to a rope, as shown in the sketch. The cot is 5 feet 8 inches long by 21 inches wide. The main feature in this lift is a double inclined plane placed under the buttocks, thighs, and legs of the patient, thus preventing during his

CHAP. VI.
The Gorgas lift.

transit, slipping down in the cot, while his body is still further held by means of a breast strap. The proportions of the inclined plane are such as to adapt it to tall and short men, or even boys.

The cot is principally suspended by a whip attached to the

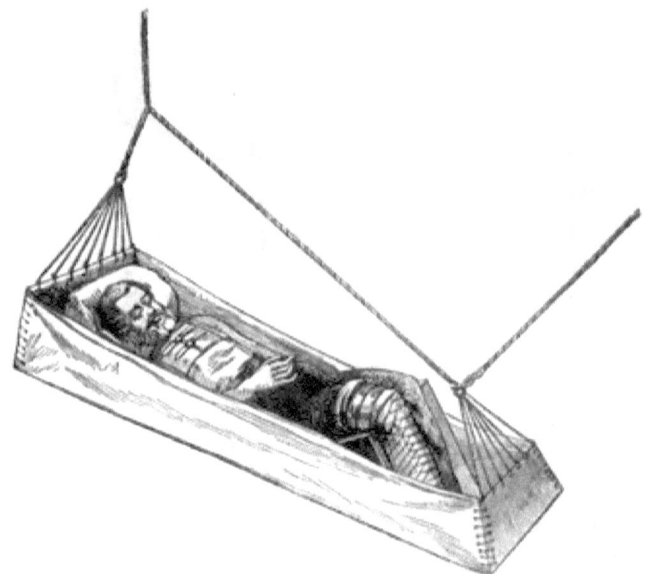

Fig. CLXXV.—Ambulance cot of Dr. Gorgas, United States' Navy.

head clews, while a guiding line is connected with those of the foot, by which means the descent is regulated as required. It is recommended to have canvas loops or beckets on the sides of the frame of the cot to act as handles for ordinary lifting, and through these handles may be passed, converting the cot into a stretcher.

This lift is a safe and reliable means of ambulance transport, and can be readily extemporised on any occasion.

The following extract of a letter by Dr. Gorgas is of considerable interest:—

"*Ambulance for Ships of War.*

"U.S. NAVY YARD,
"Portsmouth, New Hampshire,
"*December 6th*, 1869.

"SIR,
"While serving on board the 'Juniata' in 1864, I had in preparation for the battle of Fort Fisher two apparatuses made from the ordinary ships' cots similar in principle to this one,

which answered the purposes for which they were designed so well that I think it a matter of professional interest sufficiently important to report to the Bureau, in response to the invitation contained in its circular to the Medical Officers of the **Navy** dated July 7th, 1869.

"The inconvenience of transporting sick **and wounded** from one deck to another is especially due to the **fact** that hatches are usually too small to permit a cot or stretcher to be hoisted or lowered through them in the horizontal position.

"If the cot be inclined the patient within it is liable **to** slip downwards to its foot, which is always inconvenient, and in cases of fracture of the lower extremities is apt to cause displacement of the fragments and other serious complications.

"To provide against this on the occasion to which I have alluded, I had a double inclined plane fastened upon the cot frame, and a band of canvas secured to the upper part of the **same.** The thighs and legs of the patient **are** flexed **over the** double inclined plane and the canvas **band is tied around his** chest beneath his arms, his head resting upon a pillow.

"The ring in the clews of the head of the cot was, on **board the 'Juniata,'** hung upon a hook attached to a whip, which was **made** fast to the fish davit over the fore hatch, to the lower **clews a** line was secured. The patient being placed **in the cot, the upper** end of the latter was raised to the proper **angle by means of** the whip; the foot of the cot, by the line **attached to** it in **the** hands of one man, was swung over the hatch and allowed **to** pass through it, and the whole apparatus was lowered together at the proper inclination.

"In **this** ambulance the sliding down of the occupant is arrested by his **buttocks** and thighs being supported by the upper surface of the double inclined **plane,** and his body is **still** further held by **the strap.**

"In the common cots used on board the '**Juniata**' **this** arrangement was an entire success. In the first day's bombardment, when 13 men **were** wounded at the same time by the bursting of a gun, much delay was avoided in getting them **below** by the excellent working of the ambulances, and the propriety of having two, so that the whip had only to be unhooked from the empty one on its return to **the** upper deck and applied to the other, in which a wounded man **was** all ready to be sent below, was clearly shown.

"While I was attached to the U.S. s. '**Brooklyn,' the flag-ship** of Rear-Admiral Godon, on the Brazil Station, **the** same ambulance **was** used, and it was part of the drill at "general quarters" to designate a man as wounded, when the men detailed for that purpose would place **him** upon an ordinary canvas stretcher and convey him to **the cot** in which he would **be sent** below. On **that** ship the whip was made fast to the mizzen stay, the steerage hatch being directly over the surgeon's quarters.

"On board the '**Juniata**' **there** were no gratings over the fore hatch, it being covered by **a** tarpaulin only. On board the

CHAP. VI.
The Gorgas lift.

'Brooklyn' the gratings were left off on one side of the hatch, through which opening the ambulance readily passed.

* * * * *

"A Commander in the Navy, to whom I showed this ambulance, informed me that he was wounded in the ankle on board a monitor during the late war, and that to remove him from the vessel it was necessary to lash him in the most uncomfortable intricate manner to a common cot in order to get him through the narrow hatchway, and that although his lashings, when the cot was inclined, gave him great distress, he did not get through without slipping down upon the injured limb sufficiently to occasion considerable increase of pain. In cases of injuries aloft this ambulance with the staff attached would secure the safe and comfortable descent of wounded, the whip being made fast to any convenient part of the rigging.

"Very respectfully, your obedient servant,
"ALBERT C. GORGAS,
"Surgeon U.S. Navy.
"Surgeon W. Maxwell Wood, M.D.,
"Chief of Bureau of M. and S.,
"Washington, D.C."

Macdonald's Ambulance Lift.

Macdonald's ambulance lift.

This "lift," together with the "lowerer" which, in reality, is a lift, for the word naturally implies lowering (the description of which follows), are the invention of Inspector-General Macdonald, M.D., F.R.S., &c., R.N.*

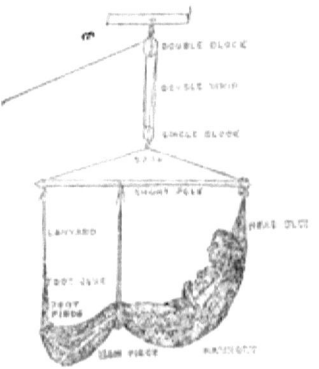

Fig. CLXXVI.—Macdonald's Naval Ambulance Lift.

It will be observed that in this lift the sailors' hammock forms the principal feature, and the patient is secured in the

---

* See "Macdonald's Naval Hygiene," p. 286 et seq.

following way. The head and foot clews are secured to a short pole (between 4 feet and 5 feet long) to which again a spar is attached above, with an eye in the middle for the lower hook of a double whip, or fixity to a longer pole when the apparatus is used on shore. The easiest possible movement is thus effected, either in lowering a patient from one deck to another, or carriage from place to place on shore. Nothing more is required when the injuries are confined to the head, trunk, and upper extremities; but by the addition of a small transverse ham-piece placed under the hammock, and connected by a lanyard at each end with the pole above, provision is made for fracture of the leg or thigh, with the whole effect of the **double** inclined plane.

The arrangement **for** carriage by a pole is of great service in tropical countries, and an awning can be quite easily extemporised.

Macdonald's Ambulance Lowerer.

Dr. Macdonald devised this lift apparatus, as shown in the figure, for being kept in the "tops" of a ship.

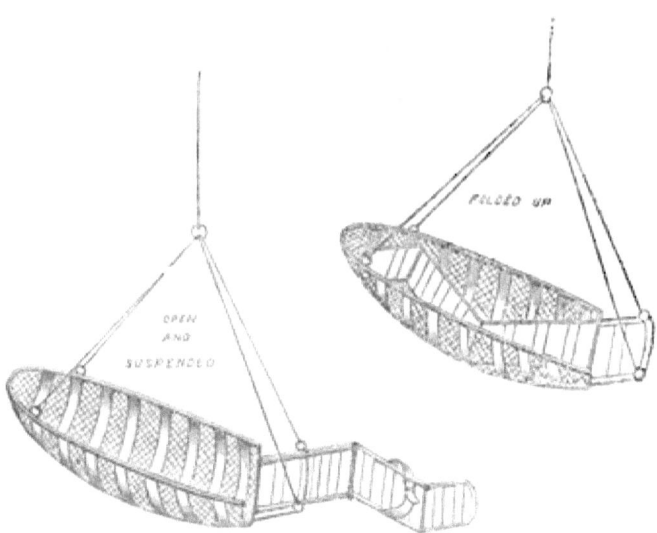

Fig. CLXXVII.—Inspector-General Macdonald's "Ambulance lowerer," **for use in** the tops **of** war vessels.

It consists **of** a cradle with a leg-piece arranged on a double inclined plane, and in which a sailor injured in the "tops" of a ship, and unable to descend, can be lowered with safety. Four lines support the conveyance. It is ingenious, safe, and com-

CHAP. VI.

fortable, but owing to its breadth it **cannot pass through a hatchway** of much less than 4 feet.

This is important, for **in** action in **some ships, if a man is** wounded in the turrets, he can only be carried **off by the ammu**nition shoots, which are only 19 inches in **diameter.**

An Extemporised Lift.

An extemporised lift.

This consists of an **ordinary lifebuoy which** is passed over the trunk of the body **close up to the armpits.** Two short stays support a seat, and two or three more are attached to a block

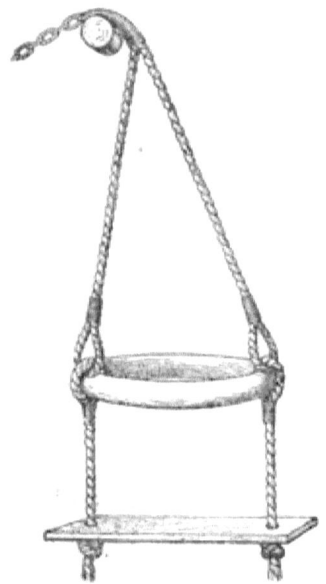

Fig. CLXXVIII.—An Extemporised Lift.

and single rope **working** over a block at the end of a spar. It **is a** useful and **safe way to** lift a man into a large ship. It is an **extemporised** apparatus and is only suggested as a means **when better** apparatus is not obtainable.

MOWLL'S FOLDING SHIP AMBULANCE CHAIR.

This **is the invention of** Fleet-Surgeon **Mowll, R.N.** The want of an ambulance which can **be used** in confined spaces, and hoisted **or** lowered down hatchways, or in and out of a ship, with comfort and security, has long been experienced, and this contrivance, fulfilling all necessary conditions, is invaluable in troop **and** passenger ships.

It is a light iron frame supporting a piece of tanned canvas, which by passing over a padded roller, forms a comfortable and secure seat on the double-inclined plane principle. For convenience in carrying, the extremities of the handles are covered with leather, and it has been found by experience that for short distances, as in ships, the carrying straps are unnecessary.

Straps for securing an injured leg are attached in a suitable position, and a similar one of webbing buckles across the patient.

Fig. CLXXIX.—As a Chair.

The principal feature of this ambulance is the rapid way in which by moving two sets of handles the chair can be converted into and carried as a stretcher (as in Fig. CLXXX).

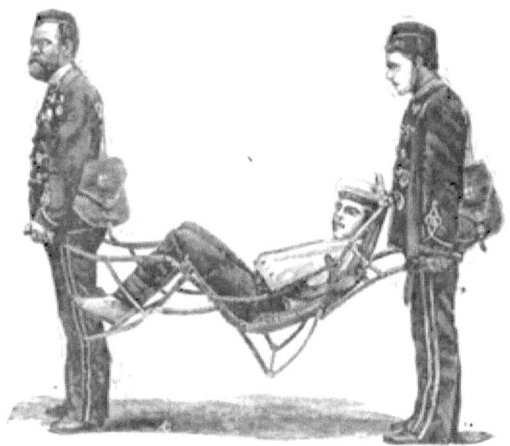

Fig. CLXXX.—As a Stretcher.

To hoist or lower it wire rope slings, so hinged in the middle as to fold up compactly, and fitted with spring hooks, are provided, and can be instantly fastened to the shackles at

CHAP. VI.
———
Mowll's chair.

each corner of the chair. When not in use the folded slings are contained in a pocket behind the seat.

By shortening the after legs of the slings the chair can be suspended in such a way as to pass and transport a wounded and insensible man through a ship's hatchway of three feet square.

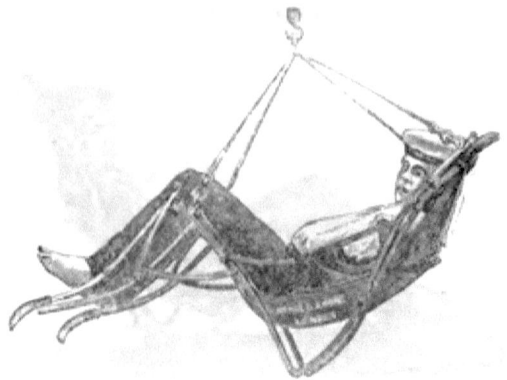

Fig. CLXXXI.—Slung ready for hoisting or lowering.

Beyond the four small leather straps which confine the sides of the chair when folded there are no loose parts. The chair being secured by a half turn of the thumb screws.

It is sufficiently light to be easily carried under the arm, by one hand, and only a few moments are required to prepare it for use.

To hoist or lower it neat wire-rope slings can be readily attached to shackles at either corner of the framing, as in Fig. CLXXXI. When not required, these slings fold up, and are carried in a pocket behind the seat.

Having removed the loose straps round the framing, to open the chair :—

1. Lay the chair, leg straps downwards, on the ground, and unfasten the small seat straps.
2. Then standing the chair upright, roller upwards in front of you, push open the fold and hook the long side stays over the studs, the thumb-plates of which should be in the same line as the framing. One half-turn from you secures them.
3. Allow the chair to fall back on the ground, and walking round to the front, pull open the fore legs, securing the short stays in the manner described above.
4. Place the fore legs on the ground and the chair is ready for use.

To close the chair the reverse obtains :—

1. Standing behind the chair, turn back the thumb plates of

the studs to the original position, pull on the roller, and allow the stays to slip off.
2. Pull up the fold, unfasten the fore stays, close the fore legs, and turn over flat on the ground, leg straps downwards.
3. Fasten the small seat straps and secure the framing by the loose straps. It is then ready for carrying.

To convert the chair into a stretcher, it is necessary to lower the rear handles and fix the brackets, raise the fore handles and hook the stays over the studs. By reversing the motion it at once assumes its original form. Slings for hoisting or lowering the chair are carried in the pocket behind the seat.

MACDONALD'S AMBULANCE LIFT AND STRETCHER.

It will be most convenient to notice, first, the ambulance lift, *per se*, and then, the manner in which it is converted into a stretcher for carrying in the ordinary way.

The Ambulance Lift.

This consists of three principal parts, viz.:—

1. A back or body-piece.
2. A seat or middle-piece.
3. A leg or front-piece with A supplementary or foot-piece (4).

The parts 1, 2, and 3, are composed of wood or of steel tubing, hinge-bolted together, after the manner of a folding-up couch; and by means of two metallic supports, *c*, the fore, and *d*, the after brace, on each side, any required inclination can be given to 1 and 3, the back and leg-pieces respectively. The available positions are four in number, as shown by the small figures, 1, 2, 3, and 4. The first (1) approaches a right angle (90°), the second (2) an angle of 60°, the third (3) an angle of 30°, and the fourth position (4) is complete extension. Corresponding with these four positions, four buttons are placed on the outer side of the back and leg pieces, so that the *order* "Number 1," "2," "3," or "4," will be readily understood by the bearer in preparing the lift for the reception of a patient.

The free extremity of each brace is furnished with a slot to receive the selected button, and when placed *in situ*, the parts are secured automatically by a hook with a spring-pin-catch.

The extremities of two transverse iron rods form the pivots of the principal hinge-joints (*a* and *b*) of opposite sides. To the

Chap. VI.

The lift.

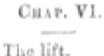

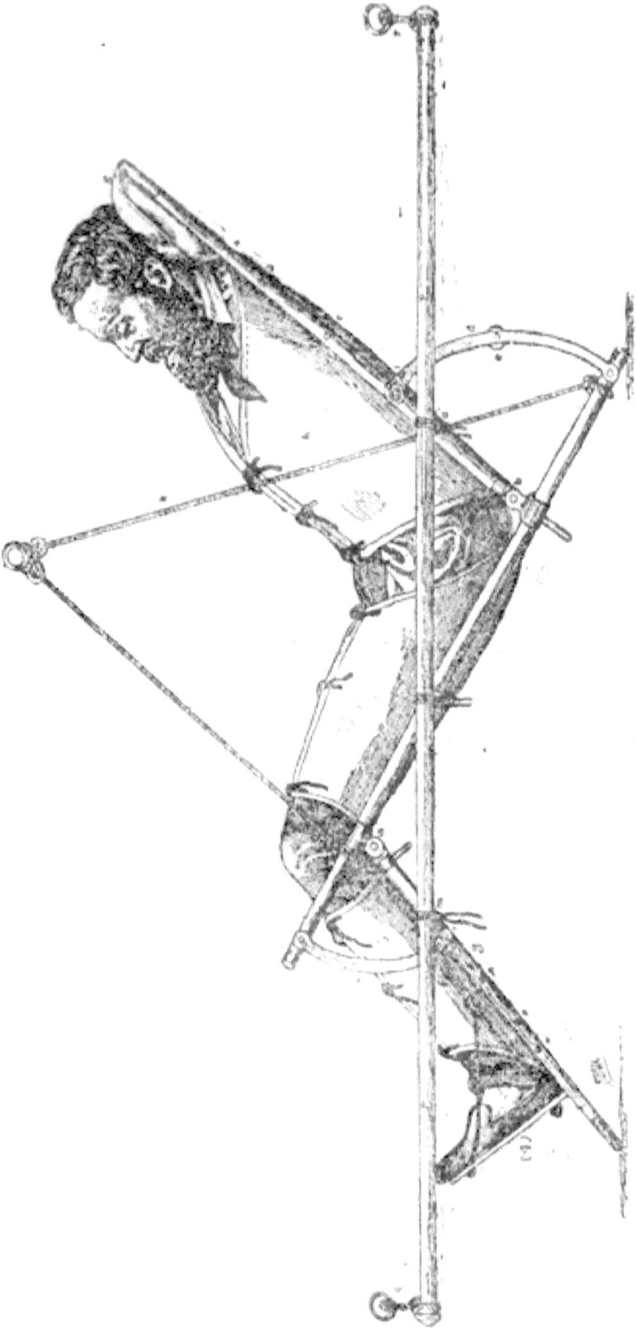

Fig. CLXXXII.

foremost of these rods the upper end of the suspensory rope (*f*) of the foot-piece is connected by loop and thimble, and the length is adjusted by a running eye, nearly as in the case **of** a tent-rope.

The arrangement of the canvas in the **lift** is similar to that of the patent stretcher, **but** the lapels (*h*, **i, and** *j*) are made sufficiently large to enwrap and tie over **the** patient, and pillow flaps (*g*) are supplied to extemporise a pillow if necessary.

The side slings (*k k*) are about five feet long, carrying a running eye (**1**) on the bight, and when a patient is secured in the lift the point of suspension is readily determined by bringing the two running-eyes together and balancing the weight in the hands. By now drawing up the bight, and having twisted it once, passing it over the neck of the eye, the latter will be ready for attachment to the suspension rope by a bowline knot, or with the hook of a double or single whip, for hoisting in the usual way. Provision for this may be readily made even where there is no well in the staircase, in hospitals and **asylums,** and for the convenience of invalids in railway carriages.

CHAP. **VI.**
The lift.

The Stretcher.

By simply **attaching a** pole (*p p*) on either side, with a separate lashing (*m n o*) for each segment of the lift, it can be carried by bearers like an ordinary stretcher. The lashings or stops are permanently attached to the lift by a clove hitch or noose, and the two free ends of each are passed round the pole **from** underneath, **crossed** under **the** standing part and tied **above** in **a** reef knot.

As ringstraps **or rope** (*q r*) are fixed to the poles the **combination slings can be used** with advantage in this case also, **or,** the whole apparatus may be raised upon wheeled trestles, specially designed for the purpose, and so carried with ease and comfort to the patient to any required distance.

All further details connected with this appliance will be made clear by reference to the drawing.

Particulars of construction, in the combination lift and stretcher, **and** rules for manipulating and arranging it for use :—

The stretcher.

1. **As a** lift simply.
2. **For** carriage by suspension.
3. **For** carriage with stretcher poles and slings.

The general form and character of this ambulance are sufficiently given in the illustrated paper describing it, but, for its practical working, notice of some further details will be necessary under the three above-mentioned heads.

1. As a lift *per se*.—In this case we have only to consider

specially the arrangement of the "rope slings." On each of these will now be found two sliding eyes, of which the hinder ones alone are to be connected with the tackle rope as described in the paper referred to, while with the foremost eye is permanently connected a suspension strap, to be noticed under the second head.

2. For carriage by suspension between two bearers, a leather **strap** as weft band is supplied. This strap or band, connected with the sliding eyes, is simply passed over the outer shoulder of each bearer, and when the proper level is determined the carriage will be easy, especially when the support of the inner hand is given to the middle piece, which can be grasped between the lashings of the canvas. By this arrangement both taking up and setting down will be easier for the bearers than would be possible with the stretchers in ordinary use for very obvious reasons.

3. For carriage with stretcher poles and slings, instead of the hempen lashings figured, three pole straps with buckles are fitted on each side. The front pole-strap is secured permanently to the leg piece just above the first canvas lashing. The middle pole-strap is fixed in the same way to the middle piece, while the after pole-strap **is looped round** the hinder part of the middle piece, just in front of the stay, and when not in **use is placed** sufficiently **out of the** way by connection with its fellow **of the** opposite side.

Simple rounded **poles, 6 feet 8** inches long, with ring straps as ropes at the extreme ends, will answer their purpose perfectly, for, although complete extension may be given to the ambulance in the few cases requiring it, more or less flexion of its three parts will be usually permitted, with greater comfort to the patient.

INSTRUCTIONS FOR BEARERS.

1. In opening out the lift, loose the fore and middle pole straps, lay the ambulance down with the transverse irons upwards. Next unlock the stays of the leg piece and lay them forwards, give the required inclination, and lock the stays on the corresponding buttons. Lay down the ambulance with the transverse irons downwards, unlock the stays of the back piece, and lay them backwards, to give the required inclination, and lock again on the appropriate **button,** when **all will** be ready for the reception of the patient.

2. In closing the ambulance, first roll up the canvas **flaps from** within outwards, and tie the ends with part of the **nearest lashing.** Though this is a little improvised, it will be **found to** answer very well. Next loose the hinder end of the suspension strap, and carry it with the rope sling behind the after hinge, then pass it from below upwards once round the opposite segment of the middle piece, and connect it again with its own sliding eye. Finally, when the ambulance is folded up and the

stays are fixed to the closing buttons, connect the front pole-strap with the middle piece, the middle pole-strap with the back piece, and the after pole-straps with each other, if not already buckled together.

3. When the ambulance is to be used as a lift the after frog of the leather slings must be released from the sliding eye, crossed out of the way beneath the middle piece, and connected with one of the pole-straps on the opposite sides.

4. For carriage by suspension the rope slings are drawn out on each side, and the after frog of the suspension strap is readjusted to the sliding eye. Lengthening or shortening of the strap may be effected at the fore sliding eye. Finally, when the balance of the ambulance with the patient is once determined it should be carefully preserved by the bearers.

5. The position of both rope and leather slings when the ambulance is folded up need not be altered for the application of poles, when the ambulance is to be used as a stretcher.

Singleton's Chair.

Singleton's Ambulance Chair is made of sailcloth, stiffened at the back with leather; at the sides are fixed leather straps

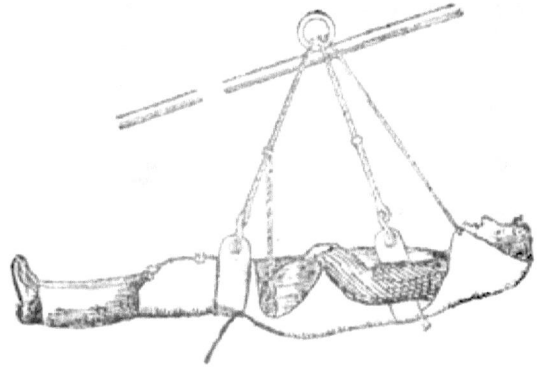

Fig. CLXXXIII.—Patient horizontal.

and buckles, by means of which a disabled person is secured in the chair. There are brass eyelet holes at the front and back of the chair, to which iron clip hooks and rope slings are connected, and these slings join into an iron ring. By simply fastening a rope to the ring, the chair, with the patient, can be raised or lowered by two persons hand over hand, or, more easily, by means of a block and tackle. In the act of raising or lowering, the patient is prevented from coming into contact with any obstacles or projections by a person holding the guide rope attached to the chair.

Chap. VI.

Singleton's chair.

Fig. CLXXXIII shows the chair with a patient in the act of being raised in a horizontal position; this position is particularly suitable for a person suffering from an injury to the thigh or hip. Fig. CLXXXIV shows the patient in what might be termed a

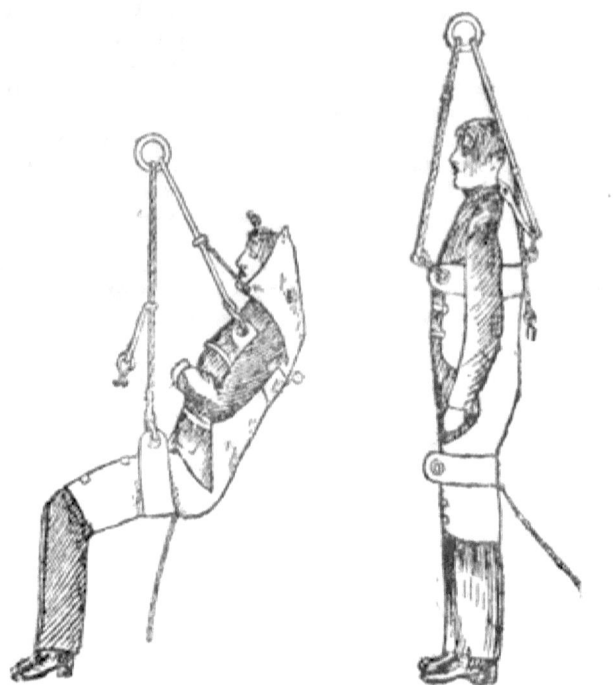

Fig. CLXXXIV.—Patient sitting.   **Fig. CLXXXV.**—Patient perpendicular.

sitting posture. In Fig. CLXXXV the patient is represented in a perpendicular position, which is assumed for the purpose of raising or lowering the person through a very small or narrow opening. When the disabled person has been raised or lowered to the required spot, he need not be removed from the chair if further transport be necessary, but if a stretcher be at hand can be put on it with the chair still attached. If a stretcher be not obtainable, the patient can be carried by simply removing the chair and slings from the block (if one has been in use), and then by passing a handspike, pole, plank, or batten, or a boat's oar (see Fig. CLXXXI), through or under the ring for the slings, two men can conveniently move the patient to any distance. The chair can also be made use of in shipwrecks in cases where a sick or disabled person has to be brought ashore by the rocket life-saving apparatus.

Ambulance Launches.*

Ambulance launches.

These are a very necessary part of marine ambulance transport, for the conveyance of sick and wounded from the shore to a ship, as at Suez or Malta, and for the transference from ships in harbour to the hospitals on shore. The ordinary steam pinnaces do not answer for the purpose, nor are they to be always obtained when required.

At Portsmouth Dockyard there is an ambulance launch used for carrying sick and wounded from the ships to the Royal Naval Hospital at Haslar. It is an ordinary service pattern launch, 42 feet in length, housed in, and divided into two compartments, the smaller for four officers lying down, the larger for eight men in the same position.

There is also room for others not needing lying down accommodation. There is a cot-hatchway in the centre of the roof through which the sick men lying in their cots can be lowered and placed under shelter on the cot-stands in the cabin. When all the cot-stands are filled, the portable seats can be drawn out and further utilised for lying-down accommodation. This launch has no steam aid of its own, and has to be towed. It is well lighted and ventilated, and a stove can be fitted in winter time.

The absence of steam aid is a drawback to an otherwise excellent form of transport, as it is not always possible to depend on being towed. Electric launches would serve the purpose of ambulance transport in harbours, and are not so costly in the end as those which burn coal, and require at least two men to work.

The "Red Cross."

This is the name of the ambulance steamer of the London Metropolitan Asylums Board, and used for the conveyance of infectious cases of disease from the London receiving wharves to the hospital ships off Dartford.

The "Red Cross" is a paddle-wheel steamer, 105 feet long, 16 feet wide, and 6 feet 9 inches deep, made principally of iron with a strong keel. It has a silent discharge steam apparatus to prevent the noise caused by the safety-valves blowing off steam when the engines are at rest.

The vessel is built in six water-tight compartments, but consists mainly of two portions: one, the forepart in front of the funnel, devoted to the reception of infectious cases, and the stern portion which has a saloon or waiting-room for the use of patients returning cured from the hospital ships.

---

* The description of these launches is drawn from Brigade-Surgeon Lieut.-Colonel J. H. Evatt's work "Handbook of Ambulance Transport," published by Messrs. Clowes and Son.

Forward of the infectious section, but separate from it entirely, is a small room for the crew, and the captain has a cabin near the saloon or stern end of the vessel.

The infectious disease portion of the steamer is divided down the centre by a partition into two parts, one for males and one

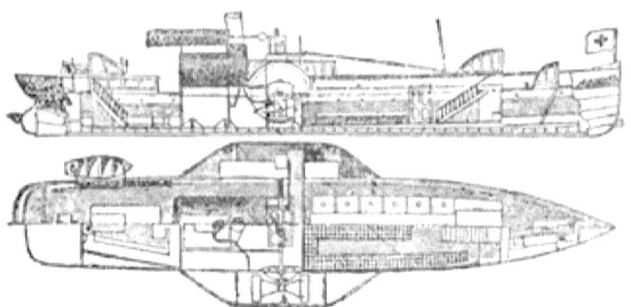

Fig. CLXXXVI.—Ambulance steamer "Red Cross," Metropolitan Asylums Board, London (after Evatt).

for females—with a doorway between for the medical staff and nurses.

The lying-down accommodation consists of couches or settees running continuously round the sides of the hospital, and on these the patients lie covered by blankets.

APPENDICES.

APPENDIX I.

THE SANITARY TRAIN OF THE SOCIÉTÉ FRANÇAISE.

This train consists of the following:—

1. Locomotive **and tender.**
2. Guard's **van.**
3. Surgeon's wagon.
4. Wagons for the wounded—twenty.
5. Cooking wagon.
6. Store wagon.
7. Magazine wagon.
8. Guard's van.

The train is arranged so that the doors at each extremity of the wagons open towards each other, forming a passage through the entire length. These doors are of a sufficient width to allow of the free passage of a stretcher with a severely wounded soldier upon it. The passage between each carriage, i.e., over the couplings, should be protected by a screen from the weather.

In arranging this train, as many carriages as possible should be allowed for the wounded. These occupy the centre of the train, but are equally divided by the wagon arranged for the medical officers, while at each end of the train are, respectively, the store and guard's van, and the magazine and cooking wagon.

The Carriage for the Wounded.

In the time of war these wagons receive at once all the necessaries for the transport of the wounded. Four wooden posts, to be found in the roof of the wagon, are detached, lowered, and put in their places, and in the holes with which they are provided, are placed iron rods, which are kept in a box under the floor of the wagon. The rods support, one above the other, three beds, which can be instantly put into position for the reception of the wounded. A latrine is furnished on one side for the use of the sick, and there is a stove placed alongside of it. The loading and unloading of the wounded should take place by the end doors, but if necessary those at the side can be opened for this purpose.

APPENDIX I.

The wagon for those not requiring lying-down accommodation is arranged by turning down seats from the sides, and fixing them to the posts, which support **the beds**. There **are four** sets of **seats**, sufficient to accommodate 40 wounded.

If **it is** necessary to carry wounded, both lying **down and sitting** up, **in the same** wagon, the arrangement is obvious.

In **order** that the balance of the stretchers **shall be maintained they are fixed** to the wall of the wagon.

If necessary, the wagon can be readily converted into a refectory, by screwing legs into the seats previously alluded to, and thus making tables; the wagon is lighted by lamps, and the light is regulated by sliding covers.

Each train contains 20 wagons for wounded, **and** is able to carry at one time nearly 300 lying down, or 500 sitting.

Inventory of a Wagon for Wounded.—Each contains 15 beds complete, with mattress, 1 pillow with case, 2 sheets, 2 blankets (woollen), 1 night shirt, 1 cotton night cap, 1 pair of slippers, 1 folding chair, to each bed; besides these are 1 stove, with sand bath, to hold hot drinks, 1 **poker**, 1 shovel, 1 pan of charcoal, 1 w.c. at partition, 1 bucket for **drinking** water, 1 mug, 1 enamelled iron basin, sponges, hand towels, **dish cloths**, cups, spittoons, boxes, thermometer, and **lanterns**.

Wagon for Medical Officers.

This wagon **is arranged for 4** Medical Officers, and possesses all **the** comfort rendered necessary by the laborious and prolonged fatigue **of the service**. This service of evacuation of the wounded by train is composed of long journeys, lasting many weeks, at all times and in all seasons. These 4 doctors have continuous charge of 300 or 400 wounded, and they are held responsible that a record and a register of the observations on a large proportion of the patients is regularly kept.

These remarks are sufficient to answer any reproach relative to the comfort of the wagon made by individuals ignorant of the conditions of active service, the difficulties of the journeys, the continual monotony, the frequent stoppages, countermarches, &c., which are borne by the medical officers managing this kind of service.

The interior of the wagon is in the figure of a cross. The two **longitudinal arms of the** cross represent the passage from end to end **of the vehicle, the two short arms contain, on one side the** w.c. and **the other the** stove. The passage **is** lighted by day **by a** skylight, **which can be** opened, if necessary, for ventilation, and **by** night by an ordinary lamp placed in the roof of the carriage.

The stove is heated by hot water, and it is so arranged that the water contained in the roof to supply the offices and the w.c. is prevented from freezing. The same apparatus, by a series of hot-water pipes conveyed under the carriage, keeps it at an equable and agreeable temperature.

The furniture in each medical officer's compartment includes a press for linen and clothes, upon which rests a wash-hand basin with the usual accessories, and a tap for water. Above this is a small bookshelf for medical works. At the opposite end of the wagon, facing the press, there is a seat for two persons, on raising which a comfortable bed is disclosed.

At the back of the seat and just above it, is a cupboard with shelves.

There is a folding table, with an inkstand let into the wood, and a moderator lamp, which can be placed either by the linen press or on the table.

Each room has, further, a clock, with a thermometer and barometer attached.

Over the door is inscribed the name of the medical officer, and a small hand lantern is suspended day and night before that of the medical officer on duty, to avoid disturbing those officers who are resting.

The following is the exact inventory of each officer's compartment:—

- 1 bedstead with mattress attached, pillow, sheets, and blankets.
- 1 portable lavatory.
- 1 writing table.
- 1 linen press.
- 1 clock and thermometer and barometer combined.
- 1 medical library
- 1 oil lamp.

The Kitchen Wagon.

In this wagon is combined all the apparatus, utensils, and necessaries for the cooking for 300 or 400 sick and wounded, and also for the Ambulance Staff of the train. In this carriage it is necessary to be able to prepare, not only the ordinary diets and drinks, but all kinds of nourishment required for sick and wounded soldiers.

The material is arranged thus:—

A large range is placed in the centre of one side of the wagon. It has 2 large boilers, each holding 75 litres (9 gallons) for the preparation of soup and broth,—2 large bain-maries for coffee and hot drinks.

When the train is moving, broad covers are put on these boilers, and fixed by wooden bars, to prevent splashing.

A shelf placed above the range carries the cooking pans, and some are hung up in such a manner that they can be easily removed, but are, at the same time, fixed so as to prevent noise with the shaking of the train.

Two beds, one for the cook and one for his assistant, are fastened by hinges to the side of the wagon opposite to the cooking range.

These beds during the day are raised up against the side of the wagon. By a simple method one of them can be converted into a dresser.

The scullery, sink, and drain are also placed on the same side. Cupboards are arranged for the reception of glass and ware, after the fashion common in the Navy. They are contained in the four corners of the wagon, while above them are tanks of water, holding altogether 1,800 litres, i.e., 225 gallons. These are filled by a simple opening in the roof, and the water is distributed by means of taps to the kitchen.

The wagon is lighted by a large lantern and 4 sliding windows.

There is a clock at one end of the wagon.

This wagon contains:—

APPENDIX I.

1. A cooking range, with the necessaries for preparing the diets and drinks.
2. A large coffee pot.
3. Two large soup boilers.
4. A large shelf.
5. Hot-water reservoir.
6. Cooking utensils complete in tinned copper.
7. Box for charcoal.
8. Sink and drain.
9. A butcher's hook and meat chopper.
10. Reservoirs of cold water.
11. A large table.
12. Two folding chairs.
13. Two beds with mattresses, pillow cases, **sheets**, and woollen blankets.

The plates and dishes, and necessaries are:—Plates, forks, tablespoons, teaspoons, knives, glasses, salts, water-bottles, teapots, teacups, covered baskets, bottle baskets, butcher's knives, meat chopper, and a clock.

APPENDIX II.

AMBULANCE TRAIN OF THE KNIGHTS OF MALTA—AUSTRIA-HUNGARY.

This Train, constructed on Mundy's system, at the expense of the Knights of Malta of the Grand Priory of Bohemia, is composed of 15 wagons, arranged in the following order:—

Engine and tender.
Guard's van with brake.
1 carriage for the Commandant and Medical Officers.
1 provision wagon.
1 kitchen wagon.
1 dining wagon with break.
5 ambulance wagons.
1 store wagon with break.
5 ambulance wagons.
1 signal van with break.

The guard's van and signal van at the ends of the train are each furnished with a break, which the railway companies have to provide in accordance with regulations, so that it is not necessary to adopt breaks to the ambulance wagons.

The Commandant's and Medical Officers' Carriage.

Considering that the Commandant and Medical Officers attached to the ambulance trains of the Knights of Malta may have to serve for several weeks or even months at a time without interruption, it is absolutely necessary that they should have the same comforts that are enjoyed by the ambulance employés on most of the railways, who are, in addition, frequently relieved.

At the four corners of the carriage to the right and left of the centre passage are four cabins, two for the Knights of Malta and the Commandant and two for the medical officers. The free space between the cabins to the right of the centre passage is utilised for a latrine and the space opposite is used as an office for the medical officer on duty.

The partitions and the platforms are of plain wood without any veneering. The floor is covered with oil-cloth with a plain carpet above it.

The end doors are glazed and the centre passage is lit up during the day by the lantern in the roof and at night by electric light.

The cabins have each a lateral window cut in the outer wall of the wagon, and at night electric light is used

Furniture of the Cabins.

APPENDIX II.

In consequence of the restricted space in the cabins it was necessary to have a seat which could also be utilised as a bed, and to this end some armchairs have been arranged for the wagons.

By day this seat looks like the ordinary armchair used in railway carriages. In front of the cushion on the seat are two tags, by means of which the seat can be drawn out to form a bed.

The empty space above the chair can be closed by two doors and it contains a press for linen, clothes, &c.

The writing table is made with a hard wood frame and a white wood panel covered with green cloth and is fastened by hinges to the wall of the cabin in front of the chair, and can be raised and lowered at will, and there are two arms fixed to the wall, which serve as supports.

Opposite to the cabin door is a toilet table composed of a square cupboard with two doors, it contains shelves for linen and small toilet necessaries.

Above the cupboard is a water-tank and an enamelled iron basin fixed in a hinged slab which can be lowered when required. A tap from the tank is fixed above the basin, and a cup fastened to the wall holds the soap. The slab which holds the basin serves as a door for enclosing the space, and when it is turned up the water in the basin flows down a drain pipe.

Each cabin is further provided with a mirror, folding stool for trunks, 2 hat hooks, 1 folding chair, 1 daily calendar, 1 cup, 1 water bottle, 1 lamp, 1 inkstand and writing materials, and a complete toilet service (see Inventory).

The hot-air system of Thamm and Rothmüller has been adopted to heat the carriage, and the apparatus is placed horizontally across the wagon in a space under the flooring. It is composed of a sheet-iron cylinder separated by a door which incloses an iron fuel basket—the lower part of the cylinder is pierced with holes, whilst the upper part is trellised and can be taken to pieces. The air necessary for combustion enters by the holes in the cinder box and passes through to the fuel. The copper funnel, which has a suction pipe at the end, carries off the gases. The sheet-iron cylinder has an outer iron casing from which the heat is conducted to the cabins. The openings serve to draw in the current of cold air which passes through the heating apparatus to the cabins. The protecting plate placed above the apparatus prevents the woodwork from being affected by the heat. The ventilators above the cabin windows carry off the foul air and regulate the temperature. The fuel used for the heating apparatus is coke and charcoal broken up to the size of large nuts.

The special advantage of this system is the circulation of air which results from it, as the cold air from the floor of the cabin flows to the heating apparatus and returns as hot air, so that the temperature of the floor of the cabin is one degree higher than in any other part.

The enclosed space between the two cabins on one side of the passage contains a latrine with water-pipe. There is also a shelf for the baths and urinals. On the opposite side of the passage is the office of the medical officer on duty, in which there is a folding table **similar** to those in the cabins, with an inkstand, also **a horse-hair chair** and a folding chair, barometer, thermometer, clock, **alarm bell**, and signals.

On the walls are portraits of the Emperor and Empress of Austria and the Grand Masters of the Knights of Malta from 1099 to 1118.

The wagon with its fittings complete weighs 9¼ tons.

Inventory of the Wagon.

Two cabins inscribed "Medical Officers," one "Knight of Malta and Commandant of the Train," and one "Knight of Malta and Sub-Commandant," each contains the following articles.

One chair-bed with red wool counterpane and 1 thin ditto, 2 sheets, 1 feather pillow, 1 horsehair ditto, 1 folding stool for trunks, 1 framed mirror, 1 daily calendar, 1 cap, 1 wicker-covered bottle holding 2 qts., and 1 wooden shelf, 1 lamp complete, 1 inkstand, 1 complete toilet service, comprising 1 hair-brush, 2 tooth-brushes, 2 large combs, 1 small ditto, 1 clothes-brush, 1 bottle of gum with brush, 1 bottle of ink, 1 gross of steel pens, 2 penholders, 3 pencils, 1 roll of blotting-paper, 1 piece of India-rubber, 1 ink-eraser, 1 wash-hand basin, 1 brass tap, 1 stick of sealing-wax, 1 night lamp and box of night lights, 1 match holder and 1 packet of matches, 1 flat candlestick, 1 carpet with eyelets and pins, 1 green spring-blind, 1 window strap, 1 double brass window ring, 1 folding chair, 1 folding table, 1 teapot, 1 pair of slippers, 1 spittoon, 3 towels, 1 two-handled box, 1 list of sick and wounded.

In the Latrine.

One complete water-closet, 1 towel holder, 2 quires of indispensable paper, 1 umbrella stand, 4 baths, 1 hat stand, 4 urinals, 1 spring-blind, **1 window strap,** 1 double brass window ring.

In the Corridor.

Eight green curtains to the skylight, 3 spring-blinds, 1 window strap, 1 railway time table, 1 folding table, 1 pair of scissors, 1 clock with key, 1 barometer, 1 thermometer, 1 shoe-brush, 1 alarm and 1 signal bell, 3 lamps, 2 inside and 1 out, 4 writing card holders, 1 folding chair, 1 leather foot-stool, 1 dark lantern, 1 carpet with eyelets and pins.

Outside **the** Wagon.

One heating apparatus, by Thamm and Rothmüller, 2 alarm clocks and 1 thermometer.

Provision Wagon.

APPENDIX II.

The construction of the exterior of this wagon is similar to that of the ambulance wagons. The interior arrangement of the wagon allows of the sliding doors being removed for loading provisions.

The four corners are thus occupied, in one there is a cabin for **sick** or wounded officers, fitted up like the medical officers' cabin, with the exception that the inner partition can be removed in case of necessity for the reception of a seriously wounded officer. In another **corner** is a cupboard for storing **charcoal, wood, and wines** in **bottle**. A cupboard in the third corner holds in the upper part provisions, such as semolina, pearl barley, dripping, preserves, oil, soap, candles, chocolate, sugar, dried vegetables, &c., and below beer and wine in cask. A third cupboard in the other corner holds the fresh meat provisions, fish, vinegar, peas, potatoes, and ice, which latter is kept in a box placed on rails. The same cupboard also contains the electric battery.

The two remaining spaces on either side of the sliding doors contain folding tables fixed to the walls. The wagon contains, in addition, a thermometer, daily calendar, 2 dressers, 2 baths, &c.; under the floor of the officers' compartment is a stove which is filled from the interior of the wagon, but cleaned and emptied from the exterior by means of a small door at the side. The hot air enters the wagon by a grating, and the chimney is isolated by means of a double pipe to prevent all danger of fire. All the precautions prescribed for the heating of passenger wagons are strictly observed.

The provision wagon with its fittings complete weighs $9\frac{1}{2}$ tons.

Inventory of the **Wagon**.

The reserved compartment for sick or wounded officers is furnished in the same manner as that of the medical officers.

In the Corridor

Two lamps inside and 1 outside, 1 electric bell, 24 green curtains to the skylights, 2 folding tables, 1 thermometer, 1 slop-pail, 5 baths, 1 tool box, 2 dressers, and one stove with its accessories under the floor.

The different cupboards contain 2 complete electric batteries (1 in use and 1 in reserve) 15 elastic pipes, 1 oil can, holding about 2 gallons, 1 ditto, holding 5 pints, and one of machine oil (5 pts.), 1 pot of **grease**, 3 **cakes** of toilet soap, 3 sticks of cosmétique, 2 boxes of **night lights (10 in** each), 4 metal plates, each with 6 movable **meat hooks, 1 ice** box, complete with double bottom in trellised wood, **3 marked** casks, 1 barrel stand, 3 bottle holders, 3 tin funnels, **1 ice** machine with knife, 1 flat candlestick, 12 bath-bricks, 12 sink brushes, 3 dusters, 3 scrubbing brushes, 2 clothes brushes, 3 shovels, 2 urinals, **4** linen baskets, 4 market baskets, 4 cwt. of coal, wood, and shavings.

Kitchen Wagon.

This wagon is built in the same way as the ambulance wagons, except that there are no lateral sliding doors, on account of the range and other fittings. Against one of the side walls is placed the kitchen

APPENDIX II.

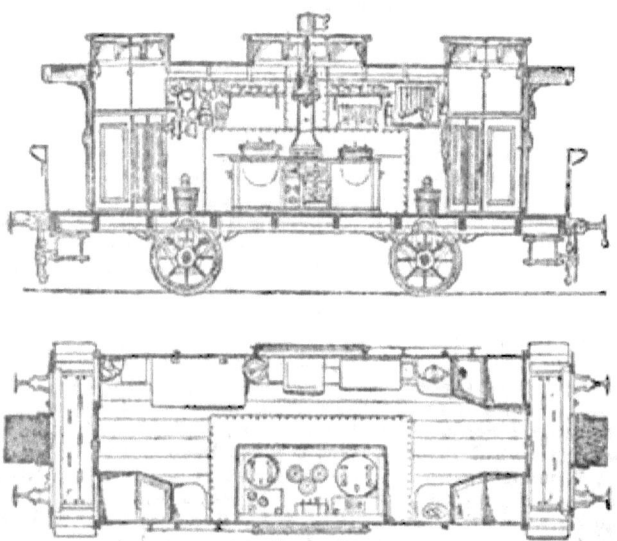

Fig. CLXXXVII.—Railway Kitchen Wagon of the Austrian Ambulance Trains of the Knights of Malta, Austrian Branch.
Upper plate—section; lower plate—plan.

range, calculated to cook for 150 men; it is 7 feet 2 inches long by 3 feet 6 inches broad and 2 feet 6 inches in height. To the right and left are 2 large soup boilers, the one containing about 16 gallons, the other about 32 gallons, the covers of which fit tightly; there are also a reservoir of hot water, a bain-marie for saucepans, with 3 openings, 3 fire-holes between the 2 boilers for cooking and preparing extra dishes, 4 ovens for roasting and 3 fire-grates.

Several experimental journeys have proved the excellence of this range, which answers perfectly for all that can be required. Herr Edward Sacher, the celebrated Vienna restaurant keeper, personally superintended the kitchen during these journeys, and is of opinion that in the space of from 2 to 3 hours the most **simple** as well **as the** most luxurious nourishment can be prepared for **150 men**.

Three corners of the wagon are occupied by cupboards **for** keeping the kitchen accessories. Above each of these cupboards is **placed** a reservoir of water, each holding 56 gallons, and furnished with discharge taps. They are filled from inside the wagon; the fourth corner contains a sink; near it and facing the range is a folding bed for 2 persons, the cover of which serves as a dresser in the day-time.

APPENDIX. II.

By the side of the bed are placed a marble **mortar** and pestle and a chopping board; a large folding table fixed to the wall of the wagon; a larder (or safe), and finally another chopping board. Opposite the range, and running the whole length of the wagon, under the roof is a shelf.

In addition to the cooking and other necessary utensils mentioned in the inventory, the wagon contains a wall-clock, thermometer, daily calendar, and 2 lamps.

The wagon, with its **fittings** complete, weighs 9 **tons 11 cwt.**

Inventory.

One kitchen range with 2 soup boilers, reservoir of hot water and bain-marie for coffee in copper, 3 china coffee pots with covers, 2 pokers, 2 cinder shovels, 1 pair tongs, 2 frying-pans, 1 coal scuttle, with shovel and poker, 1 fish fryer in copper with cover, 1 copper mould, 3 copper stew-pans with covers and 2 handles in sizes, 6 block-tin ditto with covers and 1 handle in sizes, 3 soup ladles, 3 gravy spoons, 3 large zinc reservoirs holding about 60 gallons each, with 2 taps, 1 for the kitchen and 1 below; 1 meat safe with 3 drawers, 1 bed with **2 folding mattresses** stuffed with wrack, **2** bolsters, **2** feather pillows, 2 sheets and 4 blankets, 1 sink with portable tripod, 3 zinc cups to place under the reservoir taps, 2 wooden mats, 1 chopping stool, 1 square chopping board, 1 pestle and mortar, 1 wooden stand for the mortar, 1 folding table, 3 round carving dishes, 4 small square chopping boards, 1 rice mould, 1 Charlotte ditto, 1 baba ditto, 1 cutlet pan, 2 salt grinders, 2 round graters, 1 whisk basin, 2 whisks, 1 double chopper, 1 single ditto, 2 American hatchets, 1 pepper pot, 1 balance with brass trays, 1 set of **weights of** $2\frac{1}{4}$ **lbs.**, 2 butter pats, 1 large chopping knife, 6 large kitchen ditto, 3 dish covers, 2 French meat forks, 2 lemon squeezers, 1 dripping-pan, 1 rolling pin, 20 ladles, 3 block-tin colanders, 3 wooden sieves, 3 strainers, 1 coffee mill, 2 covered wooden tubs, 1 rack for the covers, 1 grindstone complete, 1 box of skewers and larding pins, 2 skimmers, **3 oak** pails for washing dishes, 1 zinc ditto, 3 **wooden bowls**, 2 meat safes, 2 large candlesticks, 1 cucumber pot, **1** grease pot, 2 salt boxes, 2 cucumber slicers, 2 meat choppers, 1 soup strainer, 1 purée ditto, 1 drop funnel, 2 flat brioche pans, 2 almond biscuit moulds, 1 butter pump, 1 cake platter in hard wood, 12 tasting spoons, 1 tin spoon tray, 4 wooden measures, 2 butter knives, 2 milk pans, 1 porringer, 1 washing bucket, 1 cinder box, 1 thermometer, 1 calendar, 1 signal bell to the dining-wagon, 1 electric alarm bell, 1 wall clock with key, 3 lamps, 2 inside and 1 out, 24 green stuff curtains to the sky-lights, 2 towels, 2 dish-cloths, 1 water can for filling the reservoirs, 1 cwt. of coal, wood, 2 earthenware jugs, 2 china ditto, 2 earthen pans.

Dining-Wagon with Break.

It is necessary that there should be a place apart from the ambulance wagons where the Commandant, Medical Officer, Quartermaster, nurses and convalescents, can take their meals, and for this reason a dining-wagon has been built for the Austrian ambulance trains of the Knights of Malta. The exterior of this wagon is the same as that of the ambulance wagons, and if needful it **can be** adapted to the same purpose.

The interior of the wagon contains 4 long tables and 4 benches; 3 of these latter **are** placed the full length of one side of the table and 1 on the other side. On the same side as the **1** table and bench is the stove already mentioned, some shelves **on** the wall, a cupboard for crockery, &c., and a side-board. The empty corner has a complete douche surrounded by a curtain, so that it is quite private. In addition to these, the wagon contains everything necessary for a dining-room.

Above the seats and just under the roof is a shelf running the full length **of the wagon**.

The service for the use of the Commandant **and Medical Officers** is kept **in** separate cupboards.

The wagon, with its fittings complete, and including the break, **weighs** about 8 tons.

Inventory.

Two buffet-cupboards, 4 portable tables, 4 folding benches, **1** Meidinger stove, with accessories (4 pieces), 1 coal box, 3 lamps, 2 inside and 1 out, 1 electric alarm bell, 1 ditto for Medical Officer, 1 ditto for the kitchen, 24 cotton curtains to the sky-lights, 1 cotton curtain to the douche, 4 green stuff curtains for the buffets, 1 complete douche, comprising water tank, 1 detachable rose, 1 lever, 1 basin, 1 wooden bath mat and 1 wooden chair, 1 thermometer, 1 daily calendar, 1 long carpet with eyelet holes and pins, 4 padlocks, 12 wood napkin rings, 1 varnished bucket, 4 water bottles, 4 wine decanters, 7 tankards, 7 champagne glasses, 7 port ditto, 7 claret, 7 sherry and 7 liqueur, 7 beer tumblers, 2 jugs, 7 finger-bowls, 6 large wine glasses, 120 enamelled iron soup-plates, 120 plates, 120 porringers, 144 knives and forks, 144 table-spoons, 144 tea-spoons, 2 cases of carvers, 6 cases **of** salad servers, 6 marrow spoons, 6 fine table-cloths, 6 silver spoons, 1 large Britannia metal spoon, 1 ditto vegetable spoon, 2 butter knives, 6 soup spoons, 1,000 tooth-picks, 6 glass carriers holding 36 enamelled iron cups, 24 wood-topped corks, 2 tea caddies, 2 small enamelled iron cups, 1 water bottle and 4 glasses, 2 salt-cellars, 2 nut crackers, 2 sugar sifters, 4 bread baskets, 2 bronze coffee **urns,** 12 soup tureens, with stands in Britannia metal, **10** pepper **pots, 4 stone**ware jugs, 6 mustard pots and spoons, 12 oak trays, 12 **glass holders**, 6 covered baskets, 24 egg-cups, 3 cork-screws, 2 bottle rinsers, 3 **tea** urns, 1 rinsing bucket, 1 water pitcher, 1 china soup tureen, 1 large china tea-pot, 1 sauce boat and spoon, 1 large oval ditto, 1 small ditto, 1 **china** dish, 3 large china plates, 1 sauce ditto, 2 cream jugs, 1 coffee pot, **2** ditto with lids, 8 small china plates, 8 tea-cups and saucers, 8 large coffee cups and saucers, 8 small ditto, 21 plates, 8 soup plates, 10 broth bowls in enamelled iron, 6 little china cream jugs.

Ambulance Wagons.

These wagons, representing *par excellence* the idea of a sanitary train, that is to say, the transport of sick and wounded from the first-dressing station or nearest ambulance on the battle-field when too encumbered, to the hospitals in the interior of the country, are only

APPENDIX II.

covered goods wagons, used as such in time of peace, and consequently furnished with lateral sliding doors in use for this sort of wagon.

The double doors at each end of the wagon, the platforms with movable hand rails, as also the skylights, are no doubt unnecessary accessories in ordinary goods wagons, but when one considers the cause of humanity involved in this question, this cause seems to be perfectly served by building a wagon answering in time of peace for the carriage of goods, and in time of war as an ambulance wagon, built and furnished on rational and hygienic principles.

The distance between the wagons when coupled is sufficiently great to allow of their being easily loaded and unloaded when the hand rails are raised.

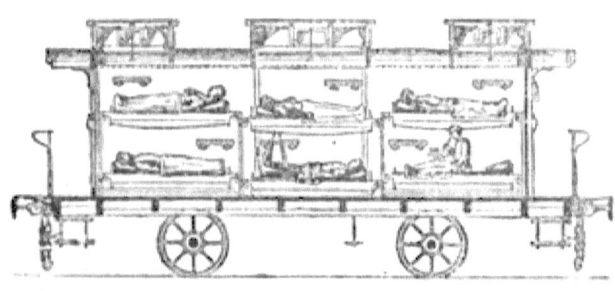

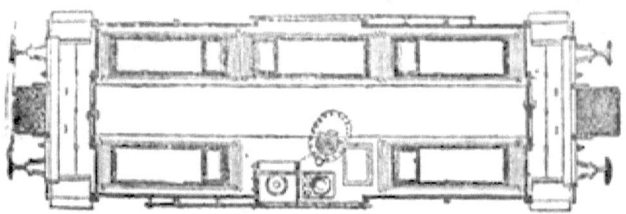

Fig. CLXXXVIII.—Ambulance Wagon of the Austrian Branch of the Knights of Malta, for ten patients lying down.
Above—the section ; below—the plan.

In order to load or unload through the end doors the 10 beds occupied by the wounded and sick simultaneously, 4 men are needed for each bed ; this work can be easily carried out in 6 minutes, as has been proved by numerous trials.

The 10 stretchers in each wagon are each fastened to 4 wood or iron uprights placed on the floor of the wagon, and not requiring any other fixings.

These 4 uprights on feet are placed opposite to each other at a convenient distance, to enable the stretchers to be easily fixed, and are joined together to form a single piece by a beam below and two round bars above.

At the upper end of each upright there are transverse joints, in which the round bars are inserted in such a way as to form one immovable piece with the uprights. The inner side of each upright has transverse supports for 1 stretcher below and 1 above. Between these are other supports on to which the stretchers can be raised or lowered in order to facilitate the medical attendance.

For the stretchers in the middle of the side facing the latrine and stove there is no necessity for a special framework, as these stretchers are placed on other supports fixed to the uprights. The ends of these supports are sufficiently hollowed out and padded with leather to receive the handles of the stretchers.

The new iron frames which are to be used in **all the** sanitary trains of the order of the Knights of Malta (which **will** eventually be increased to the maximum number of 12 trains) are arranged on the same plan as the wooden frames, but they take up less space, and each weighs 11 lbs. less than the wooden frames.

Above the foot of each stretcher when fixed to the framework is a movable shelf for the wounded man's effects; by the side of each stretcher is a shelf which forms a bed table; it is fixed by iron eyelet holes fastened to the wall of the wagon and can be easily removed.

The latrine is placed on one side of the wagon between the stretcher frames by the side of the stove. There is a nurse's table on the **same** side. The latrine, which also serves for emptying slops, is partitioned off and covered by a green stuff curtain. The seat **is** made in such a manner that on raising the lid the valve of the pan closes and opens when the lid is shut down. By the side of the stove is a fuel box, which serves as a seat for the nurse.

To facilitate the inspection, dressing of wounds and washing of the sick and wounded in the upper stretchers, without having to remove them each time, the ambulance wagons are provided with folding ladders, which can be kept under the lower stretchers when not in use.

Each wagon is furnished with a bench and 2 folding-stools to allow of convalescents sitting up a little. These can be folded up together and stowed under the lower stretchers. In order to have all the sanitary appliances to hand, a table is placed behind the stove on which are arranged a basin, 11 drinking cups, bed-bath, urinal, spittoon, water-bottle, 10 tooth brushes, 4 combs, 1 hair brush, 1 stick of pomade cosmétique, some cakes of soap, candles, and an **inkstand.** In addition **to** these each wagon has 3 coat-hooks fixed **to the wall of the latrine,** a daily calendar, **thermometer, 1 large** water-jug, 1 bucket, 1 scrubbing brush, 1 match **holder, 1 broom** 1 brush, 1 shovel, and a carpet. The weight of an ambulance wagon with its complete equipment is about 8 tons.

Its capacity is 36.726 cubic metres. The superficial air space with the windows open, is about 0.375 square metres.

Inventory.

Four frameworks, each with 2 supporting straps, 10 stretcher beds, 10 mattresses, 10 bolsters, 10 pillows without cases, 20 sheets, 20 blankets, 10 bed-tables, 10 shelves, 1 table for the nurse, 1 basin, 11 drinking cups, 2 bed baths, 1 spittoon, 1 wicker-covered water bottle holding about 3 qts., 1 stove with accessories, 1 fuel box, 1 folding footboard, 1 ditto bench, 1 footstool with straps, 1 long carpet with eyelet holes and pins, 1 date indicator, 1 thermometer, 3 coat hooks, 3 lamps, 2 inside and one out, 4 padlocks, 1 electric **alarm** bell, 1 ditto for the medical officer, 10 hand cords covered with **green** leather, 1 latrine partitioned off with planks **and a** curtain,

24 green curtains to the skylights, 1 large water can, 1 rinsing bucket, 1 scrubbing brush, 10 tooth brushes, 4 combs, 1 hair brush, 1 stick of pomade cosmétique, 1 cake of soap, 1 match holder, and 1 packet of Swedish matches, 2 candlesticks, 1 complete writing-case, 1 carpet broom, 1 brush, 1 shovel, 1 inkstand, 2 urinals.

Store Wagon with Break.

This wagon is constructed, as regards fundamental conditions, in the same way as an ordinary goods wagon, with the addition of skylights, end doors, sliding lateral doors, platforms with steps, detachable handrails, and movable trap-doors for establishing the necessary intercommunication between the wagons of a sanitary train; it has also a break.

In one corner of the wagon is a compartment for the Quartermaster, fitted up like those of the medical officers, save that the inner wall of the cabin can be raised for the reception, in exceptional cases, of sick or wounded officers.

On the same side and forming a continuation of this compartment is a small library with a toilet basin attached to the wall; then comes the accountant's office, under which is placed an iron cash box.

At the side of the office is a wardrobe with drawers and shelves for keeping paper, various games, blankets, pillow cases, sheets, napkins, towels, table-cloths, &c.

On the the opposite side of the wagon are cupboards for the stretchers, mattresses, additional pillows, the dispensary, bath-room, sitz-bath, and foot-bath. The space above the cupboards is reserved for the uniforms and other military equipments, shirts, drawers, and socks, and also for the dispensary accessories, hospital utensils, and dressings.

The heating is **on the same principle** as that of the provision wagon.

The store wagon with its complete equipment weighs about 9 tons.

Inventory.

One complete chair-bed with red wool counterpane and 1 summer ditto, 1 feather pillow, 1 hair ditto, 2 sheets, 1 pair of slippers, 1 framed looking-glass, 1 daily calendar, 1 drinking cup, 1 wicker-**covered water** bottle, 1 shelf for ditto, 1 lamp complete, 1 writing-case, 3 **coat** hooks, 3 candlesticks, 1 complete toilet set with hair brush, 2 tooth brushes, 1 clothes brush, 2 **combs,** 1 bottle of liquid gum with brush, 1 bottle of ink, 2 penholders, 3 pencils, 1 stick of sealing-**wax,** 1 roll of blotting-paper, 1 night light holder, 1 box of 10 night lights, 1 basin, 1 brass tap, 1 cake of glycerine soap, 1 match holder and 1 packet of matches, 1 carpet with brass eyelet holes and pins, 1 green window curtain, 2 pieces of wash leather, 1 folding table, 1 ditto stool, 1 teapot, 1 urinal, 1 spittoon, 1 towel, 1 box with 2 handles, 1 inventory board.

APPENDIX III.

Macpherson's Lushai Dandy Drill. (Details.)

I.—*Formation of "Dandy Detachments."*

The men who are to be instructed * are formed up in two ranks, properly sized, and "fours deep" formed. The sets of four thus formed are "numbered" as dandy detachments and the bearers "told off," and "proved" exactly as in stretcher-bearer drill. (*See* "Manual for Medical Staff Corps," para. 334.)

II.—"*Standing, two Lifting and Lowering Dandies.*"

Words of command—

(1.) "*Stand to dandies—quick march.*"—The detachments move off together on the word of command to the dandies, which should be placed ready on the ground one pace distant from one another. A detachment goes to each dandy, and its bearers halt as follows in "Standing to dandies":—No. 1 at the front end of the pole, with the pole on his right; No. 2 in front of the cover with the pole on his left; No. 4 behind the cover on the same side as No. 1, and No. 3 at the rear end of the pole on the same side as No. 2.

(2.) *Lift poles.*—Nos. 1 and 3 stoop down, and, grasping the pole, the former with the right hand, the latter with the left hand, rise together, holding the pole at full arm's length. (*See* Fig. 1 of accompanying illustrations.)

(3.) *Lift dandies.*—On this word of command the bearers act as follows:—

(*a.*) All turn inwards *toward* the pole.
(*b.*) Grasp the pole with both hands, grasping *under* the pole.
(*c.*) Raise the pole steadily and evenly on to their shoulders, fronting as they do so. No. 1 and No. 4 will thus have the pole on their right shoulders; Nos. 2 and 3 on their left.
(*d.*) Bearers then close up, and grasp the pole in the customary manner when carrying dandies. (*See* Fig. 2 of illustrations.)

(4.) "*Lower dandies.*"—This process is exactly the reverse of lifting. After the dandy reaches the ground the bearers "front," Nos. 1 and 3 retaining hold of the pole as in after "Lifting poles."

(5.) "*Lower poles.*"—This command must be given only if the dandy is empty. No. 1 and No. 3 stoop down, let go the pole, and rise to attention. The bearers can now be made to "stand at ease," or if

---

* As this drill is an adaptation of stretcher-bearer drill, dooley-bearers must first undergo the prescribed instruction in that drill. Dooley-bearers so trained pick up the drill with dandies at once, one drill (or at the most two) being quite sufficient to teach it to them.

426 Macpherson's Dandy Drill.

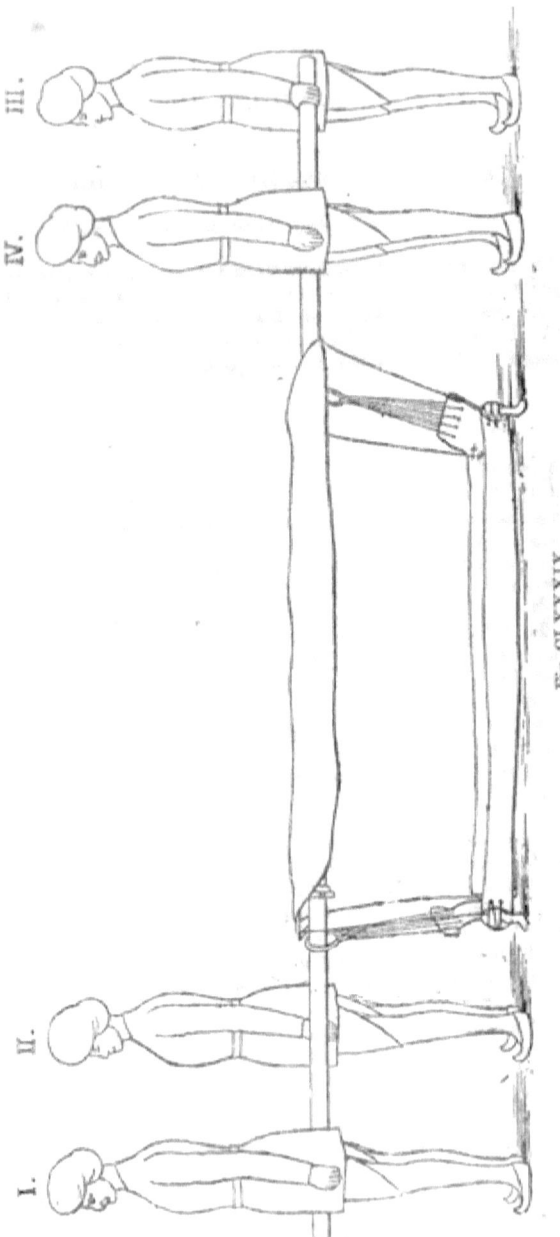

Fig. CLXXIX.

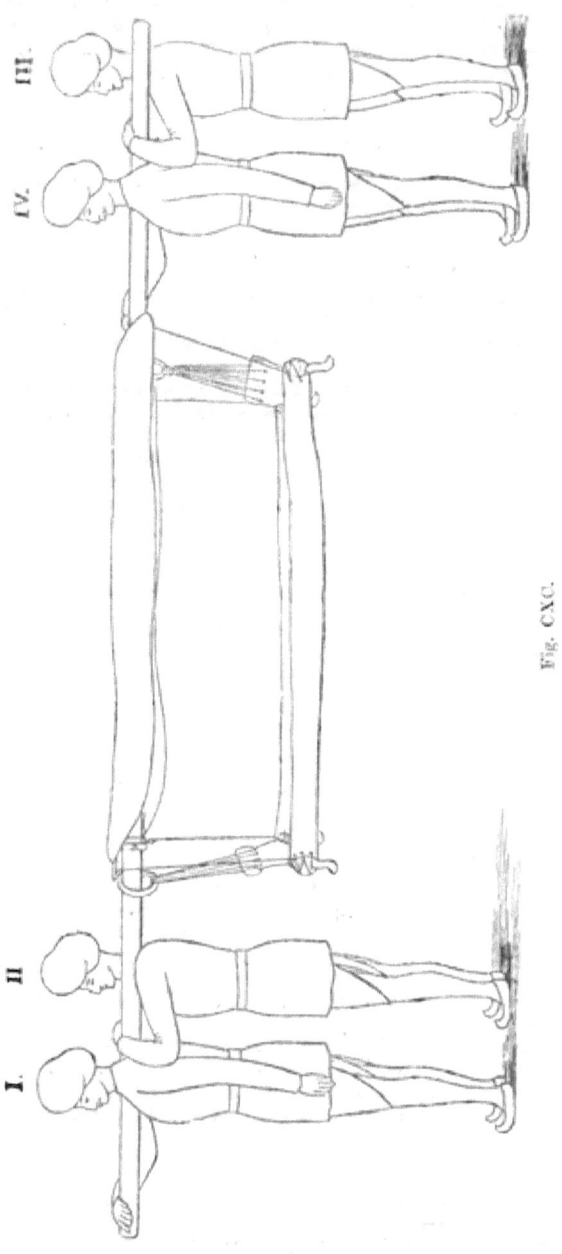

Fig. CXC.

the company is to be dismissed, they can be marched away from the dandies by "right-about turn," "quick march," &c. If the dandy is loaded the bearers must "prepare dandies," as detailed below, before they are allowed to "stand at ease or rest."

III.—*Marching with Dandies.*

The words of command are the same as in marching with stretchers prepared for use, viz., "Advance" (for movement towards the front), "Retire" (movement to rear), "Right turn," "Left turn," "Right incline," "Left incline."

The following points to be attended to in marching:—

(1.) The bearers should use their usual quick shuffling step.

(2.) No. 1 should invariably lead going down-hill. The exception to this rule with regard to the carriage of severe fractures of the leg being attended to.

(3.) In changing direction No. 1 will bring his end steadily round by the right-about or shortest way, while No. 3 marks time on his own ground till the change is completed.

(4.) If a bearer wishes to change shoulders he should give the word to the other bearers, and then all should change together. On halting, however, the bearers should invariably change the pole on to the proper shoulder.

IV.—*Extending and Closing a Company of Dandy Detachments.*

For the purposes of instruction it is necessary to adopt some method of extending the detachments after "lifting dandies." The following method is suggested and explained in Fig. 5 of the illustrations.

Words of command—

(1.) "*In file from the right or from the left or centre extend.*"—The flank named stands fast. The detachment on the opposite flank immediately makes the necessary left or right turn, and moves on to the left (or right). The remaining detachments make the necessary turn one after the other, and move on in file, keeping one pace behind the detachment in front of them.

(2.) "*Advance—Halt.*"—When the instructor sees the whole thus moving in file, after the first word of command he gives the command "Advance." The dandies are thus brought round in the direction of the front, and *halted* whenever the change of direction is completed. If this has been done correctly it will be found that the dandy detachments are fully extended one pole's length from one another.

In order to close the company after extension the usual word of command, "On the right (left or centre)—close," is sufficient. The detachment named stands fast, the remainder turn towards it, No. 1 advancing his end as he comes up on the flank named, and No. 3 closing in to the proper position.

V.—*Removing and Replacing Covers and Poles.*

This is the special feature of the drill with Lushai dandies, as it is by means of removing the covers and poles that the drill for loading and unloading stretchers can be applied to the dandy.

The process of removing the covers and poles is therefore called "preparing dandies," and bearers stand to "prepared" dandies in the same way as they stand to stretchers carrying out the drill from that point exactly as they carry out stretcher drill.

A.—*Removing Cover and Poles.*

"*Prepare Dandies.*"— Before the word of command is given bearers should be in the position they are in after "lifting poles" (Fig. 1). On the word of command bearers act as follows :—

(1.) No. 1 and No. 2 right-about turn; No. 1 transferring the pole from the right to the left hand.

(2.) Nos. 2 and 4 stoop down and untie the strings that attach the corners of the cover frame to their ends of the dandy. Then rise and remove the straps that attach the cover frame to the pole, buckling them loosely round the end sticks of the frame.

(3.) No. 4 then seizes the cover frame at the centre and carries it to the rear, placing it evenly on the ground, about 1½ poles' length distant from the dandy, while No. 2 catches hold of the rear ring with his right hand.

No. 1 at the same time, without letting go the pole, keeps the front pole ring raised with his free hand.

(4.) No. 3 now draws the pole steadily away,—Nos. 1 and 4 assisting in passing it evenly through the rings, taking care, however, not to let the rings down until the pole is clear of them. No. 3 carries the pole to the rear, and places it on top of the cover while Nos. 1 and 2 lower the pole rings on to the ground.

(5.) All the bearers at once take position by the dandy as in "Standing to stretchers" (*see* Fig. 3 of illustrations, and for illustration at the intermediate stage of removing the cover, *see* Fig. 4).

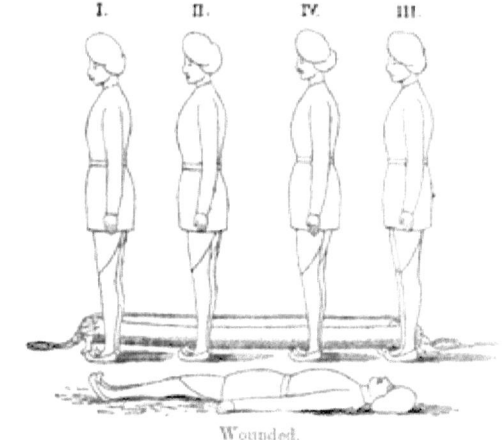

Fig. CXCI.

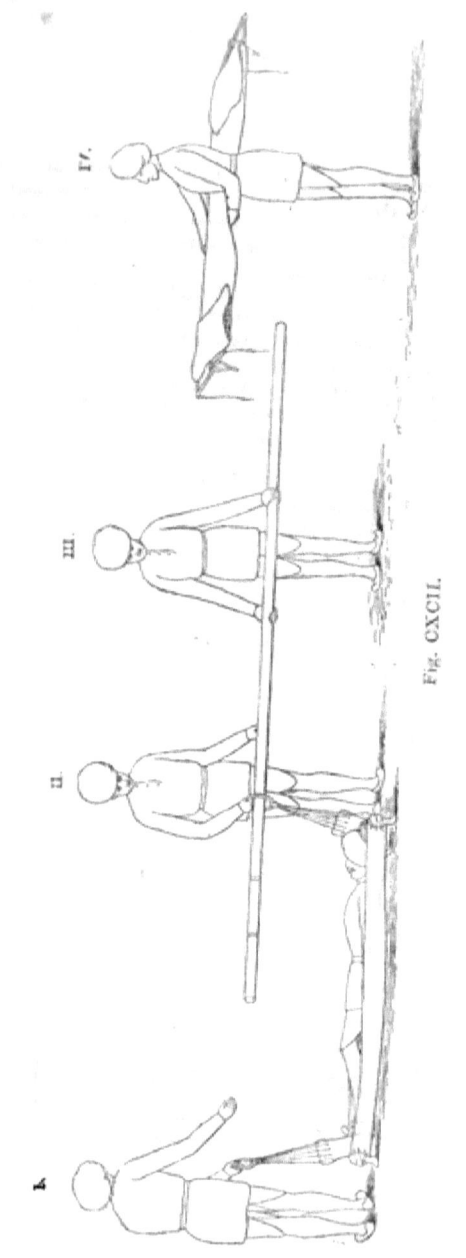

Fig. CXCII.

B.—*Replacing Covers and Poles.*

Word of command—
"*Fix Covers and Poles.*"—(This process is exactly the reverse of "Prepare dandies.") Bearers starting from the position of "Standing to stretchers," as in Fig. 3, act as follows:—

(1.) Nos. 3 and 4, right about turn and double up to the pole and cover, No. 3 going to the off side and No. 4 to the near. No. 2 doubles round the foot end of the dandy by a right about wheel, and raises the rear pole ring with the right hand. No. 1 turns inwards and raises the front pole ring with the left hand.

(2.) No. 3 carries the pole to the dandy, and assisted by **the free hands** of Nos. 2 and 1 passes it horizontally through the rings into its proper position. When it is in position, Nos. 1 and 3, holding it **at** full arm's length, stand to attention; No. 1, however, will remain turned to the rear, holding the pole with his left hand. It should be the duty of No. 1 and No. 4 to fix the pegs that keep the rings from slipping on the pole.

(3.) No. 4 will now place the cover evenly on the pole in position, and No. 2, having let go the pole ring, will resume his position at the front end of the cover, and proceed simultaneously with **No.** 4 at the rear end to fix the straps and corner strings.

(4.) When covers and poles are completely fixed all the bearers rise to attention, No. 2 facing the rear. Nos. 1 and 2 then front together by the left about, No. 1 making the left about turn, so as to transfer the pole from the left to the right hand. Bearers and dandy will then be as in Fig. 1.

APPENDIX III.

VI.—*Taking* **Post at** *Wounded and Loading and Unloading Dandies.*

These processes **are** carried out by the same words of command, and in exactly the same way as in the corresponding exercises with field stretchers (*see* Manual for the M.S. Corps, para. 339), with **the** addition only of "Prepare dandies" before loading or unloading, and "Fix covers and poles" **after** loading or unloading.

In taking post the body of **the** dandy should be halted alongside the patient on his left or right, according to the word of command. The words of command that follow will be: "Lower dandies," "Prepare dandies," "For loading, lift wounded," "Lower wounded," "Fix covers and poles," "Retire," &c.

VII.—*Carrying Dandies over Obstacles.*

A dandy can be carried **over a wall** or ditch on **the** same principles **as** a stretcher **is** carried over **them** (*see* Ante, p. 158, *et seq.*).

The dandy **is** halted **and lowered a** few paces from the obstacle. It is then "prepared" by word **of** command, and the prepared dandy lifted as a stretcher over **the obstacle.** Nos. 3 and 4 then double back, carry **the** pole and cover over, and "Fix **covers and poles**" is then carried **out** by all four **bearers** before lifting **and continuing the** march.

APPENDIX III.

VIII.—*Placing Dandies in Hospital Tents, &c., on the Line of March.*

At the end of a march, or at a rest stage, the dandy is lowered and "prepared." In order to carry the dandy into its place in the hospital tent bearers are ordered to "lift dandies." They then lift the prepared "dandies" as in crossing obstacles, and on the word "advance" carry it into its place in the tent and "lower" it by word of command. On resuming the march the dandy should be lifted and carried out of the tent in the same way, covers and poles fixed, dandies lifted, and the command "Advance" given.

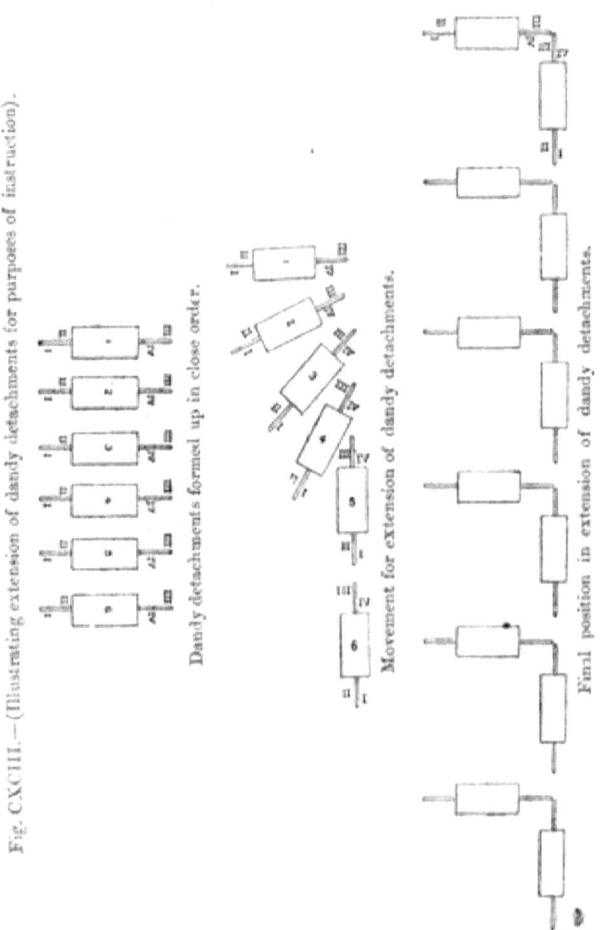

Fig. CXCIII.—(Illustrating extension of dandy detachments for purposes of instruction).

At rest stages the dandy should be first carried into a shady or sheltered place before being prepared. After "preparing dandies" thus the bearers are allowed to fall out and rest. If there is no shade or shelter, improvised methods must be adopted for keeping the pole and cover from collapsing on the patient before the bearers fall out.

IX.—*Placing Wounded from Stretchers or other Sick Transport on Dandies.*

The stretcher detachment in "taking post at the dandy" is ordered to halt a few paces in front of the dandy. After the stretcher is lowered the command "For loading—lift wounded" is given. The stretcher bearers then lift the wounded as in unloading from the stretchers, but No. 4 bearer, after drawing away the stretcher, doubles on to the dandy, which is already "prepared" by the dandy detachment, and places it under the patient.

On the command "Lower wounded" the patient is lowered on the dandy, and the stretcher-bearers then stand to their stretchers, while the dandy bearers take their place by the dandy. The stretcher detachment can be made to "lift stretchers and advance" again to the front, while the dandy detachment "fix covers and poles," "lift dandies," "Retire" to the dressing station or field hospital.

The same principles can be followed in unloading wounded from ambulance wagons, &c., and placing them on dandies.

In loading wounded from dandies into ambulance wagons, the dandies would be prepared, after taking post, and wounded loaded as if from stretchers (Manual M.S.C., para. 354).

APPENDIX IV.

Morris's Dandy Drill.

FIRST LESSON.

[It may be noted that, for the purposes of instruction, only the long bamboos of the dandies need be used.]

The dandies should be laid in a row, and the bearers told off to them; this, of course, corresponds to "sizing" in the Medical Staff Corps Drill. It is best to let the men size themselves, merely giving an order to "*stand to their dandies*." The equivalent of the word "attention" is "*kurra-rao*," and of "stand at ease" or "rest," is "*beito*." This, of course, is readily understood, and a few repetitions of this manœuvre makes them perfect in it.

The word "*kurra-rao*" having been given, the men having sized themselves and standing by the dandies (on the ground), the next word is "*dandy utao*," whereupon the men will stoop, pick up the dandy together, and place it on their shoulders, retaining the upright position, with all the dandies just touching one another at their sides. This manœuvre **must** be followed by **the** order "*dandy lagao*," whereupon the men are to place the dandies on the ground and return to the upright position,—then the Medical Officer will give the word "*beito*" and the men **will sit** comfortably by their dandies.

Exercise I.

English.	Vernacular.
(*a*.) Stand to your dandies.	(*a*.) Stand to your dandies.
(*b*.) Stand easy.	(*b*.) Beito.
(*c*.) Attention.	(*c*.) Kurra-rao.
(*d*.) Lift dandies.	(*d*.) Dandy utao.
(*e*.) Ground dandies.	(*e*.) Dandy lagao.
(*f*.) Rest.	(*f*.) Beito.

This will be sufficient **for the first day and little difficulty should be** anticipated so far.

SECOND LESSON.

Repeat **former** lesson. In this lesson the cahars are to be taught to face about **with** dandies, and to advance and retire in close order. The practical **value** of this lesson is not **so** much, **as** its utility in preserving a continuity of method in the instruction.

"*Kurra-rao*" having been given followed by "*dandy-utao*," in order to face the cahars about, the word "*ghumn-jao*" is given, whereupon the **men are** to be instructed to merely change the shoulders, and **to** face in the opposite direction: the word "*front*" must next be given to bring **them** back again. Then give the word "*dandy lagao*" and "*beito*" and another exercise is finished.

APPENDIX IV.

Exercise II.

English.	Vernacular.
(*a.*) Attention.	(*a.*) Kurra-rao.
(*b.*) Lift dandies.	(*b.*) Dandy utao.
(*c.*) Right-about-turn.	(*c.*) Ghúmn-jao.
(*d.*) Front.	(*d.*) Front.
(*e.*) Ground dandies.	(*e.*) Dandy **lagao**.
(*f.*) Rest.	(*f.*) Beito.

The expression "*front*" may seem curious, but it is most useful, and strikes the attention better than any other word that would suit the purpose.

To march the men with dandies is also very simple,—giving the words "*kurra-rao*" and "*dandy utao*," followed by "*challao*" or "*march;*" at this stage they should be taught to march in line and then halted. They may be taught also at this stage if there is time "*right and left form.*"

Exercise III.

English.	Vernacular.
(*a.*) Attention.	(*a.*) Kurra-rao.
(*b.*) Lift dandies.	(*b.*) Dandy-utao.
(*c.*) March.	(*c.*) March.
(*d.*) Halt.	(*d.*) Halt.
(*e.*) Right-about-turn.	(*e.*) Ghúmn-jao.
(*f.*) March.	(*f.*) March.
(*g.*) Halt.	(*g.*) Halt.
(*h.*) Front.	(*h.*) Front.
(*i.*) Ground dandies.	(*i.*) Dandy lagao.
(*k.*) Rest.	(*k.*) Beito.

If forming is taught, the marching may be varied accordingly. Before this exercise is complete, it should be done perfectly at the double.

THIRD LESSON.

This is rather more difficult, and consists of teaching men *to extend* with dandies from close order, from any flank or file. A file is meant four men deep, or one dandy detachment.

Number off from right to left the front rank men only. To do this it is best to number them slowly, and repeat the exercise often. Though simple, it is extraordinary how long the men will take **to** learn it. **As far as possible, the** same men should always occupy **the same file.**

APPENDIX IV.

Fig. 1. 1. 2. 3. 4. 5. 6. 7.

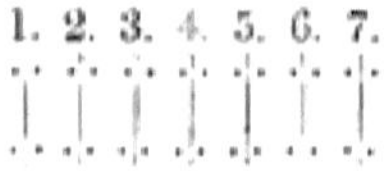

Fig. 2. 1. 2. 3. 4. 5. 6. 7.

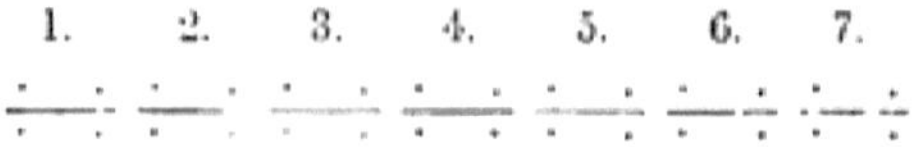

Fig. 3. 1. 2. 3. 4. 5. 6. 7.

The men being formed in close order as in Fig. 1, the word is given.

(a) From the right (*dyne*) or left (*byne*) extend, and the position of Fig. 2 will be obtained.

(b) "*Front*" turn, or "*rear*" turn, will turn them as in Fig. 3.

In addition to this, the converse must be taught.

(a) On the right or left—close.

These are about the most useful exercises a Bearer Company can learn, and when once learnt, is then appreciated.

The interval between any file may be as much or as little as possible.

EXERCISE IV.

English.	Vernacular.
(a.) Attention.	(a.) Kurra-rao.
(b.) Lift dandies.	(b.) Dandy-utao.
(c.) Number.	(c.) Number.
(d.) From *right*, or *left* or *centre*—extend.	(d.) From *right*, or *left*, or *centre*—extend.
(e.) Front turn.	(e.) Front turn.
(f.) March.	(f.) March (in extended order).
(g.) Halt.	(g.) Halt.
(h.) Right-about-turn.	(h.) Ghúmn-jao.
(i.) March.	(i.) March.
(j.) Halt.	(j.) Halt.
(k.) Front.	(k.) Front.
(l.) Ground dandies.	(l.) Dandy-lagao.
(m.) Rest.	(m.) **Beito.**

EXERCISE V.

English.	Vernacular.
(a.) Attention.	(a.) Kurra-rao.
(b.) Lift dandies.	(b.) Dandy-utao.
(c.) From *right*, or *left*, or *centre*—extend.	(c.) From *right*, or *left*, or *centre*—extend.
(d.) On *right*, or *left*, or *centre*—close.	(d.) On *right*, or *left*, or *centre*—close.
(e.) Ground dandies.	(e.) Dandy-lagao.
(f.) Rest.	(f.) Beito.

Advancing in extended order may be varied accordingly **at the** discretion of the Commanding Officer. Advance—right incline **(half right)** right incline (half right), thus bringing the dandies **into** file, as in Fig. 2. The same can, of course, be done on any flank.

FOURTH LESSON.

This very important part of the instruction can be easily taught, and becomes quite progressively the substance of this lesson. For the purpose of an exercise, the following should be carried out :—

A dressing station being formed, the Bearer Company may be divided into half companies and sections, each section being under the **command** of an apothecary, and the whole under a medical officer; some men should be sent away in a certain direction and ordered to lie down and keep as much out of sight as possible. The sections or half companies are then ordered to take ground to right and left of the dressing station, at 250 to 300 yards interval or more if necessary. Then each section shall proceed as follows :—Those sections on the left front of dressing station shall extend from the right-hand man, and those on right from the left-hand man. The effect of this movement will be that a large amount of ground **will be** covered, all having touch with the dressing station. To **advance or** retire this line, in **the** absence of bugle sounds and **so forth, the best plan is for** the warrant officers in charge of sections **to** watch **the movements** of the medical officer ; if he rides slowly forward, they **should advance;** if he turns round, they should retire ; if he halts and **raises his hand,** they should halt. This is most simple, and is readily **learnt.** Advancing the company to the neighbourhood of the wounded **to** be searched for, at a sign from the medical officer to the apothecary next **to** him, all the dandies shall be placed on the ground. The commanders of sections will then order two men from each dandy to go forward, and they will see that the ground is successfully searched. A water-carrier and a ward-servant should accompany each commander of a section to administer temporary relief, which may not have been obtainable before. On finding **a man,** the bearer will signal to his dandy, and the two remaining in **charge** will take the dandy out and lift the wounded man into it, with every precaution as far as possible, under the superintendence of a warrant officer or available officer. They will at once return to the dressing station with all despatch, where they will be relieved and ordered back to their section.

Exercise VI.

English.	Vernacular.
(a.) Attention.	(a.) Kurra-rao.
(b.) Lift dandies.	(b.) Dandy-utao.

(c.) Commanders of sections will take ground to right **and left of dressing** station, and prepare to search for wounded.

Commanders will give the folllwing orders **for the purpose of exercise, having** taken up their ground as ordered :—

(a.) No. 1 from right 30 paces extend.
(b.) **Right turn, or form.**

APPENDIX IV.

(c.) March (taking his movement from movements of the medical officer).
(d.) Halt—(ditto).
(e.) Search for wounded. **Two men** to remain with each dandy.

This last movement would probably take some **time, but for the** purposes **of** exercise, the distance to the dressing station should be made short, and when all the sick have been carried in and the bearers and their dandies have returned to their respective sections, the exercise may be completed as follows:—

(f.) On the right—close.
(g.) Right-about-turn.
(h.) March.

Then take them back to the dressing station, where they will be dismissed in the usual way.

At the dressing station men of the Army Hospital Native Corps should be instructed in dressing. All the dandies with sick, when brought in, should be placed in a line, and care taken that there is an interval between each dandy sufficient for the surgeon and dresser to get at the patient.

APPENDIX V.

TORTOISE AMBULANCE TENT EXERCISE.

To pitch Tortoise Tent, with poles in box at front of wagon, and with pegs in box at side of wagon.

1 non-commissioned Officer and 8 men.

```
                                              Rear.
                                             ⌒⌒⌒
Odd numbers take post and work throughout on near side   2 4 6 8
Even      ,,         ,,        ,,         ,,  off  ,,    1 3 5 7
                                             ⌣⌣⌣
                                              Front.
```

A.

Nos.
1 and 2. Undo traces; remove horses and pole; get out curtain poles, put halves together, and lay poles under front of wagon.
3 and 4. Facing the rear, get out pegs and mallets, hand them to 5 and 6.
5 and 6. Distribute pegs and mallets each side, and each end.
7. Get into wagon and hand out latrine tent, &c.
8. **Get** out 4 window glasses and hand to **non-commissioned** Officer.

B.

1 and 2. Jump up in front, drop curtain (and lace **to** side).
3 ,, 5. ⎧ Unbuckle from the raves and drop side curtains and
4 ,, 6. ⎩ open out the flaps.
7 ,, 8. Jump up and drop rear curtain (and lace to sides).
3 ,, 4. Put in front and off side windows to roof (and help 1 **and** 2 with lacing).
5 ,, 6. **Put** in rear and near side windows to roof (and help 7 and 8 with lacing).
3 ,, 4. ⎧ Drive peg for runner in straight line with seam at **edge**
5 ,, 6. ⎩ of wagon roof.
5 ,, 6. ⎧
3 ,, 4. ⎩ Proceed with other pegs till all are driven in.

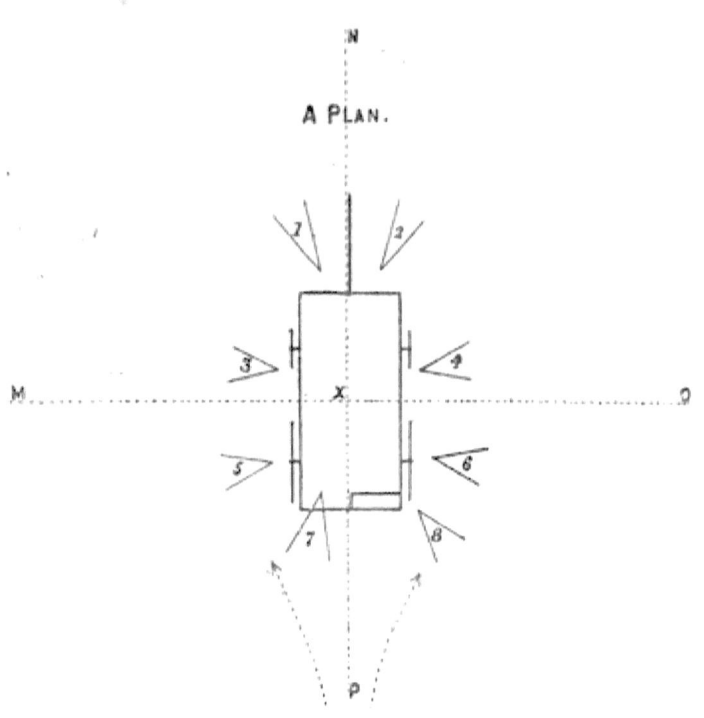

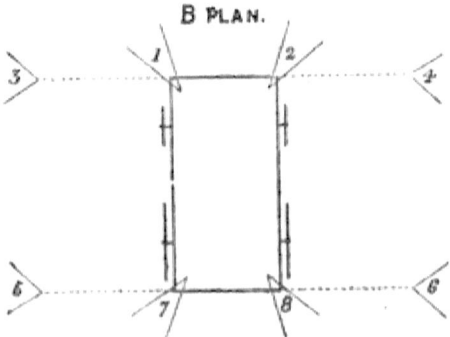

C.

Nos.
7 and 8. Get inside and place curtain poles:—(a) Where runners **are held** out by 3, 4, 5, and 6; (b) At the corners, (c) Remaining poles in the order shown in diagram.

1 „ 2. { Hold out front end while **7 and 8** place **the poles**, and direct dressing of poles at each side.

3 „ 4.
5 „ 6. { Unbend and pull out runner of curtain, in line with edge of wagon roof and hold it out until the pole is placed, then fix runner to peg.

3 „ 4. Assisted by 1 and 2, drive top corner runner pegs.
5 „ 6. Assisted by 7 and 8 (inside), drive rear corner pegs, place windows in front, sides, and rear, and join 7 and 8 in tent.

7 „ 8. Prepare inside of tent, **stretchers**, &c., **assisted by** 5 and 6.

1 „ 2.
3 „ 4. { Finish runner and curtain pegs.

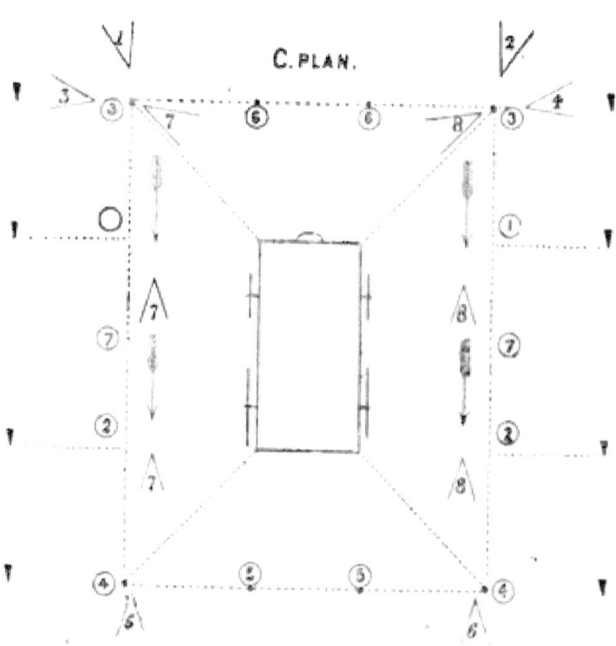

C. PLAN.

To strike Tortoise Tent. Reversing previous work.

A.

7 and 8.
5 „ 6. } Pack up and put **away stretchers**, &c.

Nos.

3 „ 4. ⎧ Slip **off curtain** loops; **loose** runners, but do not
1 „ 2. ⎨ remove from pegs until poles are collected inside;
        ⎩ collect window glasses and hand to Non-commissioned Officer.

1 „ 2. Fasten up door curtain.

B.

7 and 8. Remove poles from rear to front (unlace rear corners and ends).
5 „ 6. (Lace door).
1 „ 2. (Unlace front corners and ends).
3 „ 4. ⎧ Slip and bend up runners; fold in and buckle side
5 „ 6. ⎨ flaps; remove window glasses and hand to Non-
        ⎩ commissioned Officer.

C.

3, 1, 2, 4. Roll up front curtain.
5, 7, 8, 6. „ near „
1, 3, 5, 7. Then fold up near side.
2, 4, 6, 8. „ off „

D.

1 and 2. Separate **poles**; put **them** away; put **up pole and attach horses**.
7. Put away tent, stores, &c. in wagon.
8. Put away window glasses.
3 and 4. ⎧ Pull **out**, and put away the pegs
5 „ 6.   ⎩

To pitch the tent with wagon removed.

The tent, except the front end, must be pitched as described, but the runners must be left quite loose all round. The carriage pole should not be removed. The front end of **the** tent should be unlaced **up** to the roof of the wagon, and the **sides** then thrown back, leaving the front **clear** for the wagon to run out. The men take post:—

1. At the carriage pole ready to "near" or to "**off lock**."
2. Mounts front of wagon and sets the ridge **pole free**.
3 and 4. At the front wheels **ready** to **move the wagon.**
5 „ 6. „ rear „ „ „
7. Mounts tail of wagon and sets the ridge pole **free**.
8. Takes **rear** upright pole to receive rear end **of** ridge pole.

The wagon is slowly drawn forward until the rear of the ridge pole is sufficiently clear to be placed upon the upright by Nos. 7 and 8. The wagon is steadily drawn forward, No. 7 dismounts, and, assisted by No. 1, places the front upright under the front **end** of the ridge pole. The wagon being drawn just clear of this pole, Nos. **1 and 2 can** mount and drop the curtain (and lace **it if** not laced). **The wagon** is taken clear of the tent. The front end is pitched, and **the tent** completed.

In the new pattern tents the windows are put in the roof from inside, and can therefore be placed after the tent is pitched. In tents which are laced at right angles to the sides and ends of the wagon (A plan, lines N P and M O), the poles in line with these seams are placed first, and then the corner and remaining poles are put in position.

Note.—This is merely a scheme of drill, apportioning the work. An intelligent N.C.O. can easily modify it to suit the pattern tent or wagon he has to deal with. The directions as to lacing are put in brackets because this will generally be omitted. The tent is intended to be kept laced except when removing the wagon.

INDEX.

Abolition of regimental hospitals ; 39.
Adjustment of slings by bearers ; 164.
Algeria, French cacolet mules in ; 226.
Ambulance barrows; 188.
—— definition of ; 2.
—— carriages, transport ; 251.
—— —— adjustment of springs to weight carried ; 260.
—— —— attendants ; 265.
—— —— capacity proportioned to draught power ; 254.
—— —— carriage of medical comforts on ; 259.
—— —— double roof for hot climates ; 307.
—— —— ease of access to patients ; 264.
—— —— horses suitable for draught of 257.
—— —— injurious effects of overweight ; 270.
—— —— kits of wounded ; 265.
—— —— loading and unloading ; 264.
—— —— means of light ; 263.
—— —— need of portability ; 262.
—— —— patients carried sitting up ; 261.
—— —— patients carried recumbent ; 261.
—— —— pole system ; 271.
—— —— positions of patients ; 261.
—— —— protection against weather 263.
—— —— relative merits of 2-wheeled and 4-wheeled ; 268.
—— —— repairs on field service ; 262.
—— —— risks when loading ; 264.
—— —— seat for attendant ; 265.
—— —— shaft system ; 271.
—— —— stowage on board ship ; 262.
—— —— surgical stores carried in ; 263.
—— —— two leading forms ; 266.
—— —— variations in capacity ; 269.
—— —— classification of ; 272.
—— carts, transport, equilibrium ; 266.
—— —— British, Mark II. ; 283.
—— —— field, Cherry's ; 279.
—— —— hospital conveyance, Guthrie's ; 274.
—— —— ambulance, Larrey's ; 272.
—— carriages, La Voiture Macou ; 274.
—— —— Madras, Macpherson's ; 278.

Ambulance carriages, Maltese ; 282.
—— —— Indian tonga ; 285.
—— —— military field, Tufnel' ; 275.
—— corps, United States ; 10.
—— misuse of term ; 2, 58.
—— stretchers ; 153.
—— system, British, history of ; 28.
—— —— Baron Percy's ; 24.
—— —— Baron Larrey's ; 21.
—— transport launches ; 409.
—— —— railway ; 347.
—— —— steamers; 390.
—— trains of the Knights of Malta 415.
—— vehicles, regimental ; 256.
—— wagon-stretchers, British ; 312.
—— —— British, Mark I. and II. ; 310.
—— —— —— Mark III. ; 313.
—— —— —— Mark IV. ; 315.
—— —— —— Mark V. ; 316.
—— —— the Cairo ; 320.
—— —— Francis's ; 308.
—— —— French Red Cross ; 300.
—— —— Furley's ; 318, 319.
—— —— Howard's ; 321.
—— —— Lecati's ; 291.
—— —— Löhner's ; 298.
—— —— Macpherson's ; 306.
—— —— Baron Mundy's ; 296.
—— —— Neuss's ; 302.
—— —— New Zealand ; 304.
—— —— Rücker ; 289.
—— —— Tortoise ; 323.
—— —— "Wheeling," or Rosencrans ; 288.
Amoo, or New Zealand litter ; 141.
Apothecaries to the forces ; 39.
Apparatus for carriage en cheval ; 103.
—— —— trials of ; 104.
Appliances to aid wounded in walking ; 100.
Apron, Landa's ; 140.
—— trials of ; 141.
Arab mode of carrying off wounded ; 224.
Araba, Turkish ; 337.
—— —— resembles Indian hackery ; 338.
—— —— use in the Crimea ; 337.
Armies, estimates of transport for ; 78.
—— on active service, casualties in ; 88.
—— volunteer aid with ; 12.

Army, Austrian, ambulance transport system; 48.
—— —— bandage carriers; 49.
—— —— bearer detachments; 49.
—— British, ambulance transport system; 28.
—— Danish, ambulance transport system; 52.
—— French, ambulance transport system; 44.
—— German, ambulance transport system; 45.
—— Hospital Corps; 36.
—— medical department; 39.
—— —— reserve; 41.
—— Russian, ambulance transport system; 50.
Ashanti, cot; 119.
—— —— Director-General Sir W. A. Mackinnon's opinion of; 119.
—— hammock; 120.
Austrian ambulance trains of the Knights of Malta; 415.
—— railway ambulance system; 389.

Bandy, Burmese; 340.
—— Indian; 338.
Bareilly dandy; 124.
Barrow, China ambulance; 188.
Barrows, ordnance ambulance; 188.
Battle, ambulance transport on occasion of; 4.
Battles, care of wounded prisoners; 9.
—— deficiency of bearers in; 7.
—— proportions of killed and wounded in; 91.
—— proportions of those dangerously wounded; 98.
—— —— —— severely wounded; 98.
—— —— slightly wounded; 98.
—— returns of wounded; 91.
—— wounded left by vanquished army after; 80.
Battlefields, collection of wounded from; 80.
—— old methods of removing wounded; 5.
—— proposed aid by volunteers; 12.
—— transport of wounded from; 81.
—— wounded able to walk unaided for assistance; 99.
Bearer Companies; 7.
—— —— effects of Lord Morley's Committee; 79.
—— —— distribution of on service, in the English Army; 82.
—— —— the first, in the English army; 81.
—— —— Germans, annual instruction of; 47.
—— —— mobilization of; 83.
—— —— mounted; 84.
—— —— organization of; 81.
—— —— personnel of; 82.
—— carrying a wounded man pick-a-back; 102.

Bearer detachments of Austrian army; 48.
—— physical conditions of; 83.
—— single carriage of wounded man by; 103.
Bearers, analysis of work done by; 150.
—— ambulance, Indian; 144.
—— carriage by two; 106.
—— —— —— patient semi-recumbent; 95.
—— —— —— patient recumbent; 93.
—— ambulance, Indian cooly; 149.
—— deficiency of; 7.
—— dandy; 144.
—— dooly; 144.
—— dooly, districts where found; 145.
—— Eastern, stretchers unsuitable for; 155.
—— ambulance, Indian, entertainment of; 149.
—— Indian ambulance, experience of, in Afghanistan; 128.
—— Indian ambulance, experience of in Burma; 128.
—— four-handed seat formed by; 109.
—— how weights are most easily borne by; 161.
—— length and kind of step suited for; 108.
—— misapplication of term; 112.
—— not to carry stretchers on their shoulders; 183.
—— to break step; 180.
—— ambulance Indian, standard required; 149.
—— three-handed seat formed by; 107.
—— ambulance Indian, temporary; 149.
—— trained, special need of in modern warfare; 70.
—— work performed by; 150.
Beaufort's springs for country carts; 334.
—— stretcher; 167.
—— system, railway ambulance transport; 377.
—— stretcher rests; 336.
Bengal and Madras bearers compared; 145.
—— doolie; 146.
Berlin railway ambulance system; 360.
Brett's camel kujawahs; 206.
Borny, battle of; 88.
British ambulance system, history of; 28.
—— ambulance wagon stretcher; 312.
—— —— —— —— Marks I. and II.; 310.
—— —— —— —— Mark III.; 313.
—— —— —— —— Mark IV.; 315.
—— —— —— —— Mark V.; 316.
—— Legion in Spain, Cherry's carts with; 280.
—— field-stretchers; 169.
—— regulation stretcher, Marks III. and IV.; 172.
Bry-Annelise railway ambulance system; 377.

INDEX. 447

Blanket stretcher; 143.
Boulonnie's railway ambulance system; 389.

Cacolets, British, construction of; 229.
—— French; 230.
—— Italian; 233.
—— mule, origin of; 225.
—— to reverse; 229.
Camel, the Bactrian; 200.
—— cacolets in the Soudan; 208.
—— crates, Mosley's; 210.
—— —— —— advantages claimed by inventor; 215.
—— —— —— avoidance of side leverage; 216.
—— —— —— construction of; 211.
—— —— —— general conclusions concerning; 217.
—— —— —— girthing; 214.
—— —— —— for lying down; 211.
—— —— —— for sitting up; 213.
Camels, conveyances borne by; 200.
—— different modes of movement; 201.
—— fitness of, for carrying sick; 202.
Camperdown's, the Earl of, Commission; 90.
Cape of Good **Hope**. Ambulance wagon; 341.
Captains and lieutenants of orderlies; 39.
Carriage of stretchers, rules for; 179.
—— of wounded on saddles; 228.
Carriages, railway, effects of collisions; 349.
Cart, British ambulance, Mark II; 283.
—— field, Cherry's; 279.
—— flying ambulance, Larrey's; 272.
—— Indian tonga; 285.
—— Macon; 274.
—— Madras, Macpherson's; 278.
—— military field, Tufnell's; 275.
—— Maltese; 282.
Carts, ambulance, compared with wagons; 266.
Casualties, proportions of, in battle; 98.
Chair, Mowll's ambulance; 400.
—— Singleton's ambulance; 407.
Cherry's cart; 279.
China ambulance barrow; 188.
Classification of conveyances; 112.
—— of ships; 390.
—— of wounded; 98.
Construction of ambulance material; 15.
—— —— —— the surgeon's share in; 16.
Convention of Geneva; 56.
Conveyance carts, hospital; 275.
—— corps, hospital, failure of; 33.
Conveyances borne by camels; 200.
—— —— by men, subdivision of; 112.
—— —— by mules and horses; 218.
—— classification of; 112.
—— drawn by animals; 251.
—— —— —— —— accommodation of; 261.

Conveyances drawn by animals, aëration of; 263.
—— —— —— —— capacity of; 261.
—— —— —— —— draught of; 261.
—— —— —— —— elasticity of; 260.
—— —— —— —— history of; 252.
—— —— —— —— ingress and egress; 264.
—— —— —— —— means of communication; 264.
—— —— —— —— portability of; 262.
—— —— —— —— protection of; 263.
—— —— —— —— repairs; 262.
—— —— —— —— requisite qualities; 258.
—— —— —— —— stowage **of kits and** arms; 265.
—— —— —— —— strength of; 262.
—— —— —— —— surgical requisites; 263.
—— models of; 157.
—— railway; 347.
Collis dandy; 131.
—— —— construction of; 131.
—— —— cover forms tent for bearers; 132.
—— —— directions to put together; 133.
—— —— measurements and weight; 133.
Cot, Ashanti; 119.
—— sailor's, fitted to Furley's under litter; 195.
Crimean war, transport **system; 31**.

Dandy, Bareilly; 124.
—— Collis; 131.
—— Himalayan; 122.
—— Leake's; 129.
—— Lushai; 126.
—— Macpherson's; 134.
—— McCosh's; 123.
—— position of person carried in; 26.
Deficiency, examples of ill-results from, of ambulance transport consequences of; 6.
Definition of ambulance; 2.
Dooly-bearers; 145.
—— of India; 147.
Dooly, derivation of; 145.
—— Francis' improved; 151.
—— Porter's Indian bill; 152.
Doolys, Bengal sanitary commission on; 148.
—— essential in India; 148.
—— in China war of 1860; 155.
—— method of carrying; 146.
—— Sir H. Rose's opinion of; 148.
—— Sir W. Mansfield's opinion of; 148.
—— their useful qualities; 146.
—— universal praise of; 147.
—— why essential in India; 148.
Directions for the proper carriage of stretchers; 179.
—— for the proper use of mule conveyances; 240.

INDEX.

Directions for medical officer in charge of railway ambulance train; 368.
Draught horses, English, work done by; 258.
—— —— influence of speed on work done by; 258.
Drill, St. John Ambulance Association; 425.
—— Macpherson's dandy; 429.
—— Morris's dandy; 438.
—— Tortoise wagon tent; 443.
Drivers, training of; 269.
Driving from box, compared with riding and driving; 267.
—— with reins, training for; 267.

East-Indian mules; 222.
Elephant ambulance transport; 199.
—— —— —— objections to; 199.
—— —— —— carriage by pads; 200.
—— —— —— by howdahs; 200.
—— —— —— by charjamahs; 200.
—— the health of; 200.
Equipment for ambulance trains; 413.
Equirotal system; 315.
Esmarch's braces for hæmorrhage; 101.
—— crutches; 100.
—— —— their practical utility questioned; 101.
Evans's hand-wheeled litter; **187**.

Field equipment, risks exposed **to**; 156.
—— **stretcher,** British regulation; 172.
—— **stretchers,** Percy's views upon; 164.
—— surgeons, their duties in connection with ambulance transport; 17.
Fischer's apparatus; 103.
—— railway ambulance system; 387.
Francis' dooley; 151.
—— proposed Indian wagon; 308.
French ambulance transport system; **44.**
—— **army** regulation stretcher; 166.
—— **views** regarding mule conveyances; 226.
Furley's Cairo wagon; 320.
—— civil stretcher with telescopic handles; 176.
—— —— —— —— its advan**tages**; 176.
—— —— —— —— its construction; 176.
—— " Lowmoor" jacket; 177.
—— military stretcher; 174.
—— —— weight of; 175.
—— —— its construction; 174.
—— stretcher for police purposes; 177.
—— —— rests; 336.
—— trestles; 162.
—— ambulance wagon; 318, 319.
Furse on the importance of spreading the wounded; 348.

Galton's temporary stretcher; 144.
Gauvin's hand-wheeled litter; 190.
General observations on civil stretchers; 175.
Geneva, Convention **of, and its** badge, the Red Cross; 56.
—— —— —— abuses of; 59.
—— —— —— aim and general organi**zation** of; 70.
—— —— —— ignorance regarding, **very great**; 58.
—— —— —— in Austria and Hun**gary**; 64.
—— —— —— in France; 63.
—— —— —— in Germany; 64.
—— —— —— instituted for one reason only; 56.
—— —— —— **instances** of the abuses; 60.
—— —— —— international relations; 71.
—— —— —— steps by governments concerned, urgently required to suppress abuse; 61.
—— —— —— supplements the regular medical service; 58.
—— —— —— the sign of the Red Cross; 56.
—— —— —— the sign of the Red Crescent; 65.
—— —— —— the Red Cross of, wrongfully used; 60.
—— —— —— volunteer ambulance societies are strictly under military discipline; 58.
Geneva, Convention of, work of national societies of, in time of peace; 71.
—— —— —— —— of war; 74.
Gorgas marine ambulance lift; 395.
Gravelotte, the battle of; 88.
Great-coat stretcher; 143.
Gründ railway ambulance system; 383.
—— —— —— action of; 384.
—— —— —— construction 383.
—— —— —— Richter's modification of; 384.
Guthrie's ambulance cart; 275.

Hackery, four-wheeled; 338.
—— Indian; 339.
Hamburg railway ambulance system; 385.
Hammock, derivation of; 114.
—— officer's sash as a; 115.
Hammocks, Ashanti; 120.
—— position of person carried in; 118.
—— in railway carriages; 358.
—— Mexican twine; 120.
—— sailor's; 117.
—— soldier's, blanket used as a; 116.
—— suspended from poles; 117.
—— unsuited for certain kinds of wounds; 116.
Hand-wheeled litters; 187.
—— —— —— Baron Mundy's; 191.

INDEX. 449

Hand-wheeled litters, Bautzen's (barrows); 187.
———— ———— China ambulance (barrows); 188.
———— ———— ———— British army; 194.
———— ———— conclusions on; 197.
———— ———— ———— Evans's; 187.
———— ———— ———— Gauvin's; 190.
———— ———— ———— general observations on; 185.
———— ———— ———— Macdermott's (wheeled carrier); 189.
———— ———— ———— Neuss's; 192.
———— ———— ———— Neuss-Manley's; 194.
———— ———— ———— objects aimed at by their use; 185.
———— ———— ———— the Ashford; 196.
Hill conveyances of India; 122.
Hill's hayband stretcher; 144.
———— two-mule litter; 241.
Himalayan dandy; 122.
———— ———— its construction; **123.**
———— ———— McCosh's improved; 123.
Horses best suited for carrying sick; 222.
———— conveyances borne by; 223.
———— mules preferable for ambulance transport; 218.
———— suitable for draught of ambulance carriages; 257.
Hospital cart, Madras; 278.
———— conveyance carts, Guthrie's; 275.
———— conveyance corps; 31.
———— ———— ———— failure of; **33.**
———— ———— ———— why unsuccessful; 33.
———— ———— ———— vehicles with; 32.
———— Corps, Army; 36.
———— ———— ———— functions of; 37.
———— ———— ———— organization of; 37.
———— ships; 390.
Howard's ambulance wagon for civil purposes; 321.

India, dooleys or dandies essential in; 148.
———— hill conveyances; 122.
Indian railway ambulance transport in; **372.**
———— transport of invalids from; 372.
Indian ambulance wagons, essential qualities of; 309.
———— camel conveyances; **203.**
———— cart or bandy; 338.
———— dooley-bearers; 145.
———— hackery; 339.
India-rubber springs; 260.
———— ———— objections to; 261.
Inventors, mistakes made by; 156.
Italian war, railway transport in; 350.

Jaunting-cars for ambulance transport, defects of; 277.
Jhampans; 120.
———— system applied to stretchers; 125.

Kujawahs, camel; 203.
———— ———— Brett's; 206.
———— for patients sitting; 206.
———— Punjab; 204.
Knots for marine ambulance transport **purposes;** 394.

Landa's apron; 140.
———— ———— trials of; 141.
Launches, ambulance transport; 409.
Larrey's ambulance volante; 22.
———— ———— system; 23.
———— ———— ———— origin **of; 22.**
———— ambulance wagon; **287.**
Leake's dandy; 129.
———— ———— construction of; 130.
———— ———— peculiar mode of suspension of; 130.
———— ———— weight of; 131.
Letterman on the duties of medical officers; 18.
Leu stretcher rests for **railway ambulance transport;** 378.
Lift, Macdonald's; 398.
———— and Stretcher, Macdonald's; 403.
Line of march, ambulance transport on; **3.**
Litter, camel, Larrey's; 202.
———— Evans's hand-wheeled; 187.
———— Gauvin's; 190.
———— Hill's two-mule; 241.
———— Mule, British Mark III.; 235.
———— ———— French; 236.
———— ———— Furley's folding; 175.
———— ———— in British service; 236.
———— ———— Italian sitting; 241.
———— ———— Locati's; 243.
———— New Zealand; 141.
———— mule, peculiar motion of; 235.
———— ———— Shortell's modification of English pattern; 242.
———— ———— sleigh (travois); 250.
———— ———— to place patients on; 239.
———— ———— to prevent swaying; 238.
———— ———— to secure patients in; 238.
———— ———— United States; 247.
———— ———— Woodcock's; 246.
———— ———— weight of; 236.
Loads carried by mules, analyses of; 221.
———— ———— ———— ———— regulation limits; 221.
———— ———— ———— ———— weights of; 221.
Locati's ambulance transport wagon; 294.
———— single litter mule carriage; 245.
Looped blanket; 117.
Lorraine wagon; 336.
Lowmoor jacket; 177.
Lowerer, Macdonald's; 399.
Lushai dandy; 126.
———— ———— advantages of; 127.
———— ———— Bengal pattern; 127.
———— ———— construction of; 126.
———— ———— disadvantages of; 128.
———— ———— Madras pattern; 127.

Lushai dandy, number of bearers required for; 128.
—— —— weight of; 127.

Macou cart; 274.
Macdonald's ambulance lift; **398.**
—— —— lowerer; 399.
—— —— stretcher and lift combined; 403.
Macpherson's Indian wagon; 306.
—— —— stretcher dandy; 134.
—— —— —— advantages of; 137.
—— —— —— construction of; 135.
—— —— —— weight of; 138.
Maltese cart; 282.
Mandil de Socorro; 140.
Marine ambulance transport; **390.**
Mars le Tour, battle of; 88.
McCosh's Himalayan dandy; 123.
Medical Staff Corps, the first; 35.
—— —— —— its disbandment; 36.
—— —— —— functions of; 37.
—— —— —— organisation of; 40.
—— —— the present; 40.
—— —— —— organisation of; 40.
—— —— —— training of; 41.
Mexican twine hammocks; 120.
Military field cart, Tufnell's; 275.
Militia Medical Staff Corps; 41.
Models of conveyances, very deceptive; 157.
—— and patterns compared; 158.
Morache's railway ambulance system; 377.
Mowll's folding ambulance chair; **400.**
Mule cacolets; 225.
—— —— origin of; 225.
—— conductors; 227.
—— conveyance, Locati's single litter; 245.
—— conveyances, rules for proper use of; 240.
—— litter, British Mark III.; 229.
—— —— French; 236.
—— —— Italian sitting; 241.
—— —— Locati's; 243.
—— —— Shortell's modification; 242.
—— —— sleigh (travois); 250.
—— —— two-horse; 248.
—— —— United States; 247.
—— —— Woodcock's; 246.
—— litters, carriage of patients in; 235.
—— —— construction of, in the British service; 226.
—— —— peculiar motion of; 238.
Mule litters, to balance; 238.
—— —— to place patients on; 240.
—— —— to prevent swaying; 238.
—— —— to secure patients in; 238.
—— —— weight of; 236.
—— panniers; 247.
Mules and their drivers require training; 228.
—— analysis of loads carried by; 221.
—— Arab mode of removing wounded on; 224.

Mules, conveyances borne by; 218.
—— East Indian; 222.
—— fitness for carrying wounded; 219.
—— preferable to horses for ambulance transport; 218.
Muncheels, defects of; 153.
Mundy's ambulance transport wagon; 296.
—— hand-wheeled litters; 191.

Netley railway ambulance carriages; 375.
Neuss's ambulance wagon; 302.
—— hand-wheeled litter; 192.
—— Manley ditto; 194.
New Zealand amoo; 141.
—— —— ambulance wagon; 304.

Officer's sash, former use of; 115.
Omnibuses, Furley's mode of arrangement; 335.
Omnibuses, used for ambulance purposes; 334.
Ordnance, ambulance barrows; 188.
—— of Percy's corps of stretcher bearers; 27.
—— of Volunteer Medical Staff Corps; 42.

Palki; 152.
Paris, railway ambulance transport, experiment at; 361.
Passenger carriages; 355.
—— —— accommodation in England for ambulance purposes at the present time; 374.
—— —— generally considered; 356.
Peninsular spring wagon; 310.
—— war, transport during; 30.
—— —— —— of wounded on pack saddles; 223.
Peltzer's tables of the numbers transported by the Nancy line in the Franco-German war; 354.
—— railway ambulance; 376.
Percy's ambulance system; 24.
—— —— compared with Larrey's; 26.
—— —— distinguishing features **of**; 26.
—— —— mode of action in the **field**; 25.
—— —— objects of; 25.
—— —— vehicles, peculiarity of; 25.
—— *brancardiers* or stretcher carriers; 27.
—— corps of stretcher carriers, organisation of; 27.
Percy equipment of bearers; 27.
Personnel of English bearer company; 82.
Positions of wounded during transport; 92.

Primary stretchers; 154.
Provision of ambulance transport by Governments; 13.
Prussia, system of railway transport; 359.
—— railway transport in 1866; 361.

Quadrupeds employed in transport of sick; 198.

Railway ambulance, experiments in Paris; 363.
—— —— hammock system; 360.
—— —— luggage vans fitted for; 362.
—— —— influence on army in the field; 347.
—— —— influence on field hospitals; **347**.
—— —— influence on surgical treatment; 348.
—— —— in India; 372.
—— —— in Italian war; 350.
—— —— in Prussia in 1866; 361.
—— —— regulations for; 368.
—— —— transport; 347.
—— —— United States; **365**.
—— goods wagons; 357.
—— passenger carriages; 356.
Recumbent and semi-recumbent transport compared; 96.
—— —— relative amount required; **96**.
—— —— economical objections to; 94.
—— and sitting **transport**, wounds requiring; 94.
Red Crescent, sign of; 65.
"Red Cross" ambulance steamer; 409.
Returns of battles; 91.
Rezonville, the battle of; 88.
River ambulance transport; 392.
—— —— —— experiences on Irrawaddy; 393.
—— —— —— —— Nile; 390, 393.
—— —— —— —— Red River; 390.
Rosencrans ambulance wagon; 288.
Royal wagon train; 29.
Rücker ambulance wagon; 289.
Rugs and poles used as stretchers; 143.
Russian ambulance transport system; 50.

Saddle, the Turkestan; 217.
Saddles, carriage of wounded upon; 223.
Secondary stretchers; 154.
Semi-recumbent transport, wounds requiring; 95.
Shortell's modified mule-litter; 242.
Sillèn's statistics of those transported by railway during the Russo-Turkish war; 354.

Singleton's ambulance chair; 407.
Soldat-infirmier, instruction of; 45.
Soldier's blanket used as a hammock; 115.
Springs, **adjustment to weights carried**; 260.
—— india-rubber; 260.
Staff Corps, Medical; 40.
St. Privat, battle of; 88.
Steamers, ambulance transport; 399.
Stretchers, canvas and pillows of; 163.
—— construction of; 158.
—— feet of; 162.
—— poles of; 158.
—— preservation of; 164.
—— slings of; 163.
—— traverses of; 160.
—— weight of; 164.
—— effects of rough carriage of; 179.
—— general description of; 153.
—— importance of feet to; 162.
—— not to be carried on the shoulders; 183.
—— only suited to European bearers; 155.
—— position of patients upon; 180.
—— **proper** carriage of; 180.
—— reasons for bearers breaking step; 180.
—— rules for carrying; 180.
—— simplicity essential; 156.
—— temporary substitutes for; 143.
—— to keep level when the ground is uneven; 179.
—— trestles for, Furley's; 162.
—— wheeled; 195.
Stretcher, Austrian; 168.
—— Baron Percy; 164.
—— Baron Mundy's; 168.
—— British regulation, Marks I. and II.; 169.
—— —— —— —— III., IV., and **V.** 172.
—— "Frank"; 167.
—— French; 166.
—— Furley ordinary civil; 176.
—— —— —— with telescopic handles; 176.
—— —— military; 174.
—— —— folding mule; 175.
—— —— police; 176.
—— Italian; 169.
—— Peck's, for mines; 178.
—— general rules for the proper carriage of a; **178**.
—— Prussian; 166.
—— bearers, Percy's corps of; **27**.
System, railway ambulance, the Austrian; 389.
—— —— —— —— Beaufort; 377, 388.
—— —— —— —— Berlin; 377.
—— —— —— —— Boulemie; 389.
—— —— —— —— Bry-Ameline; 377.
—— —— —— —— Fischer; 387.
—— —— —— —— Grund; 382.
—— —— —— —— Hamburg; 385.
—— —— —— —— Morache's; **377**.

System, railway ambulance, Peltzer's; 376.
—— —— —— Zavodovsky's; 378.

Tonjons; 153.
Tonnage, how calculated; 391.
Tortoise Ambulance, the; 323.
—— —— —— plan of encampment; 331.
—— —— —— stoves of; 325.
—— —— —— stretcher bedsteads of; 328.
—— —— —— the tents of; 325.
—— —— —— wagon of; 324.
Trag-sitz, or bearing seats; 139.
Trains, ambulance railway; 350.
—— —— —— in Austria - Hungary; 389, 415.
—— —— —— England; 372.
—— —— —— France; 363.
—— —— —— Germany; 353.
—— —— —— India; 372.
—— —— —— of the Knights of Malta; 415.
—— —— —— the Société Française; 411.
—— —— —— Russia; 354.
—— —— —— United States; 365.
Transport Ambulance of Austria; 48.
—— —— —— Denmark; 52.
—— —— —— France; 44.
—— —— —— Germany; 45.
—— —— —— Russia; 50.
—— —— —— British, peculiarities of; 14.
—— —— camel, comparative economy of; 202.
—— —— —— where specially needed; 202.
—— —— deficiency of, consequences of; 7.
—— —— elephant; 199.
—— —— —— objections to; 199.
—— —— —— carriage by pads; 200.
—— —— —— —— by howdahs; 200.
—— —— —— —— by charjamahs; 200.
—— —— estimates of for armies; 78.
—— in a recumbent posture; 94.
—— in a semi-recumbent posture; 95.
—— in a sitting posture; 93.
—— ambulance, in standing camps; 6.
—— —— on line of march; 3.
—— —— positions of during; 92.
—— —— railway ambulance; 347.
—— —— recumbent and semi-recumbent postures compared; 96.
—— —— recumbent and sitting, proportions needed; 96.
Transport ambulance, economical objections to; 7.
—— —— its advantages; 5.
—— —— wounds requiring; 93.
—— sitting, wounds suitable for; 94.

Transport ambulance, system in Crimea; 31.
—— —— —— of Austrian army; 48.
—— —— —— British legion in Spain; 31.
—— —— —— Danish army; 52.
—— —— —— founders of; 20.
—— —— —— of foreign armies; 43.
—— —— —— of French army; 44.
—— —— —— of German army; 45.
—— —— —— of Russian army; 50.
—— —— —— in the Peninsular war; 30.
Traverses; 160.
Trek wagon, The; 342.
Trestles, stretcher folding, Furley's; 162.
Tufnell's cart; 275.
Turkish araba; 337.
Two-horse litters; 248.

Unification of Army Medical Department; 39.
United States army mule-litter; 247.
—— —— two-horse litter; 248.

Vionville, battle of; 88.
Volunteer aid; 42.
—— bearer companies; 43.
—— brigade-surgeons; 43.
—— Medical Staff; 42.
—— Medical Staff Corps; 42.
Volunteers, proposed aid by, on battle-fields; 11.

Wagon, ambulance, British Mark I. and II.; 310.
—— —— —— III.; 313.
—— —— —— IV.; 315.
—— —— —— V.; 317.
—— —— Cairo; 320.
—— —— Francis's; 308.
—— —— French Red Cross; 309.
—— —— Furley's; 318.
—— —— Howard's; 321.
—— —— Locati's; 291.
—— —— Löhner's; 298.
—— —— Macpherson's; 306.
—— —— Baron Mundy's; 296.
—— —— Neuss's; 302.
—— —— New Zealand;304.
—— —— The Rücker; 289.
—— —— The Tortoise; 323.
Wagons, ambulance transport; 287.
—— classification of; 272.
—— equirotal system in; 311.
—— Indian, essential qualities of; 309.
Walcheren, the expedition; 91.
War, classification of wounded in; 98.
—— Crimean transport system; 31.
—— Peninsular, transport during; 30.
Warfare, modern, special need of trained bearers for; 83.
Wars, recent statistics of; 91.
Wheeled stretchers; 185.

"Wheeling," or **Rosencrans wagon**; 288.
Woodcock's mule litters; 246.
Wounded able to walk unaided; 99.
—— apparatus for carrying "en cheval"; 103.
—— Arab mode of removing; 224.
—— carriage by a single bearer; **103.**
—— carriage pick-a-back; 103.
—— —— by two bearers; 105.
—— —— on saddles; 223.
—— collection from battle-fields; 81.
—— crutches to help in walking; 100.
—— effects of stimulus of self-preservation; 99.
—— fitness of **mules** in carrying; 218.
—— horses suitable **for** carriage of; **222.**
—— **left** by vanquished armies; 80.
—— numbers in great battles of Franco-German war; 88.
—— old methods **of** removing from battle-fields; 20, 28.
—— positions of during transport; **92.**
—— quadrupeds employed in transporting; 198.

Wounded, relative number able to walk to hospital; 99.
—— —— dangerously, proportion **of in battle;** 98.
—— —— severely, proportion of **in battle;** 98.
—— —— slightly, proportion **of** in battle; 98.
Wounds which admit of sitting **transport;** 94.
—— —— require recumbent transport; 93.
Wintz, Baron Percy's, nature of; 25.

Zavodovsky's railway ambulance system; 378.
—— —— —— **advantages of;** 382.
—— —— —— **construction of;** 378.
—— —— —— **materials required for;** 379.
—— —— —— **modification of** (Christen Smith's); 383.